Salvaged Pages

Salvaged Pages

Young Writers' Diaries
of the Holocaust

Collected and edited by Alexandra Zapruder

SECOND EDITION

Yale

UNIVERSITY PRESS

New Haven and London

Excerpts from the diary of Moshe Flinker, © 1971 Yad Vashem, Jerusalem.
Excerpts from the diary of Dawid Rubinowicz, © 1982 Norman Bolotin,
courtesy of Laing Communications, Inc.
Excerpts from the diary of Yitshok Rudashevski, © 1973 Ghetto Fighters' House,
courtesy of the United States Holocaust Memorial Museum.

Second edition 2015. First edition 2002.

Yale University Press books may be purchased in quantity for educational, business,
or promotional use. For information, please e-mail sales.press@yale.edu (U.S. office)
or sales@yaleup.co.uk (U.K. office).

Printed in the United States of America.

Library of Congress Control Number: 2015930522
ISBN: 978-0-300-20599-2 (pbk.)

A catalogue record for this book is available from the British Library.

10 9 8 7 6 5 4 3 2 1

To my dear friend and mentor, Barbara Kellum

Thou hast nor youth nor age
But as it were an after dinner sleep
Dreaming of both.

T. S. Eliot, *Gerontion*

Contents

Preface to the Second Edition

Fresh out of college, in the summer of 1991, I went looking for a first job in my hometown of Washington, D.C. Thanks to several prior stints as a research assistant, and despite knowing little about the Holocaust, I was hired as a researcher in the Special Exhibitions Department at the United States Holocaust Memorial Museum (USHMM). The museum as we now know it did not yet exist. The building was under construction, a restricted hard-hat zone where we picked our way over wooden planks and around scaffolding; the younger members of the staff, myself included, swiped loose bricks or giant nuts and bolts to use as paperweights and, more important, to keep as markers of our insider status. Until shortly before the museum opened to the public, we were scattered in nondescript suites on various floors of an office building on L Street. We worked in relative obscurity; many people had never heard of the museum and didn't know what we were doing. In fact, until the museum opened in April 1993, there was no central repository for documentation, scholarship, and education about the Holocaust in the United States.

It took several months to get my bearings in the job. In early 1992, I joined the curatorial team for *Remember the Children: Daniel's Story,* the museum's exhibition planned for young visitors. Soon after, I was dispatched to the museum's library in search of diaries written by children during the Holocaust. There wasn't much of a library yet—just a lot of books waiting to be catalogued and shelved, and a card catalogue in the form of a box of index cards. Mostly, we didn't bother with it. We just asked the librarian, Bill Connelly, for whatever we wanted; he disappeared for a while and then came back with a wisecrack and book in hand. So when I came looking for the diaries of teenagers, I asked Bill what to read. He rummaged around in the piles and then handed me a stack of books—worn and weathered copies of the diaries of Yitskhok Rudashevski, Dawid Rubinowicz, Moshe Flinker, Éva Heyman, and Mary Berg, together with a few volumes that included excerpts of young writers' diaries from the Łódź and Terezín ghettos. I had never heard of any of them. Nearly every one—except those of Anne Frank,

Etty Hillesum, and Hannah Senesh—was either out of print, only available in excerpts, or both.

After more than twenty years, I still remember the sudden, overwhelming experience of reading those diaries for the first time. From out of the vast body of historical studies and scholarly analyses, videotaped testimonies of aged survivors, and hauntingly silent photographs and film footage, there emerged a single, clear, unmistakably human voice. And another. Still another. One was chatty, another reflective, a third earnest; some were lyrical and others pragmatic; some were bitter, angry, hopeful, resigned, sarcastic, resentful, pleading, and often all of the above. Alone in my small office, these diaries *happened* to me with a visceral force, as if the writer was pulling me by the hand back in time and into a specific place, leading me through the courtyards of the Vilna ghetto or into an apartment in Brussels or on the open streets of a desperately poor village in Poland. I began to see in my mind what they saw, hear their questions reverberate in my own head, and witness, in mute sympathy, the fear, loss, and despair that dominated so much of their lives.

Within weeks of reading the handful of diaries borrowed from the library, I began asking myself a series of questions that drove most of my work over the next decade: Why hasn't the public taken notice of these writers? Why is Anne Frank the only young person we know to have written a diary? Are these diaries like hers or different? Do common themes run through them? And most of all, could it be true that in the immense universe of Holocaust documentation, only seven or eight young writers' diaries survived? I thought of them like the Roman ruins that I so loved studying in college. If archaeologists could find shards of urns and pots that were thousands of years old, surely there must be more written fragments from this more recent past. But where to find them? And how, when I didn't speak any languages but English and French, when I knew relatively little about the Holocaust, and when I myself was so young? Armed with little more than a sense of confidence in the legitimacy of my questions, I started scribbling ideas and thoughts in a spiral-bound notebook, courting what then seemed like an outlandish idea to research the subject, try to find more material, and bring these journals back from obscurity in the form of a published book.

Over the course of the next ten years, this endeavor dominated much of my life. Research in the early 1990s was much as it had been for centuries and almost nothing like it is now. With no Google to use for searching the Internet and with limited email, I read books and dug around in endnotes and footnotes. I searched through the finding aids of major Holocaust archives in Europe and Israel to chase down references to young writers' diaries. I wrote letters to authors, publishers, historians, archivists, and sometimes survivors or the relatives of the deceased, and waited weeks for letters back. The process of gaining access to the written texts was slow and laborious. It could take months to make contact with a survivor, establish trust through communication, and persuade him or her to photocopy the diary pages and send them to me. Then months more could elapse before I would have the text translated so that I could read it. Eventually, my colleagues at the Holocaust Museum became aware of what I was doing. As they gathered archival material and interviewed survivors, they began to call me when a diary was donated to the museum or mentioned in an interview. I began to receive phone calls and letters about diaries not only from my colleagues but also from complete strangers. I can still recall the excitement I felt when I opened my mailbox and found one of those unmistakable envelopes—battered from a long journey, marked with foreign stamps, addressed to me in an unfamiliar hand. Standing in the lobby mailroom of my apartment building, keys in hand, bags on my shoulder, I would tear the parcel open to find out what was inside and then walk to the elevator and all the way to my front door without looking up, furiously scanning the enclosed pages trying to decipher what I had just received. Sometimes the packages contained long-awaited copies of diaries; a few times, I opened them to find letters from strangers who had learned of my work from mutual colleagues or friends, and who had taken pains to copy and send a hand-written diary that I had never known existed.

Although the research and discovery of diaries were exciting, the process as a whole was deeply personal and often difficult, for it involved grappling with the intellectual, moral, and emotional problems these writings raised. I continued to work on and off at the Holocaust Museum during these years, except for a short time beginning in 1994 when I left Washington to pursue my master's degree in education and then briefly taught writing at a small college in Boston. There were fits and starts, setbacks, detours, and at least one attempt to abandon the project altogether. But the material had taken hold and refused to let go. In 1998, I had made enough progress to present a proposal for the book to an editor at Yale University Press. We signed a contract for publication the following year, and I left my job at the Holocaust Museum permanently, to set up shop in my home office, where I would spend the next two years turning the mass of rough translations, scribbled notes, unanswered questions, and half-formed ideas into a book.

As I gathered and sifted through diaries, setting aside the ones that didn't fit into the scope of my project, I began to struggle with the genre. How to understand the meaning of these texts within the massive realm of Holocaust literature and scholarship? I didn't want to see these writers as "other Anne Franks," nor did I want to apply the perennially positive and hopeful framework that hung around her diary to the ones that I was reading. To do so rang false and offended my sense of grief for their suffering and deaths. I tackled this problem in the introduction to the book, critiquing the habit of mind that leads us to read young writers' diaries as symbols of lost lives rather than as complicated and legitimate contributions to the historical and literary record of the Holocaust. I aimed not only to bring more young writers' Holocaust diaries into the public discourse but also to present the whole—including Anne Frank's powerful and endlessly interesting words—within a framework that reflects the inherent value of the diaries, rather than the reader's wish for a comforting coda to the stories.

Salvaged Pages was published in 2002. The long and difficult work was over, and I expected that the book would have a typical life span, generating some interest for a while and then tapering off. All too soon, it would be time to decide what to do next.

And then, something unexpected happened. Within several months of the book's publication, I began getting calls not from bookstores or reviewers but from teachers, organizers of educators' conferences, and Jewish community leaders who organized local Holocaust education. They wanted to know if I would come to speak about *Salvaged Pages,* to show teachers how to use it in the classroom, and to share how it could complement instruction on Anne Frank's *Diary of a Young Girl.* At first, I accepted these invitations with hesitation. Holocaust education in the United States was in a state of transition; although educators at the USHMM and elsewhere were working to establish and disseminate a responsible methodology for teaching the subject in an American context, there were not yet widely adopted standards and best practices. Likewise, those who labored to bring Holocaust education into their schools and communities did not share identical educational aims. Many times, I met teachers and volunteers who were driven by an emotional, and often personal, connection to the Holocaust, which often came with a moral imperative to convey a fixed set of "lessons" to the next generation. A great many people, when faced with the overwhelming breadth of the subject matter, abandoned its historical specificity in favor of generalities and, all too often, clichés about "man's inhumanity to man" and the like. Methodology and educational rationale could be equally uneven in schools. Whereas in one, the Holocaust was used as a point of entry for vague lessons about "tolerance," in another, students read Anne Frank's *Diary of a Young Girl* and regurgitated well-worn phrases about "hope for humanity" and the "triumph of the human spirit" to the satisfaction of their teachers and school administrators. In still another, misguided instructors used punitive methods to teach the history, forcing students to "reenact" the Holocaust by requiring them to "experience" the suffering of the victims or even carry out oppressive tactics against one another. As I accepted more and more speaking engagements at educator conferences, in schools, at Jewish community centers, and in synagogues, I found myself in the thick of this emerging and changing field.

Just as the collection of the diaries themselves had been a slow accretion of material that took ten years to coalesce into a book, *Salvaged Pages* gradually developed into an educational tool over the next decade. In 2005, I partnered with MTV to make a documentary film based on the book, called *I'm Still Here*, and worked collaboratively with the educational nonprofit Facing History and Ourselves to develop materials for study of the film in classrooms. The education department at the USHMM adopted *Salvaged Pages* as one of its foundational texts, inviting me to speak at educator forums around the country and giving copies of the book to thousands of teachers over the next several years.

During this time, I met teachers who were also struggling with changing norms and values within this field, and who were engaged in professional development at the USHMM, Yad Vashem, Facing History and Ourselves, and other institutions. They saw the value of the diaries in *Salvaged Pages* and drew me into dialogue about how to frame the material. They invited me to teach their students and present at their educator conferences, and pushed my thinking about how the content could be best adapted to classroom instruction. Many of these teachers became my close colleagues and friends, and their work has not only shaped the teaching of *Salvaged Pages* but also given the book its second life.

Now, thirteen years after the first edition's publication, I have traveled across the United States, teaching the book in a dizzying number of cities. My memories of these places exist as a study in contrasts. One week, I am standing at a podium in a posh, hushed auditorium in a wealthy private school in California with students quietly typing into laptops; the next, I am in a cavernous auditorium with eight hundred rowdy middle schoolers in Tucson, Arizona, when a student stands up to ask me, "Do you speak Jew?" I am speaking to a group of young Orthodox women students from Yeshiva University, all with their heads covered, in long sleeves and skirts, and I am in an inner-city classroom with water stains and peeling plaster, where fights break out in the halls and students look at me with suspicion, doubting my ability to say anything of interest or meaning to them. I am in a nondescript conference center reading a difficult diary entry about Jews who profited from fellow victims to survive in the ghetto when a rabbi takes me to task for dishonoring the memory of the dead. I am in a room filled to capacity with Christians and Jews at the Mobile Public Library in Alabama, then in the hauntingly beautiful Jewish synagogue in Birmingham, and later in a small conference center in Monroeville, with sixty non-Jewish teachers, where the group says grace before eating and thanks Jesus for our food. I've met with students in small suburban school libraries, on parochial school campuses, in progressive charter school classrooms, and in rural community schools where no one has met a Jew, let alone learned the traditions, culture, and religion of the Holocaust's primary victims. I have been in a lot of sterile conference centers and tired hotel ballrooms, where teachers come for the day and animate the space with their questions, their observations, and their deep engagement with the subject matter and its potential for students.

In every context, every time, whether I am with students or teachers, whether they know a little or a lot, we approach the diaries in the same basic way. We open the book and read diary entries aloud, lingering over the words and letting our questions bubble up. Our observations lead us to reflection, to contemplation, and to deeper understanding. Sometimes we discuss the historical reality of Nazi oppression in a particular place and time; sometimes we delve into the bottomless permutations of hunger and its reductive, devastating impact on the body, mind, and spirit; and sometimes we talk about hope, faith, and despair, or about shame, resentment, and anger, or about survival and loss. We talk about evil and God and ask who is responsible. We talk about Anne Frank and why her diary was read the way it was, and how to rethink it. The diaries never fail to provoke thoughts and questions; individually, they break down the Holocaust experience into moments that reflect the complexity of a life; taken together, they offer complementary and sometimes contradictory accounts that defy simplification and generalization. And although these texts cannot restore the lives of their writers or redeem their deaths, they can and do preserve memory and complicate, in the best possible way, our understanding of this historical past.

Far from tapering off over time, the book has continued to raise opportunities and challenges for me. In recent years, I have taught *Salvaged Pages* over several intensive days of back-to-back classes at the Maya Angelou Academy, the charter school attached to the D.C. Juvenile Detention Center. I walk through the metal detector, surrender my phone and keys, and enter lockdown to teach students who are also inmates, perpetrators of crimes who are also victims of unjust circumstances. Most of them receive me with warmth, respect, and also curiosity; others are so medicated or disengaged that they put their heads down on the desk and sleep. "You a Jew?" I am asked, and when I say yes, they laugh, embarrassed. "I never met no Jew before." "What do you think?" I say, smiling, and they laugh again, with such sweetness that it is hard to believe that they are in jail for violent crimes.

These mostly African American teenage boys, who generally read far below grade level, work hard to understand the substance of the book, but they confidently articulate deep, difficult thoughts about inequity, suffering, violence, and survival. We talk about how much of life is chance, and what we do with the cards we are dealt. We talk about fairness and justice, and what Jewish teens experienced during the Holocaust. "I could never have gone through what they went through," one boy says. "I would have killed those bastards," says another. And while I know that a forty-five-minute session discussing *Salvaged Pages* has little hope of changing the course of any of these boys' lives, I am still pained to learn how few of them will succeed in rebuilding a life outside of the criminal justice system.

On another occasion, I traveled to Shanghai to work with students at Concordia International School on personal narrative, using the diaries in *Salvaged Pages* as models and inspiration. Over the course of the week, the mostly expatriate students, who excelled in the rigorous academic environment of their school, struggled to shed their analytical skills temporarily and engage in personal inquiry, observation, and self-expression. It was not easy for them, nor was it easy for me to grasp how teaching *Salvaged Pages* in China differed from teaching in America. A small number of students thrived on the challenge; many others, raised in cultures that do not encourage sharing personal thoughts or feelings, were uncomfortable and even frustrated. Some didn't know what to write or how to tolerate the open-ended, no-wrong-answer nature of the assignment. Their teachers worked hard to make the experiment work, encouraging me to raise these issues directly. And so we did, wrestling aloud with the purpose and meaning of personal writing, and the private and sometimes painful feelings it can evoke. Although our week together did not make diarists out of most of them, it did challenge them to probe their memories and use words to make meaning of their experiences. For my part, I left with a deeper understanding of what students may need in order to go beyond reading the diaries in *Salvaged Pages* as history or literature to using them as inspiration for their own writing.

The night before I was to leave, I spoke at the Shanghai Literary Festival at M on the Bund, the fabulous, glamorous restaurant-bar overlooking the main street that runs through Shanghai. To my left, through a bank of windows, I could see the Huangpu River with barges slowly floating by, flanked on one side by elegant eighteenth- and nineteenth-century buildings and, on the other, by the ultra-contemporary, almost extraterrestrial skyline of Pudong. I briefly had time to wonder what Yitskhok Rudashevski or Moshe Flinker or Elsa Binder would think if they could imagine their words reverberating through this space, moving strangers to tears, so far away in time and space from anything they could ever have known.

Shortly after teaching in China, I traveled to Israel for the first time to speak at Yad Vashem's Ninth International Educator's Conference. In the week before the conference, I met and interviewed Sarah Kalivatsch, the first cousin of Yitskhok Rudashevski, and the following day, Leah Levy and Rebecca Schweber, two of Moshe Flinker's sisters. They had all survived the Holocaust, and they remain the only living links to these writers. In each interview, we sat together for hours as I asked question after question, trying to revive sixty-year-old memories, to catch a glimpse of Yitskhok and Moshe, not as the writers I have known through their words, but as the boys they were at the time. The following week, during a morning plenary session, in an imposing auditorium filled with 450 educators from all over the world, I read from the diary that Moshe kept while passing as a non-Jew in occupied Belgium. More than any other writer, he wrote passionately about the promise of Jewish redemption and voiced his dreams of escaping oppression in occupied Europe for life in a Jewish homeland.

> Each time I stand to [pray] I direct my whole soul to my lovely land, and I see it before my eyes; I see the coast, I see Tel Aviv, Jaffa, and Haifa. Then I see Jerusalem, with the Mount of Olives, and I see the Jordan as it flows from Lebanon to the Dead Sea. [. . .] Several times already I have asked myself whether I will ever get the chance to stand on its holy earth, if the Lord will permit me to walk about in my land. Oh, how my soul yearns for you, my homeland, how my eyes crave for the sight of you, my country, the Land of Israel.

Once again, the old words become new, as I see Tel Aviv, Jaffa, and Jerusalem not as the tourist I have been all week but through Moshe's eyes as a devout Jew and a Zionist before the State of Israel even existed. And as I read—the morning after Hamas launched its first rockets into Jerusalem, beginning yet another war—half-expecting an air raid at any time, I remember that Moshe did not just dream of Israel but taught himself Arabic in hiding so that he could become a diplomat there after the war. It was a difficult and laborious effort but a necessary one, he wrote, for to ensure peace in Israel, he would need to "be able to speak with our brothers, the sons of Ishmael, who are also Abraham's descendants." Moshe did not live to walk on Israel's "holy earth," nor did he ever speak with its Arab inhabitants in their native tongue in search of understanding and peace. He was deported to Auschwitz-Birkenau and ultimately to Bergen-Belsen, where he succumbed to typhus instead. But on that perfect, clear morning in Jerusalem, as his words reverberated at Yad Vashem, they became more than his alone; to them, we added our own lament for the dream accomplished that he did not live to see, despair for the elusive promise of peace, and grief for all that was lost in his death.

I thought I had plumbed the depths of these diaries in the years it took to assemble *Salvaged Pages*. But these experiences over more than a decade have taught me that there is no bottom. They are not static texts but dynamic ones that continue to challenge and provoke, to spark original reflection by readers in their own particular time and places. As such, we read them not only to shed light on the historical past but also to illuminate our own morally complicated present. And perhaps, in the best of circumstances, they take us one step further by challenging, bolstering, shifting, or even shaping what we think and believe and feel. And there is no telling what good may come of that.

We are in the third decade since I began to work on these writings. Much has changed since the publication of *Salvaged Pages* in 2002, in the years during which it has been adopted as an educational resource in communities around the country and the world. I pursued the idea of a new edition of *Salvaged Pages* in part because the genre itself has grown—many new diaries have been published over time—and in part because there are new things to say, thanks to countless close readings and the influence of teachers and students who have shared their interpretations and observations with me.

But more than that, the ongoing role of *Salvaged Pages* as an educational tool in a changing world began to raise questions about what teachers and students, in particular, need in order to make meaning of it. For many, educational instruction is no longer based on a written text with the occasional accompanying image. Books are digitally animated; websites provide easy access to a wealth of resources; and a variety of platforms allow students and teachers to learn, converse, and share ideas without being in physical proximity to one another. During the very years that technology was revolutionizing the way that many teach, the surviving writers were entering their last decades of life, depositing a great deal of material into archives and museums, including artifacts; historical photographs; corresponding artwork, documents, and letters; oral testimonies; and other records that testify to the events that preceded the writing of the diary or tell us what happened after the words broke off. All the while, scholarship about the Holocaust also continued to grow, providing educators and students with encyclopedic definitions of terms and events, maps, and answers to nearly every historical question that the texts might pose. And people in all fields—documentary filmmakers, scholars, educators, writers, and artists—undertook their own projects around diaries, publishing new editions, making films, creating curricula, and embarking on group projects to memorialize the writers.

This revised edition of *Salvaged Pages* reflects a new vision for its educational possibilities and, as such, exists in three related parts: this updated paperback edition, an enhanced electronic book, and an educational website for teachers. The paperback, enlarged to be easier to read, includes new details about the diaries, several additions to the list of diaries by young writers at the end of the book, and a new subject index. At the same time, *Salvaged Pages* is now available as an enhanced e-book, with text definitions, maps, images of diary pages, personal and historical photos, key documents, and oral testimony clips of some of the writers who survived or their close relatives. Finally, in partnership with Facing History and Ourselves and a team of master teachers, we created a website with wraparound educational materials that offer specific ways to use the diaries for instruction in history, reading analysis, and writing.

Far from the largely solitary project to write *Salvaged Pages* in the 1990s, this revision has been a collaborative effort across disciplines, with a team of contributors who bring a wide array of expertise and knowledge to the work. Our primary goal is to serve teachers and students, and to make the diaries in *Salvaged Pages* an indispensable tool for Holocaust education by contextualizing them so they are accessible and useful to anyone who wants to read them.

In the end, the diaries as historical and literary records of the Holocaust remain the core of *Salvaged Pages*. It is our hope that this new edition, in its multiple forms, will continue to engage and inspire new generations of readers, and that the words these writers labored to produce as refugees, in hiding, and in ghettoes throughout Nazi Europe will continue to reverberate among teachers and students, posing new questions, challenging assumptions, and sparking dialogue about the Holocaust and what it means to be human.

Acknowledgments to the Second Edition

I am immensely grateful to many colleagues and friends who made the new paperback and enhanced e-book editions of *Salvaged Pages* possible.

First and foremost, I wish to thank Ingrid Tauber and the Tauber Family Foundation for the generous grant that made this project possible. We are all in your debt. In addition, thanks go to Holocaust Museum Houston, the Warren Fellowship for Future Teachers, and the Naomi and Martin Warren Family Foundation for contributing much-needed funding late in the development process, and to David Bell and Mary Lee Webeck. The Warren Fellowship for Future Teachers is supported in loving honor of survivor Naomi Warren, by her children, grandchildren, and great grandchildren.

Words cannot fully express the depth of my gratitude to the survivors and their family members who gave their time, energy, and strength to help with this project. Thank you to Miriam Korber Bercovici, the Shek family, and Jacob Langer and his daughter Yael, who generously shared family papers, photographs, and other personal materials with me. I especially wish to acknowledge Leon Schwimmer for his boundless determination to arrange interviews with the sisters of Moshe Flinker, for answering countless questions, and for helping me secure important images to use in the e-book. I am so grateful to Moshe Flinker's sisters, Leah Levy and Rebecca Schweber, for welcoming me into Leah's home with coffee and treats, and for patiently telling me about their beloved brother and their family's story. Likewise, I thank Ilana Kazovsky for making an interview with her mother possible, and I am grateful to Sarah Kalivatsch for sharing her many memories and photographs of her dear friend and cousin, Yitskhok Rudashevski. To Chava Pressburger, I thank you again and always for your generosity and warmth, and for all the ways you have supported and encouraged this work. And to dear Peter Feigl, you are the best Chapter 3 anyone could ask for! Thank you for your incredible energy, unfailing enthusiasm, and cheerful help, and for your friendship, which I treasure.

Many colleagues helped in the development of the e-book and the educational materials. I wish to especially thank Suzy Snyder at the United States Holocaust

Memorial Museum for always going above and beyond to help me find and use the very best materials. Thank you to Judith Cohen and Nancy Hartman for help with photo research, Bret Werb for help understanding Ilya Gerber's Kovno ghetto songbook and for sharing musical recordings for the e-book, and Ann Millin for help with archival documents. I am immensely grateful to Jonathan Brent, Fruma Mohrer, Shmuel Klein, and Marek Web at the YIVO Institute for Jewish Research for unfettered access to the Nachman Sonabend and Kaczerginski-Sutzkever Collections. I also wish to thank and acknowledge the collections and archives staff at Yad Vashem, the Vilna Gaon Museum, the Jewish Historical Institute in Warsaw, the Belgian State Archives, and the Directorate Generale of War Victims in Brussels, who provided valuable documents for inclusion in the e-book and educational materials. At these archives, Agnieszka Reska, Ilona Murauskaite, Michal Feiner, Filip Strubbe, and Sylvie Vander Elst were especially kind and helpful, as was Dorien Styven at the Jewish Historical Museum at Mechelen, Belgium. My heartfelt thanks go to Eva Wymark, editor at Bodzentyn.net, who offered great help with information and materials related to the diary of Dawid Rubinowicz, and to John Braat, who deepened my understanding of the Flinker family's wartime history and shared important visual materials with me. Thank you to the USC Shoah Foundation Institute for Visual History and Education for granting permission to use survivor interview clips in the e-book. These are very special contributions, and we are most grateful for them. Thank you also to my dear friend Daphna Cohen-Mintz in Israel and Magal Lotan at Beer Sheba University for help obtaining copies of Chava Pressburger's family photos and personal papers. Finally, on behalf of Bonnie Sussman, I thank Dr. Simon P. Sibelman, Leon Levine Distinguished Professor of Judaic, Holocaust, and Peace Studies at Appalachian State University, Boone, N.C., for help with Elisabeth Kaufmann's diary.

Thank you to Shoshana Mandel for invaluable aid as an interpreter during my interviews in Israel and to Gabriel Wagon for filming them. Additional thanks go to Julie Donat, Mona Momescu, and Hana Rudnick for translating foreign-language interviews into English for use in the e-book, and to Fritz Paul Gluckstein, D.V.M., for translating Erich Langer's final letter to his son Klaus. For administrative support, I thank Ash Lago, Taly Ashkenazi, Michael Lemanski, and Elissa Gallagher. Bill Nelson created the maps, and Nancy Zibman compiled the index.

At Yale University Press, I wish especially to thank Sara Sapire, who oversaw the production of the e-book and guided me through the unfamiliar terrain of digital formats and platforms. I also thank Jenya Weinreb for her patience and diligence in copyediting the revisions to the manuscript. To my good friend and patient, steady, and clear-headed editor Sarah Miller, I thank you for seeing the possibility in this project and for seeing it through to publication. I will always be grateful to you for the countless ways in which you helped make this project a reality.

I feel very lucky to have found my literary agent, Gail Hochman, who negotiated the mindbendingly complicated publishing contracts for the new paperback and enhanced e-book editions of *Salvaged Pages* with clarity, efficiency, wisdom, and heart.

I am deeply indebted to Marc Skvirsky, Adam Strom, Fran Sterling, and the staff of Facing History and Ourselves, who always say yes instead of no when there is a possibility for collaborative work in history and education. Your team contributed material support, countless hours of staff time, and professional expertise to the creation of the educational materials, and you gave our curriculum a permanent home on Facing History's website. You are partners in the truest sense of the word, and I am so grateful for every opportunity to work with you.

I am reserving my last and deepest thanks for my co-authors in creating the e-book version of *Salvaged Pages* and the accompanying educational materials. When we began this work, we had no idea how complicated, involved, and overwhelming this project would be. For all the administrative and process-related hassles, I am sorry and I thank you for hanging in there. As a team, you gave more time, energy, and brainpower than anyone had the right to expect. And yet, somehow, I knew you would come through. You have always shown remarkable dedication to these diaries and commitment to bringing them to students and teachers. I am lucky to have such partners and friends in this work, and I thank you with all my heart for the hours you spent turning our shared vision into reality.

Bryan Davis undertook the first review of the manuscript to identify and position enhancements for the e-book, drafted the glossary terms, and worked closely with me to create and fill in the initial spreadsheets that mapped the project.

Sheila Hansen conducted extensive visual research for the e-book, locating historical and personal photos, documentation, and footage, and she researched, gathered, and identified the oral testimony clips for the e-book. I am so grateful for her endless patience and hard work.

Lisa Bauman, Colleen Tambuscio, and Bonnie Sussman created the educational curriculum for *Salvaged Pages,* which will become a permanent part of the educational website for Facing History and Ourselves. They shared resources, conducted new research, developed activities, and brought years of classroom expertise to the finished product. It was an ambitious undertaking, and I am grateful for their time, energy, and commitment.

Fran Sterling served as liaison between the teachers and Facing History and made meaningful contributions to every stage of the process. She oversaw the immense editorial project of preparing the materials for publication on the website, rewrote and polished the activities, found necessary funds, helped with permissions and access to materials, and performed countless other thankless tasks without which the curriculum would never have been completed.

A final, personal word of thanks to my husband, Craig Dye, whose support and understanding make all my work possible, and to our beloved children, Hannah and Toby, who inspire me beyond measure and who make everything matter.

Acknowledgments to the First Edition

This project would quite simply not have existed but for the kindness and generosity of people throughout the United States, Europe, and Israel. Foremost among them are the Holocaust survivors and the relatives and friends of living and deceased young writers who shared diaries with me, answered countless questions, and in small and large ways encouraged my work on this subject. For this, I am deeply grateful to Werner T. Angress, Andrea Axt, Janina Bauman, Miriam Korber Bercovici, Norman Bolotin, Aleksander Demajo, Debórah Dwork, Selma Engel, Peter Feigl, Jacob Fishkin, the family of Moshe Flinker, Raymonde Frazier, Felicitas (Lici) Garda, Helga Weissová Hošková, Lilly Isaacs, Inga Joseph (also known as Ingrid Jacoby), Helga Kinsky, Elizabeth Koenig, Clara Kramer, Michael Kraus, Moshe Kravec, Jacob Langer, Jutta Levy and Debbie Levy, Guido Lopez, Thomas Mandl, Halina Nelken, Ana Novac, Elisabeth Orsten, Mirjam Pinkhof, Chava Pressburger, Anne Ranasinghe, Macha Rolnikas (also known as Masha or Maria Rolnikaite), Lillyan Rosenberg, Tamara Lazerson Rostovsky, Eva Roubíčková and Vera Wiser, Lena Jedwab Rozenberg and Dorothée Rozenberg, Gertrude Schneider, Alisa Shek, Leo Silberman, Edith Velmans, Charlotte Verešová, Werner Warmbrunn, Susi Hilsenrath Warsinger, Denise Weill, Paul Weiner, and Leon Weliczker Wells.

Many young writers did not live to see the end of the war and their diaries are in the safekeeping of archives and museums around the world. I am particularly indebted to archives that provided documents and gave permission for their use in this work, among them the United States Holocaust Memorial Museum in Washington, D.C.; Beit Theresienstadt, Givat Chaim Ichud, Israel; Centre de Documentation Juive Contemporaine in Paris; Fondazione Centro di Documentazione Ebraica Contemporanea in Milan; the Jewish Historical Institute in Warsaw; Joods Museum van Deportatie en Verzet in Mechelen; Kibbutz Moreshet Archives in Israel; the Lithuanian Central State Archives in Vilnius; the Museum of Jewish Heritage in New York; the Vilna Gaon Jewish State Museum in Vilnius; YIVO Institute for Jewish Research in New York; the Federation of

Jewish Communities in Yugoslavia, Belgrade; Herinneringscentrum Kamp Westerbork in the Netherlands; the Jewish Museum in Prague; and Yad Vashem in Jerusalem.

In these archives, there were individual librarians and archivists whose help and graciousness went far beyond all expectations and requirements. I wish especially to thank William Connelly, Steven Vitto, Mary Ann Leonard, and Mark Ziomek of the United States Holocaust Memorial Museum, Alisah Schiller of Beit Theresienstadt, Alina Skibinska of the Jewish Historical Institute in Warsaw, Judith Kleiman of Yad Vashem, Rachel Kostanian of the Vilna Gaon Jewish State Museum in Vilnius, and Esther Brumberg of the Museum of Jewish Heritage in New York.

A small but generous group of people and foundations funded the translations for this project. I am very grateful to Diane Troderman and the Hatikva Holocaust Center in Springfield, Massachusetts, Zamira Korff and the Baruch Korff Foundation, the Pozez family, Steven Ludsin and the Remembrance of the Holocaust Foundation, my parents, Marjorie and Henry Zapruder, and Marcia Kurtz for the invaluable contribution of financing the translations that made these diaries available to the public in English.

A veritable army of dedicated translators rendered these diaries from their native languages into English. I am indebted to them for their skill, talent, and ingenuity, and for their many efforts on behalf of this project. They are Madeline Vadkerty, Ivo Řezníček, and Benjamin Herman (Czech); Małgorzata Markoff and Kristine Belfoure (Polish); Maya Popović (Serbo-Croatian); Dana Keren (Yiddish, Hebrew, and Polish); Galeet Westreich (Hebrew); Solon Beinfeld and Tina Lunson (Yiddish); Kenneth Kronenberg and Gerald Liebenau (German); Radu Ioanid and Julie Donat (Romanian); and Laszlo Szimonisz and Peter Katona (Hungarian). I wish to also extend my thanks to those who previously translated some of the diaries that appear in this book. They include Peter Feigl (French and German), Michael Kubat (Czech), Percy Matenko (Yiddish), and Derek Bowman (Polish).

I wish to express my special thanks to my many colleagues and friends at the United States Holocaust Memorial Museum who supported this work over nearly a decade. Staff members and volunteers from the various divisions—Library, Archives, Collections, Photo Archives, Registry of Jewish Holocaust Survivors, Oral History, Education, Exhibitions, and the Center for Advanced Holocaust Studies—regularly came to my aid, supplying me not only with primary and secondary source material, but with interviews, contacts, photographs, ideas, informal translations, and, perhaps above all, the kind of encouragement that makes all the difference. I wish especially to thank Vadim Altskan, Brewster Chamberlin, Emily Dyer, Raye Farr, Martin Goldman, Sara Greenberg, Jerzy Halberzstadt, Ken Haman, Patricia Heberer, Radu Ioanid, Ferenc Katona, Marvin Liberman, Genya Markon, David Marwell, Scott Miller, Susan Morgenstein, Klaus Mueller, Jacek Nowakowski, Teresa A. Pollin, Jerry Rehm, Mary Lou Riccio, Joan Ringelheim, Travis Roxlau, Diane Saltzman, Sara Sirman, Suzy Snyder, Paul Thomas, Shari Rosenstein Werb, Bret Werb, and the late Sybil Milton.

I have been extremely fortunate during the course of this project to have knowledgeable, thoughtful, and generous colleagues and friends upon whom to lean. Their contributions have taken all forms and have been material and spiritual; I would not have wanted to do this work without them. Chief among these are Michael Berenbaum, Maria Bucur, Steve Cogil, Ellen Diamond, Brian Funck, Deborah Gaffin, Alexandra Garbarini, Jennifer Gaylin, Mimi Hellman, Zuzana Justman, Anita Kassof, Barbara Kellum, Sara Lawrence Lightfoot, Frank Lawrence, Dini McCullough, Kelly McHugh, Kristy Sager, Philippa Shepherd, Jillaine Smith, Alicia Seiger, Marion Usher, Melody Wilenski, Carin Zelenko, and Rabbi Daniel G. Zemel.

My thanks also go to my very close circle of friends who offered their help, advice, suggestions, and contributions to the manuscript. I especially want to acknowledge and thank Joan Ringelheim, to whom I first confided this project, and who helped, advised, and encouraged me from the outset; François Guilleux, who listened to all my ideas and patiently read and commented on early drafts of the manuscript; Sara Hendren, who has been a true kindred spirit and devoted friend and supporter; and Michael Downing, whose friendship, solidarity, humor, and wisdom were often my saving grace.

To this, I wish to add my warmest thanks to my perfectly wonderful literary agent Jennifer Lyons, who instantly and completely understood this project, and to my editor at Yale University Press, Jonathan Brent, who lent his support and enthusiasm, and to whom I will forever be grateful for making this book a reality. Hannah Tinti and Heather Currier from Writers House and Aileen Novick from Yale University Press offered help in small and large ways, and I thank them for their forbearance and support. Finally, I am indebted to Philip King, my manuscript editor at Yale University Press, whose kindness, patience, and good humor made editing the manuscript a joy. His attention to detail and consistency, his thoughtful consideration of countless questions and issues, and his clearsighted suggestions and improvements transformed my manuscript into a book and for this he has earned my admiration and my enduring gratitude.

My friend Sara Greenberg stepped up to the plate as an impromptu research assistant during the final three years of this project, typing parts of the manuscript; researching obscure articles, books, and oral histories; correcting footnotes and miscellany of all kinds; traveling with me to interview Holocaust survivors and others; listening and offering suggestions and help at every stage of the preparation of the manuscript. She lightened the load when it was most needed and for this I will always be thankful.

I could not have completed this book without Radu Ioanid, who read every page of the manuscript as it was written, and who patiently endured countless hours of conversation about the Holocaust and every aspect of the manuscript, offering suggestions in the way of history, style, content, form, and structure. I thank him for all this, and for his generosity, sense of humor, and above all, his friendship, which sustained me during the writing of this book.

I am very grateful to my family, immediate and extended, for their enduring support over the many years it took to complete this project. I especially want to acknowledge and thank my parents for their wisdom and generosity of spirit; my twin brother Michael for his many creative and artistic ideas, his gentleness, and his unfailing encouragement; and my older brother Matthew, for his critical eye, his sympathetic ear, and his thoughtful suggestions that so often influenced this work for the better. Finally, I want to thank Craig Dye, who has lived by my side for over a decade, and whose ceaseless encouragement and unselfishness have always made it possible for me to follow my own heart.

I cannot help but close with a final note to the diarists themselves—living and dead—who struggled to leave a mark on the world in the face of obliteration. Above all, this book recognizes their contribution to history and acknowledges the grace of that gesture.

Editor's Note

This project, which I began in October 1992, included three major phases. The first centered on research and involved gathering information about or copies of as many Holocaust diaries of young writers as possible. To this end, I was in contact with Holocaust survivors and archives across the United States, Israel, and Europe (Germany, Poland, Russia, Lithuania, the Czech Republic, Slovakia, Bulgaria, the former Yugoslavia, Greece, Italy, France, Holland, Belgium, and Romania). Many of the major museums and archives related to Jewish or Holocaust history had very few or no diaries of young writers at all in their collections. Thus, my inquiries often were made as informal requests through Jewish or Holocaust survivor communities of these countries, or through letters to scholars, historians, and experts in the field. This kind of research more often yielded results, as diaries of young writers still seem to be predominantly held in private collections and known about through informal and local channels. I am certain that there is a great deal of original material still out there, and I am under no illusion that this work represents a complete or definitive study of young writers' diaries from this period. Rather, I wish to introduce this subject as one worthy of serious, continuing research, and I hope that in the years to come diaries of young writers will continue to surface and will be made available to scholars, historians, and the public.

In many cases, and thanks to the generosity of individuals and archives, it was possible to obtain copies of original handwritten diaries. Alternatively, I received typescripts or versions of diaries published in their original languages. Likewise, there were some cases in which it was impossible to obtain a complete copy of the diary; under these circumstances, I worked from publications of excerpts either in the original language or in translation. Finally, there were some survivors who were understandably reluctant to share their diaries with the public. In these cases, and with their permission, I have included information about the existence of the diary and the circumstances under which it was written even though I have not seen or read the text itself.

The second major phase involved translating the diaries from their native languages into English. Thanks to the generosity of individual and institutional donors whose financial support made such translations possible, I was able to assemble a team of translators to undertake this work, many of whom volunteered their time and expertise to review and summarize or informally translate diaries for my review. In this way, I was able to narrow down the body of material that I wished to have translated for the purposes of this work. While there is much that was translated into English for this project and not excerpted herein, because of the obvious limitations of space, there is also much that has not been fully translated into English. Just as I hope that diaries of young writers will continue to emerge, I also hope that in the future still more of this original material will be translated, studied, and made available to the public in English.

In the majority of cases, translations were made from a copy of the handwritten original diary; sometimes, however, translators worked from typescripts or copies of the text published in its original language. Only in the case of Klaus Langer's diary was the translation undertaken from a spoken audiotape of the diarist reading his text. This was due to the fragility of the original diary, which prohibited its being copied. Translators worked under my direction, endeavoring first and foremost to render an accurate text and simultaneously to make the text as readable as possible for an English-speaking audience. In a very few cases in which the writer's use of his or her native language was especially problematic, translators were asked to make the text as comprehensible and correct as possible without altering its meaning, sense, or fundamental character. In all cases in which the diarist or a surviving relative was willing or able to review the translation, it was checked, corrected, and approved. A few of the diaries excerpted herein are reprinted with the permission of the publisher from currently out-of-print English editions. Finally, a few diaries that had previously been translated into English by the writer of the diary or by a translator have been published in this volume for the first time. In all cases, I have included details about the source of the diary and translation in the section titled "Sources and Translators."

The third phase of the project involved choosing the diaries to be included in the book and editing them for publication. Given the extraordinary richness of the extant diaries, narrowing down those to be excerpted in this volume was among the most difficult tasks of all. I tried to choose the diaries based not only on their diversity of nationality, economic and social class, religious orientation, and wartime experience, but also with an eye toward the connections and relationships that existed between them. I also chose diaries that reflected varying writing styles and differing degrees of historical content. I did not want to create a falsely romanticized image of the historical significance or literary strengths of the body of material by choosing only the "best" diaries, but to provide a sample of the extant material that would begin to suggest the variations, complexities, and echoes that exist within the whole.

I organized the diaries in the collection according to the relationships that might be found among them and their logical connection to the larger history of the Holocaust. I did not choose to adopt a strictly chronological or geographical frame, as such an organizational structure tends to invite generalizations that are beyond the scope of this work. Multiple diaries from a particular ghetto, for example, may indeed reveal facets of daily life in the same place, but grouping them in this way is misleading as it seems to suggest that these diaries "represent" life in that ghetto. On the other hand, multiple diaries that echo various kinds of experiences—either by virtue of circumstances (such as life as refugees, in hiding or passing as non-Jews, or in ghettos) or when they were written (early in the war or near the liberation), or the particular orientation or focus of the diary—are often placed together as they make evident both what is shared and what is distinct among them.

The amount of material available necessitated the editing of most diaries, with the exception of a few that were so short and fragmentary that they could be reprinted in their entirety. When editing was necessary, I tried to retain the shape of each diary, pruning entries and shortening the whole without fundamentally altering its character. If I eliminated an entire entry or series of entries, there is no indication unless a note was needed to explicate a break in the text. My edits within entries are indicated by bracketed ellipses, to distinguish them from ellipses in the original diaries. Many diarists were fluent in multiple languages and laced their diaries with expressions and phrases from languages other than the primary one in which they wrote. In order to retain the flavor of the original as much as possible, I generally preserved such expressions in the language used by the diarist and added an English translation in brackets. Finally, I usually retained the punctuation and paragraphing of the original, unless it was necessary or useful to modify it for the sake of clarity.

Each diary is preceded by an introduction that includes biographical information about the diarist, its historical context, and a study of the text itself and its relevance in the context of Holocaust history or literature. For this reason, I did not heavily annotate the diaries themselves. Still, since diaries are filled with references to people, places, and events ranging from the personal to the local to the highly public, it was on occasion necessary to include essential or especially interesting information in brackets or in the endnotes. On the other hand, an unfortunate reality of working with this material is that much information is lost forever. In some cases, I was not able to establish the identities of people mentioned in the diaries, nor was I always able to clarify references to events. This missing information, and the frustration or confusion that it sometimes causes, should be understood as an inevitable result of encountering fragmentary remains from genocide.

Appendix I gives brief descriptions of the known extant diaries by young writers. Each entry summarizes what is known of the biographical facts about the diarist, the circumstances under which the diary was written, and the fate of the writer. Most significant, I hope, for research and further scholarship, I have wherever possible included information about the various versions of the diary, including the location of the original manuscript, typescripts, and duplicate versions on paper or microfilm in archival collections; and English or foreign-language editions of the diary. Because some of the better-known diaries have been reprinted in excerpts in several publications, I have not included a complete list of such reprintings but have indicated only major English or foreign-language publications. These lists should serve as a solid starting place for researchers who wish to pursue the subject.

Finally, Appendix II describes a number of works at the margins of the material included here. This includes diary-memoirs, postwar "diaries," rewritten "diaries," and the like; letters and other prose written by youngsters of the time; diaries written by non-Jewish victims of the war and Nazism; and diaries written by young adults in their twenties. This study was intended not only to briefly examine the many related materials that surfaced during my research, but also to explicate the terms by which I defined the subject matter—that is, diaries as compared to memoirs, the Holocaust as compared to World War II, and young writers as compared to adults—and to explore the rich and complicated questions that such distinctions raise.

Notes to the Second Edition

Given changes in typesetting technology between the first and second editions, it was not possible to correct mistakes or incorporate updated information directly into the text. Instead, corrections and updates are listed here.

KLAUS LANGER

"Aid to Jewish Youth" should be translated as Youth Aliyah, the organization formed by Henrietta Szolt to train Jewish youngsters for life on a kibbutz and to rescue them from Nazi persecution by sending them to safety in Palestine.

ELISABETH KAUFMANN

Peter Kaufmann was held in the French internment camp of Meslay-du-Maine.

Elizabeth and Ernst Koenig were married for just over fifty-five years. Elizabeth died in 2003, and Ernst passed away in 2005.

PETER FEIGL

Daniel Trocmé was the nephew of Pastor Andre Trocmé.

"Sec. Suisse" should be translated as Secours Suisse aux Enfants, which was a Swiss aid organization for refugee children.

OTTO WOLF

In 2010, Felicitas Garda donated the original diary to the United States Holocaust Memorial Museum in Washington, D.C. She died in 2006, and Thomas Mandl passed away in 2007.

Salvaged Pages

Introduction

During the Holocaust, from one end of Europe to the other, from before the outbreak of war until the liberation, young people kept journals and diaries. They wrote in leather or clothbound books, or in albums embossed in gold that had been received as gifts for birthdays and holidays; they carried their journals with them from their homes to hiding places, from transit camps to ghettos. When times grew difficult, they smuggled and stole scraps of paper, found pencil stubs and worn ink pens; they scribbled by carbide lamp or candlelight in school notebooks, address books, calendars, and ledgers, on the backs of cheap paper notices and thin brown bags, and in the margins of the published works of other authors. Despite fear and repression, despite hunger, cold, exhaustion, and despair, despite crowded living spaces and a lack of privacy, and despite separation from home and loved ones, young people documented their experiences and their impressions of their lives, and in so doing marked their places in the world.

As the world knows, one of these diaries surfaced in the late 1940s in Europe. Anne Frank's diary, written while the author was in hiding in an attic in Amsterdam, was as evocative and poignant as any historical fragment could be; like an ancient artifact, it had survived the passage of time and the destruction of almost everything related to it to testify to a moment in the past. When on August 4, 1944, the Frank family was arrested in their hiding place at 263 Prinsengracht in Amsterdam, the diary, containing the record Anne had kept for just over two years, was among the belongings left behind. It was only after Anne's father, Otto Frank (the only survivor among the eight who had been in hiding together), returned to Holland in June 1945 that the diary was unearthed and given to him.[1]

Less than two years later, in March 1947, the first edition of Anne Frank's *Diary of a Young Girl* was published in Holland. An edition in French followed in the spring of 1950. That summer, the American writer Meyer Levin read the French edition of the *Diary* and immediately recognized its tremendous power. Levin, who had been in Europe in 1944–45 reporting on the liberation of the concentration camps, had returned to the States with a passionate moral imperative to communicate to the world the horror he had witnessed. He came to believe that "someday a teller would arise from amongst themselves" to recount the story of the genocide of European Jewry. This teller had to be someone who had been there, who had endured the unimaginable, and who could thus form the words that the rest of the world might hear. When he read Anne Frank's *Diary* in 1950, he felt that the search for a "teller" was over. It was she who would testify to the events of the Holocaust for the millions who had not left records, who had not been able to speak.[2]

In fact, Levin sought more than just a teller of a story; he sought a way to make that horrific story comprehensible, to make meaning from the senseless. This broader impulse was reflected in his review of Anne Frank's *Diary,* which appeared on the first page of the *New York Times Book Review* on June 15, 1952, the day before the book was released in America. Both the review and the *Diary* instantly captured the American imagination. As the scholar Lawrence Graver put it, "afterward nearly everyone agreed that Levin's tribute in the *Times* was what launched *Anne Frank: The Diary of a Young Girl* on its spectacular career in America." Indeed, the *Diary* was sold out by the following afternoon, and two successive printings brought the number of copies to forty-five thousand within the very first week of its publication.[3]

Since the discovery of Anne Frank's diary, more than fifty-five diaries of young writers have emerged from all corners of Europe, written in various languages, reflecting a wide range of wartime experiences. These fragmentary remains are the subject of this work. Still, the diaries themselves require a prelude, for the popular perception of Anne Frank's *Diary* necessarily influences any reading of diaries that share the genre that she defined, created, and perfected. And perhaps the clearest point of origin for this now tangled and deeply embedded collection of perceptions, assumptions, and impressions is Meyer Levin's *New York Times* review. For in it Levin did much more than just introduce his "teller" to America; he gave his audience its first language about why the diary mattered for the girl herself, for her lost generation, and for humanity.

In his review, Levin drew on the common perception of diaries as repositories of the writer's personal thoughts and ideas, confided privately and without pretense, and committed on paper spontaneously, without revision or artifice. He emphasized the diary's personal content, highlighting Anne's thoughtful analysis of her character and personality, her reflections on her relationships with her family, her confessions of her developing sexuality and first love, and her meditations on her own coming of age. Likewise, he acknowledged the private quality of the diary, calling it "tenderly intimate" and a "stirring confession." Finally, "because the diary was not written in retrospect, it contains the trembling life of every moment," he wrote; its very spontaneity made it seem "so wondrously alive, so near."

Levin linked the attributes of the diary to its larger significance for Anne Frank herself. Unlike a photo, an article of clothing or a toy, a document or a letter, the diary—personal in its content, private in its intent, and spontaneous in its form—was a reflection of Anne Frank's own self. It was as if the diary captured something ineffable about the writer—her voice or her spirit, perhaps—and by reading it, we could come to know her. Through it, "one feels the presence of this child-becoming-woman as warmly as though she were snuggled on a near-by sofa."

But most important, Levin linked the diary's poignancy and power as an evocation of Anne Frank's self to a more transcendent meaning for her fate. While acknowledging the tragedy of Anne Frank's young life, he saw a ray of hope that shone through the desolation. For though Anne Frank had perished in the Holocaust, the survival of her diary could guarantee the symbolic survival of the writer herself. "There is anguish in the thought of how much creative power, how much sheer beauty of living, was cut off through genocide," Levin concluded. "But through her diary, Anne goes on living. From Holland to France, to Italy, Spain. The Germans too have published her book. And now she comes to America."

The significance of the diary did not end with its relevance for Anne Frank. She was, in Levin's words, "a born writer" whose literary talents allowed her not only to express her own thoughts and feelings, but also to reach beyond the narrow specificity of her own story. In this, Anne's voice was literally "resonant" in two distinct ways; first, she eloquently captured in her diary the universal experience of coming of age. "Little Anne Frank," Levin wrote, was "spirited, moody, witty, self-doubting, [and] succeeded in communicating in virtually perfect, or classic, form the drama of puberty." Second, her account of her own imprisonment and its punishing nature gave voice to the fear, loneliness, insecurity, longing, restlessness, desire, curiosity, and pain of all those who were oppressed like her. So much so, Levin asserted, that "Anne Frank's diary succeeds better than [novelist John Hersey's] *The Wall* in bringing us an understanding of life under threat." In this, the specific selfhood of Anne Frank—as a young person coming of age, and as a victim of unwarranted persecution—was linked to the millions of young people who shared similar experiences but had ostensibly not left records behind.

Levin thus saw her voice as the potent echo of all those of her generation who had suffered and perished. The attributes of her diary captured parts of her self, and through reading it we could come to know the girl, and she could "live on"; in a similar way, her writing was so evocative that she could actually speak for other young victims, and could symbolically stand in for the missing, and hold their places. In turn, we could hold them in our memories, just as we held her, overcoming abstractly the annihilation that was their fate. "Anne Frank's voice becomes the voice of six million vanished souls," Levin wrote.

As Levin presented it, the importance of the diary reached even beyond its relevance for Anne Frank herself and its significance for her generation. The young writer spoke not only to the circumstances of her own life, and by extension to the experiences of those like her, but in one extraordinary line she voiced a still broader reflection on humanity itself. Toward the end of his review, Levin quoted this by-now famous passage: "in spite of everything, I still believe that people are really good at heart." This trusting and beneficent sentiment was a prelude to Levin's final salvo, his summation of the meaning of Anne Frank's diary for humanity. For while there were many exceptional things about Anne Frank (her humor, her cleverness, her insight, her honesty, and her gift for writing), none were more meaningful and lasting than her perennial hopefulness and her conviction in the essential, fundamental goodness of humanity. "Surely she will be widely loved," he concluded, "for this wise and wonderful young girl brings back a poignant delight in the infinite human spirit."

The very existence of Anne Frank's diary—a document written by an innocent young girl oppressed, imprisoned, hunted, and ultimately murdered under the authority of the government of a modern nation—had by definition implied a dark and frightening question about the nature of humankind. But, for Levin, her belief in the goodness of humanity could be read as a hopeful, encouraging answer. As Levin framed it, her reflection spoke not only for her but for us as well, restoring *our* hope and reminding us of a "human spirit" that forgives, that believes in good, and that remains triumphant and victorious over evil. She thus gave herself—and, more important, the reader—an existential position to occupy, one all the more uncontestable as it was uttered by the most innocent and tragic of victims, not an adult, but a child, and not a survivor but an unwilling martyr.

Much has been made of how aptly Levin's review reflected the culture of the 1950s that gave rise to it. Indeed, its optimistic and positive spin is easy to dismiss as hopelessly transparent and out of date. But the seemingly obvious language of the review belies the alluring power of the ideas he presented. In the review, Levin built a relationship between the concrete qualities of the *Diary* and the symbolic meaning he assigned to it. His ideas were not vague generalizations or abstract notions applied to a text that could not support them. To the contrary, he sought and found in Anne Frank's death and in the survival of her diary the attributes, qualities, and passages that could bolster his assertions about its meaning for the writer, for her generation, and for humanity. Rooted in the facts of her life and death, and grounded in Anne Frank's own writing, Levin's ideas were not only compelling, they were persuasive, credible, and convincing.

It is not surprising, then, that variants of Levin's original ideas—that the survival of Anne Frank's diary could speak for the writer, represent her generation, and rekindle hope in humanity—pervaded mainstream discourse about the *Diary* in the 1950s and beyond. Over time, the specificity of Levin's assertions grew increasingly diffuse, diverging from a direct relationship to the diary's content to a generalized sense about it. But though the ideas became divorced from their origins, the impression of Anne Frank's diary as a hopeful testament remained, influencing the creation of the 1955 Broadway play that catapulted Anne Frank to stardom, and in turn shaped the way millions of audience members thought of the diary, the writer, and the Holocaust itself. Indeed, as Lawrence Graver put it, "Most theater-goers adored the Goodrich and Hackett *Diary* because they felt it transformed horror into something consolatory, inspirational, and even purgatorial: the characters may have been doomed, but the play was full of hope, energy, humor, lyricism, and 'ineradicable life.'"[4]

It would be overly simplistic to place too much weight on the significance of Levin's review. Although it was surely one central element, there was a confluence of factors—the nature of Anne Frank, the potency of her text, the temperament of the audience, and the culture of the era itself—that contributed to the fame of the *Diary* and to the way it was understood. Still, its main importance is that it provided the readers of Anne Frank's diary with a construct for approaching the Holocaust. Ultimately, though the review was forgotten, its message—a terrible tragedy occurred, *but* something positive and hopeful could be gleaned from it and celebrated despite it—was repeated again and again, in endless permutations of Anne Frank's story over the decades to come.

Echoes of this antithetical and paradoxical understanding that gleans hope from desolation, good from evil, and celebration from tragedy have reverberated throughout the published diaries of young writers who perished in the Holocaust just as Anne Frank did.[5] But more and more the assertions floated away from their original relationship to the diary; no longer tied to the text, they became a series of absolute truths about what any such diary would mean, regardless of its attributes, the literary talent of the writer, or its content. Thus, it no longer mattered whether the diary reflected the internal life of the writer, whether the writer spoke to circumstances or truths larger than his or her own experience, and whether the diarist expressed hope for humanity. Indeed, many writers who introduced diaries of other murdered children no longer sought meaning from what was *in* the text at all, but simply applied the familiar frame of Anne Frank's diary to each new one that surfaced.

Thus, the survival of a diary written by a young person who perished has come to be the symbolic equivalent of that writer's survival. "Come, meet David, Moshe, Yitzhak, Éva and Anne," wrote Patricia McKissack in the foreword to the children's book *We Are Witnesses*. The diary of Ruthka Lieblich, we are told, "remains a living monument" to its writer. And Louise Jacobson's letters, written in the French prison of Fresnes and the Drancy transit camp, "allow their readers to witness the resurrection of Louise," wrote Serge Klarsfeld in his preface to the published volume. "As soon as one reads her, she vanquishes death and overcomes time."[6]

On the next larger scale, the existence of a diary speaks not only for its writer but for the millions of young people who perished. The diary of Dawid Rubinowicz "speaks for the thousands, indeed millions, of his Jewish contemporaries," according to its introduction. In his book for young readers about children's diaries of the Holocaust, Jacob Boas wrote, "The diaries of the Jewish teenagers spell out the anguish of an entire generation." Serge Klarsfeld said of Louise Jacobson: "Louise, murdered, has remained young forever, example and representative of all those who were her age and who were murdered as she was. Louise speaks, testifies, and lives for all of them." And Ruthka Lieblich's diary is described as "the voice not only of Ruthka, but of a million and a half Jewish children who perished."[7]

Finally, the existence of a diary not only speaks for the writer and his or her generation, it reaffirms the triumphant human spirit that transcends all evil. On the jacket cover of Laurel Holliday's *Children in the Holocaust and World War II*, we are told that the diarists' "voices and their vision ennoble us all." Likewise, the jacket cover of *We Are Witnesses* reads, "we see the largest truth [the diarists] left for us: Hitler could kill millions, but he could not destroy the human spirit. These stark accounts of how five young people faced the worst of human evil are a testament, and an inspiration, to the best in the human soul." In the introduction to Dawid Rubinowicz's diary, Derek Bowman wrote, "Although the reader is saddened to see an innocent young life subjected to such repeated atrocities, only to be cut short so soon, he is again and again impressed by the moral caliber of the diarist: this terse account bears lasting witness to the nobility of the human spirit in the face of man's inhumanity." In Moshe Flinker's long out-of-print diary, the introducer shares a similar sentiment: "The final impression is not of tragedy or despair but of the transcendence of the human spirit and the eternity of the Jewish message."[8]

One may be tempted to dismiss these passages as marginal, for they are printed in the pages of diaries that barely flickered on the popular scene before going out of print and disappearing in used bookstores and libraries. Still, they reflect the paradigm by which the Holocaust has been presented in America, despite the fact that such a framework obscures the irrevocable atrocity of genocide by applying to it a hopeful veneer. Indeed, even as late as 1991, in the "definitive edition" of Anne Frank's *Diary* (with differences in the sophistication of the form if not in the essence of the content), her work "continues to bring to life this young woman"; she "emerges more human . . . than ever"; and her diary "remains a beloved and deeply admired testament to the indestructible nature of the human spirit."

That Meyer Levin and others of his generation saw Anne Frank's *Diary* as a lone testimony emerging from the decimation of the Jewish communities of Europe is understandable. That he and others read into it what they wished it to be is likewise comprehensible. Still, it is plain that Meyer Levin saw Anne Frank's *Diary* not as a document that could shed light on a facet of the history of the Holocaust but as a symbol, capable by its intimacy of rescuing the girl; by the resonance of her voice, rescuing her generation; and, by its seemingly dominant theme of hope for humanity, rescuing all of us in the process.

Even as new fragments emerged, other writers throughout the intervening decades continued to apply the same frame to each new diary, suggesting that Levin's ideas cannot be so quickly written off as products of the 1950s. Nor can they be exclusively ascribed to the fact that the fragment in question was a diary, which because it is the work of a single hand lends itself to such fantasies of rescue. For while Levin's *words* may reflect the culture and the style of the 1950s, his idea that something positive can, indeed must, be found in the tragic remains of the past touched a more universal chord. It was not only a compelling notion, it was an appropriate antidote to the disgust and despair that comes with confronting genocide. Indeed, it was the fact that these fragments emerged from genocide—from an era of which we are ashamed rather than proud—that was perhaps the most relevant factor in shaping the way these diaries have been framed over time. For it is genocide itself—that unspeakable damage caused by human beings to humanity, and the shame that comes with it—that stirred the impulse to try in whatever way possible to rectify the damage, to see in what we do in the present a way to undo what was done in the past.

Many critics, writers, historians, and scholars have examined the American popular understanding of the Holocaust as it was defined by Anne Frank's *Diary* (and the Broadway play) and have explained, critiqued, and deconstructed those notions in their work. Many have made much broader arguments that attack the clichés and comforting fictions that have for so long been applied to the study of the Holocaust in mainstream books, films, educational materials, and the like. Their works have in many cases served as a foundation for the ideas developed in this introduction.[9]

Still, the pervasiveness of these ideas in the mainstream, especially throughout the permutations of Anne Frank's *Diary* and others like it, suggests how difficult it would be to approach the diaries in this book without those assumptions and how tempting it would be to automatically apply them to this material. It is not enough, then, to continue to accumulate and publish new diaries written by young people during the Holocaust without reexamining the conventions that have for so long been associated with them. Although publishing more diaries may seem to move the dialogue forward by suggesting that Anne Frank wasn't the only writer and that young people all over Europe kept diaries, the meaning we glean from them remains locked in a consolatory mold that obscures rather than elucidates what they contribute to our understanding of the Holocaust.

Although many diaries can give the tempting illusion that the reader is in the presence of the writer—because they are written in the first person, and are often intimate in tone and spontaneous in form—it is unfortunately not so. Whether personal or not, private or public, spontaneous or crafted, the content of the diary does not allow us to come to know the writer, its survival does not permit a deceased diarist to "live on," nor does its existence confer literary immortality upon the person who penned it. Being at best only a few hundred pages of the writings of a young person, each diary can be only a fragmentary work of the writer's hand. And a collection of pages written over a few months or years—no matter how intensely personal, confidential, or immediate—can be little more than a pale shadow, a wretched fragment from which to try to capture the immeasurable complexity, likes, dislikes, dreams, wishes, desires, contradictions, and stories that compose a whole, complete person.

Indeed, the tragedy of a diary that survives its writer is not that we can read the text, come to know the writer in some concrete or abstract way, and grieve his or her death. Instead, the tragedy is that no surviving fragment of genocide can reconstruct the person who created it; and that once dead, a person can never be known again. The essence in confronting the diaries in this book, then, is exactly *not* to confuse the reading of them with the rescue of individual lives, even symbolically, but to allow them to be seen as the partial records that they are; and to contemplate at one and the same time what is before us and what is lost and unrecoverable.

In the same vein, though many diarists expressed compelling, evocative, and poignant reflections that reach beyond their own particular circumstances, no collection of their words can speak for those who did not write or whose writings are lost. Just as an individual diary is only a fragment left from the life of the writer, a surviving group of diaries—no matter how rich, eloquent, powerful, or historically relevant, no matter how aptly they capture a remote and foreign aspect of the Holocaust or a seemingly universal one—is but a set of fragments from a generation that lived, endured, and ultimately perished. Seen in this context, the surviving diaries must not be imagined as symbolic stand-ins for the vanished children. Instead, they must be seen for what they are—a few extant records stranded in a sea of missing material—evoking but surely not representing the vast, uncountable, incalculable loss.

Finally, though many diarists expressed hope at one time or another in their diaries, the words they wrote do not give us, as readers, final answers to the questions we must ask ourselves after genocide. While all their words—positive and negative, hopeful and despairing, encouraged and resigned—give rise to meditation about what they endured, it is unfortunately up to us to assess this past in the full context of history, judging humanity's crimes by a critical review of the past, not by the would-be absolution or the condemnation of its victims. And though it is tempting to find in the survival of these diaries a core that transcends the evil that gave rise to them, they nevertheless do not redeem humanity for that evil, nor do they celebrate a vaguely articulated "human spirit," which is slanted to include only the saints and not the sinners.

There are many fragments from history that can be regarded as evidence of humanity's achievements and its progress; these diaries unfortunately do not fall into that category. For they were not created in celebration of beauty or in praise of progress but were produced in response to an overwhelming evil that threatened to engulf their writers. No praise for the writer of a diary can undo the fact that the task was undertaken in the context of annihilation, and that the diary is a cry to hold on to a place in the world in the face of erasure. No celebration of the courage or grace of the writer's gesture can cover up the human fallibility and frailty that is captured within the diary's pages. And no glorification of the diary (as the vehicle by which we are reminded of the "noble," "triumphant," and "indestructible" human spirit that we, by implication, share with the diarist) can alter what these diaries represent. At best, for the survivors, they are a record of years denied; at worst, for the perished, they are all that is left from a single life that ended in brutality. It is fair to allow the historical fragments that represent humanity's greatest successes to be treasured and cherished; it is also only fair to allow the remnants from genocide to serve not as a consolation or a comfort, but as a censure and a warning.

If the habits and platitudes of the past fall away, if we outgrow them and reject them, they must be replaced by something else. For the purpose of this work is not to apply a nihilistic frame to these diaries, suggesting that because they do not rescue lives, speak for the lost, or redeem humanity, they mean nothing and have no value. Nor would it be enough to deconstruct the familiar ways in which we have been taught to consider this material without looking to the fragments themselves to help us construct a new frame.

In this, we must cease to treat these fragments—because they come from genocide—as qualitatively and fundamentally different from all the other remains of the past. The study of history always begins with fragments. Buildings crumble; frescoes and paintings fade and crack; objects break apart and their pieces are scattered; documents are lost, found, and lost again; and the ephemera of daily life vanishes, leaving only those remnants that happen to survive. The pieces may be recovered intact or in parts; they may come from eras and places about which we are able to construct a great deal or only a little. Time and fate play their part in this; ancient civilizations and their cities have almost vanished or have been reduced to small fragments, their pots, paintings, scrolls, or utensils destined to be examined divorced from their original context. Other civilizations left more substantial traces; the tombs of the Egyptian pharaohs, or the remnants of Pompeii and Herculaneum, held their mysteries intact, though the world that gave rise to them had long since disappeared. And artifacts, documents, and images remain from more recent places in time—Florence and Siena during the early Renaissance, London during the Victorian Age, or New York during the Great Depression—which, though they reflect more familiar languages and more recognizable cultures, are not without their own puzzles and enigmas.

These diaries, then, are broken and unfinished fragments from the Holocaust. Not imbued with special gifts, overlaid with precious attributes, or assigned a sacred role, they belong to the vast body of historical fragments that testify to our collective past. And, like a fragment of an ancient pot that we may turn over in our hands to admire for its beauty, to examine for its clues as to the past, and to ponder for its suggestion of the passage of time and an era, these diaries are replete with their own information and potency. Each reflecting specific circumstances and each with its own measure of fact, truth, or insight, these diaries nevertheless make their contribution to an understanding of the history of the Holocaust.

It is worth noting that this kind of contribution is one for which adult diarists of the Holocaust are widely recognized. While adults' diaries have long been depended upon to yield useful information about the Holocaust as it was recorded at the time, the diaries of children have been reduced to rescuers of meaning or evokers of emotion rather than repositories of information. This misguided perspective equates these diaries with accidental fragments, like baby shoes or dolls, whose power is symbolic, rather than acknowledging them for the intentional records that they are and the literal contributions they make to an understanding of daily life during the Holocaust.

It is also worth noting that this is a framework that applies to all the fragments—those written by children who perished *and* by those who survived. For the habitual way in which we have spoken about these diaries as symbols is, paradoxically, a narrow frame, applying only to the deceased. It would not make sense, for example, to suggest that a diary written during the Holocaust stands in for or speaks for a person who survived and went on to live a life after the Holocaust. Nor would it follow that such a diary represents the millions who perished. Nor would it be assumed that the diary reflects the "triumph of the human spirit" if the survivor did not him or herself choose to assign that value to the diary (which almost none of them did). Indeed, attaching this redemptive meaning to the diary makes sense only if the diarist perished, and thus is a perennial victim in need of rescue. And in that case, what do the diaries of the survivors signify and reveal? Certainly we cannot apply different standards to the same kinds of fragments, depending on whether the writer lived or died. It implies once again that the value we have traditionally placed on them does not stem from what they actually describe, recount, or suggest, but that it grows from what we wish or want them to be.

Like any assembly of historical fragments, the diaries that have emerged thus far represent a range of literary quality, historical significance, evocative power, and compelling interest. To fail to recognize that fact and to refrain from interpreting and judging them based on what they yield would be to simply romanticize and glorify these diaries in a different way. Still, the framework of this book makes room for all of them, whether they were written by children who perished or children who survived, by great writers or mediocre ones, by those who limited their diaries to their internal lives and those who turned their gaze to the wider persecution of their communities and people, by those who expressed hope for humanity and those who condemned it.

The diaries in this collection, then, are treated as historical fragments that shed light on aspects of the Holocaust as it was lived by individual young writers. It endeavors to include a wide range of writers, whose social, cultural, and religious backgrounds and whose wartime experiences reflect a multiplicity of perspectives. Likewise, it includes diaries that echo one another by virtue of content, background, or circumstance, providing a nuanced rather than monolithic understanding of the experiences they recount. And it includes a variety of writings, with the implicit understanding that some writers were more talented in their craft than others, but that even those whose diaries may not be defined by their literary brilliance may contribute something to an understanding of this history.

The introductions to the diaries excerpted in this collection, therefore, do not address them as symbolic evocations of their writers, but as remnants that have survived to testify to a moment, an experience, a feeling, or an idea in the context of the European genocide of the Jews. The introductions focus on what the diary may reveal, whether it touches on a current of experience that was shared by many—hunger, deprivation, or loss, for example—or whether it is specific, such as an account of daily life in a particular ghetto or hiding place, or a description of the outbreak of war or the liberation. This approach seeks to construct a different frame—diaries as historical fragments instead of diaries as rescuers of lives—and apply it to a real, concrete body of material that may move both our knowledge *and* our interpretation forward, allowing us to see and experience these diaries in a new way.

In the end, these fragments stand, but surely not to rescue individual writers from death, to rescue a generation from oblivion, or to rescue ourselves from confrontation with the final, disconsolate truth of genocide. To the contrary, at its most pragmatic, each diary fits into the stream of history, constituting a more or less valuable, more or less lyrical, but nonetheless valid contribution to the historical and literary record of the Holocaust. At its most evocative, each diary not only suggests all that was lost for the individual, and for his or her missing generation, but also stands as a mark of the writer's place in the world, a gesture undertaken against obliteration. Still, even that is thin and faded as a silver lining. As Primo Levi wrote of his friend Sandro, who was killed during the Holocaust and whom he tried to characterize in his book *The Periodic Table:* "Today I know that it is a hopeless task to try to dress a man in words, make him live again on the printed page, especially a man like Sandro. He was not the sort of person you can tell stories about, nor to whom one erects monuments—he laughed at all monuments: he lived completely in his deeds, and when they were over nothing of him remains— nothing but words, precisely."[10]

1

Klaus Langer

E S S E N ,   G E R M A N Y

Klaus (later Jacob) Langer was born on April 12, 1924, in the city of Gleiwitz, in Upper Silesia, which at that time was part of Germany. His father, Erich, had also been born in Gleiwitz; his mother, Rose, was born in Odessa and emigrated to Germany in 1912, where she and Erich Langer married in 1922. Klaus's grandmother, Mina, joined the family in 1927, when he was three years old. After successive moves from Gleiwitz to Wiesbaden, then to a small town near Gelsenkirchen, the family settled in Essen in 1936.[1]

Klaus began his diary in his native German shortly after his bar mitzvah in March 1937. According to the author, the first part of the journal consists mostly of descriptions of the family's apartment, his aquarium, books, and notes about friends, "hopeless loves to girls," and the like.[2] It was not until 1938 that he began reporting consistently on the political situation in Germany and its effect on him and his family. The segment of the diary included here opens in April 1938, at about the time Klaus turned fourteen years old. The early part of the diary shows that life was relatively normal for him—he was still attending school, was part of a Zionist youth group, and was living at home with his parents and grandmother as he always had done. Despite signs of instability—the emigration of many of his Jewish friends and the occasional restrictions against Jews (closing of Jewish-owned businesses and prohibitions against Jews attending the public pool)—the Langers were still living in a relatively recognizable world.

Much of the early part of Klaus's diary was devoted to recounting the events, activities, and discussions held in the Zionist youth group of which he was a part.

He participated in Maccabee Hazair, which together with Hashomer Hazair and Habonim constituted the predominant Zionist youth groups in Germany. Although there were political differences among these groups, they all shared the same basic goal of promoting interest in Jewish matters and encouraging emigration to Jewish settlements in Palestine. Indeed, like many students of his generation, Klaus sought shelter in the security of the youth group in part as a response to the growing hostility around him.[3] Group meetings focused largely on discussions, often oriented toward distinctly modern and nontraditional topics, among them Zionism, assimilation, anatomy, modesty, and sex. Most central to the movement, however, was preparation for emigration to Palestine. Because life there was geared toward building Jewish settlements, there was an emphasis on outdoor activities, nature, and, above all, communal existence and agricultural and manual labor.

Klaus's involvement in the Zionist youth movement gave rise to a faint but unmistakable tension with his father that emerges in the diary. Klaus's family was an archetypal German Jewish one, having had a long history of residence in Germany. His father had fought on the French front in World War I, joining the German army as a volunteer in 1915. After the war, he went on to become a judge in the German court system. Like many German Jews of that generation, he and his family were nationally, culturally, and socially embedded in mainstream German civilization. For Erich Langer in particular, who had successfully assimilated into German society, the culture of the Zionist youth movement was diametrically opposed to everything he envisioned for his son. Life as a pioneer among Jews in an underdeveloped country, living in communal dwellings and performing physical labor, was seen as a step backward, a loss of the very entitlements he had struggled so hard to achieve. It was for this reason that he was reluctant to allow Klaus to immerse himself in the youth group, and only permitted him to attend meetings if he did not neglect his studies and his music.

Klaus's relatively normal life came to a crushing halt with Kristallnacht, the Nazi attack on synagogues, homes, businesses, and private property of Jews in cities throughout Germany and Austria on November 9–10, 1938. It was a dramatic turning point in the history of Germany's Jews, a shocking display of violence in which the property of Jews was destroyed, their synagogues burned, and their businesses vandalized. Klaus's longest and most detailed diary entry is about this event; he documented the damage to home and property and the fear, sleeplessness, and chaos of those days. The famous Essen synagogue and the Jewish youth center were both destroyed. Thirty thousand Jewish men throughout Germany were arrested by the Nazis during this pogrom.[4] As Klaus recorded in his diary, his father was among those arrested in Essen.

Kristallnacht, for the Langer family as for many German Jews, signaled the severity of the situation as no previous passage of laws or decrees had done. The gradual escalation of restrictions, humiliations, and exclusions had culminated in an unexpected and drastic pogrom reminiscent of those perpetrated on Jews in the Middle Ages. Further, a new onslaught of decrees followed Kristallnacht, almost completely limiting the movement and freedoms of Germany's Jews. Among them were the orders expelling all Jewish children from German schools and banning Jewish youth group activities.

For the Langer family, Kristallnacht served as a powerful catalyst for emigration. Ultimately, this is the main subject of the diary—emigration itself—and the family's increasingly desperate efforts to get out. "I can sing a song on that subject," Klaus wrote dryly on January 14, 1939. His diary entries reveal the overwhelming difficulties and bureaucratic mazes that faced those trying to flee. The Langers tried to find safe passage to Chile, India, Palestine, Holland, the United States, the Dominican Republic, Peru, Uruguay, Shanghai, Argentina, and England; each try was met with evasions, further requirements, or outright refusals. Further, Klaus listed in his diary the various "paper walls"—personal papers, physical exams, travel documentation, employment assurances, visas, affidavits, and letters of credit—that made emigration virtually impossible.

Klaus's diary captured the excruciating recurring cycle that plagued would-be emigrants. It began with a hopeful lead, the frantic gathering of materials, promises, assurances, packing, and then, ultimately, seemingly inevitably, the plan would collapse, undermined by a technical detail or a missed deadline. Klaus's diary entries, filled as they are with requirements, regulations, and restrictions, seem to mirror the confusion and bureaucratic entanglements of the process itself. His personal story typified that of hundreds of thousands of German Jews who were faced with the fact that throughout the 1930s, few European countries eased quotas, lifted restrictions, or simplified existing procedures to allow for Jewish emigration. As a result, many families who were willing to emigrate found that they had nowhere to go.[5] This failure on the part of the European nations and the Americas, including the United States, resulted in the entrapment of hundreds of thousands of families in Germany. Beginning in the fall of 1941, these individuals and families were deported to ghettos and concentration camps in the German-occupied Eastern territories.

While much of the diary is filled with the pragmatic details of the Langers' search for a safe haven, there are traces in the diary that reveal a still deeper issue that also lay at the root of the emigration process. Beyond how the Nazis approached the problem, how the European nations addressed it, or even how the individual families attempted to maneuver within the bureaucracy, there remained the question of how assimilated Jews like the Langers understood themselves and their place in the world, and consequently how quickly, efficiently, and aggressively they attempted to flee. In the case of the Langers, they deliberated over where they should go, weighing such matters as the transfer of Erich Langer's pension and the likelihood of finding work, rejecting potentially viable opportunities in their quest for the best choice. Further, there are subtle clues in the diary that suggest how difficult it was for the Langers to fully accept their altered circumstances and to comprehend the nature of the move that confronted them. In particular, Klaus on occasion seemed to view the matter of preparing for emigration as if he were moving to another country by choice, rather than fleeing for his life. Most notably, he calmly made preliminary arrangements to bring such impractical items as an old typewriter, his bicycle, his cello, and even the family's grand piano with him in exile.

These allusions, faint as they might be, suggest the depth of the Langers' ties to established German society. For even as they faced the once unthinkable question of leaving Germany and accepted the necessity of flight, that stubborn root—the image they had of themselves in the world—remained at least partially intact and entrenched. These last ties were not only a tragic illusion in the context of Nazi Germany but were, in some cases, another impediment to emigration itself, as people unwittingly delayed, deliberating over choices and exercising rights that were no longer theirs. The truth, which is easy to see in retrospect but was incomprehensible to many at the time, was that emigration was not a choice, it was an imperative—the last hope to escape unharmed as Germany unraveled, bringing the rest of Europe with it.

World War II broke out on September 1, 1939, when Germany invaded Poland. Ultimately, it was the Aid to Jewish Youth (Jüdische Jugendhilfe) that succeeding in getting Klaus, with a group of three hundred other Jewish youngsters, out of Germany on September 2, the day after the war began. The Danish Ministry of Justice allowed them to enter Denmark as a result of pressure from Danish women's groups, which were also busily recruiting Danish farm families to house the children temporarily.[6] Klaus wrote his first diary entry in Denmark on September 8, 1939, shortly after his arrival. In stark contrast to the erstwhile vision he had of bringing his bicycle, cello, and piano, Klaus found himself very much alone, with only the barest possessions. He had been abruptly separated from his parents and grandmother, none of whom he ever saw again. At age fifteen, he began a new life in exile.

In January 1940, Klaus and the other youths from the group left Copenhagen for Amsterdam and then traveled to Marseilles by train, and on to Beirut by boat. From there they took a bus to Haifa, arriving in Palestine after a journey of two weeks. Upon arrival he changed his name from Klaus to Jacob and ended his diary. His parents and grandmother were not able to emigrate from Germany. His mother died of blood poisoning on September 8, 1941, in Essen. His father was deported on April 21, 1942, to the Izbica Lubelska camp in the Lublin province of Poland. By the end of that year, the local Jews from Izbica and those who had been forced to settle there from other localities had been taken to the death camps at Belżec or Sobibór, or had been shot. Klaus's father was surely among them. His grandmother was sent to Terezín (Theresienstadt) on July 15, 1942, and only a few months later was deported to Minsk, where she perished.[7]

April 19, 1938

There was great excitement over the past few days since two of our comrades in the group, Paul [Rolman] and Lobi [Lother Bierhoff], left. There was still much to do and we spent much time together. On Saturday, Bambus, the former leader of the group, had one more meeting with us before the two departed. On Saturday, April 25, they left for Berlin to the Beit Maccabee in order to train for the emigration, but not in farming. Our group in the Bund [youth movement] now consisted of only six members. Fifi is sick at the moment. He had his appendix removed and is still in the hospital. Kumo [Kurt Mohr] was fired from his job and will probably attend a trade school, probably after the summer vacations. Kume's [Kurt Melchior] parents are going to emigrate to the U.S. and he obviously will go with them. Rotzig's [Wolfgang Rapp] parents also are thinking of emigrating to the U.S. Kume thinks that they will leave in October at the earliest. In Rotzig's case no date has been set. By Easter 1939 our group will be dissolved since Bobby [Ferse] and I want to make *aliyah* [emigration to Palestine]. Our group reached its maximum size a long time ago. We are now going downhill. Saturday a seminar was held. In the morning we studied Jewish history and the Maccabee movement. In the afternoon a physician talked about anatomy and first aid. Instead of listening we fooled around and drew pictures. At the end we sang a few songs.

April 26, 1938

On April 25, yesterday, it was two years that we have been living in this apartment. I hope that we shall remain for a long time. Bachrach, the owner of the house, had to close his store since such business under Jewish ownership no longer was permitted. Perhaps they will be able to hold a final sale; if not, they will fall on hard times. I have to work hard in school. I have to prepare myself well in Latin and have already started. I have kept my teachers.

May 9, 1938

Two more boys joined our group. [. . .] One is still quite immature, the other seems like a nice fellow, but he has problems getting to our meetings. A large *pegisha,* a large gathering, was held on May 8. Almost three hundred members attended from various cities. Our former leader, Hans Bloch, also came from Cologne. In the morning we had study groups and in the afternoon a long discussion about assimilation.

May 18, 1938

[. . .] The situation with Rotzig is still uncertain. His brother is going to America. His parents and he probably will follow. This will only leave Bobby and me from the original group. Since I am writing my diary at night and in bed, I always have to be on the lookout for my parents and often have to interrupt my entries. It looks like I shall be going to school until Easter 1939. I shall then enter some kind of agricultural institute. Hopefully that will lead to my making aliyah. My parents still don't know to which school they will send me.

July 10, 1938

Today we had a test on Jewish history, the youth movement, Zionism, and similar subjects. Now that I have passed the test it seems like a great weight was taken off me. There was a great deal of excitement and work over the past few days. I was busy every free minute with preparing for the test. Our total average was 62¾ points, which made us the best group in the Bund. The girls had only 62 points, which is just a little less than our average but we came out the winners.

September 8, 1938

I must say that we accomplished very little since Easter at our meetings and in our discussions. Aside from *sichot* [group meetings] that did not start on schedule, also, Horst terminated the meetings too early. Much time was spent on organizational matters and there were only a few political discussions. They only thing we accomplished was that all of us read Stefan Zweig's book *Brennendes Geheimnis* [The Burning Secret]. If it continues like this after the vacations, I am going to submit a complaint. I have considerable problems getting permission at home to go to the meetings.

We went to the pool a few times. After my cousin left, Bobby and I went with girls from the *Lehava* group to the pool. However, there was a sign saying that Jews were not desired. That meant that we no longer could go swimming. Bobby's mother consequently called a Jewish banker from Essen. Their house was in a large park with a private swimming pool. She asked permission for us to go swimming there, which the family granted. The girls from the *Lehava* group also went. The pool was located in a very pleasant part of the garden, surrounded by trees and bushes. [. . .] We had a lot of fun there and got along very well. I swam five hundred meters in about seventeen minutes. It was no great achievement but good enough for a start. We also practiced lifesaving and jumping into the pool. Once we had a team race, and once we even played polo, but that was very tiring.

One day I suddenly received an invitation from a friend who was one of Mother's violin students. The family invited me to come to Paderborn in Westphalia where an uncle had a house in a small village. I really did not feel like going but to be polite I accepted the invitation. I was gone for two weeks, which meant that I missed several meetings, for which I was very sorry.

November 11, 1938

The past three days brought significant changes in our lives. On November 7 a German legation member was assassinated in Paris. He died two days later. The day following, on November 10 [*sic*], came the consequences.[8] At three o'clock the synagogue and the Jewish youth center were put on fire. Then they began to destroy Jewish businesses. During the morning, private homes also were being de-molished. Fires were started at single homes belonging to Jews. At six-thirty in the morning the Gestapo came to our home and arrested Father and Mother [. . .] Mother returned after about one and a half hours. Dad remained and was put in prison. In the morning I went to the Ferse home. Bobby was at the synagogue and at the youth center in the morning and saw how they burned. Later we went to the day care center where the children had been brought from the community home, which they had to flee during the night.

We [. . .] returned to our neighborhood by two o'clock. Not far from us we saw a gang vandalizing a home, throwing things out of the window. When I went around the corner and looked up my street there was nothing to see. It looked peaceful. I, therefore, returned directly to our house. When I turned into the front yard I saw that the house was damaged. I walked on glass splinters. In the hallway I met Frau Baum, who lived upstairs. I ran into our apartment and found unbelievable destruction in every room. It was the same in the apartment of the caretaker below us. Mother and Grandmother were there. My parents' instru-ments were destroyed, the dishes were broken, the windows were broken, furni-ture upturned, the desk was turned over, drawers and mirrors were broken, and the radio smashed. The kitchen and the bathroom were untouched. The up-stairs room also was left alone, including my father's cello. The cellar also was not disturbed. The apartment of the caretaker, Bachrach, was in much worse condition.

In the evening, mother brought gold and other valuables for safekeeping to Christian acquaintances. We wanted to spend the night at home, but the care-taker, Frau Bachrach, urged us to go to her relatives, the Herzfelds, where we spent the night. I read until late. In the middle of the night, at 2:30 A.M., the Storm Troopers [Sturmabteilung, or SA, also known as the Brownshirts] smashed windows and threw stones against store shutters. After a few minutes they demanded to be let into the house. Allegedly they were looking for weapons. After they found no weapons they left. After that no one was able to go back to sleep. Everyone sat in one room. I tried but could not sleep. After a while I went back to where they were sitting and found they had dozed off. The time passed terribly slowly. Then we thought there was still another person in the house who was making noise. Finally, at 5 A.M. I saw a policeman outside who walked back and forth. I shall never forget that night.

The next day, rumor had it that children under sixteen years of age would also be arrested. I wanted to flee and ride my bicycle to Christian friends of my parents who lived in the Rhineland. Mother objected, however, and I remained at home, of course. The next night we all wanted to sleep at home, but we were too upset. At nine-thirty at night we went to the Kosmanns' where the gangsters had already been, that is, they had destroyed everything. We had calmed down somewhat and slept there quite well.

Books could be written about all that had happened and about which we now begin to learn more. But, I have to be careful. A new regulation was issued that the Jews in Germany had to pay one billion reichmarks for restitution. What for? For the damage the Nazis had done to the Jews in Germany. I shall return to that subject later. My room will stay as it is. I am not going to go to school as long as Dad is not at home. I now want to get to Erez Israel as quickly as possible, maybe with the first Youth Aliyah.[9] The plan for making aliyah was made some time ago. The Bund of course has come to a standstill. Its leaders were arrested.

November 16, 1938

A number of events occurred since my last entry. First, on November 15, I received a letter from school with an enclosed notice of dismissal. This became superfluous since that same day an order was issued that prohibited Jews from attending public schools. I did not realize at first that I no longer had to attend that awful school, with the "Heil Hitler" at the beginning and end of every lesson, with the boring algebra, the terrible Latin, the way the teachers talked. Each day that I did not have to attend school, I considered myself lucky. I was not in the least bit sorry.

The pupils were mostly acceptable, but they are not at the same level as I am. They were only interested in girls and talked mostly about sex. Musically, they were only interested in hits, nothing more. Their literary interests ran only to science fiction or bad movies. The youngest pupils played with small model cars of any type. So, I am free from those rascals, [. . .] free from that politicizing biology teacher who explained that Germany needs a high rate of birth because it will have to fight in the future against Russia. No more problems with grades. Of course, I could not have any interest in such a school.

Even though the boys in that school had to participate actively in the Hitler Youth they did not do so happily. When service in that organization became inconvenient their love for the fatherland subsided quickly. Such an environment is not one in which I could be comfortable. I was not a model student and once even received a 5 in my report card. I could have been a good and diligent student, but what happened, happened. I am no longer angry that I was thrown out of school; in fact I am happy at this turn of events, even if it is not quite right.

[. . .] Grandma and Mother went to the prison [to see Klaus's father] but were not allowed to enter. Meanwhile Bobby and I went to the Gestapo office and asked whether our Bund was outlawed. The answer was affirmative. We did not become intimidated, however, and since there was no lack of funds and things in the girls' group were going well, we met unofficially. [. . .] At the first meeting we played games and talked. Unfortunately, I missed the second meeting at which sexual matters were being discussed. Discussions between us and the girls, who were younger than we, became easier. At the third meeting we talked about kissing, and although it was something that should not be prohibited the general consensus was against it.

November 28, 1938

[. . .] The Jewish youth center building is still standing, albeit burned out. Even the steps leading upstairs were burned. The gym looks terrible. Half of the ceiling is hanging down. At first the police were there to guard the building, but later anyone could enter it. One evening, Rotzig, Bobby, and I went in. After we walked around a while we entered Sternberg's apartment. He was the caretaker. It was totally burned out. We also looked into the hallway and tried to go into the basement. We retreated, however, when we heard steps below.

On Wednesday, fourteen days after he was arrested, Father was released from jail. There was great joy. Afterward Father talked about his imprisonment. The food and treatment were quite tolerable.

November 28, 1938 [second entry on this date]

On the first day of his arrest, Father was left all alone, which made him very nervous. Later he was placed into a small cell with two others. [. . .] They [. . .] were allowed to walk outside their cell, which brought them in contact with prisoners in other cells. Most disturbing was their lack of communication with their families. The same applied to us. Before the second visit to the prison, Grandmother was up at 3 A.M. wanting to know whether it was time to leave for the prison. The women were harried to no end. They had to run from one place to another to get permission to leave packages for their husbands and relatives, which left them no more than ten minutes for visiting. Mother always returned from these visits most discouraged. The last two days before the prisoners were released were the worst.

On November 23, Father came home and immediately began to work on the emigration process. The only two countries to which Father's pension could be transferred were Chile and Palestine. By his calculation, his income would not be enough to make a living in Palestine and the question then arose whether he would be able to supplement his pension. There was also the question whether the Nazis would continue to send his pension abroad. As an amateur musician it was almost impossible to make a living in Palestine because of the many other Jewish musicians who had emigrated there. In Chile the situation was somewhat better and it would have been possible to live there on the pension. [. . .]

Yesterday I applied with several others for making aliyah. I don't know which of these opportunities will work out, but I plan to take the first one that comes along. There also is a chance to attend a trade school in England. If the opportunities in Holland fail to come true, I may have to go to England, whether I like it or not. Father had to give up hope for emigrating to Argentina. He is now hoping to get a business license for Palestine. It would be best if we could all go to Palestine.

December 1, 1938

The two boys, my former friends who gave me the book in which I am writing this diary, emigrated to the U.S. before Kristallnacht. We had seen very little of each other lately, since they were not members of the Bund.

December 3, 1938

Taking up this diary again is not for any pleasant reason. Today, the day of National Solidarity, Jews were not allowed to go outside from noon until eight at night. Himmler (who I wish were in *Himmel* [heaven]) issued an order by which Jews had to carry photo identity cards. Jews also are not permitted to own driver's licenses. The Nazis will probably soon take radios and telephones from us. This is a horrible affair. Our radio was repaired and the damaged grand piano was fixed. I hope we can keep it. But one can never know with these scums.

December 8, 1938

In Berlin, Jews are no longer allowed to live or walk on certain streets, usually along the grand avenues. This order does not yet affect the rest of the country. Yesterday, Fräulein Haag came to visit us. She is a Christian acquaintance of my parents. She lives in St. Goar on the Rhine and often played music with my parents. In 1937 she had come to visit us here and my parents went to visit her in her home. She is about thirty years old and has played violin in public. However, she is now in some trouble since there are rumors she had played music with Jews. Among such friends also is a minister in Biebernheim near St. Goar. He is the one with whom I would have sought refuge if I had had to flee. Dad had asked Fräulein Haag to come and discuss emigration. He thought of going to India;

she suggested Madras, in India, saying that few Europeans and Jews live there. I wonder whether they will allow immigration. Our apartment is almost back to normal.

December 14, 1938

Except for a new foreign currency regulation no new orders have recently been issued. According to the new law, Jews are allowed to take only essentials with them when they emigrate. The new regulation requires rehabilitation to the German government for the destruction caused over Kristallnacht. In the afternoon, my parents met with Frau Ferse and later Herr Ferse joined them. One hour later they hurried back and told me that I have to have a physical examination. I had to wait for hours until my turn came but it was too late for Mother to take the result with her to Cologne where she had gone to speak with the director of the *Jawne,* the Jewish middle school, whether I can attend the school and then leave for England.[10] However, while this is not a bad idea, the primary course at the school is in Hebrew, which I don't know very well. I am also poor in English, but otherwise it would be a good idea to go there. I would have to work very hard and have little time. I would leave by train for school very early and return late, getting home at four o'clock in the afternoon.

December 19, 1938

Regarding the emigration of my parents I have the following to report. First came two refusals from Argentina for lack of letters of credit. The rich uncle in America is unable to assume such a financial responsibility. We don't have an affidavit for the U.S. India requires firm employment there, or a contract. Father is now trying to make connections in India to obtain a contract. He also wrote to Peru and he was told to go to the Uruguayan consulate. Allegedly the Dominican Republic would take ten thousand Jews and provide them with visas. However, nothing further is known about that. It probably makes no sense to turn to them. However, with a Dominican Republic visa it is possible to get a half-year visa for Palestine. Shanghai also accepts Jews, even without a visa, but it is questionable how one can live there. The mail also brought no news from Palestine. We had submitted a request for a "commercial certification."

December 20, 1938

The kind of cold spell that we experienced over the past few days is very uncomfortable, particularly since one of my ears was frozen. It should not have been a surprise because I was riding a bicycle in minus-fourteen-degree weather without a hat. The things that can happen to a person who should know better. Dad is in Lorch at Dr. Jung's, who owns a wine cellar. He is a very decent person and an anti-Nazi. My parents often played chamber music with him. He is trying to help Father with his patent and with my parents' emigration.

December 23, 1938

I have to make some additional entries regarding my emigration. England no longer is a possibility for me. I was not accepted because I was registered in Holland. My acceptance at the Jawne school in Cologne is in question. It might work out that we shall have enough money since we rented my room and that of Grandmother for forty marks per month. In addition, Herr Bachrach reduced my parents' rent by twenty marks. That means that my attendance at the Jawne school is not totally out of the question. My frozen ear still keeps me at home. Outside there is wonderful new snow and we had planned a snow fight.

January 5, 1939

There is again a lot to report, but nothing of particular importance. My emigration situation is about the same as before. My attendance at the Jawne school is no longer feasible. Holland offers my best chances since I am registered with the committee and also have a private offer. There still is a very small chance for my going to England, for which we submitted the required documentation. Then there is still the Youth Aliyah, which will take much time. Finally there is Schniebinchen, the agricultural training center in Germany, which is holding a place for me.[11] Bobby also will go there. I am registered there and therefore am not giving up all hope. So much for my emigration. My parents had to all but give up hope for South America. However, India is still an open possibility. If they can get there it would be very good. Their chances for emigrating to the U.S. also are very slim because they have a very high waiting number, 25,000.

All attempts at getting an affidavit have been to no avail. On December 31, my grandmother and I moved to the lower rooms in our apartment. After one woman had agreed to rent the room, she canceled when she learned that she did not have to vacate her apartment. A few days later a family by the name of Kern rented the room. I am sorry to have to give up my comfortable room. It is the first time in my memory that I no longer have my own room. I now sleep in the living room. Dad stowed away the books in his wardrobe. I also lined and repaired the large desk drawer. Grandmother now sleeps in the dining room. The new tenant pays forty marks. This reduces our rent to sixty marks per month because Herr Bachrach lowered the rent on his own by twenty marks.

January 12, 1939

Since my last entry I have to make another addition, not a very pleasant one. Regarding the papers for England, the documents were all returned from Hamburg where we had sent them. I am now back where I was two weeks ago. Dad returned from Lorch and there seems to be some possible income from the patent. Regarding their emigration, my parents have not progressed one step. As of January 1, 1939, we are required to have an identity card.[12] In providing personal information the official asked my father's hair color. My father is bald. I must really admire my parents. Despite having been rejected, disappointed, having suffered hardships and daily aggravations, they did not lose their good humor. It is a miserable situation and it looks just as bad for me. I have the following possibilities:

1. England with the help of ?
2. Holland with the help of a committee
3. Holland through Rosalinda Rosenberg
4. Wieringen (also Holland)[13]
5. Jawne (high school in Cologne) perhaps to England
6. Youth Aliyah (through Schniebinchen)

Wieringen not available (full) and Jawne, no hope to emigrate through the school. Youth Aliyah is the most hopeful, but will take time. So, I sit here at home and, after all, have a good life. I am studying a little English and French and practice the cello while our piano has not yet been returned. I sleep late and listen to the radio until late at night.

Today I received my final report card from high school. The bums and scums who call themselves National Socialists [Nazis] lowered my grades from "good" to "fair." I am sorry in particular about the grades in mathematics and French. The principal listed my name as "Klaus Israel," although the law requiring "Israel" did not take effect until the first of the year.[14]

January 13, 1939

On January 12, that is yesterday, I was informed by telephone that I shall be able to go to Erez with the Youth Aliyah without any special preparations. The date has not yet been set, but very soon. The dice that determine my life have been thrown.

January 14, 1939

A topic on which books can be written is "emigration." I can sing a song on that subject. During a discussion that Herr Ferse had with someone at the community center in Cologne and in which he mentioned my name, the topic of Schniebinchen came up. Father wrote to Cologne and received an immediate response. The documents from Essen were not at the Cologne community office. My mother was told in Cologne that I had to get a medical statement from my doctor. I then obtained a form that had to be filled out and also had received a letter from Berlin in which I was told that I was almost fully accepted in Schniebinchen. We then walked to the doctor's office for a physical exam, but he had moved. When we finally located his new office he no longer had office hours. I then went to our cantor and asked him to fill out the form for me. It was actually to be filled out by the youth leader, Löllbach, but he does not like me very much. Ogutsh, however, still sent me to Löllbach, who was in a good mood. He wrote me a decent report.

January 15, 1939

I left Löllbach and went to the community office where my papers were still being held instead of having been sent forward. I was told that the papers were at my English teacher's. When I had my lesson that evening I finally received my papers and sent them off. That afternoon I saw the doctor, who gave me a medical statement, and dog-tired I came home at five. After I had taken a nap my parents told me that I received a telephone message from my English teacher, who said that I would be sent to Erez Israel with twenty-four other youths without any further preparations. It was seven-thirty in the evening. It should not be difficult to imagine what effect that news had on me. My parents were at first not too happy but then saw that it was best that I leave as soon as possible to where I would be well cared for.

January 18, 1939

The wonderful story about my making aliyah immediately is only a dream. My name was stricken from the list of twenty-four. I am not in the mood to tell the whole dumb story again. In any case, it is finished. Perhaps I shall still be able to go to Schniebinchen.

January 24, 1939

It is ironic that while waiting to go to Erez Israel I am sitting here waiting for authorization to go to Schniebinchen. At this point I am only on a waiting list. It is terrible. The damn youth committee removed me from the list for the Youth Aliyah and now lets me wait. [. . .] I have been awaiting authorization for two weeks and will not be surprised when I am also stricken from the list for Schniebinchen.

No meetings of our group had been held since the beginning of the year. Complaints were registered that we only held meetings under the auspices of the Bund, the youth movement, so that we could while away time and flirt with girls. This was absolutely not the case. [. . .] Our last meeting was at [Bobby] Ferse's birthday party. We read something and finally agreed to hold a farewell party for Lotte on January 15. [. . .] There was an uproar caused by Anneliese Katz and a number of people [. . .] because they had not been invited to our meetings. [. . .]¹⁵

January 29, 1939

Finally, finally it came. The call to leave for Schniebinchen. It came late, but it came. Then the excitement started. What do I need? What is there still to do? For example, the official departure notice, the identity card, purchases of small items. I already had boots, long trousers, gym clothes, and a raincoat. Bobby will go with me on Monday and spend the night in Berlin at Aunt Kate's. We plan to arrive in Schniebinchen on Tuesday at three in the afternoon. It will take about three months until we go abroad. However, we still don't know where that will be. England is still in question and then there is Holland and Erez Israel. It can also take longer than three months. Tomorrow then we leave. I still have to run from one place to another. That is known as saying good-bye. Rotzig received the first letter from his girlfriend. The opposition, Anneliese Katz, left for England. We now have hardly any enemies left. Lobi has not been heard from. Melchior is too lazy to write. The same is true for Rolman. It is very sad. [. . .] That is about all there is new.

The emigration of my parents has not progressed. India requires not only a contract for work, but also someone to vouch for you. There is no chance for an affidavit. Generally, the situation is very grave. The political situation is becoming increasingly tense. More on that later.

[Klaus was at the agricultural training camp *(hachsharah)* of Schniebinchen from February 1 until April 2, 1939, when he returned home for a short vacation.]

April 4, 1939 [Essen]

I came home on leave lasting from April 2 to April 12. That means that on my birthday I am returning to Schniebinchen. I had some foot injury over the past few days. It was a festering wound that already made itself felt in one gland. On Saturday, with my foot in bandages, I left for Berlin and then continued the journey from there. The emigration plans for my parents did not progress. There is a question whether India should be considered since it is unlikely that one can make a living there with music. The earliest they could emigrate to the United States is in 1941. My parents are now trying to get to England by some means.

In my case it looks like I will leave either for England or Holland in two months. Emigration to Palestine does not look good for the moment. [. . .] If, according to one British proposal, only seventy-five thousand immigrants will be authorized to settle in Palestine over a five-year period of time, and the purchase of land for the most part is prohibited or restricted, then the outlook is not very good.

The political situation also looks strained. Spain has now come totally under Franco. Everywhere countries are arming. Czechoslovakia has become a German protectorate. Memel has become German. Now German pressure is on Romania. English–Polish discussions are under way about a mutual security treaty. The situation looks very tense. In China, the Chinese and Japanese are at each other's throats. The United States also is arming itself. In other words, there is unrest everywhere. Palestine also is in turmoil, but we still shall go there.

April 8, 1939 [Essen]

My leave is coming to an end quickly. There are only three days left. My leg is well again. Rotzig visited me a few times. He is the only one left from our Maccabean group. He feels very lonesome. For the time being he is staying in Essen. Today I received mail from Edit, my girlfriend. My parents must have found this out, since they showed a lively interest. Edit also sent me a good photo of herself. I must leave on April 11 and will again spend the night in Berlin at my Aunt Kate's place. I expect to arrive in Schniebinchen on April 12 late in the evening.

April 9, 1939 [Essen]

The leg is still bothersome when I get up. Today it is swollen again. Once in a while I play the piano to get back into practicing. I don't know how my cello playing is coming along. After a two-month hiatus it may not go so well. However, my piano skills are still quite good. The political situation also has changed. Albania was occupied by Italy. My preparations for emigrating to Palestine have almost been completed. I just bought a few more things, a leather jacket, a good pair of gym shoes, and underwear.

When I consider the effect that Schniebinchen had on me I must say that I have changed much. I have become less inhibited and my interests have changed. I am no longer much interested in collecting stamps. I read better books there than I do here, when I find time for that. Life there is much more natural and I like it better. Life there also has disadvantages. For example, it is impossible to be alone. The group consists of good and bad people and one has to find a way to deal with the bad ones.

April 10, 1939 [Essen]

Two days ago I learned that Bobby is going to England through private arrangements. On April 13 he will leave Schniebinchen and travel to England on the nineteenth. This means that of the original Maccabean group everyone has been scattered elsewhere. Kume is in Chicago, Lobi in Montevideo, Paul now lives near Amsterdam. He wrote a short while ago. Bobby is going to England, but does not know the exact location. If he is lucky he will get to Scotland where a hachsharah was organized by Balfour for training youngsters from Germany. Rotzig is attending a locksmith school in Cologne. There is no one left in Essen.

[On April 12, Klaus went back to Schniebinchen, where he remained until late June 1939, when he returned again to Essen.]

April 29, 1939 [Schniebinchen]

Confirmation was received by our group leaders for the emigration to Palestine. Consequently, there was a great deal of excitement. A few people still had not received their confirmation. Kurt Goldman [head of the Aid to Jewish Youth] came from Berlin and we learned that the final decision would be made tomorrow. A list was prepared by us, the boys, and we discussed every person. Nineteen were confirmed by us immediately, five were questionable. We presented that list to the *madrichim* [youth group leaders]. It is interesting to note that we, the youth, applied a stricter standard than the madrichim, who were far kinder in their confirmations. Perhaps it was because of the urgency to leave Germany as quickly as possible.

July 1, 1939 [Essen]

[. . .] I am again in Essen. I must catch up with my diary for all the time that I failed to make entries. In about four or six weeks I shall finally leave for Palestine. That means that I am now on an aliyah vacation.

So as not to create greater gaps in my diary, I shall write about the current situation. Later I shall write about the last developments in Schniebinchen while I still resided there. I think that I shall really leave in about four or five weeks. I am maintaining an extensive correspondence with all the members of my group at Schniebinchen as well as with people who are still there. Bobby did not reply to my last letter and I just wrote him an extensive letter about the situation here.

July 9, 1939 [Essen]

First, a short overview of the current situation. I wrote to the Youth Aliyah in Berlin and asked them to send me all the necessary forms so that I can begin processing. I shall try to take the grand piano and an old typewriter with me. However, we still don't know when we are going to leave, and I am beginning to see things more negatively.

July 15, 1939 [Essen]

Finally the response came from the Aid to Jewish Youth. I should take along my bicycle and cello. The word has yet to come about the piano. I am waiting daily for news. My things are almost fully packed. The other Schniebinchen youth group, Kibbutz Me'uchad, received their notice to leave on August 7. Bobby, my friend in England, is leaving on July 26 for Palestine via Marseilles. I hope to see him soon in Erez. Rotzig visited me again. He likes the locksmith school in Cologne. He is learning a lot there, although the people there are not worth much. He may go to England, or to the United States. For the time being he is not going to Erez Israel. My parents finally have something that might work with regard to their emigration. A Chilean visa costs about seventy pounds, which my parents somehow obtained. Unfortunately, all the ships for Chile are booked until December. However, that still represents a possibility.

July 28, 1939 [Essen]

There is little to report about the situation at home. My aliyah has been put off, as I learned from Moritz, with whom I had been good friends, and who wrote from Schniebinchen. We must be there by September 30. A few days later, Bert Königsbuch, the *madrich* [youth group leader], came to Essen for a visit. I asked him to visit me and he came. He said that we shall leave at the end of August or by early September, which is sooner than I had feared. This visit at least was a short break in the days that I am staying here. I am bored. I practice at the piano, play the cello, read the newspapers and also read a lot of other things. I also had a few visitors who did not interest me much. The emigration of my parents is making progress. They finally have the seventy pounds for Chile.

We hope that the Chile application will work. We also have an affidavit for the U.S., but it helps little because of the long wait for the consulate to act. My baggage for Palestine is ready. I am also taking many books. There were problems with those of the group who either were Polish nationals or stateless. We even expected a police raid. Finally we succeeded in pressuring the authorities to provide them with identity cards. Then the question arose [regarding] where these young people were to go. Some were to go to Palestine, others to England, and some quickly to Sweden.

August 8, 1939 [Essen]

Finally, on August 5 the authorization came to leave for Palestine. [. . .] I had to be in Munich on September 5 and depart from Trieste by boat on September 6. There was great joy at home. It also was Mother's birthday. In the afternoon came the official announcement with all the arrangements that had to be made. I saw to it that we received the foreign currency exchange instructions. That same day we began packing to see what had to be shipped and what could be taken as hand baggage. We packed and repacked several times and finally divided my belongings. We worked on the lists for two days until late at night and I had to obtain a statement attesting to my legal status. This took a lot of effort since the Nazis made this a very complicated procedure. The gold discount had to be paid, as well as various other fees that were required. The head of a family had to pay as much in taxes as a single person and then there were additional payments that we Jews had to make. Finally, after three days I sent the completed lists to the customs office.

August 19, 1939 [Essen]

Today I received the news that my aliyah has been postponed, for technical reasons, as was said. These people have no idea how nervous all this makes me, and I have already waited for months. [. . .] My parents are still trying to get papers for Chile. At the moment it does not look good. My parents also are hoping that once I get to Erez I will be able to bring them there as well.

August 21, 1939 [Essen]

My old friend Manfred came to visit yesterday. His mother had returned from Poland and they are about to dissolve their residence. His emigration efforts have met with no success. My parents are very angry that my aliyah was postponed, but I learned from a girl in Essen that the entire transport was delayed. It shows again the incompetence of the Aid to Jewish Youth and the Palestine Bureau when it comes to organizing. One has to get used to that and be patient.

During the past few days the political situation has dangerously worsened. It looks like war. How much that will affect the Jews is obvious. I shall try to describe the situation briefly. For some time now the German press was agitating about Danzig. There is an English, French, and Polish defense pact as a counterweight and German press agitation because of that. There are also English and French negotiations with Moscow and at the same time secret negotiations with Germany. Most of the hatred spewed by the German press is against Poland. There is an increase in tension. Poland and Germany have mobilized. France and England also are ready to mobilize. Italy clearly is on the side of Germany. Spain's position is in question.

Today, the twenty-sixth of August, the English ambassador in Berlin is flying to London after discussions with Hitler. Presumably he is bringing proposals. In the meantime I received my baggage authorization without having to pay duty. On August 29 the customs official is coming, and packing has to be done in his presence. Everything has been prepared and I hope nothing will happen in between. The political situation also has somewhat eased with everyone waiting for results from London.

September 8, 1939 [Denmark]

Since my last entry the situation took a turn for the worse so that I did not have an opportunity to write until today. I am sitting here in a room in which there is a bed, a table, a box, my suitcase, and in the corner there is a curtain, which comprises all the furnishings. [. . .]

[. . .] On August 29 I received a letter from the Aid to Jewish Youth in Berlin. Efforts were under way to get us into Denmark. We were to prepare to leave. My hopes were not very high since we were disappointed so many times before. However, on September 2, the second day of the war, a telegram arrived that instructed me to be in Berlin the next morning because we would be going to Denmark. That meant I had to leave that day and spend the night in Berlin. We asked the customs official to come and in his presence we packed a large suitcase and a backpack. I also took a bread bag. The doctor also had to come because I still had a gland infection in my leg. That afternoon at four o'clock I left Essen. Dad had called Aunt Kate in Berlin who was to pick me up. The departure from my parents was very short and difficult. I had no idea when I would see them again, especially because the war is on now. To be in a war in Germany as a Jew means to be ready for the worst. When I sit here all alone, I often think of my parents and grandmother and then only sad thoughts come to mind.[16]

End of September [Denmark]

I find that I have kept my diary very one-sided. I shall now try to avoid anything unnecessary and not overlook anything. [. . .] When I have time I shall briefly record later what happened in general. And now to the most recent past.

On September 2 I arrived late in Berlin and went to Aunt Kate. The Youth Organization had already sent instructions. I slept badly and had to leave very early, at six o'clock, from the Stettin railroad station. There was also a group from Schniebinchen. Not all were there, partly because of their age, and also because some were cut off by the Germans from their homes in East Prussia. There also were many from Vienna. The total transport included forty-eight people. Half came from Vienna. We traveled to Warnemünde on the Baltic coast. We had no problem crossing the border. We then traveled by ferry about one and a half to two hours to Gedser in Denmark. It was a beautiful crossing. As we learned later, it was the last boatload to leave with Germans. A few hours later war was declared by England and France. Although ships crossed between Germany and Denmark, only foreigners were allowed on board.

End of November 1939 [Denmark]

More than two months have passed since I made my last entry. Not much has changed in my situation here, although I feel that in that time I have learned something. As I noted above, several of my entries in this diary were not correct; rather, I left many gaps. I recorded only facts, and these are often one-sided and not complete. I shall now try to compose my diary in a different manner and hope that I shall be successful in doing so.

I shall begin with my parents and with my attitude toward them and toward my grandmother as I see that relationship today. I have noted that things have changed and that I now see them in another light. Whether this is due to the situation in which I found myself when recording my diary or for having grown older is something I don't know myself.

My parents were married in 1922 in Gleiwitz, Upper Silesia. My mother was born in Odessa and my father in Gleiwitz. They lived in Gleiwitz where I was born in 1924. As I recall, my grandmother lived with us. One year after I was born she gave up her position in a factory in Berlin owned by a Jew and moved to Gleiwitz where she helped with the household and with raising me. She lived with us. She fed, stuffed, and pampered me just as grandmothers are supposed to do. I was just as fond of my father as I was of my mother and grandmother. [. . .] I must also say that my mother, and my father less so, showed their feelings openly. My parents were not strict but were not as giving as my grandmother. Despite that, I don't think they made any mistakes with me. When I compare myself with friends I can see that I had a better relationship with my parents than they had. [. . .] My father always wanted me to learn while my mother was more concerned about my upbringing. My grandmother, on the other hand, was mostly interested in my physical and mental health.

In general I must say that I was, and still am, very close to my parents, especially during the recent past. With regard to my average school performance, my father was always saddened while my mother did not take it so seriously. Later, however, I did not trust my parents as much as I trusted my grandmother. This was mainly because of the youth group, which filled me with ideas that my parents did not share. My father permitted me without hesitation to make aliyah but he wanted me to learn something useful. I see now that he did not want me to go through life as an ordinary worker in a kibbutz. I talked with him about that over the recent past, often without reaching any conclusions.

End of December [Denmark]

I now want to continue after the last interruption. My mother is an ardent Zionist and dearly wanted to see me go to Erez, which means, first to Denmark. Grandma is neutral on that score. I already wrote that my parents had very good ideas with which in earlier times I did not agree, but which I now recognize as very valid. I was allowed to join the youth group but was not to neglect school and music. I was obviously more interested in the youth group than in school and I did not tell my parents everything, which sometimes was unjustified. Often not much was being said in the sichot and when I was asked, I told stories. Even if something of importance was discussed, I did not always share that with my parents. For example, discussions on kibbutz morale, matters of sex, and friendships. I don't know what my parents might have said if I had told them.

New Year's Eve, 1939 [Denmark]

I really have nothing to record for this day since New Year's for me was not a special holiday. [. . .] During the past year I have learned, experienced, and seen a great deal and it was not always pleasant. Objectively speaking, I can say that I have progressed in every regard. In general, the year was filled with thoughts about making aliyah and preparing for it. In November 1938 I reported to the Youth

Aliyah and in January I arrived in Schniebinchen and in September I was suddenly in Denmark instead of Erez Israel. [. . .] Instinctively, the question comes to mind of what the future will bring. Where and under what circumstances will I be next year at New Year's? Soon it will be midnight and a new year will begin, even if only by the calendar. I shall wait for it in my sleep.

2

Elisabeth Kaufmann

PARIS, FRANCE

Elisabeth Kaufmann (later Elizabeth Koenig) began writing in her diary in her native German in February 1940 in France, just before her sixteenth birthday. She and her family had arrived in France one and a half years earlier as one of the thousands of refugee families fleeing Austria after its annexation by the Germans in March 1938. Born to a well-established family on March 7, 1924, Elisabeth spent her early childhood years in Vienna with her parents and her older brother, Peter. Her family was cultured, sophisticated, and well read. Her father held a doctoral degree in international relations and was a prominent journalist. Her maternal grandfather was a pediatrician, and her paternal grandfather had been a lawyer until his death. The family was well off, living in a large apartment, frequently attending concerts, the theater, and the opera, and enjoying summer vacations together. As a little girl, Elisabeth went to the Czisek Art School, which had been created especially for gifted children. In 1933, the family moved to Berlin, where they remained until 1936, when Elisabeth's father was blacklisted by the Nazis and forced to leave the country. Upon their return to Vienna, they lived with Elisabeth's maternal grandparents.[1]

In March 1938, Germany annexed Austria. The first weeks of occupation were characterized by mass arrests of opponents of the Nazi regime and mob violence directed against Jews. Confiscations, looting of businesses, vandalization of apartments, and humiliations followed one another in rapid succession. The sudden Nazi takeover of power in Austria stripped Austrian Jews of their rights and entitlements as if they had never existed. The terror prompted the Kaufmanns to flee in the fall of 1938, reducing them to refugees stranded in France, without funds or a permanent home in which to live.

By the time she began to write in her diary, Elisabeth had already been a refugee for two years. Although much of the diary reflects the struggles, hardships, and complexities of life as a refugee, it also shows the mark of the writer's hand, suggesting the particular educational, social, and cultural milieu in which Elisabeth had been raised. Possessed of a subtle and refined sense of style and culture, Elisabeth was on occasion precocious, calmly stating that a performance of the Comédie Française only matched the level of the municipal theater in Vienna, and dismissing the Paris ice skating rink as "quite pathetic" compared with the one in Vienna. She was fluent in both German and French, moving easily between the two languages in her diary, and was tutored in English by a young friend of the family. The value she placed on education, books, foreign languages, politics, and art comes through in the diary, as she criticized those around her whose intellect or sophistication failed to meet her standards of excellence. Among these were several of her schoolmates and her "boss," as she called the man for whom she worked informally to earn extra money handling correspondence in French and German.

For Elisabeth, as for most Central European refugees of this period, there was a tremendous gulf between the life she lived prior to the Nazi takeover of power and her status as a refugee. From time to time, she directly articulated the disconnect between her middle-class past and the realities of being a refugee, often with surprising poise, self-examination, and humor. In particular, when she was expected to bring a "Viennese cake" to a party, she delighted in finding a way to get around the problem without letting on to her friends. But, on a more serious note, she remarked time and again how difficult, even embarrassing, it could be to accept and acknowledge her family's poverty among her friends who had no such worries. "It is difficult to maintain a middle-class front while totally without funds," she wrote.

Beyond the normal problems facing refugees in any time and place—lack of money, security, stability—the Jewish refugees in France faced a rising tide of xenophobia that further complicated their lives. Like many refugee families, the Kaufmanns had turned to France for shelter and asylum because of its long tradition of tolerance and hospitality for the oppressed of Europe. In particular, it held a reputation for acceptance of Jews, having been the first European country to emancipate its Jews during the French Revolution in 1789. During the 1930s, however, with the onset of the Great Depression, a sharp rise in unemployment, and economic and political instability in France and throughout Europe, resentment of foreigners grew. They were presented by right-wing politicians and newspapers as usurpers who took jobs from the French and parasites who drained limited French resources. Further, the German refugees fleeing Nazism were accused of straining the French economy. Throughout this period, the French tradition of liberalism and tolerance toward foreigners was undermined by an inward-turning xenophobia directed at refugees in general, and at Jews in particular.[2]

With the onset of war in September 1939, the tide of fear and suspicion of foreigners that had been gaining ground in France throughout the 1930s came fully to the fore. Thousands of refugees who fled to France to escape Nazi oppression were now considered "enemy aliens" because of their German or Austrian nationality. They were viewed as a threat to French national security and were summarily rounded up by French gendarmes and sent to internment camps such as Le Vernet, Gurs, and Saint Cyprien. Elisabeth's father and brother were among those arrested and detained in a camp called Melay-du-Maine, located about 150 miles west of Paris.

Despite the upset and anxiety that came with this forced separation from her father and brother, much of the first part of Elisabeth's diary reflects the odd calm of the so-called *drôle de guerre,* or "phony war," the period from September 1939 to May 1940 during which there were no open hostilities between Germany and France. Indeed, her life seemed rather pleasant; she attended school at the Ecole des Arts Décoratifs, rode her bicycle through Paris, enjoying the parks, "broad avenues," and passersby, ice skated and attended picnics with friends, and spent short vacations with her boyfriend, Ernst Koenig (who returned to Paris on leave from duty in the Czech army in exile).[3]

But Elisabeth's life was to change once again when the "phony war" came to an end. In early May 1940, the sudden and swift German attack on the Western countries began. Holland, Belgium, and Luxembourg were occupied almost immediately. The invasion of France was imminent. The political developments prompted the French to undertake another roundup and internment of German nationals; this time Elisabeth and her family were exempt because they were Austrians. But as the German invasion and occupation of France loomed nearer, more and more people began fleeing Paris for the provinces.

Elisabeth's diary captures the rising tension in Paris, the accompanying "Parisian migration," as she referred to the panicked columns of those fleeing the capital, and her own struggles as she joined them, becoming a refugee for the second time in her young life. Elisabeth and her mother made preparations to leave Paris on June 12, joining the giant columns of refugees fleeing south. As her diary shows, her efforts to get out of Paris (first as an au pair with a French family, and eventually with her mother) were time and again complicated by the paranoia and suspicion of foreigners that were rampant in France at the time.

The third and final notebook of the diary comprises Elisabeth's description of the first three days of the journey and its hardships. The days seem much longer, so filled are they with confusion, unexpected events, and uncertainty. Elisabeth took her bicycle, and her mother found room in a car. The first day they traveled to Rambouillet, then to St. Remy, then to Chartres. At each stop, Elisabeth and her mother, who had traveled separately, tried to find each other as well as a secure place to spend the night. Elisabeth's diary is filled with scenes of the thousands of refugees on the road, and the exhaustion, hunger, panic, and confusion of the flight south.

This chaos and upheaval in combination with the continuing scrutiny and suspicion of foreigners culminated in the arrest of Elisabeth and her mother by French police. Among Elisabeth's "suspicious" papers was a small volume of German poems, her boyfriend Ernst's identity card, and his diary. Apparently suspected of being spies, they were interrogated, imprisoned, and held overnight at the gendarmerie in Chartres. They were released the next morning as panic broke out over the imminent arrival of German troops in Chartres. The diary ended suddenly the following day, June 14, when Elisabeth was in Chateaudun waiting again for her mother.

After much confusion, crossed signals, and weeks of separation, Elisabeth found her parents and they settled in Saint Sauveur par Bellac, which was in the southern zone of France, and consequently not under German occupation. In the summer of 1941, Elisabeth was contacted by Hilde Höfert, her former Latin teacher who had lived with the Kaufmann family in Paris, who invited her to come to Le Chambon sur Lignon, to be an au pair for the family of Pastor André

Trocmé.[4] In November 1941, after spending the summer and fall with the Trocmé family, Elisabeth received a letter from her father telling her to go directly to Lyons because the family had obtained visas to travel to America.[5] The family arrived in Virginia Beach in early 1942.

The rest of Elisabeth's family—grandparents, aunts, and uncles—were equally fortunate to escape Europe; although they were far-flung, they had all made it to safety. Elisabeth's maternal grandparents were in Cuba, her paternal grandmother and an aunt and uncle were in England, and another aunt and uncle were living in San Francisco. Once in America, Elisabeth's brother Peter, who had married in the States and was expecting his first child, returned to France as a soldier in the American army fighting the Germans. He lost his life in France in 1944, at the age of twenty-four. In 1947, Elisabeth and Ernst Koenig were married and have remained so for more than fifty years. The three volumes of Elisabeth's diary remained in her own possession until she donated them to the United States Holocaust Memorial Museum in Washington, D.C., in 1990.

February 26, 1940 [Paris]

[. . .] I finally succeeded today in convincing the director of the Ecole des Arts Décoratifs that it is unjust to regard the children of an Austrian mobilized in France as enemy aliens and not accept them in school. Tomorrow I will start school. The Comité will do the rest and pay for my studies.

Based on my experience last year in school, when there was no war yet, I believe the atmosphere will be even more xenophobic. Besides, a newcomer arriving in the middle of the school year will always be the object of criticism. In short, as much as I look forward to a regular course of study, I wish the first school days would be behind me.

February 27, 1940 [Paris]

I was happily surprised at the reception by professors and schoolmates—no trace of xenophobia. By the way, there are only five other girls in class: Jeannette, Joanne, Gabrièle, Nicole, and Simone. They are all very nice and between sixteen and eighteen years old. The intimacy among the classmates is unusual; it reflects the whole character of the school. We call ourselves by our first names and even the director calls me Elisabeth.

Unfortunately, I did not understand much of today's lesson on perspectives. The half year that I lost in schooling is noticeable.

The battles in Finland must be almost unbearable given the cold climate.

February 28, 1940 [Paris]

My class schedule is as follows:

> Monday mornings: practical perspective.
> Tuesday mornings: charcoal drawing, letters in the afternoon.
> Wednesday mornings: charcoal drawing.
> Thursday mornings: charcoal drawing and letters in the afternoon.
> Friday: the theory of perspectives.
> Saturday mornings: water colors or modeling.

According to this schedule it will be possible for me to continue working for my "boss" on two afternoons and, besides that, make the few *sous* [pennies] that are hard-earned but make for handy pocket money.

March 1, 1940 [Paris]

[. . .] Since it takes almost three-quarters of an hour to get to school, even by Métro, I cannot go home at noon for lack of time and money. Therefore, I eat a sandwich somewhere, be that in the Trocadéro Park, which really is a pleasure, or at the post office, which is much less comfortable. However, I can go to the park only when the weather is somewhat pleasant, and I can read or watch the children play, or look in the direction of the Eiffel Tower and far into the city. If the weather is bad I go to the post office to eat my sandwich and spend the time until two o'clock writing.

My greatest wish, therefore, is for a bicycle with which I could ride to the library, eat and read there at the same time. The ideal situation.

March 2, 1940 [Paris]

Three new girls arrived to attend the three morning charcoal drawing lessons: Olga; Tchiquie, a Spanish girl; and Hélène. I feel better all the time. Everyone is pleasant, and in terms of my class work I am among the three best.

March 3, 1940 [Paris]

I hope my wish for a bicycle is moving toward reality. I know about a second-hand bike in excellent condition with a generator and back-pedal brake. The only big drawback is that it's a man's bike, but it costs only two hundred francs and I don't think I could get a bike at that price again. [. . .]

March 7, 1940 [Paris]

It is evening, seven o'clock, and I am "celebrating" my birthday. I really never had such a sad birthday; I have never been alone on my birthday before. Dad is in the camp. Until today, I had thought for sure that he would be released. He has now been away for seven months and I have not seen him once during that time. Peter has been in the camp for just as long and we have seen him just as little. Mother has just accepted a job as a nurse for a woman who lives outside Paris. The grandparents are still in Vienna. The other grandmother along with Uncle Paul and Aunt Edith are in London, and Uncle Arthur, Aunt Annie, and Hederl are in San Francisco. Everyone is scattered around and no one is with me. I received very nice letters from them and Peter sent me a poem and from London I received a package. Every year, even the last when we were in Paris already, we celebrated my birthday somewhat. Today, I cooked my own birthday meal and, sitting in the kitchen, I am writing in my diary and I am sad. Today I am sixteen. [. . .]

March 9, 1940 [Paris]

It is unbelievable. Dad is free and will come home. This evening I found a letter that confirmed it. And just now, Mother is not here. I plan to go early tomorrow morning, on Sunday, and get the bicycle and ride to Mother and bring her the news.

March 10, 1940 [Paris]

I went by bike to Mother. She will return in two days.

In the afternoon I went to my "boss." I think he is a grotesque-comical person. I worked two and a half hours on his correspondence, partly in German but mainly in French, and then gave him a French lesson for one hour . . . and for all that he paid me ten francs and thought he made me happy. Moreover, I was to be thankful and devoted to him! A person who cannot tell the difference between Latin and Greek, but not only that, he cannot speak German properly and no French at all. In short, he cannot speak any language accent-free or without making mistakes. He does not like music and finds *Faust* terribly boring. He finds his pleasure in coffee houses and in reading detective stories . . . and I am supposed to get used to such a person. Slowly the hours I spend with him are becoming torturous. . . .

March 12, 1940 [Paris]

Dad should be coming within the next few days. Permission to visit Peter at the internment camp was rejected. It's unbelievable. I would like to know what harm it would do if we were to visit him. We are going to apply for permission once more.

March 14, 1940 [Paris]

Dad came this afternoon. Mother came in the morning. I was home alone when Dad came and he immediately climbed into the bathtub. Now we will talk, embrace, talk . . .

March 16, 1940 [Paris]

Although Dad is now here, we still have one bed and a place, the one vacated by Peter. We therefore asked Vilma to stay with us, and she moved in today.

Vilma is twenty years old and at the moment all alone in Paris, without any relatives or money. Her husband is in the same camp as Peter, and she has not seen him for the past seven months either. We cram ourselves into bed every evening; she sleeps next to me. [. . .]

March 17, 1940 [Paris]

[. . .] I keep myself busy with politics. In school we talk of nothing but politics. The more so since the various political opinions are represented here. Tchiquie, the Spanish girl, is not, as I had assumed, a refugee from Franco. To the contrary, her father is an attaché at the Spanish embassy and she is an enthusiastic nationalist who is ruthless and unfair in her opposition to anyone else's opinion. [. . .] At the other end of the spectrum is Gabrièle, the Italian girl, a refugee from Mussolini and an anti-Fascist. The two are in each other's faces almost every day.

Meanwhile, two new students have arrived. Francine, who at first glance seems to be an ardent French nationalist, claims that it would not be such a bad idea if Hitler brought some order into the country and protected it from the danger of Communism.[6] Sabine is anti-Fascist, as are Nicole and Jeannette. Simone is anti-Hitler but not anti-German. The most heated discussions are taking place almost uninterruptedly and the studio, unfortunately, is split more and more into two parties.

If the girls were serious and would first think through what they are saying it could be very interesting. As it is, they are totally unschooled politically and they simply repeat whatever they pick up at the dinner table without forming their own opinions.

I love political debates. To participate in these discussions, however, is nonsense. I therefore take a mediator position between the debating parties, although that does not reflect my character. As a result of our immigration, political questions obviously affect me much more directly than they do the other girls, and I have learned to occupy myself much more with politics. [. . .]

March 17, 1940 [Paris]

It has been almost one week since I have received any news from Ernst. I learned today to my dismay that various companies of the Czech army were sent to Norway, so I am very concerned should Ernst be among them.

March 19, 1940 (evening) [Paris]

Ernst is coming tomorrow.

March 24, 1940 [Paris]

Since Ernst came, I have had no chance to get to my diary. We are constantly together. We went on two very nice all-day excursions. When walking through the woods in this spring mood, telling each other stories, and making plans for the future, one could almost forget that there is a war, and that all this joy will be over in four days. It is good that his leave lasted through Easter vacation so that we have the whole day together. We take full advantage of these eight days. [. . .]

My parents know Ernst very well and [have known him] for as long as I have because I introduced him as soon as we met. Therefore, my parents know with whom I go out and Ernst can visit us as often as he pleases. We have known each other for almost a year. Before he went into the service he came to us often to eat because his family is in Czechoslovakia and he lived alone in a small hotel room. He came to France to study, and after Czechoslovakia was ceded to Germany he was unable to return home.

March 29, 1940 [Paris]

Ernst returned yesterday afternoon. We spent the last four days together uninterrupted, like the first four. The day before yesterday we went with my parents for a late birthday celebration to the Comédie Française and saw *Madame Sans-Gêne,* a very charming piece. But in terms of artistic performance it only comes close to performances at the Burgtheater [municipal theater in Vienna]. We were also often at the phonograph record salon where we heard Beethoven, Schubert, Mozart, Schumann, et cetera.

April 4, 1940 [Paris]

We had a picnic at school and everyone brought something special to eat or drink, and then we went to the movies to see a very stupid film. "Peter," that's what they call me, "apportes un beau gâteau viennois, ah, oui, nous adorons les gâteaux viennois!" [Peter, bring a good Viennese cake, oh, yes, we love Viennese cakes!]

That we have a small problem never enters the minds of these girls. Since I have been in Paris Mother has never made a "Viennese cake" because it requires all kinds of things that we do not have, a cake form, for example. Everything would have to be purchased. It is difficult to maintain a middle-class front while totally without funds. However, we shall overcome! And "Peter" did bring her "beau gâteau viennois." How that was done was her business.

April 20, 1940 [Paris]

We have been given the authorization [to visit Peter in the internment camp] and will travel in a few days over the weekend. I am already terribly happy. Because the camp is twenty kilometers from the closest railroad station I shall combine the trip with a bicycle tour. I shall travel alone, and when I return my parents will go. It is always more pleasant for the internee to have company for an entire week and to visit with us individually than to have us all come at the same time.

April 27, 1940 [Melay-du-Maine]

It is twelve-thirty at night. I am sitting in the small Hôtel du Cheval Blanc, three kilometers from the internment camp for Germans, Austrians, and those from the Saar. I left the camp about fifteen minutes ago by bicycle. I spoke with Peter and all the others. I am still under the spell of the night ride, which, although quite short, was wonderful. Peter accompanied me past the guard to the camp gate. (Theoretically, visitors are allowed to stay only until 5:00 P.M., but the guard simply said, "Bon soir, Monsieur-dame.")

[. . .] Today, early in the afternoon, after a much more uncomfortable bike ride than the one later at night (hills and valleys), in the burning heat of the midday sun, I arrived at the camp. I saw a field surrounded with barbed wire guarded by soldiers carrying mounted bayonets. I presented my visitor's pass and was allowed to enter. In front of the barracks I saw a number of indifferently dressed, gesticulating men standing and sitting. The sight of so many men made me somewhat nervous at first because I could feel that I attracted their attention and knew they looked at me critically. (A permit to visit is not easy to obtain and is available only to the closest family members. For that reason there are never more than about six women in the camp among about three hundred men.)

I went up to the first man and asked whether he knew my brother, Peter Kaufmann, who is with the Fourth Company. The man knew him and gave me a friendly greeting and asked how my father was doing [and if he was] still free. He then told me that Peter would be at roll call. First I saw Otto, another acquaintance.

[. . .] Then another person joined in and finally I saw Peter. Since he did not expect me, he was particularly pleased. [. . .]

I ate supper with Peter and the others at the common kitchen, which provided neither good nor plentiful food. Then they dragged me into their homemade movie theater where, dead tired from the train and the bicycle ride, I fell fast asleep . . . Then I rode back to the hotel. Tomorrow morning I shall return.

April 28, 1940 [Melay-du-Maine]

I should have gone back home this afternoon but Peter and the others asked me to stay. How often does one get permission? Il faut en profiter. [One must take advantage of it.]

With the weather so nice, the internment camp does not seem as bad as it really is. It now seems like a vacation camp. The internees had made a kind of tennis court, soccer field, and sunbathing area. There is a "coffee house" and a pond in which one can allegedly swim and go boating. They have a theater and movie house, and because there are a number of artists among the internees they often have serious as well as amusing presentations. The barracks, which on closer examination really are not fit for humans, are more like ski huts.

However, such impressions should not influence one's judgment. It is horrible to be confined for seven months in a limited space, behind barbed wire, without having committed any crime. Seven months without work and nothing useful to do. Seven months without being alone for one minute. Yes, I believe that despite all the deprivations, despite the poor food, and the rough and shoddy accommodations, that is the worst of all. Not to have one minute to oneself. [. . .]

There was a farewell party in the evening for a group leaving for military service.[7] There was singing, but the voices of those remaining behind were quite wistful. [. . .]

April 30, 1940 [Paris]

When I came home today I found Dad busy packing to leave. It must be terrible to have to leave his family and his work for a second time in his life.

May 2, 1940 [Paris]

Dad is gone again. He was assigned as a "Prestataire." This company, Compagnies des Prestataires Etrangers, is composed of Spaniards, Saarlanders, stateless Germans, and Austrians. They are men seventeen to forty-eight years old. Since the French government refuses to allow foreign soldiers, they formed this [labor battalion] to perform service without weapons.

That has both an advantage and a disadvantage. They are not sent to the front and, therefore, are not exposed to life-threatening danger. But they can never attain a grade higher than common soldier, second class. Besides, those assigned to factories must work for twelve hours a day [. . .].

May 5, 1940 [Paris]

Isn't it funny to go ice skating now when the weather is so warm that the authorities have decided to open the swimming pools? Jacqueline, Nicole, Tchiquie, Francine, and Olga had the idea and I went along. We just went ice skating. The first time in one and a half years. The pleasure is out of all proportion to the cost. The rink is indoors, of course, small, and quite pathetic when I think of the Vienna Ice Skating Club.

Sport in France is commensurate with wealth . . . particularly ice skating. How can these girls ever understand that while I can skate, and have my own skates that I brought from Vienna, I don't have the money to pay the entrance fee? None of these girls will understand that this is the reason I am not going to join them the next time, pretending that I don't enjoy going. But why did I go this time when it would have made more sense to buy a pair of stockings?

To a large extent, the Austrian middle class was a class with exaggerated ambitions. When I lived in Vienna I was not aware of this, but it has now become clear that we already then were living beyond our means and that we afforded ourselves pleasures that were not commensurate with our material situation. We children studied at *gymnasium* [high school], our parents and grandparents frequently went to the theater, and in the summer we went on vacations.[8]

My parents tried in every way to give my brother and myself the same education and cultural exposure that they had enjoyed with their parents who were truly well off. In Vienna, this outward facade was somewhat supported by some possessions dating from the past and by established connections. Here in the emigration, the desire to maintain culture and tradition have not ceased, yet the means for it are practically exhausted. Thus, we are satisfied with less expensive food but not resigned to count ourselves among the poorest.

We continue to try by all possible and impossible means not to give up such "luxuries" as the Comédie Française, our own bathtub, a good book, presentable clothing, and so on, all those things that we cannot truly afford. That is how I was not able to refuse to go ice skating. It was more or less seen as a social obligation.

May 6, 1940 [Paris]

Peter also has been called into the service as a Prestataire and before he begins active duty will be able to spend one or two days in Paris. Today I started with a new

English teacher. He is the son of one of my mother's acquaintances and accepted the task as a matter of friendship. I already had one lesson and hope to be able to speak decent English quickly.

May 8, 1940 [Paris]

Peter arrived yesterday. He is hardly to be seen during the day and only for a short time at night. Understandably, he does not want to waste a minute of the two days that he is here without having fun. His motto is, "Not a minute without a girl."

May 9, 1940 [Paris]

Holland and Belgium are being occupied by German troops. The long-expected spring offensive begins. All leaves are being canceled. The German troops seem to advance at lightning speed while the Allies issue protests. Bombs are being dropped and the Dutch and Belgian civilians must flee. Once again the fighting takes place on neutral grounds.

May 11, 1940 [Paris]

The Dutch give up and the Germans march through the country. Hitler's success with his policies and pressure on the small countries is unbelievable.

May 13, 1940 [Paris]

As a result of the political developments terrible measures were taken today. [Quoting the newspaper:] ". . . Tout les ressortissants de l'Empire Allemand et les Dantzigois, Sarrois, Rheinians [*sic*] de deux sexes de 17 à 55 ans vont être internés . . ." [All nationals of Germany, Danzig, the Saarland, the Rhineland, male and female, age seventeen to fifty-five are going to be interned.] [. . .] Across from us lives a German family. The mother is in her late forties, the father in his mid-fifties. They have two daughters, eighteen and twenty years of age, and one son who will be seventeen next week. The members of the family will be completely separated for the duration of the war. The father will be the first to go into the camp although he was only recently discharged [from the camp] as "loyal." His son will follow him in a few weeks. The mother with her two daughters must go into another camp. I should add that the mother is almost totally deaf and not well.

We, as Austrians, are in a great state of anxiety. The official decree does not clearly state whether Austrians fall under the internment order, or whether we have been excepted. Mother and I—I skipped school today—are running from one office to another and are being given evasive answers. One commissioner says "yes" and another "no." They play with our nerves as if they were toys. This kind of day is nerve-wracking and filled with doubt about losing in the next three days what one values most in life, what is left of our personal freedom.

Should I now really go to school? One can go crazy. I am going to see whether the people at the Austrian Committee on the Madeleine know anything. They should have been given some instructions, but they usually know nothing when it comes to something important. [. . .]

[Elisabeth and her mother were not required to enter an internment camp at this time.]

May 14, 1940 [Paris]

Our neighbor's two girls left today . . . it is an indescribably deplorable situation, how pitiful. Two young, beautiful girls . . . and such people are thrown into those inhuman camps where their lives will be ruined. Ilse, the older, recently had obtained a good position taking care of a spoiled child of very rich parents. She turned over the job to Vilma, who is very happy with the pay.

Gabriella said the Germans had advanced so far that she and her mother would evacuate into the province in a few days. Sabine and Odilie already left.

My "English teacher" [a young man who informally tutored Elisabeth] was also interned as a German, so my studies did not last very long. Poor boy, he was only recently released from the camp.

May 17, 1940 [Paris]

I am very afraid for Ernst. It is now quite possible that after General Sikorsky's [prime minister and head of the Polish government-in-exile in London] resounding appeal to the Polish Legions, the Czechs will be next. We shall not see each other in the foreseeable future.

Vilma came home today with the news that the family for whom she now works eventually would like to employ a young girl in case they were to leave Paris, and that I would be considered. In that case, I would have to leave school, which I would never have done had the offer not been so tempting from a financial standpoint. Also school itself may close soon. Every day another colleague leaves for the provinces.

May 18, 1940 [Paris]

The Germans are at the Somme. For some weeks the strategic importance of this river has become clear. This region played an important and sad part in World War I and it seems as if that tragedy will be repeated. A large army concentration is under way to wage battle and it is hoped the Germans will be stopped.

The Arnold family for whom Vilma works appears to have decided to leave and they asked me to come for an interview tomorrow. In addition to the material benefits the job also gives me the opportunity for a free evacuation. However, the advantages that I gain have to be weighed against Mother having to remain in Paris alone.

May 20, 1940 [Paris]

This family is so crazy that neither Vilma nor I are happy [in this position] even though the pay is good. Departure from here becomes more certain as the Germans are advancing, and I think the family would like to take us with them. Theoretically we are not allowed to leave here without permission granted by the Préfecture [of police] to foreigners who wish to change their residence. [We need] the kind of pass that we had to obtain to visit Peter at the camp. Since then, times have changed. The officials are now so busy with their own internal affairs that control over foreigners no longer is of such great concern. But there still is a great risk in leaving without a permit. Yet it is impossible to have the officials grant a permit in less than two or three months without paying them or some intermediary large sums of money as a "gratuity." Taking this risk also is justified by the fact that the opportunities for leaving will diminish in time. Our situation is relatively favorable because we would be traveling in a private car with a French citizen who has a permit to travel. The whole situation, however, also has to be considered from another aspect, which is separating from Mother.

The advantages are great. I will be completely taken care of and in addition will earn a large salary that might help Mother stay alive, or, if she can earn money herself, she would be able to save. The disadvantages are that I will not be able to attend school to the end. (This disadvantage is not serious because the school will dissolve itself.) Separating from Mother for an uncertain period of time is more grave, since these are abnormal times during which we may lose each other, when, for example, the mail no longer functions. On the other hand, I am keeping Mother from working. Now, for example, she has an opportunity to take a position as a nurse in the American hospital in Neuilly.

May 22, 1940 [Paris]

Since the Germans have already taken St. Quentin and Amiens, last night the [Arnold] family decided to leave quickly. At 7 A.M. Vilma and I were to be at their house with packed suitcases, although they had not told us until the evening before that we were leaving and we could not get home until 10 P.M. There was not much time to consider the situation. Mother absolutely wanted me to leave, so

Vilma and I got up very early and each of us packed a suitcase with the most important things. At 6 A.M. we stood in front of the house searching for a taxi, because the Arnold family did not live directly in Paris, but in a villa. [. . .] This was not easy because almost all the taxis had been commandeered. It was difficult for us to find one and with our running back and forth we attracted the attention of the concierge, who told us that she was ordered by the police not to allow any foreigners to leave. She could not be persuaded that we did not intend to drive away either with arguments or with twenty francs, which she pocketed. Instead, she ran to the nearby police station and we were forced to [go with the] policeman. Although they were unexpectedly friendly, they insisted that for the time being we leave the suitcases at the station.

This delay lasted until eight-thirty, and we now fully expected to arrive at the villa and find the doors locked. This turned out not to be the case. [. . .] When we told them of our misfortune they said that their departure had to be delayed by one day because of some official problems and that we could spend the rest of the day getting permission from the police to travel. Should we fail they would be forced to leave without us.

As expected, we did not succeed. It would have been the first time that the police would have helped foreigners. This afternoon we ran from the police station to our house and from there to the office of the commissioner, and from there twice back to the police station and then back to the commissioners and finally back home. Nothing. All that rushing around was for nothing. [. . .]

May 24, 1940 [Paris]

The Arnolds are gone. Vilma and I no longer have work. It was a short-term job. I continue in school and it is becoming increasingly desperate.

According to the official news, the Germans are being driven back at Amiens. Overall, however, I doubt the French will be able to do much damage to the Germans. Nevertheless, all my hopes lie in an eventual Allied victory. A lost battle does not mean that France will lose the war.

The newspapers are carefully preparing us for the Italians to take an anti-French position. Tension is mounting daily. It can be assumed that if the current battles are won by Germany, Italy will join Germany. "Don't burn your fingers," Mussolini tells himself.

May 28, 1940 [Paris]

Leopold, the Belgian king, declared an armistice. There is talk and there are newspaper articles that this is the greatest betrayal in memory. Leopold made peace with the Germans without first having warned France or England to pull back their troops that are in the country. The Belgians give up to the Germans without a fight.

The French papers write that the Allies were sold out. They report that this was done so secretly that the French and British officials had no idea this was going to happen and continued sending troops, which are now lost, falling captive to the Germans. The result: another loss, one more defeat.

Nothing, however, is definite. I don't really believe that there are so many [Allied] troops in Belgium that the damage will be all that great. This can all be overcome. In 1914 the Germans stood forty kilometers outside Paris and were still pushed back. It is unthinkable that the Germans will win *à la longue* [in the long run]. [. . .]

Ernst writes that they were issued new uniforms. That is like being given one's last meal. It means departure. . . . It is now a matter of days. We are in the middle of the battles at Abbeville and Amiens.

May 29, 1940 [Paris]

The weather is so nice that often at lunchtime I feel sorry for myself for having to sit in the library. I then take my bicycle and ride around the streets to observe the people. Many already know me from having seen me before. [. . .]

I ride along the big broad streets next to the Seine from the Trocadéro to the Place de la Concorde. To cross it is particularly tempting since it is a little dangerous and one has to pay close attention because cars come from the left and right, from the front and the back. The broad avenues, on the other hand, with their beautiful parks and homes, give me a special delight, and since the traffic here is not so heavy, I can look at the lovely homes, the well-cared-for palaces, and observe the faces and dress of the passersby.

At the Place de la Concorde I decide whether I want to ride through the busy rue de Rivoli, where businesses since the war have suffered heavily because the luxury items meant for rich foreigners, the English, Swedes, and Americans, no longer are there to be sold. Other stores must close "pour cause de la mobilisation" [because of the mobilization]. [. . .]

The Jardin des Tuileries reflects the unusual wartime conditions. The lawns, usually so well kept, look like a meadow and the stalks of grass are long and dried out. Instead of the tulips that usually are magnificent there is earth waiting to be turned. [. . .]

When I walk through the entire park in the direction of the Louvre I go around the big pond, which at other times is crowded mostly with children and their governesses, the former playing with sailboats, motorboats, or rubber animals, the latter watching that their charges don't slip into the water. [. . .] I continue along the broad, shaded promenade to the fountain and then through the low iron gate across the path flanked by stone figures toward the Arc du Carrousel. I always go right through the arch, never to the right or the left of it. [. . .]

It is difficult to say what I love most about Paris. Only one thing is clear, and that is that I love it. Whether it is the broad, generous, and modern grounds of the Tro-cadéro, the symmetrical avenues, the magnificent gardens, or the colorful Latin Quarter. I don't know which—it could be all of that together, the multitude that affects me. I love Paris because in merely looking one can be distracted and find excitement. One has to lack all imagination to be bored in Paris, even without spending any money.

It is peculiar that right now, when the whole world is in a state of constant turmoil, I can make such "peaceful" observations to note in my diary. Daily life continues, although diminished in every sense. However, the charm of Paris has not disappeared as much as it may have been reduced, and I have not become insensitive, although my feelings have been relatively dulled. Paris still gives me pleasure.

Saturday, June 1, 1940 [Paris]

Yesterday I received terrible news. Ernst wrote that tomorrow or the next day he is departing training camp to be sent to the front lines. For a long time to come, this will be the last communication. I am terribly afraid. [. . .]

Poor dear Ernst. I ache in my stomach. That was a true farewell letter. How long before I will receive mail again? Ernst wrote almost daily. My eyes hurt as if I had been looking too long into a strong light.

June 3, 1940 [Paris]

An air raid alarm this afternoon made life a little more interesting. I spent one hour in the shelter with my excited neighbors. Only later did I learn that heavy bomber attacks took place in many quarters, particularly in the nearby suburbs. There were at least eight hundred wounded and two hundred people killed.

The war now becomes personal and more real from day to day. There lies a certain tension in the Paris air—understandably so. Almost everyone has someone "out there" for whom he is worried, a concern that increases measurably as the Germans advance. And their advance is imminent. [. . .]

June 8, 1940 [Paris]

I don't think that enough attention is being paid to the political situation. It is acknowledged indifferently that the Germans are barely a hundred kilometers from

Paris. For several days now cannon fire could be heard. Yet people already have become used to it even though the air during the day is shattered by the resounding noise. [. . .]

The days are warm and lovely. The evenings are long and clear. I often sit at the window in the dark to enjoy the night air. Across from my window in the middle of the square a huge spotlight is searching the sky for enemy planes. The light that periodically sweeps across my window keeps me from sleeping and reminds me of the war. They are fighting even at night.

No news from Ernst.

June 9, 1940 [Paris]

Already many refugees from the north are seen in the streets. All the schools are being evacuated from Paris, as well as many factories. A great defensive operation can be expected similar to what took place in 1914. Many of our acquaintances are leaving. Yesterday I received a letter from Gabriella, who left for Brittany some time ago. She writes how happy she would be if I were to join her. It is something to think about, but [it isn't] practical. It would be impossible for me to find work in a resort town, especially given the attitude toward foreigners and with so many French people who would be available to do the kind of work I would do. How would I live? Evacuation is for those with plenty of money or for those who own property.

Aside from that, I am not afraid of the bombings. That may only be because I lack imagination. I cannot imagine that something would fall on my head. Paris is probably well defended, the Germans are not yet in the city, and there is no panic.

The Beaufils family, our friends, also left today. They rented a small house on the Atlantic coast, near Biarritz. Mother, who was there when they left, said they mentioned that if things went badly with us, we could join them.

June 10, 1940 [Paris]

It happened. Today the Italians declared war. One must grant them that they are true heroes, those gentlemen from Rome. [. . .]

June 10, 1940 [Paris, second entry on this date]

[. . .] The Germans are said to be in St. Germain. The newspapers have stopped. All the world is leaving Paris. The streets are filled with refugees from the north. Optimism has no place here. But I am not going to allow myself to panic. Not me. I am staying in Paris. The Germans are not in the front door yet. In any case, my bag is packed. Not all the Parisians are leaving. What are Mother and I going to do?

In any case, I am going home to see what Vilma has to say about this Parisian migration. [. . .]

June 11, 1940 (evening) [Paris]

[. . .] Vilma is leaving tomorrow morning between five and six. It would be better if she sneaked out so that the concierge would not hear her. She is leaving on foot and is carrying a white linen sack on her back in which she has all her things. She is going to look like I imagine the Jews must have [when they] wandered from Egypt . . .

Mother and I also will be going on foot. We shall be leaving tomorrow sometime in the morning. We were lucky to have found two wax-lined bread bags in a small store, an article that can probably no longer be had in Paris, nor can anything else that would be of use for us. This *musette* [sack] will hold quite a bit. I am going to tie the "baggage" on the back of my bike, which I plan to take along. That way the bike instead of being a burden will help me carry our things and I don't have to leave it in Paris.

Tomorrow we shall leave Paris on foot. Our intermediate destination will be Dad, who is only about one hundred kilometers from Paris. Our final destination is the Beaufils family, who suggested that when nothing else works to take refuge with them. They are seven hundred kilometers away. The idea is fantastic—seven hundred kilometers on foot! If we walk on the average thirty kilometers a day it will be an uninterrupted march that will take twenty-three days. Not to think of it, give it no thought . . . Only away from Paris.

This afternoon I still took time to hurry through the Latin Quarter. Although excited I tried to fix everything in my mind, the houses, the plazas . . . and I asked myself for how long? Forever . . . or will it be for only a short time? [. . .]

June 13, 1940 [Rambouillet]

I am sitting on the steps of the Rambouillet Mairie [town hall] some forty kilometers from Paris. The weather is wonderful, the sky is clear, and the sun is shining. Next to me sits a family with many children. They look like Belgians. Just now a few troops marched by, pulling a small cannon. I am waiting for Mother.

Yesterday, after we had already become quite tired from walking, we found another means of getting away. The traffic on the road had finally come to a full stop because the never ending line of cars and trucks had come to a crossing over which an equally heavy stream of traffic was coming from another direction. A soldier was posted at this crossing to direct traffic, which he did by stopping traffic from one direction for fifteen minutes and allowing traffic from the other direction to cross. Then he stopped the traffic from the other direction for fifteen minutes. However, we did not see that from the place where we decided to go our separate ways. We only saw an endless line of vehicles moving forward periodically at a walking pace.

I went from car to car and asked whether they had a small space for a lady with some baggage. It took a while until I found a car that was not totally filled up and whose driver was also willing to take Mother. I ran back quickly and showed Mother the car, pushed her a little to make her go faster, and then climbed on my bike and rode away. At the last moment I remembered that I had no idea where the car was going. I turned around, but at that moment the line moved ahead and when I yelled and asked where the car was going the driver had only time to yell back "St. Remy." I did not know the place but then learned that it was not far, some twenty kilometers from Paris.

Because the cars actually were standing still more than moving, I was well ahead of the one in which Mother was riding. Meanwhile the weather turned bad and it looked like rain. I also had to pay attention while riding my bike because the only place was on the sidewalk; the road was packed with cars with no space between them. [. . .]

As I approached St. Remy, I remembered that I had made no arrangement for a meeting place with Mother and I had no idea how in this chaos of cars and people I could find her again. At last I thought of standing under the town sign, St. Remy, and waiting until the car carrying Mother arrived. As paradoxical as it may seem, I had come much farther with my bicycle than Mother had in the car. I guessed that I was about a half hour to an hour ahead of her and could rightly assume that she would have to pass by the town sign.

The place that I chose was not very quiet. I sat on the edge of a wall to avoid the danger of a car running over my feet, or being stepped on by a passerby. I stared at the road crossing and did not dare take a step away from it, or look away. Soon soldiers arrived and started to talk to me. They wanted to go to a bar and wanted to take me with them. When I explained to them that I could not leave, they went away. Then others came. After one hour Mother still had not come and I started to worry, but I remained seated motionless on the wall. Then it began to rain. I did not know what to do with my loaded-down bike, which was being ruined while the packages were soaked. I decided to push the bike into a restaurant, but did not [want to] leave my post. I therefore ran to the soldier who was directing traffic and asked him for the next three to five minutes to look for a woman in a small dark car who seems to be searching for someone. That would be my mother. He was to tell her that I would be back in a few minutes.

Elisabeth Kaufmann

I pushed my bike along in a heavy rain and then put it in some corner under a big tree without locking it, or having it watched, just counting on people being honest. Then I ran back to my post. Nothing had come to the soldier's attention. I was soaked through and through and was thinking that I had never been in such rain before. The constantly changing traffic, the cars, trucks, people, bicycles, noise, rain, soldiers, all made my head swim, and soon two hours had passed. [. . .]

A third hour passed during which [. . .] I became increasingly afraid and anxious. The rain continued to come down heavily. [. . .] It was already seven, then eight, and then nine o'clock. [. . .] It got later and later, and wetter and wetter. Suddenly I saw Mother getting out of a car . . . I ran to her.

After I picked up the bicycle we went to look for a place to sleep. It was dinner time and we were very tired and hungry. However, there seemed to be no possibility for stopping or to find a place to sleep. It was still raining, although not as heavily. We asked for a room at a hotel but were turned away by the owner as if we had asked for the head of his first-born. They obviously had no need to be polite. Their business flourished and they could rent every space in their place for a high price. It seemed quite hopeless. The streets were all packed with people from everywhere and it was as crowded as at the exit of a movie theater. But then we got lucky. While other refugees were looking for a place to lie down for the night on the wet pavement in narrow side streets, a young Polish worker led us to her apartment, which consisted of a kitchen and one room. She gave us the room with a double sleeping couch.

The next day we had learned from our experience. We decided to go separately for half a day. Mother had to stop cars that might get her to the next place faster, but she also might have to wait for two hours before she could get a ride. I rode ahead on the bike and we agreed to meet every thirty to forty kilometers so that we could spend the night together. Whoever arrived first at the agreed-upon town would have to wait for the other. However, we would no longer wait under the town sign but at the local Mairie, either outside, if the weather was good, or inside. This is how we hoped to cover the distance best, not become too tired, and still stay together.

This morning, after one and a half hours of trying, I was able to get Mother a place on the back of a motorcycle. I was very proud of myself since it really was a master stroke, if one considers the number of people and the few empty seats in any vehicle. I had some advantage in that I did not care where the vehicle went as long as it was more or less in the right direction. The motorcyclist only told me hurriedly that he would be going to Rambouillet and then disappeared down a side road. Rambouillet is about twenty kilometers from St. Remy, in the direction of Chartres along a side road where traffic was not heavy.

[. . .] I am now sitting in front of the town hall and am waiting for Mother. I can't understand where she might have gotten stuck for such a long time, but she cannot be far behind. [. . .]

June 13, 1940 (at night) [Chartres]

Chartres, some seventy kilometers from Paris. This is an unusual place for writing my diary, at the police station. It is eleven-thirty at night and we are sitting on a bench at a long table. The light is poor. Across from us sits a man in his mid-thirties, well dressed, who wants to extract "my secrets." He is a detective. Mother is sitting next to me. A few meters farther on the same bench sits a gendarme [policeman], writing. Behind us is another table, like the one in front of us, and also a bench like ours. On it an old man is lying, seemingly asleep. The man who wants to extract secrets from me now looks a little skeptical. He probably wants to know what I am writing. [. . .] [S]ince I really have a lot of time, I might as well begin at the beginning.

. . . [T]his morning, we sat down in the coffee shop and began to write post-cards. We wrote to Grandmother in England, to my uncle and his wife, to Dad in the camp, and then I wrote to a mutual friend of Ernst that news from Ernst should be sent to me at the Beaufils'. We did not really count on the mail being forwarded. Then we decided to continue to Chartres, another thirty kilometers, to spend the night.

[. . .] I accompanied Mother to the road leading to Chartres and within ten minutes a car with some space stopped and the driver promised to take her to Chartres. I knew that she would arrive at least two or three hours before me and asked her not to go first to the post office this time, but to wait right there [at the town hall] no matter how long.

[. . .] I finally arrived in Chartres. It overflowed with refugees. I asked for the Mairie. It consisted of three blocks of houses attached at right angles to each other, a courtyard closed off by a wrought iron gate. The gate was open and I dismounted my bike and led it into the courtyard. I noticed that my knees were shaking. A woman approached me from the door of the building on the right, looked me over, and then asked: "Are you the daughter of a lady speaking with an English accent and wearing a gray suit?" [Elisabeth answered:] "English accent? No . . . maybe, the gray suit is right." [The woman replied:] "She left for a moment to get something to eat. Don't be upset. She will be right back."

I followed her into the room where others were seated and waited. When I stood my bike against the wall, I suddenly collapsed and found myself seated on the floor. I was very shocked but pulled myself together, stood up, and sat down on the bench. My knees were trembling, my hands and eyes hurt, and I could feel myself starting to cry. I was very ashamed of myself and struggled against this attack. I scolded myself for becoming hysterical until I calmed down a little. Only then I noticed the heavy shoes hanging from my feet and how much they hurt. I took off my shoes and placed them next to me. The others who were waiting hardly noticed me. Most of them were crying.

Suddenly there were shots and sirens, which, I noticed, were different from those in Paris. Someone slammed the door shut. Then the room became very dark, which I did not mind. The attack that I presumed to have taken place was over in two minutes. The door was opened. I was concerned where Mother might have been all this time. Then she came. She also was worried where I might have been and then we both were happy to be together again.

But we did not have much time to be happy. At the moment when we wanted to leave for the shoemaker Mother had found, who was to give us soup—I had not eaten the entire time except that little bit at lunch and now it was already eight o'clock in the evening—the sirens began again. "Everybody into the shelter." We ran into the neighboring building and went into the cellar. After a little while we were told it was all over. However, no sirens announced the end of the raid. We left and went back to our old seat in the waiting room of the Mairie. [. . .]

I was very tired, but also very hungry. Mother took me down the street to a house. I put my bicycle in the entryway and we went into a dark room with a table and two armchairs. Mother told me to sit down and that the owner knew I was coming. She was going to get our provisions. Just as she was leaving two policemen came and said, "Come along." [. . .] They grabbed us under the arms and pulled us along. When we asked what this was all about they gave no answers. They hurt me. They walked with long strides. I was perplexed. I stammered, "my bike . . ."

Soon we arrived at the Commissariat. They led us into the room where we are now sitting. Only then they let go of us. "You are Germans?" "No, Austrians." They laughed. "Your papers." We showed them. "Give me your bag, and that one too." [. . .] They wrote everything down carefully . . . the names, et cetera. Then they went through my bag. They made two piles, probably one for things they considered indiscreet, for example a small volume of German poems, selected for classroom study. I took it along when I was rushed because it was very dear to me. It contained beautiful poems. Then came Ernst's passport and carte d'identité [identity card]. Before Ernst left for his regiment the last time, he gave me these two important documents, in addition to his diary, and asked me to safeguard them. I promised to do that for him and saw it as my duty to take them with me.[9]

Then the interrogation began. [. . .] First they asked us what we were doing in Chartres, where we had come from, and where we wanted to go, as if we had answers to all those questions. Then they asked about our backgrounds. All the answers we gave, however, seemed not "dangerous" to them. [. . .]

Shortly thereafter they were through with us, at least for the time being. They pointed to the bench on which we were to sit. After all that, we obviously were very depressed, particularly since we had not eaten and it was already nine-thirty. When we complained they brought us some provisions, but not much.

We were in the middle of eating, each of us shelling a hard-boiled egg, when the man who is now sitting across from us came, smiling cheerfully while sitting down with us, waiting for us to finish eating. He seemed quite friendly and he still is, but I was suspicious of him. He looked at me and must have thought, "the little one will confess." He asked me about this and that, about Paris, my studies, and Ernst, whose diary was lying in front of him.

I did not give him short replies, no, I told him everything he wanted to know at great length, and why not? I don't have to hide anything from him. I think he is not very pleased that the "little one" is talking so much and gives a straight answer to every question. [. . .]

June 14, 1940 (the third day of our flight) [Chateaudun]

After the detective had realized that he could not get anything out of us, he left. The light was turned off, and we stretched out on the bench and tried to sleep. We were very worried about what would happen to us. Naturally, we asked the detective whether he would let us go in the morning since he must have been convinced of our innocence, but his answer was very vague and left us with little hope. [. . .]

I never thought that wood could be so hard. Lying on the narrow bench was torture. I was filled with [the desire for] revenge. From time to time I muttered "pigs." I wish I had the power to burn down the whole police station. But I wanted to torture in particular the one who treated us so badly. [. . .] I tried repeatedly to find a way to lie so that the wood would hurt me the least. In the end I reconciled myself to dying of leprosy while being locked up with hungry, poisonous rats.

Then I thought how mean this is and considered the injustice in this world. As if it is not bad enough to be chased on foot like that, poor and without a destination, and without a home! And then, to be accused of being a spy for no reason at all. As if someone with Austrian documents, with no proper authority, and with no passport would be a spy. How absurd. If I were a spy, the Gestapo would have seen to it that I had a proper nationality, a Swiss passport, or French papers. What a dumb idea to make two Austrian refugees into spies, two women!

Elisabeth Kaufmann

Suddenly, at about four-thirty in the morning, the friendly gendarme from last night stormed into the room, full of energy and fear. "The Germans," he stammers, "the Boches are fifteen kilometers from Chartres—all the men are officially ordered to leave and the women are advised to do so also. The city is being evacuated." [. . .] [Then] another policeman entered loaded down with our baggage, which he threw at our feet. "Run, run, the Germans are coming," he said.

And then we ran. My bicycle was downstairs and we went to the town square. A damp, gray morning hung over the square, crowded with vehicles and people ready to depart. I went around and asked for a seat for Mother. It was useless. The people were so excited that they failed to hear me. I begged for a seat, but there was none. A gray, wet morning, a city is leaving, a city in flight. The Germans are coming, the Boches, the Boches . . .

Mother said that I should ride ahead and that she would continue to look for a ride and would follow quickly. We agreed on Chateaudun, sixty kilometers from Chartres, as the next meeting place. We figured that it would be noon or afternoon before we would see each other again. I climbed on my bike and left hesitatingly and unwillingly. It was the first time that I did not see Mother secure in a car.

The air felt like rain. Human shadows moved along the road. Then I had to laugh to myself that thanks to the Germans we were freed and also laugh at the illogical French police. If we were really spies, we would now have it easy. After I rode one kilometer I saw a well in which I washed myself and also quickly took care of other toilet matters. [. . .]

Then I continued to ride. After a few minutes I came to a house where coffee was being passed out. Warm coffee, or warm water, it was all the same to me, it was warm. I got off the bike and remembered that I had nothing warm in my stomach since Paris. I stood the bike against a wall, left it with a worried look, and entered the room. It was almost impossible to breathe for all the people who were there. I had to wait a long time before I could find a place to sit. Then everything went quickly. A dirty bowl was placed in front of my nose and a woman poured a black brew with one hand while collecting two francs with the other. I had a headache, was afraid about Mother, the hard, narrow bench from last night still hurt. I drank with one gulp, first because I was hungry, second because other people were standing in back of me, and finally, because I had left my bike hardly secured for a long time. [. . .]

[I] arrived in Chateaudun at about three o'clock. [. . .] I had to go to the Mairie where I am still sitting and waiting for Mother. [. . .]

3

Peter Feigl

FRANCE

Peter Feigl was born Klaus Peter Feigl on March 1, 1929, in Berlin, Germany. His father, Ernst Feigl, an Austrian national, was a mechanical engineer working in Berlin; his mother, Agnes (née Bornstein), stayed at home to raise their young son. Ernst and his family were fully integrated members of middle-class Austrian society. He had served in the Austrian navy during World War I, and his family had lived in Austria for many generations. The family was well off, with servants in the house, a Mercedes automobile, and summer vacations to the North Sea or Switzerland. Like many assimilated Central European Jews of the period, the family did not practice Judaism, nor was there any Judaica in their home.[1]

For reasons connected to Ernst Feigl's business, the family moved to Prague in 1936 and to Vienna in 1937. During that year, sensing the rising threat of Nazism in Europe, Ernst Feigl had Peter baptized as a Catholic, hoping to protect him from the Nazis' anti-Jewish policies. Peter, who had never had a Jewish upbringing, recalled that he immediately began taking catechism classes and serving as an altar boy. According to Peter's recollections, from that point forward he considered himself a Catholic.[2] In March 1938, the *Anschluss* brought Austria under German domination. Ernst Feigl had at a certain point refused to cooperate with the Nazis, who had wanted his help in bringing machinery forbidden by the terms of the Versailles Treaty into Germany. He now suspected that he was on a Nazi "blacklist" for not aiding them in their illegal schemes. This in combination with his Jewish identity did not bode well for him and his family with the Nazis in power in Vienna. He consequently wasted no time fleeing Austria for Belgium, taking the family and leaving most of their property behind.

There they remained until the outbreak of German hostilities in Western Europe in May 1940. With the invasion of Belgium, the Netherlands, and Luxembourg, Peter, his mother, and his grandmother fled to France. The xenophobia that had so plagued Elisabeth Kaufmann and her family as refugees in France affected Peter and his family as well. Upon arriving in France, they were promptly interned in the camp at Gurs, as were many Austrian Jewish refugees. They endured the miserable living conditions—overcrowding, lack of food, poor sanitation, no running water, and wretched barracks—for six weeks before they were released. They eventually settled in the unoccupied southern zone of France in a town called Auch, located in the Gers department. Meanwhile, Peter's father had been arrested in Brussels on his way to work in Antwerp and was subsequently held in two French internment camps. Due to his extremely frail health, he was eventually released on a thirty-day convalescent leave (which was extended month by month) and he was able to join his family in Auch in late 1941. Peter's grandmother bid farewell to the family in Auch and ultimately emigrated to the United States via Spain and Portugal.

In mid-July 1942, amid deportations of foreign Jews in France, Agnes Feigl succeeded in having thirteen-year-old Peter enrolled in and sent to a summer camp sponsored by Catholic charitable organizations at the Château de Montéléone in a town called Condom. A few weeks later, Agnes and Ernst Feigl were arrested and sent to the internment camp at Le Vernet. It was this devastating news that prompted Peter to begin writing a diary, "intended for his dear parents," as he put it.[3] The diary, comprising two journals, is sparse and much of the text seems at first obscure and difficult to decipher. Names and phrases are abbreviated; references to people, organizations, and situations are often vague; and most activities, events, or plans are not explained in detail. This may have been deliberate, to camouflage various aspects of his life in hiding; it may have been a reflection of his own lack of complete information; or it may have simply been a form of shorthand that he made up.[4] Despite its terseness, it is filled with information that reveals what the young Peter Feigl experienced during the years that he lived more or less on his own, shuttled from one refuge to another, without parents or a stable home.

Peter's primary concern throughout the first diary was the whereabouts and well-being of his parents. In fact, his diary entries were addressed to them, written as a sort of letter in which he informed them of his news, worried about them, and reminded them that he was thinking of them. The first entries of the diary reveal that there was a short exchange of letters and postcards between the Feigls and Peter; their vague and hasty nature left Peter suspicious and confused. In mid-September, the letters from his parents ceased entirely. His separation from his parents and their vanishing without a trace gave rise to a mixture of emotions, principally extreme anxiety and increasing suspicion about their whereabouts. At the same time, on occasion he expressed some hope for the future, looking forward to the possibility that one day the family would be reunited, perhaps in America, where he hoped to emigrate.

It is abundantly clear from the diary that whatever his fears, Peter had no real knowledge at the time of his parents' fate. While he knew that they had been interned in Le Vernet, and he discovered in mid-September that they had been sent to a place he called "Transi" (actually Drancy, the transit camp outside of Paris), that was the last news he heard of them. The Feigls are listed among those on Convoy 28, which departed Drancy on the morning of September 4 and arrived in Auschwitz-Birkenau two days later on September 6. They were most probably murdered on arrival, together with all but about fifty-four of the thousand Jews from the same transport.[5] Thus, most of the entries that Peter so earnestly addressed to his parents were written after they had already been killed. The Feigls were among the seventy-five thousand French and foreign Jews deported from France by Nazi design and French collaboration between 1942 and 1944.[6]

In addition to his worries for his parents, Peter was himself hiding from the French police who were looking for him. Consequently, he spent a good deal of time in bed, pretending to be ill, a fiction that was supported by a false medical certificate. Additionally, there are many diary entries recounting the necessary details of reclaiming his parents' remaining possessions from their apartment in Auch, where they had lived until they were deported. Above all, Peter recounted in his diary the efforts undertaken on his behalf to get him on a ship bound for America and safety. Although many of the details of the emigration application process are sketchy in the diary, it is clear that Peter understood the urgency to leave. The efforts to get Peter out of France, however, collapsed just before he was scheduled to leave. The November 1942 Allied landing in North Africa precipitated the German occupation of the previously "free" southern French zone; consequently, the Marseilles port was closed and the ship did not sail. "Tomorrow is the day when the ship was to sail. Good-bye ship," wrote Peter. He and a number of children who had been scheduled to leave on the same voyage ended up in Les Caillols instead, which was a temporary refuge for these children, run by a Monsieur and Madame Brémond.

In January 1943, Peter had the good fortune to be sent to Le Chambon sur Lignon, the Protestant village in the Haute-Loire, where Pastor André and Magda Trocmé, among thousands of others, were sheltering and harboring Jews and refugees, especially children. The inhabitants of this Protestant enclave were descendants of the Huguenots, who had been bitterly persecuted by the Catholic Church in France throughout much of their history. With their collective memory of oppression and suffering and their profound conviction of the sanctity of human life, this community refused to cooperate or collaborate with the Fascist Vichy government or with the Nazis. Their resistance took the form of sheltering those in need of refuge, without regard to their religious, racial, or national identity.[7] Peter was welcomed at Les Grillons, a home for young refugees financed by American Quakers and run by Daniel Trocmé, the cousin of André Trocmé. There are only a few entries written in Le Chambon before the first notebook of his diary abruptly ends on February 1, 1943. Peter believes that Daniel Trocmé or one of the adults there took it from him because it was too dangerous for him to have it in his possession. It could have compromised not only Peter but some of his friends, as well as the network of people and institutions involved in rescuing and hiding Jewish and refugee children. He was not to see his diary again for more than forty years.[8]

Peter remained in Le Chambon for about ten months, during which time he was given false identity papers, as were all the refugee inhabitants there. His new name was Pierre Fesson, born in Auch on March 1, 1929.[9] The inhabitants of Le Chambon ran a sort of "underground railroad" that continually supplied newcomers with false identity papers and then sent them on to new destinations, allowing still more people in need to take their places.[10] So in September 1943, Peter left Le Chambon and was sent to the Collège Champillion, a boarding school in Figeac (Lot department). Those who operated the school knew that Peter was Jewish (as were some of his schoolmates), but with his false identity papers and a ration card he was able to "pass" as a non-Jewish French citizen.

The second notebook begins in January 1944, a few months after Peter arrived in Figeac. Although less than a year had passed since the end of his first diary, the tone of the second diary is completely different. He was three months away from his fifteenth birthday, but he seemed decidedly older. He emerges as tough and self-reliant, fighting with other students and getting into trouble at school, taking risks that seem out of character for the young writer of the first notebook. At the same time, despite his toughness, traces of his loneliness emerge, especially around the time of his birthday or in relation to arguments with other boys in the school.

Like many other young people who wrote diaries at the time, he was preoccupied with his schoolwork, carefully marking his grades, test results, and class rank in his diary, as well as listing and keeping track of the books he read and the movies he attended. Beyond recording the day-to-day routine of classes, friends, books, movies, and such tasks as mending, helping arriving refugees, or making his bed ("Slave labor!" Peter called it), he also kept track of the progress of the war, noticing the movement of planes, air raids, and the sounds of gunfire. Further, he remarked on the activities of the resistance fighters (the Maquis) and the increased movement of German troops, which endangered those Jewish students who were passing as non-Jews. In marked contrast to the first diary, Peter only once mentioned his father in his second diary. In an interview given in 1995, he recalled that while he was in Le Chambon, even before arriving in Figeac, "day flowed into day, occasionally I would inquire whether anything had been heard from my parents . . . and so as time went on, let's say that my hopes faded . . . and I just kept on."[11]

In May 1944, Peter's escape into neutral Switzerland was organized. He and some of his schoolmates were taken to the Swiss border, where they met up with a *passeur,* someone who helped people cross the border, usually for money. The children were given instructions on what to do and how to cross, and on May 22, 1944, Peter made a break for it and ran from France into Switzerland. With him he carried his false identity papers, his diary, some photographs from Le Chambon, and, sewn into the lining of his jacket, his baptismal certificate from Vienna, testifying to his conversion to Catholicism. He and the other children who made it across the border were taken by a Swiss army truck to the Claparède refugee camp in Geneva, where they spent their first nights in the safety of a neutral country.

Peter's consistent and often ardent practice of Catholicism is a striking thread that runs through both notebooks, despite their differences. The diary shows that he attended Mass, served as an altar boy, took communion, and went to confession. Indeed, his second entry in the diary after learning of his parents' arrest was, "I went to communion and I prayed for you, my loved ones." He echoed these sentiments time and again throughout the diary, seeking comfort for his separation from his parents and praying fervently for their well-being and safe return. Across the span of both diaries, Peter emerges as a practicing Catholic with no personal ties to Judaism, through either religion or upbringing. In fact, the few references in his diary to Jews are, perhaps surprisingly, oblique and fairly hostile. In one instance, after a Jewish boy called Liverand punched him, Peter wrote, "I see that DAD WAS RIGHT and I'll get even." This was most likely a veiled reference to his father's dislike and mistrust of religious Jews, which was not an entirely uncommon attitude among highly assimilated Central European Jews, and which was inevitably communicated to Peter. As an adult, Peter recalled that many of the Jewish students at Figeac picked fights with him for the very reason that he did not consider himself Jewish. Further, in one of his last entries, written in the safety of the refugee camp in Switzerland, he referred to the Jews in the camp as "kikes." Years later Peter recalled that he had heard rumors that the Jews would be sent back to France and that he wrote this "shameful entry," as he put it, in part because he wanted to convince the authorities that he was *not* Jewish, and to confirm the veracity of his claim to be Catholic. In this, the whole diary not only reflects the hardships that Peter endured during the war years but begins to suggest the deep internal wounds he carried into his new life. Orphaned and homeless, Peter was left to grieve his losses, untangle his own deeply confusing identity, and struggle with a morally complicated ambivalence about Jewishness itself.[12]

Peter remained in Switzerland until July 1946, when he came to the United States. He had lost his first diary, but kept his second one throughout the years after the war. In 1987, he was contacted by a David Diamant, who had published the diary in 1986 and had not known that Peter survived. He learned about Peter because he appeared in Pierre Sauvage's documentary film *Weapons of the Spirit,* which recorded the wartime history of Le Chambon sur Lignon. Mr. Feigl eventually regained possession of the first diary and donated both notebooks and his collection of photographs from Le Chambon to the United States Holocaust Memorial Museum in the early 1990s.

Diary Intended for His Dear Parents

Belonging to FEIGL Pierre, August 27, 1942

This diary is written for my parents in the hope that it will reach them both in good health. Their son: Pierre FEIGL. Condom, August 27, 1942.

My Diary as of Thursday, August 27, 1942

Mr. Weissmann had mentioned it to me. It was before lunch that the [summer camp] directress, returning from Condom, called me to her office and told me what had happened to you, my dearest!

It was the Sec. Suisse [Swiss Aid Organization] which wrote her that they had come for you. I thought I would go mad. At the same time she gave me the last letter dated the twenty-fifth, together with the ration [coupons] and five francs.

I immediately wrote to the Sternefelds asking them to look after you, our possessions, me. I went out with the [Boy] Scouts. Later, returned and went to fetch the milk. I thought about you a great deal while waiting to hear from you.

Friday, August 28, 1942

I went to communion and I prayed for you, my loved ones.

Saturday, August 29, 1942

The mailman was here. I run to ask if there is something for me. Praise the Lord. A postcard from you telling me that you are together at the Camp du Vernet—Quartier H—Barrack 66/Ariège [Le Vernet—Section H—Barrack 66/Ariège county]. I am happy and hope that you will be released in view of Dad's poor health. The Di. [directress] also got a postcard.

Tuesday, September 1, 1942

The start of a new month. I wait to hear from you. Nothing for me. At noon, Mrs. C. [Cavailhon, director of the summer camp at Château de Montéléone in Condom, Gers] orders me to bed and tells me that they (3 gen.) [three gendarmes] want to pick me up. She has a cert. [medical certificate]. At two o'clock, they come. But thanks to the cert. they leave me.

Wednesday, September 2, 1942

I am in bed. Nothing from you.

Thursday, September 3, 1942

I am deeply concerned. Mrs. C. has received a letter with my baptismal certificate and three shoe ration coupons and nothing else. Sender: A. Feigl—Limoges, and addressed to Château de Montéléone, Condom/Gers, written in great haste (the postmark is from the first or second, from Limoges). I am worried. I fear that you have left. I am still in bed. I fear for you; my dearest parents.

Saturday, September 5, 1942

I am bedridden. At last I got your second postcard dated the thirty-first. I recall the strange letter of the third. But let's not get discouraged. I also got a very nice letter from Charles because I also had written to him.

Sunday, September 6, 1942

Nothing. I am in bed.

Monday, September 7, 1942

Nothing from you. Still in bed. Another letter from Charles who had the kindness to send me one hundred francs.

Tuesday, September 8, 1942

I am in bed. Nothing from you. I often think of you.

Thursday, September 10, 1942

Nothing from you. I got a postcard from Lex who is already in Madrid. He is lucky. I wrote you a card and another to Charles.

Friday, September 11, 1942

Still nothing. I wait.

Saturday, September 12, 1942

I receive a card from Ch. [probably Charles]. I have written you a card every other day just as you asked. But the directress tells me that she got a letter from a J. aid group [probably a Jewish Aid organization] saying that you were in the occupied zone and that you wanted to hear from me. I am afraid for [you]. I don't mail the card. It's useless. Tonight I cried. Who knows where you were taken to? . . .

Peter Feigl
{ 70 }

Sunday, September 13, 1942

Mrs. Lapper came to visit me. She says that you left (for Transi near Paris) [Drancy]. She is kind and says she stood by your side. She had brought me three morsels and the address of Siegmund [Peter's great-uncle then living in England]. We must be brave and wait. I think of you a lot.

Monday, September 14, 1942

Willie came to see me at noon. He told me he had the key. He brought me a package [. . .]. He received 300 francs from Dr. Koen and sold the animals. All told he brought me 1,003.80 francs. He is handling everything and I trust him. He was pale and haggard.

The directress showed him your letter, which she had just received, forwarded by the Quakers. I hope, despite everything, that you will leave with me. Perhaps you'll still be freed? She also said there was hope for my leaving. I think she got a letter from Charles.

Thursday, September 17, 1942

This morning Mrs. Cavailhon received a telegram from Vichy to the effect that everything was arranged for me and all those in similar circumstances. She and I are pleased.

Friday, September 18, 1942

Nothing. This evening, during dinner, I was sent to bed. Again the gendarmes. The telegram is of no interest to them. They want an official document or alternatively a medical certificate within forty-eight hours saying that I still cannot be moved. I was scared and thought of you. They left again.

Sunday, September 20, 1942

Nothing. I still could not go out. On one hand I wish I could be with you, on the other hand no. If only I knew where you are. What is happening to you? And Dad, his health.

Monday, September 21, 1942

I am sad and weary. During rest hour Mrs. Cavailhon called me. She received a letter asking whether she wanted to send some children to a very nice school in Haute-Loire at an elevation of one thousand meters.[13] She selected me and another boy. I'll be able to go there but she is afraid that perhaps I won't be safe there (gendarmes). Ah, what a life? . . . I'm still hoping. I got a postcard from Lex. If only I could go to this school. I would be very happy. I'll work hard to please you. Lex is in Portugal. Those who were left behind in France will join him on the thirtieth in Portugal.

Thursday, September 24, 1942

I cried a lot thinking of you. Miss Mariette of the S.S. [Secours Suisse] came to see me. She will send all my personal belongings to me. Mrs. Cavailhon told me in her presence that it was only a matter of a few weeks and that I will be leaving for America on the first ship (in October). I would have wanted to take you along. But once over there, I'll be safe and I'll be able to bring you over.

Monday, October 5, 1942

I phoned Willie and he told me that Mr. Lapp went to Fourrier's and took the bicycle. What a (bastard) he is. This evening Mrs. Cavailhon came back. She brought some forms for America and said it was now a certainty that I'll be leaving and she won't be sending me to school, either here, or in Haute-Loire. How often I have kissed your photo.

Tuesday, October 6, 1942

Nothing from you.

Wednesday, October 7, 1942

I filled out the forms for America. A ship leaves on November 25. It's the one I am to take, because Mrs. Cavailhon said that I would be leaving on the first one. The second one will leave before Christmas. What a joy this will be for you and for me, too. You'll know that I am safe. And you?

Thursday, October 8, 1942

Still nothing.

Friday, October 9, 1942

Mrs. Cavailhon has just gotten permission from the Ministry of Interior and from the préfecture [county government] for me to remain under the protection of the Quakers and that I am allowed to go out while waiting to leave for the United States. It's certain now. Yet I can't bring myself to believe it.

Tuesday, October 13, 1942

I asked Mrs. Cavailhon whether she'll accompany me to Marseilles and when (because she had promised once to take me). She said that she'll have to go there on November 5 and she said that she would take me because I must go to Marseilles a few days before the departure to the U.S.A. since the ship is to leave around the twentieth or twenty-fifth of November.

Saturday, October 17, 1942

Nothing new.

Sunday, October 18, 1942

Nothing. I am now able to go outside.

Monday, October 19, 1942

We went to Auch. I had time to take all my personal effects. [. . .] I brought back the papers, et cetera. No letter. Nothing from you. I languish. The doctor made me fill out another form, similar to the first one, for the emigration and he said that we will have to appear before a board in Toulouse.

Wednesday, October 21, 1942

Nothing. I got a postcard from Charles. How I would love to hear from you. If only the war would soon end. Not one aid organization knows where you went.

Thursday, October 22, 1942

I think of you and often pray for you.

Friday, October 23, 1942

The emigration forms were returned from Marseilles to Mrs. Cavailhon saying to wait for the board in Toulouse and as far as the young Feigl is concerned, if he is Catholic, it is not certain whether he'll be able to go. [14]

Saturday, October 24, 1942

The gendarmes came again. They asked if I was still at the home.

Thursday, October 29, 1942

At six-thirty this evening Mrs. Cavailhon got a phone call to send me in the morning to Toulouse with the other boy for the [board] hearing. At last, tomorrow we will be told whether I leave on the first or second ship. If only I could have you near me.

Friday, October 30, 1942

On our arrival in Toulouse, we went to the Quakers' office across from the railroad station. We were admitted right away. A man, an American, questioned me about you, Grandmother, et cetera, then I was given a number and I was taken to the doctor. He listened with the stethoscope and asked me questions (to determine intelligence). I was given an overall score of 18/20 [90 percent]. I went back to see the man and he said that I would [leave] with the first convoy around November 25. We ate very well there. We took a short walk around town while waiting to leave and then we returned to Condom.

Saturday, October 31, 1942

I am to get my things together because Mrs. Cavailhon is going to Marseilles Wednesday and she will phone whether she is to take me along. So I must have all my things in readiness.

Tuesday, November 3, 1942

I phoned Willie this morning to say good-bye to him and to thank him because tomorrow I leave for Marseilles with the directress.

Wednesday, November 4, 1942 [Marseilles]

All the [female] counselors cried on [my] leaving. A taxi came to pick us up at 9 A.M. to take us to Agen. From there we took the Agen–Marseilles train, the directress, her daughter and I, by way of: Agen, Montauban, Toulouse, Carcassonne, Narbonne, Sète, Montpellier, Nîmes, Arles, Marseilles. We arrived in the evening and I slept in the Quakers' office, 108, Boulevard de Paris. (*Furchtbar* [awful])

Thursday, November 5, 1942 [Marseilles]

[. . .] [A]t seven o'clock [. . .] I was told I would have to leave immediately in order to catch up with some other children going to a colony [home], "La Rouvière," near Marseilles, while waiting to depart [for the United States]. We did not catch up with the others and the man who accompanied me had never been there. Instead of making us get off at La Rouvière, they made us get off before, at La Rougière. So after a one-hour hike in darkness, we arrived at a colony [home] (Les Caillols) where it was decided to keep me.

Friday, November 6, 1942 [Les Caillols]

Nothing. I am getting to know the children. The directress, Mrs. Sarboer, is a Belgian from Brussels and is very kind. The director, Mr. Brémond, also. This evening I got sick. I am running a fever of forty degrees. The nurse, Irene, is taking care of me. But she doesn't know what ails me. I think of you.

Sunday, November 8, 1942

Sick.

Monday, November 9, 1942

Sick. Nothing. The ship is to sail on November 25.

Wednesday, November 11, 1942

The English and Am. [Americans] attacked North Africa. We were able to read the leaflets. They were everywhere. The gendarmes came to collect them.

Thursday, November 12, 1942

Sick. The Germans came to Marseilles.[15] I am a little bored. People think that the Anglo-Saxons will land. The director, Mr. Brémond, and the directress, Mrs. Sarboer, are very nice.

Friday, November 13, 1942

I still have no information about you.

Sunday, November 15, 1942

N.n. [Nothing new]

Monday, November 16, 1942

N.n.

Tuesday, November 17, 1942

N.n.

Wednesday, November 18, 1942

N.n. . . . T. of Y. [Thinking of You]

Thursday, November 19, 1942

N.n.

Friday, November 20, 1942

N.n.

Tuesday, November 24, 1942

Tomorrow is the day when the ship was to sail. Good-bye ship.

Wednesday, November 25, 1942

It will soon be Christmas. Who knows whether we will ever meet again.

Thursday, December 3, 1942

Nothing.

Friday, December 4, 1942

Nothing from you.

Sunday, December 6, 1942

I prayed for you in church.

Friday, December 11, to Tuesday, December 22, 1942

N.n.

Wednesday, December, 23, 1942

On a table, we set up a manger made of clay. The spirit of Christmas is everywhere. This will be a very sad Christmas for you as well as for me.

Friday, December 25, 1942

Noël, Noël, Noël, this is the day that is normally so joyous. But you are far from me; where? If we could only celebrate our Christmas quietly around a very modest Christmas tree, in Auch! Oh well, perhaps next year we will be together again?

We ate well at noon and also in the evening.

Sunday, December 27, 1942 [La Rouvière]

Mr. Brémond sent me to La Rouvière because I talked to the Germans. I cried a lot but he promised me that I would be allowed to return to Les Caillols.[16]

Monday, December 28, 1942

I am very unhappy; there's hardly anything to eat; there are nothing but Spaniards here;—and lice. I am very bored and think of you. I wrote Mr. Brémond and begged him to come back (water chores).

Tuesday, December 29, 1942

Nothing new. I'm bored.

Wednesday, December 30, 1942

Nothing.

Thursday, December 31, 1942

Nothing.

[At the bottom of this page, Peter pasted passport photos of his mother and father taken in Auch on May 15, 1942, when they applied for U.S. immigration visas. The first notebook of the diary, written in French to this point, from here on is written in German.]

Friday, January 1, 1943 [La Rouvière]

Today marks the start of a new year. We celebrated at Les Caillols with a stage play. We went there and had afternoon tea. Mr. Brémond promised me that he would take me back.

Monday, January 4, 1943

Mr. Br. [Brémond] came to La Rouvière today. I practically flooded him with tears. Then he told me to pack my things within five minutes because he is taking me along. I can tell you that I was happy.

Tuesday, January 5, 1943 [Les Caillols]

Mrs. B. [Brémond] (they got married) wrote a letter to Mr. Trocmé in which she asked him if he did not have an opening for me at his place.[17] I had asked her to allow me to go to school. She gave this letter to a young girl, Simone Fullenbaum, who lived previously at Les Caillols and now lives at Les Grillons with Mr. Trocmé. I hope that I'll be able to go there. The food there is fit for kings (butter, potatoes, et cetera). Whatever is happening to you? . . . Your son is thinking of you.

Friday, January 15, 1943

We were told that we'll have to get out in two or three days. When I returned from Marseilles at noon, Mrs. B. told me that she received a telegram from Mr. Trocmé. He has a vacancy and expects me as soon as possible. Once again I am in luck. I quickly packed my suitcases so as to be able to leave early Saturday at 7:20 A.M. At the same time, the thing from the UGIF [Union Générale des Israélites de France] arrived.[18]

Saturday, January 16, 1943 [Le Chambon sur Lignon]

I took leave, took the first streetcar at 6 A.M. and at 7:20 A.M. I left aboard the Marseilles–Paris express (travel = change train, bus, wrong [place?], Lavoulte bridge, telephone, fast train, Cheylard local train, St. Agrève). I arrived at St. Agrève at 11:49 P.M. The train did not go beyond there.

Mr. Trocmé came on his bicycle to meet me (still a young man and very nice). Now we still had to cover fifteen kilometers through the snow and a moonlit night. We arrived at Les Grillons at 2:30 A.M. There we ate something warm and then I went to sleep in the annex (I only saw Mr. T.).

Sunday, January 17, 1943

I got up at the stroke of nine [in the morning] and little by little got acquainted in the kitchen. It was really very nice and clean. Later, I went to see Amedée, the boy who was to come here with me.[19] I played and thought a lot about you. There are children here in various situations (some like me). [Here Peter drew a heart in the original.]

Monday, January 18, 1943

Mr. T. [Trocmé] gave us school textbooks and notebooks. Tomorrow we'll go to school. I changed my room and I now sleep on the second floor.

Tuesday, January 19, 1943

Today I went to school for the first time. Every day we have to cover twelve kilometers in the snow. It is much colder here than in Marseilles. I attend fifth class but no Latin. I got here one trimester too late.

Wednesday, January 20, 1943

I go to school. Often think of you. I found an Austrian with whom I get along well and practice speaking German. His name is Kurt Grossmann. His mother disappeared like you. His father [is] in [the French internment camp] Gurs. Later Mr. T. left for Vichy where he has [contacts] and his father was released in one week! Lucky! Lucky!

Friday, January 22, 1943

The UGIF now sends me three hundred francs every month. Mr. T. however takes them.

Sunday, January 31, 1943

Again another month begins and I am still without news from you.

Monday, February 1, 1943

[The first notebook breaks off here, the point at which Daniel Trocmé apparently took it from Peter, not long after his arrival in Le Chambon. The remainder of the diary is from Peter's second notebook, written entirely in French, which he began almost a year later, several months after leaving Le Chambon for the Collège Champillon in Figeac.]

January 1, 2, and 3, 1944:

Was a little bored. Left at two o'clock and arrived at Collège on Tuesday, January 4, in the evening. Despite assurances that the portal would be open, it was closed. After waiting a half hour and banging (on the door), at last it is opened for us. I fall asleep around midnight.

Sunday, January 16, 1944

The new class monitor [Mr.] Vigne punished me. Together with the other punished ones, I hiked out on the road to Aurillac where I was really bored. I read a book *(Première Without Jenny Graan).*

Thursday, January 20, 1944

During the night of Wednesday to Thursday, around midnight, guys from the Maquis [French resistance fighters] blew up the Ratier factory in Figeac after first stealing tobacco and gasoline. There was only one death. The most important machines were destroyed. (eight explosions). [. . .]

Friday, January 21, 1944

[. . .] To date, I have read: *The Young Eagle* (Rostand), *Colomba* (Mérimée), *The Mutineers of Elsenor* (London), *Koenigsmark* (P. Benoît), *For All the Sea's Gold* (G. Toudouze), *From One Spying to the Next* (?).

About five o'clock I noticed that something was being plotted against me. I wonder what it could be. But I think I can guess. Yes, this evening at dinner they were being pretty obvious about it. They [the other students] have decided, I don't know yet for what stupid reason, to ignore me. It doesn't bother me. But they didn't have the courage to say it to my face. I'm not afraid. So I'll be the one to go and ask them for the reason. What a sorry lot.

There is one among them who has not been bitten by the bug. It's because he is not one of them [not a Jewish student]. He (Claude Mathé) is really swell toward me and is in my class. Verilhac has been crying because someone took who knows what from him. I asked the oldest (Siroît) [one of those in hiding] why this silence is being maintained around me. Evasive and hardly honest answer: "Because." You gotta admit they're real gutsy. I just finished [a game of] naval battle with Mathé. I'll get even! I just filled out my leave pass.

Sunday, January 23, 1944

This morning I went to mass by myself. During mass, an airplane flew by very low. After lunch I went with Mathé to Pezet [a monitor] (coffee). Then to the Rex movie *(The Big Battle)* and to the Vox *(Viennese Blood)*. After the second film everyone wants to do the waltz. Especially the [student] monitor (Bros). Everyone dances a little, then we calm down. I read *The Burnt Pavilion* and started on *The Adventures of Till Eulenspiegel and Lamm*.

Monday, January 24, 1944

Only geography class was held. This afternoon in singing class we were together with the third [grade], a mere seven [students]. The teacher played for us waltzes, et cetera. . . . Then I read and tended the stove. They're still not talking to me. Mathé got news that he was to return to Paris because his mother, like nearly everyone else by the way, fears an [Allied] landing before April. Finally, before going to bed, Simon told me why they ignored me. It was because of the box. Well, that was settled.

Tuesday, January 25, 1944

[. . .] The weather is not fit for man or beast. It rains and the wind howls. Mathé leaves tomorrow evening. [. . .] This morning the bread was like JOB paper [as thin as cigarette paper]. Not until four o'clock and in the evening did I eat well.

After the meal, while going up to study hall, Mathé knocked over the stove pipe. The result: Vigne bitches and we make him bitch even more than before. He again promises detention for us, puts us on report; throws out two, et cetera. . . . You have to admit: We're having a ball. Siroît brought me a knife. Since Friday we haven't had any biscuits. Carrot Top [a Jewish refugee named Wolf] is immersed in his stamps [collection].

Friday, January 28, 1944

The German teacher lent me a book [. . .] . (Edgar Wallace, *The Yellow Snake*). This morning I asked someone to buy me some tracing paper. I read some Mickeys [comics] and in study hall I started making a map of the Scandinavian countries.

This evening some slob needled me, then hit me in the face with his fist (Liverand). I had a nosebleed and my lips are swollen. I see that DAD WAS RIGHT and I'll get even. And the older ones are taking advantage by making fun of me. Their tongues are untied as well as that dear little café waiter and vegetable peeler "carrot top" = Verilhac. It could well be that he won't be laughing much longer [. . .].

Sunday, January 30, 1944

I first went to mass. There I helped a blind man whom I already had helped last Sunday. Then we went to study hall. I read *Odd Story of Flight,* a small, pretty good book. At the Rex [cinema] I saw *Business Is Business* (not bad) and at the Family: *The Raven* which was a bit boring. [. . .]

Four guys arrived too late for dinner. The principal threw them out without eating and he revoked their permission to go out next Sunday. A good number of interns already are back. More will probably arrive at nine-thirty. No more school closing. It won't be long until carnival and then Easter. When will the [Allied] landing occur??? At noon there was an air raid alert.

Monday, January 31, 1944

Most of the students have returned, even my best friend Bernard. We talked together about the Ratier factory. This afternoon I went with him to choir. I'm in the second voice [probably singing baritone], as I was in sixth class, and we sang "The Old Chalet."

Wednesday, February 2, 1944

I borrowed from the library *Cyrano de Bergerac* by Rostand. I've decided to go visit Bernard at his home on Sunday if the weather is good. At present it is raining. A classmate will lend me a bike.

Thursday, February 3, 1944

[. . .] Bouzou lent me his bike and I decided to go see my friend Bernard whom I found home. At least I think he is [my friend].

We played nain jaune [yellow dwarf], then we had a tea break (three slices of bread spread with jam and some good tea). With his help I was able to find twelve cheeses (twenty francs) and he gave me a piece of bread to take along. I got back to the Collège, all sweaty, at five-thirty after covering a good twenty-eight kilometers.

I think I'll go back on Sunday with Schiltz's bike, spend the afternoon and get to know him better. I had a good time.

Friday, February 4, 1944

Today it was announced in the Official Bulletin that all young males between the ages of sixteen and sixty must report for forced labor assignment. Lots of excitement. I checked out a German library book and I read *Outpost at the End of the World.*

Saturday, February 5, 1944

Yesterday I got chewed out by Mr. Verbié. I made a mistake in the "equality case," and I must copy the first case fifty times. I did it. We had English composition, easy; I read *Kai Out of the Box* [*Kai aus der Kiste*], which wasn't bad.

Sunday, February 6, 1944

We went to mass, played ball, et cetera. . . . I got better acquainted with Tascali and Wittelson. I read *The Eleven Lemoyne Brothers* and was unable to go see Bernard because of the bikes. Hence I saw *Forbidden Love* (totally stupid) at the Vox cinema and *Sacred Fire,* which wasn't bad, at the Rex. After a dash, I got back to the Collège just in time.

Monday, February 7, 1944

I read *The Pyramid of Atlantis.* In the afternoon I went to choir. The grades for the compositions are: German first with 15—French fifth with 9½ [both out of twenty]. My ranking is unchanged. I did not get my cakes. I'll get them Thursday. There are two new interns. One from Nice, one from Montpellier. I believe that on Thursday nearly two thousand people will be evacuated here [to Figeac].

Tuesday, February 8, 1944

We had dictation (awful). I made nine errors. It's shameful. [I am] in the midst of reading *Chancellor Martin Paz* by Jules Verne. It's a bit boring. I spoke with Mr. Verbié and I'll get my first lesson Friday from 5 to 6 P.M.

Friday, February 11, 1944

It is raining and hailing this morning. Winter is back. [. . .] This morning I got a 5 [25 percent] and a 0 in Math. Furthermore, I'd like to master the multiplication table before my fifteenth birthday. Tonight my sinusitis started again. I took an inhalant. [. . .]

Sunday, February 13, 1944

This morning I felt well again. After going to mass, at ten o'clock I went to the youth home in place of chief Delbos. (It's for teams being organized for Saturday's arrival of refugees). In theory, the refugees are to arrive here on Tuesday the fifteenth, that is on a market day (what a great mess that's going to be). I got back about eleven-fifteen.

After lunch, I went to the ice cream parlor (coffee) with Durand and Benne. I read a newspaper. Then around two o'clock I went to the movies. At the Rex: *Snow on the Footsteps* by Henry Bordeau and at the Vox I again saw *Salvator Rosa, The Black Mask* which I had seen in Marseilles about one and a half years ago. We got back on time.

Monday, February 14, 1944

Mr. Pujolle is back and therefore we had geography class. This afternoon we had only singing class and we had a lot of fun. The refugees are due to arrive tomorrow morning. In English class I rank first and together with Verilhac have a grade of 16.5/20 [82.5 percent].

Thursday, February 17, 1944

The refugees arrived. We spent the entire day at the railroad station (it was snowing and we did not have classes), we hauled furniture. Tomorrow we'll continue.

Monday, February 21, 1944

I saw three airplanes this afternoon. I did some mending. For the past two or three days it has been freezing.

Tuesday, February 22, 1944

The sink is frozen and leaks. I went to see Schiltz and together we went to see the abbot (the scouts' chaplain). Loupias was there. With him we played a game of Monopoly, which I won. He lent me some newspapers.

Sunday, February 27, 1944

I went to the movie and celebrated a little my [coming] birthday. At the Family [cinema] I saw, together with Sendic whom I invited, *Grim Fate* with Zarah Leander and at the Vox: *Am I a Criminal?*

Tuesday, February 29, 1944

Yesterday I bought some blue Parker ink. We had math. Tomorrow is my birthday. I'm curious to see who'll congratulate me. Today I did one-tenth of the English preparations in advance. It snowed.

Wednesday, March 1, 1944:

I couldn't drag myself out of bed this morning. I went to class. In the morning, Iffernet wished me a happy birthday. I must admit that I was really surprised, it coming from him of all people. Then Jean-Claude gave me a book, *Is That a Crime?* Other than that no one said anything. [. . .] The weather is beautiful and the snow has melted. That's practically my only consolation. This evening we won't have study hall because the windows are broken.

Thursday, March 2, 1944

Well, no one wished me a happy birthday. In the afternoon we went to study hall because it's raining.

Wednesday, March 8, 1944

We had history composition: Christianity. It was a snap.

Sunday, March 12, 1944

I went to the movie. Around four o'clock I saw three airplanes. Lately there have been air raids during the night (midnight, 12:30 A.M.).

Tuesday, March 14, 1944

Geometry composition. It was fairly easy; I got a 14½. That raises my overall average to 12½ and I think I rank eighth in class.

Wednesday, March 15, 1944

We got our history composition grades. I ranked first with a grade of 13. Monday we'll have geography [test]. I had a lesson with Mr. Verbié. I read *Surcouf the Pirate* by Karl May and *The Pioneers* by Fenimore Cooper.

Thursday, March 16, 1944

I read *The Heroic Life of Guynmer* by Henry Bordeaux, *The Death Mob* (a terrific crime novel) *Across New York* and *The Zeppelins* (written by a German). [. . .] Since Tuesday we are all required to fold our sheets and our blankets and make up our bed at 1 P.M. only. Slave labor! Fortunately I found a gimmick. The weather is great today. It's none too soon for the arrival of spring.

Friday, March 17, 1944

I got my math grades today (eighth, 12½). Many guys are saying that our summer vacation will start around the first of May. It's possible because this afternoon Germans came to look over the Collège. It seems they want to use it as a hospital.

Tuesday, March 21, 1944

There was an air raid during the night. Verbié told us that there would be a girl in our class.

Wednesday, March 22, 1944

She came and her name is Régine Veissier. She is from Marseilles and she is bright as a tack. I'll have my work cut out for me.

Thursday, March 23, 1944

She sits next to me in history, geography, English. We got the geography results. I got an 11 and rank eighth. In the afternoon we went into the La Capelette woods. I had a lot of fun with Wittelson.

Friday, March 24, 1944

I read *The Life of Napoleon* by Louis Bertrand.

Sunday, March 26, 1944

I went to mass and this afternoon I'll go to the movie. The juniors [aged eleven to thirteen] of our Collège will play rugby against the public [primary] school this afternoon. At the Family [cinema] *Two Young Girls*, it was sad, and at the Vox *Adrian* with Fernandel, it was very funny.

Tuesday, March 28, 1944

It rained punishments in German and in math. Twenty-five sentences to copy in German and seven theorems to be copied ten times in math, due by Friday. Tonight there was a fire in the countryside.

Wednesday, March 29, 1944

I completed the punishment assignments. This afternoon I went to confession and tomorrow morning at eight o'clock I'll go to communion.

Thursday, March 30, 1944

This morning I went to communion at eight. The Reverend Father P. Nicolas spoke. He is a very good speaker and he also spoke last Sunday. I read *Jerry on the Island* by Jack London.

From Friday, March 31, to Wednesday, April 26, 1944

Vacation, ate well on Easter Sunday; visited acquaintances. On returning, the incident with the trucks (tires), expelled and really chewed out.[20] Chewed out again because of the music teacher. X was there and gave me a severe reprimand. Last Sunday there were major roundups [probably by the Germans and the Vichy police]. The prison raid with the Maquis [resistance fighters].

    I read: *Napoleon Bonaparte, Dream Music, Lights in the Night.* I read *Mystery of the Garage, Raffles Return, The Good Life of Airline Pilots,* [. . .] *The Coral Vessel, The Black Cruise, Robinson's School.* Lost the chess championship match. [. . .]

Wednesday, April 26, 1944

Yesterday we had German composition (Beethoven version and three questions). Today it's French composition. Idiotic topic. I played chess with Delbos and I won. [. . .]

Thursday, April 27, 1944

We got the results of German composition. I am first with 17. Did they ever make some dumb mistakes.

Thursday, May 4, 1944

I saw another airplane. I went out in the afternoon. I received the letter in which I am informed that I'll probably leave.

Sunday, May 7, 1944

I went out this afternoon. This morning I was told that I must leave tomorrow morning at eight o'clock. I went to the movies and saw *Water's Prey* and *Cupola of Death.* I threw away all my notebooks. After dinner, all is ready. That's when I'm told that I don't have to leave. Damn!!!

Thursday, May 11, 1944

This morning the Germans came through riding on tanks et cetera. . . . An inspector was here. The first and second grades passed their scholarships. In town and in the surrounding area things are hopping and are really getting hot. Rumors are running wild. [. . .] I also went to the movie at the youth center. I saw: *The Heroic Struggle.* I hope I'll be able to leave soon because I have had it. We heard machine-gun fire this evening in study hall.

Friday, May 12, 1944

The town is flooded with Krauts. The Maquis is fighting. There are Krauts and armored vehicles everywhere. All the males between the age of sixteen and fifty-four must report to the gendarmerie. It was said that they would return right away but they were all taken away with the "cuckold." The Germans came searching, et cetera. We played [Peter's code word for hiding].

Saturday, May 13, 1944

We played [hid]. It is believed that they [the Germans] are in Cahors.

Sunday, May 14, 1944

Mass. It was learned they [Germans] are in Montauban. I was able to go out. The [drawing of a swastika in the original, meaning Germans] finally left. Denise [a rescue worker] did not come.

Tuesday, May 16, 1944

Denise finally came yesterday evening. She tells me that I leave tomorrow morning at eight. I had my baggage checked in.

Wednesday, May 17, 1944

At eight o'clock, at the very moment I was to leave, Wham! I won't leave until tomorrow. There is no train. [. . .]

Thursday, May 18, 1944

At last I leave for Clermont-Ferrand by way of Aurillac. Arrival at 12:30 A.M.

Friday, May 19, 1944 [Clermont-Ferrand]

As there is a curfew, I am given a pass and I go to the hotel. I stay in Clermont. Maybe I'll leave tomorrow.

Saturday May 20, 1944 [Clermont-Ferrand]

I cannot leave yet. The weather is bad. I went to the fair.

Sunday, May 21, 1944 [Lyons]

The weather is still lousy. I leave at 12:30 P.M. in the direction of Lyons by way of Vichy. I arrive at 8 P.M. I sleep at the red [drawing of a cross in original, meaning Red Cross] and will continue onward tomorrow morning.

Monday, May 22, 1944 [Geneva]

Leave at 6:30 A.M. from Lyons Brotteaux to Viry via Culoz. Arrival at 12 P.M. There, half of them don't get off [the train]. I jump off the running train. The two passeurs [guides who help people cross national borders clandestinely] tell us to hide in a grass field. Cops go by. At 1 P.M., the others who got off at St. Julien rejoin us[.] The column starts walking behind the passeurs. We are marching along a road. While no one could be seen on the road, at a sign from the passeur we cross in double time a grassy field and then a plowed field. We see the railroad track. The barbed wires have already been cut. No one on the tracks. We go through at a gallop. Then we enter high grasses and a small forest. There the two passeurs get lost; we run around in circles three times then he finds the way again. There is a young kid who's screaming and the passeurs are furious. We go through a woods. We see the border. No Krauts, no French. He makes us lie flat on the ground. It rained and it's not pleasant. My feet are soaking wet. The signal for us. On the run we get nearer to the barbed wires. We throw our backpacks over the fence and we cross wherever feasible. A Swiss guard is watching us. We cross at Sorral II. We are well received. An interrogation (the first one) already started. I pull out my real [identity] papers, which had been sewn into my jacket [lining].[21]

A truck came to pick us up around 3 P.M. It took us to Geneva to the "triage" camp of Claparède. Everybody along the road waves to us. There the interrogations start. We eat well. At 11 P.M. I take a shower and they inspect our scalp [for lice]. Then I sleep soundly in a free country.

Tuesday, May 23, 1944 [Geneva]

Interrogations all day long. (Police, photos, doctor, et cetera . . .) In the evening after dinner (7 P.M.) I left with a lady and her two children and another young man. We are rid of the kikes who are sent elsewhere.[22] It is said that the camp is the best of all of them.

From Thursday, May 25, to Tuesday, May 30, 1944

Nothing special, camp life, we eat well. I wrote to Mr. Gersonde [a business associate of Peter's father who had given him his name earlier]. Yesterday I got two francs fifty [centimes] plus a collection that was taken up for me. I received my bank account today.

Monday, June 6, 1944

Letter from Mr. Gersonde. Very happy. Rome fell [to the Allies]. Interrogation by the commanding officer.

Tuesday, June 7, 1944

Wrote Mr. Gersonde with two photos.

Arrived Bern June 26, 1944, 1:30 P.M.

4

Moshe Flinker

Moshe Ze'ev Flinker was born in The Hague on October 9, 1926. He had an elder sister, Esther Malka, and five younger siblings: Leah, Gittel, Rivka, Rochel, and Chaim Aharon. Moshe's father, Noah Eliezer Flinker, was originally from Poland and had deserted the Polish army to settle in Holland, where he married his wife, Mindel, and became a wealthy businessman. The family was devoutly Orthodox, living comfortably in a beautiful home and rigorously observing Jewish law and custom in all aspects of their lives. The children attended secular schools and studied Jewish subjects at home with a Rabbi Grabel. Moshe, in particular, as the eldest son, studied intensively and was remembered by his younger sisters as exceptionally bright, serious, and hardworking.[1]

After the German invasion and occupation of Holland in May 1940, the Flinkers remained in The Hague, subjected to an increasing series of restrictions against Jews. Moshe wrote in his diary of being expelled from public places, being forced to wear the yellow star, and hearing news of the concentration of Jews in Amsterdam. In July 1942, while Noah Eliezer was on business in the nearby border town of Roosendaal, Mindel Flinker received deportation notices for all nine members of the family. According to Moshe, he left that very day for Roosendaal, followed by his mother, brother, and sisters the following morning. From there, the family hoped to flee to Belgium and then find permanent shelter in neutral Switzerland. Hank Raats, Noah's longtime friend, took on the complicated and dangerous task of finding shelter for nine Jews in the border town. He and his wife took Esther Malka and Leah in with their nine-year-old daughter, Corry. The others were placed with families nearby. Within a few days, the family illegally traveled again, crossing the border into Belgium and taking up residence in an apartment at 1 Pikar St. in Brussels. Thanks to Noah's wealth, they were able to obtain false identity papers that allowed them to pass as non-Jews and residence papers permitting them to remain in Brussels.

They had escaped the Nazi snare in The Hague, however, only to arrive in the midst of another one in Brussels. Like their Dutch counterparts, the Belgian Jews were living under intensely repressive measures and were being routinely deported to the East (under the Germans' propaganda story of being sent to work in the Ukraine or Russia). But the Flinkers were unknown in Brussels, and not listed on any records stating that they were Jewish. This, together with their residence papers, allowed them to live, if precariously, in Belgium. Like Peter Feigl in France, Moshe Flinker found himself passing as a non-Jew, evading deportation to the East with the help of false papers. Unlike Peter, however, who was Catholic according to his identity papers and by conviction, Moshe was, as Shaul Esh put it, a "quasi 'Marrano' of the 20th century in the heart of Europe," concealing a strong Jewish identity and devout religious conviction beneath the guise of a non-Jewish persona.[2]

Moshe began his diary in November 1942. His early entries read less like those of a diary and more like a treatise on the subject of the persecution of the Jews under the Nazis and its meaning in a religious Jewish context. His ideas are difficult to understand and impossible to appreciate unless seen in the context of his larger world view, which was entirely defined by his faith. Indeed, as the diary reveals, he was first and foremost a deeply religious young man, who believed that everything that happened in the world was an expression of God's will and his divine plan for his chosen people, the Jews. Further, Moshe defined his world by what he saw as the ultimate truth of the word of God, expressed in the Tanach, the Hebrew Bible. In this, he understood the experience of the Jews in the present as part of the continuum of Jewish history, and their life in the Diaspora as a continuation of the story that began with the destruction of the Temple of Jerusalem and the exile of the Jews from there two thousand years earlier. While he vaguely attributed this punishment of exile to the sins of the Jews, he also firmly and concretely believed that eventually, with repentance and prayer, the Messiah would come, bringing about the final redemption of the Jews and a return to Israel.

Faced as he was with the unprecedented persecution of the Jews of Europe in his own time, Moshe endeavored to reconcile these deeply held religious beliefs with the troubling reality that surrounded him. But whereas the monumental suffering of the Jews caused many young writers to question or doubt the existence of God, Moshe's belief in God was as absolute as his belief in the suffering he witnessed and experienced. The diary does not reflect a struggle for faith, or a battle to maintain belief in God in the face of suffering. Instead, it is the effort to reconcile two truths—the existence of God with the existence of suffering—not by questioning the existence of one or the other, but by asking a different question entirely: what is the meaning of this? As Moshe voiced it in the diary, "What can God intend by all these calamities that are happening to us in this terrible period?"

At the outset of the diary, Moshe put forth his answer, which had begun to develop in The Hague and was, as he acknowledged, still "crystallizing." At its core was Moshe's view of this particular persecution in relation to those of the past. He rightly recognized the dramatic differences between the persecution of the Jews by the Nazis and those that had preceded it, remarking on its basis (racial versus religious persecution), its scope (Jews across Europe versus localized persecution), and its potential threat to Jewish existence (modern technological means of killing versus rudimentary ones). These distinctions suggested to Moshe that God intended the outcome of this persecution to be different, too. Though there are many complex parts and nuances inherent in Moshe's theory, the crux of his belief was that this persecution could not be just a "link in a long chain of suffering," without an end in sight. Rather, the very extremity of its scope and the threat it posed to Jewry signified the opposite: it was the penultimate moment of redemption, "the birth pang of the Messiah." It was to be the final suffering before the Jews would be saved and redeemed once and for all from their long history of persecution, oppression, and torment.[3]

Still, in Moshe's understanding of the world, the coming redemption was not a foregone conclusion; rather, it depended on the fulfillment of certain conditions. One of these was the forsaking of sin on the part of the Jews; another was the accumulation of sin on the part of the Jews' enemies, which would "only intensify [the Jews'] right to salvation," as he later put it. Although these notions may seem stilted or foreign to a secular audience, Moshe did not invent them from whole cloth; he drew his ideas from his reading of the Tanach and its commentaries. All around him he saw encouraging signs that the moment was drawing near, as more and more of the essential conditions for redemption seemed to be falling into place. But, he concluded, "there is still one small detail that could spoil all this. But on this subject I shall write tomorrow, God willing, for I am most weary (it is past 1 A.M.)."

The "detail" is, in fact, the very heart and soul of Moshe's theory. It is that "most Jews" saw their persecution and the struggle for liberation not as a divine matter but as a secular one. Instead of placing their faith in God, they were entrusting their lives to such secular agents as diplomats or the military. And instead of praying to God for redemption, they were wishing for an Allied victory, liberation from this persecution, and a return to normal life. For Moshe, this was not only short-sighted, but misguided. For in this case, the pain they had endured would indeed have been nothing more than a "link in a long chain of suffering," with true deliverance eluding them. Further, the way would be paved for more persecutions in the future and the continuing existence of anti-Semitism in the world.

While Moshe devoted much of his energy to his own deeply inward and reflective analysis of his ideas, the diary is also filled with reports on all aspects of his daily life and the world around him. Moshe had initially articulated the purpose of the diary as follows: "It is because I hate being idle that I have started this diary, so that I can write in it every day what I do and think; in this manner I shall be able to account for all I have done each day." To this end, Moshe reported on how he passed his time—reading books and articles, studying the Bible and Talmud, teaching his sisters French, and the like. He also described the worries of renewing permits and residence papers, the family's close calls with the police and Belgian authorities, and the deeply upsetting disappearance of those who were deported. Most poignantly, he mulled over questions of his own character and moral conduct, and took up the question of his future, considering what he would do as an adult, when he would have to "earn [his] own living." In a testament to his determination to live according to his convictions, Moshe declared that he would become a diplomat in Israel, and undertook the monumental task of teaching himself Arabic.

Moshe was a gifted linguist, having studied eight languages by the time he began writing in his diary at age sixteen.[4] Further, he chose to write his diary not in Dutch, his native language, but in Hebrew, despite the challenges and problems it presented. He had undertaken the study of Arabic because it formed a central part of his preparation to become a diplomat in Israel. He wrote: "I have begun—and hope I may finish—to study this language because a large part of the inhabitants of the land of Israel and the surrounding countries speak it. . . . It is obvious that we shall have to live in peace with our brothers, the sons of Ishmael, who are also Abraham's descendants. . . . And therefore I am trying very hard to learn the language."

As the months wore on, information about the outside world gradually filtered through to Moshe in Brussels. As it did, he continually returned to his ideas, reshaping and refining them in light of what he learned. In many cases, the information was faulty, influenced both by the general unreliability of news in wartime and by the deliberate efforts of the Germans to cover up their crimes. From the beginning, Moshe, like many others, believed that the Jews deported East were being sent for labor, and had no knowledge of the death camps or the murder being perpetrated there.[5] In late December, however, Moshe heard the first rumors that massive numbers of Jews were dying in the East. And though he did not know how many (he heard one hundred thousand had died, when in reality more than three million Jews had already been killed by the Germans) and he did not know the cause (he believed it was due to disease and death from hard labor, not outright murder), the news was devastating.[6] His shock and disbelief spilled onto the pages of his diary, as he turned in despair to the Bible, searching for a text that might bring him understanding or comfort. He eventually turned to Lamentations, "that elegy on the earlier calamity that befell my people," as he put it, finding consolation for his sorrow in the echoes of the biblical past.

After the grief of the first days subsided, Moshe turned again to his ideas, reexamining them in light of the news he had heard. Thus, an idea that had been faintly expressed in the beginning of the diary began to take shape, gaining in clarity and force. Moshe had always believed that "most Jews" were wrong to place their trust in the Allies instead of in God, but as the crisis deepened he came to believe that salvation itself depended on the reversal of that position. Indeed, it was only a collective Jewish shift in belief—in essence, a return to true faith in God—that would be the decisive factor in bringing about the redemption. In an entry written on December 28, 1942, he articulated the point most clearly, writing: "The idea is that salvation will come only when the whole world, and especially the Jews, give up all hope for a victory by the Allies. Then will the Lord have mercy upon us, and His light shall shine upon us, and His salvation will come."

Further, from the outset, Moshe had insisted—without explaining why—that the Germans would appear victorious until the very end of the war, and that their defeat would only come suddenly and at the last moment. As he clarified his ideas toward the middle of the diary, he returned to this notion, explaining it as God's final test for the faith of the Jewish people. If the Jews could not only abandon their hope in an Allied victory and place their faith in God, but also maintain that faith even when all seemed lost—that is, when Germany appeared to have won the war—God would save them once and for all. He would manifest his power with a dramatic reversal of fortune, overthrowing the Jews' enemies and demonstrating once and for all that it was God, and not humans, who determined the fate of the world, and that salvation depended on his divine grace.

Throughout the diary, Moshe had struggled to distinguish himself and his view from those "other Jews" who, as he saw it, had abandoned a true belief in God by assimilation into mainstream European culture. While they wished for the end of the war, Moshe prayed instead for salvation. Indeed, it is only by understanding this delineation that much of Moshe's text can make sense, for he repeatedly (and indeed stubbornly) refused to acknowledge the Allied victories as signs of hope. When on occasion he was tempted to be pleased by such events, he chastised himself, reminding himself that this was not the sort of liberation he sought. "One may practically say that it is forbidden to entertain such a hope," he wrote.

The question of merit and sin, both on the individual and collective level, also shifted as Moshe refined his ideas throughout the writing of the diary. Indeed, he became increasingly literal about this notion—measuring the good and bad deeds of the Germans, watching for their "accumulation of sins" as further signs that the redemption was imminent. Further, he came to believe that the Allies knew of or were somehow aware of the mass death of the Jews and, perceiving them as indifferent to the circumstances of the Jews, he turned his rage and hostility on them. The Allies, who until this time were neutral but irrelevant (because dependence on them was a misplaced form of loyalty that rightfully belonged to God), became the Jews' enemies as well. Their "sins" (the continuing war and the death of innocent people by bombs and artillery) were measured too, as Moshe waited for them to accumulate enough sins to bring about Jewish redemption.

Moshe's literal measurement of "merit" and "sin" as it applied to the Germans and the Allies likewise spilled over to the individual realm. The grief he felt for his suffering "brethren" in the East soon transmuted into guilt for escaping a similar fate, such that he even suggested volunteering for "labor" in the East. Indeed, as the diary progressed, his helplessness, guilt, and grief gave him no rest. His heart told him that he was abandoning his people, and he came to believe that he would be punished for this "sin," writing, "it sometimes seems to me that only those Jews who have suffered, who have carried the heavy and bitter burden of exile, will be saved in the redemption of our people; but those who remained here, hidden, will perish like the Jews who perished in the darkness of Egypt."[7]

The stream of information that reached Moshe over the course of the diary eventually tested his convictions. His doubt, however, was never in the existence of a benevolent God or the promise of Jewish redemption. Rather, the essential issue was timing—whether this oppression was indeed "the 'birthpang' of the Messiah" or simply "a link in a long chain of suffering." As the diary progressed and Moshe's uncertainty escalated, his emotional and spiritual well-being deteriorated, giving rise to an extraordinary struggle to maintain hope in the face of almost all-consuming despair. In late January 1943, Moshe wrote: "I have begun to doubt whether the time has really come for the end of our two-thousand-year exile. . . . Maybe the whole thing is a figment of my imagination." As he continued to write, Moshe vacillated between reiterating his theory and doubting it, fine-tuning his convictions and then wondering if perhaps he had been mistaken all along. His despair (which had existed faintly in the diary from the beginning and had increased with the news of the mass death of the Jews) continued to mount throughout the course of 1943. He tried to understand the causes for this—pinning it on his helplessness, his guilt at having "abandoned" his people, and his loneliness in hiding. But as his "isolation" and "inner vacuum" grew, so did his fears, the latter entries in the diary forming a cyclical pattern of hope, doubt, and despair.

Not even the study of Arabic, which had sustained him throughout the long months of depression, held up under his unrelenting gaze. For his ideas—which centered on an abandonment of all hope in human action and a total faith in God—came into conflict with his goal to become a diplomat in Israel, in which the mastery of Arabic was a primary step. With perfect logic, he demolished his own rationale for having begun the study of the language in the first place, explaining that the redemption could only come about through the grace of God, not through human action. In giving up Arabic, he wrote, "nearly all the positive content to my life is shown to be pointless, and I am left with almost nothing."

Moshe's ideas may not ring true to many readers, but they hold a place for the devout believers who understood their experience of suffering and persecution in religious, not secular, terms. Moshe struggled to reconcile the incomprehensible, and to understand his world in light of his beliefs, even as he acknowledged that they were unconventional and perhaps far-fetched. "Obviously my outlook is a religious one," he wrote. "I hope to be excused for this, for had I not religion, I would never find any answer at all to the problems that confront me." In this way, Moshe complicates the image of the "believer," for he was neither inflexible nor dogmatic, and he did not hang rigidly on to blind faith. Although some beliefs were never negotiable—his faith in God and his conviction that the Jews would ultimately be redeemed—he continually adapted his ideas when confronted with new information, and continued his search for understanding even though it brought with it an extreme spiritual and emotional crisis. Though his pain, confusion, and grief infuse the diary, Moshe nevertheless maintained his struggle against nihilism, fighting doggedly to find meaning in a world that no longer made sense.

Moshe ended his diary in September 1943. Though he was engulfed by desolation, he ended his diary affirming his faith in God, closing it with the words, "the end of my diary, thanks to the Lord."

The Flinker family's life together in hiding came to an end on the eve of the first night of Passover in April 1944. Informed on by a well-known Belgian Jewish collaborator known as Jacques, Mindel and three of her children, Esther Malka, Moshe, and Leah, were caught by the Gestapo in their home, and taken from there to the transit camp at Malines.[8] A mug shot made by the German authorities for "Mozes (alias Maurice) Wolf" still exists; the grim, harrowed expression on Moshe's face testifies to his terror and exhaustion. At the time of the family's arrest, Rivka, Gittel, Rochel, and Chaim Aharon were at the public baths and Noah Eliezer was on an errand preparing for the holiday. As Noah approached the family's apartment, the landlady signaled to him not to enter, and he waited in secret to intercept his four other children. He immediately placed them in hiding; they eventually found refuge in the Tieffenbrunner orphanage, where they survived until the end of the war. Noah was apprehended two weeks later and sent to Malines, where he found his family. On May 19, 1944, the five imprisoned members of the Flinker family were deported from Malines to Auschwitz-Birkenau. Esther Malka and Leah endured the selection process and entered the women's camp, but Mindel was sent immediately to the gas chambers. Although Leah recalled having seen her brother once across the barbed wires that separated the men from women, they never met again. On November 17, 1944, Moshe and Noah were sent to the Echterdingen work camp near Stutthof, where they were put to work repairing landing strips. After two months in hellish circumstances, amid a typhus epidemic that ravaged their fellow prisoners, Moshe and Noah also contracted the disease and were sent to Bergen-Belsen on January 20, 1945. They both succumbed to death there.

Esther Malka and Leah survived and returned to Brussels, where they found their siblings and began the process of rebuilding their family. They returned to the family's apartment to find Moshe's diary among the belongings that the landlady had preserved for them. The six surviving siblings fulfilled the family's lifelong Zionist dream by immigrating to Israel shortly after the end of the war. The elder sisters, who had taken on the role of parents to their younger siblings, refused to settle on a kibbutz. They insisted on remaining together in Jerusalem, where they could carry on the devoutly religious Jewish tradition in which they had been raised. They all eventually married and had many children and grandchildren. Moshe's diary has been published in Hebrew and in English; the original diary has remained in the family's private possession since they reclaimed it from their hiding place in Brussels.[9]

November 24, 1942 [Kislev 15, 5703]

For some time now I have wanted to note down every evening what I have been doing during the day. But, for various reasons, I have only got round to it tonight. First, let me explain why I am doing this, and I must start by describing why I came here to Brussels.

I was born in The Hague, the Dutch Queen's city where I passed my early years peacefully. I went to elementary school and then to a commercial school, where I studied for only two years. In [May] 1940, when the Germans entered Holland, I had another two years to go until graduation. They issued a decree forbidding Jewish students to attend schools staffed by gentile ("Aryan") teachers, and so I was prevented from finishing my course. The exclusion of Jews from public schools is just one of a long list of restrictions: they had been forced to hand over their radios, they were not allowed into the movies, et cetera.

In the big cities, where many Jews lived, special schools for Jews were opened, with only Jewish teachers. One such school was opened in The Hague. Our school was a high school with three departments: classical languages, modern subjects, and commerce. I, of course, continued my commercial studies. During the year I attended [1941–42], the number of restrictions on us rose greatly. Several months before the end of the school year we had to turn in our bicycles to the police. From that time on, I rode to school by streetcar, but a day or two before the vacations started Jews were forbidden to ride on streetcars. I then had to walk to school, which took about an hour and a half. However, I continued going to school during those last days because I wanted to get my report card and find out whether I had been promoted to the next class. At that time I still thought that I would be able to return to school after the vacations; but I was wrong. Even so, I must mention that I did get my promotion.

[. . .] I forgot to mention that during that year [May 1942] we had been forced to sew a "Badge of Shame" on the left side of our outer clothing. This "Badge" was a Star of David, on which the word "Jew" was written in Dutch. Halfway through that year [1942] the Germans began gathering Jews into the big cities, particularly Amsterdam. Jews were not permitted to move anywhere except to Amsterdam. When there were enough Jews there, the Germans began sending them to destinations which are still unknown to me today. [. . .]

Once a German official spoke to a gathering of his comrades. In his speech he touched on the Jews and said that they hate Europe and wish to humiliate Germany and the rest of Europe. That is why he had—in self-defense—to send them to the Ukraine. He went on to tell the Dutch that there was no reason to pity them, for they would come to no harm. He was only returning them to the countries from which they had originated, and since they arrived in Western Europe poor, they must leave poor, and that was why they were not allowed to take anything with them. He added that the fate of the Jews there (in the Ukraine) would be extremely hard. When we read this speech we were in despair. Amsterdam had always been a dangerous city for Jews but we had hoped that conditions might be better elsewhere. Nevertheless, we still continued to hope that, by the grace of God, we might be saved before we were forced to flee. But our hopes were in vain.

[At this time] the Germans [. . .] controlled almost all Europe. The only neutral countries were Sweden, Spain, Portugal, and Switzerland; all other countries were occupied by Germany or her ally, Italy. There was one refuge still remaining—that part of France as yet unoccupied by the Germans. Those who had enough money, and who did not want to be sent to the Ukraine, fled from Holland to one of the unoccupied countries. My father, who also has money, did not want to be deported by the Germans, and so he went to Roosendaal, a border town, to investigate the possibilities of crossing the border. He was already in Roosendaal when my mother received the letter ordering us to report at the station at eleven the next day. I went that very day to Roosendaal. It was already 9:30 P.M. when my mother informed my father that she had received the documents (she told him by telephone that she had been "invited to the wedding").[10]

Early next morning my father sent three women to The Hague to escort my mother, brother, and sisters to Roosendaal. Traveling by train was then most dangerous because it was forbidden by the Germans: if anyone dared travel and got caught, he was sent to one of the concentration camps, which no one could hope to leave alive.[11] The feat was difficult from another point of view too, for our family consists of nine people: my father and mother, my five sisters, my small brother, and myself. However, with the help of the Lord, we all reached Roosendaal safely. [. . .] Then began the search for people who guide refugees across the border. The search was fruitless until the Friday when an acquaintance of my father's told him that he knew a route that was not guarded by the police. I went first with my oldest sister. We left Roosendaal on Friday at three. The Lord caused our trip to be successful, and we reached Brussels, the capital of Belgium, after having traveled by bicycle, trolley, and train. That night my mother and my young brother also crossed the frontier; my father had found a woman willing, for eighteen hundred gulden, to guide them over. On Sunday my father and my three sisters also crossed, and so, by Sunday, all of us except my youngest sister had reached Brussels. She arrived ten days later. [. . .]

Although Belgium is also occupied by the Germans, we were not afraid here as we had been in Holland, because no one (except a few Jewish friends) knew us. So we ventured out into the streets without wearing our Jewish badge and did other things forbidden to Jews. During this war period, through which we are living, it is almost impossible to buy anything without ration coupons: there are bread coupons, coffee coupons, soap coupons, and so on. In addition, everyone must have an identity card, stating who he is, where he works, where he lives, and so forth. Anyone found without this card is immediately taken to the police, and it is extremely dangerous of course to go about without this document. For this reason my father made a great effort to get us registered at the city hall. Naturally, he couldn't simply go there and say "here we are." Had he done so, the clerk in charge of registering people who have moved from another city or country would have asked him how we got there and he would have wanted to examine our visas. Therefore my father went to a man recommended by someone and this man got us a permit to stay in Belgium for three months. Naturally this cost my father a lot of money, but he doesn't care about the money so we are living in Brussels.

I am idle all day long, and have nothing to do. A few weeks ago I registered in the lending library for Hebrew and Yiddish books. I read a lot—all sorts of Hebrew books—but this does not cheer me up. I feel that I am sinking lower and lower. I have tried to study the Bible (I brought with me a small Bible, without commentaries) but I am unable to concentrate. I shall try to borrow a volume of the Talmud. It is because I hate being idle that I have started this diary so that I can write in it every day what I do and think; in this manner I shall be able to account for all I have done each day. Now the introduction is over, and I shall begin my diary tomorrow.

November 26, 1942

[. . .] The newspaper said today that things aren't going too well for the Germans in Russia. The Russians have opened a great offensive south of Stalingrad. Maybe they will succeed, and the Lord will save us from our present plight. I think that the time has come for us to be saved. If the Lord wishes to save some of the Jews deported by the Germans, now is the time to do so, because if they will be forced to spend the winter in Russia, then, it seems to me, not many of them will be able to survive, God forbid. [. . .]

We are in a very bad situation. Our sufferings have by far exceeded our wrongdoings. What other purpose could the Lord have in allowing such things to befall us? I feel certain that further troubles will not bring any Jew back to the paths of righteousness; on the contrary, I think that upon experiencing such great anguish they will think that there is no God at all in the universe, because had there been a God He would not have let such things happen to His people. I have heard this said many times already—and indeed what can God intend by all these calamities that are happening to us in this terrible period? It seems to me that the time has come for our redemption, or rather, that we are more or less worthy of being redeemed. (Tomorrow I shall continue further in a search for an answer to this last question, because now I am very sleepy, and it is after midnight.)

November 30, 1942

As I thought, I was unable to follow through my plan for "tomorrow," nor for the day after tomorrow nor the day after that. I thought that even today (after four days) I would not be able to continue writing, because I had to let so much time go by, but I gathered courage and told myself not to be weak, and so I now continue what I have begun. I hope I shall not keep continually interrupting myself, and, the Lord willing, I shall write in my diary every single evening.

Now I return to the question mentioned above and its solution: what can God mean by all that is befalling us and by not preventing it from happening? This raises a further question, which must be settled before we can proceed further with the main problem. This second question is whether our distress is part of the anguish that has afflicted the Jewish people since the exile, or whether this is different from all that has occurred in the past. I incline to the second answer, for I find it very hard to believe that what we are going through today is only a mere link in a long chain of suffering. I find it difficult to believe this primarily because of the effect that the restrictions and persecutions are having on me, but I know that it is very difficult to base the solution to a problem of such importance solely on personal feelings. [. . .] We should therefore compare our sufferings and theirs in order to find the difference between them.

First of all, we see that in former times the persecutions were always localized. In one place Jews were very badly treated, while in another they lived in peace and quiet. Second, and perhaps more important, is the official character of our oppression today, and the organization created solely to persecute us. This difference is really very obvious. Unlike the Spaniards [in the Spanish Inquisition], for instance, who gave our religion as their reason, the Germans are not even trying to justify their persecutions; it is enough that we are Jews. The fact that we were born Jews is sufficient to explain and justify everything.

Moshe Flinker

To the first difference, we may add another; that today it is quite possible to destroy the entire people of Israel. The following example may explain this better. In the Middle Ages when an enemy besieged a city, he attacked it with fire and hurled stones into it, and also tried to breach the walls with large and sturdy battering rams. The strongest of the soldiers would grasp the ram and begin smashing at the walls. The people of those times thought that this was the height of strength and power. At the most, when a few dozen more men came to demolish the walls, the enemy reached the limit of its manpower and strength. But today we see that even a small child could destroy a whole city. One only has to connect a bit of dynamite to an electric current, and a mere touch of a finger can destroy the strongest wall in an instant. So it is with respect to our sufferings.

In olden days—for example in Crusader times—our ancestors thought that the climax of persecutions had been reached; but today, without swords or weapons, we see persecutions a thousand times more severe. The explanation is that today everything is highly organized. They arrange and organize, organize and arrange, until perhaps only one in a thousand is able to flee or hide. And why can they now organize everything in a manner that was not previously possible? The reason is, and here we return to our second main difference, that with the Germans everything is official, everything is done according to the law. The law condemns us. Just as there is a law against stealing, so there is a law to persecute the Jews.

So we thus see that there really is a difference between our sufferings since our exile and our anguish in these terrible times. And because of this difference we have reason to ask: Why does the Lord not prevent this, or, on the other hand, why does He permit our tormentors to persecute us? And what can be the result of these persecutions?

The answer to these questions does not seem difficult to me. We know that we were expelled from our country for our great iniquities; therefore, if we wish to return we must first completely repent of our evil ways and then we shall be able to go back to our land. However, the prophet foretold that we would not return because of our righteousness, but as a result of the evildoing of our enemies and of our agony at their hands (such as happened in Egypt). [. . .] We must therefore hope that since most Jews do not dwell where they used to and that most of them wish to be redeemed, the hour of redemption has come and with the Lord's help we shall soon be saved. Maybe even on the forthcoming feast of Hanukkah the Lord will perform this miracle and return us to our land. There is still one small detail that could spoil all this. But on this subject I shall write tomorrow, God willing, for I am most weary (it is past 1 A.M.). However, before I conclude I should like to pray to the Lord of Israel that He may fulfill in the near future the prayer: "Return us unto Thee, O Lord, and we shall return; renew our days as of old."

December 2, morning [1942]

The small detail I mentioned above is the following: most of the Jews think that redemption and salvation depend on the victory of England. Now if England wins, most of the Jews (even those who wish to be redeemed) will be able to say that not the Lord but England saved them. The gentiles will say the same. I mention this because I think the gentiles too will learn something from this war. For although I don't care about them [*] we must nevertheless not forget that they too have lost much in the way of people and property, and the time has come for them to learn something from all the wars they wage, especially from the last two world wars. The victor in this war that we are living through will not be either of the opposing sides, but God; not England and not America, but the Lord of Israel will triumph. I think that before this final victory, Germany will win on almost all fronts, and when it will seem that she has almost won, the Lord will approach with His sword and will conquer. Obviously my outlook is a religious one. I hope to be excused for this, for had I not religion, I would never find any answer at all to the problems that confront me. [. . .]

December 3, morning [1942]

Yesterday nothing important enough happened to write about here. [. . .] The Russian offensive on the eastern front continues, but I think nothing will come of it. No news from the other fronts. Today is the eve of Hanukkah but I have the feeling that this Hanukkah will pass, as have so many others, without a miracle or anything resembling one.

December 7, night [1942]

During the past few days nothing important has occurred, either to me or around me. We lit the fifth candle tonight, and Hanukkah, the Feast of Lights, is drawing to a close. I cannot hope any longer for miracles on this Hanukkah. Every day more and more Jews are being deported—now from one place, now from another. They say that the Germans have special personnel who go round town trying to find out where Jews are living, and they show the Germans these locations, and the Ger-

---

* Asterisks in brackets [*] indicate where portions of the original diary were omitted from the English translation published by Yad Vashem in 1971.

mans come and take our brothers away. Already many times the Germans have said that they would continue deportations only until a certain date, after which they would stop. They have given such dates many times—but still it goes on. The Germans have not ceased deporting Jews. [. . .]

These days I don't want to do much. When you are waiting for miracles, and nothing happens, you can't find any drive or willpower within yourself. I have so often wondered whether Germany will really win this war. The Jews seem so sure that England is stronger than Germany and that she will win. The real reason they think this way is because if the Germans win we shall not be permitted to live. But such a reason is no proof that one side or the other will win. Whoever wins is no longer important to me. The main thing is that we Jews will be redeemed and rescued from the troubles of our times. [*] With this I conclude because I am very tired. Good night, my people!

December 8, night [1942]

Shortly after we came to Brussels and found an apartment, my mother began to question my father about my future. I was spending my days idly. At times I read Hebrew, but Mother considered that this would lead nowhere. The first times she expressed her views, I laughed and even Father paid little attention to them. I wondered how she could worry about a happy future at a time when we were faced with the problem of life or death. My father gave her a similar answer whenever she broached the subject to him.

During the past few days when my mother raised the question of my future, my reaction was again one of laughter, but when I was alone, I too began to ponder this matter. What indeed is to become of me? It is obvious that the present situation will not last forever—perhaps another year or two—but what will happen then? One day I will have to earn my own living. At first I wanted to drive such thoughts away but they kept coming back. So I started thinking seriously about the problem. After much deliberation, I've decided to become . . . a statesman. Not any sort of statesman, but a Jewish statesman in the Land of Israel. Even though it would take a miracle to free us now, the rest of my idea—living in our land—isn't so farfetched. Then, perhaps, the rest of the world might slightly change its attitude toward us. The relations between other nations may also alter a bit. But our people are so exile-minded that many generations would have to pass before we became a free people physically and mentally (the latter is the main thing). That is why we will need leaders to guide us on the road to true spiritual freedom.

[. . .] Therefore, from today on, everything I do will be directed toward this aim. Of course, I will continue to study the Bible, because only according to its spirit can Israel survive. In addition, I will learn as much as I can about Judaism and about my people.

[. . .] But now it seems that difficulties have arisen in renewing our permits to stay in Brussels. Tomorrow our three months are up, but my father is hopeful that we will get our extensions. It's late, so I'll go to bed. I'll close with this verse from the Bible: "Though your dispersed were in the uttermost part of heaven, yet will I gather them from thence."

December 10, morning [1942]

Yesterday my father came home and said we would have to wait until Friday to have our permits renewed. I don't think we'll get them at all this time, but my father is full of hope. [. . .]

December 12, Saturday evening [1942]

Thursday was the last night of Hanukkah. My father, young brother, and I lit the candles that we had obtained, though not without difficulty. While I was singing the last stanza of the Hanukkah hymn *Maoz Tzur* [Rock of Ages] I was deeply struck by the topicality of the words:

> Reveal Thy sacred mighty arm
> And draw redemption near
> Take Thy revenge upon that
> Wicked people (!) that has shed the blood
> Of those who worship Thee
> Our deliverance has been long overdue,
> Evil days are endless,
> Banish the foe, destroy the shadow of his image
> Provide us with a guiding light.

All our troubles, from the first to this most terrible one, are multiple and endless, and from all of them rises one gigantic scream. From wherever it emanates, the cry that rises is identical to the cries in other places or at other times. When I sang *Maoz Tzur* for the last time on Hanukkah I sang with emphasis—especially the last verse. But later when I sat on my own I asked myself: "What was the point of that emphasis? What good are all the prayers I offer up with so much sincerity? I am sure that more righteous sages than I have prayed in their hour of anguish for deliverance and salvation. What merit have I that I should pray for our much-needed redemption?" And then I thought about our first and best leader, Moses. He too was all alone [. . .]. Nevertheless, he reached the status of Prophet of Prophets and Prince of Princes. He did not attain his stature easily as he had to work and enslave his spirit for eighty years, as our teachers have carefully pointed out. Only after eighty years was he worthy.

And so I must learn from his enlightening example. I am irritable by nature and lose my temper easily, but by the example of the man whose name was the same as mine, I must make an effort to overcome this side of my nature. But every time I have resolved to do this I have got into an argument or fight with one of my sisters and forgotten all my good resolutions. But now I am writing down in black and white that I will strive not to lose my temper easily or, better still, not to lose my temper at all. [. . .]

December 14, midnight [1942]

Yesterday I went to the movies with my sister. When I was still in The Hague, before it was occupied by the Germans, I didn't go to the cinema much. After the Germans had been in Holland for some time, they forbade the Jews to go to the cinema. Then they began showing anti-Semitic films. I wanted very much to see these movies, but I didn't dare, because my identity card was stamped "J" for Jew, and I could have been asked to show my papers at any time, and for such an offense I could have been sentenced to six months' imprisonment. But here, in Belgium, where I am not registered as a Jew, I can go to the movies. In any case, there is not the same strictness here. When we arrived, only the anti-Semitic cinema proprietors had notices posted in front denying entrance to Jews. Now, however, in front of every theater is posted: "By order of the Germans, entrance to Jews is forbidden."

Even so I went to see the film *Jud Süss*.[12] What I saw there made my blood boil. I was red in the face when I came out. I realized there the wicked objectives of these evil people—how they want to inject the poison of anti-Semitism into the blood of the gentiles. While I was watching the film I suddenly remembered what the evil one [Hitler] had said in one of his speeches: "Whichever side wins the war, anti-Semitism will spread and spread until the Jews are no more." In that film I saw the means he is using to achieve his aim. [. . .] One thing I know [is] if we are not saved now by some miracle from heaven, then our end is as sure as I am sitting here. For not only the body of Israel is being attacked, but also its spirit. The Jews are being made so hateful to the world that nothing that anyone can do will be able to undo his work. [. . .] [*]

December 15, 1942

Today we received our permits. [. . .] The permits we received this time are, according to the interpreter, good until the end of the war. After three months we have to go to the city hall and renew them for six months, and after these six months go by for another six, and so on. All foreign residents have such permits. [. . .]

December 18, morning [1942]

For the past few days I have done nothing concerning Judaism. I haven't read the Bible, or any articles, or anything else. However, a week ago I began learning Arabic. But because I was afraid that I wouldn't persist and continue, I didn't write about it. But now that I can already read Arabic and have mastered the first lesson, I am making a note of the fact. But because I've begun learning Arabic I haven't been able to study anything else. At first it was very difficult; I would read something and understand it—but when I tried to read the piece again, it was as though it were completely new to me. I had to go over it three or four times before I knew, understood, and remembered it. But there is a great satisfaction in finally mastering it. [. . .]

As far as my study of Arabic is concerned, I am not learning it simply because I like it or anything like that. I have begun—and hope I may finish—to study this language because a large part of the inhabitants of the land of Israel and the surrounding countries speak it. And, in view of my plans, I see that I will need this language more than any that I studied in school. It is obvious that we shall have to live in peace with our brothers, the sons of Ishmael, who are also Abraham's descendants. I am sure that the terrible riots in the Land of Israel before the war were incited by Germany and Italy; such terrifying outbreaks must not recur. I think that had the Jewish leaders learned Arabic and so had been able to speak with the Arab leaders, that violence would not have occurred. And therefore I am trying very hard to learn the language. [. . .]

December 22, 1942, morning

Last Friday afternoon, as I was about to finish my Arabic studies, my father came in and told me that he had some bad news. He had heard that many Jews were dying in the East, and that a hundred thousand had already been killed. When I heard this, my heart stood still and I was speechless with pain and shock. I had been fearing this for a long time, but I had hoped against hope that they really had taken the Jews for forced labor and that therefore they would have to feed, clothe, and house them enough to keep them alive. Now my last hopes have been dashed.

And as if my father had wanted to rub salt on my wounds, he added the further bad news that England, America, Russia, and eight other countries [text unclear] this savagery. They, who regard themselves as privileged, good, and superior, are really not a whit better than Germany. It is only through them that such a disaster could have befallen us. Cruel Russia, for instance, has already forgotten the many myriad of Jews murdered under its rule, most of whom lost their lives by Russia's intention. Through this war which is desolating her land she is getting what she deserves. It is as if everyone is laughing at our plight.

My anguish and pain are so great I don't know what to do. I have been quarreling with everyone. Because of my brothers' torment I, too, wish to die because I can not bear to hear of our terrible afflictions. [*] Oh, how great are our troubles, how great, how great! I took up my Bible, the only book I salvaged from my home, to find some consolation. I went through the Pentateuch [the five books of the Torah], through Joshua, through Judges, and further, but not the slightest consolation did I find there. I went further and further until I finally reached . . . Lamentations. "How doth the city sit solitary, that was full of people,"—here I found consolation. Not in the Pentateuch with its exalted commandments, nor in the books of the Former Prophets nor in Isaiah with his lofty poetic eloquence did I find comfort for the anguish of my people, but in Lamentations, that elegy on the earlier calamity that befell my people, did I find it. Never did I think that I would draw sustenance from the agony of my people in bygone days. [. . .] And likewise the last verse of that prayer, which seems to have been intended solely for today: *Thou hast been exceedingly wrathful with us, even unto loathing.* Yes, You have been exceedingly wrathful with us. Exceedingly! Exceedingly!

I have done what I said I would do—study the Bible each day—but I have found nothing in it. The terrible events of these days make everything seem tiny, as if viewed through the wrong end of a microscope; the greater the troubles, the smaller everything seems. I thought: "What is there for me in the whole Book of Genesis?" Everything now seems pointless, worthless. [. . .] [*]

December 24, 1942

For the past few days I haven't had anything to write. Nothing has happened to me and nothing has made any impression on me. I am indifferent to everyone and everything. Nothing I read arouses interest. [. . .]

Winter has begun here in Brussels. This morning, when I went out, I felt for the first time the cold of winter, and I immediately thought about what my brethren will do in this cold. We need supernatural help, if the Lord still wishes to save us. If He will not grant us this miracle of salvation, not many Jews will live to take part in our redemption. But the Lord will not be able to forsake His people. Undoubtedly He will save us, he must save us.

December 28, 1942

[. . .] This morning it snowed for the first time this winter; the snow froze hard. I think the temperature was nine degrees below zero. I felt the cold when I had to leave the house to go and fetch potatoes—about ninety pounds—and suddenly I thought again, even more sharply than before, of the fate of my brethren in the East. I am always thinking of them, I never forget them all day. I silently pray for the salvation which does not seem to want to come, and I hope that it will speedily arrive, that God will have mercy on His people, who are in so terrible a plight.

During the past few weeks the Russians have increased their attacks all along the front. During the past few days they have begun a new offensive, with even greater intensity and power, in the region between the Volga and the Don. And they have been successful. The German army headquarters has unprecedentedly been forced to admit that the Russians have succeeded in breaking through the German lines. And it was also in the newspapers that never in all the Russian wars had so many Russian soldiers and weapons been concentrated in one place as now. Everywhere that one Jew met another or even when a German-hating gentile met another, they said: "All is well in Russia; they are retreating from hour to hour."

When I heard all this I said to myself: "Perhaps the Lord has not forgotten us and at the last minute will save us from these terrible troubles." But after considering this idea I went deeper into it and thought further and then said: "What will happen if the Russians defeat the Germans? Our troubles will cease and . . . then there will be room for more troubles." For in a short time, after we calm down from all the unrest and confusion and anguish, we shall suddenly realize that we are still in exile and all that has happened was for nothing—only part of a long chain of pain has now passed and before us is another very long chain and the end is not yet in sight. That is how it would be if the Russians were victorious. And I realized that what I had thought of as a hope was not really a hope at all. One may practically say that it is forbidden to entertain such a hope. It is not yet time for joy. For as I have shown, this war, and all the troubles it has brought, marks the end of our exile; it is the "birthpang" of the Messiah. Therefore we should not look to Russia, England, or America, because salvation will come from a completely different source. This brings me back to the theory I had while I was still in The Hague. At that time it was only a vague notion, but now it is gradually crystallizing. The idea is that salvation will come only when the whole world, and especially the Jews, give up all hope for a victory by the Allies. Then will the Lord have mercy upon us, and His light shall shine upon us, and His salvation will come. [. . .]

Moshe Flinker

January 4, 1943

Almost nothing worth noting has happened to me recently. They say that in Russia all goes well. The Germans are retreating on the southern front. [. . .]

My father often tells us these days that we don't know how lucky we are!—we have everything we want to eat and we can go wherever everybody goes. I have thought about these words of my father, and it seems to me that I am not at all lucky. Even though I thank the Lord every moment for the miracles He performs for us at all times, and despite all the grace He bestows upon us, I often have a great yearning for my brothers who are in Poland and elsewhere. The Lord alone knows where they are. Often have I felt this yearning and the need to be with them and participate in their sufferings. I realize that it is actually possible to reach them. The Germans want many workers everywhere. The more they have, the more they need. In Holland, Belgium, and France they have already taken hundreds of thousands and even so they need more. They also need workers in Poland and the lands of the East, so that should I go to the Germans and say that I wish to go and work then they would doubtlessly take me. But at least for the time being I am sure that my father would not let me do any such thing.

I continue my studies in Arabic, and although the work is becoming more and more difficult, I persevere. I have already reached the ninth lesson.

January 7, 1943

Last night my parents and I were sitting around the table. It was almost midnight. Suddenly we heard the [door] bell: we all shuddered. We thought that the moment had come for us to be deported. The fear arose mostly because a couple of days ago the inhabitants of Brussels were forbidden to go out after nine o'clock. The reason for this is that on December 31 three German soldiers were killed. Had it not been for this curfew it could have been some man who was lost and was ringing at our door. My mother had already put her shoes on to go to the door, but my father said to wait until they ring once more. But the bell did not ring again. Thank heaven it all passed quietly. Only the fear remained, and all day long my parents have been very nervous. They can't stand the slightest noise, and the smallest thing bothers them. [. . .]

January 13, 1943

Last Sunday my father went to the butcher's to buy a fowl and have him slaughter it. The butcher told him that people have again been deported in his neighborhood. And among those taken are acquaintances of ours, with whom we had spoken only a few days ago and to whom we had given our address. The family whom we know and who were taken is named Keller. [. . .] I think that it was Thursday that [Mrs. Keller] was deported, together with her husband and three children. [. . .] The Kellers were not deported alone—more than sixty people were taken. [. . .] Since the Kellers were taken, my parents feel themselves in danger at every moment. They think it impossible to hide from the Germans and that some day they will be deported. [. . .]

January 19, 1943

Last Sabbath I was beginning my prayers, but as has often already happened, I found I could not concentrate and I started to leaf through the prayer book. When I reached the penitential prayers I started to read more closely and I saw there a prayer that made a very strong impression on me. This prayer is read on Mondays and Thursdays and starts with the words: "Angels of mercy, servants of the Highest." [. . .] This verse impressed me as being very topical, as if the author had just finished writing it. From this I saw again that the troubles of the Middle Ages and our troubles today are identical. And I thought to myself: "But the troubles passing over us today are already the end of our troubles in exile," an idea I have had in my heart many times. Despite this, I had a doubt: perhaps this is only one link in a long chain of anguish that will continue in the future? And from this I got thinking: why is our suffering so drawn-out and why does the end not come? You have only to go out for one moment and meet one Jew and you hear of enough troubles for the whole day, and sometimes you can't find peace of mind for the rest of the week. [. . .]

This past week I read in a German newspaper an article about a certain German, his wife, and children who all work for the German army. From morning to night they all work hard. The writer of the article asked his hard worker if the work were not too much for him, and if he did not find it too strenuous. The man answered that he was not at all afraid of hard work because he knew what it was to be without work—he had been unemployed for about seven years. [. . .] It is true that Hitler gave the people work almost exclusively in arms factories but this does not much decrease the credit due him. The merit he accumulated in those times is indeed great; it is true that this merit is decreasing, but most probably he has a great deal and thus does not yet have to pay for his sins. Also, while his merit is decreasing rapidly, the English, Americans, Russians, and their allies have no great merit themselves.

When I was still in The Hague I went with my sister to Roosendaal, the border town, for the first time, but my father did not permit us to cross the frontier. And when I returned to The Hague my teacher asked me: "Why did you not cross the border? [. . .] Any girl or boy who can flee from the Germans is saved for our people, and can be a hope for the future." When I heard this I thought that here was the answer to the question I had often asked myself: "How can I flee from my people while they are in such terrible trouble?" And now, when I am here in Brussels, far from where my people is suffering, I feel that this answer is a rationalization, a dialectic justification. In theoretical matters one may employ such justifications, but in spiritual affairs only the feelings may speak, only the heart is important. Now I feel that I have not been saved for the future of my people; on the contrary. I see myself as if I were a traitor, who fled from his people at the time of their anguish. Moreover, it sometimes seems to me that only those Jews who have suffered, who have carried the heavy and bitter burden of exile, will be saved in the redemption of our people; but those who remained here, hidden, will perish like the Jews who perished in the darkness of Egypt. [. . .]

Last year, while still at The Hague, I went to a Hebrew school. In that school I found the two images by which I symbolize all Israel. The first is of the girl I loved and still love. She almost never spoke to me, nor did I speak to her; nevertheless, I still feel that I could recognize her glances of love toward me. Who knows where this girl is now? And now, in my free moments, when I am doing nothing and my mind starts wandering, her image floats up before my eyes; she appears to me in all her beauty. Last week especially, not a night passed without my seeing her in my dreams. And when I envision her, then almost always the image of my dearest friend in The Hague appears also. I used to talk with him a lot, and during our lunch hour, from twelve to two, we would sit together and study the Talmud. He was an amiable, open-hearted boy. He also was in love with a girl in the school, but he was not fearful, as I was, to go up to her and tell her that he loved her deeply. [. . .] And when I remember these two Jewish souls, who to me are the symbol of all my people, then I can cry at our situation. And on Friday evening, while lying on my bed, I really wept when I remembered them. I asked myself: "Where are they? Where is my people, the chosen people of God?" May the Lord have mercy on his people. Save us, O Lord, please have mercy on us, for we shall soon perish. If we ourselves are not worthy of salvation, then do it for the sake of Thy name which is being defiled by the gentiles. [. . .]

January 22, 1943

Yesterday my mother told me to go to the beadle [an official of a synagogue or congregation] to buy coupons for clothing and bread, if he had any. I was mildly happy. [. . .] When I got to his house I rang once, twice, three times, but the door did not open. Until then I had been ringing the bell he had made for himself, so that if his visitors rang they would not disturb the other tenants of the building. Then I rang the house bell. After I had rung twice, someone came to the door. The door opened and a woman appeared. I saw that she was shaking all over, and I asked her whether the people I had rung for were at home. She answered me in French that yesterday these people had been taken away in a car. When I heard this terrible news I was very badly shaken. My heart was pounding and I felt as if face to face with the Angel of Death. [. . .] I thought: "This man took so much trouble in hiding from the Germans, and now, despite all his labor, he is taken away—he, his wife, and his two children." The younger child was a four-year-old girl. While I was walking back to the train station I still felt violently shaken; I did not know what to think. This time it seemed to me that I had myself witnessed their deportation. [. . .]

What little happiness I had while going there disappeared, and anguish and sadness took its place. While going to this man I had told myself that I would take a walk [. . .] in a forest close by my home, but upon returning home I put aside my walk and everything else I was planning to do. I did not want to enjoy anything; I wanted to stay at home all day and be sad. Not even the slightest happiness came to me; I only looked for ways to torture myself. With all my body and soul, I wish to be with my people and share their bitter fate. When trouble befalls them so shall it befall me. I wish to be a part of my people. I do not know if I can succeed in chasing the small joys from my heart, but I shall find ways. [. . .]

While saying the afternoon prayers that day I wanted to open my heart before the Lord by means of the Eighteen Benedictions. But I find that this form is much too small and constricting. I was unable to put into it all that I had in my heart. I do not know in whose name to pray. Our forefathers are too far from us. Our people? It looks as though they have no merit at all, otherwise so many troubles could not have befallen them. Maybe the prayer that will be most effective will be about the magnitude of our pain. As great as our sins have been, our troubles have already surpassed them. A little more and we shall perish.

January 26, 1943

Last Saturday evening I went to get the paper. When I bought it I saw the headline: "Tripoli Captured by the British." When I came home and told my father he was delighted, and said several times: "The end is in sight," "That taught them a lesson," and similar expressions. As I listened to my father I thought to myself: "Is their defeat really near? Is our people's salvation approaching?" And a voice within me answered: "No! No! Judah will not be saved by the English or by any other nation." I told my father that what the English have conquered is really nothing; with a little luck the Germans could recapture all the territory they have lost as a result of the English attack. My father answered that I am silly and stubborn, and finally he got mad at me, and we didn't talk about it any more. But when I went to sleep I was unable to free myself from the thought I have written many times, namely, that salvation will not come to us through an Allied victory. Even though I love my people dearly, I cannot hope for any such salvation, for the simple reason that it would not be true salvation. An Allied victory will put an end only to our momentary troubles, those from Germany, but along with this it will mark the beginning of troubles far greater than the present ones, because instead of coming from one source, Germany, they will come from everywhere in the form of unlimited worldwide anti-Semitism. For this poison, which the cursed Hitler has injected into humanity, is spreading, and after the war—ended by such an Allied victory—it would not be limited to the vanquished Germany, but would cross the borders of the victorious nations as well. The victors will have to find some scapegoat to blame for the innumerable crises that will come after the war, and who will be more suitable than the Jews for such a role?

No, not from the English nor the Americans nor the Russians but from the Lord Himself will our redemption come. And for that I pray always. Therefore I see in every victory of the Allies a prolongation of our troubles. Already after reaching this conclusion, I have begun to doubt whether the time has really come for the end of our two-thousand-year exile. [. . .] Maybe the whole thing is a figment of my imagination; perhaps all my ideas are a result of our infinite pain; every day brings a new agony and new tortures. [. . .]

February 12, 1943

During recent days an emptiness has formed inside me. Nothing motivates me to do anything or write anything, and no new ideas enter my mind; everything is as if asleep. Although I do not know from where this emptiness has come, I can feel it with my whole body. When I pray I feel as if I am praying to the wall and am not heard at all, and there is a voice inside me that says: "What are you praying for? The Lord does not hear you." (A few times already there has flashed into my mind the verse which I think I heard on *Simchat Torah* [Jewish holiday celebrating the Torah], "And the spirit of Thy holiness do not take from him.") Yes, I think that the holy spark I always felt within me has been taken from me, and here I am, without spirit, without thought, without anything, and all I have is my miserable body. I don't know what I will do. [. . .] Whenever I pray I beg the Lord to return His holy spirit to me, but up to now I feel nothing but this numbing emptiness, which has lasted for two weeks. [. . .]

In the past few days the Germans have been continuously retreating, as they themselves admit. [. . .] Now everyone is thinking that the war will end soon. Prices of merchandise have gone down. My own views I have already written—and they are unchanged. My father is full of hope. But despite the fact that all, and especially the Jews, are hopeful and even a bit joyous, the Germans continue to pick up Jews as if nothing had happened. Nearly all the Jews we knew when we came here have been deported.

There is no other news. I continue studying Arabic, concentrating mainly on grammar. I hope I can get a textbook with a better grammatical section. I have now reached the twenty-second lesson. [. . .]

A few hours ago I heard a speech made by the German propaganda minister, Goebbels. [. . .] The main part of Goebbels' speech was about the workers. He said that women should go to work in factories, thereby freeing men for military duties, and that next spring Germany will be ready to attack Russia and conquer her completely. I think that he is correct, and that the Germans will succeed in subduing Russia. As I have already written, the Jewish people should not pin their hopes on an Allied victory. Germany is now retreating only to be able to advance later with increased strength, until victory will be ninety-nine percent in her grasp, and then she will start to fall. And the greater her triumph, the greater her fall. That, in my opinion, is the only way that salvation will come. Nor will our salvation be a mere relief from suffering such as has occurred many times during our exile; no, the salvation will and must come after this war, otherwise we are doomed. And now I understand the feeling of joy I felt when I heard of Germany's victories, and my hatred for England, America, and their allies. Then I felt, and now I know, that the way to redemption will not be measured by England's victories but by Germany. For then shall we be saved by the Lord Himself and our two-thousand-year old exile will come to an end.

March 9, 1943

What shall I do? The emptiness has spread within me and now fills me completely. For a few days now, no new thought or idea has come to me. I have tried various measures and nothing has helped. I tried going to bed very late, and went to bed at three, but nothing changed. For two weeks I have reduced my daily meals from three to one, but this, too, has been to no avail. Maybe these things will yet help, but so far I am completely in the grip of this nothingness, this lack of will and thought. I have tried to find a reason for all of this, but I have been unable to settle on anything for sure. Maybe it is due to the fact that I am living a life of peace and quiet while my brothers are in a situation so bad that God alone knows its full horror.

Maybe this void will disappear soon; there are some signs of this, but I cannot be sure.

[. . .] Each time I stand to say the Eighteen Benedictions I direct my whole soul to my lovely land, and I see it before my eyes; I see the coast, I see Tel Aviv, Jaffa, and Haifa. Then I see Jerusalem, with the Mount of Olives, and I see the Jordan as it flows from Lebanon to the Dead Sea. I also see the land across the Jordan—I visualize all of this—when I stand to pray. And when I pray and do not see my beloved country before my eyes it is as if my prayer had been rejected and as if I had been praying to the wall. Oh, I love all of it so much! My people and my country do not leave my thoughts for even a moment; all day long they are in my mind. Several times already I have asked myself whether I will ever get the chance to stand on its holy earth, if the Lord will permit me to walk about in my land. Oh, how my soul yearns for you, my homeland, how my eyes crave for the sight of you, my country, the Land of Israel.

April 7, 1943

The last time I wrote in my diary I wrote things that, when I finished them, I myself did not know from where they had come. I had wanted to write something quite different, but it was as if the words came out without my knowledge. I had meant to write about my terrible loneliness. During recent days I have been gripped by terrible sensations of loneliness, isolation, and dejection. I believe that the reasons for this are that I think so often about my people—from which I am so far removed—and that the tragic image of the girl in The Hague crosses my mind so frequently. I also suffer from the fact that there is no one here to whom I might talk and expect to be heard with understanding.

When I was still living in my first exile, in The Hague, I used to laugh when someone would tell me or when I would read in a book that some persons have a great need to pour out their hearts to a friend. I always would tell myself that I, at least, have no need for such things and that it is only a manifestation of a kind of soft-heartedness that I have always despised. In those days I used to say that if, at rare intervals, I should ever feel the need to pour out my heart I would pour it out to myself. But from then until now I find myself completely changed. I didn't know then what it was to live without knowing anyone even a little, without having anyone, to be as lonely as if one were in a desert. Oh, how I wish I could see some of my old friends; how my soul longs to talk with my friend Finkel.

All day long, thoughts of my people never leave my mind, not even for a minute. They are with me everywhere, whether I am standing or sitting, eating or talking, or whatever I am doing. I try so hard to deprive myself of the numerous pleasures that are to be found all around. I walk in the street and the sun is burning hot and I am covered with perspiration, and then I think of going for a swim—immediately afterward I remember where my people are and then I cannot even dream of going swimming; or I pass a pastry shop and I see in the window some attractive, delicious looking cream-cakes and I am just about to enter the shop—and then the situation of my brothers flashes across my mind and my desires are destroyed, and I am overcome with shame for having forgotten their plight.

May 19, 1943

MY FUTURE

I have written several times about a question that has been bothering me for some time; namely, what I will be when I am on my own, which I imagine will be in about five or six years. I thought at one time that I had answered this question, and that I would be a statesman, a Jewish statesman, and in that way work for my people and my God. [. . .]

When I first got this idea and wrote it in my diary, I tried to do all I could to bring it about. Everything I did and thought was, as far as possible, related to this aim. [. . .] [T]o further this object, I studied a lot of Arabic. But as the war grew more and more terrible, I came to feel that if results of lasting value were to come out of it, that is, if we attain the redemption for which our people has been waiting and hoping for two thousand years, then these cannot occur through diplomacy or other deceit or by the grace of the great powers. In that case, there is no longer any value to the Arabic I am studying and my activities in this direction would appear to be useless. Thus nearly all the positive content to my life is shown to be pointless, and I am left with almost nothing.

My great complaint is against this terrible emptiness. I now understand that ideas and thoughts are worthless if one cannot convert them into action. My inner vacuum, moreover, is giving rise to all kinds of thoughts, which are expressing themselves in strange desires. For in life one cannot be neutral, neither positive nor negative; if one has nothing positive, then all sorts of negative tendencies appear unhindered. So now all day long I do nothing but search for some positive content for my life, so as not to be entirely lost. In every single thing I hope to find a meaning that will fill me and satisfy me, but it is as if I heard a voice inside me always saying: "You are deceiving yourself if you think this is of value for you; it can at best fill only part of your spiritual void." This has been my situation for quite some time; I am lost and seek in vain, for meaning, for control, for purpose. But so far I have found nothing.

[. . .] In my prayers I ask that the Lord take pity on me and bestow on me His lovingkindness and that His holy spirit fill me that I might live again. [. . .]

[Undated entry]

THOU HAST CHOSEN US

Yesterday was Shavuot, the festival of the first fruits. The people of Israel, who are living through their greatest crisis, who are in exile and who have been exiled dozens of times, celebrated this harvest feast. At this time in former years synagogues would be decorated with flowers, tree branches, ferns, and the like, but of course it was impossible to do so this year. The reason is perfectly clear: this year the Jews find themselves in an exile totally unlike all previous exiles. It finds itself in Belgium, France, Holland, Romania—wherever Jews are exiled—and not merely exiled but they are persecuted as only Jews can be persecuted. [. . .]

Well, it was Shavuot, and so with perhaps a bit more than usual fervor, I said this holiday-prayer; and when I reached these words, my head reeled as I thought of how many generations of Jews have said them. In how many times of trouble have we repeated these words, so full of meaning, "Thou hast chosen us." Yes, Thou hast chosen us. In everyday life we laugh to ourselves when we think of those words, and yet they have accompanied us for two thousand years, and I think they will go with us into the future, too. Then I wondered whether it were really worthwhile to belong to such a "chosen" people; but even as I thought, I realized that such thoughts were useless. Whether it be worthwhile or not, we were chosen once and that is all there is to it. There were times when I was proud of being a son of the elected people, but those times have long since passed. I can't say that I hate this chosenness, but I am still very far from loving it. When, oh when, shall we see the fruit of all our toil? When, O when?

June 13, 1943

For the past few weeks I have not written in my diary. The main reason for this is difficult to explain, but here it is: all this time I have been hoping for something. I am almost ashamed of myself when I think of what it was that I hoped for, but anyway I hoped, day by day, for—a miracle. What this miracle would be and what could come of it did not concern me, I just hoped for it, but day followed day and week came after week and my miracle did not come. This showed me that one should not rely on a miracle. [. . .]

Nothing important has happened lately. While it is true that the Germans and Italians have been chased out of Africa, this, in my opinion, does not bring the end of the war much closer. I intentionally write the "end of the war" rather than "our salvation" because, in my opinion, as I have already written several times in my diary, the "end of the war" and "our salvation" are not synonymous. And I cannot see the approach of redemption in Allied victories, but rather the contrary. I had formerly thought that I detected disagreement among the Allies, and that such fallings out were signs of the coming redemption, but this has come to nothing. There are, however, other signs which are promising.

As I have written, I think that this war will end with the downfall of most of the world because all have tortured our people. As I see it, the only thing that is delaying the approach of our salvation is that certain countries have not committed enough sins to blacken their names completely. The most important of these nations are England and America (the sins of Germany and Russia are now sufficiently enormous). Now, when England and America every day drop bombs on defenseless towns, on women, children, and the aged, their list of sins must be getting longer and longer. There is another sign—the increasing anti-Semitism was the exclusive property of Germany, but slowly, the poison has been spreading to the other side, and while it does not as yet exist there with official sanction, it is only a short step until that will happen. Undoubtedly this step will be taken, for after all it can only serve to intensify our right to salvation. In the meantime, however, and despite all these "good" signs, our people continue to suffer, especially here in Europe, in an almost intolerable fashion. [. . .]

Sabbath eve, June 17, 1943

During recent days, more than I can write has happened to me. Everything is in a state of decline, I feel as if I am descending lower and lower. I have promised myself that next week I shall make a complete, radical repentance. I hope and pray that God will help me and have mercy on His people and on me. Perhaps He will change everything for the better, and every descent will serve only to accentuate the ascent.

The situation of our people has not changed much. Every passing day different "kinds of Jews" begin to share our troubles. For instance, the Romanian Jews, previously not subject to deportation, are now also being rounded up. By decree, a family of six, whom we know very well and whom my father used to visit almost daily, was deported. When I heard the news I trembled all over. But several hours later I felt a sort of relief. Somehow from my point of view all this is quite understandable. Though I feel the sorrow with all my soul, from another point of view I feel that salvation is nearing. At the same time I am not yet ready to be saved and I seem to decline further and further. Perhaps the Lord will have pity on me and assist me. Have mercy, O Lord, and pity Thy faithful servant.

July 4, 1943

It has again been two weeks since I last wrote in my diary, despite all the promises I made to myself last time. What can I do? Several times during the past two weeks I took my diary in hand but I did not open it because I had nothing to write. I still am hopeful from day to day and from week to week; despite the repeated disappointments I have suffered I shall never stop hoping, because the moment I stop hoping I shall cease to exist. All I have is hope; my entire being depends on it. And at the same time I have nothing. What will these useless hopes bring me? I don't know what to do. Everything is becoming hollow. Formerly, when I took up my Bible and read it, it was as if I had returned to life, as if the Lord had taken pity on me; even in my darkest moments I found consolation in Him. Now even this is denied me, all seems lifeless, it does not enthuse me. [. . .]

July 14, 1943

[. . .] [C]hanges have occurred in the world situation that can affect the outcome of the entire war. The Germans have started a great offensive against the Russians, and a few days after this offensive was launched the Allies landed in Sicily. This last is especially important. If the Allies succeed in conquering Sicily, then the war will end soon, in an Allied victory.

Such is the military situation today. As far as my opinion concerning the end of the war goes, I have not changed it; rather, I am more convinced of it than ever before. My conviction does not rest on military developments or anything like that, but it comes because I feel inside myself that all we have suffered and continue to suffer cannot be in vain, and that it is nothing more than a preparation for greater and more terrible troubles, the likes of which we have never experienced since we became a nation. I realize, however, that it is possible that, in spite of what I think, a completely different situation from the one I foresee might come about. As far as I am concerned, however, there can be nothing more certain than the feeling I have within me. The days to come will show whether all that I have thought up to now, all that has simmered in my heart, and has become a deep and strong conviction, will be falsified or will prove correct. If I am proven right, then that will be the strongest possible justification of the goals that I set for myself a long time ago. I do not beseech the Lord on my own behalf that all should be as I have thought, but rather for the sake of my beloved people and that an end might come to our exile of two thousand years.

Moshe Flinker

September 6, 1943

[. . .] Now that I have reached the end of the first notebook of my diary, feelings of thankfulness come over me: first to our Lord, the Lord of Israel, who has protected me and my family in such terrible times, and who has given me the privilege of understanding and knowing His divine guidance and heavenly protection; and second, my thoughts turn to my teacher, my master, and my guide—Mr. Grebel— whose memory has not left me from the moment I left The Hague, and about whom I have written little because I did not feel that my soul was pure enough to speak of this most beloved and dear man.

My Lord, so close art Thou to me and yet so far. I search for Thee constantly, my thoughts go out unto Thee, and my acts as well. My Lord, my Lord, do not abandon me. Hearken to my pleading voice, and have mercy and compassion on me.

Twilight, the hour of the Minha (afternoon) prayer. [Undated]

[. . .] I am sitting facing the sun. Soon it will set; it is nearing the horizon. It is as red as blood, as if it were a bleeding wound. From where does it get so much blood? For days there has been a red sun, but this is not hard to understand. Is it not sufficient to weep, in these days of anguish? Suffering stares at me as on every side and in every direction, and still further troubles appear before your eyes. Here a man and woman, both over seventy, are taken away. There you meet a Jew who has been hiding and has no money to live, and elsewhere you meet a Jew whose fortune has gone because he invested it in dollars, which for some unknown reason have become worthless. Trouble never ends . . . and every time I meet a child of my people I ask myself: "Moshe, what are you doing for him?" I feel responsible for every single pain. I ask myself whether I am still participating in the troubles of my people, or whether I have withdrawn completely from them. Some three or four months ago I would have had no trouble at all in answering these questions, because then I was attached to my brothers with all the fibers of my heart and soul, but now all has changed. From the moment I became empty, I have felt as if all this no longer concerns me. I feel as if I were dead. [. . .]

The end of my diary, thanks to the Lord.

5

Otto Wolf

OLOMOUC, CZECHOSLOVAKIA

Otto Wolf was born on June 5, 1927, in Mohelnice, Moravia, the youngest child of Berthold and Růžena Wolf. He had two older siblings, Felicitas (nicknamed Lici or Licka), born in Lipník nad Bečvou on March 27, 1920, and Kurt, also born in Lipník, on February 13, 1915. Berthold and Růžena, married on July 20, 1913, instilled in their children a strong sense of their Jewish identity, but their daughter Felicitas recalled that before the war they did not rigorously observe the Jewish holidays, rituals, and laws, nor did they keep kosher at home. Indeed, like many Czech Jews of their generation, they were very much assimilated into mainstream culture, living a middle-class existence until the German takeover of Czechoslovakia. Throughout most of the 1930s, the family lived in the Moravian city of Olomouc, where Berthold was a businessman. Otto attended middle school there, as did Felicitas, who completed her studies as a tailor and went on to attend a technical design school. At the same time, she taught apprentices in dressmaking about textiles and worked as the manager in a clothing boutique. Meanwhile, Kurt was studying medicine at the nearby university in Brno.[1]

On March 15, 1939, the Germans annexed Czechoslovakia, their troops crossing the border from Germany and marching into Prague. They immediately dismantled the country, setting up a nominally independent Slovakia (in reality a puppet state under Hitler's control) and establishing the so-called Protectorate of Bohemia and Moravia with the remaining part. The Protectorate (including the capital city of Prague) became part of Nazi Germany, its citizens subject to the laws and decrees of the Reich. This development prompted Kurt Wolf to flee Czechoslovakia, seeking safety in exile in the Soviet Union. Less than seven months later, Germany attacked Poland, bringing the Protectorate with it into the massive European conflict. The repercussions for the Wolf family were immediate. The battery of anti-Jewish decrees, the harassment of Jews, and the prospect of imminent danger at the hands of German occupying forces and the Gestapo drove Berthold, Růžena, and Otto from Olomouc to the small town of Tršice, where they had friends and acquaintances from before the war. Felicitas went to work as a farm hand to help her parents with their declining financial resources, concealing her Jewish identity for as long as possible.

Less than two years later, in June 1941, Germany attacked the Soviet Union, beginning the war in the East. At the same time, Reinhard Heydrich, the top Nazi official in charge of implementing the "Final Solution of the Jewish Question" throughout Europe, was appointed Reichsprotektor of the Protectorate of Bohemia and Moravia. This sinister development marked the beginning of the expulsion, concentration, and annihilation of the Czech Jews. The Terezín ghetto was established in October 1941 in a former eighteenth-century military fortress thirty-five miles outside Prague. According to Nazi design, it was to be a concentration point for the Jews, from where they would be dispatched to the killing centers of the East. The deportations from Prague to Terezín began in December 1941. In January 1942, Kurt joined General Ludvik Svoboda's Czech military unit, which was being formed to fight against the Germans in the Soviet Union. Just about six months later, in the summer of 1942, the rest of the Wolf family received a call-up notice ordering them to leave Tršice and report to Olomouc for deportation.

As Felicitas later put it, the family decided to "decline this invitation" and instead went into hiding in the woods surrounding Olomouc.[2] Unbeknownst to the inhabitants of Tršice, a local gardener, Jaroslav Zdařil (called Slávek in the diary), had arranged a hiding place for the Wolfs. Motivated largely by an ardent (but unrequited) love for Felicitas, Slávek had undertaken the monumental task of providing for her and her family, as well as trying to conceal their existence in a small town where people inevitably watched, discussed, and gossiped about every aspect of one another's lives. The climate of fear, insecurity, and suspicion caused by the German occupation further exacerbated the situation, making such a deception even more perilous and difficult to carry out. Despite this, Slávek was determined, establishing the Wolfs in the first of their many secret dwellings in an improvised shelter near his fields in a section of the forest called Amerika, about a kilometer from Tršice. He remained the Wolf family's primary protector for almost two years, providing them with shelter, supplies, food, and occasional news of the war and the outside world.

Otto began his diary on June 22, 1942, with an account of the family's departure for the collection point for deportees, located in a school in Novy Hodolany, near the main railway station, and their disappearance into the underground life in hiding. He was fifteen when he began, and he wrote more than a thousand entries over the course of the next three years, sustaining his chronicle outside or in makeshift shelters, in the cold, rain, and dark, pestered by vermin, harassed by the unwelcome presence of those who might discover them, and combating escalating hunger, fear, frustration, and helplessness. Its very existence not only testifies to Otto's determination to record his family's experiences, it evokes a kind of defiance of the "disappearance" itself, as if Otto wanted to account for himself and his family from the day they vanished until the day they would be able to resurface from the underground world in which they had been forced to dwell. The resulting account is an extraordinary one, its details capturing the mundane and highly specific character of each day, and its almost epic longevity reflecting the entire arc of the Wolf family's three-year odyssey to survive.

Otto wrote in a generally neutral style, for the most part limiting his entries to terse, detailed notes about the immediate circumstances of his family and usually staying away from deeply reflective or overtly emotional subjects. From the outset of the diary, he reported the specific details of each day: the time they rose in the morning, the food they ate, and the status of supplies. He noted the annoyances of ants, mice, and bugs; the perils of illnesses or health problems; the details of the weather, and described their many makeshift innovations. He marked special occasions or small exceptions to the daily routine, as when he found tulips, raspberries, or cherries to bring to his parents; when they received extra food or a treat from Slávek; or when they celebrated an anniversary or birthday. He also remarked on particularly interesting or unusual events. ("Last night, an eclipse of the moon occurred. Pretty weird, that. Our little moon!")

Similarly, he noted their individual and collective moods, their boredom, and the regular routine of prayer that marked most of their days in hiding. Although Felicitas recalled that they were not observant before the war, once in hiding, their father (who had been brought up in a very religious family, and had been trained as a cantor) insisted that they meticulously observe the Jewish holidays and rituals. Most of all, he led the family in offering daily prayers of thanks for their food, meager as it was, and for their shelter, precarious though it may have been. Finally, as often and regularly as possible, Otto also recorded the news of the war as they heard it from the outside world, noting the progress of the battles, the movement of troops and the front line, and the capturing of towns and villages whether by the enemy or by the Wolfs' would-be liberators.

Otto's daily reports of the family's routine are punctuated by news of contact with members of the outside world. Slávek was their primary link to that world, their total dependence on him a source of frustration and anxiety for both parties. While he did much to shelter and care for them, he also sometimes disappeared for several days, leaving them without food, news, or provisions. At the same time, unwelcome members of the outside world sometimes encountered *them,* as they inevitably left traces of their presence in the woods. Over time, former friends and neighbors began to suspect or find out that the Wolfs were in the forest. This ever widening circle of often unwilling "accomplices" was a kind of double-edged sword for the Wolfs: while it increased the risk of betrayal, it also increased the number of people who could potentially provide the family with supplies or shelter. The most important of these other "helpers" was a man named Alois Pluhař, who ultimately became a second provider for the Wolfs, bringing them food, provisions, and books to lessen the stagnation of their days.

Above all, however, Otto's diary captures the ambivalence that their presence engendered in their former neighbors. Whereas in most diaries the tension exists primarily between the victims and their oppressors, in Otto's diary the Germans are an oblique menace, for all practical purposes completely absent. Instead it is the relationships between the victims, their would-be helpers, and unwilling outsiders that are at the center of the diary's narrative. Far from presenting a rosy, romanticized view of the beneficent rescuer or the equally exaggerated stereotype of the unfeeling, indifferent bystander, the diary begins to suggest the immense complexities of an ordinary group of people forced by unprecedented and life-threatening circumstances to decide how and whether to act. In this, the Czech locals who helped the Wolfs were not like the inhabitants of Le Chambon, who are now famous for their collective commitment to protect and hide Jews as a reflection of their conviction of the sanctity of all human life. No such cohesive or intentional imperative bound the random but nevertheless interconnected individuals who sheltered the Wolfs. Instead, the diary paints a picture of a group of people who exhibited a whole range of human conduct, including altruism and generosity, indifference and opportunism, impatience, selfishness, and cruelty, and whose conduct itself shifted and changed over time, defying all attempt at simplification or generalization.

As the war dragged on and the strain of hiding increased, the Wolfs' relationship with Slávek deteriorated. His long absences and lack of consistent food deliveries frustrated the Wolfs, who began to suspect that he might be taking advantage of their helplessness for his own financial gain. To further complicate matters, Slávek seems to have resented the intrusion of Pluhař, and in return Pluhař repeatedly warned the Wolfs that Slávek was not to be trusted. Over the course of 1943–44, as the Wolfs remained for the second winter under Slávek's protection, the tension grew almost unbearable. Begrudging the fact that Felicitas did not share his feelings for her, and aggravated by the demands of caring for the Wolfs, Slávek fought with her almost constantly; meanwhile, Berthold Wolf grew ever more impatient with Slávek's recalcitrance and indifference. Many of Slávek's friends and family who knew of the Wolfs' whereabouts also began to show signs of hostility and frustration. Otto reported that a friend called Vladya was heard referring to the Wolfs as "goddam bastards," Mrs. Pluhařová became reluctant to do their laundry, and the generally kindhearted Pluhař blew up at them in a drunken rage.

The rising tensions between the Wolfs and Slávek exploded in the spring of 1944. In desperation, the Wolfs decided to seek shelter elsewhere and made contact with Mrs. Ludmila Tichá, a dentist in Tršice, and with Maria Zbořilová, their former maid, who promised to rescue them from their desperate plight. On the night of April 13, 1944, the Wolfs moved from Slávek's hideout into the attic of the Zbořils' home, and another circle of protectors took over the task Slávek had begun two years before. In the new hiding place, Otto continued to report in much the same way as he always had, generally restricting himself to daily reports on food, tasks, visits from the Zbořils or Mrs. Tichá, the well-being of the family, the progress of the war, and the like. Initially, the Wolfs were overwhelmed by the kindness they received. Maria Zbořilová (called Mařenka) was described as "so very pleasant—the very salt of the earth"; likewise, Mrs. Tichá, who lent the family one thousand crowns, "wouldn't hear of a receipt." It is clear from the diary that the Wolfs were heartened not only by the increase in food and comfortable surroundings but by the dignity and respect with which Mařenka and Mrs. Tichá treated them.

Although conditions in the Zbořils' attic were markedly better than those in the forest and huts (the food was better and more plentiful, their "hosts" kinder and more friendly, their movements less proscribed), certain inevitable parallels emerge between both experiences. While Mařenka and Mrs. Tichá expended great effort to provide for the Wolfs, the fear of discovery and the accompanying strain surfaced in this setting as well. Mařenka's husband, Mr. Zbořil, was deeply ambivalent about hiding Jews in his attic, repeatedly threatening that they would have to leave, then relenting and allowing them to stay. Even Mařenka occasionally lost her patience with them. The Wolfs, paralyzed by their helplessness and dependence, sometimes complained or criticized their hosts in ways that seem surprising, given the risks that were being taken to protect them. Finally, just as in the forest, a new circle of outsiders emerged, among them passersby, visiting relatives, and others who noted with suspicion the odd goings-on in the Zbořil household and began to whisper and gossip that the Zbořils were sheltering Jews.

The Wolfs remained with the Zbořil family for one year, until Mr. Zbořil, who had always been uneasy with the Wolfs' presence, lost his patience entirely and demanded that they leave. The Wolfs uprooted themselves again, this time to nearby Zákřov to stay in the attic of the Ohera family. Still under the protection of Mrs. Tichá, and also aided by a new helper called Andela Chodilová, the Wolfs left for the new hiding place on March 5, 1945. Initially, their circumstances were promising, with the war clearly at an end and a new set of kind, generous people to look after them. The new hiding place was comfortable, food was plentiful, and their "landlord" was able to listen to a secret radio almost every day, transmitting a steady stream of encouraging war news to them.

With the exception of a miserable but mercifully brief stay in the forest prompted by house searches, presumably conducted by the Gestapo, days at the Oheras' house passed much like those at the Zbořils': Otto reported on the clothes Felicitas made to barter for food, and the meals, visits, moods, fights, tasks, and news of the war that filled their days. The more unsettling aspects of life in hiding emerged in this place, too; almost immediately, nosy neighbors and others began to suspect that someone was hiding there, generating yet another round of anxiety-provoking rumors and gossip. In particular, the indiscretion of the Oheras' maid caused tension and insecurity for the Wolfs and their helpers.

In the waning months of the war, instability in the region of Olomouc (including Tršice and Zákřov) mounted, as partisan activity in the forests was high and the Gestapo increased its efforts to find and uproot this anti-Nazi activity. On April 18, 1945, there was a raid on the village of Zákřov. So-called Vlasovites, a group of Soviet POWs who fought alongside the German army under General Vlasov, swept into the village in search of partisans or local villagers who were protecting them. During the raid, twenty-three young men, including Otto, were caught and taken away.[3] Almost immediately after his capture, Felicitas began writing the diary in her brother's stead, starting with an account of the details of the roundup and Otto's disappearance.

Devastated by Otto's capture and terrified to stay in town, the Wolfs sought shelter yet again in the forest. Felicitas's entries are filled with the shock and loss the family experienced as day after day passed with no word about Otto's fate. Added to their grief, conditions in the forest were horrendous, with unseasonably cold and wet weather plaguing them, forcing them to move from outside into a shed and back again. Their supplies grew dangerously low, reducing them to spare meals of bread and jam or shmaltz. Further, the ongoing chaos in the town prohibited contact with their helpers except on rare occasions. Amid the confusion, terror, and deprivation of their final days in hiding, the fear for Otto's well-being and the gulf created by his absence are the predominant subjects of the diary. Day after day they prayed for liberation, thinking constantly of Otto and Kurt. But as the long-awaited liberation eluded them and the days dragged on, depression, grief, and apathy began to take hold, making it difficult for the Wolfs to do anything but wait for the end to come.

Liberation finally arrived on May 8, 1945, almost three years after the Wolf family went into exile. Upon emerging from the hiding place, however, the Wolfs learned of Otto's death. After his capture, he had been denounced as a Jew by a local Fascist named Hodulík and was tortured by the Gestapo, refusing to reveal the whereabouts of his family or the identity of those who had sheltered them. On

April 20, 1945, he and eighteen other young men caught in the roundup were taken to a nearby forest and shot, their bodies burned where they lay.[4] Kurt, too, perished during the course of the war, having fallen in battle fighting the Germans in Sokolovo on March 9, 1943.[5] Mrs. Wolf, undone by the loss of both her sons, news of which she received on the same day, suffered a massive stroke that left her partially paralyzed and from which she never fully recovered. She died in 1952. Both of her sons were posthumously awarded the Order of the Silver Lion by the Czechoslovak government. Berthold eventually remarried, giving Felicitas a stepbrother, Thomas Mandl, with whom she remains close to this day. Felicitas married and she and her husband, Otto Garda, emigrated to the United States in November 1968. In 1995, she donated Otto's diary to the United States Holocaust Memorial Museum in Washington, D.C.

June 22, 1942. Monday, first week.

We depart Tršice at 2 P.M. en route to Olomouc. We are being moved out. Josef Lón takes us, because Mrs. Zdařilová could not get anyone else. Farewells are tough, and we are all quite upset. We make good time, and get to Olomouc around 4 P.M. Before we left Tršice, I turned in our apartment key at the district office, and also got identification papers for Licka [Felicitas, Otto's sister]. We get off in Olomouc-Hodolany and tell Lón that we are going to see a doctor and some friends. We enter an apartment building. Just to make it look legitimate, Dad asks where Mr. Hanzlík lives. We rip the stars from our clothes right away. Around 4:30 P.M., we leave Olomouc-Hodolany to go back to Tršice. Lón had turned in the packages at the school, and we go on foot. We march tirelessly until 11:45 P.M.—we only take about an hour of rest en route. We go through Veliký Týnec around 7 P.M. Anyway, we reach the forest around midnight. Slávek had already been here with the backpacks, but because we are so late, he had gone back with them and then they carted the sewing machine and the box with stuff that has been prepared to the house of Zdařil the painter. We don't sleep much—we just lie there. We feel like we'd been whipped.

June 23, 1942. Tuesday, first week.

In the early morning, around four-thirty, we go lie down in the haystack because we could not locate the place that we had found for ourselves earlier in the forest. We get some water at the spring and bed down in the wheat. The weather is beautiful and the temperature is climbing, reaching fifty-six degrees by noon. We are running out of water, but we are brave and stick it out. Jenofa Vybíralová is working in the field not three meters from us, but she has no idea that we are that close. The heat lets up in the afternoon. We stay in the wheat until 10 P.M., and then we return to the forest to get some sleep and to wait for Slávek. He does not come until eleven, but without the backpacks. He stays with us until 4 A.M., then goes home.

June 24, 1942. Wednesday, first week.

At 4:14 A.M., we look for a stable hideout and manage to locate one. It is in thick bushes, so that we can't even sit up in there, just lie down. At five, Lici [Felicitas] and I go get some water at the spring by the forest. Only then do we lie down to sleep and sleep until eleven, bothered by hundreds of ants. Dad is cooking the first warm meal in two days: soup and meat with bread. [. . .] In the afternoon, we lie down again with the ants, and stay down until evening, and then have eggs and bread for dinner. We are waiting for Slávek. He is supposed to bring our backpacks today. He brings them around 11 P.M., and Dad makes coffee around eleven-thirty. Slávek sleeps with us all night until 4 A.M.

June 25, 1942. Thursday, first week.

At quarter after five, we go for water, then put away things from the backpacks. Right afterward, we have breakfast of warm coffee and then sleep until 10 A.M. Dad is improving the camouflage on our hideout: he cuts down two small trees with his pocket knife and uses them to hide the entrance well. Lunch consists of soup and rabbit with bread. In the afternoon, Dad cuts off all my hair and then, for the first time in his life, he shaves off his beard. We can't recognize him. [. . .] Slávek does not come, and no one seems to be looking for us yet. [. . .]

July 4, 1942. Saturday, 2nd week.

We fetch water at half past four, then lie quietly until eight. We have bread and black coffee for breakfast. We have practically no kerosene or bread left. We have no idea why Slávek has not come. We have bread and bacon for lunch. That is the last of our bread, and it's only noon. We have no idea what to eat in the evening and the next morning. In the evening, we have lentil beans softened in water and boiled just a little, because we have no kerosene left. Slávek did not come.

August 25, 1942. Tuesday, 10th week.

We go at half past four in the morning and then we have breakfast of coffee and bread. We then take a nap. At eight we start snapping beans. As soon as we finish our lunch of garlic soup and bread, we continue with the beans. We are done at 2 P.M. We have a tidy pile of them. Dad puts them on the roof of the hut [a makeshift shed in the forest] to dry. In the afternoon, something scares us terribly. We hear a noise in the hut and assume that someone had found the beans on the roof and is pawing them. Later we found out that some man had merely put some fresh chaff into the hut. We were really scared at the time. In the evening we have dinner of bread with jam and then sleep a little and then take off at quarter past ten to pick up food. But apart from some trifles there is no kerosene at the drop-off point, and we are almost out. Dad is the angriest because of it: he doesn't sleep one bit during the night. We don't know what we will cook and eat.

September 10, 1942. Thursday, 12th week.

[. . .] It is cloudy in the afternoon. Dad tells me to go to the hut and rake the chaff into a pile. I go in there and start raking the chaff into one corner. When I look behind me my blood goes cold in my veins. Mr. Bláha's brother is standing behind me. He says: "I've been wondering what the rustling noises are." I immediately make a face and reply: "Oh, I lost a knife here somewhere." He says: "Well, it'd be a pity if it's a nice one." I say: "Oh, I've got it," and start walking away. He stares after me quizzically but says nothing. I hide a little distance away and wait to see what he will do. He starts walking off, but stops and listens periodically to see if he could hear us. Meanwhile, I get back to the tent. Dad is just coming back from the latrine. I meet him and tell him what happened to me. Mr. Bláha's brother probably did not recognize me. While I am telling all this to Dad, we hear whispering by the hut. Dad quickly ducks into the hideout, and I run down into the forest. It is Mr. Bláha and his brother. They are listening for us. Then they suddenly let the dog go. The dog sniffs and sniffs and even sticks its head into our tent. It does not bark, though, and does not give us away. [. . .] After a while, everything is quiet again. We live through hours of terror. Then suddenly someone walks up to our hideout with something that is ringing in his hand. [. . .] Then suddenly Mr. Bláha's brother looks into our hideout and says: "This looks like some prisoners live here." They go to the entrance and try to get inside our hideout. At that moment Dad comes out and begs Mr. Bláha not to denounce us. To our surprise, his behavior is honorable, and he assures us that he will not mention us anywhere as long as we do the same for him.[6] His brother's behavior is exemplary, too. We can continue to use the hut, but only when it is raining. He reassures us that the war will be over soon. We should pray that it turns out okay. They then leave. That was at quarter to eight in the evening. That means that we were living in horror since half past five. [. . .]

Otto Wolf

September 15, 1942. Tuesday, 13th week.

[. . .] Mr. Bláha comes at 7 P.M. and tells us to look for a new hideout. The chief forest ranger could come and find us. Because of this, I go into the bushes to meet Slávek. To be able to meet him, I go at quarter to eight. Fortunately, I don't run into anybody on the way. I wait, and he finally comes at nine. I tell him everything, and he says that he will have a word with Mr. Fiala. I am to meet him here again tomorrow at 9 P.M., and he'll come over with me. I go home, but run into the rest of the family. We go off to get the food. We find croissants, spinach, eggs, tomatoes, salt, and some other things. [. . .]

September 16, 1942. Wednesday, 13th week.

We already have water at home, and sleep until nine. We have breakfast at seven. Lici is making a tomato spread. We're waiting impatiently to find out who will take us: Fiala or Herinek. We have bean soup and bread with the spread for lunch. The soup is great. In the afternoon, we go searching for another hideout but cannot find anything that fits the bill. At a quarter to nine, I go to wait for Slávek in the bushes, but run into him on the way. Herinek won't take us and Fiala is not sure, but Tandl is okay. He will reportedly take us, but only a month from now. Slávek will ask Fiala to take us for this month. Slávek will come again tomorrow.

September 18, 1942. Friday, 13th week.

[. . .] We have coffee and bread for lunch. We are all packed and waiting [to move to a safer place]. It begins to drizzle. Today we'll probably move to the Fialas'. We have bread and cheese for dinner. We are waiting for Slávek, who is to help us move. He doesn't show up by one o'clock, and I and Lici therefore go to the Fialas'. I tap on the living room window and they come to open up, all frightened. I ask if we can stay with them. They say that they are scared to do it and it would kill her and that we shouldn't ask it of them. They'll do anything for us: all we have to do is to tell Slávek. They give us a pot of milk and four large apples. We take the bread that Slávek had left with them. We get back around two. Dad tries to cheer us up by saying that this must be G–d's will.

September 19, 1942. Saturday, 13th week.

We sleep until ten, and then pray. We have bread with jam for lunch. I and Lici go for water. We are depressed, wondering how things will go. Who will give us sanctuary? [. . .] We have cheese and bread for dinner. They go to the bushes at 8 P.M. and wait for Slávek until half past ten, but in vain. Slávek does not come. We don't know why, and hope that he will come tomorrow.

September 29, 1942. Tuesday, 15th week.

We go for water at 6 A.M. and then immediately have coffee and bread for breakfast. [. . .] Dad has a fight with Lici and Mom and wants to leave again because he can't stand it anymore, and so forth. He wants to write a letter to Mařenka Zbořilová but the others don't want him to. Dad is very angry and doesn't talk to anybody. Mom has a breakdown. She doesn't even go for food with us. I and Lici go for food alone at half past eight. We find kerosene, denatured alcohol, onions, vegetables, potatoes, and pears. We get back at 9 P.M. and find our parents already asleep.

October 17, 1942. Saturday, 17th week.

Around quarter past five, the rain intensifies. We therefore pack up our things and sit under the Billroth paper [an impermeable paper developed as a covering for burns and other oozing wounds]. We have a piece of dry bread for breakfast. It is cold. We have to move into the hut at 8 A.M. It continues to rain until 1 P.M. When it stops, we all go for a walk on the path because we're cold. [. . .] Around 5 P.M., we hear some rustling: we think it's Slávek, but it is some forester who keeps walking around our hideout. After a while we hear rustling again: we think it's the same forester returning. We are very disappointed to find out it is the head forester himself. We therefore decided to pack up all our things and tell Slávek that we must leave here. Dad and Lici are done packing by quarter after seven in the evening. I and Mom meanwhile get the rest of our things. Slávek comes to the bushes at quarter after eight. [. . .] We load ourselves up and happily leave the forest. Dad is very happy to have a roof over his head. We sleep until morning sitting up.

November 8, 1942. Sunday, 20th week.

[. . .] Slávek comes at half past seven, very unhappy. Mrs. Fiala told Pecek [about the Wolfs] and he, in turn, trumpeted it in a pub. Tandl leaked it to Pluhař. So, we don't know if Tandl will do it [shelter them], or what will come of it. Lunch consists of dumplings with jam. In the afternoon, we keep watch. We have bread soup for dinner. Slávek comes at 8 P.M. with very good news from the front. [The Allied landing in North Africa.] The English are advancing and have taken a lot of ground already. He sleeps with us until 3 A.M. I spend the whole night downstairs with my parents; we do not sleep, just talk politics.

January 11, 1943. Monday, 30th week.

I go for water. It is cold. It is minus twenty degrees [Celsius] outside. Downstairs where my parents are staying it is minus eight. We'll never make it without the down comforters. Slávek's got to bring some. The water and the coffee have frozen

Otto Wolf

{ 133 }

solid. We have breakfast at eight. We sleep until eleven, and have potato soup for lunch. At least it warmed us up a little. In the afternoon, we all sit upstairs. By early evening, it gets very cold. It is minus ten downstairs; Mom and Dad, who sleep there, are cold. Slávek comes at 10 P.M. [. . .]

February 4, 1943. Thursday, 33rd week.

Dad and I go for water at 3 A.M., then we sleep until six and have breakfast right away. [. . .] Today Stalingrad fell; also today, the Czech legionary unit took part in fighting for the first time [units under the command of General Ludvik Svoboda]. Maybe our Kurt is there, too. Slávek sleeps here until five in the morning.

February 12, 1943. Friday, 34th week.

[. . .] We have yesterday's blood sausage and potatoes for dinner. We invite Slávek in honor of brother's Kurt's birthday. We drink tea, and eat croissants and pastry (i.e., gingerbread from L.). Licka had embroidered "We all wish you, dear Kurt, a speedy return" on a red pillow. Kurt's photo is in the middle. We talk a little, and Slávek then goes home. The situation is excellent. Slávek goes home at 3 A.M.

February 18, 1943. Thursday, 35th week.

[. . .] It is freezing. The situation is great. The Russians are kicking the Germans' butts. Just let the war end already. Slávek doesn't come today, either. We have no idea what happened to him or why he isn't coming.

March 19, 1943. Friday, 39th week.

Dad and I go for water at 1 A.M. We then go for a walk in the forest. We're back at four—we've been away for three hours. We breakfast on bread and coffee (which is really just colored water, and bitter to boot). There is very little hope that Slávek will find any milk. [. . .] Purim is coming on Sunday, but Hitler isn't hanging yet. We're waiting for Slávek. He comes at ten with bread and croissants. He goes down below to lie down right away, and Licka says that "she'd love to drill that jerk's teeth without anesthesia." The weather is nice during the day, but we need rain.

April 18, 1943. Sunday, 43rd week.

At a quarter after four, we take off for the forest for the second time. We have two backpacks, a briefcase, carpets, water. Day has broken already. We're in the forest at half past five and immediately get to work. We cut small branches. We're done by eight and put them inside the hideout. It is great. We then get busy on the camouflaging. We go off for small trees. We're done by half past eleven, then eat bread with coffee, and sleep until 2 P.M. It's very nice here. The morning was cloudy, but now it is clear. We pray at half past six. [. . .]

April 20, 1943. Tuesday, 44th week.

We turn off the burner and the light and close the hut and literally run back to the forest so the food will stay warm. [. . .] We warm up the soup. Dad spills it, also the kerosene. A tree catches on fire, but Dad coolly picks up the dumplings and only then puts the fire out. He said that the forest isn't his but the dumplings are. [. . .]

April 28, 1943. Wednesday, 45th week.

[. . .] We celebrate Mommy's birthday with a holiday meal—bread, meat, and canned fruit. It is an excellent lunch. We then stay out in the sun, and afterward go into the hideout. We have bread for supper, but there is very little left of it, so each of us only has an eighth of a slice. We go into the hut to cook at 9 P.M. We found bread and various things and Slávek's birthday wishes to my mother. [. . .] We go home at quarter past two and get back at three. Just as our parents start eating, we hear branches rustling. Someone is climbing up here from down below. At three in the morning, if you please! He keeps mumbling something under his breath. He goes right past the hideout, but didn't find us. Dad says that this is very bad, that he had to have tracked us back here all the way from Slávek's, and that we have to make ourselves scarce right away.

May 2, 1943. Sunday, 45th week.

[. . .] At nine, we go to cook and to wait for Slávek. He comes at half past midnight, bringing bread and goat meat. Our parents had come with us in the evening, but because there was no bread, they'd gone back again. They are hungry, poor souls. As soon as Slávek shows up with the bread I go back to bring it to them, and they are very happy. I return to the hut immediately because I have to fix the burner in the hut. Lici and Slávek had an argument. We cook potato soup (a big potful) and bread dumplings. Slávek goes home at 4 A.M. and we head out at quarter to five.

June 1, 1943. Tuesday, 50th week.

A new month begins today: hopefully it'll bring us more luck. We go back to the forest at a quarter to four and eat soup with dumplings there. I picked a few strawberry leaves for Dad near Slávek's—he'll try to smoke them since there are only twenty cigarettes. [. . .] He had tried them and said that wild strawberries are excellent. At noon, we have white coffee and bread. It's delicious. In the afternoon, I and Lici go for strawberry leaves, and manage to get a lot. Dad is carrying them with him so they'll stay warm. We'll cut and dry them. [. . .]

July 6, 1943. Tuesday, 55th week.

We return to the forest at half past three. [. . .] Around five-thirty in the afternoon, we hear rustling. I climb a little higher up and see a person. He straightens up and sees me. When he recognizes me, he comes straight to us. It is Pluhař. He promises not to tell anyone, not even his wife. Then he leaves. We theorize extensively, and are really concerned that he went to turn us in. We wait to see what will happen next. The women are down below, and Dad and I go into the clearing. We hear more rustling around 8 P.M. and conclude that he is returning with a policeman. What a surprise! He comes with a loaf of bread and a little shmaltz. He is assuming that we are hungry. What an outstanding deed! Dad gives him his black pants, and he is very happy. He says that he will return in the morning and bring milk and cigarettes. We are overjoyed and thank God that that's the way things turned out. At ten, we go cooking. There is bread as well as laundry soap there. We make caraway soup with bread. The sky is glowering.

July 7, 1943. Wednesday, 55th week.

We return to the forest through a drizzle. We polish off one and a half pots of soup, and then Dad and I go into the clearing to wait for Pluhař. The poor man shows up at 7 P.M. with three-quarters of a liter of goat milk and a cup. He goes home immediately. It begins to rain. We eat bread with shmaltz. In the worst of the rain, we hear rustling and someone calling: "Where are you?" It is Pluhař and his wife! They are bringing pots of hot soup, meat, cherries, and gingerbread. This is to warm us up, they say. We should move into their spare room, they insist, instead of freezing out here. They spend a little while with us and then go home. We are very nearly speechless. They advise us to watch out for Slávek. We eat the soup, bread, and delicious white coffee. [. . .]

July 8, 1943. Thursday, 55th week.

[. . .] Pluhař comes again at half past eight bringing milk and a small pot of thickening. He sits with us for about an hour and talks. We'll be getting milk every day. We eat white coffee and bread. Dad tells him that we would like to live with them and that Slávek already knows about it. It is raining again. We eat bread and vegetables and white coffee. We have more coffee and a little soup for dinner. At ten, we go cooking. There is food already there, but only bread and new potatoes. We cook caraway soup with bread. Slávek didn't leave a note: maybe he'll show up. He comes at half past one in the morning, in the rain. He did guess that it was Pluhař. He's against it: says he doesn't trust him. He won't bring us food there. Maybe he'll mellow out. [. . .] In Russia, the Russians have launched an offensive. Slávek brought milk.

July 20, 1943. Tuesday, 57th week.

We cross the creek to get home, where we eat soup and dumplings with mushroom sauce. We sleep until eleven, then have bread with shmaltz for lunch. In the morning, right after eating, we congratulated our parents on their anniversary. Dad gave Mom a piece of paper on which he summarized the events of the past thirty years in verse. I gave them a small poem too. [. . .] To celebrate, we have bread with shmaltz for dinner. [. . .]

July 25, 1943. Sunday, 57th week.

[. . .] In the afternoon, we have a small bit of bread with shmaltz. Today, Lici will go to the Pluhařs. We go to the hut at 10 P.M. and find bread and meat in a glass. Slávek has left me a nasty letter. Lici puts on Mom's coat and kerchief and goes from the hut to the Pluhařs. They were sleeping already, but [Mrs.] Pluhařova comes to open the door anyway. He is drunk and sleeping in the back room. They hadn't come because Slávek had visited them and told them not to help care for us, that we have enough of everything and that he keeps bringing us baskets full of stuff. He threatened them that if anything happened, we won't protect anyone. They should not put themselves in danger: it's enough that he has. They'd all be shot. Well, that's the kind of back-stabbing jerk our Slávek is! Our parents are waiting by the shed. Lici brings back delicious cakes and says that Pluhař is going to come to us tomorrow. We cook potatoes, caraway soup, and mushroom sauce.

July 31, 1943. Saturday, 58th week.

We go back to the forest while it is still dark, then eat soup and goulash with potatoes and cabbage. We sleep until quarter past ten and then pray. We have goulash with bread for lunch. We spend some time in the clearing and some in the hideout. A storm moves through the area in the afternoon and dumps some rain on us. We have bread with honey for dinner. We take all our things into the clearing at half past seven. [. . .] Dad is grumpy because he hasn't got a newspaper. We feel like we're stuck behind some barrier. [. . .]

August 15, 1943. Sunday, 60th week.

[. . .] Pluhař is supposed to show up today. The sky is still gray, and it even sprinkled in the morning. For dinner, we have bread with mustard. It's cloudy, and we therefore go cooking at half past nine. Licka had made a scene again today, and what a beauty it was! There are provisions in the hut: bread and twenty cigarettes. I go to meet our parents. I get water and bring them hot coffee. We cook bread soup and warm up the beans. This morning, only parts of the sky are cloudy. Last night, an eclipse of the moon occurred. Pretty weird, that. Our little moon!

September 8, 1943. Wednesday, 64th week.

[. . .] We go cooking at half past eight. The moon is veiled in fog. We find provisions in the hut, namely bread, salt, matches, and three small pieces of gingerbread. Slávek had stuffed himself with the rest and couldn't polish off what we found. He has been an incredible jerk lately! I go to meet our parents. We also find the Sunday paper. I bring coffee to our parents and get water. The sky is cloudy. We cook cabbage, caraway soup, potatoes, and apples. [. . .]

September 28, 1943. Tuesday, 67th week.

[. . .] Tomorrow is Erev Rosh Hashanah. For dinner, we have plain bread. [. . .] I go to the Pluhařs' to ask if Papa and I can come there. Pluhař isn't home, and she is asleep. I go back to the hut. Dad wants Lici and Mom to go to the Gandis' [code name for Slávek's parents]. [. . .] I go there, and she [Mrs. Zdařilová] answers me from the window that Slávek isn't home. I ask her to come outside for a moment because I need to tell her something. She turns on a light in the yard and comes out. I say: "It's me, Mrs. Zdařilová." She comes closer, and when she recognizes me she hisses right in my face: "Damn you, man, shut up!" I wait a while, and then Gandi [Mr. Zdařil] comes. I tell him that Slávek hasn't given us bread or potatoes. He says that he'll give us potatoes, but I want bread. He goes to look and brings a basket of bread and croissants that Slávek had prepared for us. [. . .] Gandi apologized for her, that she got the scares and is shaking like a leaf. That poor Gandi: he can't do a thing when he has to deal with a beast like that. I beg a newspaper from him. There isn't much new. I go back to the hut. [. . .]

October 2, 1943. Saturday, 67th week.

[. . .] We go to the hut at half past seven. All we find are two loaves of bread and a newspaper. I go to the Pluhařs' to get some cigarettes, but they are not home. I go back at 10 P.M. This time, I find them both home. He gives me five cigarettes: the engineer supposedly brought him only forty-five. They seem a little scared today. They probably don't want us to come by so often. It's understandable. [. . .]

October 15, 1943. Friday, 69th week.

In the forest, we eat cauliflower soup, cabbage with potatoes, and goulash, then lie down to sleep. After that, we have some plain bread, and pray. [. . .] Today, only Dad and I go cooking because it is wet and we don't have shoes. All we find in the hut is bread. Slávek writes that he won't get the hut ready [for the Wolfs to move] until next Tuesday: he doesn't have the time earlier. [. . .]

October 19, 1943. Tuesday, 70th week.

After we eat at 1 A.M., we lie down to sleep and stay asleep until half past five. We then start disassembling the roof. We carry the sticks to the edge of the forest. From there, I carry them to the Gandis' meadow. [. . .] We then pack [to move to Slávek's hut]. We eat plain bread and pray. [. . .] Pluhař comes to see us in the afternoon. We are to come and get cigarettes on Friday. We eat plain bread, and carry our things up to the clearing at half past five. We schlep the first load at six. [. . .] Slávek still hadn't come, and we therefore put the things downstairs and sit down upstairs [in the hut]. Slávek ends up not coming at all. We'd crossed the creek while moving. We all got wet. Dad uses a knife to fix the boards.

October 20, 1943. Wednesday, 70th week.

We have a miserable time sleeping sitting up. [. . .] It is stifling hot inside the hut again. [. . .] Slávek isn't coming, and we all need to relieve ourselves. At 8 P.M., Dad finally jimmies the hasp from the inside, goes to the bathroom, and waits for Slávek.[7] It is incredibly windy. Slávek and Dad stand in the garden, screaming at the top of their lungs. I'm sure they hear them in the neighboring houses. Slávek has had a few too many, and wants to go to the police station. At long last, they patch up their differences. Slávek gives Dad cigarettes. Apparently, he is sobering up a bit. Slávek then brings bread, a newspaper, sausage, and a piece of home-baked bread for Dad. He then spends some time in the hut, and goes home at quarter after eleven. [. . .]

November 5, 1943. Friday, 72nd week.

Papa hasn't been sleeping nights: that's how angry he is at Slávek. We have breakfast at half past six. [. . .] For lunch, we have soup made from the last of our potatoes. Slávek hasn't brought more, even though we have been asking him for three days now. Yesterday he gave us red beets, celery roots, parsley, cabbage, and a few onions. It is windy again. In the afternoon, we sit around. [. . .] Papa is incredibly upset. He and I go for a walk. At half past eight, I take a bag and go to the Pluhařs' to borrow some potatoes. I tell them that we are hungry. They lend me some, and we cook them in the hut. We then go for water and afterward to bed. We hope that Slávek will bring some bread or potatoes in the morning. It is sprinkling. Hunger.

November 18, 1943. Thursday, 74th week.

[. . .] In the afternoon, Slávek surprises us by putting in an appearance. He is angry because I'd gone to the Pluhařs' on Tuesday. Pluhař supposedly screamed at him like a baboon that we shouldn't come there anymore and his head feels like it's going to explode and he's going to go nuts because of it and so on. Well, that was our last visit there, then. [. . .]

November 29, 1943. Monday, 76th week.

[. . .] [Slávek] hasn't shown his face here since Saturday: another example of his beastly behavior. Dad is out of tobacco. We go to the irrigation ditch at five. I cut some boards to make a table. We then return to the irrigation ditch, hammer the pieces together, and presto, I have a handy little table. Now housework is a different story. [. . .] We are all mad at Slávek because of his conduct toward us. We go to bed at half past nine. It is very muddy outside.

December 13, 1943. Monday, 78th week.

We have breakfast at eight. I munch on dunked bread crusts. Dad and I rise at ten. [. . .] In the afternoon, we sit. We hope that Slávek will show up today. We wait and wait, but in vain. Dad and I have some dunked bread crusts for dinner. [. . .] [We] then go outside. While we are taking our walk, we decide to wait one more day, but tomorrow we will tell Slávek—that is, if he shows up—that we managed to hold on only by eating everything in his last delivery. [. . .] When we get back, poor Dad is so hungry that he eats some bread crusts and a croissant. He can't sleep, and he and Lici go for more water at a quarter to midnight. Mom and I stay in the hut. She is in a slightly melancholy mood this evening. Dad and Lici are back at quarter to two, and we go to bed.

December 16, 1943. Thursday, 78th week.

We have breakfast at eight, then sleep until half past eleven. Dad is busily cooking barley soup for lunch. He has nothing to smoke, only that homemade stuff, and that has no nicotine in it. Pluhař said that they'll get fifty extra cigarettes for Christmas and the same for New Year's, but after that they'll only be able to get twenty-five per ration. I am curious if Slávek will give Dad more cigarettes. In the afternoon, we sit. [. . .] Mom and Lici go out at half past six. It is pretty dark. They are back at eight, and Dad and I go at half past eight. We are out until eleven. We bring back water. When we return, we find Pluhař sitting in the hut. He came just a while after our departure, totally smashed. Lici made him some mocca. He evidently had an argument with his wife. Maybe they even fought, because he is calling her every name he can think of. He says that he'll have a Christmas bread [a sweet, plaited bread, similar in texture and shape to challah] made for us at Christmastime. He goes home at half past two. We go to bed. It is bright outside. Slávek didn't show up.

December 18, 1943. Saturday, 78th week.

We have breakfast at half past seven, and we pray at ten. For lunch, there is noodle soup. [. . .] Slávek said yesterday that there was some talk about a special Christmas cigarette ration but that nothing came of it. Pluhař, on the other hand, said that he'd gotten one hundred cigarettes. So Slávek had kept the ones he got. In the afternoon, we just sit. For dinner, we have garlic toast with coffee. It is nice outside. [. . .]

December 24, 1943. Friday, 79th week.

[. . .] Around quarter past ten, we hear footsteps and a voice calling: "Open up, it's Pluhař!" And it is really him, with over two and a half liters of beef soup, four pieces of boiled meat, barley kasha, liver sausage stuffing, pastry, a Christmas bread, and two books. Just as he sits down, Slávek shows up. Pluhař quickly slips into our beds downstairs and sits there. Slávek brings three loaves of bread, a newspaper, cigarettes, and about a kilo and a half of pork from Lipňany that costs 180 crowns per kilo. This means he must have paid about 270 [crowns] for it. He stands around for a while. He is tipsy. He says that he is on watch today. When he leaves, Pluhař crawls out. [. . .] Those Pluhařs are really being fantastic: they are poor but are willing to give, whereas others, better placed, are not. Pluhař goes home soon. He doesn't want his wife to be alone on Christmas Eve. She supposedly wanted to bring the stuff herself but was not sure how we'd receive her. Pluhař says that he'll come tomorrow, so we'll see. Dad and I go for water. In the evening, we finish up the meat soup. Thank G–d we now have enough bread. [. . .] Dad gives everyone a pastry. The Christmas bread is very nice and the whole hut smells of it. [. . .]

December 25, 1943. Saturday, 79th week.

We go to the bathroom at six and have breakfast at half past six. We pray. For lunch, we have noodle soup. Dad skimmed the fat from the meat soup and added it to the beef soup, and the beef soup was nicer and fatter than anything we have had in exile. Slávek was smashed yesterday. He kept chuckling. Pluhař was probably in a rage because he has nothing to drink and Slávek was literally floating in alcohol. [. . .]

December 31, 1943. Friday, 80th week.

The last day of the old year. [. . .] At seven, Dad and I go outside. We meet two unknown people as well as Holubář. At that point, we see someone coming over from the Herineks'. We hide behind the tomato patch. We assume it is Slávek, but the person goes to the compost pile and literally smashes something down on it. We call out: "Slávek, Slávek!" The person walks on but stops a good distance away. Papa and I go to him and he says: "It's not Slávek, it's me." It turns out to be Vladya. As soon as he says that, he turns around and leaves with the parting words: "Goddamn bastards." We have no idea what this behavior is supposed to signify, and why Slávek didn't come himself. The briefcase contains chicory, matches, cigarettes, and light bulbs. [. . .] Naturally, we are upset. We assume that Vladya is drunk. They are celebrating New Year's Eve at the Herineks', and there is a lot of shouting. We have bread and goulash for dinner. We wait for Pluhař until midnight, but he does not show up, and we end up going to bed. So, these were our last impressions of the year 1943. Good riddance!

1944

January 1, 1944, Saturday, 80th week.

[. . .] Pluhař comes around half past eight, bringing Christmas bread and pastries so we know—so he says—that it is a new year. He forgot the newspaper. He goes home at quarter to ten. I follow him a while after he leaves. His wife is in bed already, but she welcomes me pleasantly and talks a lot. They serve me Christmas bread. There is nothing new. There is heavy fighting near Zhitomir and Vitebsk. The Germans are admitting that the Russians have launched an offensive during the holidays, so we are curious what the Anglo-Americans will do. [. . .]

February 12, 1944, Saturday, 86th week.

We eat breakfast, sleep until ten, then pray. [. . .] Tomorrow is Kurt's birthday. Lici made a drawing on a sheet of paper. She wrote on it: "G–d give our Kurt health and may He return him to us soon." A photo of Kurt is in the middle. Lici is sewing Pluhař's vest. It is taking her a long time. I make some thickening at half past ten. To celebrate the birthday, Dad makes a caraway soup with thickening and barley. I go for water twice alone. It is windy, and there are snow drifts. We go to bed at half past one in the morning.

March 24, 1944, Friday, 92nd week.

We get up at half past nine and pray. It is Rosh Chodesh Nisan. Mom and Lici pray after us. For lunch, we have soup with potato dumplings that we prepared yesterday. In the afternoon, I start unraveling my sweater. Mom wants to re-knit it, and we will try to exchange it for food. I wash and then change pants. That means that I get out of the rags that pass for my pants and get into shorts. The weather outside is absolutely horrible—snow, rain, and strong wind alternate. [. . .]

April 3, 1944, Monday, 94th week. Summer time.

We rise at noon. Bread soup constitutes lunch. In the afternoon, we sit. [. . .] Toward evening, we hear someone tap on the pipe. After a while, someone behind the hut calls: "Mr. Wolf!" It is Slávek. He tells Dad to come for a visit tonight at eleven, and to bring Lici along. We assume that Slávek has some financial matters to discuss. [. . .] At half past ten, I go to Slávek's [. . .] Dad and Lici join me [there]. We all go inside. What is at first a lively discussion turns into a screaming match. Slávek wants power of attorney so he can get our gold and hold it as security. He says that he ran out of money, that Orel doesn't want to give him bread except for once a week for sixty crowns. Slávek uses some pretty foul language. He gets up from his bed and slaps Lici across the face. Dad gets up and says that he is going to the police station. Slávek takes off after him, calling back to Tandl and Vladya to keep Lici and me in the room. Papa reaches the fence gate before Slávek catches up to him. I break loose, pull Slávek off Dad, and open the gate. It takes everything we have to keep Dad from going to the police. Malcha and the old woman, who are in the kitchen, keep telling us to stop shouting and go home. Tandl is falling down drunk. Slávek has had a few as well. Only Vladya is sober. Slávek wants Dad to certify that he, Slávek, will be fully reimbursed after the war. He doesn't seem to know what he wants. [. . .] We finally manage to calm Dad down and we slowly walk home. [. . .] Slávek said that as long as Dad doesn't hand over some money we are not getting anything to eat. There is a lot that could be said on that theme. We go inside the hut at 3 A.M. I make mocca. We go to bed at half past four, wondering what to do next. Even Gandi is talking differently than he did before.

April 4, 1944, Tuesday, 94th week.

[. . .] We decide that Lici has somehow got to get to Mrs. Tichá today. We'll go to the Oheras' and ask where she is living, and then we'll visit her. [. . .] At half past eight, Lici and I go through the forest to the Oheras'. When we get there, Lici rings the bell, but no one answers. Just as we turn to go home, some woman comes walking by. We ask her if Mrs. Tichá doesn't happen to live here. She asks what we want. Lici asks her if she doesn't happen to be Mrs. Tichá. She says yes: this has got to be the coincidence of the century. Lici goes up with her. Mrs. Tichá is very pleasant with Lici. She immediately promises help, financial and material. As much bread as we want, she says. She invites us for Thursday after the holidays. We return to the hut happy. As we relate our experience, Pluhař comes in, drunk, bellowing, and cursing like a sailor. At first he says that we have to give him his books and that, from now on, we don't know each other. We are pigs, oxen, asses, snakes, and so forth. After he has sat a while and sobered up a bit, he is sorry for what he said. He goes home at half past two. [. . .]

April 7, 1944, Friday, 94th week.

Dad and I get up at quarter to ten and pray. It is Pesach [Passover]. After that, Mom and Lici pray. For lunch, we have noodle soup that we cooked yesterday. In the afternoon, we just sit. We have decided to start keeping watch during the night, since these kinds of people are capable of anything. When I go for food, I will always have my pocket knife open in my pocket. In the afternoon, Slávek goes by. He even comes up to the hut to take two saplings. Naturally, he doesn't say anything, the boor! We pray. For dinner, we have the rest of the noodle soup. [. . .]

April 12, 1944, Wednesday, 95th week.

We rise at one. Dad shaves. For lunch, we have garlic soup with crusts. One bag of crusts is now gone. [. . .] We keep praying to G–d that Mrs. Tichá will come through for us. We have bread with margarine for dinner. Dad and I go outside from quarter to nine to ten. I then go to see Slávek. He has readied flour and bread. [. . .] From the day we moved, the day counter stands at 719.

April 13, 1944, Thursday, 95th week.

Dad and I get up at ten. We pray. Mom and Lici pray after us. For lunch, we have egg drop soup with bread crusts. In the afternoon, I pack backpacks and various other things. It is warm. We are curious if G–d will hear our prayers today. For dinner, we have the rest of the soup. Lici gets dressed at quarter after eight and goes with G–d to the Oheras' at 8:35. [. . .] Lici shows up at half past nine with good news. She is carrying a loaf of homemade bread, one and a quarter kilos of honey, a quarter kilo of margarine, and two large noodle soup cubes. Mrs.

Oherová supposedly apologized extensively and said that Lici should come back on Monday. Mrs. Tichá supposedly wanted to give us some lard, but didn't get around to finding it. Next time. Lici begged her not to abandon us and she said that it goes without saying. Whatever is in her power to do for us, she will do. We can have as much bread as we need. She lent us a thousand crowns and wouldn't hear of a receipt. This says more than lengthy panegyrics about the goodness of her heart.

[Later], Lici comes running in to tell us that everything is all right, that the Zbořils will take us. We are ecstatic. [. . .] Dad leaves a letter in the hut, stating that, because of his violent behavior, Slávek has forced us to look for a safer environment, that we succeeded in finding it, and that Dad and Slávek will meet again after the war to settle accounts. [. . .] Dad is overjoyed when we get there: they are fantastic people. [. . .] We sit in the kitchen until half past two: the daughter is asleep. Then [Mrs.] Zbořilová and Lici go upstairs to the attic and put our things up there. Odessa has fallen.

April 14, 1944, Friday, 95th week.

We then go up to the attic to lie down, but cannot sleep. At half past six, Mařenka Zbořilová comes up and greets us with a "Hell-l-l-o-o-o!" [. . .] Yesterday was Mom's mother's yarzheit [the anniversary of her death]: maybe it was she who had planted a word in G–d's ear on our behalf. In the afternoon, we lie down for a while. We are curious when Slávek will find out that we are gone. [. . .] We tell the Zbořils how roughly we had lived, and she is agog. I, Dad, and Lici then go to the creek to wash ourselves. Young Mařenka is home by this time. We chat for a while and go up to the attic at ten. In the afternoon, we did some repairs to the attic: I made a kind of wall from straw so we would be invisible. In the night, we hear sirens from Přerov.

April 16, 1944, Sunday, 95th week.

We get up after six. [. . .] At quarter to nine, we go downstairs. Mařenka tells our parents that Mr. Zbořil had been thinking about it through the night and has concluded that he doesn't want us there because he is afraid of being shot. [. . .] Dad talks to Mr. Zbořil about the situation, but he says that he isn't throwing us out, that he is only talking about things. Well, we have no idea what to think. Mařenka gives us soup with a lot of delicious grease, but we are so distraught that we have scarcely a thought for eating. [. . .] We force down a few spoonfuls and then go upstairs. We decide not to go downstairs to the kitchen anymore. Mařenka will bring us food in the attic. We are very upset.

April 19, 1944, Wednesday, 96th week.

We have breakfast at half past six. Mařenka is in a hurry: they are going to Laznický to attend the funeral [of Mr. Zbořil's father]. Dad gives her fifty crowns to hand out to beggars as a way of thanking G–d for delivering us from Slávek's claws. Afterward, she brings us a small cup of leftover milk. [. . .] We ask her if Mr. Zbořil has had anything more to say about us, and she said that he only told her to bring us up some long straw so we won't be cold. Seems like he has made up his mind. [. . .]

April 20, 1944, Thursday, 96th week.   *7 [days at the Zbořils']*

We sleep until half past five. I then look at the newspapers and find papers from last Sunday as well. The situation is excellent. [. . .] At noon, Mařenka cooks potato soup for us and again puts in so much fat that fat rings float on the surface. She also gives us a little skillet of delicious cabbage, supposedly "just to have a taste." The poor thing really cannot do enough for us to make our lives more bearable. She keeps telling us that she feels terribly sorry for us. The young Mařenka keeps echoing the sentiment. [. . .] At half past eight, the young Mařenka comes up and tells us that she was feeling lonely without us. [. . .] Today is that asshole Hitler's birthday.

April 24, 1944, Monday, 96th week.   *11.*

We are up at quarter to six. Breakfast is at quarter to seven. Mařenka then shows up with a beautiful long velvet coat. It is very nice indeed. Lici is going to sew lining into that suit of hers using fabric from my coat. [. . .] [Mrs. Tichá] said that she had heard that Pluhař has been saying that we are no longer with the Zdařils and are most likely at the Zbořils'. We are very perturbed, and wonder how Pluhař could have come up with the Zbořils' name. I keep hoping that Pluhař will realize that it is very much in his own interest to keep quiet. We still find it very unpleasant, because Mařenka is a bit upset by it. [. . .] The world situation is supposedly great: things can be expected to collapse just about any time. [. . .] They are all a bit upset over Pluhař's conduct, especially the little one. [. . .]

June 4, 1944, Sunday, 102nd week.   *52.*

I dump the bucket at two. We sleep until quarter after six, then have breakfast. For lunch, we have pea soup. Mařenka gives us five cakes. Again, she loans us a newspaper. The situation is great. "Ours" have already reached the outskirts of Rome. Foreigners are supposedly writing that the invasion will happen any day now. The young Mařenka comes up to the attic for a while in the afternoon. She brings a piece of cake. She then returns downstairs. Dad and I spend some time in the other attic. For dinner, we have bread, half an egg each, and salad. My family wish me all the best for my birthday. Lici gives me a hat that she'd sewn for me. It is really stylish and I love it. [. . .] I ask Mr. Zbořil to come up with some material for a hat. He comes up a little while later and tells Lici that Mařenka will give her some old gloves to make into a hat. The two of them, Mařenka and Mr. Zbořil, are not exactly seeing eye to eye on things. We go to bed at ten.

June 9, 1944, Friday, 103rd week.   57.

I dump the bucket sometime after one. We sleep until half past six, then have breakfast. Mařenka has lent us an atlas. [. . .] The situation is fabulous. The Anglo-Americans have landed between The Hague and Cherbourg on a 400-kilometer front and are holding on. May G–d give them strength to succeed! For lunch, we have garlic soup with potatoes. [. . .] Mrs. Tichá shows up at half past eight with a pot full of buttermilk and a cake. She comes up to the attic for a while and we chat. We go to bed at half past ten. It is raining.

July 7, 1944, Friday, 107th week.   85.

I dump the bucket at half past two. Breakfast is at quarter after six. Dad is making noodles. Mařenka leaves, and Lici goes downstairs to sew. Around half past eleven, we hear a horrible noise: the tiles on the roof are ringing. It turns out to be aircraft, flying high and in several waves. Later, we are told that they were American. One aircraft dropped about eight bombs near Grygov, and the forest caught on fire. So, that's how strong German air defenses really are! We thought at first that those were German planes, but they turned out to be American. Not a single German fighter challenged them: they were free to just "stroll" across the sky. There were more than two hundred of them. This is the first time we have seen "our boys" anywhere near us. All the people in Tršice were reportedly outside. [. . .]

August 7, 1944, Monday, 112th week.   116.

Breakfast is at half past six. In the morning, I go downstairs with Lici to cook. Mařenka is at work. Around quarter past eleven, we see Americans flying overhead. There are huge numbers of them. It is very pretty, all glittering in the sunlight. For lunch, we have smoked noodle soup, cabbage, potatoes, and smoked meat. It is great. [. . .] After seven, Tichá returns. She has bought us soup again, and also brings a piece of bread with chicken slices. She has also baked us apple strudel, and has brought Dad six cigarettes and yesterday's and today's newspapers. She leaves almost right away. Before she goes, she says that the radio reported that the Russians are fifteen kilometers from Cracow. The papers say that they are west of Mielce. Things are really looking up in France now: the American breakthrough is now a hundred kilometers deep. Just let it go on like that! Mr. Zbořil comes home at half past nine. He brings us a loaf of bread and forty crowns. We go to bed at 10 P.M.

August 13, 1944, Sunday, 112th week.   122.

Breakfast is at half past six. [. . .] I peel potatoes. We have potato soup for lunch. Mařenka gave us five pies. [. . .] Lici is embroidering polka dots on Tichá's sweater. Mom is knitting. Mařenka borrowed a newspaper for us. The situation is great, especially in France. Mařenka sends up a cake. For dinner, we have bread with Limburger cheese—smelly but delicious. In the evening, Mařenka and the young Mařenka go to the movies. I go down to keep Mr. Zbořil entertained. Our parents are in the garden. We go to bed at half past ten.

August 21, 1944, Monday, 114th week.   130.

We have breakfast at quarter after six. Mařenka and Mr. Zbořil go to the fields to bring in the harvest. Lici goes downstairs. I prepare dumplings upstairs. Just before noon, they return with straw. Jakeš sees Lici in the kitchen and recognizes her. He asks Mařenka how come she's got Miss Wolfová in her kitchen. Mařenka tells him to shut the hell up, and he assures her that he is not stupid. For lunch, we have garlic soup and plum dumplings. I spend the afternoon downstairs, making hangers. [. . .] For dinner, we have bread with buttermilk. Mom has an upset stomach. [. . .]

September 6, 1944, Wednesday, 116th week.   146.

We eat breakfast. [. . .] We hope that Mrs. Tichá will come today. We have no bread left. We weigh ourselves again today: Dad weighs sixty-one and a quarter kilos, Mom fifty and a half, Lici fifty-six and a quarter, and I sixty-six. We have all gained weight since the twenty-second of June: Dad two kilos, Mom three, Lici one, and I four. This is obviously because the supply system here is much different from Slávek's. [. . .] The situation could not be better. "Ours" are almost finished with Belgium: they've taken <u>Brussels, Antwerp, and Sedan</u>. Down south they captured <u>Lyons. Finland and Bulgaria have capitulated to the Russians</u>. Simply superb. [. . .]

September 16, 1944, Saturday, 117th week.   156.

[. . .] Tonight is the eve of Rosh Hashanah. At six, we pray. For dinner, we have noodle soup, thickened sauce, bread, and beer. We keep waiting for Mrs. Tichá.

We hope that Kurt will remember G–d in tough times; we pray for him and for his early and happy return. Bedtime is at nine.

September 28, 1944, Thursday, 119th week.   168., 26th week.

[. . .] Mrs. Tichá shows up at half past six with a loaf of bread and a newspaper. She has to go soon, but will be back on Saturday. She says Mařenka complained that we want her to get everything for us and that she has a hard time finding anything. That's an incredible lie. We haven't asked her for anything except for those vegetables that she got at school, and vegetables are easy to get. It's just lack of willingness talking. [. . .] We have bread with honey for dinner. We go to bed at eight.

October 3, 1944, Tuesday, 120th week.   173.

We have breakfast at quarter after six, then go to the other attic. Lici goes downstairs. We pray. While downstairs, Licka was taken by surprise by Klimešová, but fortunately she doesn't know Licka. Mařenka told her that this is Licka Slávková, the cousin of [illegible word], and the matter was thus resolved. Still, Mr. Zbořil already has visions of himself on the gallows. [. . .]

October 9, 1944, Monday, 121st week.   179.

Breakfast is at half past six. Lici goes downstairs, the rest of us to the other attic. We pray since it is Simchat Torah. [. . .] Marta K. took our atlas yesterday: it's like cutting off a hand. Mařenka searches for some map, but in vain. We asked Mrs. Tichá, and she will try as well. For dinner, we have bread and coffee. We go to bed at seven. Mr. Zbořil calls me downstairs to chat. I return upstairs at nine and go to bed.

October 27, 1944, Friday, 123rd week.   197.

After breakfast, Mom goes downstairs to do laundry. When she returns upstairs, I go down and peel potatoes. Before noon, Mařenka goes out for a newspaper. When she comes back, she says that the Gestapo is going crazy in Tršice, that they are ripping up the floors in the city offices and in the police station, looking for weapons. They may have picked up senior policeman Mičulka. Amazing, their pride: their world is falling apart all around them, but they are still acting like lords. Poor Mičulka. We are all upset over it. For lunch, we have potato soup. [. . .] We wait for Mrs. Tichá. She came yesterday, bringing Dad's chompers [new teeth] for him to try out. She leaves at six. For dinner, we have mushroom sauce over potatoes. We sit for a while, then go to bed at seven. It is raining.

October 31, 1944, Tuesday, 124th week.   201.

We have breakfast at quarter after six. We stay up in the attic. It is raining. I peel potatoes. Mařenka goes out for bread. Mrs. Tichá called to her that she will come tonight. They'll have to take it easy with the coming and going so it won't get too suspicious. [. . .] In the afternoon, we see Vladya Zdařil drive a wagon past us to the mill. He has sacks covered up with our carpet. So, that's how they take care of our things. Mrs. Tichá said that she will bring a newspaper in the evening. From now on, Mařenka should avoid going out to get it. [. . .] Lici keeps insisting that Mrs. Tichá is somehow not herself, but I don't know. We go to bed at eight. Lici is up all night with a toothache.

December 11, 1944, Monday, 130th week.   242.

Breakfast is at seven. I go to the creek for two watering cans of water. Lici is dyeing that fabric (that coat). Dad is upstairs. He refuses to talk to Mom or to Lici. For lunch, we have caraway soup with bread and potatoes with meatloaf. After lunch, Dad goes upstairs again. I go with him. I pray and then return downstairs. Dad goes to lie down at half past three. The rest of us stay downstairs until half past seven, then go to bed. For dinner, we had bread and coffee.

December 31, 1944, Sunday, 132nd week.   262.

We eat breakfast at nine. Mr. Zbořil is in a bad mood. For lunch, we have barley soup, pork, cabbage, and dumplings. Mr. Zbořil then leaves. In the afternoon, we read the newspapers. We have white coffee and bread for dinner. We go to bed at eight. <u>Fare thee well!</u>

January 2, 1945, Tuesday, 133rd week.   264.

[. . .] Mařenka says that Pluhař was here yesterday, drunk. He said that he was on his way to wish Mr. Wolf and Otto a happy new year. He was here until twelve. As he was leaving, he told Mr. Zbořil not to tell anyone or half of Tršice will be wiped out. We are all agog. We have breakfast. For lunch, we have caraway soup, carrots, and potatoes. Mr. Zbořil comes at half past seven, this time in a good mood. Mrs. Tichá comes at seven to try out a dress. We go to bed at eight.

February 13, 1945, Tuesday, 139th week.

We have white coffee for breakfast at seven. For lunch, we have farina soup with croutons and potato dumplings with poppy seeds. It is to celebrate Kurt's birthday—he is thirty today. We have his photo on display in the living room. [. . .] For dinner, we have bread with cottage cheese. Mrs. Tichá comes after dinner with fish and five Vlastas [cigarettes]. She sits here until seven. She says that the situation is great. According to the newspapers, the Russians have captured the German city of Lignitz. We go to bed at half past seven.

February 17, 1945, Saturday, 139th week.

We have white coffee for breakfast. [. . .] In the afternoon, we sit downstairs. Lici is sewing. As we talk, Dad remarks that he only wants a place where there is water. We had been talking about the outhouse at the Herineks'. We eat bread with herring, then go to bed. Lici goes back downstairs to go to the toilet. On her way back upstairs, she overhears Mařenka tell Zbořil that no one will be willing to take us into an apartment regardless of what we do or say: we don't even want to go get our own water or even to take a shit. "Why did you even bother to ask him what he did with the money for the summer cottage, you old asshole?" she asks Mr. Zbořil. "He's been sitting on his ass all his life, doing nothing, living from what he had, and now he doesn't have shit left." Dad had confided in them that we had a summer cottage but had sold it for 165,000 [crowns]. Well, at least now we know the true nature of her "sincerity." Naturally, we are angry, and feel very bad about it. We go to bed.

February 18, 1945, Sunday, 139th week.

We eat breakfast. Lici doesn't go downstairs but stays in bed upstairs. Dad tells both Mařenkas that they need not bake any more cakes for us, that we can do it ourselves. Mařenka practically makes herself ill wondering what she could possibly have said again to make him so brutal to her. This morning, the partisans raided the village. They struck the post office and the police station. The policemen shot at them. [. . .] They supposedly pulled down pictures of [Emile] Hácha [briefly president of Czechoslovakia before the German establishment of the Protectorate of Bohemia and Moravia] and Hitler and trampled them, and ripped off Hitler's head. [. . .] German might seems to have turned into something from a comic opera. [. . .] For dinner, we have bread with shmaltz. We go to bed at quarter to seven. It is freezing.

March 3, 1945, Saturday, 141st week.

We have white coffee at half past six. Mařenka goes out for a newspaper. [. . .] As soon as she is out the door, Mr. Zbořil turns the place into a madhouse. He is all angry that we are there, and he does not want us anymore. If we don't leave, he will, or else he will take an axe and knock out doors and windows. We are to find a place to live elsewhere. Why did the devil dump us on their doorstep anyway, and not on some prosperous farmer's or peasant's or millionaire's? We are to clear out by tomorrow. Our parents go upstairs. Lici and I wait for Mařenka. She returns with thirty kilos of potatoes, quarter kilo of butter, twenty-four small Limburger cheeses, ten Sfinx [cigarettes], and a newspaper. We tell her about Zbořil, then go upstairs.

March 4, 1945, Sunday, 141st week.

Mařenka brings us breakfast upstairs, and we eat. Mr. Zbořil is carrying on like a madman: he does not wants us here, and so forth. He goes to church, and we venture downstairs. For lunch, we have noodle soup. Mr. Zbořil comes home at noon, raging. He looks like a beast. We therefore think it wiser to retreat upstairs. Mařenka goes out to borrow a newspaper. When she returns, he rips the paper out of her hand and bellows that we had better be gone by morning. He even comes up to the attic to tell us that we must go, everyone in all the huts allegedly knows about us. [. . .] We can't even eat dinner. Tonight, I sleep with my parents. During the night, Mr. Zbořil was out in the yard three times, cursing like a sailor.

March 5, 1945, Monday, 142nd week.

[. . .] Mrs. Tichá shows up at noon and comes upstairs to see us. She and Andela have managed to find us a place at the Oheras'. [. . .] Mrs. Tichá and Andela show up with a sled at quarter to nine. I load up the comforters and Dad's backpack, and they are off. Lici helps them out by pushing. We go up the hill through Bránka and around Burianka. [. . .] We get there around ten-thirty. It is very nice there: a bed, curtains, and even a freshly scrubbed floor, courtesy of Miss Andela. She is very good. Our landlords then come: very good people, too. They had heated the place and made white coffee and set out a liter of milk for tomorrow morning, all in anticipation of our arrival. [. . .]

March 6, 1945, Tuesday, 142nd week.

We have white coffee for breakfast. In the forenoon, we organize our things. Mrs. Oherová brings us water. For lunch, we have slaughter soup with chunks of bread. I update my notes. In the afternoon, it is pretty cool in here: Dad and Mom stick their feet between the sheets on the bed. Miss Andela comes to check up on us around six. She gives Dad two Tatras [cigarettes] and says that Mrs. Tichá will come tomorrow. We are to heat up the place right away and not sit in the cold. [. . .] [Mr. Ohera] returns at half past ten with buttered cooked potatoes, a few dumplings, a liter of full-fat milk, and over a quarter kilo of sugar. This is very nice of them: they are wonderful people. And Miss Andela is outstanding. [. . .]

March 13, 1945, Tuesday, 143rd week.

We have breakfast at quarter to seven. I then peel potatoes. [. . .] In the evening, Mrs. Oherová comes back from Tršice with the following report: they have been searching apartments in Tršice today, and will come here as well. For this reason, it would be best for us to disappear temporarily, perhaps into the forest. Of course, we could come back in the evenings to get warm. [. . .] We are practically shaking. We keep thinking that Mařenka could let us stay in the attic during the day, and at night we would return here. We can't even eat dinner. At half past eight, Mrs. Tichá and Miss Andela arrive. Mrs. Tichá talked with Mařenka. Going there is out of the question. We had left on Monday, and the very next day Frantina Houšt'alová came to visit Mařenka and immediately headed for the attic to see if we were there. Fortunately, we weren't. Miss Andela says that we need to go into the forest for at least four days, until it is determined whether the inspectors will come here, too. We suggest that we could go to the Pluhařs' for two weeks. Mrs. Tichá says that Pluhařova had told her that she wished she knew where we are, since she has a lot of things that need sewing and fixing. They would be in favor of our coming there, too.

Lici and I therefore go see them in Tršice. It is quarter after ten. The Pluhařs give us a remarkably cool welcome. They say that they cannot take us because they don't have the room, and so forth. We tell them that we are staying in Přáslavice, but they say that they don't believe it. They insist that we are at the Zbořils', that Licka was seen there at the sewing machine, and that even Hajtlová and all the others know about us. We say that it must be some mistake, but they don't believe us. We leave without having accomplished anything. [. . .] Well, we must go into the forest tomorrow after all. We return home sometime after midnight. We lie down for a while, but Papa doesn't—he can't. He stays up, sitting. We rise at 4 A.M., get dressed, and at five we take off along the linden tree alley to the forest. [. . .]

March 14, 1945, Wednesday, 143rd week.

We find a suitable patch of reasonably dense bushes before dawn. The location is between Zákřov and Laznický. There is a lot of snow in the forest, up to eighteen centimeters in places. We cut armfuls of small branches and stand there for a while. We can't walk around there. Everything is frozen. [. . .] It is really miserable in the forest now: all wet and terribly cold. For lunch, we eat bread with meatloaf. Around half past one, we must run and hide since they are out collecting dry sticks. All our shoes are completely wet. [. . .] The day lasts forever, and we are cold. These will be a nasty four days. [. . .] Darkness begins to fall. At half past six, we venture to the edge of the bushes. At seven, Mom and Lici go to the Oheras'. Dad and I follow them at half past seven. Miss Andela is already there, waiting for us. She says that we won't have to go to the forest anymore. She asked what is going on, and they are not allowed to quarter troops in private homes. Naturally, we rejoice, because the conditions in the forest are horrible just now. Miss Andela already has the stove going for us. When she leaves, we eat barley soup. Mrs. Oherová is all upset over everything. We go to bed at half past ten.

March 17, 1945, Saturday, 143rd week.

We have breakfast at half past six. In the morning, we pray. Lici sews, Mom is darning socks, I peel potatoes. For lunch, we have farina soup with a whipped egg mixed in, and potato goulash. [. . .] At quarter after ten, Mr. Ohera appears with a plate containing three large chunks of cooked meat, liver, and horseradish. When he leaves, Mrs. Oherová comes in with half a liter of wine "to make it go down better," and Miss Andela brings pepper. We eat like pigs. What a feast this is, and how wonderful of them to have treated us so! [. . .] I still have a toothache.

March 21, 1945, Wednesday, 144th week.

We rise at six and eat breakfast. Mr. Ohera brings Dad a little tobacco from Miss Andela. I clean and lubricate Mr. Ohera's bicycle. [. . .] At one, Mrs. Oherová brings a sausage with cabbage and potatoes and a loaf of white bread from Miss Andela. [. . .] After that, Mrs. Tichá shows up, bringing about a liter of milk and five Vlastas. [. . .] Mrs. Tichá says that the very day after we visited the Pluhařs, Pluhařova told Božena about us. Jarka Kotlabová supposedly ran to the dairy and announced that they are missing their potatoes and that it is a sure bet that they were taken by those Jews hiding out at the Zbořils'. Hajtlová supposedly knows about it, too, because she saw us there. [. . .] Bedtime is at eleven. More Russian aircraft overhead.

March 24, 1945, Saturday, 144th week.

Dad stokes a fire and starts cooking at half past four. We stay in bed until half past six, when we rise and have breakfast. We then pray. Miss Andela comes at half past eight, bringing a loaf of bread, baked potatoes, a glass of shmaltz, about three kilos of barley, thirty-five decagrams of sugar, a newspaper, and flyers. [. . .] We see someone by the window, as if listening. After a while, Mrs. Oherová comes in, all upset. She says that the maid had heard the sewing machine and is convinced that someone has got to be here. Well, we will see what develops. For dinner, we have bread with cooked meat. [. . .] More Russians fly overhead. We go to bed at half past eleven.

April 11, 1945, Wednesday, 147th week.

Lici is up and sewing by four. She wants to make sure that Miss Andela's outfit is ready for a fitting. They should be here this morning. We get up at seven and have white coffee for breakfast. We then pray: Rosh Chodesh Iyar. [. . .] Just before eight [in the evening], Dad sees a truck full of people drive by. People are running to the pub. The Oheras unlock us at half past eight. Russian aircraft are overhead. At half past nine, Mr. Ohera comes by to tell us that the whole village was full of partisans. Now they have all returned to the forest. One of our lieutenants was in charge of them. They stay until eleven. We couldn't even listen to the radio. I go get water and wood, and we go to bed at half past eleven.

April 12, 1945, Thursday, 147th week.

At seven, we have black coffee for breakfast. Mom and Lici sew, Dad and I pray. [. . .] Miss Andela comes by. That maid is supposedly trumpeting all over the village that as soon as Miss Andela and Mrs. Tichá come to the Oheras', they head to the back. They obviously have someone back there. At noon, Mr. Ohera had a frank talk with her, so hopefully she will shut up now. [. . .] Mrs. Oherová brings us some baked sausage stuffing and potatoes. She says that the forest is full of Vlasovites. They are hunting partisans. Mr. Ohera won't even take a chance on listening to the radio now. They supposedly conducted a door-to-door search in Stameřice. I go out for wood. We go to bed at quarter to eleven.

April 13, 1945, Friday, 147th week.

At seven, we have black coffee for breakfast. Mrs. Oherová brings us water. For lunch, we have leftover cabbage soup, some soup from the Oheras, and leftover potato dumplings with poppy seeds. Lici is stitching away on Miss Andela's outfit. Mrs. Oherová brings us eight pancakes and a bowl of soup. She says that there were thieves in Tršice last night. They took fat, meat, and a cow. Mrs. Oherová doesn't know where, but probably at Orel's or in the communal farm. Probably partisans. Dad spends the morning lying down. He has nothing to smoke.

[On April 19, Otto was arrested during a raid on the village of Zákřov. From this point on, Felicitas kept the diary.]

April 19, 1945, Thursday.

At 6 A.M., they [the Vlasov troops] ask us all for personal identification. They confront our Otošek [diminutive for Otto] first. He is at a loss for words, and finally says that he is visiting the Oheras and that he is from Telč. The Vlasovite com-

mander does not believe him, though, and simply says: "You're coming with me."
Otto rises to his feet resolutely and goes, although his face is as white as paper. The
rest of us feel like knives are being driven into our hearts. They demand identification from Papa, too, but he says that he has special dispensation and besides is
sixty-one already, so finally they leave him alone. They don't even bother Mommy
and me. [. . .] After a search, they line up all their prisoners. There are about fifteen
of them, including Mr. Ohera, our Otošek, Michlík, Hodulík, the two Závodník
boys, and some others we don't know. Papa is the last to glimpse them as the Vlasovites lead them, double file, toward Újezd where they have their headquarters. We
are all half-dead with anxiety about what will happen next. [. . .] Papa decides that
whatever happens, we cannot afford to stay here and must go off to the forest,
though unfortunately without our beloved Otošek. We take nothing with us except
a piece of bread and some shmaltz. [. . .] We are all so crushed by events that none
of us has eaten anything since yesterday, and we all feel emotionally exhausted.
Each of us tries to hide sadness, pain, and tears from the others. Papa laments and
weeps terribly, and we have our hands full keeping him calm. Just before I returned
from the Oheras' in the afternoon, he had gone off to cut some branches so we have
something to lie on in our hideout: a job that used to be Otík's [diminutive for
Otto]. It made him so sad that he had to return to Mommy. He was so weak that he
could not talk or even breathe. Mommy immediately gave him some medicine to
calm him down. The weather is changeable and somewhat cold. We go to sleep at
seven without having eaten anything.

April 20, 1945, Friday.

We wake up at quarter after five and go to a clearing to move our feet a little since it
has been dreadfully cold during the night. We have no blankets. We then pray: it is
Yom Kippur Qatan. We fast until 1 P.M. At noon, I take the basket and go back to the
Oheras' for the most indispensable of indispensable items. When I get there, I find
Mrs. Oherová running around as if she had lost her mind. She says that I must
leave right away, that the criminal police have already been here twice and that they
had left just before I arrived. [. . .] Each one of us has a tiny piece of bread with a
little shmaltz for dinner. Before noon, an old woman roaming around the place
scared us. We go to sleep at seven.

April 21, 1945, Saturday.

We rise at 7 A.M. Breakfast consists of a tiny piece of bread with a hint of shmaltz.
The weather is very cold now. At noon, I crawl through the forest toward Mrs.
Tichá's, who is already waiting for me with a loaf of bread. [. . .] She doesn't know

anything about our men: all Tršice men are home already but none from Zákřov. She says that I shouldn't even think about going to the Oheras' because the Gestapo is showing up there constantly. The Vlasovites may also be roaming around Tršice all the way to the Korábko looking for us. She is afraid that they may find us. She looks terrible: she can barely walk. [. . .]

April 22, 1945, Sunday.

The rain lets up in the morning, but the wind continues. It is terribly cold. We have lunch of a small piece of bread with a tiny bit of aspic that was still left in the bag from the attic. In the forenoon, the rain returns. We have to hide in a shed because our little tent is completely soaked and so is everything inside. The cold is more intense than anything we remember during our three-year exile. When a break in the rain occurs, we hope it is permanent and move outside the shed again because we don't feel safe inside. But the rainstorm returns four more times, bringing with it hail and such terribly cold wind that we keep moving back and forth between our hideout and the shed. Everything is so wet that we have to spend the night in the shed. We sit down on a narrow perch and huddle close together. The hut is very drafty, so we hang a raincoat in front of us to cut down on the cold wind. During the night, we have to get up several times to stretch because all our bones hurt terribly from sitting on that perch. We actually squat more than we sit. All our clothing and shoes are completely soaked, which adds to the cold. We shake like leaves. We keep praying and thinking about Otošek, wondering what he is doing now. At times, we simply cannot explain to ourselves how such a misfortune could possibly have befallen us. At half past six, we pray and go to sleep.

April 23, 1945, Monday.

We rise at seven, pray, and each breakfast on a tiny piece of bread with a few molecules of shmaltz. We fix up our hideout. Papa uses his knife to cut branches from about ten trees and uses the branches to make a roof. I help a little, but in everything we do, we sorely miss Otošek's able hands. At quarter to twelve, I go to see Mrs. Tichá. She provides two loaves of bread, half a jar of jam, ten hard-boiled eggs, a little shmaltz—about five decagrams, six to eight decagrams of butter, nine pies, ten apples, a little over a liter of milk, and medicinal drops. She also sends Papa twenty Zorkas [cigarettes] and a little tobacco, two boxes of matches, and two newspapers. She says that we have to make it last for two weeks. [. . .] Our dear ones have already been transported from Újezd: no one knows where they are now, but the guess is Přerov. [. . .] At noon, I go for water. I feel helpless with grief when I remember that I used to walk through here with Otošek. I have to monitor myself carefully so our parents don't notice anything. The weather is very cold now. We shiver at night, and get up in the morning nearly frozen.

April 27, 1945, Friday.

We pray at eight, then eat a little bread with shmaltz for breakfast. [. . .] Dad has stopped shaving: he is growing a beard. We don't even feel like washing in the morning: we just splash a few token drops of water on our faces. All we can really focus on are our prayers to G–d: we beg for liberation and for Otík's and Kurtík's [diminuntive for Kurt] safety and well-being. [. . .] We have bread with jam for lunch, the same for dinner. Tomorrow will be Mommy's birthday. [. . .]

April 30, 1945, Monday.

The temperature dips below zero during the night. We are <u>terribly cold</u>. We scramble out of the bushes all stiff and frozen. I go down to get water. Everything is frozen stiff and gray with rime. [. . .] We are pessimistic. We hear very little shooting. We are cold and hungry. Papa says that we will only eat twice a day, and smaller portions to boot. We are desperate because our situation is not improving at all. I decide that I have to go see Mrs. Tichá tomorrow. We sleep in the shed. Dinner consists of a tiny piece of bread with shmaltz.

May 1, 1945, Tuesday.

[. . .] [A]t a quarter to one, I see Mrs. Tichá going by to the huts. I come out of the forest and call to her. At this point, I just don't care anymore. Mrs. Tichá comes to me, but it is clear that she is not very pleased with the encounter. She says nothing to pump up my hopes. She says that she is scared, that Tršice is full of fleeing German soldiery. And those Vlasovite animals are going crazy everywhere. Last night, they burned three buildings in Přáslavice and shot fifteen people on the spot. She doesn't know anything about our poor people. [. . .] I am terribly worried about our Otošek. We keep praying for his safe return. [. . .] We crawl inside our hideout, toss out all the wet branches, and replace them with dry ones from the shed. We throw Mrs. Tichá's canvas over the roof. In the evening, when the rain starts, we don't go into the shed. Dinner consists of a piece of bread with butter.

May 5, 1945, Saturday.

We pray. A new month has arrived. The weather is gloomy. Every now and then, we hear rifle shots. We assume they come from the sentries along the road where the DPs are retreating. We have a little bread with butter for breakfast. Lunch consists of bread with jam. We pray again. Our thoughts and prayers are constantly with our Otošek and with the prospect of liberation for all of us. [. . .]

May 7, 1945, Monday.

I go to Božka's at quarter after five. She welcomes me warmly. I come back with half a loaf of bread, some cakes, two liters of sweet white coffee, two spoonfuls of shmaltz, and a quarter kilo of sugar. [. . .] It rains throughout the night, and we hear terrible artillery fire. We think that this is the beginning of the real thing. It quiets down in the morning because of the horrible rain. They had told me at Božka's that things are great, but they didn't really know much.

May 8, 1945, Tuesday.

Breakfast consists of a piece of bread with shmaltz and a cake. We slept in the hide-out, but we were very cold during the night. The weather starts out nice, but be-gins to worsen. We hear some shooting every now and again. Papa says that things may really get going tonight. We hope that since they have already taken Přerov, our Otošek is already free, with the help of G–d. [. . .]

There is fighting in the forest, bullets are ricocheting off trees near us. We duck them as best we can, but finally conclude that we have no choice but to hide inside one of those half-collapsed hideouts. Finally, we hear shouts of HURRAAH! and HELLOOO! We simply cannot believe that, after three years, it could finally be over for us. Mommy and I don't want to come out because we don't want to show ourselves too early, and we scuffle with Papa in the hideout until we finally emerge, all covered with yellow mud and in terrible condition.

6

Petr Ginz and Eva Ginzová

TEREZÍN GHETTO

Petr Ginz was born on February 1, 1928, in Prague, the first child of Otto Ginz and Maria Ginzová (née Dolanský). Two years and three weeks later, on February 21, 1930, his younger sister Eva came into the world. Although Maria had been raised in a Catholic family (and had left the church in her twenties, declaring herself an atheist), she and her husband maintained a liberal but traditional Jewish home, keeping kosher, attending synagogue on major holidays, celebrating Petr's bar mitzvah, and sending their children to a progressive Jewish school. Part of a close-knit family, the Ginzes spent Christmas with the children's maternal grandmother, Růžena Dolanský, in the Bohemian province where she lived; they visited almost every Sunday with their paternal grandmother, Berta Ginz, and their aunts, uncles, and cousins, who lived in Prague. The Ginz children were especially close to their Uncle Miloš, his wife, Nad'a (who had not been born Jewish but had converted to Judaism), and their first cousins Pavel and Hanka.[1]

On March 15, 1939, the Germans annexed Czechoslovakia and four months later, in June, legislation modeled after the Nuremberg Race Laws (defining who was and was not a Jew) was put into practice.[2] Petr and Eva were classified as *mischlinge* of the first degree—children of a mixed marriage in which two grandparents were Jewish. Though in a better category than "full Jews" in the terms of anti-Jewish legislation, the Ginzes were subject to a battery of restrictions that limited almost all aspects of their daily lives. Circumstances worsened with the outbreak of war between Germany and Russia and the subsequent appointment of

Reinhard Heydrich as Reichsprotektor in the summer of 1941. In September, the Nazis imposed the requirement that all Jews wear a yellow Star of David marked with the word *Jude*. Only those mischlinge who were "privileged" (that is, not raised as Jews) were exempt from this regulation; thus Petr and Eva were forced to wear the star.[3]

In December 1941, shortly after the establishment of the Terezín (Theresienstadt) ghetto, deportations from Prague to Terezín began. The Ginz family was gradually broken up according to the Nazi rules for dealing with Jews in mixed marriages and their offspring. The children's Uncle Miloš was the first of the family to be deported to Terezín, probably in late 1941. He was followed in early 1942 by the children's grandmother Berta Ginz, and Miloš's son Pavel. Petr's turn came shortly thereafter, in October 1942, when he was fourteen and a half. Pavel's younger sister Hanka arrived in 1943 and Eva herself in May 1944. Otto Ginz was sent to Terezín last, arriving in February 1945, just three months before the liberation of the ghetto.[4]

Eva's diary opens on June 24, 1944, when she was fourteen, with a description of her arrival in Terezín six weeks before. She wrote until the liberation of the ghetto in May 1945, recording all aspects of her daily life there. In particular, her diary reflects the living circumstances of the young in Terezín, who lived not with their parents but in collective "children's homes." The Jewish ghetto administration had created these homes in part to provide for clandestine schooling, as well as to try to shelter the children as much as possible from their surroundings.[5] And while their efforts did much to improve children's lives, nothing could shield them entirely from the bitter deprivations of the ghetto. It is the harsher side of life in Terezín that is most powerfully reflected in Eva's diary, as she observed and recorded the brutal realities that assaulted her and her friends daily.

In her diary, Eva described the barracks in which she and her bunkmates dwelled; they were overcrowded, cold, filthy, dark, and infested with bedbugs and fleas. Their primitive sleeping arrangements often consisted of straw mattresses with only a single blanket to cover each of them. To make matters worse, the constant influx of new arrivals in the ghetto necessitated frequent moves, undermining even a minimal sense of stability. Time and again Eva and her friends were uprooted and moved, only to find themselves ordered to move again just as they got settled. The lack of decent shelter in combination with frequent exposure to new rooms led inevitably to illness. Eva herself suffered from a bout of scarlet fever and diphtheria that kept her in the hospital for six weeks. As if all this weren't enough, there was the plague of hunger, which grew increasingly worse as time went on. "Sometimes I also feel so hungry that I want to cry," Eva wrote.

As Eva's diary poignantly illustrates, the strain of her life in Terezín was exacerbated by intense loneliness and homesickness. In entry after entry, Eva voiced the plaintive cry of a little girl far from home, deprived of her parents' love and protection, mourning the lost small joys of her former life. Many of her entries were written in the form of a letter to her parents, as if she wanted to conjure up their comforting presence in the alien and threatening world around her. Further, her homesickness and anxiety were amplified by the overcrowding in the barracks. There was almost never the possibility for solitude; time and again she reported that she cried "under the bedclothes" or "in such a way that Hanka wouldn't hear." Even her attempt to find some privacy within the pages of her diary was violated by the prying eyes of her roommates. At the same time, the crowding inevitably led to snappishness and bickering, which made her feel lonelier and more isolated than ever. "Hanka and some other of our girls snapped at me a moment ago because of some silly little thing. I feel so homesick," she wrote.

Work was another relentless aspect of life in Terezín. Eva reported on the various labor tasks to which she and the girls in her group were assigned, many of them miserable ones, forcing the girls to stay outside for long periods in the cold. At the same time, she noted with relief her days off, and wrote about those rare assignments that were interesting or even pleasant, giving her an opportunity to be in the fresh air with her friends. In one philosophical entry, she reflected on an unexpectedly positive by-product of her life in Terezín, which allowed her to learn new skills such as building or cooking. "I'm sure that Daddy will be really surprised when he finds out how good I am at hammering nails," she concluded. "At home I didn't have a clue how to do it."

Eva's diary offers glimpses of daily life in Terezín, but there is something still deeper to be found within it. Across entry after entry, week after week, and month after month, Eva returned to the subject of the separation of her family—children from parents, siblings from each other, husbands from wives, cousins from one another, aunts and uncles from nieces and nephews, grandparents from grandchildren. She not only grieved for herself but shared the sorrows of all her family members, marking holidays, birthdays, anniversaries, dates of death, and dates of parting, each one prompting recollections of the past and a renewed lament over the loss and pain of forced separation. The image that thus emerges from Eva's diary is that of a family decimated by war and oppression, its members scattered, left only to mourn their losses and worry for the fates of their loved ones.

In this context, Eva's adored older brother Petr was her lifeline. She proudly noted his excellent reputation among the young people in the ghetto, writing: "Petr is really an extremely clever boy. He [always] had the reputation of being the cleverest at school." She looked up to him, admiring his unusually serious and thoughtful nature, and endeavoring to live up to the standard he set. At the same time, she was also protective of him, worrying about him, fretting over his emotional and physical health. Indeed, it was she who often sounded like the older sibling, time and again expressing her sense of responsibility for him, and holding herself accountable to their parents for his well-being.

Petr kept a journal of his own in Terezín beginning in October 1943. Unlike his little sister, Petr did not make daily, dated entries in his journal, nor did he write it in the form of a narrative. Rather, it is a terse list composed of two parts: "plans," noting what he intended to accomplish for the month, and "reports" listing his actual achievements for that month. He annotated his "plans" with plus and minus marks, which seem to indicate whether or not he was able to complete his proposed assignments. In this regard, the journal does not provide an account of daily happenings in Terezín, the character of the persecution to which Petr was subjected, or the events of the Holocaust per se. Instead it is a record of the fifteen-year-old writer's efforts to expand his intellectual and artistic capabilities in spite of, or perhaps because of, his confined existence. It is a colorful and impressive chronicle on its own, but it is rendered still more poignant when seen against the backdrop of his sister's diary, which captures so fully the harsh daily life in Terezín from which no one, including Petr, was immune.

Petr's "plans" were ambitious, even by the standards of an adult or someone living in freedom. Among his tasks for November 1943, he included "Get to know perfectly a brief history of humankind." He listed specific works he intended to read and general areas of interest to study, and the artistic projects he planned to undertake, including drawings, linoleum cuts, and bookbinding. If his plans reflect his great ambition, however, it is his "reports" that testify to his astonishing level of intellectual, artistic, and creative accomplishment. He listed the many books he read each month, his interests spanning philosophy, literature, geography, religion, science, history, and art. He further noted his own creative projects, including the completion of various elaborate and fully colored maps and the mastery of a wide variety of subjects. In June 1944, he rattled off the following, "I've learned: Antiquity (Egyptians, Assyrians, Babylonians, Indians, Phoenicians, Israelites, Greeks, Persians, et cetera), the geography of Arabia, Holland, and the Moon." The range of his artistic interests was as varied as his literary endeavors, prompting him to experiment in various media, including drawing, painting, and graphic arts. His choice of subjects was equally broad and imaginative, including such whimsical titles as "an inter-stellar rocket called 'Brave as a lion, fast as a thought.'" Inasmuch as this list speaks to Petr's interests and drive, it also communicates *urgency:* to learn, do, absorb, and create as much and as quickly as possible.[6]

Still, throughout the journal, traces of the external realities of Terezín occasionally emerged. In March 1944, he included among his plans, "Try to get my weight up to 65 kilos" (143 pounds), a reminder that health and well-being depended in part on keeping strong. Similarly, in July 1944, he wrote, "Finish and return the history book and then do something different depending on what books will be at hand." This easily missed line suggests the makeshift nature of his studies, quite unlike a normal school environment. The backdrop against which Petr lived and worked comes through still more in his reports; in November 1943, he wrote, after listing his accomplishments, "I couldn't do more because of unsettled conditions at the end of the month (German visits, call-ups to do labor)." Likewise, in the following month of December, a chilling line is embedded among his notes: "At the beginning of the month, transports to Birkenau (the Schenks), great chaos, I couldn't do more."

One of Petr's projects, noted in both the "plans" and "reports," was to begin keeping a diary, in February 1944. Its first date wistfully reads, "from February 8, 1944, till ? (I wish it was soon)." He saw the diary as a place to record details and anecdotes about his life in Terezín, so that he might later "reproduce the events as they happened with appropriate colorfulness." To this end, he described various occurrences in his life—events he witnessed or experienced, conversations overheard in his bunk, what he ate, how much he studied, fragments of news from home, and rumors from within the ghetto. A scant eight days after the opening of his diary, however, he wrote in disgust, "I hereby declare that keeping a diary is stupid because you write things in it that one should keep forever to oneself and uninvited jerks can stick their noses into it."

Although Petr decided that his diary was not the best vehicle for recording aspects of life in Terezín, it was in the pages of a more public form of communication, the magazine *Vedem,* that this commitment was most fully realized. *Vedem* [In the Lead] was a secret publication undertaken by the boys of Home 1, produced every week between December 1942 and September 1944, and read aloud on Friday evenings. Contributions included poems and prose essays of all kinds, "quotes of the week," inside jokes, and, in one instance, a wry list of the most embarrassing mistakes made during the course of an "intelligence test." Petr occupied a central role in the production of the magazine, serving as its editor. In this capacity, he solicited articles from contributors, edited and corrected them, assembled the magazine, and generally oversaw the operation. It was by all accounts a huge job, and one that Petr took seriously. He was not only the editor of *Vedem* but a contributor as well, and his literary gift is amply evident on its pages, where he penned his most eloquent, wry, and lyrical prose and poetry. His commitment to *Vedem* apparently knew no bounds, for according to his friend Kurt Jiří Koutouč, when Petr was unable to extract enough articles from his friends, he simply wrote the issue himself, disguising his authorship under various pseudonyms.[7]

In late September 1944, Eva noted in her diary that a transport of men between the ages of sixteen and fifty was being assembled, ostensibly to perform manual labor in Germany. She worried that Petr and Pavel would be called up even though they were both half-Jews. Five days later, Eva wrote in her diary, "So Petr and Pavel are on the transport. . . . When I found out that Petr was in the transport, it made me feel ill. I ran from here to the toilet where I cried my eyes out." Ever protective of him, she added, "I try to keep calm in front of Petr—I don't want to make him feel worse." Her diary entries are filled with despair and panic, laced with the familiar combination of her worry for Petr and her fear at being left alone in the ghetto. She prayed that the train would not depart and that some miracle would prevent her separation from her adored older brother, but to no avail. When the boys boarded the train, Eva and Hanka brought them bread for the journey, and in her diary Eva described her last moments with her brother. "I pressed

Petr Ginz and Eva Ginzová

through the crowd . . . and passed Petr the bread through the window. I had enough time to hold his hand through the bars before a guard drove me away."

Petr's last journal entries were written in September 1944, the month he was deported. For his plans, he wrote, "Do lino-cuts, drawings, stenography, and English. Take a good look at *Vedem,* and its standards, and if necessary, really shine at something, but if I do, make sure that it's worth it! (possibly a lino-cut)." Petr's life came to an end in Auschwitz, where, at the age of sixteen, he was murdered in the gas chambers. Pavel, slightly stronger than his younger cousin, entered the camp and worked at slave labor before succumbing several weeks later.[8] Petr's journal, diary, hundreds of pages of *Vedem,* and his watercolors, drawings, and graphic arts testify not only to his determination and creativity in the midst of terror and deprivation, but also to his extraordinary potential and the future that was brutally robbed from him.

If Petr's diary is a reminder of promise denied, Eva's diary begins to suggest the high price of survival. The shock of the separation from Petr, the loss of his comforting presence, and her fear and desperation for his well-being dominate the rest of the diary. Although Eva continued to report on other aspects of her life—work, health, goings-on in the ghetto—she returned again and again to the familiar refrain of worry for Petr. She often addressed a few lines to him in her diary; these entries, penned weeks and months after he had already been killed, read with painful irony. At the same time, her worry escalated as she received no word from him. "There hasn't been any news of Petr," she wrote on November 13, 1944; "I'm so unhappy."

Adding to her fear and insecurity was the fact that her Uncle Miloš was deported from the ghetto at the very end of October. He too was sent to Auschwitz, where he perished. Although Eva knew no more about his fate than she did about Petr's and Pavel's, she was painfully aware that she and Hanka were alone in Terezín, their small circle of protectors still further reduced. And though Eva's father arrived in Terezín in February 1945, this development did not comfort her. To the contrary, she worried about his well-being in much the same way as she had Petr's in the years before, fretting over his health, whether he had enough to eat, whether he was working too hard. Most of all, however, his presence in the ghetto raised the terrifying possibility that he too would be "sent on" to the unknown.

As the months continued to roll by and Eva continued to hear nothing from her brother, her worry for his fate developed into a deeper, more suspicious kind of fear. From time to time, she dared to voice the possibility that he might be in mortal danger, or to wonder whether he was still alive at all. In April 1945, as liberation was imminent, surviving prisoners evacuated from concentration camps in the East were brought westward by the Nazis. In ten short days, more than twelve thousand of these death camp survivors flooded into Terezín, shocking the ghetto inhabitants with their terrible physical and emotional state.[9] The very sight of them and the horrendous information they brought about Auschwitz shook Eva to the core, not only for its own sake but also for its implications for Petr. "Children under fourteen, people over fifty, went straight into the gas chambers and were then burned," she reported. "I'm so worried about Petr and whether he's still alive."

Terezín was liberated by the Soviet army on May 8, 1945. A few days later, Eva and her father returned home to Prague and were reunited with Eva's mother. Though Eva was disappointed that Petr was not waiting for her at home, she closed her diary on a hopeful note: "when Petr comes back I'll write it here." Almost two years later, on April 14, 1947, Eva, then seventeen, made one additional and final entry in her diary, "Petr hasn't come back."

The Diary of Petr Ginz
from February 8, 1944, till ? (I wish it was soon)

After thinking about it for a long time, I decided to write a diary. I'm doing it for my Mom, Dad, and Eva, to whom I cannot write everything I would like in a letter because, first, it is not allowed and, second, my German is not good enough. I'm also writing it for myself so I won't forget the great number of incidents and types of people that I have come into contact with.

February 8, 1944

I'm lying in bed. Next to me on the bunk are my neighbors Kalíšek and Cuml. [. . .] Since I had already wanted to start writing the diary yesterday, my head is full of thoughts from yesterday.

I went to the Magdeburg [barracks] to get some coal for the cooks and I stopped by at Boby Munk's to give him a letter and also to pass on a message that he should send some potatoes. So he gave me a full sack and I put it into the suitcase I had for the coal and made my way to the exit. There was so much fog you couldn't even see a step ahead of yourself. Then suddenly a *křipák* [member of the criminal police] appeared right in front of me and said: "What are you carrying there?" I muttered something confusingly and handed him the empty suitcase. The křipák felt for its weight and reached for the other one. "What, is this one empty?" And he took the suitcase and opened it. I was getting ready to run away and the křipák told me importantly, as if he could read my mind: "Stay there."

But I disappeared like the fog that was all around and I almost merged with it. I managed to tell Munk about it and then, taking up a defensive position, I disappeared through the narrow window used for distributing food rations. My [. . .] coat got caught in it, however, and so I was left shaking in the little window, unable to move in any direction. I finally managed to get loose and rushed home to attend the program [clandestine school] because it was already late (half past nine [in the morning]).

At noontime, I went to see the cooks as usual but when I got there I was greeted with great laughter. There was no way I could have known that they had bribed all the křipáks, *vorpáks* [those in charge of deliveries], and *kupáks* [those in charge of the kitchens]. Apparently, the křipák asked Otto Bloch if he knew whose briefcases they were. He naturally recognized them and took them away from the křipák. The křipák got the best out of it because he was given a huge portion of potatoes. And the cooks then made fun of me for "going on the defensive." [. . .]

I [. . .] was late for the program. They were in the middle of writing a geometry test. Professor Kolm dictated the problems to me. I did three out of five, in fact I got only the last two easiest ones right. Since we didn't manage to finish the test in three hours, we were told to hand it in that evening but we had to promise not to look into our exercise books and not to cheat. I like that. That's how a professor should be! [. . .]

Then I went to visit Uncle Miloš. This time, everyone was at home—Uncle, Pavel, Hanka, Mr. Weis, and Mr. Oplatka. Then I went home and was greeted by an assignment to write an essay on one of the following topics: (1) The Life of an Inanimate Object, (2) Me (My Character), (3) Reflections on Work. I chose the first topic and wrote about insults.[10] Then I tried to finish the geometry but somehow it is not going too well. And so now I'm lying and writing, since the flickering light has stopped flickering so much. I'm going to stop in a minute and go to bed because it's almost half past ten. Cuml is talking to Kalíšek about literature and inverted word order. I'm stopping now and going to bed. I'm wondering what my family is doing in Prague. I can't even remember Eva's face properly anymore.

9.2. [February 9] 1944. Wednesday (evening, in bed)

Nothing special. At lunchtime we had *gebäck* [bread], soup (a good one, with meat, I would accept no other), and porridge in the Magdeburg [barracks]. There are no potatoes in the ghetto. I cleaned the cooks' shoes for the first time. I do not intend to write here any rambling essays like I saw in Wolker's diary, but only little things [that are] to the point, which I will be able to use as points of reference that will help me remember and reproduce the events as they happened with appropriate colorfulness. At eight o'clock we had a Chinese poetry evening organized by Jelínek. The most important idea of his introduction: People are the same everywhere. Chinese poetry is a poetry of the people.

10.2 [February 10, 1944] Thursday (half past eight in the evening)

Nothing special. Everyone is studying for the poetry and literature exams. I'm not studying anything because, being in the fifth form, I do not want to admit to myself that I should need to do more studying while the others, even the ones who work, will learn in a short time what I studied for almost a whole year. I received a letter from my parents, which I was very pleased about. I was particularly pleased by the news about Eva and the news from Hradec.

11.2. [February 11, 1944]

Everything's "all right." [Karl] Rahm, the new German [commandant] in the ghetto [. . .], is doing an inspection of the ghetto. . . . I have seen Rahm twice in person. There's a *bonkes* [rumor] going round at the moment that all half-Jews will be allowed to talk to their mothers in the commander's office under the supervision of a German soldier. I'm afraid that unfortunately it's not true. I'm writing this at quarter to twelve. I was working on *Ceylon* until now. I wrote about [. . .] the Highwayman and how he was really making it.

16.2. [February 16] 1944

No news—today I wrote two letters home. [. . .]

I hereby declare that keeping a diary is stupid because you write things in it that one should keep forever to oneself and uninvited jerks can stick their noses into it.

Plans:

FOR OCTOBER 1943:

Finish *Ceylon* –
Good marks in the program +
5 pictures +

FOR NOVEMBER [1943]:

Finish *Ceylon*–
~~Get to know perfectly a brief history of humankind.~~

Petr Ginz and Eva Ginzová

To write my contributions (the better ones) from the magazine [*Vedem*] +
5 pictures–
Instead of the history of humankind: Plato +

FOR DECEMBER [1943]:

Finish reading Plato +
finish *Ceylon*
devote more time to drawing–
Continue bookbinding. +

PLANS FOR JANUARY [1944]:

Do more writing and drawing, not just capturing other people's thoughts. Quickly finish *Ceylon* and devote the rest of the month to writing and editing my own work. +

PLANS FOR FEBRUARY [1944]:

Leave *Ceylon* and do my own things.
For that purpose start a diary. +
Attend lectures.–

PLANS FOR MARCH [1944]:

Work on *Ceylon* at the same pace.
Try to get my weight up to 65 kilos.
Prepare for exams. +

PLANS FOR APRIL [1944]:

An extensive study of Buddhism. +
Get rid of all the silly little things that I feel sorry about throwing away, under the influence of the leading article by Nora Fried. +

PLANS FOR MAY [1944]:

Quickly finish Ceylon +
finish book C + and read and revise all my notes so that I can again spend more time on general studying. For that purpose, return Ceylon and get back [H. G.] Wells's *The Outline of History*. +

PLANS FOR JUNE [1944]:

Quickly finish studying the East and devote most of the time to general studying. +

Petr Ginz and Eva Ginzová

Also, do lots of drawing and write articles, according to what [Emmanuel] Chalupný says on page 39 on the subjective truth of culture

PLANS FOR JULY [1944]:

Finish and return the history book and then do something different depending on what books will be at hand.

AUGUST [1944]:

Return the history book +
borrow a stenography textbook +
Make up what I have missed in the program.

SEPTEMBER [1944]:

Do lino-cuts, drawings, stenography and English.
Take a good look at *Vedem,* and its standards, and if necessary, really shine at something, but if I do, make sure that it's worth it! (possibly a lino-cut).

Reports

OCTOBER [1943]:

Ceylon not finished because of exams.
4 pictures:
    About a man who tore his trousers
    The thief who stole the orchids

NOVEMBER [1943]:

Continued to work on *Ceylon* (all together 136 pages of manuscript already)
Bookbinding
Picture: (*From the Feast*)
Lino-cut: *A Medieval Mythological Ship*
Have written down the best contributions from the magazine [*Vedem*]
New contributions [to *Vedem*].
Have read: Plato's *Euthyphro, Crito, Apology of Socrates,* part of *Phaedo.*
I couldn't do more because of unsettled conditions at the end of the month. (German visits, call-ups to do labor, *Strassenreinigung* [street sweeping])

DECEMBER [1943]:

Have read Plato's *Phaedo, Crito*
Continued work on *Ceylon*
Picture: *Prague at Night*

Bookbinding

At the beginning of the month, transports to Birkenau (the Schenks), great chaos, I couldn't do more.

Lino-cut: *At the shores of the Adriatic Sea.*

JANUARY 1944:

Continued working on *Ceylon*. Finished the notes from Úlehla's *Beyond Life's Curtain* (C) Lecture on Buddhism (Ceylonese and Lamaism). Hired as the cook's assistant. This job takes up most of my free time. Honoré de Balzac, *Eugénie Grandet.* [illegible.] I started to learn Russian and stopped studying trigonometry.

FEBRUARY [1944]:

Continued working on *Ceylon,* but quite poorly. Articles: "Freedom or Prosperity?" and "Insults." Our building is having exams, which were not on the program. I got 66/96 in literature, grammar, and poetry, which is a below average result; 66/100 (second place) in general knowledge; 51/60 in English; 34/60 in German; /60 in Latin; /60 in Esperanto; /60 in Singhalese; /60 in Sanskrit; 43/60 in Russian and 24/25 in composition.

Drawing: Orchid painting.

For Pepek Tausig, I wrote an article: "The cook from Terezín" but I lost it. Found it. I started a diary. I concluded that I have put on thirteen kilos in Terezín.

MARCH [1944]:

Arguments with Prcek. I decided to move to Uncle Miloš's attic room. I did not write any article for the magazine.

Exam results:

(Average: 1.71, which is down by 0.21 on my average from previous exams)

English:	1
Czech:	1
Geography:	2
History:	2
Latin:	3
Maths:	1
Geometry:	[1]
Judaism:	
Hebrew:	2

Lino-cut: *An Inter-stellar Rocket called "Brave as a lion, fast as a thought"*

Petr Ginz and Eva Ginzová

APRIL [1944]:

Have moved to the attic room. The program is a mess. I spend the time saved working on *Ceylon*. I read it for the third time and made about ten pages of notes. Besides that, I also made notes from *The Adventures of Marco Polo*—eight pages. I read *Marco Polo, Ceylon, Through the Country of People, Animals and Gods II*, several *Selected Works*, [Jirásek's] *A Student Story*, [Capek's] *Tales from Two Pockets*. Harris Franck: *Around the World Without a Penny, Part I*.

I studied the most important part of my notes, namely Book C. I managed to cover only Taoism, Confucianism, Hinduism, and superficially Buddhism. [. . .]

MAY [1944]:

Eva arrived. I finished making notes from *Ceylon* and bound them. *Ceylon* has been returned. I haven't yet finished reading all the notes but I have done preparatory work for my studies: I read Chalupný's *System of Sociology*, in which he divides the sciences. Based on this division, I have made a plan to briefly go through each individual science. I read Gwen B. *Burning South;* Franck: *Around the World Without a Penny I, II;* a detective novel [called] *Velvet Face;* Chalupný: *A System of Sociology;* Wells: *The Outline of World History*, Pedagogical Bulletin; Jiri Valja: *Story-Teller*.

—I drew: A Brewery.

JUNE [1944]:

I'm working in the Lithography (Department). I made a geographical map of Asia and started a map of the world according to Mercator's projection. I read: Otáhalová-Popelová: *Seneca's Letters;* Arbes: *Crazy Joe, My Friend the Murderer, The Devil;* [Jack] London: *Lost Face;* Musil: *Desert and Oasis;* Cosmos, two volumes of *Selected Works;* H.G. Wells: *Christina Alberta's Father;* part of Descartes' *Discourse on Method*.

I've learned: Antiquity (Egyptians, Assyrians, Babylonians, Indians, Phoenicians, Israelites, Greeks, Persians, et cetera), the geography of Arabia, Holland, and the Moon. I have drawn: *Behind the Sheep-pen, Vrchlabí*. I made an overview of zoology mentally and on paper. I attend evening lectures (about Rembrandt, Mastičkář, and others). I don't visit the cooks anymore.

JULY [1944]:

I have read: Honoré de Balzac: *Eugénie Grandet;* Gorky: *Stories, Fairy Tales, and Accusations;* André Theuriet: *The Last Refuge;* Valenta: *Uncle Eskimo, Embers*.

I have drawn: *Behind the Brewery, Houses*

Petr Ginz and Eva Ginzová

{173}

I'm still working in the Lithography (Department), but next month I'm only going to work half a day every day and follow the program the other half. I'm improving my English. Eleven-twelfths of the map of the world is inked over. The only
thing that still needs to be done is the coloring and writing in of the towns and
cities.

AUGUST [1944]:

I've read: Dickens: *[A Christmas] Carol;* Hloucha: *The Sun Vehicle;* [Nyklíček]:
Miracles on Every Step; Fight in the Settlement; Trojan: *Little People in Court, Boy
Scouts of the Good* [rest of the line illegible]

Flammarion and Scheiner: *Is There Life on Stars?;* Lidman: *House of Spinsters;*
Stolba: *From the West of India and Mexico I and II;* Tomek: *Jewish Folk Stories
and Legends from Prague* and *The Theory of Man*—a booklet.

I work in the Lithography Department for half a day and the other half I attend
the program. I have a lot of catching up to do in Latin and math. I do stenography
and I also do a bit of English and zoology every so often. I have spent most of my
time on drawing and lino-cuts: two flowers, *People, This Is the Typical Czech Dove-
like Character, Behind Kavalíř,* and various small sketches. Five-sixths of the map
of the world is colored in.

In the Lithography Department, I have disagreements with Master Schrimski.
He doesn't like me going to the program in the morning. I'll wait to see how things
work out and then I'll make a decision. I might go next door to the Zeichensaal [art
room]. They have already expressed an interest in me. Next month I'm supposed
to bring my drawings for them to see (Master Heilbron). That wouldn't be bad at
all.

SEPTEMBER [1944]:

I've read: Schweitzer: *From My Life and Thought;* Dinko [Šimunovic]: *The [Vin-
cic] Family;* [Theo de Vries]: *Rembrandt;* Thomas Mann: *Mario and the Magi-
cian;* Dickens: *A Christmas Carol;* Daneš: *The Origin and Extinction of Aborig-
ines in Australia and Oceania;* Milli [Dandolo]: *The Angel Has Spoken;* Karl May:
Son of the Bear Hunter; Oscar Wilde: *De Profundis* and other novels. [. . .]

The Diary of Eva Ginzová

June 24 [1944]

On Wednesday, it will have been six weeks since I first arrived here. We came here
by train where we had the whole carriage to ourselves. [. . .] Our bags, large and
small, were with us in one carriage and were also transported with us to Terezín by

truck. As we were going through Bohušovice (a large village with clean houses), people stopped and looked at us. We could already see Terezín in the distance with its church tower rising above it. I was already really looking forward to seeing Petr, Uncle, Pavel, and Hanka and all those I knew. The first person I recognized in Terezín was Petr Fischl ("Cokl") [the pooch], who used to go with me to the shelter. We drove along a street with one- and two-story buildings packed with an enormous number of people. We actually arrived just as transports were leaving for Birkenau. Seventy-five hundred people left this time—the poor things.[11] They took us to the Hamburg barracks where we were held locked up for three days. They took our bags from us and didn't give us any food. We suffered from extreme hunger. We were able to look out the window and when Petr came there to see me and talk to me through the window, he brought me something to eat. [. . .]

I must just add a couple of lines. This writing makes me feel a lot better since I've felt all the time that I have been writing a letter to you, dear Mummy and Daddy. It seems such a long time since we saw each other last when we parted on Dlouhá Avenue. [. . .] I'm sending you a big good-night kiss, Mummy and Daddy.

June 26 [1944]

I've got *toranut* [cleaning duties] today and I've already had enough. We had a good cleanup this morning and now it's a complete mess here. You see, room 27 is moving in here and they are all messy girls. I won't even make [it to] lunch because I will still be clearing up after them. Hanka and some other of our girls snapped at me a moment ago because of some silly little thing. I feel so homesick.

I'm learning English now with Mrs. Popper as a part of my program. Harry [Mrs. Popper's son and a friend of Petr's] is ill—he had a nervous breakdown because he was so upset about the transports to Birkenau. We had peeled barley with tomato sauce for lunch today. I haven't eaten yet. I'm hungry as a wolf.

July 1 [1944]

Another new month! When I arrived here, I thought I would definitely be back home within two months, but I'm now starting to lose hope because Uncle Miloš keeps saying that we will definitely still be here through the winter. I probably wouldn't be able to last that long. I've already had enough of it here—all the grown-ups who came here with me are leaving today for Birkenau. They were the poor things that had been released from prison and were mostly all skin and bones. They can only take with them what they can carry themselves and people in their state won't be able to carry much. We now are on holiday from our program. We still have a history test on Monday and I haven't yet [done] anything [for it].

Petr Ginz and Eva Ginzová

August 16 [1944]

Yesterday, I came back from the hospital. I had scarlet fever and diphtheria. Early on July 3, I went to the clinic because my throat hurt terribly. [. . .] At midday, I had a fever and my temperature was 38.5 degrees [Celsius] when I measured it. I lay down immediately and asked for the doctor to come to see me on his rounds. In the afternoon, the doctor came into our room and discovered that I had scarlet fever. My temperature was 39.2 degrees [Celsius]. They took me to the hospital in Vrchlabí in the evening. I can't remember the details anymore since I was so ill that I only noticed that they carried me away on a stretcher. The first week in Vrchlabí was terrible. I was very ill—I couldn't eat at all, and even if I wanted to, I wouldn't have been able to swallow it. I would only drink milk, tea, and strong soup that my relatives cooked for me. My glands were all swollen—it hurt a lot and I could neither move my head nor sit up nor lie down. I thought it was going to drive me crazy. I cried for days (under the bedclothes, of course, so that the patients and nurses wouldn't hear). I thought of home and what Mummy would have probably done if she had seen me so ill.

I started feeling better within a week and within three weeks I was able to get up for the first time. There were seven cases of scarlet fever throughout Terezín at that time, three of whom had left, leaving just the four of us. I was in the hospital for six weeks and one day in all. After three weeks I was already allowed to go to the window. Petr came to the window to see me twice, sometimes even three times every day. Hanka usually came to see me every other day. I always really looked forward to someone coming to see me—Uncle and Pavel also came to see me sometimes. [. . .]

When I got back from the hospital, Uncle complained about Petr to me that he [. . .] had totally stopped taking care of himself and had become terribly forgetful. Uncle doesn't know what else he can do. [. . .] I really regret it—Petr definitely needs to go home so that our parents could keep an eye on him. Otherwise, though, Petr is really an extremely clever boy. He [always] had the reputation of being the cleverest at school. When I arrived, one girl asked me whether Petr Ginz was my brother, and [said] that he was the most intelligent boy from the *heim* [children's home]. I was very pleased and I was very proud of him. [. . .]

August 18 [1944]

I have already been here three months as of yesterday. When I left Prague, I didn't think that I would be here so long. People said two months at the most. I cried in the evening, but in such a way that Hanka wouldn't hear me. We were sleeping in number 23 (in the entrance hall) on the ground. We put our mattresses down there and our blankets and pillows on them. We can't put up with our room any longer, what with all the bedbugs and fleas there.

August 20 [1944]

Today we made our beds here in the room on the floor. We tried in vain to get to sleep and regretted that we don't have a place for lying down in the corridor or in the courtyard. We were bitten by bedbugs and fleas (as were the other girls who had stayed and slept in the room). We caught forty-eight bedbugs on our mattresses, not even counting those we caught on the floor and on ourselves. We had the lights on all night and we hunted bedbugs. I can't even properly imagine going home again and sleeping in a clean bed with nothing there to bite me.

Today they are moving everybody out of the building where our folks are so that they can fumigate it. They are going to fumigate our building on the twenty-fourth. I can't wait for it to be clean in here again.

August 24 [1944]

There's a great commotion here. We're moving to the attic in the Hamburg [barracks] today. We'll sleep on the floor and we'll move back here once it's been completely fumigated, which will be in about ten days' time. Then it's also going to be painted in here and then we'll clean the place properly. I can't wait for everything to be clean here. It was about time, too—there are so many bedbugs now that it's more than one can stand. We've just caught two bedbugs on the bedclothes (or rather Hanka has, since I don't try to catch them anymore) and, when I had a look to see what was biting me, I found a fat bedbug on me. It was full of blood.

Petr and I have come across something new. We're studying shorthand. Petr got hold of a textbook and exercise books and I'm thoroughly enjoying it.[12] When Hanka saw us learning, she joined in. Pavel also said that he would learn, but he didn't continue.

I got a letter from home the day before yesterday, and yesterday as well. I was so pleased to get them—I hadn't received anything for at least two weeks before then. Daddy wrote that the birthday greetings had arrived and he was very pleased to get them. Dear Mummy [. . .] I'm always thinking of you! I'm going to have to make an effort not to burst out crying now, I miss you so much! I'm sorry for ever being horrible to Mummy and Daddy, but I'll make it up to them for everything once I get back home. [. . .]

August 25 [1944]

We've finally moved in here to the attic at the Hamburg [barracks]. It's an enormous attic separated into small sections by wide beams. Several girls sleep together in each section. I'm with Hanka, Rutka Weberová, Miluška, and Helzicka. It was filthy here when we arrived. We had to give it a good sweep, sprinkle it with water, and wipe it. When we were finished and went to get the straw mattresses (obviously, we sleep on the floor), there wasn't enough of them for us five. Every girl with a straw mattress who didn't absolutely need it gave it to us so that we didn't have to sleep on the bare floor. I was cold the next morning—each of us was only covered by one blanket. We want to make a little hole in the roof, since we don't have much light in here, but we're worried about a brick falling off and hitting a passer-by on their head. We might do it in the evening since no one is outside at that time. [. . .]

September 6 [1944]

Finally we're out of the attic! We moved in here hastily the day before yesterday, since the whole of Hamburg had to move. A big transport of Jews arrived from Holland and they will be moved into the Hamburg barracks, so we had to move out of the whole barracks. I'm really sleepy—it's nine o'clock and I will finish my writing tomorrow. Good night, Mummy and Daddy!

September 16 [1944]

I haven't written for a long time—I couldn't get to it. Petr was ill—he had a temperature of thirty-nine degrees [Celsius]. There's a sort of epidemic now in Terezín. Temperature, nothing hurts, and then it's gone again. I was extremely concerned about him going down with something—it's just the two of us here, Petr and me, and if something were to happen to him, how would I explain it to my parents? This isn't the case with the Miloš family. Hanka and Pavel at least have their dad here—but I wouldn't like to have mine here. I dreamed not long ago that Daddy had come to Terezín and I woke up covered in sweat. Anything but that!

There's a prayer room in front of Uncle's attic room. The Jews always go to pray there on Friday evening, Saturday, or when there's some holiday. Uncle always jeers, sneers at them and insults them for disturbing him, and all three children always join in with him. And Petr does it too. I regret it thoroughly—I feel more of a Jew than almost ever before. Petr declared that he'll renounce the faith as soon as he gets home. I couldn't do that! I wonder what Daddy will tell him when Petr gets home. Pavel says that he's related to Jesus and doesn't want anything to do with the Jewish faith even if Jesus was a Jew, too.

September 21 [1944]

It was Milenka Mandelíková's birthday. Hanka once found a celluloid plastic doll in the toilet. Her arms were missing, she was all dirty and lying on the window sill. We boiled her thoroughly, cleaned her, made her cloth arms, and then made some clothes for her, a coat, et cetera. We gave her to Milenka for her birthday. She was so happy—a real doll is extremely rare here—people only make rag dolls. [. . .]

September 22 [1944]

I have to go to the *ambulanz* [clinic]—I'm getting an injection to put on weight. I'm supposedly terribly thin. I lost three kilos at the hospital. I'm getting Trisalin. It hurts quite a lot. Dr. Stern is very rough—he always thrusts it into my arm and then it hurts a lot. A transport's leaving—men aged from sixteen to fifty going to work in Germany. I'm concerned about Petr or Pavel having to go as well. I don't know if half-Jews are protected from this.

September 27 [1944]

So Petr and Pavel are on the transport. They got their notice the day before yesterday. They said that they were leaving the next day, but for the moment they are still here because the train hasn't yet arrived. They are living in the attic of the Hamburg barracks, but they are here in Uncle's attic room the whole time. It's not as strict here as in Prague. There, you wouldn't be able to get away with someone leaving the *šlojska* [collection point for deportees] to go for a walk around town. We're hoping that the transport will stay here. The word is that there's a strike throughout the Protectorate, so the train won't even arrive.

When I found out that Petr was in the transport, it made me feel ill. I ran from here to the toilet where I cried my eyes out. I try to keep calm in front of Petr—I don't want to make him feel worse. They are supposed to go somewhere near Dresden. I'm really worried that there will be bombing there and that something may happen to the boys. Petr's not used to a lot of [manual] work and there's bound to be hard labor there. My dearest boy! We haven't quarreled at all since I arrived here and I don't know what I'd do if he left! Uncle isn't on the transport, but he might still be called up. He thinks, though, that he won't be now, because he has a leading status and would be difficult to replace. At first, he wanted to volunteer and go with the boys so he'd be with them together, but then he changed his mind—they might have gone to one place and he to another place. But the main reason was that Hanka and I would be left here completely on our own.

I'm very hopeful that none of them will go. Uncle wants us to move into his attic room if (God forbid) the boys and the other two in his room left. I don't want to even contemplate being here without Petr.

[. . .] Mummy and Daddy, I really miss you, especially now that my only support is leaving. Who knows if we'll all get together again? Oh, if only the war would end—it's a bit too much for us! What will my family at home say once they find out that Petr's gone! Maybe they already know—Karel Müller wrote about it in his letter home. Poor Mummy and Daddy!

September 28 [1944]

The train's already here and both boys have already got on it. Petr's number 2392 and Pavel 2626. They're together in the same car. Petr's terribly calm and Uncle is full of admiration for him. I hoped to the last minute that the train wouldn't come, even though I knew it would. But what can be done? Just this morning Hanka and I were with them at the šlojska. It was a horrible sight that will stay with me forever. A crowd of women, children, and old men were pressed around the barracks to get a last look at their son, husband, father, or brother. The men leaning out of the windows were pressed one against the other to catch a glimpse of their dearest ones. But the barracks were guarded by police guards so that no one would escape. The *Ghettowachmanns* [ghetto guards] stood by the building and drove back people who came too close to it. The men from the windows waved and said good-bye to their relatives with their looks. The sound of crying came from all around. We quickly ran home and brought the boys two slices of bread each so that they wouldn't be hungry. I pressed through the crowd, crawled under the rope that separated the crowd from the barracks, and passed Petr the bread through the window. I had enough time to hold his hand through the bars before a guard drove me away. At least it worked out all right. Now the boys are gone and the only thing left from them here is their empty beds.

October 13 [1944]

Tomorrow fifteen hundred people from mixed marriages are supposed to be arriving here from Prague. I'm expecting Daddy and I'm very upset about it. When Petr left, I thought that it was an end to all that suffering—and now this! I hoped that Petr would come back safe and sound and even that we would survive it here until it was all over and that Mummy and Daddy would wait for us at home. I'm concerned about Daddy having to do hard labor here and not getting enough to eat. And what about poor Mummy at home! She's probably suffering. Oh, if only I could have a cuddle with them and be with them and Petr together! [. . .]

Petr Ginz and Eva Ginzová

October 24 [1944]

Apparently, another transport is leaving tomorrow. Mrs. Friedmann, who knitted my sweater, is also on it. Grown-up children up to sixteen years old are on it as well as orphans who are defenseless, which is why they put them on it!

Half-Jews are on *Spervermerk,* which means that they're not allowed to leave. So that goes for Hanka and me, too. If the boys had stayed here until the registration of half-Jews, they'd be here and wouldn't have had to be sent on. That is fate. Dear Petr, what can you be doing?

October 26 [1944]

The transport left. The streets are a lot emptier—they used to be full of people before. In our room, there are only eleven out of twenty-one girls left—just half-Jews. Helzicka, who's a Jew, was the last to leave. Her mom was seriously ill. She has had three strokes here and her dad has an infection of the lungs. Her mom won't survive the journey, I'm sure. Her brother went away on one of the first transports. Helga is desperately unlucky! I really feel pity for her! We haven't slept in our heim for some time now, but here in the attic room instead. [. . .]

I wonder what you're doing, Petr. What work are you doing, dear boy? I really miss you and our parents in Prague. If only the war would end! It was Uncle Miloš's nineteenth wedding anniversary. I felt so sorry for him, he was so sad! [. . .]

October 28, 1944

Oh dear, today's another sad day! Uncle reported to the šlojska a moment ago. At about midnight last night, he received a notice to report for the transport at two o'clock. He already knew about it at midday, however, so we had enough time to get him ready. Apparently, [Hans] Günther [head of the Central Office for Jewish Emigration in Prague] arrived and was very cross with Rahm [the camp commandant] for allowing so many Jews to stay here. That's why the whole of the *Wirtschaftsverwaltung* [management], the deliverers, all the Ghettowachmanns, OD [Ordnungsdienst, or order police], and Kripo [Kriminalpolizei, or criminal police] got *weisung* [orders]. Uncle will now apparently be called in by Rahm who might wipe him off the list. It's only a small hope, however. [. . .]

Dear God, please let Uncle come back from the šlojska and let us go back to living as before. All the way to the šlojska and back, I was praying for Uncle to be sent back.

November 2 [1944]

Uncle's been away for five days.

I found Petr's diary yesterday. When I read it, I couldn't make myself stop crying. Poor boy! The Miloš family were wrong about Petr when they said he didn't think about home once. I can see from his diary how dearly he thought about home. I feel so homesick here, but I won't let it show to Hanka, I don't want her to worry about it. My dearest Mummy and Daddy, I so wish to go home!

November 11 [1944]

A few days ago, it was a year since Granny died here. And it was Pavel's birthday yesterday. Oh, I want to go home so much that I can't even describe it. Dear Granny!

November 13 [1944]

Today I received two letters from home. Mummy writes that she was in bed for a week, she was ill, poor old Mummy. I'm so worried about Mummy, whether she has completely recovered now and what was wrong with her. Dear God, why does the war have to go on for so long? My dearest Mummy, I love you so much. You must take good care of yourself so that you'll be well when we come back! There hasn't been any news of Petr, I'm so unhappy. I hope that Daddy won't come here, otherwise Mummy would be left at home all on her own. The day before yesterday, I received a parcel, I don't even know where from; there was no sender written on it and the postmark was illegible. There were apples, dried biscuits, sweets, and vitamin C in it.

I'm working in the cadre and I like it a lot. These ten days we're working at the *Bauhof* [building yard]. We're taking wood to the *Reitschule* [riding school], or even out of the ghetto to the *Zeughaus* [a building where tools and equipment are kept] and to the Bohušovice valley. It isn't hard work, on the whole. It's only hard work when we have to carry big planks. There are twelve young girls in our group and we have a lot of fun. I can at least partly forget about all my worries when I'm with them.

December 19 [1944]

I got a letter from Uncle Miloš the day before yesterday! He writes that he's well and sends us his best regards and kisses. We managed to decode that the letter was dictated to him and that he is unwell.[13] Poor old Uncle! I loved him so much. He looked after us so well, our own father couldn't have done it better.

[. . .] A man who left from here wrote that he met the first transport in Poland. Everything was coded, of course. It seems they are digging trenches there. I can believe that, that they let Jews do it, such a dangerous thing. I'm so upset, I've been thinking about it all day. I'm so worried. I wish this awful war were finally over!

We also celebrated Hanukkah with Bertička Justitzová. It was very nice but sad at the same time. We thought of home and how we used to celebrate it all together.

December 27 [1944]

It's been five days since Mummy's birthday. I sent her a letter with my best wishes already at the beginning of November, and I hope that she's received it by now. I wonder how she spent her big day, poor old Mummy. I've been thinking about home the whole day, about how last year I went around to the shops with Daddy to buy Mummy a present and how sad we were that Petr wasn't there too. God knows what has happened to him. Sometimes I'm so overcome and I miss him so much that I feel like crying all day. But I must control myself. If I want to cry, I have to cry into the pillow. And there is still no end to the war. I'm so desperate!

January 3, 1945

Today I did *Putzkolonne* [outside cleaning duties] for the first time. It was totally unfair. In the morning—as usual—we turned up for work at Magdeburg [barracks]. Our group leader, Hanka Zentnerová, got ten days in the kitchen and that's why we're on our own. Hanka Fischerová (the leader of another cadre group) took her place. She sent some of her girls to the builders, others to the painter, and us (from Hanka Z.'s group) to the Putzkolonne. It was beastly of her to choose the best places for her own group and to send us to do such nasty work. But we were lucky. We didn't have to clean anything, we were asked to scrape ice away from the long pavement in front of Dresden and to salt it. We did it as piece-work. It was nasty work, it was cold and windy . . .

[. . .] Yesterday I got a letter from home, unfortunately from November. My parents wrote that they are all right, but that they missed us a lot. When I got the letter I buried my head in the pillow and cried.

January 7 [1945]

It's Auntie Nad'a's birthday today. Poor Auntie! Her husband and both children are gone, scattered in different places! It's even harder for her than for our parents. At least Mummy and Daddy are together and can console each other.

January 16 [1945]

Tomorrow, I will have been here for eight months. It's almost unbelievable how fast time flies. I feel desperate when I imagine that our parents are at home alone and that Petr is God knows where.

We have been doing *Altmaterial* [recycling] the past two days. It's an awful job, something completely inhuman. You stand outside in freezing temperatures for ten hours, picking tin plate and black plate from a pile of scrap metal and then sort it. I was so frozen I thought I'd go mad. There was nowhere to warm yourself up. They threw us out of everywhere because they were afraid that if [Rudolf] Haindl [deputy camp commandant] arrived they would get into deep trouble. On top of that, we had a very nasty group leader who kept on pushing us to work harder. He warmed himself up in his shed and let us freeze outside. [. . .]

February 2 [1944]

Our Petr had [his] birthday yesterday. I wonder if someone over there remembered him and gave him something. How beautiful it used to be when we were still at home! I would search for something really nice for him a long time before his birthday. My dearest brother, I'm sending you a big kiss for your birthday.

A transport will definitely arrive tomorrow or the day after tomorrow. They say that all the remaining Jews from the Protectorate will arrive. Now I've got another thing to worry about. What if they sent transports from here and Daddy was in it? I would probably go mad. I want to go to the *Einsatz* [work allocation group] tomorrow morning to ask Mrs. Külová to put me on the *Transporthilfe* [transport assistance]. I'd like to save Daddy his luggage but I don't know how. I hope that Egon will help me.

I wonder what Daddy will say when I tell him that there hasn't been any news from Petr. It scares me, I have a strange feeling about it. On one hand, I think that Daddy is better off at home at the moment, but on the other hand, I'm looking forward enormously to seeing him. I would be happiest, however, if a miracle happened and Daddy stayed at home!

February 3 [1945]

Stranger! Don't be nosy next time and keep off my diary! Otherwise, something nasty will happen to you. I can tell immediately if someone has been reading it.

It's seven in the morning. I'm still in bed because we're doing an afternoon shift at the *Barackenbau* [building one-story wooden huts]. [. . .] Barackenbau—that's very interesting work. [. . .] I've already done a ceiling. We're starting a new building now so I'm going to do the floor. To be in Terezín has some real advantages as well. At least I can learn something completely new, which I wouldn't have a chance of doing at home. So when I'm working in the bakery I'm learning how to make bread. In the cabinetmaker's workshop, I can learn various kinds of things. When I worked for the roofers, we also went to repair a stove and so I have a chance to learn at least a bit in a lot of trades. I'm sure that Daddy will be really surprised when he finds out how good I am at hammering nails. At home I didn't have a clue how to do it.

February 9 [1945]

[. . .] Today I'm really in the mood for writing. I'd like to have someone to whom I could tell everything, absolutely everything, someone to open my heart to. My Mummy is the only person I could tell everything to, but, unfortunately, I'm not with her so I'll have to confide in my diary. [. . .] I must write a short story.

EXPECTATIONS

Wave after wave was throwing itself on the steep rock with a roar. The sea was rough. Its awesome shades reflected in the eyes of a young man who was clinging with great difficulty on to the small ledge in the rock. He couldn't sleep. He was expecting a boat to come early in the morning with his little sister on board. She was far away over the sea in an orphanage and now she was coming to stay with her big brother forever. He was waiting for daybreak. It was dawning. The sea went to a mellow red and then blazed with gold. The young man trembled with anxiety.

Will Marika come? His little, sweet Marika about whom he didn't know whether she was still alive?

A mast appeared and within a moment the whole boat. The tension was extreme. At last! A white scarf waved from the boat. The young man ran down to the small port. The boat anchored. A loud hooray greeted the land. The already big girl rushed to the young man.

"Marika!"

"Dan!"

Brother and sister fell into each other's arms.

February 15 [1945]

Daddy has been here for four days already. I have absolutely no time to write.

February 28 [1945]

I got a letter from Mummy yesterday and Daddy [got one] today. I'm so happy. It's been five months today that our Petr is away. I'm so unhappy. Dear God, I wonder what's happening to him, whether he's still alive. There have been air raids in Prague now. I'm so scared that something might happen to Mummy. You can't avoid being worried.

I'm doing a night shift at the Bašta today and tomorrow I'll have the whole day off. It's no use to me, though; I tried to sleep a bit now but it was impossible because of the girls who wouldn't stop talking. I'm sure that tomorrow it will be the same. They are all inconsiderate, without exception.

I had a bit of a quarrel with the girls today. We were telling each other our Jewish names. There were Rachel, Rézi, Cipora, Rivka, and so on. All the girls were laughing at what funny ugly names they were. I told them it wasn't right to laugh about it, that, for example, in Palestine names such as Liselotte or Antonia would also seem ridiculous. I'm so angry with the girls sometimes when I hear them saying such stupid superficial things. I always think of our Petr and how different he [always] was from all the other kids. I really think that it's difficult to find such a clever, intelligent boy. Even Hanka is sometimes like them.

March 22 [1944]

This morning I had a delivery note to collect a big parcel, but, unfortunately, I can't go and pick it up now because there's an alarm at the moment and I won't be able to go to the post office. We really needed it this time, we have hardly anything left. It's awful to see that Daddy would like to eat some more and I have nothing to give him. Sometimes I also feel so hungry that I want to cry but I won't let it show. I'm ashamed. [. . .] Moreover, I still think that Daddy is suffering from hunger. The food he gets here is nothing for a man doing heavy work. Daddy keeps reassuring me that he gets enough food here but I don't believe it anyway. Hanka has just started singing. I don't know, at the moment everything gets on my nerves. She's singing some silly love song.

March 30 [1945]

Two more days and a new month starts again. Oh God, I've been here for almost a year! All the things that have happened during that time, it's awful. Petr's gone, God knows where, Mummy's alone at home, Daddy's here. I wish it was over soon.

> Hanka, I know very well that you've been reading this diary. It's awfully nasty and dishonest of you. Don't think that I won't find out about it!

April 14 [1945]

We're now living here, at L 414. A lot of things happened since I last wrote. Both Hanka and I have received a parcel. Hanka's expecting another one. But the other big thing is that the Danish king has asked for all the Danes to be allowed back.

They're leaving either tomorrow or tonight. They're supposed to go via Germany and Denmark to Sweden. It has never happened before that someone should return home from here.[14]

April 23 [1945]

[. . .] My God, the things that are happening here now, it's difficult to describe. One afternoon (on Friday, April 20), I was at work when we saw a freight train go past. There were people sticking their heads out of the window. They looked awful! They were pale, completely yellow and green in the face, unshaven, emaciated, with sunken cheeks and shaven heads, dressed in prison clothes . . . and with a strange shine in their eyes . . . from hunger.

I ran to the ghetto straightaway (we're working outside at the moment), to the railway station. They were just getting off the train, if one can call it getting off. Very few could stand on their feet (bones, covered in nothing but skin), others lay on the floor, completely exhausted. They'd been traveling for two weeks with hardly anything to eat. They came from Buchenwald and Auschwitz (Oświęcim). Most of them were Hungarians and Poles. I was so upset I thought I would collapse. I was still looking for our Petr among them since some of those who arrived now were those who had left from here. But our Petr wasn't there.

One transport after another started to arrive now. Hungarians, Frenchmen, Slovaks, Poles (they had spent seven years in concentration camps), Czechs, too. No one from our family. And the number of dead among them! A whole pile in every car. Dressed in rags, barefoot or in broken clogs. It was such a terrible sight that hardly anyone had seen before. I wish I could express on paper all the things that are happening inside me. But I'm not talented enough to do that.

And how the poor people threw themselves at any food they were given, whatever it was. How they fought over it—awful! A woman gave a lump of sugar to a sick boy, he was about seventeen. He burst out crying. He was sobbing terribly, kept looking at the piece of sugar and the bread the woman had given him and kept on crying: "Sugar, sugar, sugar, *weissbrot, weissbrot* [white bread]." Then he ate it. God knows how long it had been since he had seen any. Some have spotted fever and many other nasty diseases.

And those who arrived from Litzmannstadt [Łódź] and from Birkenau told us awful things. They said Oświęcim [Auschwitz] and Birkenau were made into one. They used to be two concentration camps right next to each other. Now it has been liberated. Every transport that had arrived in Birkenau had had everything taken away and been divided immediately. Children under fourteen, people over fifty, went straight into the gas chambers and were then burned. Moreover, they always selected some more to be gassed from those who remained. And the food was lousy. Coffee, soup, coffee, and so on. I wouldn't believe any of it if I wasn't told about it by those who themselves experienced it. I'm so worried about Petr and whether he's still alive.

April 25 [1945]

A peace conference is supposed to take place today. I wonder what will come out of it. I'm so unhappy now. Everything gets on my nerves, everything makes me angry and I want to go home. I'm unable to look forward to anything, except me going home. But I've stopped hoping that it will ever happen.

May 2 [1945]

Apparently, Hitler has croaked. They're flying a flag on the field hospital and the fortress. It's flying at half mast, which means mourning. I've been so disorderly lately. I can't concentrate on anything, everything gets on my nerves, it's awful. There's been talk that the first ones to leave here will be mixed marriages [. . .] .

They say that seven thousand Jews came to Prague from Germany. How I wish Petr would come to Prague. Mummy could go and see him. Oh God, that simply can't be true!

I can't even write anymore, I'm so upset; they say the war is over. Dear God, I beg you, let it be true!

May 9, 1945

The Russians occupied us at half past nine yesterday. Well, they didn't get inside Terezín, only to the roads surrounding it. They came to the former commander's office to announce (without weapons) that we have been occupied. But I was more frightened yesterday than I've been for a long time. All of a sudden, I could hear banging noises, it seemed so awfully close. Daddy was on duty behind the Dresden [barracks] by the Aryan road at that time. The Germans often fired at the ghetto from there (when they were passing by) and so I was scared that something might happen to Daddy. He's all right, thank God.

There was so much joy when the Russians came. People stood along the roadsides, waving at them, and they stopped and shook their hands. Well, it was beautiful! I'm happy!——Watch out!! What's going on?

—I've just got back from the cellar where I went to find shelter from an air raid. We could hear bombs falling so close we thought it was in Terezín. But it was somewhere quite close to the ghetto, somewhere near Litoměřice, or even closer. I'm so frightened now.

May 14, 1945

Yesterday morning (May 13) I arrived back home. Petr wasn't at home (I was secretly hoping he would be). We're now expecting him every day, for him to come back or at least to have some news of him. Mummy looks well, thank God.

The Russians occupied us on May 8, at half past nine at night. I was in my room when I suddenly heard cheering and shouting: "Long live the victorious Red Army!" They went to Prague to help. It's hard to describe what was happening there—Germans were murdering Czechs, Czechs were murdering Germans. I'm glad I wasn't here when it happened.—I sleep and eat all day, nothing else.

This is the end of my diary since I only want to have my memories from Terezín in it. But when Petr comes back I'll write it here.

HOME

April 14, 1947

Petr hasn't come back.

7

Yitskhok Rudashevski

VILNA GHETTO

Yitskhok Rudashevski was born in Vilna (Vilnius), Lithuania, on December 10, 1927. His father, Elihu, was a typesetter for the *Vilner Tog*, the daily Yiddish newspaper, and his mother, Rose, originally from Kishinev in Bessarabia, was a seamstress. He was an only child, living together with his parents and his maternal grandmother. Yitskhok went to school in Vilna, having completed his elementary education and one year of high school at the city's well-respected Realgymnasium before his studies were interrupted by the German invasion. One of the few surviving photographs of him from this period shows him standing on a busy street in Vilna on his way to school. Dressed in a dark overcoat, with his briefcase in hand and his shoes perfectly polished, his serious gaze directed at the camera, he is the very picture of a thoughtful young scholar.[1]

At the time the photograph was taken, Vilna was under Polish rule, as it had been since 1920. In August 1939, however, the terms of the Molotov–Ribbentrop nonaggression pact stipulated that the entire Baltic region—including Lithuania, Latvia, and Estonia—and the eastern part of Poland (including Vilna) belonged to the Soviet "sphere of influence." A little more than one month after the occupation of Vilna by Soviet forces on September 19, 1939, the city and its environs (which formed a sort of strip along Lithuania's eastern border) were ceded by the Soviet Union to Lithuania. This began a short period during which the city of Vilna was part of Lithuania, as it had been prior to its 1920 takeover by the Poles. But in mid-June 1940, the entire country of Lithuania, including the recently acquired Vilna province, was annexed by the Soviet Union.[2] Such were the circumstances in

Vilna until the end of June 1941, when the Germans invaded the Soviet Union, breaking the nonaggression pact of August 1939 and signaling the start of war between the two giant powers.

The German army quickly overran and occupied all of Lithuania. In early September 1941, the Vilna ghetto was established. One year later, as he approached his fifteenth birthday, Yitskhok began writing his diary in Yiddish. The entries that compose the main part of the diary span the period of September 1942 until April 1943. A shorter, stylistically distinct part recounts an earlier series of events, those of the first seven months of German rule in Vilna, from late June to December 1941. Although the diary was written by a single boy, the editors of the English edition aptly titled it *The Diary of the Vilna Ghetto*, for it is as much a portrait of a community and its collective fate as it is a daily record of the life of its writer.[3]

Yitskhok, whose literary gift is evident from the very first pages of his diary, chronicled all aspects of the ghetto and its character, capturing not only the appearance of its streets—on a Jewish holiday, at night, in the snow, or as spring arrived—but reflecting on all that those "little narrow streets" evoked of suffering, nostalgia, and loss. He sketched the ghetto inhabitants, highlighting passers-by on the streets, child vendors, and others, capturing their collective pathos, desperation, and humiliation. From time to time, he turned his gaze to the painful presence of the Jewish ghetto police, whom he saw as collaborators, helping "the Germans in their organized, terrible work of extermination."

If there is one predominant subject in Yitskhok's diary, however, it is the intellectual and cultural life of the ghetto's youth. "Finally I have lived to see the day," he wrote on October 5, 1942: "Today we go to school." Classes covered a range of subjects, including languages (Latin, German, Yiddish, and Hebrew), math and sciences (physics, chemistry, and biology), history, Jewish history, geography, and drawing. In addition to school, "the club," which had been organized for the young people in the ghetto, was the center of an extraordinary cultural, intellectual, and artistic life. Yitskhok documented the club's activities proudly in his diary: its members had literary, nature, and poetry circles, in which lectures were given regularly by intellectuals and artists in the ghetto; they performed puppet shows, dramatic presentations with full costume and lighting, gave recitations, and sang songs; they created an exhibition to honor the Yiddish poet Yehoash (with

documents, manuscripts, letters) and had a memorial for the Yiddish poet
Mendele. They also held an occasional party or social gathering, sometimes for an
important holiday such as Purim, and sometimes because they just "felt like having a little fun," as Yitskhok put it.

Yitskhok frequently reported on the progress of two club circles to which he
was particularly devoted, reflecting on their challenges, rewards, and significance.
One circle gathered aspects of "ghetto history" (he was assigned to research the
courtyard at Shavler 4), and the other collected "ghetto folklore." Of the colorful
ghetto folklore project, he wrote: "In the ghetto dozens of sayings, ghetto curses,
and ghetto blessings are created before our eyes; . . . even songs, jokes, and stories
that already sound like legends. . . . [T]he ghetto folklore . . . must be collected
and cherished as a treasure for the future." Yitskhok was equally dedicated to the
ghetto history project, though, as he reported in his diary, it posed a different set of
challenges. He recorded the painful aspects of some visits, noting when residents
reproached the interviewers for their attempts at objectivity. In another meeting,
however, the interviewees encouraged the young ghetto historians, and Yitskhok
noted in his diary the parting words of one of them: "This will be a history of us.
Write, write, children. It is good this way."

In his diary, Yitskhok often reflected on the significance of this intellectual
and creative work for the youth of the ghetto and for the Jewish community as a
whole. In part, he saw it as sustenance for the embattled youths living under Nazi
repression. "Our youth works and does not perish," he wrote on October 22, 1942,
after noting some of the accomplishments of the club members. But, as he remarked time and again, this creative impulse played an even more important role:
it was the very foundation on which the future life of the Jewish youth of Vilna
would be built. "Our spirit, which we bear proudly within the ghetto walls," he declared, "will be the most beautiful gift to the newly rising future." Throughout
these many entries, Yitskhok sounded a note of defiance, seeing in his friends' creative efforts a refusal to succumb to the imprisonment, suppression, and stagnation that the ghetto represented. Indeed, for many diarists, to work and to create as
if they were *not* in the ghetto was an achievement in itself, a sign that they were living as fully as they could given the confines of their oppression.

From the beginning of the diary, Yitskhok reported on his own work—the
books he was reading, the papers he was assigned to write, the daily projects that

occupied him, and his grades in school. But as the diary unfolded, he began to reveal a growing sense of himself in his world, seeing himself not only as a student but as a contributor to the intellectual and literary life of his community. At an evening memorial service held for Yankev Gershteyn, a beloved educator in the Vilna Jewish community, Yitskhok was asked to read aloud an essay he had written in his teacher's memory. His surprise at being included among the speakers was evident; but even more significant was his nascent awareness that others had noticed his talents as a writer. The entry is laced with a mixture of pride and embarrassment, modesty and self-consciousness. At the end of the entry, he wrote proudly: "At night we go home in a group. They tell me I read well, a fine essay. While lying in bed my cheeks still burned. . . . I shall never forget that evening, sitting at the dais, my reading, just as I shall never forget my teacher Gershteyn."

The shorter segment of Yitskhok's diary, which covers the early period of Nazi rule in Vilna (from late June to December 1941), is not a daily account, like the main part, but a retrospective one, written after events had occurred. A few clues—the writer's knowledge of the systematic mass murder of the Vilna Jews at Ponar (which he would surely not have known about before November 1941 and was unlikely to have known about before January 1942), and several veiled references to a clandestine Soviet youth group that was formed in February 1943—suggest that Yitskhok wrote most of this text when he was already in the ghetto, and possibly after he had been there for well over a year.[4] At the same time, the text was not written entirely in the past tense, as are most retrospective accounts. Rather, he used a mixture of past and present tense, as if he wrote in stages, perhaps over a long period of time. Yitskhok may have taken notes during the initial period of the German occupation (writing in the present tense) and later went back and added to them (recalling events in the past tense). Or he may have begun his account after the establishment of the ghetto and deliberately adopted the present tense as a literary device to recapture the feel and immediacy of the moment. In either case, this first part of the diary must be read in the context of Yitskhok's life in the ghetto, in which two powerful elements were coming together: his growing ideological commitment to maintaining a record of the history of the Vilna Jewish community, and his own developing sense of himself as a writer.

The young man who wrote in his diary, "I consider that everything must be recorded and noted down, even the most gory, because everything will be taken into account," did just that in this segment of his text. He not only recounted what happened to him and his family—how they came to be in the ghetto—but documented the broad assault on the Vilna Jewish community, recording virtually every major event of the collective experience of invasion, occupation, repression, and mass murder. Further, it is clear that Yitskhok carefully shaped and constructed the story he wanted to tell, beginning with a brief allusion to the "joy and freedom from care" of the "Soviet summer of 1941" (setting the stage for the oncoming invasion); covering a specific historical period (the first seven months of German rule, during which the Nazi order was violently established and the initial wave of mass killings were carried out); and ending with the events of December 1941, when the chaos temporarily subsided and the so-called period of stability in the ghetto began.

From a literary standpoint, it is the product of the young executive of the literary circle, the writer beginning to come into his own, recognized by his peers and by his mentors. Though some of the historical details of the moment had faded with time, Yitskhok nevertheless endeavored to capture the character, if not the specifics, of the events he recalled. Thus, of the imposition of the yellow star, he wrote, "for a long time I could not put on the badge. I felt a hump, as though I had two frogs on me." Similarly, he described the night before the Jews were to leave for the ghetto as a "beautiful, sleepless September night, a sleepless, desperate night, people like shadows." And he captured the pathos of the move to the ghetto itself, depicting a woman who "stands in despair among her bundles and does not know how to cope with them, weeps and wrings her hands. Suddenly everything around me begins to weep. Everything weeps."

Throughout this section, Yitskhok used his literary talents to advantage in his text, rendering events and scenes in their most tragic and poignant light. During his long account of the roundups that took place in the months following the establishment of the ghetto, Yitskhok recounted the story as it must have seemed to the victims—chaotic, nightmarish, and unreal—mirroring the confusion of the situation. There are jumbled references to yellow, white, and pink certificates (the "blood-drenched delusion" as he called them, referring to the illusion that such papers could protect their holders), to registrations, to moves from one place to another, to periods of time spent in hiding. He sketched the people crowded in the hiding place, who were "lying on the bricks like rags in the dirt," and captured the terror of a moment when it seemed they might be discovered. "The hunter on all sides: beneath us, above us, from the sides," he wrote. "Broken locks snap, doors creak, axes, saws. I feel the enemy under the boards on which I am standing." The description of these early months in the ghetto is itself an onslaught, ending only as the roundups ceased and the survivors settled down to life in their new surroundings. Though the first part of Yitskhok's diary is filled with references to the roundups that emptied the ghetto and the disappearance of family and friends, he could not have known that more than thirty-three thousand Jews were murdered by the Germans during the assault he described.[5]

Yitskhok ended his long narrative of the first months of German occupation with a nod toward the advancing Russian army, asserting his faith in its eventual arrival. His buoyant hope in the certainty of liberation is carried throughout the main part of the diary, as he reported regularly on the progress of the war, the battles won by the Soviet army, and the liberation of towns and cities. "We who live in the ghetto read the reports daily, are eager for good news," he wrote. "Everyone is waiting for the yearned-for peace when the weary world will straighten its back." For Yitskhok, attachment to the Red Army was linked not only to the wait for liberation, but also to his devout commitment to Communism and the Soviet Union. During the period of Soviet rule, he and a number of his friends had been enthusiastic participants in the Soviet youth organization called the Young Pioneers. Although participation in this group was mandatory under the Soviets, the diary shows that Yitskhok and many of his friends were true believers whose involvement was by choice rather than by obligation. All Soviet organizations were officially disbanded throughout the German occupation, but Yitskhok and his colleagues continued their activities clandestinely, sharing Soviet leaflets, celebrating the twenty-fifth anniversary of the Red Army, and, late in the ghetto's history, establishing a secret youth movement (which Yitskhok called a "pioneer project") modeled on the Young Pioneers. Yitskhok initially described their purpose as follows: "At the meetings we shall also train ourselves, because we must prepare for the life that is in store for us. The future will require dedicated people who will have to guide the masses toward great renewal." Such activities were, of course, strictly banned by the Germans. If Yitskhok or his friends had been discovered engaging in such anti-German activity, they would have faced severe punishment and perhaps even death.

From the beginning of the main part of the diary in September 1942 until mid-March 1943, there is an unflagging, upward sweep of hopefulness, an ever increasing anticipation of the long-awaited arrival of the Red Army, bringing liberation and deliverance. But during the week of March 26 to April 2, 1943, Jews from several small ghettos around the city were moved to the Vilna ghetto. A few days later the ghetto inhabitants learned that a transport of five thousand Jews, who were supposed to have been sent to the Kovno ghetto, had in fact been taken to Ponar, where they were murdered.[6] As Yitskhok's diary shows, the news of the resumption of the killing operations came as a violent blow to the ghetto inhabitants. "It has begun again," he wrote. "It is terrible, terrible. People walk around like ghosts. They wring their hands." The renewal of mass murder prompted a shift in the nature of the "pioneer project"; from this time forward, its young members treated it as a resistance movement. Yitskhok wrote, "No! This time we shall not permit ourselves to be led like dogs to the slaughter! We have been discussing this lately at our (. . .) [pioneer meetings] and are prepared at any moment. This thought strengthens our nerves, gives us courage and endurance." Still, in the final entries of the diary, Yitskhok plunged into despair. He noted the anxiety and terror of the ghetto, even while he and his friends tried to maintain a hopeful mood, singing together at the club. The main part of the diary breaks off ominously on April 7, 1943. "We may be fated for the worst," he wrote.

Yitskhok and his friends were never able to carry out their plans to resist the Germans. Six months later, on September 23, 1943, the liquidation of the ghetto began. Yitskhok and his family went into hiding, where they remained for two weeks. The only surviving account of Yitskhok during this time is that of his cousin and friend Sore Voloshin (called Serke in the diary), who recalled him sitting and reading in a corner of their attic, "still and silent, speaking only infrequently." According to Serke, they were discovered on October 5 or 7. Yitskhok and the rest of the inhabitants of the hiding place were taken to Ponar, where they were shot to death.[7] The only member of the group to survive was Sore Voloshin, who managed to escape and flee into the forest, where she joined a group of anti-Nazi partisans. When Vilna was liberated, she returned to the hiding place, where she found Yitskhok's diary. She gave it to Avrom Sutzkever, one of those who had encouraged and inspired the young writer in the ghetto, and Shmerke Kaczerginski, who in turn gave to the YIVO Institute for Jewish Research in New York, where it remains to this day.

It is Sunday [actually Saturday] the 21st of June [1941]

A beautiful summer day. Our "ten" [unit in the Young Pioneers] is supposed to meet today. I am going to Gabik [Heller] to have him announce it to some comrades.[8] I met him in his garden busy with a garden bed. Our cheerful conversation was interrupted by the howling of a siren. [. . .] Bombs are bursting over the city [. . .]. It is war. People have been running around bewildered. [. . .] It has become clear to all: the Hitlerites have attacked our land. They have forced a war upon us. And so we shall retaliate, and strike until we shall smash the aggressor on his own soil. [. . .]

I think about our future life. I think that we pioneers will not remain aloof in the struggle. I feel that we shall be useful. — Soon, at six o'clock, a meeting of our "ten" was supposed to take place. I decide that we must attend it. I had a foreboding that hard tasks await us. The struggle is beginning, the Soviet Union will arise. [. . .] I approach the little park. No one is there. A little later Serke [Sore Voloshin] comes. We talk about the latest events. We were dispersed immediately by the first German bombs. Of all the comrades, two of us came, and that because we live near the railroad. Now as I write I think we have become quite different pioneers. I feel that if they will need us, we shall come, even if it will be our last pioneer meeting.[9]

Serke and I sit for a while in the little park. The bombing stopped as if the sky had cleared. Suddenly we hear the siren again. We run home. Explosions shatter the air again. Outside there is a banging and howling. In the cellar I see before me frightened people with bundles. No one knows what is in store for us. The anxious evening arrives. People await the coming evening with terror. I go out into the street. Autos keep moving. The black sky is aflame with red light. There must be a great fire somewhere.

Monday was also an uneasy day. [. . .] People say with despair that the Red Army is abandoning us. The Germans are marching on Vilna. The evening of that desperate day approaches. The autos with the Red Army soldiers are fleeing. I understand that they are leaving us. I am certain, however, that resistance will come. I look at the fleeing army and I am certain that it will return victoriously. The night was a restless one. Autos are roaring in the street. From time to time a burst of shooting begins. A neighbor notices a red star [symbolizing solidarity with the Soviet regime] in my lapel. He tells me to take it off. I cannot make peace with the thought: is it really so? I am full of sorrow and pain that is ending thus. I feel that he is right.

Yitskhok Rudashevski

It is Tuesday, the 24th of June [1941]

I observe the empty, sad streets. A Lithuanian with a gun goes through the street. I begin to understand the base betrayal of the Lithuanians. They shot the Red Army soldiers in the back. They make common cause with the Hitlerite bandits. The Red Army will return and you will pay dearly, traitor. We shall live to see your end [. . .] . At dawn a motorcycle rides through the street. A gray square-rimmed helmet, spectacles, a greatcoat, and a rifle. Unfortunately, the first soldier of the German usurping army that I have caught sight of. The helmet flashes coldly and evilly.

A little later I go down to the street. Today at ten o'clock we were supposed to have a meeting of the "tens." Today the school library is open. I know that I will find no one there. However, I go to the school anyway. All this has happened too suddenly. It is hard to comprehend that everything has actually come to a dead stop. I approach the school. The school is sealed up. I meet a comrade. And we walk like strangers over wide streets. The German army is marching. We both stand with bowed heads. A black mirage of tanks, motorcycles, machines. [. . .]

Weeks drag on. I returned from the summer, from its surroundings, chained to the house, to the yard. We do not see our gang. There is absolutely no contact among our gang. Everyone is occupied with his day-to-day concerns. Jews are humiliated and exploited. One must stand in long lines to receive bread and other products. Jews are ousted from them. German go to the rows, throw out the Jews. Jews receive less food than the Aryans. Our life is a life of helpless terror. Our day has no future. We have one consolation. The Red Army shows a fighting spirit. It has become concentrated. It gives blow for blow, it is offering resistance. The Germans have realized that they will not accomplish this in short order. They are dealing with a courageous fighter who does not abandon our struggle. [. . .]

Our hearts are crushed witnessing the shameful scene where women and older people are beaten and kicked in the middle of the street by small bandits. A performance. I stand at the window and feel a sense of rage. Tears come to my eyes: all our helplessness, all our loneliness lies in the streets. There is no one to take our part. And we ourselves are so helpless! so helpless. Life becomes more and more difficult. People do not go anywhere. On scores of streets a Jew must not show himself. Only in the morning do frightened Jewish women slip out to do some shopping. The men go off to work. It rains incessantly. We are so sad, so lonely. We are exposed to mockery and humiliation. [. . .] The mood becomes worse from day to day. People talk about the ghetto. In the rainy evenings we gather at a neighbor's house and talk about the news, the situation in the ghetto that has now become a reality. [. . .]

Yitskhok Rudashevski

The 8th of July [1941]

The decree was issued that the Vilna Jewish population must put on badges front and back—a yellow circle and inside it the letter J.[10] It is daybreak. I am looking through the window and see before me the first Vilna Jews with badges. It was painful to see how people were staring at them. The large piece of yellow material on their shoulders seemed to be burning me and for a long time I could not put on the badge. I felt a hump, as though I had two frogs on me. I was ashamed to appear in them on the street not because it would be noticed that I am a Jew but because I was ashamed of what [they were] doing to us. I was ashamed of our helplessness. We will be hung from head to foot with badges and we cannot help each other in any way. It hurt me that I saw absolutely no way out. Now we pay no attention to the badges. [. . .] [We] are not ashamed of our badges! Let those be ashamed who have hung them on us. Let them serve as a searing brand to every conscious German who attempts to think about the future of his people.

It is the end of the summer of 1941

We do not know what is in store for us. Never did I feel the coming of autumn as I did at that time. The days became more and more turbulent. The furniture of the Jews is being confiscated. People are talking about a ghetto. Suddenly the terrible news spread about the provocation on Daytshe, Shavler, Mikolayevske, Disner, and other streets. At night the Jewish population of these streets was led out, we do not know where. Later it became known: to Ponar, where they were shot to death.[11] The situation has become more and more strained. The Jews in our courtyard are in despair. They are transferring things to their Christian neighbors. The sad days began of binding packages, of sleepless nights full of restless expectation about the coming day. It is the night between the fifth and the sixth of September, a beautiful, sleepless September night, a sleepless, desperate night, people like shadows. People sit in helpless, painful expectation with their bundles. Tomorrow we shall be led to the ghetto.

It is the 6th of September [1941]

A beautiful, sunny day has risen. The streets are closed off by Lithuanians. The streets are turbulent. Jewish workers are permitted to enter. A ghetto is being created for Vilna Jews.

People are packing in the house. The women go back and forth. They wring their hands when they see the house looking as if after a pogrom. I go around with bleary eyes among the bundles, see how we are being uprooted overnight from our home. Soon we have our first view of the move to the ghetto, a picture of the Middle Ages—a gray black mass of people goes harnessed to large bundles. We understand that soon our turn will come. I look at the house in disarray, at the bundles, at the perplexed, desperate people. I see things scattered that were dear to me, that I was accustomed to use.

We carry the bundles to the courtyard. On our street a new mass of Jews streams continually to the ghetto. The small number of Jews of our courtyard begins to drag the bundles to the gate. Gentiles are standing and taking part in our sorrow. Some Jews hire gentile boys to help carry the bundles. A bundle was suddenly stolen from a neighbor. The woman stands in despair among her bundles and does not know how to cope with them, weeps and wrings her hands. Suddenly everything around me begins to weep. Everything weeps. [. . .]

The street streamed with Jews carrying bundles. The first great tragedy. People are harnessed to bundles, which they drag across the pavement. People fall, bundles scatter. [. . .] I walk burdened and irritated. The Lithuanians drive us on, do not let us rest. I think of nothing: not what I am losing, not what I have just lost, not what is in store for me. I do not see the streets before me, the people passing by. I only feel that I am terribly weary, I feel that an insult, a hurt is burning inside me. Here is the ghetto gate. I feel that I have been robbed, my freedom is being robbed from me, my home, and the familiar Vilna streets I love so much. I have been cut off from all that is dear and precious to me.

People crowd at the gate. Finally I am on the other side of the gate. The stream of people flings me into a gate blocked with bundles. I throw down the bundles that cut my shoulders. I find my parents and here we are in the ghetto house. It is dusk, rather dark and rainy. The little streets, Rudnitsker, Shavler, Yatkever, Shpitalne, and Disner, which constitute the [first] ghetto look like anthills.[12] It swarms with people. The newcomers begin to settle down, each in his tiny bit of space, on his bundles. Additional Jews keep streaming in constantly. We settle down in our place. Besides the four of us there are eleven persons in the room. The room is a dirty and stuffy one. It is crowded. The first ghetto night. We lie three together on two doors. I do not sleep. In my ears resounds the lamentation of this day. I hear the restless breathing of people with whom I have been suddenly thrown together, people who just like me have suddenly been uprooted from their homes.

The first ghetto day begins. I run right out into the street. The little streets are still full of a restless mass of people. It is hard to push your way through. I feel as if I were in a box. There is no air to breathe. Wherever you go you encounter a gate that hems you in. [. . .]

I decide to hunt up my friends in the courtyard. I have an idea that all of us will be there. I soon find Benkye Nayer, Gabik, and several others. The first day is spent in settling down, hunting up one another. The second evening in the ghetto people feel a little more at home, calmer. My chums are figuring out how many weeks we shall be sitting here. [. . .]

The first ghetto days speed by

Like many others I go hunting for firewood. We break doors, floors, and carry wood. One person tries to grab from the other, they quarrel over a piece of wood, the first effect of these conditions on the human being. People become petty, cruel to one another. Soon we notice the first Jewish policemen. They are supposed to keep order in the ghetto. In time, however, they become a caste that helps the oppressors in their work. With the help of the Jewish police, the Gestapo accomplished many things in the course of time. The Jewish police help to grasp their brothers by the throat, they help to trip up their brothers. [. . .]

Two weeks of ghetto life have passed. The workers of the most important German working units receive professional worker's stamps on their working certificates. Those who do not receive such a certificate must move with their families to the second ghetto. The mode of life that has just become settled is once again shaken up. Again troubled people with bundles go to the second ghetto.[13]

Today it is Yom Kippur [the Jewish Day of Atonement]. I am not well. I have fever. Today the ghetto is full of storm troopers. They thought Jews would not go to work today, so they came to the ghetto to take them. At night things suddenly become turbulent. The people get up. The gate opens. An uproar develops. Lithuanians have arrived. I look at the courtyard and see them leading away people with bundles. I hear boots pounding on the stairs. Soon, however, things calmed down. The Lithuanians were given money and they left. In this way the defenseless Jews attempted to rescue themselves. In the morning the terrible news spreads. Several thousand people were uprooted from the [first] ghetto at night. These people never came back again.[14]

Later we learn about the liquidation of the second ghetto. The same thing that happened to us happened to them, and is still going on there.[15] [. . .]

There is a great deal of restlessness also in our ghetto. The white certificates are being exchanged for yellow ones, of which, however, very few are issued. Thus was born the yellow certificate, the blood-drenched delusion, this little piece of paper constituting such a tragedy for the Vilna Jews.[16] [. . .] Like animals sensing the storm, everyone is looking for a place to hide, to save his life. They register as members of the family with the owners of the yellow certificates. Fate suddenly split the people of the ghetto into two parts. One part possesses the yellow certificate. They believe in the power of this little piece of paper. It bestows the right to life. The second part—lost, despairing people—people who sense their doom, and do not know where to go. We do not have a yellow certificate. Our parents are running around like hundreds of others, as though in a fever. Something terrible is hovering in the air. Soon, soon something will explode. A troubled evening approaches. The streets are full of people. The owners of the yellow certificates are registering.[17]

Whoever can do so hides. The word "maline" [hiding place] has become relevant. To hide, to bury oneself: in a basement, in an attic, to save one's life. Scores of people plead with those who are standing in line, the chosen ones, to be registered on their yellow certificate. People offer money and gold for the privilege of being registered. The tenants of the house go into a hideout. We go with them. [. . .] Many people have gathered in the two stories of the hideout. They sneak along like shadows by candlelight around the cold, dank cellar walls. The whole hideout is filled with restless murmuring. An imprisoned mass of people. Everyone begins to settle down in the corners, on the stairs. Pillows and bundles are spread out on the hard bricks and boards and people fall asleep. The candle lights begin to die out. Everything is covered in darkness. You hear only the snoring of the sleepers, a groaning, a restless murmuring. It is stifling. An odor of a cellar and of people crowded together. From time to time someone lights a match. By the light I see people lying on the bricks like rags in the dirt. I think: into what kind of helpless, broken creature can man be transformed? [. . .]

The dawn brings a new piece of news. Persons with yellow certificates must leave the ghetto with their families. They will leave and now the game will begin. I look at the mass of people with bundles that is streaming to the gate. [. . .] I wish like them, the people with the yellow certificates, to go away, to leave the storm behind me, to save my life. I meet my friend Benkye Nayer. He is pale, has not had enough sleep. He too spent the night in a hideout. It was the last time that I saw him.

We are in the hideout again. We expect something any moment. While lying thus on bundles I fell asleep. A noise, the sound of people crowding each other woke me. I understood that the Lithuanians were already in the ghetto. The hideout is becoming fuller and fuller. We are finally so tightly crowded together that we cannot move. The hideout is being hammered up. My parents are somewhere upstairs. I am downstairs with my uncle. The hideout is full of a restless whispering. Candles are being lit. [. . .] [G]radually everything becomes still. Everything becomes completely enveloped in a black, dreadful silence, a silence from which there shouts forth the great tragedy of our helplessness, the destructive storm that is now pervading the ghetto. You hear a faint sound, as though a tempest were being rent with shouts, with shots. My heart beats as though with hammers to the cadence of the storm outside. Soon I feel that the storm is approaching us. My head is dizzy, a cold perspiration oozes forth, my heart stops beating entirely.

We are like animals surrounded by the hunter. The hunter on all sides: beneath us, above us, from the sides. Broken locks snap, doors creak, axes, saws. I feel the enemy under the boards on which I am standing. The light of an electric bulb seeps through the cracks. They pound, tear, break. Soon the attack is heard from another side. Suddenly, somewhere upstairs, a child bursts into tears. A desperate groan breaks forth from everyone's lips. We are lost. A desperate attempt to shove sugar into the child's mouth is of no avail. They stop up the child's mouth with pillows. The mother of the child is weeping. People shout in wild terror that the child should be strangled. The child is shouting more loudly, the Lithuanians are pounding more strongly against the walls. However, slowly everything calmed down by itself. We understand that they have left. Later we heard a voice from the other side of the hideout. You are liberated. My heart beat with such joy! I have remained alive!

To save one's own life at any price, even the price of our brothers who are leaving us. To save one's own life and not to attempt to defend it . . . the point of view of our dying passively like sheep, unconscious of our tragic fragmentation, our helplessness.

We creep out of the hideout after a six-hour imprisonment. It is eight o'clock in the evening. Everything resembles the aftermath of a catastrophe. The tenants' belongings are scattered over the courtyard. Smashed locks lie around under our feet, everything is turned upside down, topsy-turvy, broken. All doors are wide open. The house is unrecognizable. Everything is scattered far and wide, many things are broken. A bottle of spirits lies smashed in the middle of the room. The bundles are ripped with knives. I go out into the street. It is dark. The street is full of the tragedy that has just happened here. On the pavement lie bundles, a bloody reminder of the people who have just been dragged away to their deaths. I enter the courtyard where my cousins live. I notice two large bright windows. I look inside. A house in the wake of a pogrom. Electricity is burning and no person is to be seen. It is so terrible. I enter my uncle's house. It is dark. I step on things. It is quiet. A clock strikes forlornly. No one is here. I go back home. Frightened people crawl out of the corners. They too have found deliverance.

In the middle of the night the owners of the yellow certificates begin to return. How dreadful is the dawn! About five thousand persons were forcibly carried off yesterday evening. They were led away to the Lukishki Prison. The ghetto is full of lamentation. Sobbing, dejected people. One has a father, another a mother, a third a child. Families have been torn apart. One left to save his life, a second was carried off by force. I run to Benkye Nayer. He is not to be found! So many young lives have been cut off. I have lost such a good friend. I am constantly thinking about this fine fellow. We miss him now, Benkye Nayer. In the ghetto he always thought about our present condition. He said, "I shall not go to Ponar." But he apparently went there after all. I shall always remember you, Benkye! We shall avenge your blood. On the street I met Gabik. We went to teacher Mire. Here too there is a fresh wound. Teacher Mire's parents have been taken away.[18]

Several days have passed. The wound is still bleeding. Some of those taken were led away to the second ghetto. The largest part to Lukishki, and from there to Ponar. Ponar [is] a slaughterhouse for thousands of Jews. The district of Ponar is soaked in Jewish blood. Ponar is the same as a nightmare, a nightmare which accompanied the gray strand of our ghetto-days. Ponar is passive death, the word contains the tragedy of our helplessness. No! We shall not go to Ponar. [. . .]

Mother went away to a work unit. Perhaps it will be possible to obtain a yellow certificate there. [. . .] Toward evening, mother returned empty-handed. We are uneasy, have not had enough sleep. We do not know what more to do. [. . .] The next morning, people set forth again to the second ghetto. Mother went to the work unit. [. . .] Toward evening mother returns again empty-handed. She tells us that the activity [roundup] in the ghetto goes on without a break.[19]

[The next day] In —— I meet mother. She brought a yellow certificate, which grants the right to life. And I passed over to the group of more or less calm people, to the yellow certificates. We received a letter from Uncle from the second ghetto. They are sitting there in a hideout. The liquidation of the [second] ghetto continues unabated. [. . .]

It is daybreak. The owners of the yellow certificates are leaving the [first] ghetto together with their families. [. . .] We take little bundles and join the stream of lucky ones who are leaving the [first] ghetto. We are accompanied by our cousins who are registered with us. [. . .] We learn that old people who are registered as parents are not admitted through the gate. Grandmother cannot go with us. We are in despair. People are no longer admitted into the hideout that is in the courtyard. They have locked themselves tightly inside. What is one to do? [. . .] We quickly say good-bye to Grandmother—forever. We leave her alone in the middle of the street and we run to save ourselves. I shall never forget the two imploring hands and eyes that begged, "Take me along!" We left the ghetto. We emptied it to enable the wild Lithuanians to break into the defenseless little streets. We go to the gate, a crowded mass of specially selected people who are running away from their closest relatives, and are leaving them to God's mercy. [. . .] We see the execution-ers. Our hearts pound. Detachments of Lithuanians encircle the ghetto. Very soon they will slip inside. [. . .] We lie on the chairs in the house where Uncle lives. We are frozen and weary. Mother is crying. We cannot forget that we have abandoned Grandmother. With heavy hearts we lie down to sleep in the new place.[20]

The little streets in the second ghetto are full of people. They chat about the lat-est news of the first ghetto. They tell about the terrible raid, that many hideouts were discovered. Hundreds of people were wrenched away from that ghetto to Lukishki. [. . .] I walk around over the little streets of the second ghetto, the little streets of the old Vilna ghetto. Never was there vented on them so much devasta-tion, desolation, as now. The old synagogue courtyard is pogromized. Phylacter-ies, religious books, rags are scattered under one's feet. Everything in the second ghetto is demolished, broken and abandoned. [. . .] After staying three days in the second ghetto we return to the gate of the first. We are not checked.

In the ghetto there is devastation. Overturned doors, torn-up floors. We come home. Everything is gone to wrack and ruin. From the hideouts people emerge like corpses, pale, dirty, with black rings under their eyes. For three days people lay choked up in holes and cellars. Grandmother is not here. The house fills with weeping and shouting. I run away from the house. I walk over the little streets. A feeling of pain, of resentment burns in me. I feel we are like sheep. We are being slaughtered in the thousands and we are helpless. The enemy is strong, crafty, he is exterminating us according to a plan and we are discouraged.

[. . .] Winter is approaching with its new daily cares: warm clothes, wood. Along with the winter there appeared a new certificate: the pink family certificate, which was received only by family members of the owners of yellow certificates. Things became troubled again. And at the end of December a new raid was launched, which wrenched away another few hundred people. A frosty day. We are not permitted to walk in the streets. Lithuanians walk through the houses and take away those who do not possess pink certificates. We sit in the house and see through the windows how people are being led to death.[21]

After that things calm down again. A hard winter has descended upon us. [. . .]

The only consolation has now become the latest news at the front. We suffer here, but there, far in the East, the Red Army has started an offensive. The Soviets have occupied Rostov, have dealt a blow from Moscow and are marching forward. And it always seems that any moment freedom will follow it.

[This marks the end of the first, retrospective part of the diary. Yitskhok ap-parently did not write any dated entries during the nine months from the end of December 1941 to September 1942, with the exception of a single entry dated March 23, 1942. The main part of the diary, written contemporaneously, begins with the following entry, on September 12, 1942.]

Saturday the 12th [September 1942]

Today is a holiday. The Jewish New Year, Rosh Hashanah. It is a cool day, like all other days recently. The sky is clear. In the morning I go down to the street. A holiday spirit that is anything but cheerful is diffused over the few little ghetto streets. Something somehow is missing. I am reminded of the past. From somewhere a sound of loud, quick praying is heard. Here and there Jewish women walk past with festive kerchiefs on their heads, with prayers books under their arms. I recalled my grandmother, how she too used to go to synagogue this way once a year. [. . .]

It is twilight. I go out into the street. The streets are lively. People are walking around dressed up. Today is a holiday. This is evident in every house you enter; the poverty has been scrubbed away. Formerly this would not have made an impression on me. However, now I felt strangely good because the everyday gray day is so much in need of a little holiday spirit, which should drive away for a while the gray commonplaceness of life. People walked around until late on the little Vilna ghetto streets. A strangely sad holiday mood. And now the crowds thin out more and more. A cold starry sky overhead. From time to time a star flies past across the sky on its silvery way and suddenly falls down. [. . .]

Thursday the 17th of September [1942]

It is getting colder and colder. How dismal and dejected the ghetto looks! A cold rain whips through the small narrow streets. You become sad and bored during the long hours that you hang around in one place. We do not go to school on account of an epidemic. It is a terrible time when you cannot settle down to some kind of work and you waste days on nothing. Toward evening when people return from work they sit down in their confined quarters and tell one another news—political and ghetto news. They tell that here and there people have secretly heard the radio and other such matters. [. . .] We who live in the ghetto read the reports daily, are eager for good news. Everyone's attention is now directed toward Stalingrad. Everyone is waiting for something tangible, for the final defeat of Germany. Everyone is waiting for the yearned-for peace when the weary world will straighten its back.

Saturday the 19th of September [1942]

It is cold and sad. When in the world will we get back to our studies? When I used to go to my lessons, I knew how to divide the days, and the days would fly, and now they drag on for me grayly and sadly. Oh, how dreary and sad it is to sit locked up in a ghetto.

Sunday the 20th [September 1942]

It is Yom Kippur Eve. A sad mood suffuses the ghetto. People have such a sad High Holy Day feeling. I am as far from religion now as before the ghetto. Nevertheless, this holiday drenched in blood and sorrow, which is solemnized in the ghetto, now penetrates my heart. In the evening I felt so sad at heart. People sit at home and weep. They remind themselves of the past. [. . .]

Monday the 21st [September 1942, anniversary of the so-called Yom Kippur aktion, in which almost thirteen hundred Vilna ghetto inhabitants were taken away and killed at Ponar]

The Holy Day is evident in the ghetto. It is quiet. The day is sunny and cold. Now and then an old Jew walks by with a prayer shawl. [. . .] Toward evening I walk with other friends over the dark little streets. "It was just such a night," one of them relates. Yes, a year ago at this time we had the terrible Yom Kippur night. It becomes dark. A round dull moon wanders between the black little clouds and lights up the spires of the church that looks into the ghetto across the crooked black roofs. [. . .] Long after the whistle we disperse to our homes.

Sunday the 27th [September 1942]

Today I woke up with a high fever. I feel very ill. [. . .] Toward evening as I lay with high fever, I learned of the great misfortune: our beloved teacher [Yankev] Gershteyn has died. The painful news struck me like a clap of thunder. Teacher Gershteyn is dead. [. . .]

I thought a long, long time about our teacher Gershteyn. He stands before my eyes. He appears so beautifully, so freshly before me from the midst of our gray, dreary life. Forever and ever will we remember you as a dear friend, the image of your proud figure will remind us of something that is precious and dear. What you have given us of yourself will always flourish among us.

Friday the 2nd of October [1942]

I am almost well now. I walk around in the street. Since new districts that border on our Disner Alley have been added to our ghetto and since our little street is full of ruins that run through the whole of Yatkever Street, these ruins are being torn down. [. . .] Now demolished walls stand. In the daytime you can see blue sky and at night the stars through the black holes that serve as windows. Strange feelings come over me as I look at the black ruins shattered by the bloody storm that used to sweep over our ghetto. I look at the black holes, at the fragments of stoves. How much tragedy and anguish is mirrored in every shattered brick, in every dark crack, in every bit of plaster with a piece of wallpaper.

Here the murderers, the Lithuanians, broke in like animals with axes and with crowbars and sought their prey: women, children, men. . . . Through here hungry people used to crawl outside the ghetto and bring in some food. Here in the ruins the people, like enraged animals hunting for prey, broke and pierced the walls, tearing boards to cook their meager midday meal. [. . .] [Here] Germans stood and laughed at the horror. . . . And Jews walked around near the ruins and bit their lips until they bled in misery and shame. . . . Here, here, here on the black walls is inscribed in blood and tears all our tragedy and pain. As I look at the ruins an uncanny feeling comes over me to see how Jews putter around there. I too crawl between the bricks, pieces of wallpaper, tiles, and it seems to me a lamentation ascends from the black crevices, from the stale holes. It seems to me that the ruins are weeping and importuning as though lives were hidden here . . . [. . .]

Monday the 5th [October 1942]

Finally I have lived to see the day. Today we go to school. The day passed quite differently. Lessons, subjects. Both sixth classes were combined. There is a happy spirit in school. Finally the club too was opened. My own life is shaping up in quite a different way! We waste less time, the day is divided and flies by very quickly. . . . Yes, that is how it should be in the ghetto, the day should fly by and we should not waste time.

Wednesday the 7th [October 1942]

Life has become a little more interesting. The club work has begun. We have groups for literature, the natural sciences. After leaving class at seven-thirty I go immediately to the club. It is gay there, we have a good time and return home in the evenings in a large crowd. The days are short, it is dark in the street, and our bunch leaves the club. There is a racket, a commotion. Policemen shout at us but we do not listen to them.

Saturday the 17th [October 1942]

A boring day. My mood is just like the weather outside. I think to myself: what would be the case if we did not go to school, to the club, did not read books. We would die of dejection inside the ghetto walls. We do not go to school today. To make up for it, however, when people return from work, things become gayer. People tell the news, of course, good news. The Soviets have forced the Don. [. . .]

I go out into the street—there is a disturbance near a bakery. A woman has snatched a pot from the bakery and has run away. She was pursued and beaten. It aroused a feeling of disgust in me. How terribly sad! People are grabbing morsels from each other's mouths. I am overcome with pity for the hungry woman, how she is being insulted with the dirtiest words, how they beat her. I think: what peculiarly ugly things occur in the ghetto! On one hand, the ugliness of stealing a pot of food, and on the other to strike a woman crudely in the face because she is probably hungry.

Sunday the 18th [October 1942]

A historic day in the ghetto. People are moving to added "districts," Oshmene Alley. People can walk freely in the new courtyards. [. . .] I go out to look over the new "districts." [. . .] I have a pleasant feeling crawling over the few new courtyards, seeing new places, the large ghetto brick walls that have just been built, what a pleasure! A simple emotion of a prisoner, who has found another new corner in his cell. He examines it and is pleased for the moment: to discover something new lying in his cell. [. . .] Now I see the free world: the church near the barracks on Lidske Street bombed out, black rain-soaked ruins in its place. Nevertheless, today I feel a little as though we had gone out of the ghetto. After all, people are walking, flocking together. I do not feel the joy but I feel the pleasure of taking a step behind the gate, as if in spite of the yellow wooden one with the strong barbed wire.

I make the first round in the ghetto, a second, a third, and I soon feel the same prison, only a little larger as if someone were teasing us. The feeling aroused by the anticipated departure from the ghetto vanishes. On the contrary, I have a feeling of bitterness. [. . .] For a long time I walk around among our new places. The empty dwellings, ruins, abandoned cellars, evoke an unpleasant feeling in me, and my mood becomes worse and worse in harmony with the weather, which becomes more dismal and more muddy. The rain disturbs me. It is cold. The wind wails over the ruins. It seems that the entire ghetto is swimming in dark mud.

Toward evening a new sensation. Suddenly one bright day Jewish policemen donned official hats. I walk across the street and here go some of them wearing leather jackets, boots, and green round hats with glossy peaks and Stars of David. [. . .] I hate them from the bottom of my heart, ghetto Jews in uniforms, and how arrogantly they stride in the boots they have plundered! The entire ghetto is stunned. Everyone feels the same way about them and they have somehow become such strangers to the ghetto. In me they arouse a feeling compounded of ridicule, disgust, and fear. [. . .]

Monday the 19th [October 1942]

The news in the ghetto spreads like wind: today thirty Jewish policemen are leaving for the small towns for a certain kind of work by order of the Gestapo. A sorrowful mood prevails in the ghetto. Insult and misfortune have reached their climax. Jews will dip their hands in the dirtiest and bloodiest work. They wish simply to replace the Lithuanians. Our Jewish policemen are now leaving for Oshmene. They take along certificates. The Jews from the neighboring towns will be transported to Oshmene and there raids will probably occur, the same sad, bloody story as in Vilna, and our police will be the most active participants in all of this. [. . .] The Gestapo people will thus kill two birds with one stone: first, they will carry out another bloody piece of work, certificates, ghettos, packing one's things. We who have suffered understand what that means. Second, they will demonstrate that Jews in uniform drive their own brothers to the ghetto, distribute certificates, and keep order with the knout. [. . .] How great is our misfortune, how great is our shame, our humiliation! Jews help the Germans in their organized, terrible work of extermination!

Thursday the 22nd [October 1942]

The days pass quickly. Having finished my few lessons, I began to do a little housework. I read a book, I wrote the diary, and off to class. The few lessons run by quickly: Latin, mathematics, history, Yiddish, and back home again. After eating I go to the club. Here we enjoy ourselves a little. Today there was a final rehearsal under the direction of [Grisha] Yashunski (the director of the educational division [of the Vilna Jewish Council]). They also presented the (puppet) theater of the club Maydim arranged by two boys. It is quite nice, although very primitive. The literary part is very weak, but it does not matter as long as one sees creativity. Our youth works and does not perish. Our history group works. We listen to lectures about the great French Revolution, about its periods.

The second section of the history group, ghetto history, is also busy. We are investigating the history of Courtyard Shavler 4. For this purpose questionnaires have been distributed among the members, with questions that have to be asked of the courtyard residents. [. . .] The residents answer in different ways. Everywhere, however, the same sad ghetto song: property, certificates, hideouts, the abandonment of things, the abandonment of relatives. I got a taste of a historian's task. I sit at the table and ask questions and record the greatest sufferings with cold objectivity. I write, I probe into details, and I do not realize at all that I am probing into wounds, and the one who answers me—indifferent to it: two sons and a husband taken away—the sons Monday, the husband Thursday. . . . And this horror, this tragedy is formulated by me in three words, coldly and dryly. I become absorbed in thought, and the words stare out of the paper crimson with blood. . . .

Sunday the 25th [October 1942]

People are moving from our room. Uncle and his family who lived together with us received a permit for a room in the recently added courtyards. A turbulent day: the little room is in disarray. Nevertheless, I am glad. It was impossible to live in such suffocating conditions, one on top of the other. Seven persons lived in a little room of nine square meters. [. . .]

Tuesday the 27th [October 1942]

[. . .] In school I learned that since my essay for the Gershteyn memorial was very beautifully written, teacher Lubotski proposed that I read it at the memorial in the ghetto theater today, eight-thirty in the evening. I was almost unprepared and it came unexpectedly. Arriving half an hour early, I practiced reading a little. I was edgy as usual. The hall was crowded. [. . .]

It turns out that of all things I was asked to sit at the speakers' table. It seemed very strange to me: the artists, the speakers, make room for me and arrange with me the order of the speeches. I feel my cheeks burning. [. . .] Finally I read my essay. The edginess that filled me until now disappears. I feel quite free. I make an effort to read loudly, with expression. The moments fly by swift as an arrow. [. . .] And finally I read the conclusion, "The name Yankev Gershteyn will always flourish among us, and remind us of the dearest and the best." I take my seat. I feel myself blushing again. I felt such exalted [emotions] as I was reading. As I was reading I sensed my teacher Gershteyn in the depths of my being.

At night we go home in a group. They tell me I read well, a fine essay. While lying in bed my cheeks still burned. . . . I shall never forget that evening, sitting at the dais, my reading, just as I shall never forget my teacher Gershteyn.[22]

Saturday the 31st [October 1942]

[. . .] Toward evening our neighbor who works with my parents brought a Soviet leaflet. A holiday spirit broke out in the room. One person sits at the table and reads. All those around him open-mouthed and with bated breath. Such a little treasure, which originates from far, far away, across battlefields, cities, and finally across ghetto gates entwined with barbed wire. [. . .] The leaflet encourages the brothers and sisters of the temporarily occupied regions. [. . .] Our neighbor handed me the proclamation. I run with the leaflet to the club to show my friends. I keep it in my bosom. It seems to me that the writing warms me. The words are so close to me, so friendly. We stand in the corners of the club and read. Everyone felt for a while so joyous and cheerful—we received regards from our liberators.

Monday the 2nd of November [1942]

Today we had a very interesting group meeting with the poet A[vrom] Sutzkever. He talked to us about poetry, about art in general, and about subdivisions in poetry. In our group two important and interesting things were decided. We create the following sections in our literary group: Yiddish poetry, and what is most important, a section that is to engage in collecting ghetto folklore. This section interested and attracted me very much. We have already discussed certain details. In the ghetto dozens of sayings, ghetto curses, and ghetto blessings are created before our eyes; terms like "vasheven," "smuggling into the ghetto," even songs, jokes, and stories that already sound like legends. I feel that I shall participate zealously in this little circle, because the ghetto folklore, which is amazingly cultivated in blood, and which is scattered over the little streets, must be collected and cherished as a treasure for the future.

Thursday the 5th [November 1942]

[. . .] Today we went to Shavler 4 with the questionnaire for investigating the ghetto. We did not get a good reception. And I must sadly admit that they were right. We were reproached for having calm heads. "You must not probe into another person's wounds; our lives are self-evident." She is right, but I am not at fault either because I consider that everything should be recorded and noted down, even the most gory, because everything will be taken into account.

Saturday the 7th [November 1942]

[. . .] In the morning Gabik came to me. Today I arranged with him to do our lessons together. It is cold in the little room. Gabik tells me about himself. His father is in the hospital. He has a heart condition. Times are hard for them. I witnessed all their hardship from the start of the ghetto when they arrived with small bundles. Gabik is emaciated. He works in the library and receives a double card. His work interferes with his studies. I know quite well that Gabik seldom gets enough to eat. For some reason Gabik is rather sad and absent-minded today, yet despite his difficult situation, he is cheerful and gay. Gabik hopes that after his father leaves the hospital, he (Gabik) will find a permanent position.

It turns out that in the morning his mother was called by the hospital. Gabik stands in line to claim the ration and his mother has the cards. He looks for her everywhere and she is not to be found. And he is very uneasy. Can she still be in the hospital? But why? We do a few lessons and Gabik leaves again to look for his mother. Later Gabik returned, again bewildered and dejected. He did not find her anywhere. We continue to do the lessons. We began to feel cold. Gabik was worried. Like him I sensed some impending trouble and this evoked an uncanny feeling in us. The cold outside penetrated our spirits. We closed our notebooks. I was very hungry. So was my friend. We had a snack consisting of hot plates of soup and began to feel warmer.

Meanwhile Lute Shrayber [a friend of Yitskhok's], who lives with Gabik, came in and called him home. His mother had returned and asked him to come home. Gabik became bewildered, left his notebooks, inquired anxiously what had happened. I exchanged glances with Lute. I understood there was some trouble, and Gabik felt our glances. And when Lute wanted to remain behind in the room to tell me something, Gabik had a presentiment, and tried to get Lute to go out first and [he] ran out the door with his face averted and tears welled in his eyes. . . . I felt a tug at the heart. I remained alone in the little room. There was no one at home. It was quiet, cold and terribly uncanny, and sadness hovered about me. I became so gloomy and dejected. I reflected, I felt somehow the terrible thing that was to come.

[. . .] Toward evening I learned the expected ending. Gabik no longer has a father. I sensed how much misfortune [there is] in this world. How will Gabik see it through, he who is so gay, so frivolous. With what suddenness was he dealt such a painful blow before my very eyes! In the evening we decided to visit him. Gabik was already lying down; we left him in peace. We remained for some time in the next room and mourned the misfortune. [. . .] I feel great pity for Gabik, for his mother. How terrible is the lot of these quiet, lonely people! How honestly, how poorly they did live, how quiet and refined they were! How hard will it now be for Gabik, how he loved his father! Gabik's misfortune struck deep into my heart.

Sunday the 8th of November [1942]

[. . .] The walls are plastered with obituary notices: Dr. Moyshe Heller, the teacher and scholar, has died. [. . .] The funeral takes place at three o'clock today. I want to see Gabik. I imagine what a hard time he has by himself. I am still under the heavy impression of all I witnessed yesterday. During the day they began to admit people to the hospital where Dr. Moyshe Heller was lying. There I also met Gabik. When he saw his friends, however, his eyes filled with tears. But he soon calmed himself. We entered the room. Two candles are burning at the head of the bed. Gabik stands with us. I cannot look him straight in the eye. I become mute. We all stand thus in oppressive silence that compounds our anguish. I kept thinking all the while what Gabik would look like, what I would see at our first meeting after the misfortune.

Gabik is bearing up exceptionally well. His face expresses a woeful sadness, a slight bewilderment. He is calm and looks very bad, pale, with dark rims under his eyes. It looks as though he has already become accustomed to it and bears it in silence. A crowd of people is gathering in the room: pupils, teachers, fellow workers. [. . .] The room becomes crowded [with people] pressing around the coffin.

Yashunski and the teacher Kaplan talk about the deceased and characterize him as a versatile and gifted person, a disseminator of culture, a man devoted to the Jewish school and culture. Gabik's father, a cripple, was nevertheless a man with a healthy spirit, a strong character. He loved what was fine, genuine, and natural. He hated the hypocrisy of his people and of all mankind. Gabik would often tell me about his father, his outings with him, the healthy education he received from his father. Our ranks are becoming more and more depleted. Four of our greatest and best have left us: Pludermakher, Khayimson, Gershteyn, and Dr. Heller was the fourth. Victims of the ghetto.

The coffin is shut tight. We want to take Gabik out but he prefers to stay. He looks calmly on as the coffin is carried out, but I perceive in his sadness how deeply he feels his misfortune. We return from the gate. It is getting rather dark. It is cold. Today there is almost no school. We are not in the mood.

Tuesday the 10th [November 1942]

It is a cold day today. [. . .] People run huddled up with cold. It is dark and forbidding. It is livelier at the dark, sad ghetto lanterns, at the street corners. Like flies around a little lamp poor ghetto vendors, mostly children, cling to the light. The bluish, dull light illuminates the rags of the children or women, illuminates the little hands red from cold which are counting money and giving change. Frozen, carrying the little stands on their backs, they push toward the tiny corner that is lit up. They stand thus until they hear the [curfew] whistle and then they disappear with their trays into the black little ghetto streets. Next day you see them again at the sad light, how they knock one foot against the other and breathe into their frozen hands. I run through the cold, sad little ghetto street and run home straight to bed, to fall asleep as soon as possible, because in sleep you dream and have sweeter hopes than when awake.

Wednesday the 11th [November 1942]

In school and in the club we now have a lot to do. We completed our textbook in Yiddish. We have to prepare three papers: 1. "Scenes of Deprivation in Avrom

Reisen." 2. "Jewish Children in Avrom Reisen." 3. "Jewish Children at Work." Furthermore, in Jewish history we are preparing the trial against Herod. The trial will be a public one. We have a court, prosecutor, defense counsel, defendant, and a whole succession of persons from history who serve as witnesses. We have already apportioned the work. Now the hardest task is in store for me [as the prosecutor]—to work out the indictment and to prepare a series of questions for the witnesses on behalf of the prosecution. You have to study Graetz, Dubnow, and others. A lively and interesting activity is now proceeding in our school.

Sunday the 15th of November [1942]

Today there is an upheaval in the house. Our neighbors are installing an iron stove. [. . .] Everything is topsy-turvy. A locksmith is busy switching the locks in the house today (we shall now have a separate entrance through the kitchen), a carpenter repairs the padlocks of the windowpanes, glaziers repair the windows. Everyone is banging, shouting. It is a real hell.

Monday the 23rd [November 1942]

This evening they installed a range in our house. It just happened that the electricity broke down. People work at the range by candlelight. The room is full of clay and bricks. And here I am with my scribblings in the midst of the hubbub. Lately I have a pile of work from school and the club. We spend whole days on historical books. We are preparing various reports and trials. In addition, I am the person responsible for the circle of creative writing in the club, under the direction of the poet Sutzkever, and I have to be in constant contact with him. The study period in the morning is quite a pleasant one. However, the rest of the day flies past quickly. I do not even have time to finish my book from the library. I am burdened by piles of reports in Yiddish, in history. And everything comes up at the same time. Every evening I go to the club as usual, visit the history circles, the nature circle, the literary one.

I often remain for the auditions of the dramatic circle. It is gay, cheerful. We wait impatiently for the completion of our premises on Disner Street.

Tuesday the 24th [November 1942]

The ghetto is in a cheerful mood and so are the children. The ghetto resounds with good news, the ghetto radiates with hope: we almost begin to imagine that presently . . . we shall leave our jail. . . . [. . .] The most important thing: the German army suffered a defeat at Stalingrad. [. . .] Thousands of fallen and captured Germans. The Soviets are strongly attacking the central front: the ghetto feels with all its senses that the end is approaching or, rather, that our beginning is near.

Yitskhok Rudashevski

In the evening I took a walk along the little ghetto streets. [. . .] The ruins on Yatkever Street glisten in the frost as though studded with diamonds. It is quiet and deserted. The snow-covered ruins stand under a frosty, blue sky where a great round moon hovers and appears intermittently through a different crevice in the wall of the ruin. [. . .] [E]ven though I come across a ruin on the way my heart feels strangely good, because on such a night I can conceive of something new happening very soon. . . . I feel it is close at hand. I grope for it in the frost with my hand.

Saturday the 5th [December 1942]

[. . .] I have a lot of work in the evening. I am rewriting my indictment against Herod. There are many lessons. Chemistry and geography have been added to our subjects at school. However, I do not feel like sitting in the house. I want to take a walk. I go up to the sport square. I stand alone under the gray, starry sky. By the light of the moon you can see how diamonds fall from the sky. The square is white with snow. I take a deep breath. [. . .]

It is late. Soon time for the [curfew] whistle. A few vendors stand at the street corners with their crates fastened on them. There are three of us in the lane. I go home and a passer-by buys something from a poor girl. By the light of the lantern she gives him change with her frostbitten blue little fingers, and I see by the light of the lantern how her hands tremble, her whole little body shakes, she is absolutely incapable of counting out the money. I hurry home because I hear the whistle.

Sunday the 7th [December 1942]

In our circles on ghetto research we decided once and for all to complete the spadework, that is to say visiting homes with the questionnaires. We want to get started on processing the answers, to make history on the basis of the data.

Today my friend and I visited a new apartment. We received very good answers. [. . .] They poured their hearts out to us, explained in full detail all their misfortunes, the complicated tragedies. [. . .] "What do you say, children, this is what [the] Führer made of us. May the same thing happen to him. This will be a history of us. Write, write, children. It is good this way." We finish questioning a family and thank them. "Oh, do not thank us. Promise us that we shall leave the ghetto, and I shall tell you three times as much, wretched folk that we are." We assured the woman ten times that we shall leave the ghetto. [. . .]

Wednesday the 10th of December [1942]

It dawned on me that today is my birthday. Today I became fifteen years old. You hardly realize how time flies. It, the time, runs ahead unnoticed and presently we realize, as I did today, for example, and discover that days and months go by, that the ghetto is not a painful, squirming moment of a dream that constantly disappears, but is a large swamp in which we lose our days and weeks. Today I became deeply absorbed in the thought. I decided not to trifle my time away in the ghetto on nothing and I feel somehow happy that I can study, read, develop myself, and see that time does not stand still as long as I progress normally with it. In my daily ghetto life it seems to me that I live normally but often I have deep qualms. Surely I could have lived better. Must I day in and day out see the walled-up ghetto gate, must I in my best years see only the one little street, the few stuffy courtyards?

Still other thoughts buzzed around in my head but I felt two things most strongly: a regret, a sort of gnawing. I wish to shout to time to linger, not to run. I wish to recapture my past year and keep it for later, for the new life. My second feeling today is that of strength and hope. I do not feel the slightest despair. Today I became fifteen years of age and I live confident in the future. I am not conflicted about it, and see before me sun and sun and sun. . . .

Thursday the 11th of December [1942]

Today we had a club holiday in the kitchen of Rudnitsker 6. We felt like having a little fun. So we wangled a hundred kilograms of potatoes out of the administration and we have a baked pudding. This was the happiest evening I have spent in the ghetto.

At nine o'clock we met in the kitchen. People are already sitting at the tables. Many, many guests came. And here we sit crowded together. I look around at the crowd, all of our kind teachers, friends, intimates. It is so cozy, so warm, so pleasant. [. . .] Club members came with songs, recitations. Until late into the night we sang with the adults songs that tell about youthfulness and hope. Very beautiful was the "living newspaper" in which the club with its chairman and speakers was humorously criticized.

We sat at the meager tables and ate baked pudding and coffee and we were so happy, so happy. Song after song resounded. It is already twelve o'clock. [. . .] We do not want to go home. Songs keep bursting forth, they simply will not stop. We disperse late at night. [. . .] Today we have demonstrated that even within the three small streets we can maintain our youthful zeal. We have proved that from the ghetto there will not emerge a youth broken in spirit; from the ghetto there will emerge a strong youth which is hardy and cheerful.

Sunday the 13th [December 1942]

[. . .] Today the ghetto celebrated the circulation of the hundred thousandth book in the ghetto library. The festival was held in the auditorium of the theater. [. . .]

Hundreds of people read in the ghetto. The reading of books in the ghetto is the greatest pleasure for me. The book unites us with the future, the book unites us with the world. The circulation of the hundred thousandth book is a great achievement for the ghetto and the ghetto has the right to be proud of it.

Monday the 21st [December 1942]

Tonight finally at eight in the evening the trial against Herod takes place. In our temporary club a large crowd of guests, club members gathered. I made the first speech for the prosecution. The trial had certain faults. The discussion between the parties was weak and there was evidence of coaching in the rejoinders. On the whole, however, our trial succeeded. Our chairman, the court, the interrogation of the witnesses for the historical personages, was quite impressive. The speeches contained much rich material and were well realized. I accused Herod of a policy of ambiguity, of playing the role of a Roman agent, of introducing into the land Roman customs that were hostile and foreign to Jewish spirituality. I accused him of murdering the people. The defense showed Herod's positive deeds, explained that Herod had lived in a tempestuous time, that his behavior was contrary to his will, and that many of his deeds were for the benefit of the Jewish people.

The court selected a committee of experts consisting of teachers and historians that had to answer the question whether Herod's deeds were in the interest of the people. A great discussion opened among the adults and this was the most interesting part. Various opinions were expressed. [. . .] The concluding part of the trial and the discussion in the hall were very interesting and continued until late into the night. The verdict was pronounced: Herod was declared guilty. I was satisfied with the verdict. [. . .]

Sunday the 27th [December 1942]

A memorial for [the Yiddish poet] Mendele was held today in the ghetto. We are now reading Mendele in school. The ghetto is commemorating the twenty-fifth anniversary of the death of Mendele. The memorial began at twelve o'clock. The speakers dwelt upon Mendele as the grandfather of Yiddish literature. Mendele loved the people, he chastised, criticized them, yet for all that a father. He believed in the people, he had high expectations of the masses, of the common people whom he liked so much. They stressed that Mendele was a critic of Jewish society. [. . .]

Monday the 28th [December 1942]

Today is a sad evening in the ghetto. The little ghetto streets are full of trouble and suffering. [Franz] Murer [deputy head of the German civil government in Vilna] is playing his game at the gate. [. . .] Uncle enters. He comes sadly from the gate. Eight hundred rubles were taken from him. Probably the last money he had. Weary and embittered he tells of the horror and anguish that are now in evidence. He had hidden the few rubles in his boots. They were forced to pull off their boots, and so he threw the money away in a corner. And to whom did this have to happen? To Uncle, who lives in such poverty! Uncle's troubles settle so heavily on my spirit along with all the last-minute news of the hell at the gate, a dreary evening, a ghetto evening. . . .

Friday the 1st of January 1943

The first day of the year 1943. In honor of the New Year the world adorned itself overnight in white. A white, clear winter day. Today the new year begins. The ghetto meets the New Year with one wish: to be liberated from the odious ghetto. The ghetto looks upon the New Year as the redeemer, the longed-for liberator.

Elke, the son of Khone Rone, lives on Shavler 4 (they lived with us). He slips out every day and brings in potatoes, flour, through a hideout. The family is a large one and so the little boy looks for a way to survive. On one of these days the Jewish police seized him and the small, frail Elke was given twenty-five lashes. Four policemen held him and [Meir] Levas himself, the commander of the gatekeeper [commander of the Jewish police who guarded the ghetto gate], beat him so mercilessly, so murderously. The little breadwinner was brought home badly flogged. [. . .]

Sunday the 3rd [January 1943]

At school today they are giving us oral marks for the first third of the school year. I have A's in Yiddish, Jew[ish] history, history, and biology. I have B's in mathematics, Hebrew, drawing, and physics; in Latin, German, C's. My grades could perhaps have been better but even those mentioned above are proof that my time is not being frittered away.

Thursday the 7th [January 1943]

Today they give five deca[grams] of pork on the ration cards. I waited in line a short time and at last found myself inside the store. There is so much injustice evident among us Jews in the ghetto, so much that is not right, so much that is disgusting. For instance, in the distribution of meat on the ration cards. People freeze and stand in line. Policemen, privileged persons, walk in freely. During the distribution the butcher throws the piece of meat to the person in line as if he were doing him a favor, exploiting a child, a person who is less vituperative, by giving him the worst.

On the other hand, those who have "pull" with the butcher (for "pull" the ghetto person lowers himself into the merest nonentity, because in the ghetto the vitamin P, as it is called, is victorious; "pull" or "pleytses," in other words, *strong shoulders*) get a somewhat fatter piece. [. . .] The butcher extends his sweet, wheedling face to them in such a disgusting manner, cuts out a piece of thick, white fat for them (I think that they have enough even without that at home). The crowd of frozen women stands in "line," hushed, wrathful, devouring the meat table with their eyes. They remain silent as they watch one person receive the fat and the second bones. People are already used to it.

"It is probably too good for you!" the butcher shouts to a poor young woman who also wants a piece of meat! With a sanctimonious air a policeman wraps up a piece of fat meat in some paper.

Friday the 8th [January 1943]

New students are being accepted in the technical school in the ghetto. I am now going through a big struggle, whether to learn a trade or continue to study in the high school as I have done until now. I cannot make up my mind. On one hand, there is war; it is easier at the moment for the person who has some kind of trade or other. I am growing up and sooner or later I shall have to go to work. On the other hand, I imagine that attendance at the technical school means an interruption of one's studies. For after the four-month vocational course the goal is to go to work, and once I start working I shall never return to school again.

After long hesitation and long reflection I decided to make use of every moment. I need to study; I still have suitable conditions, so I must not interrupt my studies. My determination to study has developed into something like defiance of the present, which hates to study, loves to work, to drudge. No, I decided. I shall live with tomorrow, not with today. And if for every hundred ghetto children of my age ten can study, I must be among the fortunate ones, I must take advantage of this. Studying has become even more precious to me than before. [. . .]

Saturday the 9th [January 1943]

This evening the great club festival takes place. Our fresh clubrooms are full of members and guests. Our auditorium prides itself on having a stage of its own, with transparent curtain and reflectors. There are some beautiful pictures on the wall. It is warm and pleasant in the auditorium. [. . .] "Within the walls yet young" is the headline of our wall newspaper, which shines down from the wall. A splendid newspaper. The articles are in the form of walls and a street leading to the ghetto gate. [. . .] A beautiful bulletin gives an account of the work that has been done.

Finally people take their seats. Up on our own stage, our own people on the dais, our young club manager, Leo Bernstein, through whose efforts the club has become a reality, our heroic chairman Avreml [Avrom Zheleznikov], Reyze [Stolitski], our secretary, and a whole group of lecturers. The mood is an exalted one. Greetings and speeches. A present is given to Leo Bernstein and Reyze. [. . .]

Until twelve at night our dramatic circle showed what it could do. It is a pleasure to see how well our members are performing. We have every right to be proud of them. Such beautiful numbers, decorations, costumes, and everything accomplished so well, so consistently.

A present is also given to [Eliohu] Pilnik, the favorite of the club, the chimney sweep director, who set up the performance. We remained in the club until half past two, intoxicated with youthful joy. After the program some entertainment, a living newspaper, songs, recitations. Pilnik presents one song after another. We are young, the young hall is saturated with youthful joy and work. Our spirit, which we bear proudly within the ghetto walls, will be the most beautiful gift to the newly rising future. Long live youth!—the progress of our people.

Sunday the 7th of February [1943]

We have good news. The people in the ghetto are celebrating. The Germans concede that Stalingrad has fallen. I walk across the street. . . . People wink at each other with happy eyes. At last the Germans have suffered a gigantic defeat. The entire ninth German army is crushed! Over three hundred thousand Germans killed. The staff taken prisoner. Stalin's city is the enemy's grave. The winter offensive of the Soviets produces splendid results.

I walk in the street . . . Winter is beginning to take leave of the little ghetto streets. The air is warm and sunny. The ice on the streets melts and oozes and our hearts are filled with spring. The snow within us melts too, and such a sunny feeling envelops us. Liberation is near. I feel its proximity with all my blood.

Sunday the 27th of February [actually Saturday]

Today was an unusual day for me. In the past two weeks new elements generally have been added to my life. We, some fifteen of us, have begun a p. [pioneer] project in the ghetto. The teacher M. [Mire Bernshteyn] and comrade Mu. [Musye Saginor] are our leaders. We considered whether in general there was a need for such an activity in the ghetto. We reached the conclusion that there was. [. . .] At the meetings we shall also train ourselves, because we must prepare for the life that is in store for us. The future will require dedicated people who will have to guide the masses toward great renewal. [. . .]

Yitskhok Rudashevski

For today we prepared a celebration in honor of the Red Army's twenty-fifth anniversary, which fell on Tuesday the twenty-third. We secretly collected money among ourselves, potatoes, beets for refreshments. [. . .] The conspiracy is great. Our fellows stand at the club and at our comrade's gate. We transport ourselves over one by one. Finally out comes the salad; bread and cookies are brought as a present from the older comrades. [. . .] On the table there is a salad in the form of a star. Near it stands Stalin's picture. The door is locked. Teacher M. also comes in and a few more of our people.

I open the celebration. I greet the festive gathering of the pioneers, dedicated to the twenty-fifth anniversary of the Red Army, our favorite whom we are awaiting and of whose victory we are certain. [. . .] We sing Soviet songs. Comrades read essays about the Red Army, about its leaders. We now all live passionately bound by our love for the Red Army, by our love of Soviet life. Teacher Op. [Leyb Opeskin] reads his poems written for the Soviets: "To the Red Tankman." The adults' wish for us is that we ride on the victorious red tanks over the liberated streets. They read Stalin's order of the day, under the slogan: "Death to the conqueror!" Thus, on the twenty-seventh of February, we pioneers celebrate in a gay and intimate mood the twenty-fifth anniversary of the Red Army!

Wednesday the 10th of March [1943]

Spring is more and more evident in the ghetto. The sun warms us. Near the walls grown-ups and children are already standing in the sun. Children raise their pale little faces toward the sun. I am busy for days at a time. In the morning at school, in the afternoon, lessons. I keep busy with housework, toward evening with meetings and at the club. At the p. meetings we now talk about the national question. We also obtained a digest of the Sov[iet] communiqués of the winter offensive. From them it has become clear to us that the Soviets are marching courageously forward, have occupied Stalingrad, Kharkov, Rostov, Kursk, and dozens of other points. The attack proceeds on the Don—Caucasus sector. The Red Army has reached a point fifty kilometers from the Dnieper. [. . .]

Work is now also being done at the club. We are preparing a Yehoash evening. I have written an essay, "On Reading Yehoash in the Ghetto." In the evenings we prepare a magnificent exhibition with Friend Sutzkever, who is directing the work. Sutzkever had brought many valuable materials, manuscripts, books, photographs, from the YIVO [the Yiddish Scientific Institute, founded in Vilna in 1925]. We shall display this in a beautiful Yehoash exhibition. We have also set up a beautiful Yehoash newspaper. The preparations for the Yehoash celebration are proceeding at quite a pace, they are interesting and will certainly bring good results.

Thursday the 11th [March 1943]

I was at the club until late at night. We are preparing for the magnificent Yehoash evening. I do not get enough sleep.

Sunday the 14th of March [1943]

Today the Yehoash celebration as well as the opening of the Yehoash exhibition took place in the club. The exhibition is exceptionally beautiful. The entire reading room in the club is filled with material. The room is bright and clean. It is a delight to come into it. We are indebted for the exhibition to Friend Sutzkever, who smuggled into the ghetto from the YIVO where he works a great deal of material for the Yehoash exhibition. [. . .]

People entering here forgot that this is the ghetto. Here in the Yehoash exhibition we have many valuable documents that now are treasures: manuscripts from Peretz to Yehoash, Yehoash's original letters. We have rare newspaper clippings. In the section—Bible translations into Yiddish—we have old Bible translations into Yiddish from the seventeenth century. Looking at the exhibition, at our work, our hearts swell with enthusiasm. We actually forget that we are in a dark ghetto. The celebration today was also carried out in a grand manner. The dramatic circle presented Yehoash's tableau, *Saul.* The members read essays on the writings of Yehoash, on Yehoash the poet, on beauty, sound, and color.

The mood of the celebration was an exalted one. It was indeed a holiday, a demonstration on behalf of Yiddish literature and culture.

Thursday the 18th [March 1943]

I am busy for hours at a time. It is so hard to accomplish something at school and in the club, and at the same time to be involved with cooking and cleaning. First of all reports sneaked up on us. At school we are now covering the theme of Vilna in geography. I am preparing a report "On Jew[ish] Printing in Vilna." For several months now there is no light in the evenings. In the evening we lie around in the workroom, the reading room. I often reflect, this is supposedly the ghetto yet I have such a rich life of intellectual work: I study, I read, I visit club circles. Time runs by so quickly and there is so much work to be done, lectures, social gatherings. I often forget that I am in the ghetto.

Sunday the 21 of Ma rch [1943]

[. . .] Toward evening there was a Purim party in the club. We were in the mood for Purim, so let it be Purim. We were the ones who set the tone. We sang songs, presented a "Purim play" [. . .] . Comrade Shmerke [Kaczerginski] sang with us. Pilnik, our dramatic director, was tipsy and joined in. We laughed our fill and went to sleep. We are waiting for the real Purim. Next year we shall eat Hitler-tashn.[23]

Thursday the 25th of March [1943]

A command was issued by the German regime about liquidating five small ghettos in the Vilna province. The Jews are being transported to the Vilna and the Kovno ghettos. Today the Jews from the neighboring little towns have begun to arrive. It is rainy and gray outside. Sadly the peasant carts ride into the ghetto like gypsy covered wagons. On the carts Jews with children, their bag and baggage. The newly arrived Jews have to be provided with dwellings. The school on Shavler 1 has been preempted for the newly arrived Jews. The school on Shavler 1 was moved into the building of our school. They are teaching in two shifts. Today we went to class in the evening. Our studies somehow no longer have any form. We are all depressed. We are in a bad mood.

Sunday the 28th [March 1943]

The mood in the ghetto is a very gloomy one. The crowding together in one place of so many Jews is a signal for something. The transportation of food through the gate has become very difficult. Several people have already been arrested on Lukishki. People walk around gray and worried. Danger is hovering in the air. No! This time we shall not permit ourselves to be led like dogs to the slaughter! We have been discussing this lately at our (. . .) [pioneer project meetings] and are prepared at any moment. We have to improve ourselves. This thought strengthens our nerves, gives us courage and endurance.

Monday the 5th [April 1943]

Sunday at three o'clock the streets in the ghetto were closed off. A group of three hundred Jews from Sol and Smorgon have left for Kovno with a large transport of provincial Jews that arrived at the railway station. As I stood at the gate I saw how they were packing their things. Gaily and in high spirits they went to the train.

Today the terrible news reached us: eighty-five railroad cars of Jews, around five thousand persons, were not taken to Kovno as promised but transported by train to Ponar where they were shot to death. Five thousand new bloody victims. The ghetto was deeply shaken, as though struck by thunder. The atmosphere of slaughter has gripped the people. It has begun again. [. . .]

The ghetto is depressed and mournful. We are unprotected and exposed to death. Again there hovers over the little Vilna ghetto streets the nightmare of

Ponar. It is terrible, terrible. People walk around like ghosts. They wring their hands. Toward evening an urgent gathering [of the pioneer project]. The situation has been confirmed. We have no one to depend on. The danger is very great. We believe in our own strength. We are ready at any moment.

Tuesday the 6th [April 1943]

The situation is an oppressive one. We now know all the horrible details. Instead of Kovno, five thousand Jews were taken to Ponar where they were shot to death. [. . .] We did not study in school today. The children run away from their homes where it is terrible to stay on account of the mood, on account of the women. The teachers are also despondent. So we sit in a circle. We rally our spirits. We sing a song.

In the evening I went out into the street. It is five o'clock in the afternoon. The ghetto looks terrible: heavy leaden clouds hang and lower over the ghetto. A darkness as before a storm. Our mood like the sky is heavily overcast. People are out in the little streets.

[. . .] It becomes darker and darker. Suddenly a clap of thunder, a flash of lightning and it begins to rain. The restless, sad people are whipped out of the few little streets. The rain lashes with anger as though it wished to flush everything out of the world. . . .

At night I am in the club. It is dark. The light is lit at nine o'clock. People sit in the dark. Fellows are singing a song. We have a feeling of oppression and anguish. The situation is still very strained. We are on guard. This thought relieves the heavy hours.

Wednesday [April 7, 1943]

Our mood is a little better. A happy song can be heard in the club. We are, however, prepared for everything, because Monday proved that we must not trust nor believe anything. We may be fated for the worst.

8

Anonymous Girl
ŁÓDŹ GHETTO

"There is no justice in the world, not to mention in the ghetto." So begins the diary of a young girl writing in the Łódź ghetto in late February and March of 1942. Her identity is unknown. The only clue as to her first name is a note copied into the diary addressed to her and her sister that begins "Dear Esterka and Minia," but nowhere else is there any hint about which name belonged to the diary's author. She did, however, introduce the members of her family: her father, who worked as a painter in the construction division of the ghetto; her mother, who worked as a machine operator in the leather and saddlery department; her sister, age seventeen, and brother, age sixteen, who also worked in the same workshop as their mother. She did not mention her own age, though her indication in the diary that she was not employed suggests that she was probably the youngest member of the family. The language of the diary is Polish; the diarist and her family were most likely native Poles, but whether they were originally from the city of Łódź or settled from a smaller village nearby is likewise unclear. There is no information about the diarist and her family apart from what is written or can be deduced from the diary itself.

The diary is fragmentary, beginning in the midst of an undated entry and ending abruptly in the middle of a sentence. The rest of the entries are dated, covering a three-week period beginning on February 27 and ending on March 18, 1942, during which time the diarist wrote every day. In the few pages that have come down to us (surely only a part of what was once a longer diary) the writer dwelled almost entirely on her immediate world, recording the details of her own daily life and that of her family. Her account is filled with reports about her activities for the day, the errands and tasks she accomplished, and the encounters she had with friends, family members, and acquaintances. Far from reflecting a diverse and varied existence in the ghetto, however, these activities and conversations revolved almost exclusively around two primary subjects: food and deportations.

This is in itself a reflection of the particular character of the Łódź ghetto, which differed in important ways from other ghettos in the occupied territories. Located in the part of Poland that was partitioned and incorporated into the German "Reich" (and thus ultimately intended to be completely "free of Jews"), the Łódź ghetto was conceived as a provisional dwelling place for the Jews after a series of expulsions was called to a halt in December 1939. As the only major ghetto to exist on "German" soil, it was completely segregated from the ethnic German population and the Poles still residing there. Consequently, there was virtually no smuggling or trading of food, medicine, or provisions between the ghetto residents and the outside world. Whereas in other places the existence of a black market allowed for supplemental supplies to flow into the ghetto, the inhabitants of Łódź were forced instead to depend almost entirely on the allocations from the German authorities, which were drastically inadequate in quantity and often substandard in quality. For this reason, hunger, starvation, and death due to malnutrition were rampant in Łódź, dramatically more so than in any of the other major ghettos.[1]

It is not surprising, then, that the diary is first and foremost about food and hunger. In her first entry, the diarist described the situation plainly as "a struggle against death from starvation." The diarist's perspective is not that of witness, observer, or commentator on other people's hunger; rather, it was the diarist herself who was struggling with the daily agony of starvation. That torment took multiple forms; most notably, the text reveals the obsessive hunt for food, the hours and days spent in line as the diarist stopped at various distribution points and waited to get a "back ration" owed to the family, to get a supplemental ration, or to buy bread or beets on the street. She noted the counting, weighing, and measuring of food and her own daily food consumption, marking down the amounts of bread, noodles, raw parsley, or beets in decagrams, and often describing the appalling quality and condition of the occasional vegetables or meat the family received. Indeed, the ration lists copied into the diary serve as a record of the inconceivably paltry amounts of food on which the ghetto dwellers were forced to subsist. She recorded, too, her own physical suffering, complaining bitterly of her aching stomach, teeth, and head, her weakness, and, worst of all, the indescribable and by all accounts excruciating sensation of unrelieved hunger. So meager were the food supplies that an extra bowl of soup brought to her by her father sent her into "seventh heaven."

The diarist wrote not only about her own personal world—the daily hunger and despair that she experienced—but also the consequences of hunger and want on her family as a whole. In a world where each bite or slice or spoonful mattered, the sharing of food among family members had to be governed by rules of equality and fairness; at the same time, the all-consuming physical and emotional torment of hunger could not always be controlled. And while the diarist recorded the generosity of her parents, who often gave up their own bread and soup for their children, she also reported on the outbreaks and fights in the family that resulted when she "sneaked" a few bites of bread or an extra spoonful of noodles. Her diary thus suggests the internal, irreconcilable conflict she faced between the desire to satisfy her hunger (and the instinct of self-preservation that gave rise to it) and the obligation to obey the unwritten rules of conduct that govern communal life, no matter how those rules have changed or how desperate the circumstances have become. Most of all, however, the diary captures the bitter irony of families breaking down in conflict over a spoonful of noodles, a slice of bread, or an extra turnip.[2]

Even over the course of the short three weeks during which the diarist wrote, the food situation grew dramatically worse in the ghetto. Initially, her family's bread ration had to last for six days. On March 16, upon receiving two loaves of bread, she learned that they would have to be stretched still further. "Bread for seven days! Horror!" she wrote. Hunger naturally took its toll on the physical health of the diarist and her family. In her diary, she frequently commented on the appearance of family and friends; indeed, it is a reminder of the fragile state of people's health under such conditions. The slightest sign of illness, weakness, exhaustion, or malnutrition was carefully watched, guarded against lest it signify an imminent decline toward death. Mortality rates from this period in the ghetto's history place these individual struggles in the larger context of the ghetto as a whole. On February 1, 1942, the ghetto population numbered 151,001 people; 1,875 died during that month. On March 1, the population count was 142,079; of these,

2,244 people died in that month. These deaths, the highest numbers thus far in the ghetto's two-year history, were overwhelmingly caused by starvation and related illnesses.[3]

If food is the primary subject of the diary, the deportations of Jews from the ghetto is only minimally secondary. "There is no end to the deportations; starvation grows and grows," she wrote. Beginning in January 1942, the Nazi authorities had undertaken the first so-called resettlements from the ghetto toward the eventual goal of emptying the ghetto and ridding the region entirely of Jews. The deportees at this time were predominantly German, Austrian, and Czech Jews who had only months before arrived in the ghetto from their homes in the West, as well as those on welfare, the sick, the elderly, and those caught dealing on the black market. The unfortunates were sent to the death camp at Chełmno, some thirty-five miles away, where they were killed, suffocated by carbon monoxide poisoning in so-called gas vans.

The diarist reported on all aspects of the deportations, sketching the scenes of the ill and elderly being dragged along the street and the general panic and chaos among the ghetto population. She also penned a chilling record of the deportation of her sister's friend, Hania Huberman, who was among those deported in March 1942. In the midst of her reports on the dismal preparations, the diarist mentioned that Hania had applied to the medical commission for an exemption from deportation on the grounds that her father was simply too ill for the journey. In a line that is deeply significant but easily overlooked, the diarist wrote, "I'm sure she will stay because her father cannot walk." The writer was not alone at this moment in the ghetto's history in believing that those who were being deported were indeed (as they had been told by the German authorities) being sent to work on farms in rural areas and, consequently, in assuming (or hoping) that someone who was ill would not be sent away.

In fact, that Hania Huberman's father was too ill to walk was far more a reason *for* deportation than a reason for exemption. Indeed, those unable to work — that is, to be exploited for the benefit of the German economy and war effort — were among those at the greatest risk of deportation. For in Łódź, as in many other ghettos and camps, the principle was simple: the right to live was determined by the ability to work. But while the diarist's entries show that deportation was a thing to be feared, dreaded, and avoided if at all possible, it also reveals that the fate of the deportees was far from common knowledge among the ghetto inhabitants. For the moment, the sealed ghetto was cut off from news and information as dramatically as it was cut off from food, supplies, and medicine.[4]

The diary ends in the middle of a sentence on March 18, 1942. In an article about the diary, the historian Lucjan Dobroszycki wrote that the diary was found in an abandoned apartment on Dworskije Street in July 1945.[5] The apartment, occupied by a Helena Rabinowicz during the Nazi period, was apparently used as the meeting place for an anti-Fascist youth organization. Other documents relating to the work of the organization were found in the apartment, together with a working radio that had been hidden under the stovetop. Dobroszycki suggested that since the diary was found in this apartment, the young writer may have been a member of this clandestine youth group. No concrete information is contained in the text itself, but it is possible that she joined the organization after she wrote her diary. Nothing specific is known of her fate or that of her family, although they are all presumed to have perished. Her diary is currently in the archives of the Jewish Historical Institute in Warsaw.

[Undated entry]

nobody sends the community officials away. There is no justice in the world, not to mention in the ghetto. Right now they are deporting people on welfare. People are in a state of panic. And this hunger. A struggle against death from starvation. Life is terrible, living conditions are abominable, and there is no food. It's our bureaucrats who should be blamed for this. They were stealing from our provisions and let food rot. So nobody could get it. And now we are under sentence of death from starvation and are at the mercy of fortune. We see how death takes new victims every day. You need a vast amount of money to buy anything. How do you get it? Everything is so costly. On the street bread costs seventy reichmarks. It's the deportees from Germany who make money from this. We receive a six-day ration of bread. They distribute it twice a week. We get our bread and other provisions at Rembrandt 13. At first everything was very orderly here. Now it's only connections and confusion. Mr. Mazur is the manager of the cooperative. On the same street, but at number 12, we get our vegetables using the vegetable booklet. My father knows the manager there.

I'm very upset about the whole situation, because how can you be indifferent to so much suffering? How can you watch indifferently when they deport people you know, the sick, the elderly, and the children?

Friday, February 24 [actually February 27], 1942[6]

Today's kitchen ration (that included sugar):

1½ kilograms of pickled beets
½ kilogram of sauerkraut
10 decagrams of vegetable salad
60 decagrams of rye flour
20 "   of *zacierki* [egg noodles]
50 "   of sugar
15 "   of margarine
10 "   of coffee

How can you survive on this for two weeks? We cook once a day, only in the evening, but it's not enough because the beets are frozen, and when they thaw what's left is only water.

Our family consists of five people. My mom and my brother are working in the leather and saddlery workshop. Mom works on a machine (she's a senior machine operator) and my brother (sixteen years old) is a leather worker. My sister, who is seventeen, works in the same workshop. At work they get fifteen decagrams of bread and five decagrams of meat. They take twenty decagrams of bread from home. This is their meal for an entire day, and they work so hard.

My father is a painter and works in the construction division. He gets some soup there—it's practically water really—and takes twenty-five decagrams of bread from home. Can a man like my father who works so hard live on this? My father looks terrible. He's lost thirty kilograms. My brother and sister also look very bad, but nothing can be done about it. I stay at home and look quite well, but I don't have more than twenty decagrams of bread for an entire day. My mother used to leave me a little soup—but recently she stopped.

Starvation is terrifying. People die like poisoned flies. Today I got one kilogram of parsley. My father, brother, and I ate it raw. O fate! O irony! Will it ever end? I'm sick of life. We live worse than animals. Human life is so miserable, but one still fights for it.

Today after dinner I got a new ration—only vegetables, because the number on my booklet is low (21). Tomorrow our household is going to pay in advance for its provisions. How impatiently we are looking forward to this March being a little warmer! Then we'll be able to open the mounds where we buried the potatoes. But maybe some food will be available sooner. Right now the winter is at its full strength and the deportations continue. Every day about five hundred people are deported: welfare recipients, black-marketeers, and small families of up to three persons.

Saturday, February 28, 1942

There was a thaw at night, it's very icy, but fortunately the freezing weather is over. Today is Saturday. Everybody except my sister works until 2 P.M. She works until six. At twelve-thirty a little girl brought a note that said, "Dear Esterka and Minia, please come as soon as possible, because we're being deported and I would like to say good-bye to you."

It was written by my sister's friend. I'm completely broken. How much she has already suffered, how much she has wrestled with difficulties. What an unhappy family. Nine months ago she lost a brother, a first-grader in the lyceum. He was a genius. He died from tuberculosis of the pharynx. Her oldest sister lives in the Soviet Union. She was left alone with her deaf-and-dumb parents. They were on welfare. It's like slow death. A week ago her mother died, so she was left with her sick father who hadn't a shirt on his back.

Nobody had come back from work yet, so I locked the door and left the key at the neighbor's. I ran upstairs as fast as I could. I saw a pitiful sight. Her father, completely helpless, lies in bed, and her friend Dorka Cymberknopf stitches a backpack. I was really indignant, because we have a sewing machine at home. She could have come to us, so we would make it for her. She explained she didn't want to come with bad news. I helped her pack a few things. I left at 4 P.M. without saying good-bye, since I promised to come back with my sister. She gave me many scientific books. In the evening I couldn't go, because I had to wash several colorful shirts. When my sister came back in the evening, she brought many books and the diaries of her friend and her friend's brother.

Sunday, March 1, 1942

March!

Finally, a longed-for March has arrived. It's warm outside, like a real spring. I'm asking myself, "What is this month going to bring us? Will there be more starvation? Will they be deporting people again? Will death prevail?" Who knows? May God help us. In my dream I saw my sister's friend Hania Huberman and her father. The day passed very quickly. At 4 P.M. I cooked dinner. My father came back from work at five. Standing by the oven, I wondered where she could be now. Suddenly, the door opened and H.H. [Hania Huberman] entered. She was with a girl, a cousin of R. Inwar, her schoolmate. I thought it was a dream. She said that her application for an exemption had been considered by the medical commission and she didn't have to show up. Tomorrow at 11 A.M. she will have a reply as to whether she can stay. I'm sure she will stay because her father cannot walk. My heart went out to her. I like her so much. She is extremely intelligent and wise. She knows life. A third-year gymnasium student, a very good girl.

Monday, March 2, 1942

It's very foggy outside. At twelve o'clock I went to see H.H. She didn't get any reply. It's supposed to come tomorrow. This day is lasting forever. I'm very hungry, and there is no food. I want the night to come. I love the night. The night is my salvation. O night! May you last forever, through all the days of hunger.

Tuesday, March 3, 1942

Today I got up at eight in the morning. I went to the co-op to see whether they are distributing any late provisions they owe us, but they aren't. Daddy left me some money, so I could pay P. Berliner from Limanowskiego Street for the paint. On the way there I stopped on Zgierska Street 76 to visit my friend Regina Wajs. She has our measuring tape. I met her on the staircase. She was crying. Her mother is very sick. I went with her to the workshop where her brother works as a carpenter's apprentice, to get a medical voucher for her mother. I also went with her to her cousin. R.W. doesn't get any welfare, because they are wheeling and dealing in homemade candies and cigarettes. And they're afraid they could be deported.

I parted from her on Drewnowska Street. The day is beautiful and the sun is shining happily. Today is Purim. Before the war the streets were so busy, so many different kinds of cakes were on display. Today nobody even remembers. I enjoyed the walk, the sun was caressing my face, but I had to go back since there was nobody at home. On the way I dropped in at H.H.'s, but she wasn't there. She had gone out to make dinner on a gas stove.

Everybody was back from work and I did the laundry. Suddenly, the same girl showed up and said that Hania H. was leaving. Where will she go with her sick, helpless father, without a shirt for him and with nothing herself? Hungry, exhausted, without money and food. My mom immediately found some shirts for her and her father. My sister and I ran upstairs. When I came back, I couldn't stop crying. I didn't stay there longer, because I had to finish the laundry. I kept crying. I couldn't find any words of consolation, I couldn't talk. My tears were suffocating me. I promised to visit her with Dorka Cymberknopf. My sister came back very late.

Wednesday, March 4, 1942

Early in the morning the sun came out, but it is very cold. At ten I went to stand in the line to get some bread. I stood there for a long time, until one o'clock. D.C. [Dorka Cymberknopf] didn't come to me, so I decided to go to her. I waited for a long time, but since I didn't see her, I had to give up and go home. There is no end to the deportations; starvation grows and grows. Fortunately, today my father is painting in the ghetto kitchen, so he can get some soup there. My mom and my brother came back late. I couldn't wait for them with dinner, because I didn't eat more than twenty decagrams of bread today, so I had to get some food. Then, my mom showed up. When will this hunger end? The whole ghetto is confused. There are rumors. Some people say everybody is going to be deported, others maintain that only people on welfare will be and that an *Arbeit Lager* [*Arbeitslager,* or work camp] will be built there. It's really crazy.

Thursday, March 5, 1942

Winter is back. A freezing wind is blowing. The deportations have stopped for a while, but only for a couple of days, because there are no wagons for the deported people. The hunger keeps getting worse. Larger food rations are only a dream. In the morning I stopped at the vegetable cooperative. They give three kilograms of beets for one ration card. But can you call them beets? They're just manure. They stink and evaporate, and what's more, they have been frozen a few times. A family of five, ten, or one gets only three kilograms of beets. My ration booklet number is 21, so I always get it first. Today they were distributing food for the highest numbers. I have nothing for dinner. All day long I was looking for something. In the evening, at last, I bought half a kilogram of rye flour for twenty reichmarks. You need thousands, millions, to buy anything. Life is impossible.

Friday, March 6, 1942

It's freezing outside. It went down to seventeen degrees below zero in the morning. The windowpanes are covered with white frost. I'm sick at heart when it's so cold. Today we have nothing to cook. We are entitled to three loaves of bread, so we'll cook a piece of bread. Unfortunately, we received a circular that only one loaf would be available. I have no idea what to do. I purchased three kilograms of beets from one lady. I paid ten reichmarks. Rotten and stinking. Today we'll cook half, tomorrow—another half. Can you call this *life?*

Saturday, March 7, 1942

Today is Saturday. My sister isn't working. My mom and my brother are working till one-thirty. My father will come back at five. It's a wonderful and sunny day. When the sun is shining, I feel lighthearted. Life is so sad. Man wants a different life, better than this gloomy and joyless existence in the ghetto. When I look at the barbed wire that separates us from the rest of the world, my soul longs for freedom—like a bird in a cage. My eyes are filled with tears. I envy those birds that can fly freely. When I write these words, my heart breaks and I see images from the past. Will I ever live in better times? Who knows? It's a difficult question. May God help us. Will I be with my parents and friends after the war? Will we have enough bread and rye flour? Right now the starvation is at its peak. Once again we have nothing to cook. I bought a quarter kilogram of rye flour for eleven and a half reichmarks. Everybody wants to live.

Sunday, March 8, 1942

The days are more and more beautiful. Sun, it's time you shone for us. Easter is coming in four weeks. They register cards for rye matzos. I registered all I had. I don't know what I did. The line was very long—nothing new, there are lines everywhere. I'm entitled to some old piece of meat, because last time they didn't have any. It's going to be a real feast today. My mother divided the meat into three portions. Today we'll have cutlets.

Dad is still working in the division's kitchen at Młynarska 32. What would he do without this job? In the evening he tells us what kind of food the staff has. How do they get the ingredients? Of course, from our soups. All the officials steal (they will not be deported). Mom bought a scale for eight reichmarks. Money has no value. It's five in the afternoon. It's warm, like in the summer. Everybody is back—like after the fast—since we didn't have any bread. I only managed to get some in the evening. They all had taken five decagrams of bread to work. There, at two o'clock they got fifteen decagrams of bread (five decagrams were cut off) and five decagrams of cold cuts. They had to live on this all day long. They work so hard. My father gets some soup, because he works for the ghetto. I didn't eat anything before three o'clock. When my father came from work, he brought me some soup. I was in seventh heaven. My brother was so upset that he cried like a baby.

Monday, March 9, 1942

The freezing weather is over. The deportations are still taking place. People are upset, the atmosphere is very tense. The starvation is impossible, people die like flies. Workers in the divisions receive the following ration: two kilograms of pickled beets, twenty-five decagrams of sugar, one tablet of saccharine. I look quite well, although for a whole day I don't have more than twenty decagrams of bread before seven o'clock. How miserable human life has been during these years, what slavery, what a struggle with difficulties. I have nothing to cook for dinner. I'm still entitled to one kilogram twenty-five decagrams of zacierki, fifty decagrams of oil, seventy-five decagrams of honey, but I didn't get it. What a misfortune struck our home! It gives me a headache, I can hardly see. The emptiness haunts the apartment. There isn't even a single crumb there or a little coffee. You may fall and nobody will pick you up. A human being is worthless, dozens of them are not important. People are disgusting. Everybody cares only for himself. Recently, I have become so tough that nothing can move me, not even the worst suffering. I learned this from people. Today I visited three neighbors—all of them are on welfare. In the evening my mom borrowed twenty decagrams of zacierki from a neighbor; also a piece of bread. We don't have enough bread.

Tuesday, March 10, 1942

My mom, brother, and sister leave at seven-thirty in the morning. My father leaves at eight. Lying in bed, I noticed that my sister had forgotten her bread. I got dressed very quickly and brought it to her. She works at Szopena Street 4. It took me half an hour to walk there. I didn't have to wait long. Their room is on the ground floor and she sits by the window, which is in the front. I knocked and she came out right away. I have no idea why I don't live more harmoniously with my sister. We fight all the time and scream at each other. I must cause my parents a lot of worry. My sister doesn't look well. She is like a stranger to me.

The hunger is getting worse. In the morning I want my father to leave as soon as possible. Then I jump up from the bed and consume all the bread my mom has left for me for the entire day. My God, what has happened to me? I [don't] know how to restrain myself. Then I starve all day. I wish I were different. God, take pity on me. During the day I drink tap water and vinegar left from the pickled beets. Eating only this I wait until seven o'clock. I have a stomachache frequently.

Today they are distributing bread. I stood three hours in the line and got three loaves. When I came back, I just had to take a piece. In the evening I promised myself not to eat, even if my mom offered me some, because I can't have someone else's bread.

I can't stay at home. I went to the cooperative to check whether they were distributing some of the provisions that we're supposed to get—but they weren't. What will we do if Mom doesn't bring any beets? I don't even want to think about it. I didn't go straight home, but I turned to Brzezińska Street. I met Mrs. Rotbard, mother of a school friend of mine. She is a very nice woman and also intelligent. She doesn't look well. I found out that Cesia R. works in the workshop. I talked to Mrs. Rotbard for a long while and quite involuntarily I let slip that I was writing a diary. She said she would like to read it. I'd made a silly mistake. I don't want anybody to know about it and nobody is going to read it.

It was four o'clock when I came home. In two hours everybody will be back. I feel very restless at home. I went out again to the cooperative. Miraculously, I got the rations:

1¼ kilograms of zacierki

60 decagrams of margarine instead of 50 decagrams of oil

1 kilogram of chocolate-colored honey.

I lit the fire and cooked twenty decagrams of zacierki on the stove. Mom came back a little earlier and brought some beets. We are lucky.

Everybody is home, except my father. He came back at seven in the evening. We could hardly wait for him. He showed up with his two co-workers. They put two rutabagas on the table and divided each of them into three. It worked out at seventy decagrams each. When they left, my father took out [a few] pieces of rutabaga from his pocket. Two rutabagas had been swiped from the kitchen, but some other scraps were given to my father by the women working there. He knew that there was nothing to eat at home, so he didn't eat them on the spot although he was very hungry. The soup had been thrown out by one of the apprentices. I can't write anymore, because my eyes are filled with tears.

Wednesday, March 11, 1942

Today I wanted to get dressed a little later because I had nothing to do. But in the morning I was called by our neighbor to go to the attic and take out the laundry. I have bad luck with this laundry. What am I supposed to do? It's still wet. She left me only two clotheslines and all the laundry had to be squeezed on to them.

When I went out to the street, I heard that there was a food ration for those who were not getting any food in the kitchen. This ration could be eaten only on the sixteenth. I was reading the announcements with a pounding heart, because two weeks of keeping ourselves alive depend on this ration. My whole body was shivering. The ration is as follows:

50 decagrams of rye flour

10   "   of peas

30   "   of white sugar

20   "   of sugar

15   "   of margarine

15   "   of honey

10   "   of coffee

2 kilograms of pickled beets

10 decagrams of rutabagas

6   "   of vegetable salad.

This ration is much worse than the previous one. Terrible hunger is awaiting us again. I got the vegetable ration right away. There is only vinegar and ice in the beets. There is no food, we are going to starve to death. All my teeth ache and I am very hungry. My left leg is frostbitten. I ate almost all the honey. What have I done? I'm so selfish. What are they going to put on their bread now, what will they say? Mom, I'm unworthy of you. You work so hard. Besides working in the workshop, she also moonlights by working for a woman who sells clothes in the street. My mom looks awful, like a shadow. She works very hard. When I wake up at twelve or one o'clock at night, I see her exhaustedly struggling to keep working at the sewing machine. And she gets up at six in the morning. I must have a heart of stone. I'm ruthless. I eat everything I can lay my hands on.

Today I had a fight with my father. I swore at him, even cursed him. It happened because yesterday I weighed twenty decagrams of zacierki and then sneaked a spoonful. When my father came back, he immediately noticed that some zacierki were missing. My father started yelling at me and he was right. But since the chairman [Mordechai Chaim Rumkowski, the head of the Jewish Council of Łódź] gave out these zacierki to be cooked, why can't I have some? I became very upset and cursed my father. What have I done? I regret it so much, but it can't be undone. My father is not going to forgive me. How will I ever look him in the eyes? He stood by the window and cried like a baby. Not even a stranger has ever insulted him before. The whole family witnessed this incident. I went to bed as soon as possible, without dinner. I thought I would die of hunger, because we have our meal only in the evening. I fell asleep and woke up at twelve. My mom was still working at the sewing machine. I couldn't stand the hunger, so I got up and took a piece of meal. We would be a happy family, if I didn't fight with everybody. All the fights are started by me. I must be manipulated by some evil force. I would like to be different, but I don't have a strong enough will. There is nobody I can talk to. Why isn't there anybody who would guide me, why can't anybody teach me? I hate my sister. She is a stranger to me. God, show me what is right. Today there was a ration of eight kilograms of briquettes for those who don't get provisions in the kitchen.

Thursday, March 12, 1942

It's cold outside. I stayed in bed until nine-thirty. Then I cleaned the house and unshuttered the windows. In the kitchen they are distributing the kitchen rations—the first one hundred numbers and the last one hundred numbers. It was eleven o'clock when I found out. My ration card has number 21 on it, and for the first hundred numbers one can pay (in advance) only until eleven o'clock. Like a shot I ran to the cooperative. I gave my cards to an acquaintance who was very close to the cashier's window. Later on, she left me her money to pay for her, because she had no time to wait to be called on. I paid fifteen reichmarks for us and nine reichmarks twenty pfennigs for her. My ration was to be picked up in the cooperative at one o'clock. I wasted five hours there. The crowd was unbelievable. I couldn't breathe and people were almost piled up on one another. There were lice everywhere. I stood under the wall, so they wouldn't get on to me. On my way home with the provisions, I saw a terrible scene. Two men were virtually dragging an old man who was unable to walk. People like that are deported. Human suffering is so great! When I got home, my dad and mom were waiting at the neighbor's because I had the key.

Friday, March 13, 1942

The sun is shining, but it is cold and the windowpanes are frozen. Today they are distributing the bread. My father told me to come to his workshop to get some soup. After all, a father is always a father. He now works at Młynarska 32, in the kitchen. He gets one soup from the division and one extra, which he gives to me. Would other fathers do the same? I was there at eleven-thirty. When I left my father, I went to get some bread. I didn't stand in line long. At four o'clock I went to the dairy at Brzezińska 24 to buy some butter. I received fifty decagrams on the meal coupon. On the way I stopped at the cooperative to register cards for coal. They told me to come back on Sunday. When my father came back from work, he lit the fire. Mom is cooking in the evening.

Saturday, March 14, 1942

Today my sister is not working. My mom, dad, and brother are working until 2 P.M. There is a ration for the workers:

1 kilogram of pickled beets
25 decagrams of sugar
20   "   of butter
10   "   of salt
2   "   of fruit
1 tablet of saccharine
1 piece of soap
1 box of matches.

My father got it right away. In the morning he gave me his soup from the division. When they came back from work, my mom cooked the beets brought by dad. She brought her ration of bread from the workshop to share with us. I don't know how she is managing. She works the hardest and eats the least. At twelve o'clock I went to R. Wajs, my former friend. What a disgusting home they have. I got all my worst habits from them. They are loathsome. The father and mother fight all the time. The mother is called "a lunatic," even in the presence of strangers. They treat her worse than a dog. She is sick in bed. Her face and legs are swollen, but they don't care. They live on the other side of the ghetto. One gets there through the gate or over two bridges. They live on Zgierska Street 74, right next to the barbed wire.

I walked home very slowly, keeping an eye on the trams dashing away toward freedom. O freedom! Will I have to stay behind this barbed wire forever? Will that sign be on that big board forever, "Wofugiebit Ver Juden betretten ferbotm" [Wohngebiet der Juden betreten verboten: Entering Jewish residential area forbidden]? Will there always be a booth with a German guard who has a rifle on his shoulder? Has it always been like this? Will it stay like this? Oh, no! But who is going to live through it? I miss freedom. Especially on a warm, sunny day. O sun! It's you who make me yearn for freedom. My heart is bleeding and my eyes are full of tears. Someone reading this in the future may sneer at me, may say I'm an idiot. But my hand is writing this involuntarily. I would like to stand there for days and feast my eyes on this sight. I came home at seven o'clock, had dinner and went to bed at nine.

Sunday, March 15, 1942

I can hardly get up. I have a terrible headache and I'm very cold. I didn't get warmer during the night. I got up at ten o'clock, put on some clothes, and went out to pay for the coal. On the way I dropped in to see Dad, but was told he had finished his work. There was a long line at the cashier's, but it was moving very fast. On the way back I dropped in again. My father was there. Perhaps they hadn't known before, because he works in a different place. He gave me some food. I ate it on the spot. I didn't get the coal, because they charged five reichmarks for a delivery. R. Wajs came to see me, but nobody was at home. I met her at the cashier's. Today Mom received her ration.

Monday, March 16, 1942

Bread for seven days! Horror!

When I went to the cooperative in the morning to get some bread, I was told it was for seven days. I shivered. I stood in line for a long time, getting cold, before they let us in. I received two loaves. There is nothing in the ghetto. One has to struggle for everything.

There is a problem with small change. Deported people took their change with them. In the cooperative they don't want to give change. People give fifty pfennigs instead of ten. Until now, they have exchanged ghetto rumkis [ghetto currency named for Rumkowski] for German marks, but nowadays people don't make any business with coins. I had to leave fifty pfennigs at the cashier's, because I didn't have any change. At three o'clock I went to get the coal, to Łagiewnicki Square 25.

At Bałucki Market German workers from the power plant were repairing the electricity and putting up a tent. A woman passed by near the tent. One of the workers pushed her to the ground and kicked her all over. People fled in fear. Nobody said a word. Hundreds of Jews may die for one word the Germans don't like. Our life is so tragic, so degraded. They treat us worse than pigs. We Jews from the ghetto work so hard, help them in the war. We make wonderful things out of rags, weave beautiful carpets, stitch military uniforms, everything they need. They treat us worse than slaves. Is this life? Isn't death better? I had to restrain myself in order not to shout some insults. You have to be quiet, although your heart is breaking.

At three-thirty I reached Węglowy Square. I had to pick up the briquettes with my hands. There was a long line waiting to use the scale and there was mud all around. A woman behind me had the same amount of briquettes (forty kilograms). I found a dry place and we both put the sacks on the ground. The woman stood there and watched them. At four-thirty I was in the street with the briquettes. It was very hard for me to carry forty kilograms from the square. I stood on the sidewalk and waited. At five-fifteen my dad came and took some briquettes. Then my brother came and we went home. On the way I met my cousin. She and her family are leaving [being deported] tomorrow. It was a beautiful day, and so warm. Before seven o'clock I hadn't eaten more than fifteen decagrams of bread. I had a fight with my father, so I didn't go to get the soup. At seven o'clock I had dinner and went to sleep.

Tuesday, March 17, 1942

There is a new ration for the workers:

½ kilogram of potatoes
1   ″   of pickled beets
½ ″   of sauerkraut
20 decagrams of peas
10   ″   of margarine

10	"	of coffee
30	"	of sugar
30	"	of meat
2	"	of paprika

At eleven-thirty I went to my father to get some soup, but it wasn't there yet, so I had to wait for one hour. There is mud everywhere. My shoes have fallen apart and my stockings are soaked. Two months ago my mom paid for new shoes in the division, but she hasn't got them yet. Today Dad paid for the rations. My mom had a terrible night, because beets disagree with her. But there isn't any other food here. We have finished the rations that were supposed to last until the first.

Wednesday, March 18, 1942

When I came back home I heard that there was a vegetable ration. I went to the co-operative, but it turned out to be a rumor. I received two loaves of bread. At four o'clock they were distributing the rations of two kilograms of rutabagas and one kilogram of carrots. It's not fair. A family of one person or more gets the same amount of rutabagas. Mine was quite nice. I took down the laundry because the neighbor needed the clotheslines. There is a lot of trading on our street. German Jews are selling everything to buy food. Sugar costs thirty-two reichmarks for one kilogram. Mrs. Berliner visited us in the evening. Before the war my father used to buy paint from her. She looks awful. She must have lost forty-two kilograms. They are deporting people all the time. Right now they are deporting families. Sixty husbands or children

9

Miriam Korber

TRANSNISTRIA

Miriam Korber (later Miriam Bercovici) was born to Leon and Klara Korber in 1923 in the small town of Câmpulung-Moldovenesc, in the southern part of the Romanian province of Bukovina. Her paternal grandparents, Abraham Mendel and Toni Korber, lived in the same town. Her grandfather and her father repaired windows and roofs for a living, and in 1927, Leon Korber opened a glass shop in Câmpulung. That same year, Miriam's younger sister Sylvia (called Sisi in the diary) was born.[1] Miriam's diary is unique among those in this collection, for although its content echoes other diaries written in ghettos and camps throughout Eastern Europe, it was written in Romania, where the Fascist regime of General Ion Antonescu carried out the genocide of its own Jewish population, creating a circumstance unparalleled in the history of World War II. Indeed, Romania was the only independent ally of Nazi Germany whose government initiated and undertook a program of large-scale massacre as a solution to the "Jewish problem," rounding up, deporting, and killing Jews under its own administration, and on its own territory.[2]

The roots of anti-Semitism in Romania run deep and reach back to a long history of hatred and persecution of the Jewish community there. During the late 1800s, by which time most European nations had already emancipated the Jews (France in 1789, England gradually between 1833 and 1871, and Germany in 1871), the Romanian state made it virtually impossible for Jews to gain citizenship, and on the occasions when it did yield it was only under pressure from the great powers. Emancipation was not granted to the Romanian Jews en masse until 1923, and even then it did not come as a natural outgrowth of modernization, but as an imposition forced on an unwilling Romanian government. Further, in a stance that was adopted yet again during the Holocaust, the attitude of the Romanians toward the Jews, and the occasional gracious gestures extended to them, were dictated largely by the opportunistic interests of the Romanian state rather than by any fundamental belief in the equality or civil rights of Jews.[3]

In the late 1930s, as Germany was aggressively implementing anti-Jewish legislation, a succession of Romanian leaders and viciously anti-Semitic political parties put in place their own legal, economic, and social restrictions on Jews, including the institution of a *numerus clausus,* or Jewish quota, in Romanian universities, civil service, and the professions, and the revocation of citizenship for 150,000 to 200,000 Jews. In August 1940, anti-Semitic legislation based on the Nazi Nuremberg Race Laws of 1935, which defined Jewishness according to "racial" criteria, was enacted in Romania. The following month, a coup d'état backed by Nazi Germany brought the Fascist leader Ion Antonescu and the Iron Guard party to power in Romania. When Romania officially joined the Axis powers in November 1940, Antonescu's government began implementing a still more systematic program of anti-Jewish legislation.[4]

It was as a consequence of these laws that Miriam Korber was forced out of high school in Botoşani, Moldova, where she had been sent as a teenager to study and live with her maternal grandparents. She returned to her hometown of Câmpulung, finding herself faced with an ever increasing battery of restrictions. She recalled that 1940–41 was a "year of humiliation," with the imposition of special identity cards for Jews, restrictions on travel by train, the seizing of hostages, and the expulsion of Jews from the villages. This year of terrors culminated with a search of all Jewish homes in September 1941 (on Yom Kippur, the Day of Atonement in the Jewish calendar), in which, Miriam recalls, members of the army, police, and even former colleagues and friends participated.[5]

The German invasion of the Soviet Union in June 1941 provided a much anticipated opportunity for the Romanians to join their German allies in the fight against Soviet Russia. This was linked (most important for the fate of the Jews in Romania) to the desire for land gains, in particular the territories of Bessarabia and Bukovina, which together with northern Transylvania had been granted to Romania at the end of World War I, then lost during the summer of 1940. Romania regained Bessarabia and Bukovina in July 1941. Against the backdrop of the war and Germany's aggressive anti-Jewish policies, Antonescu saw the perfect opportunity to rid Romania once and for all of the Jews from these provinces. Thus, he adopted as one of his top priorities the removal of these Jews through mass executions and deportations.[6]

Beginning in October 1941, the Jews from Bessarabia and Bukovina were deported to a part of western Ukraine, specifically the area between the Dniester and the Bug rivers, which at the end of August 1941 was named Transnistria and transferred to Romanian administration. Although the Romanian military authorities killed the Jews in massive numbers during the deportations (as they did in the Ukrainian areas of Odessa and Golta), Transnistria was, in general, an ethnic dumping ground where the Jews were left to die in unsealed ghettos, exposed to almost inconceivable misery in the form of hunger, cold, illness, filth, death, humiliation, and despair.[7]

Miriam and her family left Câmpulung on October 12, 1941, and arrived in Djurin, Transnistria, on November 4. Her diary, begun in her eighteenth year, and written entirely in Romanian, opens one month later. The first entries provide a long account of the family's journey from Câmpulung to Transnistria, capturing the chaos of moving and the long and painful journey from home to a strange new place. From Câmpulung, they traveled to Atachi, the crossing point over the Dniester River from Romania to Transnistria. They spent a few miserable days there before crossing the river to arrive in Mogilev-Podolski, Transnistria. "You can tell the degree of civilization by the status of the toilets," Miriam wrote dryly. From there, after placing Miriam's paternal grandparents in an improvised asylum for elderly people, they were taken via truck by German soldiers (in exchange for money) to the ghetto of Djurin. The first several days in Djurin were spent sharing a single room with thirteen people, some of whom the Korbers knew from Câmpulung. Finally, Miriam's mother found a room, but "Oh, what a room!" Miriam wrote. "We had to climb a hillside drowned in mud and climb into the room, like in a chicken coop. . . . Endless mud, in the road, in the house."

By December 13, 1941, about two months after having arrived in Transnistria, Miriam's description of the family's deportation had been completed and her diary had been brought up to date. Her daily diary entries begin at this time. While it is an account of her own life, with all its particularities, the diary also reflects the broader experience of exile shared by the Romanian Jews in Transnistria. Her diary is filled with reports of the physical hardships that plagued the exiles. There was virtually no relief from the harsh winter, made worse by the lack of decent shelter. Time and again, she returned to the subject of the cold: the ice freezing on the walls, the amount of time spent in bed (going to sleep early and getting up late) to try to stay warm, the long wait until evening when the family could light a fire, and the problem of obtaining adequate firewood. Health and nutrition were likewise an ongoing source of anxiety and obsession in the diary. In June 1942, Miriam's father became ill with typhus (an epidemic that killed tens of thousands of Jews in Transnistria), and Sisi, whom Miriam characterized as "the strong" one, suffered a fainting spell. Miriam noted several of her own bouts with illness, in August and September of 1942 and again in March 1943. Even the Korbers' relatively adequate food supply (obtained by the ongoing sale of personal possessions) did not halt the weakening of the family members, who became increasingly frail as the months and years went by.

Miriam, like diarists in other ghettos across Eastern Europe, described the rationing of food, the endless worries about the high prices of provisions, and the alarming rate at which money disappeared. The general injustice of the Korbers' situation in Transnistria was exacerbated by frequent exploitation, such as unfair "business" dealings, in which local Ukrainians charged high prices for such necessities as food and medicine or simply took advantage of them whenever the opportunity arose. The Korbers' own "landlady" tried whenever she could to squeeze still more from their limited resources. At the same time, Miriam's accounts of her family's suffering were tempered time and again by her acknowledgment of those worse off than she. She seemed to be painfully aware of their "good fortune" in comparison with the thousands of utterly desperate people around them. Still, her diary captures her own lingering sense of impermanence; even having enough food in the present did not ensure that they would be secure in the future. "When I see a beggar I become all afraid," she wrote; "it is as if I see myself, one year from now, or two."

Miriam's diary reflects the inevitable tension among family members, in particular the nervous anxiety of her father, which affected the entire household. This theme, so prevalent throughout diaries of this period, recurred in Miriam's diary as the family's situation grew increasingly desperate. Miriam candidly acknowledged in the diary that she, too, was subject to fits of anxiety and nervousness that had repercussions for her family. Of her own moods, she wrote: "I am so tense, I feel that I will crack up. And because of my nerves, I am mean to everyone. Because of my resentment and my nerves I really snap."

The diary is laced with occasional reflections on still deeper questions about life and the impulse to survive. In these entries, many of which echo those of other writers, Miriam reflected on the inexplicable desire to live, despite the misery and hopelessness of their circumstances. Similarly, she was among many writers who suffered from the paralysis of her life in the ghetto, describing the apathy brought on by imprisonment. Finally, like virtually all writers, her entries about daily life are punctuated by reflections on the future and the hope for deliverance. She wrote, "Salvation is getting close, deliverance is getting close, then they get farther away; everything is a mirage of what we want, and, like every mirage, it gets farther and farther away as time goes by."

Miriam's diary proves to be no exception to another rule of writings from this period—all share the inevitably recurrent themes of death and loss. For Miriam, personal grief came in February 1942, when she learned of the death of her grandparents, who had remained in Mogilev. As in another part of the diary, when she reported on the death of an acquaintance from Câmpulung, she reflected not only on the fact of death and loss, but on the particularly lonely and forlorn nature of death in exile. From time to time, Miriam observed and recorded in her diary the degradation of normal rituals of burial and mourning, which was yet another aspect of death in exile. In one particularly poignant entry, she remarked on the burial of the deceased in mass graves and the theft of the sheets in which they were wrapped, capturing the utter desperation of the living, which superseded even the traditional respect accorded the dead. At one point, Miriam railed against the very character of mass death, which reduced the particularities of individual lives to a blur of anonymity: "So many people have died, so many. . . . I will draw up a list of people I remember who I now heard have died. I don't think I will be able to include them all but at least I will write some of the names at the end of this so-called diary."

Toward the end of the diary, in September 1943, there is an entry that touches on a key aspect of the Romanian Holocaust. Miriam wrote of rumors that the Romanians were planning to allow some of the Jews deported across the

Dniester to return to their homes. The rumors about repatriation were not merely the wishful hopes of a desperate population; in fact, the Romanian authorities did begin, at the end of 1943, to allow some repatriation, beginning with the Jews from the region of Dorohoi (southern Bukovina) and Jewish orphans. For just as the Romanians had granted the Jews citizenship only when it met their needs (to be recognized by the great powers in 1923), so too did they cease killing when killing no longer suited their purposes. This moment came after the Battle of Stalingrad, when the tide of the war shifted, and it became increasingly clear that the Allies were gaining on victory. This reversal of fortune left the Romanian authorities with the uncomfortable prospect of being held accountable for their crimes and gave rise to a dramatic shift in their anti-Jewish policy. Self-interest once again triumphed over ideology, and the same Romanian administration that had committed itself to the elimination of the Jews turned its attention to their repatriation. Those Jews who held on until 1944 were the lucky ones; some were repatriated and others were able to survive until the liberation.[8]

Miriam's diary breaks off in October 1943. She remembers that her father was caught in a roundup and sent away to a destination unknown by the family at the time; in fact, he was sent to a forced labor camp. According to the author, she didn't have the strength to continue writing after this devastating event. A year and a half later, the Russian army liberated Djurin. Miriam returned to Romania with nine other young people, all of whom walked behind the Red Army troops as they marched through the Ukraine and into Romania. After two weeks of walking, she arrived home in Botoşani, Romania, on May 2, 1944. Of herself at that time, she wrote, "Nobody recognized in the shoeless beggar, in rags, bloated by hunger, burned by the sun and wind of the road, the well groomed and elegant student of four years before."[9] She found her father in Botoşani; he had survived the year-and-a-half ordeal of life in a labor camp and had also returned to Romania. Miriam's mother and sister Sisi also survived the Holocaust.

Miriam's diary was hidden from her for a long time, first by her mother and then by her husband, who feared the emotional repercussions of her reading the diary and remembering the horrors of life in Transnistria. After the war, she went on to become a doctor (as she had dreamed of doing since her childhood before the war), and in the 1990s she published the diary in Germany and Romania. The original remains with her to this day. Though Miriam and her immediate family survived (as did her maternal grandparents, who remained in Botoşani through-out the war), her extended family was decimated by the war. Her cousin's husband and his brother were murdered by Soviet authorities, during the 1940–41 Soviet occupation of northern Bukovina, for being Zionists. Her paternal grandparents died in Mogilev in Transnistria. An aunt, uncle, and their three children from northern Transylvania were deported by the Hungarians and the Germans to Auschwitz, where they were murdered. Another aunt, her daughter, and her granddaughter were killed under Romanian authority in a stone quarry on the Bug River. These members of Miriam's family were among the 400,000 Romanian Jews who perished at the hands of the Germans, the Soviets, the Hungarians, and the Romanians themselves during World War II.

Tuesday, November 4, 1941 [Djurin, Transnistria]

Who could have ever imagined that I would start this notebook, meant to be a po-etry album, under these circumstances. When Bondy [a friend of Miriam's] pre-sented it to me as a gift, times were different, but now?!!! Four weeks ago this Thursday, at nine-thirty in the evening, Dad came home with the terrible news of the evacuation. But nothing was for certain. On Friday people heard that we would be evacuated on Sunday. And so, the fever of evacuation set in. Crying, gloom, packing, boiling, everything in great disarray. We did not realize what the future had in store for us. On Saturday, the shops were closed and so people started to sell their things clandestinely and give them away. Just like scavengers, peasants, city dwellers, neighbors, and strangers pounced upon us and in one morning we emp-tied the house of the most beautiful things.

At three in the afternoon rumors spread that everything was postponed for six months. Uncertainty; anxiety; are we leaving or not? Mother and Father were feel-ing sorry for the things we sold and gave away; even I was seized with grief. But in our hearts we wavered; we were not certain of the rumor. We had finished packing but we packed as if we were going on a trip. We could not imagine that they could have uprooted us entirely from our homes. In the evening we went to bed and un-til tonight this would be the last time we went to sleep in a bed.

On Sunday, at six in the morning, we found out that we were leaving. We started to realize the atrocity that had been inflicted upon us. But we could not even begin to imagine what we would live through; who could have such a dark imagination? At eleven in the morning, the wagons started to roll toward the train station located at the edge of the village. It was the first sight of our exile. The long road was muddy, strewn with wagons filled with bags, bundles, children, and old people. Gypsies live better than that. They have wagons; we don't even have that. We leave Câmpulung behind and arrive at the train station. Here the scene is even more awful. Weeping, grief, bags, screams; we are loaded into cars that are actually used to transport horses. The cars had been cleaned of the hay and so we get in, thirty-eight people in a car, of whom four are over eighty years old and one is a paralyzed child. We were afraid that they would seal the cars. At the station bread was distributed to the people. From what we had thought and heard, we were going to a town somewhere in Bessarabia, Atachi; they said that we would resettle there and would be able to earn a living. We left at eight in the evening with the second transport. We spent the first night as if we were going on a trip. We were not aware of how dismal our situation was; we just sat on the luggage. On Monday, on the train, we ate old meat, drank dirty water, but still had a laugh and argued with the elderly. We were building castles in [the air], had hopes that we would be fed from the communal kettle, that we would work, that we would learn how to farm. We passed through Cernăuți and entered the steppe. How vast is the steppe, how boundless the sky in the steppe!

In the middle of the wailings, I managed to see a magnificent sunset. On Tuesday morning we arrived in Atachi. Until six in the evening we remained outside, and then, "go away, Jew," by wagon, [we] arrived in the city. Along the road we saw thousands of people. By the hundreds in each house, but what houses! They were all wrecked, without a roof, the homes of the Jews who had been killed; we saw on each wall, written with charcoal, the names of those who had been murdered. We were put about thirty in a room, together with the pharmacist Garai. It was the most awful night so far.

Friday, November 7, 1941

Only today do I start again to describe (better yet, to sketch) the horrible things that we lived through and who knows whether or not other, even more terrible things are not still ahead of us. During the first night in Atachi I saw what human misery really means. I saw people without a human face, I saw children with swollen eyes, frozen feet, helpless little hands; mothers with dead children in their arms, old people and young ones wrapped in rags—they were Jews from the Edineți camp. Chased away, infested with typhus, covered with lice, almost starved to death, they poured into Atachi, without the right to stop here. One family (the husband a lawyer, the wife a pharmacist) with two children and an old mother (what's left of a mummy) burst into our so-called home and after a real scuffle, since we were not allowed to receive them, we let them stay till the morning.

Miriam Korber

{ 250 }

That night I also saw how a person can go mad [. . .] . During that night the pharmacist Garai went mad. At five in the morning we left the house and in the afternoon we moved to Mrs. Hausvater's place on the hill, after we had moved before to a former synagogue that rumbled with people and lice. In Atachi we spent the days preparing meals. The outdoor cooking range made of stone was interesting. For firewood they used pieces torn from an old roof. The room had no windows or doors. But it was all right, at least when we did not think about it too much. At the Dniester River we washed in the cold and dirty water. For a bucket of clean water we paid twenty *lei* [Romanian currency], and for a chicken, Mother traded a ring with a stone.[10] This is because people throw their jewelry in toilets, or wherever they can, for fear of house searches.

The weather is good, the only good fortune for those who followed us, since they have to live out in the open air. We temporarily parted ways with Bondy in Atachi; he remained in the old house. Garai calmed down, after two other attacks of madness. Poor man, he just could not get used to the idea that he would no longer have a house, be a pharmacist, and that he, who had always been such a good citizen, would be pushed out in the mud with all the other Jews. In Atachi we started to ration the food: potato soup, potatoes, cornmeal, tea. In Atachi I saw that hunger knows no shame. Mr. Frigus Brecher, Mr. Kern, and others were not too ashamed to ask for a cup of tea or a slice of bread. We remained in Atachi until Sunday. We survived the inspection. The weather was miserable. It was raining and we were up to our ankles in mud. We arrived by wagon at the embarkation point on the Dniester. Mother and our grandparents went first, then Sisi and I, Father with the luggage, and pharmacist Horovitz last. And so we crossed the Dniester by boat [. . .] [and] we arrived in Mogilev.

Saturday, November 8, 1941

In Mogilev I saw that we were no longer in Romania. Everyone spoke Ukrainian and among the Romanian soldiers you could see strayed Ukrainian ones. As soon as we arrived some people were evacuated. There are camps in which people are gathered by the hundreds and from there they are driven away on foot. Therefore, we had to avoid the camps. We carried the baggage from the Dniester to a courtyard by ourselves, with much effort, and here we shivered for two hours until we found shelter. Thirty people, we stayed in one rather large room upstairs. With us were the Hausvaters, Horovitzes, Hellers, Segals, the Javetz and Tartar families. Quite an interesting gathering! We carried the luggage upstairs by ourselves and, exhausted, we slept our first night in Mogilev. [. . .] The very next day after our arrival here, we started to sell off things. We sold the brown shoes; we sold dear things: purses, blouses, sweaters, everything for a mere pittance. With each thing we sold, we gave away a piece of ourselves. Who knows when we will replace what we were losing now. Our room was not occupied but we still had many landlords. We were everyone's tenants. [. . .] Down the hall lived a Jewish woman married to a Russian. She was the only Jew we met in Mogilev who did not try to take advantage of us. She let us use her range for boiling without asking for anything in return, a rare gesture for others. [. . .] We placed our grandparents in an asylum, one that we, the evacuees, had set up for those who were truly too helpless to go on. How hard it was for them, poor people, to part from us. In the beginning it was a real madhouse there! They did not even get a cup of tea. Later on things straightened up a little bit. The saddest thing that happened to us was that, for us, death had lost its mystery. I saw dead people and did not even blink; the dead I saw in the asylum no longer made any special impression on me. Many died only because there was nobody there to give them a cup of tea. We brought food to the old people three times a day. [. . .]

Moreover, not only had civilization not progressed in the Ukraine in the past twenty years, it had gone backward by one hundred years. You can tell the degree of civilization by the status of the toilets. Well, until the present day I still have not found a decent toilet in the Ukraine. People relieve themselves wherever they can. Filth everywhere. From Mogilev I wrote two registered postcards to Botoşani and Bucharest. Perhaps they are the last sign of life I sent to the relatives. How I miss Botoşani! Will I ever see it again? Nights are terrible in Mogilev. We live close to the Dniester and every day people cross the river. But they do not cross it as we did; they are beaten up, chased away, robbed. They must cross it at night. Awful screams, mothers crying, children lost from their families; the chorus of lamentations deepened our despair. The occasional shootings by the soldiers heightened the sense of panic. Nights, like days, were spent in fear and anxiety that soldiers would come and take us away to camp. [. . .] Our departure from Mogilev was decided fast. Bondy managed to get in touch with some Germans who, in exchange for money, would drive trucks with Jews toward the interior. That is how we also left Mogilev. [. . .]

Sunday, November 9, 1941

On a rainy morning, a Saturday, we arrived in Djurin. The Germans dropped us off at a crossroad far from the village. The Ukrainians came to see us, as if they saw a miracle. The village seemed beautiful enough but the mud foreboded some gruesome things. Our first lodging was at a teacher's house; a nice woman, but she also tried to take advantage of us. We stayed there from Saturday to Wednesday, thirteen people in one room. We slept on the floor all the time and it was rather hard but still pleasant, because we were together with the Horovitzes and the Hausvaters.

Seeing that the teacher was not trying to help but only to take advantage of us, and since we had no bed to sleep in or chair to sit on at the table, Mother started to look for a room elsewhere. The first thing we did was to wash really well. I never imagined that I could feel such a delight just by washing. The problems with food started again, how to ration it so we would not starve to death in a few months. I did not go out of the house the first few days. Ceaseless rain and mud and, here as well, the problem of the toilet. On Wednesday Mother found a room. Oh, what a room! We had to climb a hillside drowned in mud and climb into the room, like in a chicken coop. Everyone else had to pass through our room. Endless mud, in the road, in the house.

We live in a room next to the Apels; in another room there is a Russian woman. Her name is Kufsinier, Jewish, a very interesting person, she could be an actress at a Jewish theater. Poor woman, she has two young children, her husband is in the army and she lost everything. And still, she hopes. I don't know, should we also have any hope? And so, days go by. [. . .]

Saturday, December 13, 1941

Yes, two months have passed since we left home. I have no words to describe everything that we had to go through until today. Days go by, each identical to the others. The daily schedule could be: get up at eight-thirty, Father first, then Mother, me, then Sisi. The days are cold, and getting up is a problem. To get out of the warm bed in a room cold as ice was impossible, but we had to get up. Sometimes before eight-thirty Oleana (Mrs. Kufsinier's maid) would go out five times, to take out the chamber pot or to fetch firewood. Well, this could be pleasant, actually. Until not long ago we had a gas lamp and would cook breakfast on it, so we did not get very warm; now we start a fire in the morning since we have firewood; well, we bought about fourteen hundred pounds for five hundred rubles, about twenty thousand lei worth, if we count the ruble at forty lei. How much lower can we get!

Right away we start to clean: we wash, make the beds, sweep. Then we start preparing the meals: we peel potatoes, onions, garlic, carrots. A rich meal: a soup with hominy, potatoes, and carrots, or a first course (onions in oil) or plums for dessert. Well, we were content with the meals. Around one o'clock the food was ready and we would usually eat the meal hot, still boiling, after which we did the dishes and again we would peel potatoes for the evening meal, since the *supe* [soups] also consist of potatoes, gruel or corn bread, hominy, et cetera.

Miriam Korber

In the afternoons, we pass the time by mending socks, I embroider, Mother is out shopping or crying, Dad deep in his moods, Sisi deep in her thoughts. Poor child, just like me, she has no girlfriend with whom to exchange a word. We eat again around seven or eight, then we spend the evening with Mr. Kive (Constantin Traktirsik), a local Jew. He is a thirty-eight-year-old man, well-built, nice, rather educated for Djurin; but rather than arriving late, he makes it a habit to extend his visits till after midnight, so I am waiting impatiently for him to leave because I am sleepy. Now it is all right, but when it was colder our room would get colder than a cellar and even in bed it was impossible to warm up. And night would fall again. We would turn off the lamp—a stable lantern with the glass broken that Dad fixed with the glass from a half-liter bottle. Still, people envy us, because they have even less than we do. The night: cold, fear, sleeplessness, thoughts, regrets, yearnings. Yes, I forgot our program before bedtime: we divide a piece of chocolate in four and we sweeten our lives. Yes, that is how days go by. Why should I write what happens every day? Days are all the same, and I am happy when evening comes and I can go to bed. At least I sleep and, for a few hours, I can forget everything.

Tuesday, December 16, 1941

[. . .] This morning I was very nervous and I almost had an argument with my parents. No wonder we quarrel, each of us is distraught and nervous. Oh, what a life! Today we baked some corn bread; everything is rationed because it must last for dinner and for tomorrow morning. [. . .] Who would have ever believed that I would ever be so disappointed with Communism and the Soviet Union. Even the locals are convinced that Communism will no longer exist, because they also realize that this regime and the way it was inculcated cannot last. No employee, from the lowest to the highest rank, would shy away from stealing from the state; money was not important, but it was easy to steal since the authorities would close an eye, they would steal as well, and how! There are some Ukrainians who, to this day, hope for a possible turn of events; they all wait for a renewal of the regime through an alliance with democratic forces. I no longer have news from the front for more than four weeks now. No newspapers.

Friday, December 26, 1941

[. . .] Will we be able to survive these times? Everyone asks himself this question, including me. Will we have the strength to get over this hardship? We manage to eat somehow, and still, everyone looks bad. Last night the north wind started to blow. A true Ukrainian north wind, the wind of the steppe; it blows into our room. It roars in squalls and we feel the gusts of wind here on the hill so much that you think that the house is being lifted up in the air. And it gets ever colder. And still, supposedly it can get even colder here. It is said that the blizzard can block the roads and the water can freeze at the pump. This morning I went for water with Sisi. I came back crying. The bitter cold had numbed my right hand, I could feel a tightness around my heart, and I almost fell down three times on the way. And in such weather Bondy went again to Morava. Poor guy, just to make a few rubles. What times we live in! Dad is nervous, Mom is nervous, we don't make any money and the money we have is just disappearing; we do have something to eat, we are used to eating better than others perhaps. Dad cannot get used to the "laziness" of doing nothing all day so he consumes his energy by quarreling with us. We are on each other's nerves only because there is nothing to keep us busy. It is two in the afternoon. It is cold in the room and I don't know how we will resist till evening without a fire. Firewood is so expensive. I can see on everyone's face the fear of tomorrow. What will happen? How will we live when we run out of money? There are good rumors from the battlefront. Perhaps salvation is closing in.

Thursday, January 1, 1942

Today is the start of a new year! Last night, for the New Year, we went to bed at seven-thirty so it wouldn't get too cold in the room, since it is awfully cold. If it goes on like this, I don't know how we will survive winter because in the past few days I could not warm up my feet anymore. Water is trickling down the walls; the shutters and the windows are covered with a couple of inches of ice. Indeed, a new year has begun. In other years, how good it was to be at home, let alone the fun! How I would love to finally warm up again, just like at home. [. . .] Today is the first day that I got up at nine-thirty because of the cold. What a night, God only knows. It was so cold in the house that I just could not take my nose out from under the covers. And today, January 1, in this cold and damp room, I sit and think of where I could go to warm up a little bit. At home the cold weather was not a problem. It was a pleasure to walk in the cold because, when I came home, a hot fireplace and a warm room would welcome me back. Here, dressed in so many layers, like Baba Dochia from the old legends, I constantly blow into my hands and I don't even want to go out to the front door. And now we are hit with another piece of "good fortune": our landlady, who seemed to be a decent person until last week, showed her claws. We agreed to pay her fifty rubles a month. Now she no longer wants money but asks for half a *pud* of flour [about eighteen pounds], and God only knows that we cannot give it to her, since we try to save each morsel of bread and each spoonful of soup. If we could only live to tell these things someday. Every day, Mrs. Fucsmann comes by and makes a big noise about how we wreck her house, that we don't make enough heat and that is why it is damp, that we don't pay her. And you must keep quiet, although your heart bursts with rage. And the nice Mrs. Kufsinier always tries to pick holes in our coats and tells the landlady everything. Well, what shape we are in, to be ordered around and led by the nose by some hysterical women who only talk about men.

Saturday, January 3, 1942

Thirty-eight degrees below zero [Celsius]. It is impossible to go outside, and inside the house it is so cold that we have our coats on. Last night we wore our coats even when we served the soup. It was so freezing cold that we could not see anything on account of the steam. It would not be so bad if Father were not so nervous. He is so agitated that I fear a disaster. Poor Mother, a martyr. She spoils him like a baby and, patient like an angel, she withstands all his outbursts. He gets overexcited at every small trifle, and not only worries all by himself but kills us as well. Therefore, we must weigh and consider each word we say. If he only calmed down a little it would be a great joy. We made peace with the landlady as well. We pay her a hundred twenty rubles a month. Indeed, money is king everywhere.

If we could only forget all these things! It is so hard when you remember the times when the house was warm and you were not hungry. Not only am I hungry but I want to eat something good. I would like to eat some pastries, something fatty. If we had some fatty foods, or at least some butter, it would be easier; like this, with no butter, with nothing nutritious, we eat only potatoes, beans, cornmeal. We fill up, but we long for some decent meals. [. . .]

Sunday, January 11, 1942

So much has happened since I last wrote about all that happened in exile. On Wednesday morning, rather at quarter to four in the morning, we had a "nice" adventure. Just as we were in the deepest sleep and dreaming about some beautiful thing, we woke up suddenly. In the beginning we thought it was an earthquake; then, when we lit the candle, we saw that a piece of the ceiling had fallen right on top of us and on Mother's bed. It was terribly cold and we moved our bed next to hers. We were lucky; we could have gotten killed or, at least, had an eye torn away. We escaped with only a big scare, and the resentment that we live in such a "beautiful" house. In the morning we cleaned out the clay that fell down on the bed and the floor. When we told the landlady that the ceiling needs to be fixed, she answered that that was our responsibility, that the house was damp and that everything that happened here was our responsibility. We were mad but could do nothing about it. [. . .]

Monday, January 12, 1942

[. . .] In Şargorod [a nearby ghetto in Transnistria] I saw so much misery, I can't believe that it could be any worse. First of all, I was impressed by the sad fate of Medy. Our poor friend! On Friday morning her grandmother and grandfather died (Thursday, after we arrived, we went to visit her and I was amazed and frightened by the shack in which she lived, among the Ukrainians and the inhabitants of Edineţi). The same day, such a tragedy! And now she is all alone, and neither I nor Margit are able to help her, to take her with us. We live like animals. We stare at someone's misfortune, yet we cannot help. Poor Medy, she is full of lice. Her uncle has died of starvation and filth since, until his death, he slept in Şargorod on three chairs. Medy is totally unkempt. It is all so strange for us. How she used to look at home, and how we saw her here! She had on a spring coat because she had covered her dead grandmother with her winter coat, instead of a blanket or a sheet. People say that her uncle was covered with lice before he died. In Şargorod there is a typhus epidemic, brought in by those from Dorohoi since only the poor people from Dorohoi were evacuated and then chased from one camp to another. And so they lost their clothes and their health and arrived in Şargorod sick and dirty, bringing with them the typhus epidemic. There are two types of typhus: the typhus caused by dirty conditions (lice) and the typhus caused by hunger, and most often the latter prevails here. Dozens die here every day, and I was told that recently forty people died in one day and they were all buried in a common ditch. Common graves are quite customary: fifteen to twenty people in one grave, not even buried in coffins or wooden boxes; it is said that the dead are wrapped in sheets but it is believed that even the sheets are stolen. [. . .]

Wednesday, January 21, 1942

A year has passed since the [Iron Guard] rebellion. It was bad then as well; we believed that it could not get any worse, but today I realize that it would have been better if they had killed us all then, in our home, rather then sending us away to this wasteland to die of cold and hunger, since this is the goal of the people who sent us here. It would have been more humane. But it looks like we are doomed to writhe in pain, and not just for a minute as by a firing squad but for months and years, God only knows for how long! Days and nights go by quickly, nights last fourteen hours and that is how long we stay in bed. If the bitter cold would only go away! It is awfully cold, we are frozen to the marrow, and the wind of the steppe bites with a fury unknown to us who lived in the mountains. And incessantly, the same concern: what will we eat today?! what will we eat tomorrow? [. . .]

Miriam Korber

Monday, January 26, 1942

It takes a lot of imagination to describe a day like today, it surpasses any fancy of the human mind. Only in the movies could there be such a day and even there it pales against reality. I am not referring to the usual cold, since for a week the temperatures have dropped to thirty or thirty-five degrees below zero [Celsius]. But last night the wind started to blow even stronger. This morning I went out of the house for the first time to relieve myself at the open pit and I could no longer see the road back home. Wind and snow; snow drifts; a blizzard that reminds me of the movie "The Hurricane." Ukraine—this word holds a new meaning for me today. It encompasses the cold, the raw wind, the starvation, and all the filth in which we live and drown. But today topped everything else. You can see a girl here who never carried water at home for sure; she goes up the hill with two full buckets and the wind will not let her breathe; or a boy and his old father carrying a piece of wood on their backs; someone else carrying a branch of a tree or a sack of potatoes on his back; everyone wants to live and the wind, as strong as it may be, cannot stifle man's will to live. And I wonder in all honesty, why do we still want to live? Only hope keeps us alive. I would have never imagined that in such cold it is possible to live in an unheated room with the ceiling half gone. And still, we live and wait. Poor Dad, he felt ill last night. [. . .]

Wednesday, January 28, 1942

Wind, snow, snowstorm, cold. Since the day before yesterday the wind has not stopped for a moment and we are snowed in. It is almost impossible to go outside. This morning I went to fetch water. I don't think there is a need to have a hell for sinners; everyone who lives through what we have to endure is absolved of all sins. There is no path, you must make your own way alone, and with my feet in the water I used a little pan to fill up the bucket. And so I reached the top of the hill with the full buckets. But once home I broke down and cried. Because of the cold and the fear; the cold bit my fingers and I could no longer move them. Why should I complain? I should keep quiet; there are others who have no clothes and they must go out in this cold. Why is there in us such a yearning for life? Why don't we cut short our torment? Is there cowardice or greatness in this ability and will to survive the hardship? And will we survive in the end? Perhaps all of these things will turn us into real human beings and in other times we will know how to appreciate the good in life.

My thoughts do not follow a normal path: they jump from one thing to another and I cannot stop them, because there are so many things I think about. People die by the hundreds, the best of them die. Mr. Wassermann passed away.

Miriam Korber

I remember him, with the cane in his hand, the straw hat on, a serene look in his eyes. I would greet him, *"shalom,"* and his calm reply would bring me a greeting from other countries; he was a Zionist and his belief in Palestine was so strong that Providence should have at least brought him to die in the country for which he longed and died in the end. And now he died in Mogilev, far away from his dead, far away from those still alive, for whom he would have sacrificed his life to his last breath. The president of the Israelite Community from Gura Humorului died; he died of typhoid fever in Mogilev. There is a terrible epidemic in Mogilev. What will happen here this summer? There is garbage everywhere hidden under the snow, and when it melts we will be swimming in filth. The main thing is to keep clean. I believe that if I read the lines I wrote again, I will laugh and tear them up since, besides the trifles I jot down, nothing has any connection to anything else. The only woman with whom we can still exchange a word here is Mrs. Kufsinier. I feel terribly sorry for her. She has no food, she has nothing to give to her children, and still she has hope; she hopes that her husband will return from the battlefield. She prays for cold weather and snow, which may stop the battle and the German advance. Perhaps nature will helps us now; it is our last chance.

Thursday, January 29, 1942

I will never forget last evening. Everything was all right, Dad was in a relatively good mood. Sisi and I went to bed. Dad went out once more and when he came back in the house, by mistake he put out the lamp of the Horovitzes (who live in the hallway), as often happens because of the draft. And for such a mere trifle as a match, Dad, nervous to the brink, started to quarrel in a loud voice until Mother barely managed to calm him down. All night long he sighed and felt sorry for this ridiculous squabble; he regretted it and realized what an unpleasant situation he had placed us in. I don't know what to do, to make excuses for him to the Horovitzes? He has an excuse, poor man. He is so nervous that I believe it makes him ill. He worked his entire life and now he sees that all that is left of it is a bundle with a few rags; even a gypsy has more. I feel compassion for Dad, but I really pity Mother. She must bear each face Dad makes, each word, each movement at night, his moods, and with the patience of an angel she bears it all and finds an excuse for them. I am ashamed for what happened and it is difficult for me. Tears are too few and too cheap to express my pain. At home Father was a man of such integrity, but here we must behave toward him as if he were ill, and he is actually very ill; if we are not saved, I don't know if we will find a cure. [. . .]

Miriam Korber

Tuesday, February 10, 1942

February is here already. The weather is better and in the last few days we no longer suffer from the cold. That, at least, is what nature has to offer to us for a while. But our troubles are not eased by the changes in the weather. Every day there are new problems, every day we hear other news that tests our nerves to the limit. Salvation is getting close, deliverance is getting close, then they get farther away; everything is a mirage of what we want, and, like every mirage, it gets farther and farther away as time goes by. The Fata Morgana of our present life: *our home.*

Every time there is talk that we will be pardoned (for what offense we don't know; for the simple reason that we are Jews), everything ends up in smoke and regrets. I did not think of Romania, or rather, of Câmpulung, as my homeland. That was because we were always oppressed and pushed to the side by the Romanians. But today, when we are far away, when hundreds of miles separate us from our small Câmpulung, I feel how much I miss and how close I feel to my homeland. *Heimat,* how much does this word say? Our mountains, our dear mountains, where are you now? Why do you pursue me even in my sleep? Fir trees, dark forests, clean houses, handsome people; homeland, I miss you. Why are we so miserable that we don't have a country that loves us as well! Our country has driven us away to a wasteland among strangers and among the words of persecution; some follow me endlessly: "go away, wandering Jew." [. . .]

Monday, February 16, 1942

Our grandparents died. They reached the end of their lives one after the other in Mogilev, Grandfather on January 3, Grandmother four weeks later. We received the sad news on Saturday. Mother was first to read the letter and from her expression I knew everything also. Poor Dad, he withstood much better than I thought the hard blow of fate. He wept silently and he carries the mourning in his heart silently. He, the only son, does his duty by saying Kaddish [the Jewish prayer for the dead] every day. Tears came to my eyes as well, and my heart was heavy when I thought about their sad death. I am not crying because they died, death is everyone's fate and they lived their lives fully; they were over eighty years old. I am crying for them because they died in Mogilev, far away from their home, from their clean bed, from the fruits of their long labor of many dozen years, far from everything they left behind at the mercy of fate. They passed away quietly, just as they lived, peaceful people who worked hard all their lives and raised their children by the sweat of their labor and made them into decent human beings. And now they died in an asylum, among strangers, far from the children for whom they worked so hard; only one daughter was with them, Aunt Roza; they died unknown to any-

one. Grandfather passed away on January 3, just when, I believe, I went to Şargorod, where I had told everyone who asked me about them that they were well.
And now they died.

I dream about them every night, and Dad, especially Dad, dreams about
them all the time. He even wanted to go to Mogilev, he had a feeling that he
would never see them again and that is exactly what happened. Childhood
memories pass in front of my eyes, cherished memories, tormenting in their
beauty. In these memories, Grandfather and Grandmother hold a prominent
place because I spent the most pleasant hours, from an early age on, in their
home, with them. Dear old people: Grandfather was always busy, at the store or
in the workroom, but always had a smile and a kind word for his "Mimica," the
redheaded and freckled granddaughter who meddled in his things and got in
his way. Grandmother, a skillful cook, a master with fried potatoes and *kihalac*,
with or without poppy; Grandmother, who saved me from a beating many times
or from a scolding, always good and nice to everyone. [. . .] Grandmother was
great with stories. She made them up and told them with exceptional talent. Sisi
and I, our heads in her lap, would listen, riveted; later on, we never paid as much
attention in school or to some other important events. Stories with dragons,
Prince Charming, with fairies and enchanted birds, with good mothers and evil
people.

Years went by, Grandmother aged, lost weight, her eyesight became weaker until she lost it entirely. She could no longer work but kept clean to the end. She shuf-
fled around the house from early morning on and did not want help from anyone;
she was ashamed of her weakness. She recognized people by their voices, but she
recognized us children by our footsteps. "Mimica," that is how she would pamper
me; she knew when I came in, she wanted to know which dress I was wearing, what
I had been doing, what else was new. Grandfather had also lost weight, he was often ill. I cared for him when Aunt Ana was away in Cernăuţi.

I think of my grandparents with love and sadness. What did their life amount
to? What did they work for? For what sins did they have to die so alone? What sins
did they have to atone for, and whose? They should not have had to pay so severely, since their sins were not so great. They always worked, always thought of
and remembered God, and still, just like those who were better or worse than they
were, they met their end; and who knows when and how their children will ever be
able to come visit their graves and pay their respects. I cry for you, dear grandparents. You no longer have any sins, you atoned them in the last weeks of your lives,
in abundance. Perhaps, if there is such a thing as life after death, perhaps in a near
or remote future, we will meet again and at that time I will be again, just as I was

Miriam Korber

until now, your "Mimica," your dear granddaughter. Sleep in peace and pray for us, should the prayers of the dead be worth anything to the living.

Saturday, March 14, 1942

[. . .] Each week we hear different news, [. . .] pleasant lies that stir the blood and fill us with courage, just like a shot of camphor. They say that we will return home on the second, the tenth, or the fifteenth of the month. We are always told of dates, but until now everything has been a lie. Suddenly, rumors fly that the *Consiliul de coroană* [Crown Council] has met in Bucharest, that it is interested in our fate. We fast twice every week; we hope that this way we will be saved. Jews always resort to impossible redresses. Like fasting. Everyone knows it is only a symbol, and yet educated and intelligent people fast. You cannot be too sure, so actually, why should they not attempt everything since it cannot hurt and might be of some help. Yesterday we received some news, sad news for us, that old Gertner died; they say that Mr. Fuhrer (Dad's competitor) may have also passed away. Everything seems unreal and still, the best people are dying, so many of them! For how much longer? How much longer will we be able to hold out against this wave that carries us to our death? Especially we, who have not received any letter or money from our family. How much longer? [. . .]

Thursday, March 19, 1942

It is seven in the morning. Dad gets up early, he goes in search of a place to say the Kaddish, but even for this there is no room—we are forbidden to go to the synagogue (because of the diseases, but people no longer want to get together, either, for the same reason). [. . .] In the past few days there is talk that we will be driven farther away, toward the Bug River. This will be the end, for sure, I think. Isn't it enough that so many are dying and dead already: forced to march on, I believe, even the strongest among us would no longer make it. How hard it is to survive everything anyway. I should have been in eighth grade by now [. . .] .

Saturday, April 11, 1942

[. . .] Dr. Leopold Tanner became the doctor of the Şargorod district and came for an inspection yesterday. He is from Câmpulung as well, so he brought us news from our acquaintances who are in Şargorod. I cannot conceive, I cannot understand how people can die so easily. And if they die so easily, why do the deaths of those I knew and were dear to me no longer impress me more? So many people have died, so many. Good people, children, women, death has cut down all of them mercilessly. I heard this news, and it pained me but I was still glad for the sun that was shining up in the sky, for the light that brightened up the town, so dark on other days. I will draw up a list of people I remember who I now heard have died. I don't think I will be able to include them all but at least I will write some of the names at the end of this so-called diary. I am so tense, I feel that I will crack up. And because of my nerves, I am mean to everyone. Because of my resentment and my nerves I really snap. [. . .] And still, I wrote some good poetry in the past and the teachers predicted a future for me. But everything was wiped out, together with the past, with the good old times when we also were human beings. For months now, for six months, not only have we no longer been humans, but sometimes we have been worse off than dogs. Even stray dogs are cared for by the dogcatchers, who provide them with a dignified death; but who cares for us? Hundreds of our people are dying and nobody is accountable. How many of us will return from here? How many and when? Home, how I miss my home.

Saturday, May 2, 1942

[. . .] When I see a beggar I become all afraid; it is as if I see myself, one year from now, or two. [. . .] Yesterday I read a good book, a very good one, even for back home, not only for Djurin: *Amock,* by Stefan Zweig. How I would have loved to read it at home, stretched out on the sofa by the electric light, not by this oil lamp on the hard bed and the mattress stuffed with hay. But I should not complain; there are others who are many times worse off, who don't even have shelter. Many die, unknown to others; whenever we get to go home, perhaps fewer than half of those who left their places will return. The typhus and starvation are decimating the deportees. We were called *the Jewish colony from Transnistria.* Indeed, some settlers we are, without any land, without a home. We have colonized the air, prey to disease and hunger.

I would like to have a sweetheart—rather, a "headache" like Lida, who has Mr. Kiva or Iboi—it would be better and easier. Since I left home, I cannot even think of a boy but as a comrade who carries the baggage. Actually, nobody has thought of me or become interested in me; it seems that I lost my sex appeal once I crossed the Dniester. Mail arrived today but, again, we received no letter. I cannot believe that the family does not write and I cannot understand why we receive no news from them. [. . .]

Saturday, June 13, 1942

It has been about a month since I wrote in my journal. [. . .] Three weeks ago this Tuesday Dad became ill. I was terribly affected by this. At first, he had only headaches, then a fever of 105 degrees. We immediately suspected that he had typhus. Unfortunately, we were right. From Wednesday until Sunday, Dad remained sick at home. Instructed by the doctor, we knew right away what he had. On Sunday, he was taken to the hospital for contagious diseases, a hospital that was set up by us deportees. I don't know from whom or how he got the disease. Some say that he got it at the synagogue, but I know that is not so. At Raia's, almost everyone in the house was ill. First, the people from Hotin who were staying there fell ill; then, two people from Cernăuți; Mr. Feiden, his wife and son; then Sonia (Raia's cousin), her sister and a child; then another younger cousin. Since Raia made it a habit to visit us daily, that is where all the trouble must have come from. When I saw how Dad was carried on the stretcher I started to cry; and because we are our own worst enemy the darkest thoughts started to cross my mind immediately. Until the day before yesterday we had very sad days, full of troubles: we would go up and down the hill dozens of times each day, not to mention the money we spent! Money for the shots of camphor and caffeine, for doctors, for the night shift, money for this, money for that, but even worse, the fright, the fear of doom. Dad was very weak but, thank God, for the past three days he has no longer had a fever. I think he is out of danger, but it was hard for him and for us as well. He is still exhausted from the illness but with some good care he will get back on his feet. I almost envy him that he got rid of this illness and that now, immunized, he will go to town without being scared. Anyway, I so wish that no one gets sick anymore. I am not thinking of the money that flows away like water; you can actually be content that you spend money and you can do something with it; more dangerous is when you lose strength and you don't know what the future holds for you. Anyhow, we are rather weak, we are barely making it.

In winter we still had some provisions from home. Now these are finished as well and we are weak, without a drop of energy left in us. [. . .]

Tuesday, June 23, 1942

Since Saturday Dad has been back in the hospital. He is so weak that he can no longer keep his head up. The typhoid fever forgives no one; not only is the illness long but the weakness that follows is extremely severe. Even we did not suspect how ill he was. For two weeks he was unconscious, his hearing was weak, his memory as well. The doctor, however, hopes that he will get better soon. The illness, the hospital, the doctor cost us a fortune, but at least our efforts were not in vain. Until now I had no idea that this disease could destroy a healthy body in a relatively short time. [. . .]

Friday, June 26, 1942

This week was more special than the preceding ones. In Djurin, as I may have mentioned before, lived an acquaintance from Botoşani: Ernestina Rosenfeld-

Klipper. She was married in Bukovina. She did not live under the Russians but she ended up in the camp in Edineţi, from where she was evacuated with her child over the Dniester River. Her story deserves a more detailed description. In brief: she has relatives in Botoşani who did their best to help her since she lived a very hard life then as now, without clothes, no money, not even a loaf of bread. Until now they sent her 260,000 lei, from which she received only 19,000, paid to her in the camp and from which she lost some more (I don't know what percentage), as the profiteers took most of her money. Last week she received a postcard from her brother-in-law, Dr. Talik—a physician in Botoşani, at the present time in concentration in Transnistria, who wrote that he will try his best to come visit her. And indeed, he came on Wednesday. He is now in a military hospital in Tulcin, about twenty miles from Djurin. Although he is Jewish, he is treated rather well. Mother talked to him immediately after his arrival; she recognized him when he passed by our place. He brought with him a breath of fresh air from home, from Botoşani.

Things are relatively good in Romania. For the Jews it is hard; they have to put up with humiliating restrictions, but they are in their homes. Our other grandparents are well. Dr. Talik says that it is impossible that they did not write us; just that at the post office, at the censorship office, they destroy the letters from and to Transnistria. In Bucharest they are working hard to improve the situation of the Jews in Transnistria. They are working on it but meanwhile thousands and thousands are dying. We will be free one day, but who knows who will get to enjoy a good life or what will come after these hard and evil times. He promised to give our greetings to the people of Botoşani since he hopes to get a short leave in about eight days. Perhaps we will thus be able to get in touch with those at home.

Another important event this week: the Jews and the Ukrainians will only be allowed to go out in the streets between the hours of six and nine in the morning. Also on Sundays all day, on Fridays until noon, on Wednesdays and Saturdays from two to four in the afternoon, to go to the baths. We hope that soon they will rescind this order, but for now the gendarmerie takes the order seriously. They can beat us and people are also afraid because they say that the gendarmes are allowed to shoot anyone who does not obey the order, at least so they set an example. It is sad, even more so than before. Not that I used to go out for walks so much, but it sufficed to know that you were allowed to go anywhere. Now, I must get up at six in the morning to carry the water for the rest of the day and then, from nine in the morning to nine at night, I stay home and get bored. My spirits are down. Physically, I feel relatively well, but my spirits? No girlfriends, no one to talk with, no work, no books. My mind is deteriorating and my nervous fits, in fact, real crying fits, are getting more numerous each day. And just now we had to also get these restrictions from going outside. I don't seem to want anything new for myself; all I want is to sleep. Some days I just want to die and wish for death to come with the same passion that I once wanted to study medicine. There are days in which I wish to live to see the end of this war, to live beautiful days as in the past. But death is kinder, all still and peaceful, without tears. [. . .]

Saturday, July 4, 1942

It is July already: nine months we have been away from home and the end is not in sight yet. Such a change in temperature as happened here on the Ukrainian steppe is not often seen. A July with no heat waves, with a cold sun, wind. Everything is upside-down. The latest restrictions exceed everything so far. What is even more humiliating: rumors are that they want to set up an even more restricted ghetto; that is, everyone who lives in Zavod would be interned in the Jewish quarter. What may happen in this case presents a new danger for us: people crowded one on top of another, frayed nerves, filth. The result: diseases, epidemics. Isn't it enough for them that so many have died so far, that hundreds go begging, that other hundreds fast more often than they eat, only so that they will not beg. This is not enough for them. They want to kill us all! And what could be easier than to kill helpless Jews? There are terrible stories about the brutal ways in which thousands of Jews were killed in the villages and towns in Ukraine. I could have never imagined that the civilization of the twentieth century would allow such horrors to happen. Quo vadis, the agony of the first Christians and, before them, the agony and tortures inflicted upon the blacks by the ancient Egyptians, nothing can compare with the present. Mothers and fathers killed in front of their own children or the other way around, children thrown alive in the ditches where their parents lie dead, stoned to death. And people keep silent; they keep silent in front of only one man, an evil genius who terrorizes an entire world and carries on a battle against a handful of powerless Jews.

Yesterday, Sisi, the strong one, passed out, a fainting I never saw in my entire life. She looked dead, white, breathless. She is anemic and weak, like Dad; I believe that at the next more serious effort we will all go to the dogs.

Tuesday, July 15, 1942

I know that all my writing is meaningless. Nobody will read my journal and, as for me, should I escape alive from here, I will throw into the fire everything that will remind me of the damned time spent in Djurin. And still, I write.

The most important event last week was not the fact that we received mail. I was just coming back with Sisi from Ruty's, with whom we sat down by the water's edge. It was Monday afternoon. I saw people happy, excited. I was prepared that we would not receive any news this time, either; I was expecting a new disappointment. But we had barely entered the house when Mother waved at us and shouted the good news. Joy, pain, laughter, tears, I felt this whole range of emotions go through my heart. Three postcards: one from Botoşani from Aunt Pepie, writing for our grandparents; one from Bucharest from Pepi Rudrich, mother's cousin; and one from Aunt Rosa from Mogilev. At first I did not even know how to express my joy. You see, we are not completely forgotten, as we thought; we are in touch with Bucharest and learn that they sent us money, five thousand lei in April and ten thousand in June.

The next day, Mother, with amazing confidence, went to see the list of the people who had received money. We received eighty-three marks, the equivalent of the five thousand lei sent in April—actually only seventy-eight marks, five of which had been taken by the Community. No need to mention our joy. [. . .]

Wednesday, July 16, 1942

Today is a sad day, very sad, just like at home, the day before the evacuation. Rumors are that a great number of the Jews from Djurin will be evacuated; first those from Djurin, then those from Hotin and those from northern Bukovina. Such panic in town! People are desperate, sounds of quarrels everywhere. What did you hear? What shall we do? Nobody knows anything for sure. Some say that it is only a move of the Committee, to squeeze some money out of us, because they ask for huge amounts from those from Djurin and Bukovina. It seems that they must pay seventy thousand marks from the Djurin people and two million lei from our people. That comes to about one thousand marks for a family from Djurin, money they don't have, even if they could sell all their possessions. When I look at their faces I can almost see myself before the evacuation. It is said that those from southern Bukovina have nothing to fear, but who knows? An evacuation now would be sure death. People's strength and the resources they brought from home are long gone. We are now tired, worn out, sapped of any energy; even if they left us alone, I think that many would not survive to see the end of the war. And as weak as we are, we are still a thorn in their eye, they try to destroy us. What an uneven battle. The German colossus and a handful of worn-out Jews.

According to the Jewish calendar we are in the three weeks before the ninth of the month of Av, three weeks in which many misfortunes befell the Jews. A week ago Bondy's father, as if he had a foreboding, said that if these three weeks pass fairly well, we may live to see better times. I am not very observant, but I see things that turn out to be true. When I think, however, that once again people will pack up their things, will leave their homes and will start, just like us, to wander among strangers, I shudder with fright—I don't even wish this upon my enemies. "Go away, wandering Jew"—these words ring in my ears constantly. But where shall we go? Why don't we have the courage to die? Are we cowards? How many have died, how many will still die, how many talents will be lost? And this is the civilization of the twentieth century!

Saturday, March 20, 1943

[. . .] Today I was very ill; I had jaundice and a high fever for six weeks; every day, excitement and nerves for no reason, with mother's recent illness, with her bile attacks, everything just happened and became part of our daily lives. [. . .]

Friday, September 3, 1943

General unrest. Since morning, one lie after another. Now we leave, now we don't, lists of people, new lists. Nobody knows. Everybody offers his opinion, which shortly after turns into a new lie. People are worried. In the afternoon it is said that we'll leave for sure, but no one knows to where. At six in the evening, Dr. Katz, the president of the Committee, calls a meeting. People are nervous. Immediately any illusion is shattered. We aren't going anywhere now. We are all disoriented. The majority claims, however, that any denial is actually an affirmation. So, who knows?

Saturday, September 11, 1943

Hopes have come to an end; rumors have also quieted down. We are no longer going home! Last week everyone knew that we would be leaving on the fifteenth. There was talk that railway cars were waiting in Lipnic and that the Jewish Office was sending assistance for the trip. Others claimed that everything was due to an amnesty from September 6, and that the first to leave would be those from southern Bukovina. A flurry of activities followed. People were packing their bags and trunks, were buying ropes and provisions, were washing laundry; it was general madness and today everything came to an end.

The first cold shower was the fact that they took one hundred men to forced labor. Nighttime was sheer terror. Fortunately, we knew nothing. On Wednesday, at six in the morning, Ernestina Klipper, her hair uncombed, ran over to see what we were doing. We knew nothing, however, of what had taken place. In town people were going mad. They could barely collect those one hundred men and on the second night eighty girls also left for labor. We did not know anything about this, either. The girls did not sleep in their homes and it was impossible to find them. At six in the morning Judith woke us up and told us to go hide. It was funny, we hid in the shed of the neighbor from whom we got milk. Sisi, Judith, Rita under the hemp, a boy in a pit; I climbed on a ladder to see if anyone was coming up the road. But they were not going to take us, only the girls from Djurin and Hotin. Today the girls came back already. I hope things will calm down. [. . .]

Saturday, October 2, 1943

[. . .] On Rosh Hashanah and on my birthday we were extremely sad. The weather is so wonderful, as if we were in the middle of summer. But our future is bleak, very dark indeed. What will happen? Will we perhaps be evacuated because the front line is getting closer, will we be put into a harsh ghetto? Will we be killed? What will happen? This is the question on the face of everyone. [. . .]

Sunday, October 10, 1943

Yesterday was Yom Kippur, an important day for Jews. Almost everyone fasted, either for observance, for atonement, or for fear, but people did fast. It is interesting what an overwhelming atmosphere prevails on a holiday. I felt the same on Rosh Hashanah. On Kol Nidre [the eve of Yom Kippur], hurried people, stooped over too soon under the weight of the times, head for the improvised synagogues: a large hallway; a spacious room; even the renovated temple in Djurin. The Jews have set up some places of prayer as well as they could. With stable lanterns, with wax candles, with oil lamps they managed, in extraordinary sadness, to light up these places of prayer. Their faith is strong and nobody can shake it, neither human beings nor the times.

During last week, as terrible as it was, nothing whatsoever kept them from praying. On the contrary, they pray with even more zeal, more passion and more hope. Perhaps the suffering is not over yet, but they pray, they beat their breasts, and they wait, they hope and nobody can make them lose hope. It is a wonderful people, that knows its mistakes, and yet repeats them over and over again. It has such a will to live; it has not vanished until now and I believe that even this time, the times will not subdue it. Many will still die, although very many have been sacrificed on the so-called altar of European civilization; enough will survive to carry into the future the memory of the dead and the hope of a life in freedom. I don't want to forget and therefore I write about the horror and disaster of last Saturday.

[. . .] In the afternoon, by chance, Sisi saw that there were too many people on our street, which was a sign they were rounding up people for work. Right away we sent Mother to town to see what news there was. In the beginning everything seemed normal. Supposedly each head of a family, man or woman, must sign their name on a list at the Community, in front of the head of the gendarmes, and pledge not to leave the ghetto, which would be punishable by death. Since people got scared, the group leaders, policemen, even the head of the colony, Dr. Rosentrauch, went into town and on their word of honor urged people to come out of their homes. Nobody came to our house, because we live farther away. But Mother, reassured by their words, came to call Dad. We did not let him go. If they did not call us, it meant that he did not have to go.

My heart told me that things would not go well, and indeed, that's how it went. After people gathered around a table in town, they drew up lists of names on the spot and, under the terror of loaded weapons, women and children were pushed home and men, young and old, were taken to the gendarmerie and from there to a labor camp near Odessa. If the cries of the women could only reach the heavens and their tears gather in the sea, perhaps then heavenly compassion would pour out to those wretched people who were taken first to Mogilev, without any pity, then to Oceacov, Trihati, and God knows where else.

Many escaped through slyness, others with money, protection, or courage, but many fell into the trap, since the trap was devised in a diabolical fashion. Sunday and Monday were, again, two awful days. Until we found out what it was all about, people had hidden from view. Then we found out the reason. They had arrested the group leaders from a district where during an inspection a doctor did not find the place clean, and it is said that they were taken to the labor camp in Oceacov.

Again, decent people from our midst, men who did nothing bad, on the contrary, men who used to help others, were taken away by force. And Nemesis, the goddess of revenge, deemed fit to take revenge on them. For what sins, I wonder? For sure, not for their sins—they only did good to others. Who knows? Indeed, these were days full of anxiety, when we lived in great fear. Still, we did not lose hope and, again, we started to give credence to the silly rumors of repatriation. Poor and persecuted Jewish people! So tormented and so ingenious in giving itself courage through its own lies, born from desires unfulfilled by a God of revenge or of compassion.

10

Dawid Rubinowicz

KRAJNO, POLAND

The first of Dawid Rubinowicz's five notebooks opens on March 21, 1940, seven months after the German invasion and occupation of Poland. Born in the Polish city of Kielce on July 27, 1927, Dawid and his family, including his parents Josek and Tauba, younger brother Herszel, and younger sister Malka, had moved to the provincial village of Krajno, where they were living at the time of the German attack on Poland in September 1939. Dawid's family was poor, his father eking out a living as a dairy farmer with a single cow and a wagon. To bolster the family's meager income, Josek also ran a small shop in the village. One of only a few Jewish families in the village, they were surrounded by their extended family—aunts, uncles, cousins, and a grandmother—who lived in Jewish communities in the towns and rural villages nearby, some in Bodzentyn, others in Bęczków, and still others in Kielce itself.[1]

Like the fragmentary diaries of Esterka or Minia (the anonymous girl) in Łódź or Elsa Binder in Stanisławów, Dawid's diary opens without an introduction. Indeed, it is as if Dawid simply picked up his pen one day and began to write, the rhythms of daily life caught seamlessly on the page, uninterrupted by the literary device of an introduction, a summary of recent events, or a declaration of the diary's purpose. He began by reporting on the latest restrictions leveled against the Jews, among them a prohibition on traveling by vehicle. He also heard and noted the news of the deportation of Jews from the nearby district capital of Kielce and the establishment of a ghetto there. While Dawid lamented his own life and the state of the world in general, he also savored the small daily pleasures that time and freedom still allowed, noting his enjoyment at picking mushrooms and berries, gathering kindling, and enjoying a sunny day after a bout of the flu.

At twelve years old, Dawid was one of the youngest diarists whose writings have surfaced thus far. Far from fulfilling the stereotypical image of an innocent little boy, however, Dawid emerges with all the true complexity of a young boy coming of age. Although in the early part of the diary he often seemed very much a child, proud at learning to ride a bike and fearful of a violent thunderstorm, he was at the same time surprisingly unfazed by the sight of a dismembered body and often asserted his bravery in the face of such terrors as raids on the family home or nearby bombings. As the diary progressed, however, Dawid often seemed older than his years, fulfilling an important role at home as the eldest son of a farming family; it was he who drew up a list for the distribution of a flour ration, ground corn and rye at the neighbors', and carried messages to people in various towns as needed. Possessed of a mature sense of the world around him, he consistently watched the weather, remarking on the importance of rain for the crops or observing that the work on the harvests had not begun on time. Similarly, he showed a clear understanding of the effects of the war on the economy, frequently noting the consequences of inflation and food shortages for the local population, Jews and non-Jews alike.

Like the diarists penning their observations and reflections in cities and towns throughout Europe, Dawid reported on all the major threats to the safety and security of the Jews in his town. What emerges most dramatically from his account, however, is the Germans' systematic exploitation of the Jews, which exhausted their material resources, leaving them beleaguered and impoverished. Dawid reported time and again on the allegedly "legal" fines, taxes, and expropriations levied against his own family and their neighbors and acquaintances. Random raids on the villages were a still more terrifying version of spoliation, as gendarmes (German police stationed in rural areas throughout the region of occupied Poland called the General Government) swept through the streets, entering homes at will and confiscating possessions and food. Dawid's own accounts of these searches and his family's frantic attempts to evade them by hiding with neighbors, fleeing into a field, or doubling back down a street are often confusing and fuzzy on the details, capturing perfectly the sense of chaos and panic that such raids engendered. And though it was the Jews who bore the brunt of German cruelty, Dawid also faithfully reported on the oppression of the Poles and the expropriation of their property.

Yet another form of exploitation was the seizure of Jewish men and boys for forced manual labor. More than just a convenient way to secure workers, it was also an opportunity to terrorize the Jews, to keep them insecure and fearful, off balance and vulnerable. Dawid himself was caught several times and sent to do various tasks, including bricklaying and snow removal. Sometimes he described the work as nothing more than "unpleasant," but in the winter those pressed into service were ordered to shovel snow day after day in freezing weather until they were, in Dawid's words, "weeping with cold." In time, the cumulative effect of fear, degradation, and humiliation effectively inculcated the Jews as the community's de facto labor force. One day Dawid wrote in his diary, "After breakfast we went out to shovel snow, even though no one had ordered us to, but the highway had got covered with snow during the night."

More perilous than any theft, humiliation, or labor was the threat of random arrest or murder. Dawid summed it up succinctly, writing, "Nowadays a person can be arrested for any trifle." Dawid's father was arrested several times for various alleged infractions. The first time, he wrote: "All sorts of ideas went through my mind—whether they'd been arrested, whether such gendarmes didn't really exist. In the end I didn't know what to think." The obscure reference to whether the gendarmes "really existed" is testament itself to the insecurity of the Jews' position; the rampant corruption and exploitation was such that one could never be sure of anything, least of all the veracity of an allegation or the reliability of the gendarmes. In another instance, the family was accused of having illegally sold its cow, a charge that was untrue. Josek Rubinowicz was taken to the gendarmerie yet again, and ultimately released, but not before the local authorities "beat him with a stick," as Dawid recounted it. In his diary, Dawid thus captured the mixture of shameless corruption, merciless humiliation, and barbaric violence to which the Jews under German domination were subjected.

Although both local populations, Polish and Jewish, were at the mercy of the Germans, brutalized and terrorized by them, they were not equal in the eyes of the oppressor. Some local Poles used the slim margin of superiority they enjoyed to exploit the Jews or gain favor with the Germans. Dawid noted these acts of indifference and exploitation in his diary, but generally without condemning them or expressing righteous indignation. Thus, he reported that it was the village police-man who time and again issued the order for Jews to perform forced labor; the parish clerk who destroyed the millstone with which the Rubinowiczes ground corn and rye, and threatened to falsely testify that they were hiding Jews from the Kielce Jewish quarter; and the mayor himself who demanded money from a local cobbler and his family. Most chilling, perhaps, was an encounter between Dawid's father and the mayor, who sat in the Rubinowiczes' home drinking their vodka and calmly announced that "all Jews would have to be shot because they were ene-mies." Though Dawid also noted in his diary those occasions when local Poles helped the Jews, these acts of solidarity were overwhelmed by the rampant hypocrisy and collaboration of the day.

As throughout Poland, the exploitation, humiliation, terror, and random vio-lence against the Jews in the region of Kielce was a prelude to the moment when they would be forced to "resettle" in Jewish ghettos. Like so many of his counter-parts, Dawid reported all the details of his family's move to the ghetto, as they dis-mantled their home, packed their belongings, and made arrangements for transport. And, as in so many other cases, traces of ambivalence and opportunism on the part of the local population emerged. On the eve of their departure, Dawid wrote that "many [peasants] don't even want to come and see us—they say they don't want to witness other people's misfortune." Although Dawid noted this, like much else in the diary, with utter neutrality, the fact remains that those peasants who were reluc-tant to "witness other people's misfortune" were not sparing the Jews from shame, but sparing themselves the unpleasantness of facing their longtime neighbors as they were uprooted from their midst. When the evening finally arrived, however, many of the family's non-Jewish neighbors came to bid them farewell, and Dawid confessed to his diary: "Thinking of how we had to leave here, I had to go out into the yard. I cried so much that I stood there sobbing for more than half an hour."

Life in the ghetto was filled with the familiar refrain of exploitation, violence, and atrocities. Dawid returned again and again to his worries about the family's fi-nances, echoing Miriam Korber's lament over the painful sale of personal items in order to subsist. Most of all, however, the diary reflects the escalation in violence afforded by the concentration of many Jews in a small space. Dawid's calm and neutral style begins to show the strain of nervous exhaustion and anxiety caused by the ceaseless killing of innocent people. "If only you could have one quiet day," he wrote. "My nerves are utterly exhausted; whenever I hear of anyone's distress, I burst into tears, my head starts aching, and I'm exhausted, as if I'd been doing the hardest possible work."

Throughout the majority of the diary, Dawid remained focused on reporting the details of the persecution of his community, only lingering over personal or family matters when they were directly related to the oppression around them (the seizure of their belongings, the arrest of his father, or the levying of fines, for example). But on May 1, 1942, an argument erupted between Dawid and his father, prompting an outraged tirade that stands in contrast to the rest of the diary not only in its personal nature but also in its emotional form. Although there were no previous indications of family conflicts in the diary, Dawid's final lines of the entry (and indeed several passages throughout the rest of the text) suggest that his relationship with his father might not always have been an easy one.

The fact of their argument might not have taken on such importance except that a few days later, Dawid's father was arrested and taken to the nearby Skarżysko Kamienna forced labor camp, which was run by a German explosives manufacturer. Dawid's fear for his father's fate and pain over the loss of his presence was compounded by guilt and shame at the memory of their argument. Of his mother's feelings, Dawid wrote: "However things may have been in the past, now she's unhappy, the whole day she goes round crying. You can well imagine how I feel." As week after week went by and Josek did not return, Dawid's panic and desperation mounted. He heard news of the conditions in the camp from a former prisoner and, while he despaired of the harsh circumstances there, he also innocently wondered if his father's imprisonment might be a form of divine punishment, writing, "Why has such a terrible fate befallen my father?—perhaps God is giving him his deserts." Josek himself apparently shared his family's ambivalence about his character, wondering in one of his letters if his family wasn't better off without him.

The last part of the diary is almost entirely taken up with the details of communicating with Josek Rubinowicz via the Krajno Jewish Council, trying to send him mail and provisions, taking care of his laundry and other needs, and endeavoring to secure his release through the usual corrupt channels. In an unusually candid and impatient acknowledgment of the corruption that was rampant around him, Dawid wrote about the frustration of trying to telephone the camp: "These people are in no hurry, they're not bothered; why should they put themselves out? If you were suddenly to give them several hundred złotys, then they'd soon be interested."

Dawid's last entry, written on June 1, 1942, begins, "A happy day." Josek was finally released due to an injured arm and returned home to his family. "I entered our flat and couldn't even greet Father, I was so glad," Dawid wrote. "No one can imagine our joy; only someone who's been through the same experience will understand." He recounted in his diary all the news from his father and, chastising himself for forgetting "the most important" thing, he added a piece of news about two Jewish women who had been shot in the woods. Abruptly, in the middle of this report, indeed in the midst of a sentence, the diary breaks off. The remaining pages of Dawid's final notebook are missing.[2]

Three and a half months after his last entry, from September 15 to 21, 1942, the Jews who had been gathered from various provincial towns and concentrated in the Bodzentyn ghetto, about five thousand in all, were marched on foot to the nearby town of Suchedniów. On September 21, they were loaded into cattle cars and transported to the death camp of Treblinka. Although nothing specific is known about the fate of Dawid and his family, they were almost certainly murdered in the gas chambers in Treblinka.

March 21 [1940]

Early in the morning I went through the village in which we live. From a distance I saw a notice on the shop wall. I quickly went up to read it. The new notice said that Jews may under no circumstances travel in vehicles (the railway had long been forbidden).

April 4 [1940]

I got up earlier today because I had to go to Kielce. I left after breakfast. It was sad following the paths across the fields all by myself. After four hours I was in Kielce. When I went into Uncle's house I saw them all sitting so sad, and I learned that Jews from various streets are being deported and I also grew sad. In the evening I went out into the street to get something.

July 7 [1940]

I've been ill now for a week; today I feel a bit better. I sat at the window and looked out at the green fields. It was nice looking out like that, when I hadn't looked out of the window for a whole week.

July 16 [1940]

Each day I get happier after this illness. Just as the days now get happier and sunnier.

August 12 [1940]

All through the war I've been studying at home by myself. When I think of how I used to go to school I feel like bursting into tears, and today I must stay at home and can't go anywhere. And when I think of how many wars there are going on in the world, how many men are daily dying by bullets, by gassing, by bombs, by epidemics and other enemies of man, then I feel fit for nothing.

September 1 [1940]

Today's the first anniversary of the outbreak of war. I remember what we've already gone through in this short time, how much suffering we've already experienced. Before the war everyone had some kind of occupation, hardly anyone was out of work. But in present-day wars 90 percent are unemployed, and only 10 percent have a job. Take us, we used to have a dairy and now we're utterly unemployed. There's only very little stock left from before the war; we're still using it up, but it's already running out, and then we don't know what we'll do.

March 24 [1941]

Today it's a bit warmer. German soldiers have been passing through. They were mostly cavalry. I stood at the window, watching the soldiers pass. My head was in a whirl with so many vehicles and cavalry. Heavy artillery was also on the move. It was fun watching the soldiers pass through; we hardly ever see soldiers in our parts.

April 1 [1941]

At ten o'clock a Jew dropped in from Kielce and said, as from today there'll be a Jewish quarter in Kielce. I was so upset by this bad news that I couldn't tell what was happening to me the whole day. The same day Jews who have relatives outside the Jewish quarter already left Kielce to go to their families. Almost all our family, however, lives in Kielce. What will they do now? And prices will go up terribly, as in other towns where there are such quarters. Today Uncle came from Kielce to consider what he should do. Papa told him he should join us for the time being; he'll do as we do. So he went to order a cart for tomorrow.

April 2 [1941]

Early in the morning Uncle had gone to Kielce to fetch the things that are there. The whole day carts were going to and fro with things. The people who were transporting them had been crying and were utterly apathetic. Uncle was supposed to be coming about 3 P.M. It got to be evening and he was still not back from Kielce. We didn't know what to think might have happened there. The whole evening we waited for them; not until 2 A.M. did they come.

April 23 [1941]

A boy from this Jewish quarter came to our house. He said two kilos of brown bread cost eleven złotys, one kilo of potatoes costs one and a half złotys, et cetera. I thought to myself, how many people are dying of hunger, how many people are eating potato skins and other things that cause diseases. It's common knowledge all kinds of diseases come from such food, and hundreds of people can die of them.

May 14 [1941]

Today's already the middle of May and spring tilling hasn't even begun. Every day everything gets more and more expensive; only recently a loaf cost five złotys and now it already costs ten złotys. In this way everything gets so expensive that you can't buy anything with money. This'll be the second war.

May 25 [1941]

It's been quite warm now for a whole week. Work in the fields will soon be over. Only food is so terribly expensive. Hundreds of people are dying of hunger, and there are thousands who don't even have a bite to eat. Almost every day letters come, asking us to buy food for this or that person, and we can't even buy anything for ourselves.

June 12 [1941]

Today the gendarmes searched a rich peasant's house because someone had reported him. [Dawid used the Polish term "Żandermerja" to refer to the German police who were stationed in Kielce and throughout rural areas in the General Government. The term is here translated as "gendarmes" for individual policemen and "gendarmerie" for the police headquarters.] They took away 2 q. [kwintal, equivalent to 200 kilograms] of wheat, 1.5 q. [150 kg] of rye, 5 q. [500 kg] of potatoes, and 2 q. of oats, and he had to transport it all to Bieliny. They jailed him for selling corn at such a high price.

June 14 [1941]

In the afternoon I was sitting at the table, when I saw a horse-drawn carriage full of gendarmes drive up. They stopped at our house, came in, and immediately began searching the place. When they'd searched every corner they said Father had to go with them on the sixteenth. We had no idea what they were looking for.

June 16 [1941]

This morning Papa went to see the gendarmes. Mama went with him. When Papa left the house we were all very sad. I looked out the window for hours on end, thinking, they'll soon be back, but the hours went by and still no sign of them. All sorts of ideas went through my mind—whether they'd been arrested, whether such gendarmes didn't really exist. In the end I didn't know what to think.

I took my sandals and went to the cobbler's for him to put straps on them. I was sitting at the cobbler's, waiting for my sandals, when a boy from Bieliny came running up and entered the cobbler's because he didn't know where we lived, and said Uncle was to go to the gendarmerie quickly, he was to say whose corn it was, because they'd taken Papa into temporary custody. We raced home with this bad news. All were alarmed. Uncle went to the gendarmerie right away, and Auntie as well. And we children stayed behind on our own, except for Grandma. We had no supper at all, at twelve o'clock I went to bed.

June 17 [1941]

Zelman came to us from Południowa. We were very curious why he came. He said a man had cycled over from Bieliny and said we must hide all our valuables, linen, and clothing because the gendarmes would be back. While he was still there we hid all our valuables. I kept on going out to see if they were coming, but there was no sign of them. There was terrible panic in the village, as if bandits were coming. And then they came. First they searched a peasant's house and then they left. When they were near to our house I thought my heart would jump out, it was thumping so violently, but thank goodness! the gendarmes didn't enter our house, though they certainly meant to. But I said, if they come back, then they're bound to search our house. We were so afraid we didn't know what was happening to us. [. . .]

While I was looking after the cow, my sister came running up saying, "Our relations are coming." I was very glad when she told me that. My cousin was already there because he'd met her on the way. I ran straight home to see if they'd arrived. After perhaps half an hour they came. You can imagine how glad we were to see them. Papa described how they'd got on in prison, who gave them enough to eat— he gave us all the details.

Dawid Rubinowicz

June 22 [1941]

It was still dark when Father woke us all up and told us to listen to that terrible din coming from the northeast. It was such a din that the earth quaked. The whole day thundering could be heard. Toward evening Jews dropped in from Kielce and said Soviet Russia was at war with the Germans, and only then did it dawn on me why there'd been that din all day.

June 26 [1941]

You can still hear the din, sometimes even better now. It hasn't rained for a fortnight. If it stays like this another two days then everything will wilt. It's already very dry; you can't walk along the highway for the sand scorching and choking.

June 29 [1941]

Today you don't seem to hear the shots anymore, only thundering from time to time. There's a cloud coming up from the north that may produce rain. Human beings are thirsting for it and so are all living plants. The cloud came and the longed-for rain. It rained for over an hour, a bit too little for the parched earth.

July 30 [1941]

While I was driving our cow home from pasture I saw a truck standing by the German's grave. At first I thought they're doing repairs. When I got nearer I saw that they were removing the remains of the corpse of the German who'd been killed at the beginning of the war. I saw all the parts of the body, each separate—the head, the arms, the trunk, and the legs. It wasn't a proper body at all. There was no smell because they'd poured some fluid onto it. On the truck there were already two full coffins, and many empty coffins as well. They filled in the grave again and sprinkled some kind of powder on the spot.

September 3 [1941]

Today the police inspector came to our house to tell us we must go to work next day. [Throughout Dawid's diary, the term "police" refers not to the Germans (called "gendarmes") but to the local Polish police force, which was subordinate to the Germans.]

September 4 [1941]

At eight o'clock I went to work—not only me, there were several boys. When we arrived, the foreman said that I and another boy were to hand bricks to the bricklayer. The work wasn't hard but I found it unpleasant. As we prepared to leave, the clerk said we were to turn up for work at seven o'clock.

September 16 [1941]

It's been fine since early this morning. After dinner we went into the forest to collect wood. While I was looking for wood in the forest I found a machine gun. I was so upset my legs were trembling.

October 7 [1941]

Last week the police discovered two peasants in possession of a slaughtered pig, and they took the meat to the gendarmerie. The peasants were told by the police to report to their local police today. One of them reported, but the other didn't turn up, so the police came to fetch him. As they entered the house they met him getting dressed, and when he saw the police he ran away. The police pursued him and when they saw they couldn't catch him, they began shooting and hit him in the right side. But he wasn't dead. The police telephoned immediately to Kielce for a taxi; it came in a few minutes and took him to the hospital. While telephoning, the policeman tore his hair, he was so sorry at what he'd done.

October 13 [1941]

Early in the morning a gendarme arrived, motorcycling to Bodzentyn. He came inside our house to warm himself. When he was inside he said that the Jews in Krajno should buy two sheepskins for him to make up a fur coat. Before returning, he went into the shop and called Mama to interpret for him. As Mother left the shop, the gendarme gave her a quarter liter of vodka.

September [actually October] 15 [1941]

Early in the morning we went to a service in Górno because today's a holiday. When we arrived at Górno we were told the Germans were in the village. After a while they arrived, saying the elders were to accompany them on a job. Several men hid behind fences and one in a loft when he saw the Germans coming. As the Germans were leaving, a woman told them the men had hidden. [. . .] They looked for them but found no one. They said nothing to Father, as he's excused from all work. When they found no one, they said everyone was to go home, there'd be no praying there that day. On our way home people told us the gendarmes were going round in Krajno after quotas and taking away cows and peasants who hadn't supplied any of their quota.

November 1 [1941]

Today notices were put up in Kielce that anyone who goes in and out of the "Jewish Quarter" will receive the death penalty. Up till now people could go in and out of the quarter. This news made me very sad, not only myself but every Israelite who heard it. These notices were put up not only in Kielce but in all towns under the "General Government" (that's the name of the area that used to be Poland).

November 28 [1941]

The postman came in the afternoon, bringing a registered letter with a writ for us to pay 150 złotys, because on September 2 our neighbor, a Jew, had come to our place to grind corn. Immediately afterward the village mayor and the parish clerk came, smashed the millstone, and testified that he was from the quarter, and now the fine must be paid today.

December 5 [1941]

[. . .] As I was going home [today], I met my sister running off somewhere. When I asked her where she was running, she said she was going to borrow money because another demand had come for 154 złotys back tax. When I got home the mayor was arguing with my father because he intended to testify that we're hiding Jews from the quarter, and that's utterly untrue. Then they stopped arguing and were in a good mood again.

December 6 [1941]

Late in the evening the cobbler's boy came running up, saying the police, the mayor, and the requisition committee had gone to the cobbler's, demanding 150 złotys, otherwise they'd arrest his father, and Papa was to repay the 100 złotys that he'd borrowed from them. [. . .]

December 12 [1941]

Yesterday afternoon I went to Bodzentyn to get my tooth filled, and intended staying there overnight. Early this morning the gendarmes came. As they were driving along the highway, they met a Jew who was going out of the town, and they immediately shot him for no reason, then they drove on and shot a Jewess, again for no reason. So two victims have perished for absolutely no reason. All the way home I was very frightened I might run across them, but I didn't run across anybody.

Dawid Rubinowicz

December 21 [1941]

Today I walked to Bodzentyn to get my fillings finished and the dentist managed to finish them today. When I got home, Father wasn't there, because he'd gone to Kielce to fetch the flour quota for the Jews in the whole district. Late at night Father came, but without the flour because the horse couldn't go any farther. He's left it with a peasant three kilometers away, and is going to fetch it tomorrow.

December 22 [1941]

Father has hired a horse and cart and fetched the flour, and I made up a list and we began distributing the flour.

December 26 [1941]

Father was just dressing when a boy came up to him and told him to go into the shop, a gendarme was calling for him, but it wasn't clear why. Father finished dressing and went into the shop. We were very frightened because we didn't know why he'd called for him. Nowadays a person can be arrested for any trifle. [. . .] Father said [. . .] an order had come that Jews were to hand over all furs, down to the smallest scrap. And five Jews were to be made responsible for those who didn't hand them over. And whoever they found with any furs would receive the death penalty—that's how harsh the regulation was. The gendarme gave till 4 P.M. for all furs to be handed over. [. . .]

December 28 [1941]

I was awakened from sleep by a knock on the window; I dressed and went to open the door. It was two Jews from Bodzentyn who were going to Kielce and had come to warm themselves. I asked them for news, and they said two more victims had been shot at Christmas, for no reason either. So not a day passes but there's bad news. They also said something had happened in Daleszyce too, but what, they didn't know. In the afternoon the clerk of the Jewish Elders' Council came from Daleszyce and said there'd been five victims that day, five Jews killed by the gendarmes because someone had reported them for hiding furs. The gendarme ordered them to be buried in a hole in their own yard. They were a father, three sons, and a daughter. In Kielce several people fall victim every day for leaving the Jewish Quarter. Under such terrible, bad conditions days and weeks pass full of fear and terror.

December 29 [1941]

In the morning I went with my brother to a neighbor's to grind a bit of corn. While [we were] grinding, a peasant came up and said they were going round the village checking inventories, because they'd made up inventories the previous months, and today if anyone has more than is entered on his inventory then they requisition it, and if the cattle that have been listed are sold, then they report it. We were sure, however, that our cow hadn't been listed because we've sold it. But the inspectors came to our house—it was listed—and when they didn't find it, they began yelling "Where's the cow? You're not allowed to sell the cow." Father apologized, said he didn't know et cetera, et cetera. But Father's excuses were no use, they were determined to write a report on the spot. [. . .]

In the evening the mayor came and called Father because the inspectors wanted to speak to him. When Father was outside, they put him onto a sledge and drove off. We didn't know where they'd taken him or why. Mother went out but they'd already gone. Mother and my brother ran after the sledge but they couldn't catch up with it. At home everyone was depressed, but what could we do? I kept on going out all the time to see if anyone was coming, but no one came. Once when I went out to look, my brother came running up and told me they'd let out Father. After a few minutes Father came. Already en route the mayor had ordered Father to go home, but the inspectors hadn't allowed him to, but in the end they told him to go, and then they beat him with a stick. [. . .]

December 30 [1941]

Mother went early on and settled the matter. She asked them not to make any written report, so that there wouldn't be any punishment, but . . .

These inspectors were going round last night to other Jews, making each one hand over a cow and take it to Kielce to the slaughterhouse.

January 8 [1942]

In the afternoon I learned that there'd been two more Jewish victims in Bodzentyn. One was killed outright and the other wounded. They arrested the wounded man and took him to the local police in Bieliny, and there they'll probably beat him to death.

January 11 [1942]

From early on there's been a blizzard and severe frost—down to minus twenty degrees [Celsius] today. While I was watching the wind blowing across the fields, I saw the village crier sticking a notice up. I immediately went out to see what was the news. There was nothing new in the notice, only the village crier said that he'd brought notices to the mayor that all Jews were to be evacuated from all the villages. When I told them at home we all got very upset. They're going to evacuate us

Dawid Rubinowicz
{284}

now in such sharp winter, and where? Now it's our turn to suffer. How long, God only knows.

January 12 [1942]

I went out first thing to clear the snow. As I was going to warm myself, the deputy mayor came and said he'd read the notice at the mayor's that all Jews were to be evacuated and that they were to take nothing with them, only what they were standing up in. We were so distressed by this news that we were utterly bewildered. When Father came we began packing bundles of things we didn't need so much, and took them to neighbors so that, if there was an unexpected evacuation, at least these things wouldn't be in the house. [. . .]

After we'd calmed down a little, we began making plans who should take which bundle, which clothes we should put on and which should go into bundles. There was nothing in the notice about where they're evacuating us and when. All it says is we're to be evacuated—that's all. [. . .]

January 14 [1942]

Father went to Daleszyce today. During the afternoon I was in the cooperative store. On the way I met a neighbor who told me her sister's daughter had come from Bieliny and had said the evacuation was postponed until May. [. . .] I went home right away with the news in order to cheer the family up. [. . .]

January 15 [1942]

Looking out the window, I noticed a horse and cart drawing up full of gendarmes who approached the house. After entering, they chased us out into the snow, but we didn't know we were supposed to go and shovel snow. We wondered where on earth they might be taking us. I, my brother, and Auntie ran off into the village, while the gendarmes were still standing outside the shop, but Uncle, Mother, and Grandma went away. I didn't go home because they were still in the shop, but went to a neighbor's and stayed there for a while. Mother had gone without gloves, Grandmother too. They'd had no dinner, even though it was all prepared—and that in such cold weather! [. . .]

[Later] I learned that they'd handcuffed a Jew and taken him to the local police, and that they'd jailed two others, ordering them to pay one hundred złotys each, then they'd be released. The village mayor had put up the bail for them and they'd let them go. I then changed my clothes and went to see what had happened to that other person. When I arrived he was no longer there. They'd tied him to their sledge and he'd been forced to run after it. Perhaps they'll shoot him—who knows? We sat there the whole evening, very sad and thoughtful. How many enemies are on the prowl after such a poor defenseless creature! Late in the evening Father came with the flour.

January 16 [1942]

During the night the father of the Jew they'd taken away came to our house. He wanted advice from Father, but what advice could Father give him? Today the whole population assembled to clear snow. While we were busy at it a girl came up with a card from Górno. The card said they'd shot one of the two they'd taken away yesterday. Who knows if it wasn't the Jew, because the other was a Pole? His sister went to Bieliny for information.

In the afternoon I went to the cooperative store to buy an electric torch. On the way back I visited a Jew. As soon as I entered his house I saw all the company had been crying, so I immediately thought the boy had been shot. I only asked briefly if it was true that he was buried in a wood. While he was tied to the sledge he couldn't run anymore, and they'd dragged him along behind the sledge and then shot him—such an unhappy fate he'd had to suffer! I returned home with the news. You can imagine how sad everyone was.

Toward evening the mayor came to our house. Father fetched some vodka and they finished it off together because he was a bit chilled . . . . The mayor said all Jews would have to be shot because they were enemies. If I could only write down just a part of all he said at our house, but I simply can't. . . . Today we were again out working in the snow, and the overseer for the Jews was the village constable.

January 17 [1942]

Today, I thought, we won't have to shovel snow. As if that made any difference! After all we've been through, all the strength we've lost, we're forced to stand outside in such a severe frost and shovel snow.

January 19 [1942]

After breakfast I went with my brother to grind some rye. On returning, I saw Jews standing in a circle in the snow by our house, with the village constable in charge. The village constable ordered us to go and shovel snow right away. [. . .] He took us right up the hill where the worst frost and driving snow was, and we had to work until sunset. We were weeping with cold; everyone had to stay till sunset. Then he returned and made us line up in twos, and we had to march. When we arrived outside the shop the mayor was still inside. It was already evening, but he still didn't allow us to go indoors. Not until it was evening did he release us, saying we had to report for work next morning.

January 20 [1942]

Very early in the morning Mother and Uncle went to the mayor to ask him to release us all from shoveling snow. They pleaded with him and he didn't give the order for snow to be cleared. Only if it started snowing again would we have to go.

January 28 [1941]

Overnight the whole highway was snowed up again, so we went in the morning to shovel the snow away. While we were working, a girl came up and said the village constable had arrested a Jew; the mayor would take him to the gendarmerie because Jews are not allowed to go from one village to another. Mother and Uncle went to the mayor to ask him to release him. Mother had a job getting him out and he had to pay a hundred-złoty fine.

February 1 [1942]

In the morning a taxi drove up and pulled up at the mayor's. [. . .] After a while a girl I knew came, saying they'd taken the mayor away in the car without giving any reason. [. . .] Then I heard that the mayor had been arrested for selling the flour quotas. [. . .]

February 2 [1942]

From early on there's been quite a stir over what happened yesterday. Most people are glad because he'd wronged many people, especially the poor. [. . .] In the evening I learned that a new mayor had been elected.

February 8 [1942]

Someone said that the members of the quota committee and a German would be making a house-to-house search for corn. They began about an hour later. I went to shovel snow. While I was shoveling snow a boy told me this German had gone to a Jew's house and turned everyone out of the place. He'd then ordered the snow to be shoveled into the house because it was so dirty inside. I didn't believe it. In the evening, however, I went and saw with my own eyes that it was really true, what he'd told me that morning. Everyone was terrified, as you can well imagine. He'd visited the house of the Jews here whose son had been shot.

February 9 [1942]

[. . .] While I was eating my dinner, the village constable came and said I'd have to go and shovel snow at the back of the school, so I went right away. On the way I called in at another Jew's to see if they were going to shovel snow too. Just as I was going there the German came out with the committee. When I entered the house it couldn't be recognized—they'd turned the place upside down. Everyone there had been beaten up; so much was obvious. The head of the house wasn't present, he was shoveling snow, so they went after him and beat him up dreadfully and cut off his beard. [. . .] Father came from Kielce just as the German and the committee entered our house. [. . .] As they were leaving they demanded two chickens and a bottle of vodka for supper. We had to hand them over a chicken and a bottle of vodka. So one day follows another—always expense and fear.

February 12 [1942]

After breakfast we went out to shovel snow, even though no one had ordered us to, but the highway had gotten covered with snow during the night. I recognized the village constable and asked him where he was going. He said he was going to the mayor with notices. About two hours later the village constable came up and began putting up a notice. It wasn't a notice but a caricature of the Jews. On it a Jew is shown, mincing meat and putting a rat into the mincer. Another is pouring water from a bucket into milk. In the third picture a Jew is shown stamping dough with his feet, and worms are crawling over him and the dough. The heading of the notice reads: "The Jew Is a Cheat, Your Only Enemy." And the inscription ran as follows:

> Dear reader, before your very eyes,
> Are Jews deceiving you with lies.
> If you buy your milk from them, beware,
> Dirty water they've poured in there.
> Into the mincer dead rats they throw,
> Then as mincemeat it's put on show.
> Worms infest their homemade bread,
> Because the dough with feet they tread.

When the village constable had put it up, some people came along, and their laughter gave me a headache from the shame that the Jews suffer nowadays. God give that this shame may soon cease.

Dawid Rubinowicz

February 27 [1942]

Father was today at Kielce to find out about the evacuation, whether it can't be postponed for two months. But he didn't succeed because the district president has already signed all the papers for the evacuation. There's just one more faint hope of postponement. Father discussed the matter with the manager of the cooperative store at Daleszyce. If he sends a messenger tomorrow, then we stay put; if not, we'll be evacuated to Bieliny. [. . .]

February 28 [1942]

From early on we waited impatiently for the messenger, but he didn't come. We've put ourselves in God's hands and are ready for anything. In the afternoon Father went to Bodzentyn, saying today or tomorrow a cart will be coming to fetch our things. In the evening Father came with the cart and I helped to stable the horse, then we began packing our things. We put the potatoes into sacks. It got to one o'clock in the morning but I didn't feel sleepy at all. We also took a bed to pieces. No one went to bed, we all just dozed a little because Father intended leaving at 3 A.M. [. . .]

March 9 [1942]

A peasant has taken various things off us that we no longer need; in exchange he's going to provide us with transport today. I went with my brother to borrow a sledge. We brought it and began to pack our things. [. . .]

March 10 [1942]

Early in the morning I went to order a cart. I arranged with a peasant for him to fetch some things from our house and transport them tomorrow. [. . .] There's hardly anyone in our village who's not sorry for us. Many don't even want to come and see us—they say they don't want to witness other people's misfortune. [. . .] After supper many peasants came to our house, wanting to visit us since we soon won't be here anymore. Thinking of how we had to leave here, I had to go out into the yard. I cried so much that I stood there sobbing for more than half an hour. When I'd quieted down a bit, I went back into the house. The peasants had already gone. [. . .]

March 11 [1942]

My brother and cousin went to Bodzentyn early in the morning. The carter came shortly before seven. Then we began piling our things onto the sledge. When the carter had gone, it was as empty at home as a tunnel—and all in a few hours. [. . .] It got very sad at home and I wished we were already leaving. After dinner Uncle hired transport to go to Bieliny; he was ready to go. It was very hard parting from them. I helped him load his few things onto the cart. This evening was very sad; there was no one here, only myself, Mother, and Father.

March 12 [1942]

Father woke me very early this morning. [. . .] We fetched the sledge and began to get ready to leave. [. . .] I went out without any armband on. As I left I couldn't say a word, my heart was so heavy. I walked perhaps five kilometers, almost unconscious—I didn't know how I managed to walk so fast. The whole way the sledge couldn't catch up with me. En route I was terribly frightened, O God, if anybody had met us, then. . . . Thank God we arrived safely. When everything was stowed away, we had breakfast. In the afternoon we carried various things up to the attic, things we don't need for the time being, that we won't be using in this house.

March 13 [1942]

Although we've only just arrived we're not strangers in Bodzentyn. Everyone treats us well, like brothers, not to mention Aunt and Uncle.

March 16 [1942]

At home everything was different from here. There was always something to occupy you. Here I go out into the street, but in no time at all I'm back—what's there for me to do in the street? Someone at home said that in Krajno four Jewish persons had been shot while walking in the direction of Kielce. Two persons had only been wounded with bayonets, and two, a mother and her son, were dead. When you hear endlessly of such atrocities how can you live calmly, without fear? [. . .] Father went to Krajno today, he's staying there overnight and tomorrow he's going to Kielce.

March 17 [1942]

All sorts of thoughts are going round and round inside my head—whether Father's pass will be signed, how on earth will he come if the pass isn't signed? Often utterly senseless thoughts force themselves upon me. I kept a lookout the whole day to see if Father was coming. Father still wasn't back even when I went to bed. In my sleep I could hear Father was back, I dressed and went into the kitchen. They've signed his pass, but crossed out Bodzentyn. It's valid only on Tuesdays and Fridays and only until April 1. This is how they intend hemming the Jews in until they all starve. A kilo of rye already costs 9 złotys, potatoes 3.20 złotys—a mark of how terribly food prices have risen. Now the poorer people will certainly die of hunger.

March 19 [1942]

Today there've been rumors circulating that on Sunday six squads of Polish police are coming, plus the gendarmes. Some say they'll be making raids, others say otherwise, no one really knows. Raids of course not on Aryans, only on Jews. Everyone goes round frightened, wondering where he can hide and find somewhere safe. But where can one feel safe nowadays?—nowhere at all.

March 22 [1942]

Today this dreaded Sunday is upon us. The gendarmes and civil police have come, but not on raids. We didn't know why they came. We waited in great fear for some terrible moment—what, we didn't know. I kept on going out of the house. It was so quiet, it was as if everyone had died, only the gendarmes kept walking up and down. Standing at the door, I heard they were making a house-to-house search of Jewish dwellings. I didn't have the courage to go out into the street. [. . .]

April 10 [1942]

They've taken away a man and a woman from across the road, and two children are left behind. Again it's rumored that the father of these children was shot two days ago in the evening. The woman, very ill, was transported to Kielce. The gendarmes were in Słupia and arrested three Jews. They finished them off in Bieliny (they were certainly shot). Already a lot of Jewish blood has flowed in this Bieliny, in fact a whole Jewish cemetery has already grown up there. When will this terrible bloodshed finally end? If it goes on much longer then people will drop like flies out of sheer horror. A peasant from Krajno came to tell us our former neighbor's daughter had been shot because she'd gone out after seven o'clock. I can scarcely believe it, but everything's possible. A girl as pretty as a picture—if she could be shot, then the end of the world will soon be here.

If only you could have one quiet day. My nerves are utterly exhausted; whenever I hear of anyone's distress, I burst into tears, my head starts aching, and I'm exhausted, as if I'd been doing the hardest possible work. It's not only me, everyone feels the same. Not enough that in the previous war the Cossacks shot Papa's father, and he was a witness, and only eleven years old at the time. That's why nowadays he only needs to see a German and he's so scared he starts shivering in his shoes.

Dawid Rubinowicz

April 18 [1942]

There hasn't been such weather as today for a long time. If only there were freedom then everything would be fine. But we're not even allowed to leave the town. We're now tied up like dogs on a chain.

They've taken away the parents from across the road, leaving two little children on their own. Next door they've again taken the husband away; if you look into their window you can see the sadness there. You can forget other people's troubles until a fresh worry comes along. Wherever you go, whether to a flat or to a café or elsewhere, everywhere people are talking about how much they've taken away from this man, how much from that, et cetera, et cetera.

While we were sitting quietly over our dinner, the policeman came to remind us we still had to pay the 150 złotys from Krajno for the corn we'd ground. We must pay up right away; if we don't hand over the money, it'll mean eighteen days' immediate detention. Mother went to the police station immediately, and the commandant said it must be paid by Monday at the latest. Of course we didn't think we'd get out of it, but nowadays in these hard times it's so difficult to pay 150 złotys.

April 20 [1942]

[. . .] Father went out to the suburbs; perhaps something can be bought there. A few minutes later my brother came, saying the gendarmes were coming. Immediately all was in confusion. I hid the hand-mill. The gendarmes were accompanied by this boy who'd reported Uncle because of the bicycle. Now he was going to inform on someone else. [. . .] We've hardly enough for necessities, and here we have to pay so much money. If we could only earn a little bit extra. To pay this fine we had to sell some of our clothes. Such hard times are upon us that people are obliged to sell their own things that they've had to work for so hard. But what can you do? Thank God there's still something to sell.

April 24 [1942]

When we came to Bodzentyn we owned a few złotys. We didn't have much capital, and now it'll soon be gone. We've paid the fine; now we're done for. Mother had earned those few złotys trading, but how far do they go? Admittedly, we don't have many expenses now, but you have to pay hundreds for every trifle; for example, even such a paltry thing as saccharine, which used to cost seventy groschen per one hundred tablets, now costs ten groschen a tablet. For saccharine alone you have to spend two złotys a day, and do you think you only need saccharine? Can anyone earn enough to cover everything? How long can we go on selling household possessions? O God, make the war end as quickly as possible. If it goes on much longer, no one will survive this terrible war and these terrible tortures.

April 28 [1942]

At daybreak Father and I went to Krajno. On the way a cart caught up with us and we were given a lift. While we were going along I felt exactly as if I was going home, and soon I found myself lost in daydreams. But shortly after I realized they were only idle reveries. Arriving, Father went to the village and I waited at our former neighbor's. Later I went to our house; there Father was waiting for me. When I went in, the dwelling seemed so strange, as if we'd never lived here. Father gave me money to pay for the potatoes he'd bought. How glad I was to run along the path I knew so well! And again I felt as if I was just running back home, that my parents were there and all the others, but then it was all over. When I got back Father was no longer there. I baked a few potatoes for myself and waited for him. Then I sat down at the window especially to recall better the moments I'd once spent here. But I didn't sit for long. Somehow I felt so sad that I went out, otherwise I'd have wept. I meant to collect a few pennies, but it was no use. While we lived here, it was easier to get things; now people won't put themselves out. I only got a liter of milk at two places. [. . .]

April 29 [1942]

Yesterday when I went to bed it was still summer, and when I got up it was already winter. It's been snowing like in January and not the end of April. As if God hadn't punished us enough, he has to give an extra punishment, a second long winter. Work in the fields should be over now, and it hasn't even started. Now everything should be cheaper, but in fact everything gets more expensive. And that's not all— Uncle and the others in the house nag at us continually. We're not even allowed to chop wood in the yard, and on top of that various trivial things that really aren't worth mentioning. But we live at a time when you can't speak out, all you can do is keep quiet and swallow everything.

May 1 [1942]

While I was in Krajno I got several clumps of chives. Today I had time to plant them in flowerpots. I still wasn't finished when Father called me to help with the grinding—I was to leave everything in the yard just as it was, my brother could clear up. After grinding I went into the flat. When Father came, he began to be very angry at me—why had I scattered the wood all over the woodshed?—and beat me. I told him I hadn't had time to tidy up the wood, and he beat me even more. I was very upset at him for beating me without cause. And finally, when he'd beaten me so hard several times with his belt buckle, I began crying, not so much out of pain as anger. I got real bruises that hurt badly. Finally he ordered me to start grinding. But how could I grind when my arm hurt me so much I couldn't move it? But for the war I wouldn't have been at home, I'd have long been out learning a trade. As it is, I must just put up with things. Father doesn't love me at all, and he wouldn't be sorry if something happened to me. All he feels is his duty; it doesn't cross his mind there might be more to it than that. All day long everyone was talking about me.

May 2 [1942]

In the evening Uncle's whole family came round and was talking about my beating yesterday. Father's always arguing with Mother over why she interferes when he beats me. A serious fight even developed. I think a married couple shouldn't argue like my parents, but today's not the first time.

May 6 [1942]

A terrible day! About three o'clock I was awoken by knocking. It was the police already making a raid. I wasn't afraid. After all Father and my cousin were in Krajno and knew what was going on. The other cousins had hidden. [. . .]

[Later] Anciel came, saying Father and my cousin had been caught as well. Only then did I start crying. They've taken Father from us, they've taken our property, and now I felt such a yearning for Father. We soon forgot the merchandise. Mother went to the Jewish Council to ask for Father's release. After all, he's ill, he can't live without medicine. It's terrible that he must now get sent to a camp to work! They said Father would be released after interrogation. We had hopes of his release. I didn't go out into the street at all for fear they'd pick me up, too; my brother and Anciel are the only ones to take them food. Anciel came in from the street, saying they'd picked up his brother-in-law as well. There was dreadful panic, everyone hid wherever he could. The relatives or wives of the arrested men wept terribly. How can you help weeping?

The Bieliny police have also made raids. When it got a bit quieter, two lorries came up and one had a trailer. When I saw it I immediately thought they were taking Father away in it, and began weeping terribly. Father told my brother he should bring him food, some clothes, and a little mug. And again I couldn't help crying when I saw him taking all those things. Mother was the whole time at the Jewish Council, making representations on Father's behalf, but all they'd say was that they'd be releasing him. My brother came to see about a warm cap, but it was already too late. . . . The truck was already at the other marketplace. I burst out crying, and as they came up I cried out: "Papa!—Papa, where are you? If only I could see you once more" . . . and then I saw him on the last truck; his eyes were red with weeping. I kept on looking at him until he disappeared around the corner, then I had a sudden fit of crying, and I felt how much I love him and how much he loves me. And only now did I feel that what I wrote on May 1 about him not loving me was a beastly lie, and who knows if I won't have to pay for suspecting him, when it wasn't true at all? If God wills and he returns then I won't be like that to him anymore. I cried a very long time, and every time I thought of Father's tear-stained face I began sobbing all over again. The dearest person in the whole world we had, they've taken from us—and ill as well. . . .

When we'd calmed down a bit, Mother went to the police station because it was getting on two o'clock. While I was sitting in the flat, thinking about Father's fate and what had happened to us all, my sister came, saying, "Go to the police; take somebody with you—they've handed back everything." [. . .] We had to make several journeys till everything was cleared. No one can imagine the joy, but it was only superficial joy; in our hearts is an indescribable sadness. Mother asked some of the members of the council to help her rescue our things, but no one wanted to go along. God so ordained it, however, that we retrieved all our things without their help.

[. . .] Mother is exhausted by today's events as if they'd been going on for a whole month. I went to bed thinking about Father. . . . Here am I, lying in a comfortable bed, but he may not even have a bit of straw in some hole of a place. I felt so sick at heart I could hold back my tears no longer and cried myself to sleep.

May 7 [1942]

I can't possibly forget yesterday's scenes—how could anyone? Mother's continually going to the Jewish Council to get them to help. One of them told Mother that they're going to Skarżysko on the twelfth to fetch the sick; Father would come then. What sort of a promise is this? God give that Father returns before they go. Everyone goes around distracted, not an instant passes but I think of Father.

May 8 [1942]

The rumor's going round that today there'll be another raid because they're still 120 men short. All the men have hidden; it's dead quiet out in the street. While I was standing on the stairs I saw three cars drive up. I recognized them right away, they were the same as on Wednesday. Immediately there was panic, all the inhabitants fled from their dwellings into the woods; the police had already begun seizing people. Auntie came, saying they're also picking up people like me. At first I didn't know what to do, but then I suddenly realized I had to hide. I went to our Polish neighbor's wife and stayed there. [. . .] I wasn't there long before the lorries drove off; only two were full, the third was empty. I went straight home; now I could be quiet at home for not a soul came in. I didn't go out into the street again the whole day.

In the evening I went to pray—after all it is Friday. We used to always go with Father; however things might be, whether happy or sad, we were still with Father, now. . . . When we returned from praying I was dreadfully sad. How could I help being sad?—supper was prepared somehow or other, the table laid; after all it is a feast day. But when I see Father's place, and he's not sitting there, then grief and sorrow break my heart. . . .

May 9 [1942]

Mother went to an acquaintance to telephone Skarżysko. She waited several hours for a connection, then they told her to come back at two o'clock. These people are in no hurry, they're not bothered; why should they put themselves out? If you were suddenly to give them several hundred złotys, then they'd soon be interested. But where from? . . . You'd have to sell the clothes off your back. No matter, the vital thing is Father comes back safe and sound.

May 10 [1942]

[. . .] As I was standing on the stairs a gentleman came and asked if a Rubinowicz lived here. I said yes. He then parked his bicycle and came into the flat. Here he took out a letter from Father and gave it to Mother. [. . .]

It wasn't a long letter, but even those few words were enough. He'd written the letter in haste; he says he's well, that the work isn't very hard, that it's tolerable, only he's very concerned about us. He writes he's very worried about me, at all costs they shouldn't pick me up, I was to see I hid well. [. . .] He asks for things to be sold off to rescue him from there. So Father knows the lay of the land; there's a reason for his writing to us to sell off things. [. . .] That evening an acquaintance of Auntie's in Suchedniów came especially to say a person could be rescued for five hundred złotys—if more persons, then more money. Mother can't go after money today anymore. Tomorrow she's going to borrow some somewhere or other.

May 11 [1942]

Mother has a piece of material for a coat. She went out to sell or pawn it. She soon returned, having borrowed the money. She gave it to the woman, then went out borrowing money from several people and returned home. [. . .] The Jewish police have also been picking up people today. I stayed almost the whole day at a Polish boy's house, I was frightened of staying at home.

May 12 [1942]

During the night the Jewish police were in our yard. They were looking for our cousins, but they weren't there. After breakfast Mother went to the Jewish Council to hand in the parcel and the twenty złotys. Mother came back from the Jewish Council, her eyes red with weeping. However things may have been in the past, now she's unhappy, the whole day she goes round crying. You can well imagine how I feel. . . . Mother talked to several acquaintances on the Jewish Council; they told her not to worry, if anyone's to return it'll be Father. Toward midday I heard the sound of a truck. My heart began to pound. People were saying twenty-five sick men were coming; perhaps Father will be among them. . . . They came—twenty-five persons—but no Father. The pain I felt—why do others come and not Father?

When the truck pulled up, they didn't let the sick men down until healthy persons had been supplied to replace them. One man from our tenement block had come back, someone from Płock. I asked him what the work was like, whether he'd seen Father. I bombarded him with questions. He told me he'd seen Father, and so far he's not been starving. The work is hard; they fell trees and uproot the stumps. They get 120 grams of bread per day, black coffee, and lots of soup—on such food no one need go hungry. Each man has a bed and Father is billeted with our cousins. He showed me several scars on his face from a whip; an overseer supervises the work. When he told me that I began to weep. Why has such a terrible fate befallen my father?—perhaps God is giving him his deserts.

May 14 [1942]

As Mother was crossing the street, a member of the [Jewish] Council stopped her and gave her a parcel. They said they'd forgotten to hand it to her yesterday. Father is sending his dirty washing, our cousins are as well. The parcel also contained three letters. Father writes that it's very upsetting for him that we don't write any letters and tell him when we send anything, or otherwise keep him informed. Obviously they haven't delivered the letter to him. He writes that I should hide, there'll be more raids; he wants me to put on girl's clothes. He asks for a few złotys to be sent, but where from he doesn't know, nor has he any idea where we're to get money for our expenses. He stresses we should sell something and save him, if at all possible. I cried my eyes out after such a sad letter. When I'd calmed down I went across to read my cousins' letters. They write the same as Father, asking to be saved. While reading the letters, I thought to myself, we're here in freedom (such a freedom as I wouldn't wish on a dog; all the same we're better off here than Father there), and perhaps Father is going short of even a piece of bread? Ah, how terrible it is! . . .

May 17 [1942]

[. . .] In the afternoon we were visited by the same man who'd come to our place the previous week on a bicycle, and he brought a letter. After reading the letter we were very worried. Father writes that we're to put pressure on the Jewish Council, and if not them, then the woman from Suchedniów, to do something. He'd been to the doctor, and he refused to release him. It wasn't a good letter—it's better not to go into detail. We don't know what to do now. Father writes we're to go to the woman from Suchedniów to whom we've given the money. We're completely at a loss. After this letter Mother's been going round as if distracted; she's been several times to the Jewish Council. There they said she was not to worry, everything would be all right. They said once the sick ones come then Father would be with them. But what sort of comfort is this?—he's still in the camp. Not until he's home will I be satisfied.

May 21 [1942]

At half past eight the truck with the Jews arrived. When I saw the truck my heart began to pound like mad—perhaps Father's with them. As it came nearer I looked for Father but didn't see him. I ran after it; the truck stopped by the Jewish Council and all the men immediately jumped out, but Father wasn't with them. I started weeping to see so many men arrive, but no Father. Some were quite healthy and yet *they'd* come back—that gave me quite a shock. [. . .] We quite forgot that today is Shavuot and made no preparations—we were entirely taken up by the one concern. It's never happened before that Father hasn't been at home for a feast day, and today he's not only not here but in a camp.

May 22 [1942]

While praying I felt a deep yearning for Father. I saw other children standing with their fathers, and the parts of their prayers that they didn't know were told them by their fathers, and who is there to tell me? . . . only God alone. God give me good thoughts and lead me in the right way. Never before have I felt my prayers to be such a burden to me as today. How could they have been so before? If only God would allow Father to return soon safe and sound. We rang up Suchedniów, and the woman said the matter's not settled yet.

Dawid Rubinowicz

May 27 [1942]

My brother brought a parcel and letter for us from the council. Father sent back his sweater, a scarf, and warm clothing and a clean colored shirt as well that we'd sent him. He'd like us to send him fresh linen. Father asks why we don't write him more often; he'd be so pleased to get a letter from home, he'd read it several times a day. [. . .] He wants us at all costs to send him this money because he can sort out everything better on the spot. If he'd had the money the previous week then he'd have come home in the second batch.

Father writes that he's sending letters every day but we don't answer. Those are his words—and we haven't received a single letter by post. Today we're bound to get a letter. I wrote him a letter right away and put it in the letter-box because the postman was just coming. The postman gave us a letter from Father and then two postcards. He writes the same in the letter and postcards as in his earlier letter, only in this letter he asks whether, knowing his irritable nature, we're better off with or without him. Mother immediately rang up Suchedniów, saying the money was to be sent to Father right away, and we sent Father another hundred złotys from us. We're sending him the money because there's nothing we can do here; he'll maybe have more chance trying to arrange something there.

May 29 [1942]

[. . .] A passing gendarme saw a Jewish woman trying to run away across a yard. He immediately ordered her to stop, but she didn't hear and continued running. When she didn't stop he fired, and his first shot hit the mark. He ordered her to be buried where all the others lie who've been shot. What a terrible fate, to be shot for no reason at all! As she lay there in the yard, not one of her children—and she has six—was allowed to go near her. Whenever one tried to approach or began to cry, the man hit it.

June 1 [1942]

A happy day. [. . .] Toward evening I went to our neighbor's to make slippers for my sister. While I was working I heard a truck approach, and singing. I immediately thought it was the Jews coming from Skarżysko. I ran out, and sure enough!—there they were, driving up. From far away you could see them waving their arms, their caps; I saw my father waving too. I threw everything down, ran to meet them, and arrived at the same time as the truck. I immediately took Father's bundle from him, and he got down from the truck. Mother took the bundle off me and I went to the police to recover the parcel. I entered our flat and couldn't even greet Father, I was so glad. No one can imagine our joy; only someone who's been through the same experience will understand. It was all like in a film, we experienced so much almost in a second. The place was immediately full of people—they all came for the good news. [. . .]

I'm so glad, I've forgotten to write down the most important and most terrible news of all. This morning two Jewish women, a mother and a daughter, had gone out into the country. Unfortunately the Germans were driving from Rudki to Bodzentyn to fetch potatoes and ran across them. When the two women caught sight of the Germans they began to flee, but were overtaken and arrested. They intended shooting them on the spot in the village, but the mayor wouldn't allow it. They then went into the woods and shot them there. The Jewish police immediately went there to bury them in the cemetery. When the cart returned it was full of blood. Who

11

Elsa Binder

STANISŁAWÓW, POLAND

In a black-and-white group photograph taken in Stanisławów, Poland, in the late 1930s, seventeen-year-old Elsa Binder sits near the middle of the second row, surrounded by the members of the left-oriented Zionist youth group Hashomer Hazair. Dressed in the organization's uniform, with a kerchief tied around her neck, Eliszewa (as she was called in the youth group) appears slight of form, her short dark hair framing her face and pulled to one side, with deep-set eyes and a shy half-smile on her face. Nearby on either side are her friends and acquaintances, many of whom would later be called by their first names or nicknames in Eliszewa's diary. Most of them smiling, looking at the camera, this fragment of Stanisławów's Jewish youth is captured on film, the moment frozen and preserved in time, only a few short years before the German onslaught engulfed them and their families, together with the majority of the Jewish community of Stanisławów.[1]

At the time the photograph was taken, the town of Stanisławów was part of Poland, located in the province of Eastern Galicia. When war broke out two years later, in September 1939, and the eastern region of Poland was annexed to the Soviet Union (as a consequence of the Molotov–Ribbentrop pact of August 1939), Stanisławów, too, came under Soviet rule. With the German invasion of the Soviet Union in June 1941, the town of Stanisławów was occupied briefly at first by Hungarian troops (allied with the Germans) and then, in late July, by the Germans themselves. Repressions, terror, and executions followed swiftly. On October 12, 1941, a massacre of ten thousand Jews took place. Two months after the pogrom, in late December 1941, the ghetto was established, and at about the same time

Eliszewa began writing in her journal. For more than fifty years, the identity of this young writer was not known; she was called only by the name—Eliszewa—that she had scrawled on the cover of her diary.[2]

Eliszewa clearly saw her diary as a place to express her deepest thoughts and feelings about herself, her family, love, friendship, and the impact of oppression and suffering on her own life. Though she worried that her family might one day find the diary, she persisted in writing, explaining: "I have to express myself more often and . . . more sincerely." To that end, she wrote about herself, her character and physical appearance, and the bitter circumstances of her life, looking back at her "twenty-one years of life, so much at odds with the gods," as she described it. Likewise, she reflected at length on her immediate family, describing her parents' and her sister's personalities, attributes, and failings, and mulling over their relationships. Finally, her penchant for analyzing herself and those around her found expression in a series of entries in which she examined in detail her first love affair, with a boy named Poldek, musing over his character, how he had treated her, and the arc of their relationship.

Though Eliszewa was drawn to matters of personal identity and character, relationships, and love, she also turned her gaze to the world around her, noting the myriad hardships that daily assaulted her and her community. The topics she described (cold, work, family tensions, restrictions, deprivations, fear, and death) inevitably echo those of writers in other ghettos, but her sharply discerning eye, her dry and clever humor, and her inimitable style set the diary apart from any others like it. In particular, though she noted with compassion, pity, and emotion the circumstances around her, she also often looked beyond the immediate pathos to see the irony and absurdity beneath, evoking not only the suffering but also the humiliation and shame that characterized Jewish life under Nazi oppression.

In particular, Eliszewa wrote with contempt, fury, and bitter sarcasm about the corruption she witnessed on the part of the Jewish Community Council. Like the anonymous girl writing in the Łódź ghetto, she remarked on the unjust distribution of food, but she did so with wry humor: "From time to time we receive some food supplies. The food mysteriously disappears the way camphor vaporizes; there must be some camphor in it." Similarly, she painted a scathing portrait of the members of the Jewish Council, alluding not only to the system of favoritism and family privileges that sustained them, but touching on the great divide between the privileged youths of the ghetto and her own circle. These privileged ghetto dwellers were the target of her heaviest moral censure, as she condemned them for betraying the poor and enriching themselves at the expense of their beleaguered community. And in a painfully clear-sighted commentary on the opportunism she witnessed, she reflected on the inequity and injustice that emerged even among those who were equally victimized by a common enemy. "Some say that people unite in misery. Probably, but not Jews. They know (some, not all of them) how to stuff themselves on the backs of their countrymen."

If there is one subject, however, that reverberates most clearly throughout the diary, it is death and its proximity. Throughout the diary, Eliszewa recited litanies of the dead, not only marking the fact of their lives and deaths in her diary, but painting an image of a community slowly shrinking, each new act of violence further reducing the already decimated Jewish population. On the three-month anniversary of the October 12 pogrom, she took stock of Stanisławów's losses, writing: "The Safirstein family was still alive three months ago. Cwijka had her parents and sister, Matylda had her family, Siamka had her sister and her family. Zyhava had her aunts and cousins, Gusta had her father, and I had more friends. But what's my point? I cannot even write down all their names in this short note."

Eliszewa's analytical side emerges in these entries too, as time and again she confronted the deepest existential questions of her young life, posing to herself the unanswerable riddle of *why?* In her reflections, she vacillated between wondering if death was preferable to life under the circumstances of Nazi brutality and alternatively finding in the deaths around her the defiant desire to live, see, and experience the world. She also observed the way death itself was transformed by war and oppression, distinguishing the violent deaths she witnessed from the natural ones that form part of the normal course of human existence. In a similar vein, she commented on the ignominious way the bodies of the dead were treated. Finally, she described the chilling omnipresence of death, writing: "The gates [of the ghetto] are guarded by Jewish and Ukrainian policemen. In the evenings they hang up purple lanterns. . . . Color of purple. Color of death. Symbol of war, starvation, and plague. Symbol of death lurking at the ghetto gates."

If matters of the present and the philosophical reflections they prompted were paramount in Eliszewa's mind, it is clear from the diary that they did not eclipse a larger perspective on her world. To the contrary, such matters were always held in relation to the past, the memory of happier times; and, more important, to the future, the hope for liberation and deliverance. Indeed, one of the great strengths of Eliszewa's diary is that it begins to suggest the frailty of hope itself in the face of helplessness and desperation. Hope was not a concept divorced from reality, but it was intimately linked to the *perception* of reality, in particular as it concerned news of the war and the liberation. As Eliszewa's diary so richly illustrates, the morale of the helpless ghetto dwellers could be bolstered or undermined by the nature of the news, rumors, and information that trickled in to them. In an entry written after a few days with no news, Eliszewa remarked: "'All quiet on the Eastern front.' As usual, when the Jews anticipate an imminent liberator, the angel of despair appears [instead]."

In Eliszewa's diary, the future is a constant and almost tangible presence, a reminder of the centrality of time itself for these young writers. While diaries are always a reflection of the passage of time (the accumulation of the minutiae of each day, days in succession, days into weeks, months, and years), diaries of this period are layered with the peculiar nature of time in the context of oppression. Unlike the apparently seamless nature of days in peacetime, the war and the violent attack on the Jews of Europe that came with it represented a break with normal life; this traumatic historical moment had a distinct beginning and, more important, an *end,* which was the central preoccupying force in the lives of all who endured it as victims.

In this context, perceptions of time infuse virtually every diary of the period, whether the writer chose to make it an explicit topic or not. Though many of Eliszewa's entries echo those of her young counterparts writing their diaries across the ghettos and hiding places of Europe, she occasionally stepped outside her immediate context to see time in a broader, more absolute light. For as much as she reflected on the concrete world around her, and the desperate wish for an end to the war and for liberation, she also voiced the philosophical notion of the inevitability of time, which would move ahead, bringing with it her fate, whatever it might be. "Time, go ahead," she wrote in one of her most eloquent entries on this theme. "Time, which carries liberation in its unknown tomorrow; maybe not for Cip, who was happy to live in interesting times, maybe not for me, but for people like me. The result is certain. Down with any doubts. Everything comes to an end. Spring will come."

Elsa Binder

On March 13 and again on March 18, 1942, another writer contributed to Eliszewa's diary. She did not introduce herself, nor did Eliszewa allude or make any reference to her; only the difference in the handwriting of the two young women attests to the shift in authorship.[3] Like Ilya Gerber, who shared his diary with friends and checked dates, incorporating information from theirs, Eliszewa may have invited this friend to borrow the diary, to pen her story and reflections on it, and to leave there a record of her existence. "I can hardly start writing again because I am out of shape," the anonymous contributor began, "but I will try to define my feelings and emotions, so that one day I will read it again and today will belong to the past." Certainly this other writer—perhaps one of the friends that Eliszewa mentioned in her diary or one pictured in the prewar group photograph—wanted to leave a mark of her place in the world too, for she wrote at length about herself, her personality, her family history, and the story of her short life, though she never included her own name, leaving her identity a mystery. Her few entries are infused with despair; and like so many diarists who struggled to endure until the liberation, she voiced the frailty of her hopes in the face of dwindling means and mounting desperation.

Eliszewa resumed the diary on March 18. On March 31, 1942, there was another major roundup in Stanisławów. Five thousand people without work certificates were seized and taken to the killing center in Bełżec, where they were murdered.[4] Shortly thereafter, all the remaining ghetto inhabitants were classified according to their ability to work: "A" category referred to "experts" working for the German economy, "B" signified people employed in "less essential" functions, and "C" was applied to those "unfit" for labor or "the handicapped and the old," as the diarist described it. Eliszewa's sister, Dora, was categorized a "C," then upgraded to a "B," and was then, according to the diary, taken to Rudolfsmühle (the improvised prison for the inhabitants of Stanisławów), where she was held with the other captives for four days. At the end of this time, she was taken away to a destination unknown to the writer.

Eliszewa did not write again for almost a month after the roundup. When she resumed her diary, she wrote about the devastating loss of Dora. "The viciousness of still objects is sometimes amazing. I'm sure that the damned walls of Rudolfsmühle appear for the sole purpose of showing me the windows in which I saw my only sister's face, pale as a wafer, for the last time." Eliszewa lingered over all the painful details, recounting the story of her sister's capture and recalling the image of the helpless Dora, who from inside the prison tried alternately to protect her family from worry and to communicate her terror and grief.

"Well, this whole scribbling doesn't make any sense," she wrote in despair on June 9, 1942. "The world will know about everything even without my wise notes." She wrote her last entry on June 18, 1942; her text ended abruptly as she was recounting a close call with the Gestapo and the Ukrainian police as she smuggled money and supplies into the ghetto. Over the course of the summer, there were shooting operations in the ghetto and another roundup that claimed the lives of another thousand people. This was followed by yet another transport of five thousand people to Bełżec in September. The liquidation of the ghetto took place in late February 1943. It is certain that Eliszewa and her family perished, although the exact circumstances of their deaths are not known. Her diary was found in a ditch on the side of the road leading to the cemetery, which was the execution site for the Stanisławów Jews.[5]

December 23, 1941

Yesterday my aunt, crying bitterly, brought a letter from her son in Italy. He was annoyed that nobody had told him earlier about his father's sickness. He declared naively that he would have come to help his father—right into the jaws of the lion. He asked that flowers be placed on his father's grave. (He has no idea what it is like here.) We will write him that his father could have lived much longer. So could his sister, who came to an even more tragic end, since she joined her husband in the grave. We'll add that we are doing as well as Kalman and that Zofka sold her dresses. Maybe it's pretty naive, but you have to tell all your relatives in the world how sweet it is for us here. [. . .]

December 24, 1941

Yesterday's newspaper said that the Great Leader [Hitler] assumed command of the army. Jews are therefore drawing the most optimistic and far-reaching conclusions. Seeing his imminent defeat and a rapid withdrawal of his undefeated army, Hitler decided to seize the reins in one hand and cheer up his soldiers. Yesterday, on December 23 (7 P.M.), they shut us up in the ghetto. Maybe because it had been anticipated or maybe because of other reasons—I'll get to them in a minute—this critical event did not surprise anybody. For a few days the Jewish community has been living in a very feverish atmosphere. Good news had been spread all over the town several times, but . . . a new disaster always followed. Since October 12 [the massacre of ten thousand Jews in Stanisławów] even the biggest optimists and prophets have been silent—until the last few days. We have just learned that the Bolsheviks were not disappointed with General Winter. (The newspapers say otherwise.) The Reds are marching ahead, slowly but steadily. It is rumored that they took Kharkov (where they didn't see a single Jew), Kiev, and Zhitomir. Some people claim to have "heard" our radio broadcast from Kiev. I wish I could believe it, although I'm trying to look into the future with hope and optimism. But I have to admit to myself that I personally don't believe in an early liberation. I want it and I fear it. From today's perspective a free tomorrow seems to be extremely bright. In my dreams I expect so much from it. But in reality? I am young, I have a right to fight and to demand everything from life. But desiring it so much, I fear it. I realize that under the circumstances such thoughts are irrational, but . . . Never mind. What really matters is liberation. What would Zyhava say, or rather what would she think, if she heard this? [. . .]

I'm working today. Because of this, I have to be happy today. Under the Soviets the question of work was a matter of bread; for Jews today it is a question of "to be or not to be." Several days ago a new law appeared stating that every "man" between twelve and sixty-five and every woman between eighteen and thirty-five (unless she has minor children) must work. The question of work will be more understandable if I add that there have been rumors about making a *lager* [camp] for the girls.

So what is the position of the highly esteemed Jewish Council and the even more esteemed councilmen, aldermen, and that whole coterie? The council consists of crooks and noisy windbags who from the very beginning smelled a good deal and flocked there together with their families and friends. Today the council is recruited from the big businessmen, the merchants, and the cunning representatives of all strata, together with their children and grandchildren. The council's offices are filled to overflowing with boys and pretty girls; both apparently treat their jobs as a fashion show. Every day they show up in a new, dazzling hairstyle or dress. What do the Germans think when they visit the council? They look at the nice, rosy faces, at the heads adorned with curly locks, at the manicured fingers, and at the looks full of satisfaction with the world around them. In any event, they come to the conclusion that our backs are very flexible and our souls are insensitive. And who knows? If it's this way, they think, one more kick won't hurt. Will a new mass murder hurt? The survivors will keep smiling anyway.

From time to time we receive some food supplies. The food mysteriously disappears the way camphor vaporizes; there must be some camphor in it. The members of the Jewish Council live very well. Today, while certain kinds of people die of starvation and cold, others enjoy marzipan, sitting by their warm stoves. I don't exaggerate! Not even a bit! Some say that people unite in misery. Probably, but not Jews. They know (some, not all of them) how to stuff themselves on the backs of their countrymen. [. . .]

December 27, 1941

Paleface exaggerates too much. There was some damage and our neighborhood didn't have electricity for a few days. Some people spread a rumor that there would be no light in the ghetto. With the exception of the few who will have access to it. Lack of electricity would mean a lot of trouble because there are no candles and lamp oil, but fortunately it all turned out to be a hoax. Today a new order came like a thunderclap—on pain of death Jews have to give away all their furs (the cheaper ones were taken a long time ago). To make sure that this order will be followed several hostages were taken. I look at my thin overcoat and think about my parents who got rid of their valuable furs earlier. I ask myself whether the Germans, surprised by the freezing winter (it has just begun here), are going to dress their army in Jewish fur coats. I would pity them if only these coats looked as shabby as mine. The collars have to be removed along with the lining. Oh well, we'll wear low-cut outfits. It doesn't scare me, but I swear I'm afraid of cold.

And Mama? We've been fighting for a few days. About trivialities, as usual. Yet no matter what moods we're in, she's the dearest person in the world for me. Not because it's the right thing to say, but because I truly feel it. Especially right now I should be more understanding with her, more loving, and so forth. But when I see how she treats my sister, my blood boils and jealousy stifles my better impulses. I don't think she loves Dora more than she loves me, but the fact is that she demands more from me and is more indulgent toward my sister. I don't imagine it's because my sister peels the potatoes. Then why? We both love her. We love her very much and I feel sorry for her. I know how she misses her relatives. She suffers because of her sister's misery; she would like to be near her, help her, console her. In other words, she would like to be with someone close. But I feel even more sorry for my dad. I look at his skinny features, at his silver hair, and my heart is breaking; I feel how dear my father is to me. And something unusual is happening. I'm grieving more over the autumn of my parents' life than over the spring of my own. I wish for their survival until the very end more than I wish it for myself. Since without them I'm not worth a thing.

I look at my father and see him shutting the door in a beggar's face. And my mother, often [. . .] unpleasant, vehemently reproaches him for it. "You know I used to help whenever I could," he keeps replying. True! But . . . what a war does to a man! But only a war? No! My father suffered a lot from [sense unclear]. When I see their way of giving thanks for Binder's righteousness, honesty, and unselfishness, nothing can surprise me. People are despicable and unscrupulous. One has to be mean! I'm afraid Dad is not always mean at the right time. I would like him to be more open and straight with people, like Mom who is sometimes disliked, sometimes insensitive, but always in the right. As a matter of fact, I'm very proud of my parents. May I be able to enjoy their company for a long time.

My sister? She's me in miniature. My way of thinking, my way of talking, my way of reacting, et cetera. Maybe that's why she managed to deprive me of the position of the elder sister and perhaps to remove me from my mother's heart. Because of her I often feel useless at home and dream about an independent life after the war is over. I don't want to be as arrogant as she is.

I also think I shouldn't be writing all this. I cannot imagine what would happen if they found it, God forbid. On the other hand, I'm so lonely. So many important things are happening in the world arena and talking to Zyhava once a week is not enough for me. I have to express myself more often and . . . more sincerely. I am reading what I have just written and it seems to be very naive and silly. But this is my way of thinking. I'm sorry that I have to put it on paper before I realize that it's like this. Regardless of this discovery I will keep writing down my thoughts, but I won't read them right away.

December 28, 1941

[. . .] Today I was visited by Frydka and Hulda [Grinszpan or Grinsztayn]. They greeted me with shouts and laughter. They couldn't stop telling me all the anecdotes and gossip from their own circle. They meet at Matylda's with Siamka and Aja. They are cheerful. Their vital humor and ability to mock everything affected me as well. But . . . Matylda lost her parents, Siamka lost her dearest and best sister together with her family. Her husband is far away, just like Aja's whose grandmother was arrested. Hulda lost her grandmother and cousins. I'm familiar with Frydka's rosy situation. Such humor in this situation? I'm baffled. Is it just youth or lightheartedness? I have no idea. Anyway, I'm jealous. I remember our gloomy meetings at Zyhava's. Laughter has deserted us. One funny word is enough to feel guilty. When I forget myself for a second, when I hum or whistle, I immediately see a procession of my friends who will never play or cry with us. Even today I still cannot talk to Charlotka about Cip [Eliszewa's friend Ciporka Safirstein] without making her cry bitterly, without feeling a sharp pain in my heart. I cannot cry anymore.

"All quiet on the Eastern front." As usual, when Jews anticipate an imminent liberator, the angel of despair appears [instead]. Today we lost our furs and several hostages (from the lower classes, of course) were jailed. What will happen to them? [. . .]

December 29, 1941

Dora has a great appetite. It is a symptom of health, but . . . when times are normal. One day my father was breaking bread for tea and, in my opinion, gave her a bigger piece. I don't care about the bread, but why should she get a bigger piece? What is more, Mother wanted to reward her and she spread some marmalade on it. Then my father realized that it wasn't fair to me and wanted to put some marmalade on mine. Mother made a gesture that meant "I want to stay out of it" and put my bread down. I thanked them for the marmalade and promised myself to never ever touch it again. Maybe it was not a mature decision but I have kept my promise.

Today, right after lunch, Dora felt like having the potato soup that was prepared for dinner. Mother was unwilling to serve it and asked her to wait. Dorota was upset and, throwing insults, gave up the soup. However, my father interfered and forced her to eat. (It is so sad that today, while people in town starve to death, others are so fussy about food.) He said a few bitter words to her. My mother took this opportunity to drop me a few hints. The atmosphere became very tense. A few words more and it's a real brawl.

Nothing can be worse. In such situations everything shrinks dramatically, even the desire to live. The atmosphere is stiff and anxious. Silence falls and only Czibi, who hides under the table when he hears the raised voices, comes out, barks, and runs around as if nothing happened. Oh, my heart aches. A few minutes later my mom went to bed. She must have thought she was very lonely and abandoned and that nobody could understand her. She's wrong. But I would think and feel the same way. I'm sorry that she is so thin-skinned, but I'm bitter that she endowed me with this disposition as well. That's why, my dear, we will always be worse off in the world than the others. It hardly matters that I'm aware of it; I can't fight it. I can't fight myself and step on what is my real "me." This is a source of the frequent frictions between us, although we love each other. When a minus meets a minus (definitely a minus) lightning is unavoidable.

December 31, 1941

Today is New Year's Eve. The last day of 1941. The end of my twenty-one years of life, so much at odds with the gods. I was endowed with a face that is basically not very impressive and rounded shoulders that charm even less. Due to the above factors I am oversensitive, weak, and acrimonious (Samek used to like my biting sarcasm). In other words, I have a difficult and rather unpleasant personality. I must add that I am demanding and arbitrary toward other people. But this doesn't mean that I consider myself a miscarriage of nature. I realize I have some positive traits and therefore I always have at least one boyfriend and one girlfriend. The durability of friendship usually depends (except for the incident with Poldi) on my will. That's why I have a grudge against my fate (perhaps unjustified) like any beautiful and shapely girl. Maybe I should prize myself less and come down a peg, but . . . I neither can nor want to. Right now all Jewish girls face the same odds. Death and prison pay no attention to external features. So many of my peers, better endowed by nature than I, have followed their call. All of us are facing death but I say I'm not afraid to die, although I long for life. It may seem naive but I'm not sure whether all my dear ones who are dead might not be better off than I am today or will be tomorrow. I see them every night together, just as they perished together and together they are resting. I see them happy, smiling, and, most of all, liberated. Really liberated once and for all. But I feel sorry about their youth, about their lost opportunities, and especially about losing such a day as September 17, 1939 [the day of the Soviet occupation of Stanisławów] (maybe I will be lucky enough to experience it once again). Because if our hearts and souls were full of happiness at that moment, what's going to happen now? It's true, we were all together then. With triumphant smiles on our faces we quickly ran toward the heavy tanks and in humble admiration and gratitude we bowed down before the red flag. With our young, really young feet we trampled the fresh blood and raised our hands in greeting. And our eyes? Our eyes were kneeling down, yes, kneeling down. There was a smell of gasoline from tanks, tractors, and trucks—we love it still—and sweeter than the fragrance of roses. But that was September 17, 1939. And today we have been balancing between death and birth for two years.

The winter is freezing. Frost knocks at the door with its skinny fingers. We have enough coal for a week and supplies for a month. "And what then, little man?" There is still a much deeper level of poverty than ours. Mom is coughing because she sleeps in an unheated room and Dad holds his back. And *juszija* [salvation] is still far away. A very long winter. Under these conditions our dreams of going out into the streets to welcome the liberators are less and less realistic. What are you bringing me, long-awaited 1942? Wasn't that my favorite heroine Catherine who welcomed the outbreak of war with the words "Welcome and be greeted, noble, happy year 1914"? So I welcome you, 1942, may you bring salvation and defeat. I welcome you my longed-for year. Maybe you will be more propitious for our ancient, miserable race whose fate lies in the hands of the unjust one. And one more thing. Whatever you are bringing for me, life or death, bring it fast.

Elsa Binder

Stanisławów, January 3, 1942

The evenings are the worst. At the orders to turn off the lights the whole family goes to bed at 7 P.M. I am the only one to waste a candle by which I read or write. Eventually I go to the cold room and lie down on the bed that is heated with a hot brick. There I have enough time to reflect over my life. I doubt whether I can even call it life. Vegetation? It can't be. I think, feel, suffer. Everything in me is just one chord of pain and hope.

I hate winter. I am afraid of freezing weather. But when I lie on my bed at this early hour, at the time when I used to get dressed and go downtown; when the moon's dull face looks through my window; when I hear the ringing bells of the sledges passing by on the street I am forbidden to walk, all my being, all my sad and lethargic self yearns for the moon, the snow, the street. And when I realize that so many of my young comrades will never see them, never feel them, I rebel against it and my instinct for life awakens.

Yes! I want to live. I want to eat well (butter appears only in my dreams and milk belongs to past memories), I want to dress well (I haven't done it for ages), I want intellectual pleasures, and here comes the nicest wish—I want to love and be loved. This is nature's law. Sad but sound. At the fresh grave of my peers I dream about such trivial things. Good God! But I don't want any fooling around, parties, and flirtations. I have never practiced them. I only dream about the essential things—like air for the plants. But milk and butter are only a dream. The order to give away boots and skis is a reality. (I would need the former myself since I have a pair of light, elegant shoes and a pair of patent-leather shoes, but my wardrobe is not appropriate for my present job.) Plays and movies are a dream, a letter from Wilk to Zyhava is a reality. He writes about typhoid in the *lager* and the ghetto and consoles himself that we will see each other soon. So gray and colorless days, brightened only by dreams, go by between a sad reality and a radiant hope. Today is very sad, tomorrow is unknown.

There are posters all over appealing to the Ukrainians. They say, "Only over our dead bodies will the Jews see the red plague spreading over Europe."[6] Should we expect a lot of sad horoscopes? The newspapers say: "Don't worry about the frost and snow. They will go away. God willing, the sun will rise the snow will melt and we will move forward." But God is high up in the sky, the sun is far away, and the Soviets are near. My heart is racing, filled with insane hope, and my soul is full of zealous prayers. Oh, God! Where are you? Help me! Help me!

January 5, 1942

They say Poldi Kriegsfeld [also called Poldek] was executed yesterday. He supposedly denounced the bakers who might have been stealing flour. If this rumor was a lie, he paid with his life. If it's true, he deserved to die. My dad, who talked to him the day before yesterday, says that he wanted to join the Gestapo. Poldi didn't say in what capacity. Is that how it was? Did your path in life pass through my devastation, then on to the scaffold? My poor, dear and lost boy! Why did you leave me in such a cruel way? Why did you brutally trample the feelings and the heart of the girl I was? I could have saved you. Did you leave me because I wasn't pretty enough for your mother—whom you and your father deserted soon after? [. . .] Finally, the end of the short, lost life at age twenty-one—for your treason. I can't recognize you. Is that you? It's been four years since you left me. After all, you're one of the Kriegsfelds—that's part of how you explained yourself.

[. . .] More pleasant news delivered by Zofka. My name is on the list of people assigned to work. I have no idea what it's all about. My father is sure that this is a mistake. I don't care. I don't think I will have to face the firing squad. I'll find out tomorrow. God, if you exist, make me strong.

January 7, 1942

I shouldn't invoke God so often. I know how he helps sheep more pious than I am. I shouldn't have gone so far in Poldek's case, either. After all, the fact that we were together in the past is not the reason for my grief today. The past: finished. Today is just sad, regardless of larger or smaller worries. In the past? In the past there was an ugly girl with a hot, naive heart and a dreaming soul. In the past there was a pretty boy with a sleeping heart and a common soul. And it happened that the pretty boy was attracted to the ugly girl and offered her his love. The ugly girl was impressed with his pretty face and readily accepted his friendship. They fell in love. She offered him all her better "self," taught him how to read and understand books, how to love the arts (in the forms that were available), and most important of all—how to think. That's what he said to other people afterward. He offered his love. They were happy together. It's true that occasionally some frictions disturbed their harmony, but they were temporary. He would make up for it with his warmth, looks, gestures, and words. He kissed her hands, sometimes her lips. He wrote her that he was never alone since her picture was always with him. It raised his spirits. Sometimes he would say, "I love you! I was drawn to you like a fly to honey. Now I flutter my wings but I can't get away." This was just a few days before the separation. The naive girl didn't understand the real meaning of these words. In her girlish vanity she was pleasantly flattered. And one day—without any reason—that means without any explanation, without a word—he turned around and walked away. Just like that! Everything has its end. For the sake of peace and quiet he comforted the despairing girl, said he wasn't worthy of her. And then the

Elsa Binder

{313}

ambiguous, or even false, "A heart can break like a fragile glass tool: can't do the job, cuts the hands of a fool." She understood. She was the only one who did! She was left alone. Her hands were still in one piece but her wings were cut off. So was her trust. Shortly after that he left the organization [the Jewish youth group Hashomer Hazair]. "Out of sight, out of mind," say the wise. Hearing about the miserable end of the once loved boy, her heart trembled again.

They say he is still in prison. But deep in my heart I know what this means. The road from prison to the cemetery is very short. The day after they had arrested the intellectuals, when I was coming from Cip's I saw . . . I saw the trucks filled with tied-up bundles. It took me a while to realize those were . . . people. I literally dragged myself into our yard where I burst into tears. I was not alone in my sobbing. I didn't know where those people were taken. I cried at the way they were transported, I guessed they were Jews. There were rumors in town that juszija is very close because some shots were heard. Oh, people are so naive! I will never forget that scene and my tears over myself and my poor people.

Monday, January 12 [1942]

Three months have passed since that memorable Sunday, October 12, 1941. Three months since the great pogrom. No! Since the great butchery that took place in our town. The Safirstein family was still alive three months ago. Cwijka had her parents and sister, Matylda had her family, Siamka had her sister and her family. Zy-hava had her aunts and cousins, Gusta had her father, and I had more friends. But what's my point? I cannot even write down all their names in this short note. They were, they lived.

Today our town is missing twelve thousand Jews, but life has to go on. Piasecki says, "Life is worthless—it starts, then it ends." What nonsense! That's the very beauty of life. But when one has to face the terror of this kind of death? And the last common resting place. I cannot write about it today. The painful and vivid memories have come back. [. . .]

Tuesday, January 13 [1942]

[Samek] used to say: "I want two things: revolution and Dora." Soon after he got his revolution and right after that . . . death. He was twenty-three, had graduated from a high school, and was very talented. Comrade Samek left me with one amateur photo and a few letters in which he asked himself and me whether I am or would like to be "the one" for him. No! I didn't want to be the one but I wanted to talk to him, listen to his eccentric opinions or pleasant descriptions of the color of my eyes, hair, et cetera. I was not only pleased but also grateful that someone liked my appearance. It's so simple. Samek, a poet and a dreamer, dedicated one of his poems to me. [. . .] I don't know whether you apprehended with some peculiar atom of your soul that you would die on such a day. I don't even know how you died. Were you hit with a sadist's brick as you stood out above the crowd? Did the crowd suffocate you as you moved back to try to prolong your life a little bit? Or maybe you were swallowed by a huge, mass grave when your chest was shot through so precisely? Or maybe . . . my God, maybe you were slightly wounded and were taking your last breaths for hours over and under the corpses? Or maybe you followed your parents voluntarily like Ciporka?

Cip: this is really hurting so much. With your open arms, lightly like a bird, you flew into the grave after your family. After the shot you fluttered your arms gently and your face fell on the chest of your father, mother, or sister. Cip. A serious girl with a schoolgirl's smile or serious eyes. Her thick braids, her figure of a healthy, hearty plant, her smile so subtle with charm and death. You loved life with so much passion. Not so long ago you were so happy that the sun was still shining and that it was so delightful to bask in its warmth. Poor little thing. Only in relation to you can I realize and understand the trivial word "never." It's terrible that you'll never find out what you meant to me. You were the only one in the world who could replace Zyhava, comfort and raise my spirits when I was hurt. But you're no more. I can hardly believe that your clear and hard-working heart is not beating and never will. [. . .]

Never again will you teach me how to be punctual in such a decisive and simple way. I'll never make you leave our company for your immodest behavior. I won't be following you, spitefully shouting out your full address—to your outrage and Tamara's amusement. We affectionately called her Tamarczyk. Delicate, black-eyed, black-browed, sweet-faced Tamara. She could fight for a winter coat by fasting for seven days. Well, she didn't wear it for too long. Full of confidence in life and in what it may bring tomorrow. Her mother went with her on that last journey. She kept fainting every time her daughters were generously whipped. (Tamara's sister, Lotka, was there, too.) Nice and polite Tamarczyk who replaced me in Jozek's heart. Samek teased me about her since all my admirers shifted their ground. I didn't treat her seriously as a rival—death treated her more seriously. I hope death was kind to her and took her right away. And that she didn't have to suffer like her companion Esterka who was seen being strangled.

Esterka. The owner of nice hands and legs that whirled in time with the lively polka lightly and proudly. She also had a useless high school diploma and an even more useless pride. Sabra with her sister, ideal Tosia, Tuska with her baby, Salka with her baby, and Gucia with her mother left with them as well. Ah! It would take volumes to describe it. The number of victims oscillates between ten and twelve thousand. Mother Earth was mourning them, wind was complaining with a moan, trees were bending their branches, and cloudy skies were crying with rain and snow. Those condemned to death were accompanied by crying, wailing, and loud cries of *Shema Israel*. But God was silent. What was left were orphaned children, mothers, entire homes and houses. Hearts full of pain, hate, and . . . helplessness.

It's strange but there is no hate in my heart, just immense pain, astonishment, and a pervasive question: Why? Why did mothers' sons and children's fathers drive old people, whimpering babies, lively young people, and pregnant women to the cemetery where fresh common graves were awaiting them? Was it in the name of the love proclaimed by their religion that they forced mothers to suffocate their children in that terrible crowd and children to trample their mothers? They say that according to international law criminals and spies condemned to death must have their eyes covered so they won't look into death's face. It's been like this for ages. But here little children, clinging to their mothers' arms and asking, "Mama, put me in front of you, I don't want to see when they kill you" (my six-year-old cousin, Zenio), are not only made to face forward but get to see how one can hold a pistol in one hand and a bun or a water bottle in the other. The crowd can see how mothers are preparing their children for death. "Mama, we want to live so much," they whine. "Children, since we can't live, we are dying together," she sobs. How fate rewards her! She can see a newborn's little head right there, crushed under a sadist's boot. And weapons aimed at the pregnant women's bellies. The crowd is silent. Perhaps it's praying. I can't understand why those people, who outnumber the oppressors, didn't attack them. It's said that they couldn't ignore those [remaining Jews] who are spread all over their territory. If that's true, how noble and . . . courageous it was. When the shooting stopped, those who were spared shouted "heil" and "danke." When they fled home, the searchlights followed them. A car stopped so they wouldn't be splashed with mud. The suffocated, wounded, unconscious, and lost were finished off the next day.

Saturday, January 18 [actually January 17, 1942]

I have been fired. I have been anticipating it from the very beginning, yet it was painful as an unexpected blow. This discharge means a loss of enough money each month to buy a pitiful five kilos of corn flour. It means a loss of one kilo of bread weekly, which under current conditions is very important. What is more, I am losing all other benefits, like ten kilos of potatoes for winter, six decagrams of oil, ten decagrams of sugar occasionally, et cetera. This big nothing put together means a lot to us. On top of everything, I am sentenced to the company of my sweet sister, bitter mother, and freezing cold.

We have had a terrible frost for some time. Obviously, all this is not going to improve the terrible atmosphere in our home. And I am remembering an incident between my father and Klocka. I hope I never forget what this man is doing to us. I know my father is quick to forgive and forget, but I'll try to get even one day. I realize this is just like howling at the moon, but it's nice to think about the revenge that may never take place. Today, with my heart filled with pain and fear I would crush him with my own feet.

So my father approached him and asked him whether I had been fired due to lack of work. (This is not true.) He replied that it was up to him to decide. He added that we shouldn't forget we are not in Palestine; and here, thank God, he can do whatever he wants. My father proposed, "Let's see what we can do. You will do all you can, so will I, so that she can stay at work." Our dear director was terribly annoyed at this Jewish chutzpah and invited my father to his office. It scares me. My father mustn't forget that he is in Hitler's country and at Klocka's mercy. Once he was a *holowa,* a boss, but now he should be as quiet as a mouse. He didn't go to the office, he was too upset. He is also waiting to be fired. He may be thrown out like a homeless dog. After he worked there twenty years. I fear other difficulties. I'm afraid to express them. Ryndycz comforted us, assuring us that the workers will all take my father's side. Should we believe him? I am afraid, I am afraid.

Sunday [January 18, 1942]

I am summarizing my impressions from this miserable day. It started with the roundup in the streets at the edges of the ghetto. Wherever the fences around the ghetto were, or even seemed to be, broken, the people living there were arrested. My father and I were passing by our courtyard when they inspected it. Fortunately, it was all right. So we avoided the fate of two hundred Jews. Although they were released the next day, they will never get their strength back.

When I was visiting Zyhava, I took a safety pin off my armband. Of course, I forgot to put it back, the band slipped down, and I walked quite a distance without noticing it. A little boy pointed it out. Fortunately, Zyhava had two bands and I was saved. Two Schupos [Schutzpolizei, uniformed German police in the cities] were walking just a few steps ahead of us. Fortunately, the only thing that happened was our fear. I missed joining Cwijka's mother by a hairbreadth—all my worries would have been over.

The last issue is my dismissal from work and my father's problem. May it end with fear only. I can't wait until Tuesday when the work week begins. There is "Jordan" [sense unclear] on Monday. I have forgotten to mention that every Jew had to give away one tablespoon, one teaspoon, one fork, and one knife for the military effort. Some say it is for the hospital that is to be established here.

My hands are totally frozen. Frost, frost, frost. I have just gotten up from the bed. Almost all the women from our town complain about missing periods. As for me, unfortunately, I have terrible cramps. Of the two evils, this is more unpleasant. That's why I had to stay in bed, which is not pleasant, either. The bedroom is freezing. Water freezes here and my hands get numb in an instant. Of course, I can't even dream of reading. I had to get up but the kitchen is extravagantly cold, dark, miserable. I'm going back to bed.

Monday [January 19, 1942]

Ryndycz paid us a visit in the morning. He brought the news that I was going to work and my father shouldn't worry since everything would be *kharosho* [fine]. He took a load off my heart. What a sly fox he is! The same Ryndycz who not so long ago was shouting that his father, a follower of [Simon] Petlura, had sacrificed his life for a free Ukraine and that he himself had always fought for her.[7] Under the Soviets he was a "Red son" and today he talks openly about getting along with everybody and keeping all his options open—just in case.

[. . .] I don't care what he talks about. He is intelligent and I respect him. He is kind and polite. I am grateful to him and mustn't forget that he has rescued me twice from unemployment. I am so happy to be able to work again. Thanks so much.

Tuesday, January 20, 1942

Poldek came home. I was done with him, had given him up for lost, and he came back. If he had been a righteous person and completely innocent, if he had been taken right from the street, he would never have seen this world again. But they let him go because of the particular reasons he was jailed for. This is a warning for "good" denunciators and a lesson for "bad" ones. Poldek and my neighbor, who was a witness, were released and that ended the bakers' scandal. Who cares that the huge shortage is made good by giving the people six decagrams of bread instead of seven? It's not surprising that the price of the stolen bread doubled. Right now bread costs thirty złotys on the black market.

Thursday, [January] 29 [1942]

For a few days I have been working in the haberdashery department. Working here destroys me physically and emotionally. I don't know whether I am less fit for this job (I realize that even under the Soviets I had to work hard to earn some bread) or whether I'm not used to it anymore. But this is nothing compared to the freezing in that place. The cold enters every single body cell, every single brain cell; it sucks them out and sterilizes them. I shiver all day, so now I know how people with yellow fever feel. There isn't a single piece of wood left at home. We burn some old furniture found in the shed.

What is going to happen tomorrow? I don't know. Anyway, I had no idea I could be so strong. I'm not hurt by the permanent specter of starvation, I'm not hurt by cold, but my Mom's pale face and my father's sad eyes virtually kill me. I don't care about myself. I'm healthy and strong. Only my head and eyes ache all the time. I have shooting pains in my ears because of the cold. I have become indifferent to everything. I shrug when I see people grabbing every bit of news like hyenas. I don't believe. January is coming to an end and . . . nothing.

Every day I see pale, skinny faces, I see people begging for bread and I see prosperity. It hurts so much! There is so much hate in me, not only toward Germans. It is not about me, about us. It's not that I am jealous. Maybe a little. It is about those homeless Hungarian Jews.[8] Along with them some twenty people who starved to death are buried in the common grave every day.

The ghetto is surrounded by a tall fence. The gates are guarded by Jewish and Ukrainian policemen. In the evenings they hang up purple lanterns. I read a book once (I forget the author's name) titled *When You Have a Purple Lantern*. "When you have a purple lantern, a purple light flickers. The bright winter evening's snow casts purple sparks and glitters." It seems to me that the author probably said that purple is the symbol of the clergy and celibacy. I don't agree with him. Color of purple. Color of death. Symbol of war, starvation, and plague. Symbol of death lurking at the ghetto gates.

Friday, [January] 30 [1942]

[. . .] When fear crawls out in the evenings from all four corners, when the winter storm raging outside tells you it is winter, and that it is difficult to live in the winter, when my soul trembles at the sight of distant fantasies, I shiver and say one word with every heartbeat, every pulse, every piece of my soul—*liberation*. In such moments it hardly matters where it is going to come from and who will bring it, so long as it's faster and comes sooner. Doubts are growing in my soul. Quiet! Blessed be he who brings good news, no matter from where, no matter to . . . where. Time, go ahead. Time, which carries liberation in its unknown tomorrow; not for Cip, who was happy to live in interesting times, maybe not for me, but for people like me. The result is certain. Down with any doubts. Everything comes to an end. Spring will come.

Elsa Binder

I can hardly start writing again because I am out of shape, but I will try to define my feelings and emotions, so that one day I will read it again and today will belong to the past. I am twenty-two. It should be the most beautiful time of my life. When I look back at my life I see that it has been so joyless, filled with sad events and experience. When my father was still alive we had a modestly prosperous existence. I don't remember it very well, but I know I was a cheerful and carefree child. It lasted until I was five; that is when my father died. My mother, at that time twenty-six, was left with three small children. I was the oldest. We owned quite a lot; my mother ran a butcher's shop and everything went along smoothly.

After a short while, however, my mother married a good-looking, decent, but weak-willed, lazy, and happy-go-lucky man. All the valuables were sold and the gold and the sewing machine (purchased by my father for his children) were pawned to pay off debts. On top of everything else, my easygoing stepfather had an affair with some shrewd elderly lady who knew how to fish money out of him. My mother was really upset. So much in love with her husband, she suffered as a wife and as the mother of her children, she suffered as an abused person. At that time I was eight, maybe ten. I loved my mother very much. I suffered with her, pitied her, and comforted her. My mother has a very good character, but she is also very irritable and hot-tempered. In addition, she is an epileptic. That's why we feel sorry for her. She is so dear to us and we constantly fear we may lose her. This is the reason I matured so early. As the oldest daughter I had to take care of my younger sisters and match my mother intellectually, so I could be her friend and confidant. I comforted her and I calculated the expenses. Living by my wits, I was her right hand. I was very serious and had no friends, since I didn't know what childhood was.

After some time my mother noticed that. She had to give up her love and think about divorce. We were ruined (one more sister had been born), had been evicted twice, and had no property. When her family saw that we were so poor and so ill-treated, they promised to help if she got a divorce. It wasn't easy because my mother and stepfather liked each other and were rather weak, but necessity prevailed. The relatives rented an apartment for us and set us back on our feet.

Then, in 1933, I joined the organization [Hashomer Hazair]. In the beginning I felt very self-conscious in the company of my peers—young, cheerful, and seemingly unconcerned people. I couldn't understand how they could laugh so much, dance, and talk about nothing. Nothing mattered but my problems at home. Anytime I was in the coffee shop I worried about home and about my mother as if I were her caregiver. At that time I used to read a lot, but I was not a good student. In our new house I met the Lebzelter family and Wilk Lebzelter convinced me to enter the *gymnasium*. I passed the exam and became a *gymnasium* student. My mother did her best so I could continue my studies and I believed in myself and became one of the best in my class. Yet my friends there came from the wealthy families and I was ashamed of my poverty, so I was angry and distant; I seemed self-confident but in reality felt inferior. [. . .]

Material conditions at home were getting worse. In 1936 we again faced bankruptcy. My mother married an old man, very unpleasant and too stingy to take the children under his roof (he owned an apartment house). The old man did not want to support four children, so my sister and I had to wander from one relative to another. My relatives were usually wealthy, but uneducated, selfish, and nasty. They made it clear to me that they were doing me a big favor. After having changed places many times I moved in with some strangers. I experienced hunger and cold, but I was free. In the mornings I went to school and in the afternoons I gave private lessons until the late evening.

One day I rebelled and left the first class of the Lyceum. My younger sisters were working in the factory to make ends meet. After many troubles and painful efforts I bought a sewing machine and took some lessons in corset making. However, I couldn't pay on time so I lost my confidence and couldn't enjoy it. All this had a very negative effect on me. I became nasty, suspicious, and skeptical, but on the other hand I was strong, resourceful, calm, and sound.

It was like that until 1939. After the war broke out my mother opened a shop and started making money. I got a job and all the money I earned was mine, so I could buy myself a few things. Overall, I was in luck—for a while. At home food was never scarce. We had our own apartment and I had money. But it didn't last long. Today I fear for my life. When we get up in the morning, we don't know whether we'll sleep in our own beds; when we go to sleep, we are not sure whether we'll live safely until the next day.

On that unforgettable Sunday, October 12, 1941, my sister Bronka and I were in the ditches. Until the very end I didn't lose my self-control. I couldn't accept imminent death so I struggled hard to save myself. Death prevailed around us. [. . .] I was tough. I didn't cry or lose my head. My cheeks were burning since my coat and sweater were torn apart. I was moving backward, slowly and easily. Trying to win some time I approached the Germans. I begged them to save our lives, to send us to the labor camps instead.

Suddenly I saw my young, dark, joyless life and was helplessly furious at the injustice of the world. Now, when my youth is blooming—and this happens only once for each human being—I am to die without having experienced anything good in life? Why? Was it a sin to be born to a Jewish mother? Have I ever hurt anybody? Why is a man, who is my peer and whom I see for the first time in my life, my deadly enemy, why can he kill hundreds of thousands of innocent people? There are some naive people who believe in God and expect his mercy, or some answer. Unfortunately, I can only see the culture and the barbarism of the twentieth century, which are reflected in such acts.

In every newspaper article, in every poster in the town, there is a promise to exterminate all the Jews. We were locked in the ghetto like lepers with no chance to earn a living. People are selling their clothes to survive. Many of us were robbed of our valuables, so what is left? Like our relatives, we have never been wealthy so we don't own many things that we can sell for money. Everything comes to an end, the selling, too. People are dying, swollen from hunger. Others are starving. There is hardly a home where regular meals are served (except, perhaps, for those on the Jewish Council, who know how to manage) since there is not enough bread nor a hearty soup that would satisfy our hunger.

We are utterly exhausted, our organisms are undernourished. We only have illusions that something will change; this hope keeps us alive. But how long can we live on the power of the spirit that also is fading? Sometimes there are rumors in the ghetto that graves are being dug. Seemingly strong people, both young and old, submit to the gossip. It is a terrible feeling. You feel you have a halter on your neck and the guards are watching you very carefully, and on the other hand you are aware that you could live longer since you are healthy and strong but without any human rights.

When I have a heavy heart, I so often wish I were dead. Maybe it is a sin to wish it, but I feel I have to come to terms with this possibility. I have been very nervous recently. I feel like having a fight with everybody. I am impatient, I can't think or reason peacefully. Everything seems to be worthless to me, unworthy of any trouble and effort. Can't I just die less wise, less intelligent, less well-read, or less elegant? Every day is a new effort for me. Our meals have been limited to a minimum. What about tomorrow when we run out of our dresses, blouses, or shirts? I cannot recognize myself as a young, easygoing person. I'm afraid I have become an old, bitter, and skeptical woman who sees everything in black. Not so long ago I said I was afraid of dying. Today I remember how many wonderful, precious, and loving people died for nothing. I am a little self-centered and fearful. I have to learn how to face the atrocities, so maybe if I don't avoid thinking about them, I will regain my faith and courage.

Elsa Binder

March 18, 1942 [unidentified writer]

Today we have had a real spring. The sun's rays were a little warmer for the first time. I got up in the morning and, looking through the window, I forgot for the moment that we are poor and miserable. I wanted to enjoy the beautiful weather so much. Just a moment later I felt something heavy on my heart, like a disturbed dream or yesterday's distress. I'm not sentimental, but I really felt it. My co-workers are mostly Chasidim who believe in salvation, strongly and blindly. I envy them when I hear them pray and confide themselves to the care of the invisible (and nonexistent) God. They hope he will help them. How about me? And my family? We are totally left to our own devices (which is not appreciated), or rather to our own trinkets. Our good humor and our dinner depend on the money our mother may get for the dress she sold a few days ago. And then what? What are our prospects when we run out of dresses and suits? Are we going to wait for juszija? When I still had some supplies I was ready to believe in some of the gossip, but today? Everything is empty, no help is arriving, and I can't live on hope.

I look at my friends, at Charlotka who has always been a very brave person. She is so pale, eats only twice a day, but she can still smile and talk quietly. And Hadaska, whose mother starved to death and whose brother is swollen: she is counting the days to juszija or to death. Rachelka, who doesn't have a rosy life, believes that you should never show your true face, that is, one should always be cheerful no matter what. I am more open as a person—I have my heart on my sleeve. I cannot pretend. That's why I am depressed and discouraged and I can't put on a happy face. Sometimes I have the feeling that everything passes by me without touching me. A while ago someone bought my skirt. I don't even miss this outfit that didn't come easy and that I liked so much. I am not even moved by any horror stories. Yesterday, for example, Elsa [Eliszewa] told me that a man who had died of starvation couldn't fit into the coffin, so his legs had to be broken. Unbelievable!

March 18, 1942

My grandfather is gone. I cannot even cry. The man who loved me and whom I loved is gone. My Grandpa. My mom's father! I don't even know how. They say it was after the operation. What operation? Because he was sick? Maybe he was hungry? My head is killing me. My suppressed sobbing fills up my throat and can't be released. We concealed this fact from Mom. She feels terrible even without it. My eyes watch her and say: "Poor thing! You don't have your father any more. You don't even mourn him as you did your mother." That's what my eyes say. My mind. My heart is silent. It's like an ice cube and trembles. This feeling is too complicated and too sacred to be said. God, what are the daughters who witnessed his death going through? My mother says she had a dream in which she saw her father among the dead and dressed in a fur coat. When he noticed her terror, he comforted her by saying it was permitted. How would Freud interpret this dream? I have no idea. I must only admire the secrets of the human heart and unconsciousness. I'm sure that Mom unconsciously senses the worst. So far we are not worse off than we used to be, but Mom—with no special reason—is terribly blue. She's a bundle of jumpy nerves. If you notice that I'm living in a constant fear that she may find out, you may realize that I'm going through hell. Maybe my reasoning is a little pretentious but I can't help myself. Sometimes I think that my sweet old Grandpa left in order to give up his place and beg for his son-in-law's life. His little daughter wrote her first words, "Dear Auntie! Help me ask God for my beloved father to come back." Words like these hurt a lot. It's possible to believe that another, more deserving messenger will be successful. And then it's much easier to go on. Man lies to himself but it's necessary.

March 21, 1942

The first day of spring. What a paradox! Spring and frost. Spring and captivity. It is not the spring we have been waiting for. It was supposed to come with bright sunshine, a fleet of silver whirring birds (I said once they gave me a feeling of security), and a clatter of tanks. They would smash the fences that are surrounded by white bands (like the one on my right arm). Above all they would bring freedom. Even the old men had these childish and naive dreams, while starving and freezing, and waiting hopefully for the spring during that cruel winter.

It has arrived. But first flocks of ravens came, those ominous messengers croaking loudly about hunger, disease, and death. A real apocalyptic beast with blasphemies written on its seven heads: "Might is superior to law." "The weak should not exist." "Be heartless if you want to be great." And so on. Four riders supposedly preceded it: "Conquest" (or "Plague"), "War," "Famine," and "Death." St. John the Evangelist, a dreamer from Patmos, preached it. He also said that a vicious cavalcade of the four riders would sweep across humanity like a hurricane. When they heard the hoofbeats of the horses of Plague, War, Famine, and Death, crazed people would flee in all directions. That's what the dreamer from Patmos said. And the Word became flesh. But the prophet didn't add that the stunned people would know the cause of these calamities. On the venerable principle, "Be heartless if you want to be great," it's enough to shout: "Get the Jews!" Here's where we find the cause of these calamities. And crazed people will turn into a beast and attack others.

Elsa Binder
{324}

The spring has arrived. In its initial attack it froze all the bogs and marshes in the ghetto, blew freezing winds, painted white flowers on the windowpanes, stirred up a blizzard, and, roaring in the chimneys, made clear that it is too early for the flowers. The time has not come yet.

[In March or April 1942, Eliszewa's sister, Dora Binder, was "selected" during a roundup and taken to the improvised prison at Rudolfsmühle, from where she was most likely taken to the Jewish cemetery and murdered.]

April 26, 1942

Whether I stay at home, go to my auntie or wherever I go, I can see the walls of Rudolfsmühle in front of me. The viciousness of still objects is sometimes amazing. I'm sure that the damned walls of Rudolfsmühle appear for the sole purpose of showing me the windows in which I saw my only sister's face, pale as a wafer, for the last time. The windows in which she was desperately signaling us to go away because we were in danger. Or she was wringing her hands, in a gesture half happy, half desperate, at the rumors that she might soon be released. She lowered her head to conceal her tears. Unfortunately, her premonition did not fail her for a second time. For the hundredth time I'm asking myself whether I can live with the memories of my sister walking with the old people and the children to her death. As she walked she made us a comforting gesture. [As if to say,] "it doesn't matter, one shouldn't be sad." And this forced and false smile. How can you forgive and forget?

Stanisławów, May 14, 1942

They say it is the way it is before the Nile floods. We are tired after the fast, which is coming to an end. Corpses and corpses. Dead and alive. It started in March. All the handicapped on the Aryan side were killed. It was a signal that something ominous was coming. And it was a disaster.

On March 31 they started searching for the handicapped and old people, and later several thousand young and healthy people were taken. We were hiding in the attic and through the window I saw the transports of Hungarian Jews leaving Rudolfsmühle. I saw children from the orphanage wrapped in bed sheets. The houses around the ghetto were on fire. I heard some shooting, children crying, mothers calling, and Germans breaking into the neighboring houses. We survived. So what that Auntie Ruchel's property was burned to the ground, that my Grandpa was taken (shot). So were Charlotka's family and hundreds of friends. Many tears were shed but . . . I was not yet struck in the heart.

On April 4 the labor department informed us that commencing next day all people over sixteen had to be registered. According to their job, health, and age they will be placed in the following categories: "A," "B," and "C." "C" was for the handicapped and the old. We were dismayed. Maybe someone is threatened with the category "B," and this means a move to another ghetto. Terrible, unbelievable. But after all, "B" is better than "C" because it doesn't smell of *Himmelkommando* [a pun on the word "himmel," or heaven]. (I was trying to be funny talking about the old people's fate.) I must admit I soon realized that in this context the word seemed to be vulgar and inappropriate.

On Sunday morning we all went. Although we knew that youngsters and children are being detained, we didn't pay any attention to Dora's fears and entered the office. I saw her trembling feverishly and in the last minute I called her a hysteric. "I have cramps, I'm so scared"—these were her last words. I told her I felt the same, although I tried to remain calm. I comforted her and said that our father and I are with her.

She went first. She was given a "C" category, which was changed into "B," so "C" was returned. We saw it with our own eyes. My father said something and they almost took him. And then the time came that I can't even write about. Black despair! What are they going to do with them? Hope. They are taking them to Rudolfsmühle. Hopelessness. Will they select them or not? Four days and four nights passed between despair and hope. We got their letters, which swung from calling for liberation and asking for help to comforting us. "Be strong," my sister wrote, "they won't shoot us, they will send us to the labor camps." And in the margin she added, "I am suffering so much."

During that period they were selecting others as well. We couldn't do anything. Forgive us, my sister. Forgive me that I didn't cheer your short life, that I was nasty and intolerant. I have realized it too late but it is so empty here without you. And our poor Mom is so sick. Forgive us that we couldn't help you. We did our best. Lucifer didn't want to buy my soul in return for your freedom. We had to watch you going away. What did you feel when you passed by our house? I was in pain. I deliberately walked away from the window in order not to watch. They say you were surrounded by a pack of dogs and the Gestapo. Who is worse? They say you were sent to work. You have to come back one day. I don't want our lives to be broken forever.

Exactly half a year after October 12, on April 12 the March *aktion* reached its peak. They were collecting "Bs," they were taking everybody. We found ourselves in great danger again. We were staying in a hidden room when they broke into the Jewish house. The ODs [Ordnungsdienst, or Jewish Police] smashed the doors and broke the windows. But they didn't find anybody. It was a difficult moment for my mom. It's over.

Elsa Binder

Once again the toll was heavy. Auntie Ruchel's husband is gone. And the *aktion* is not yet finished. Day by day transports of Jews from the provinces come to Rudolfs-mühle. Every day hundreds of people are slaughtered in its basement. And then the trucks rush to the cemetery. This week Poldek and Siomo were killed. Two people who came back home from Gestapo hell. The former was shot, the latter was torn apart by a grenade. That means that no one can escape his destiny. If something bad was to happen to Dora, it would have happened at home anyway. We are better off than the Bergstoffs. We have hope and what do they have? [. . .]

May 31, 1942

Yesterday Mom found out about her father's death. When we had decided to conceal it, we ignored her nature, so emotional and reflective. She was surprised that they were silent and didn't even mention Grandpa in their letters. So she started badgering us until she found out. Dad told her. We had wanted to conceal it because she wasn't strong enough to hear news this sad. Today she was able to. All day long she's been holding her poor liver. When Dora was taken, she had a terrible attack of gallstones and never recovered. I'll never forget how much I owe Auntie Pepa for her parcels, especially now. She helped Mom get out of bed and stay on her feet by sending her special food that isn't available here.

June 9, 1942

Well, this whole scribbling doesn't make any sense. It is a fact we are not going to survive. The world will know about everything even without my wise notes. The members of the Jewish Council have been imprisoned. The hell with them, the thieves. But what does it mean to us? Rudolfsmühle has finally been liquidated. Eight hundred people were taken to the cemetery. And they went. The head of the butcher's shop, Zygo Weiss, went too. He was shot because he stood up for some people. And Lusia Bogad. Because of her armband. [. . .] The last postcard from Drohobycz said that twelve-year-old Esta was to be registered. We don't know what came of this. But we know what we can expect. My mom is very upset. My father and I have our numbered armbands. The situation is hopeless but some people say it is going to be better. Let us hope so! Is being alive after the war worth so much suffering and pain? I doubt it. But I don't want to die like an animal.

June 18, 1942

We can't complain about a lack of excitement. My legs are still trembling. My father sold his wonderful new clothes for fifteen kilos of supplies (my God!) and 275 złotys. He sent me to the other side so I could help the *shkotzim* [non-Jewish boys] from the factory to carry them. He couldn't move around so much himself. For greater security I took Józia with me. She was supposed to hand me one sack. They gave her two sacks, each weighing five kilos. I knew I wouldn't be able to go through with them. She was afraid to help me without a wheelbarrow. So I asked her to send for someone else. I was walking around the gate on our street, kept out by the white band, the barrier, and the policemen. Time was going by. I was in a sweat. I could hardly carry all that and walk on the unfamiliar street, so close to and so far from my own people. I was scared. Shall I go through? Or maybe not?

When three Schupos and two Gestapo officers appeared I found myself between a rock and a hard place. I went! And, of course, I was stopped by a Ukrainian policeman. The Jewish policemen didn't want to have anything to do with it. They didn't know me. Apparently they were not impressed by my looks, either. (I can't help thinking that if I were prettier I would be luckier. But maybe it's only my imagination.) In the meantime my father showed up. I had called him through Moldauer. My mother came, too. The Ordnungsdiensts were given twenty złotys and they immediately changed their attitude. They appealed to that fellow to let me go.

They were in the middle of the negotiations when the Gestapo officer approached the barrier. I froze. At the last minute they pushed me into the booth. And now the climax took place. Everyone disappeared as if touched by a magic wand. Only one Ukrainian and one Jewish policemen were left, with me in the booth. My heart was racing. Suddenly I saw the pale, cruel eyes. I had seen such eyes only when Boris Karloff played in *Frankenstein.* I will never forget the look that made my blood run cold. I don't exaggerate. "Was mach diese Frau hier?" [What is this woman doing here?] I'm sure that even that OD was nervous. He said he had stopped me to check my place of work. "What is this bag?" The German made a step forward. I am lost—that was my quick conclusion. My heart stopped. I had never been so scared, not even when I had lost my armband or when I had been passed by four Germans and my band had not even been in place.

But as before, the officer believed that I only had some personal belongings in the bag and after a short while he walked away. I was so lucky! If he had bent down to check it, I would have been lost. Instead he walked away. The policeman didn't want to negotiate and took me to the guardroom. My father followed us. They took two and a half kilos of our corn flour worth one hundred złotys. This month I earned seventeen złotys, but following Jewish custom I thank God for it. It could have been much worse. And maybe we are so miserable because we keep saying "gonzi li toyva" [it's not as bad as it looks][10]

12

Ilya Gerber

KOVNO GHETTO

Little is known about Ilya Gerber apart from what can be determined from the only extant notebook of his diary and a few recollections from a former fellow student. Ilya, apparently the younger of two children, was born on July 23, 1924, in Kovno, which was at that time the capital of Lithuania. His father, Boris (Berl) Gerber, was a well-known music teacher and conductor; his mother, by contrast, is not mentioned in the diary and her name and background are unknown. The diarist indicated that his sister, Khaye, was married to a man named Shloyme, but when and where their marriage took place and any detailed information about them is likewise missing.[1]

Ilya would have been fifteen at the time of the outbreak of World War II in September 1939. The terms of the Molotov–Ribbentrop pact had put the fate of Lithuania at the discretion of the Soviet Union, which formally annexed it on July 22, 1940, proclaiming it a Soviet republic. Almost one year later, the Germans declared war on the Soviets, swiftly invading and occupying Lithuania. The first days of German occupation in Kovno (beginning on June 24, 1941) were punctuated by violent pogroms carried out by Lithuanian civilians who brutally took the lives of more than a thousand Jews in Kovno.[2]

As in Vilna and other Lithuanian cities, the German onslaught of decrees and restrictions swept like a tidal wave over the Kovno Jewish population. The mass executions that marked the beginning of the "Final Solution" in Lithuania began with the murder of almost three thousand Jews from July 4 to 6, 1941, at the Seventh Fort (one of several fortifications built around the city of Kovno during the Russian imperial period). On July 10, 1941, the Germans decreed that the Jews of Kovno were to be moved into a sealed ghetto across the Vilija River in the suburb of Vilijampolé, known to the Jews as Slobodka; by August 15 the ghetto was sealed, with about thirty thousand Kovno Jews inside.[3]

The following months brought terror to the population, which was subjected to roundup after roundup as the Germans removed intellectuals, children, sick and elderly people, "nonworking elements," and others from the ghetto and murdered them. Other people were killed in reprisals for alleged provocations. Despite the well-documented efforts of the Kovno Jewish Council (or Ältestenrat, led by the gentle and well-respected Dr. Elkhanan Elkes) to postpone, prevent, and lessen these successive blows to the Jewish community, only seventeen thousand Kovno Jews remained alive by the time the roundups of the summer and fall of 1941 ceased. The last of these was the "Great Aktion" of October 28, 1941, in which ninety-two hundred people (among them forty-two hundred children) were murdered.[4] This brought the mass executions to a temporary halt in Kovno and marked the beginning of the "quiet period" in the ghetto, dubbed so not because life was without peril or the killings completely ceased, but because during this period (lasting from late October 1941 to October 1943) there were no major roundups and executions as there had been up to that time. Ten months later, in August 1942, eighteen-year-old Ilya began writing the third notebook of his diary in Yiddish.[5]

From the beginning of Ilya's diary, it is clear that he and his family were among the small "privileged" class of the ghetto, connected to high-ranking members of the Jewish Council. The *protektsiye* (pull) and favoritism that prevailed within the upper levels of the ghetto hierarchy enabled some people to use their connections to make daily existence more comfortable, and sometimes to save their lives altogether. Indeed, the diary is filled with reports that confirm the family's closeness to some of the most important and influential people in the ghetto; these connections gained Ilya's reprieve from the arduous work detail at the Aleksotas military airfield, provided for his acceptance in the vocational school, and, later in the diary, allowed his speedy release from an arrest for shirking a labor assignment. His privilege also afforded him a social life that, in terms of food and frivolity, was shockingly excessive, standing in striking contrast to the images of poverty and want that emerge from most other contemporaneous accounts of life in the Kovno ghetto. Indeed, Ilya mentioned at least four extravagant fetes held in honor of various friends' birthdays over a course of about six or seven months, the parties complete with cakes, cookies, liquor, coffee, cigarettes, music, and dancing.

The subject of favoritism and inequity is familiar among ghetto diaries of this period. But most writers in this collection were, quite unlike Ilya, part of the "common ghetto dweller" world, unfavored by connections and privilege, and thus forced to depend on sheer luck or the mercy of fate for survival. They expressed bitter resentment, moral outrage, and righteous indignation about the system of preference and favoritism that prevailed in the ghetto hierarchy. Their fury was directed not only toward those people whose connections allowed them to bestow favors on their families and friends but toward those, like Ilya, who received such privileges as well, railing against the unfairness and corruption that allowed some Jews to survive at the expense of others.

Ilya himself was contradictory on the question of privilege, expressing throughout the diary a mixture of emotions, thoughts, and observations on the subject. Most of the time, he emerged as frank and unapologetic about the advantages he gained by his father's connections. In the many entries about attending parties or social gatherings, he seems carefree and high-spirited, puzzlingly oblivious to the massive suffering around him. Indeed, at one point he described himself as walking "about the streets freely like a dandy smoking cigarettes." At the same time, he commented frequently on the stratification of ghetto society, remarking on the lack of equality as he witnessed it, though often with an ambiguous tone, at one and the same time mildly critical but also placidly accepting of the status quo. In a particularly expressive entry about the ghetto beach (a strip of shoreline along the Vilija River), Ilya reflected on its leveling nature, as all ghetto dwellers, rich and poor, privileged and destitute, came to bathe and to enjoy a few moments of sun. "Cannot the Almighty bring equality to this people condemned to death, his people?" he wrote. "Why can the beach do it? It makes everyone equal for the moment: all are half naked, no armbands, no privileges are to be seen here!" And on many occasions, Ilya was far from insensitive to the plight of the poor and wretched around him; he witnessed and wrote poignantly about a number of ghetto dwellers evicted from their homes, and reflected ruefully about his friend Beke, whose own lack of "pull" sentenced him to deportation from the ghetto for forced labor.

Ilya Gerber

Perhaps the most direct entry on this subject, however, is one Ilya wrote recounting the circumstances of his arrest. After being called upon to show his work card to Yehoshua (Ika) Grinberg, a member of the Jewish ghetto police, Ilya wrote: "That surprises me—a close acquaintance, a former *Gimnaziye* [high school] teacher of mine, a good friend of our family—he's the one who arrests me?. . . I walk with Officer Grinberg and am amazed. For the moment I was angry with him, but later I thought to myself that if all the *yaales* [big shots] were so conscientious, if nobody had any protektsiye, as is the case with him, things would be very different. . . . In this case I respected and esteemed Grinberg." Paradoxically, his frank acknowledgment of the unfairness of protektsiye and his admiration for the principled Officer Grinberg did not provoke further comment or observation when his father simply used other connections with ghetto functionaries to get him released from jail. Indeed, he returned to his carefree self, remarking, "Papa took his 'darling boy' out of jail and transported me home."

For all Ilya's ambivalence and contradictory sentiments on the subject of favoritism, however, one thing—his sense of his place in the world—remained constant throughout the diary. Unshakenly distant from the "common man," Ilya seemed to observe rather than participate in the grim drama taking place around him. This, perhaps more than anything else, was the promise of protektsiye; it allowed for a kind of complacency, a sense of security that stemmed from the belief that connections would prevail, whether it was a matter of having enough food to eat, clothes to wear, money with which to bribe, or friends upon whom to depend. Although his circumstances did not prevent Ilya from showing compassion toward the unfortunate ones or recognizing the inequity of the system, they did profoundly shape his experience of life in the ghetto and, consequently, the content of his diary. It thus not only gives a rare glimpse of the day-to-day life lived by the small minority of privileged people in the ghetto, but it also raises (certainly without solving) deep and complex questions about the nature of moral and ethical behavior under circumstances defined by unfairness, injustice, and inequity.

While Ilya's diary offers much to consider on the question of protektsiye, it is also filled with richly colorful sketches of all aspects of ghetto life. He was a gifted chronicler who saw the world around him with a keen eye for detail, capturing in words and images the many scenes of the day. He was particularly adept at characterizing "typical" scenes of life in the ghetto, with all its particularities, ugliness, and even absurdity. He captured with dry humor the scenes of corruption that took place regularly at the ghetto gate, vividly describing the daily routine of Jews forced to bribe Lithuanian and Jewish policemen in order to bring in food for their families. Similarly, he wrote about ghetto gossip and rumors, though he was often slightly mocking, gently poking fun at the ghetto dwellers' tendency to take the smallest tidbit of gossip and build from it the most dire scenarios. His teasing tone, however, belies the significance of such rumors; whether or not they contained any truth, they were indicators of the vulnerability and fears that were justifiably omnipresent in the ghetto.

Another frequent subject of Ilya's diary was music, not surprising considering his father's prominent place as a respected musician in the ghetto. In one entry, he wrote about the persistence of musical performances: "The musical circles are working at 120 percent. They arrange concerts, they have rehearsals, they sing, they play, they blow and they tickle their instruments." He recorded, too, the controversial nature of the performances for audiences of Lithuanian or German authorities. Most notably, when his father was made the conductor of a newly formed "Policemen's Chorus," he seemed to adopt the sentiments of many ghetto dwellers who felt that these concerts were inappropriate. His own passion for music is reflected in a songbook he kept in the ghetto, which survived along with the diary. And in the diary itself it is clear that he undertook this project with some seriousness, not only recording the creation of music but categorizing the types of songs that were created, their content and subject matter, and the like.[6]

In addition to his many accounts of aspects of daily life, Ilya also documented specific historical events, such as the hanging of the unfortunate young Meck, who attempted to escape the ghetto and in the process shot at the German commander of the ghetto guard. This event impressed Ilya, partly because of a grim fascination at the sight of Meck hanging on the gallows and partly because of the unprecedented news of a Jew having a weapon in the ghetto. Similarly, he noted the seizing of people on the streets for labor in the peat bogs at Palemon and for deportation to Riga, Latvia, and sketched other important events in the ghetto, such as the much talked about ceremony for the swearing in of the ghetto police.

As in many diaries of this period, the author illustrated his text, filling it with inventive drawings, doodles, and sketches. The date for each entry is drawn as an elaborately colored heading, and important dates were often accompanied by sketches, such as a menorah (candelabra) with two candles in it for the second night of Hanukkah, the eight-day Jewish Festival of Lights; a man on a gallows signifying the date of the hanging of Meck; and a gravestone marking the anniversary of the "Great Aktion." Sprinkled among his sketches and doodles throughout the diary is a recurring image: the initials H.S., sometimes intertwined with Ilya's, sometimes inside a heart. The initials refer to Heni S., who was the great love, if not of Ilya's life, at least of this notebook of his diary. It is striking that among the diaries of the period this is a rare instance in which a writer devoted so much attention to recording the details of a budding love affair. His diary captures the arc of his relationship with her, beginning with his early memories of their first meetings and covering their courtship, his growing passion for her, and eventually (and rather suddenly) the apparent cooling of their feelings and the end of the relationship.

Although Ilya's experience in the ghetto (at least as it is captured in the diary) was shaped by a combination of his advantages and his personality, there are occasional reminders that he was no less at the mercy of the Nazis than everyone else in the ghetto. The most potent of these is an entry he wrote on New Year's Day, in which he shared the sentiments of many writers who saw in the new year an opportunity to reflect on the past year and remark on their continued, albeit precarious, survival. It is a rare instance in which Ilya's distance from the common man temporarily seemed to fall away, as he reflected on the triumph of those Jews who defied fate and somehow remained alive. "We, the Jews, stand on the threshold of 1943," he wrote. "The Jew, the people cursed by *Der Stürmer* as the criminal of all crimes, the one responsible for the world war, the betrayer of nations, the enemy of the people, the parasite who lives at the expense of others, the Bolshevik, the capitalist, the eternal exploiter, upon whose head all curses are heaped, guilty of everything—he, yes he, has survived to a new year, the year 'forty-three!'"

Ilya wrote his final diary entry on January 23, 1943. The last lines of the third notebook are as jaunty and carefree as anything Ilya had written previously. "My final concern at the moment of writing these lines is—where do I find a new notebook, a new diary?" he wrote. "Hmm?! Tell me, maybe you know where to get it? I will be most grateful to you for it. . . . BASTA [enough]!" The diary breaks off at that point, and no other notebooks belonging to Ilya have been found. Ten months later, in October 1943, there was another massive roundup in Kovno (this time the arrestees were deported to Estonia), an event that marked the end of the "quiet period." The ruthless destruction of the remainder of the Kovno Jews followed, and in July 1944 Kovno was liquidated; by war's end the vast majority of the former Kovno Jewish community had perished.[7]

It is a bitter irony of Ilya's diary that the protektsiye that played such a key role in his life was not, in the end, a lifesaving mechanism, but rather a device that could only postpone the inevitable. Protektsiye itself, in fact, was an illusion, for although it could make daily life more comfortable for the few, it had no real power to alter the outcome the Nazis intended. A few lines that Ilya wrote when he was arrested by Officer Grinberg are haunting in light of what is now known about the Nazis' plan to kill all the Jews, regardless of any distinctions they may have imagined to exist among themselves. "As a result of all the protektsiye it is only the *amkho* [common people], those with few connections in the 'well-known' circles, who suffer," Ilya wrote. "If there were no protektsiye, the 'Jewish catastrophe' would have fallen not only on the heads of the unknown, but on everyone generally." In the end, the catastrophe did fall on the heads of everyone generally, including Ilya and his entire family. They are presumed to have perished, although nothing specific is known about their fate.

August 26, 1942

A new diary—new Jewish misfortunes. Today is the seventeenth day since I left off writing. Seventeen days! Seventeen days of fear, anxiety, of panic and of a mood of madness have gone by. As can be seen in my second diary, the mood in the ghetto was not especially good. People chattered, spreading rumors that soon, soon, one more day, one more hour and of the ghetto there will remain only a heap of ashes. It seemed at that moment as if the Jews were simply racking their brains on "how to destroy the Kovno ghetto."

But if you keep talking, you may get somewhere. The peasants in the area told the Jews working there that the camps are ready for us, that they have already received from their *Butu Skirius* [Housing Department] certificates for our dwellings in the ghetto. That is one reason for the chatter in the ghetto. The other reason for the rumors is that last week the ghetto was full of high-ranking Germans. One taxi after another would drive around the ghetto and then disappear in a cloud of dust. The Lithuanian general and representative of the Lithuanian people to the Germans, [Petras] Kubiliunas, demanded nothing less than the complete annihilation of the Jews of Lithuania. For this purpose the highly placed persons came to the ghetto—such as, for example, the Kovno commissioner [Hans] Cramer, the Standartenführer of the Baltic [Helmut] Rauca (famous from the Great Aktion), [governor of the Kovno District] Lenzen, [SS] General [Lucian] Wysocki, as well as many journalists. This was the commission that was supposed to consider the situation of the Jews in the ghetto and whether it is possible to divide, to split, the Jews of Kovno. In short, more taxis and commissions, and of course more rumors as well.[8] The police (the Jewish ones, I mean) kept running around and yelling that people should disperse, that people should not stop in the street, and that small children should be kept hidden at home.

For a week the ghetto was a dead city. From time to time a small human figure would run by in haste, and gradually he too would disappear. The ghetto was hushed. The mood in the ghetto was extraordinarily bad. People were simply impatiently waiting for our day of judgment. And that day arrived. The German commission drove around the whole ghetto, visited the workshops and their departments, inspected the gardens and the better-looking areas. The commission drove away. The next morning it became known that bringing food [into the ghetto] is permitted only until the twenty-sixth of this month. After the twenty-sixth you will not be able to carry into the ghetto even one gram of food. (People talked about it for almost a whole month, but now it has been confirmed.) [. . .]

What has been taking place in the ghetto in the past few days is hard to describe. People struggled and fought at the ghetto gate; everyone wanted to slip into a better [labor] brigade in order to make a [food] parcel, in order not to starve, to be able to provide for later, for hard times. People struggle at the gate, they shove and curse (nothing unusual in the ghetto); in short, things are lively . . . The police tried to maintain order, [Benjamin] Lipzer, the *Oberjude* [top Jew] of the ghetto, brigadier of the Gestapo and darling of the SD [Sicherheitsdienst, the security and intelligence force of the SS], also tried to maintain order, but with a crowd like that you can get lost yourself. The gate sentries, the NSKK [Nationalsozialistisches Kraftfahrkorps, the Nazi Motorized Transport Corps], beat people with their whips, slapped them in their faces, socked them in their noses, but the crowd paid them no attention. If one person falls out of the line, bloodied by the German whips, his place is immediately taken. People quarrel and shove, so long as the pulse still beats, so long as the "I" wants to live. The crowd has only one thing in mind: bread, flour, a few vegetables!! I want to live. . .! That is how things were the past few days at the gate on Airiogalos Street.

And yesterday was the same, only worse. The shoving was horrendous. The square, the gathering place of the workers, was jammed and everyone pushed and shoved. The last day! The twenty-fifth! After that no food will be allowed into the ghetto! And that day, the last day of being able to bring anything home for the family, turned everyone into an animal. Nothing but "I" existed—"my children, my wife, they are hungry, they ask for food, I must bring something for them today!" That was the motto of the day.

August 31, 1942

And now some private matters. Exactly three weeks ago I entered the ghetto labor force, in the vocational school as a carpenter. Prior to three weeks ago I was a "devoted" *aerodromshchik* [worker in the brigade assigned to the Aleksotas military airfield], going off to work every day while at the same time my former friends had arranged things for themselves, this one in a good brigade in town, the other one in the ghetto itself, et cetera. My father could not countenance my getting up at four in the morning, not having gotten enough sleep, and hurrying off to work. He tried to take steps to arrange things for me. Papa several times submitted requests to the labor office to get me in a town brigade, or at least to arrange some other place for me. But the requests apparently got lost there, because we received no reply to any of them.

Then my father adopted the following tactic: My father is a singing teacher in the ghetto. That is to say he works as a teacher here in the two schools that were opened some time ago. Since he gets nothing for his teaching—that is, it is of no use to him [in obtaining food], he renounced teaching singing in the schools. Teachers used to come and beg my father to return, but Papa wouldn't budge. Dr. Shapiro himself came to our house and asked Papa to explain why he doesn't want to go back to teach. (Dr. Shapiro is head or director of the school board—all the schools are under his jurisdiction.)[9] Papa had his answer all prepared: "My whole family (here he meant my brother-in-law Shloyme and me) goes to work at the airfield and none of us goes into town, at a time when in other ghetto families as many as two men go into town. I want either work in town or an occupation here in the ghetto itself to be arranged for my son. Until this matter is settled, I refuse, as a matter of principle, to go to teach."

Dr. Shapiro took an interest in this matter and promised Papa that he would arrange work for me in the ghetto. A teacher came to our house and, in my name, wrote an application to the vocational school to be taken on as a carpenter. Not long afterward I received an invitation to present myself to the [application] committee.

I reported to the committee. I was called out. I entered a nice room. Around a round table there sat probably some ten people. Here I recognized Dr. Shapiro, [Jacob] Oleyski (he's a big shot in the vocational school, too), and many other familiar and unfamiliar noses and eyes. In a corner far to the side sat a little man with a bald pate, adorned with a big wen in the middle of his head.

"What is your family name?" I heard a voice from the corner.

"Gerber, Elye [Ilya] Gerber," I answered, enduring the sharp and unpleasant gaze of the man with the wen.

"How old?"

"Seventeen," was my answer, despite the fact that I am a year older than that.

"Where did you work until today?"

"At the airfield." At the same time I take out both my labor cards and hand them to him. He examines the expired card and the second one, which at that time, three weeks ago, already had eight weeks' attendance stamped on it.

"Yes, that is the best love letter," he said with a smile. "And have you any notions of carpentry?"

"Yes! I understand the trade more or less. I once studied with a certain Segalovitsh (a non-native)."

"Could you make a bench by yourself, or a stool or a chair?"

"Yes!" was my answer, and all the while my heart was beating wildly from telling such a big lie. I, who have spent my whole "young years" in school and *Gimnaziye*—how could I have learned a trade, and carpentry in particular? The man with the wen asked me a few more questions about tools of the trade. I answered, hemming and hawing, as they say, gave brief answers and successfully endured his look until I heard the words, "You can go!"

I had no doubt that I had been accepted. I had the best people at the table on my side. First of all, the director of all the schools and also of the vocational school, Dr. Shapiro, and second, Attorney Garfunkel, the right hand of Dr. Elkes and the most respected person in the ghetto, one who has held the highest position.[10] Could there be a better application than mine, with the signatures of the above-mentioned persons?

[. . .] I worked there for approximately two weeks. You really could learn something there, but nothing lasts forever. Up to the twenty-sixth we young newly arrived students were making progress in carpentry when all of a sudden on the night of the 25th–26th there appeared announcements [. . .] saying, "According to the order of the authorities all schools without exception (including vocational schools) will be closed." That was a blow for us. Were we now to abandon our work in the middle and go back to the airfield? But I remembered the slips that the labor office issued to us as certificates that confirm that we are working in the vocational school. The first certificate is from the vocational school. The second is from the [ghetto] police. In the latter certificate it is stated that during six days of the week I am not obligated to work. (Meaning in the city or at the airfield.) But Saturday, once a week, I am obligated. The certificate is valid till the fifteenth of September. That's not so bad after all, I think to myself. It's a long while until the fifteenth, and maybe in the meantime they will reopen the vocational school? Everything is possible.

Eight o'clock in the morning on the twenty-sixth I went off to the vocational school. The instructors were there already. They explained the situation of the school to us and expressed the hope that the school would soon be reopened. Several days went by. The school is still closed. They think that tomorrow, September 1 (Tuesday), the school will start to function again, with even greater scope. They say the work that the school puts out will be inspected. The inspector is supposedly a German.

August 31, 1942: Concerning the Beach

In the ghetto a beach!? This was already being talked about in our shtetl when the banks of the Vilija were still sheathed in ice. It was unbelievable. Do Jews, too, need a beach? Are they equating us with human beings? That would be interesting to know. The year was abnormal, perfectly suited to the abnormal and sickly times. Now cold, now hot, and vice versa. People shrugged their shoulders, stared at the sky, and did not understand: is it wintertime or spring, or—is it summer or autumn?!

I remember a winter morning, a terrible biting wind with snow, people's noses, cheeks, and ears froze, and by twelve or one o'clock they were slowly removing their coats. When summer arrived, I remember, people went to work with high fur collars. In the morning, they shivered as if feverish, and a few hours later, a heat wave, a steam bath. . . . But lately the weather here has finally been straightened out by the Almighty, and the beach season has opened. No ceremonies were held, no glasses were raised. All was quiet at the opening. People came, got undressed, bathed, got dressed, and left the same way that they had come. . . .

The best thing about coming to the beach is that you forget the situation in which we find ourselves. You cheer up, you play, you do a bit of sports. If the weather is good, the beach is filled with Jews—you couldn't fit a pin in. Little kids come, and grown-ups, as well as older men and women. They bathe and splash up a storm. For the aerodromshchik it is the ideal "bath." He comes back from work covered with dust and exhausted, and a bit of cold water, a beach, refresh the workingman. Young people find pleasure and pastime there (after all, they do not go to school). The older ones make dates at the beach (that's a pleasure, too . . .). And if older people sometimes come to refresh themselves, there's nothing wrong with that either. They are reminded of the good days of the past, of their youth, and they try to recapture their former liveliness. For each, the beach is a pleasure and an amusement.

The times of bathing are from five in the afternoon until eight o'clock. But young people pay no attention. They come when they wish, and go home when they wish.

Lately there has been talk in the ghetto that bathing in the Vilija will be prohibited as of September 1. First, because of the darkness. The days are already getting a lot shorter. And second, quite the contrary, they stretch out too long, and the authorities are afraid that in the darkness people may escape through the water to the other side of the Vilija. . . . You think that hasn't happened already? Several Jewish policemen swam over the water (or rather mostly walked over, since the Vilija is very shallow this year). On the other side they carried on a lengthy conversation with peasants and returned. And people do not just swim over from our side. We get visitors from the other side. Some time ago a man swam over the Vilija with a small valise in his hand. The police found him out and handed him over to the ghetto watch, the NSKK. They say the swimmer was a Russian soldier, a parachutist. Another time some gentile boys came to visit the ghetto beach. Jewish police took them to the ghetto watch as well. . . . A Jew arrested a superior, a Lithuanian—isn't that comic?

I am a constant, daily visitor and devotee of the beach. I find freedom here, the liveliness of youth and rest from the sounds of the ghetto. The sounds of the ghetto have no access to the beach. Here "carefree youth" bathes and doesn't want to hear about bad things. You have to grab things while you can. . . .

Even the elite of the shtetl come here. Friday practically the whole personnel of the labor office was here, Lipzer and many other big shots. At that moment, when they stood almost naked, just like all the other ordinary people at the beach, everyone was pretty equal. This one is a Jew, and the other one is a Jew. One people! One stain covers this one and the other one, the simple aerodromshchik and the higher rank of the ghetto, the elite of the town. And yet, so divided, so separated! Why is it so? Cannot the Almighty bring equality to this people condemned to death, his people? Why can the beach do it? It makes everyone equal for the moment: all are half naked, no armbands, no privileges are to be seen here! All are on one soil, all are in the same water! Here you seem to see one naked people without distinction—one nation.

September 3, 1942

Yesterday was Ida Santotski's birthday. Our group had been preparing for this birthday for quite a long time. How preparing? We hadn't done anything substantial, but we talked about it often. . . . And since we're talking about the birthday, I'll do a little writing about it.

As is known, this "company" has a membership of seven. Here I will describe the company once again—Ida Santotski, Dora Rabinovitsh, Lyusya Manevitsh, and among the boys, Avremke Tiktin, Izke Kagan, Ilik Rabinovitsh, and I. On occasion you could also add Abrashke Levin.

It all began with me. My birthday was July 23 (see Book 2, page [   ]). [On occasion, as here, Gerber referred to entries written in his previous notebooks. He apparently intended to look up the page numbers or related information and include them later, although he never did.] From that entry it can be seen that they consider me a good friend and that they expressed their friendship on the above-mentioned day.

The second birthday in point of time was Ilik Rabinovitsh's. (On August [   ] he was nineteen, a year older than I.) They "celebrated" his birthday at his house. I expressed our good wishes in the name of our group. There was cake with whipped cream, pastry, cookies, sweets, beer, liquor, cigarettes, gooseberries (not to mention coffee). In addition—records (Russian, English, German). Lights? Whatever kind you like. Do you want red ones? There are red ones. Blue? Let them be blue. In short, it was quite cheerful at his place. I smoked a lot that evening. . . . At my birthday party, which the girls had organized in my honor, there was no record player, but the gang didn't let that stop them. They stomped their feet, clapped their hands, clicked their tongues, and smacked their lips. In short, there was a beat and there was dancing, too. At Ilik's, there was plenty of dance music (he brought the records, I believe, from the Gestapo), but there was no dancing. Why? Because his father, Rabinovitsh, was taken away with the first 530 for work . . . Ilik had promised not to dance, and nobody dared to dance.[11]

The third birthday—that's Ida's. At about eight o'clock in the evening Izke and I came to her. The light shining in the house is red (evidently Ilik had brought the red lamp). Spirits were high. [. . .] I was really in form. I danced practically one dance after another; I wanted to be happy. Why? I wanted to forget something unforgettable—her. (About "her"—some other time.) [. . .]

At quarter to twelve I danced the last dance with Ida—a quick-fox. For about ten minutes, Abrashke Levin sang a beautiful potpourri of Yiddish folk songs. We all said a friendly good-bye. . . .

The night was beautiful and starry. I was reminded once again of Heni—she should have been here tonight, I thought to myself. . . .

Part of the way home from Ida's, we heard Yiddish-speaking voices.

Ilya Gerber
{341}

"Who goes there?" the three of us heard a voice. In the moonlight we recognized the armbands of the Jewish police. . . .

"Come over and let us see who's there!" we heard the same familiar voice behind us. We halted. Three policemen came over to us with papers in their hands.

"Oh, Alyoshke! Is that you?" I called out, recognizing the policeman Alyoshke Levin.

"Go, kids, go on home," he says to us. "The Lithuanian patrol might pass this way soon."

We went away. Near the housing blocks the three of us parted. I went into the suffocating little room where we, the five members of our family, sleep. Outside there remained the lovely, starry night. . . .

September 8, 1942

It was in town that I [first] saw her [Heni]. She was mostly with another group, was always happy (so it appeared to me, looking from the side) and cheerful. I found out her first name and family name, and looked upon her as a pretty girl, but you couldn't say that I cared for her a lot, since I had not seen her up close. Going past her, I would glance at her, just as I might at my former friends (some of them—even now). One look, one little bit of admiration, one stronger heartbeat, and that's it, as if it had never happened.

September 10, 1942: My Relationship with Heni

As can be seen from page 341 [of the diary] and further, it is quite understandable that in town we did not know each other personally. I knew her from a distance, and as she [later] told me, she didn't know me then [either]. In the ghetto I saw her a few times, but that too was from afar. She was in the company of Edit Gets. More than once I looked her over from a distance, and more than once I thought about her.

One morning (that was quite a while ago, but I don't remember when) on Kriščiukaičio Street on my way to work, I heard a voice behind me:

"What time is it getting to be?"

I turned around. Heni was walking next to a woman, and had asked her the question.

"I don't know," answered the woman.

"A quarter to six," I said, turning to Heni. We pulled up alongside each other. We were both on our way to our workplaces. We spoke about this and that, about news of no importance, about life at the airfield. We parted. My heart was pounding. . . .

Spring passed, summer arrived upon the earth. The beach season commenced. There I saw her again. After not having seen her for a long time, I might have forgotten her (I had liked her only as a pretty girl), but now, when we saw each other at the beach, a feeling of restlessness and longing filled my heart. I was drawn to her. Several times our eyes met between the water and the sand (on the beach). . . . But I did not greet her! She recognized me. I knew her and wanted to get to know her, but I was unable to greet her. My own lack of boldness with her seemed a bit comical to me, but that is part of my character.

I wanted to greet her, and I didn't do it! Had I greeted her, we would have had the opportunity to talk, and I was afraid of that. If I spoke to her a few times at least, I would go to pieces completely, I would fall in love! I felt it and that is why I wanted to avoid it. I already know what love means. I know what suffering is (don't laugh!) because I've already experienced it. . . . I wanted to avoid it, I didn't want any worries, any heartache. I didn't want it and I did want it! I was drawn to it as to a magnet. I felt that I would have to surrender! I cannot fight love! I knew—the period of love means jealousy and suffering and also arguments. I foresaw it all, I knew it all, but I had to bow my head. . . . For whom? For Heni! For her! Because in my heart I silently loved her, because she had conquered me! [. . .]

September 11, 1942 [continuation of above entry]

In short—I met her several times at the beach. Several times our eyes met, but we remained strangers to each other, two different people.

But I felt things could not go on like that much longer. I had to go over to her.

I waited for the right moment. After bathing, she was walking from the beach with Rivka Kaydan. I had observed that from a distance. With the excuse that I have to be home earlier today, I separated myself from my group of boys and girls and went off by myself in the direction where Heni was going. At the edge of the beach the two girls stopped. I went over to them.

"It seems to me," I said, turning to Heni, "that we have already met somewhere."

"Yes!"

"I think it was on the way to work, wasn't it?"

We both stared at each other. She smiled and I did likewise (we both understood the ploy I had used as an excuse to go over to her). Our acquaintanceship had been struck. My mood improved. I accompanied the girls to their home (they live near each other), and then I myself happily "danced" back to my house. . . .

Someone in love will always say or write (to make it more romantic) how he slept the first night after a long-awaited encounter with another person and he will

Ilya Gerber

{343}

always say that the first night was a sleepless night, a night of reflection, a night of happiness. . . . Therefore I will not write here how I slept that night, because it is self-evident. In short, I didn't sleep. . . .

So for several days in a row I accompanied Heni back home from the beach. At the beach, when we would meet, we would greet each other and then go our separate ways. Going home, we would be close to each other.

"Maybe you have some free time this evening, Heni?" I ask her one time before we part.

She glances at me. "Yes, today, I have time."

"What time?"

"Nine o'clock, here at this spot," Heni replies.

I press her hand. We part until nine o'clock. Before nine I am already at the appointed spot. Heni soon arrives. We stroll about for a bit. [. . .] So it went for several days. Short conversations, not very important, as befitted our short strolls. We got to know each other better. Time did not stand still. We strolled on Varnių Street, past the trees, tried to gaze at the stars, at the moon. There were beautiful, pleasant moments—moments when I felt happy and content. I let her know, as if in passing, that things are not so simple for me, that two together is always stronger, that two together is better [than one]. I hinted that I am not indifferent to her (I did not yet say it openly). I can truthfully say that I encountered no great resistance in her answers to my words, and this gave me satisfaction.

How many times did the [curfew] siren interrupt us? I don't remember. Very often, as we were strolling about, the siren would catch us in the middle, and then it would separate us. . . . In the days when the technical school was closed and I walked about the streets freely like a dandy smoking cigarettes, I would always be with her at twelve o'clock, and in the evening at nine. In this way I used to see her twice a day. I felt a closeness to her that she also felt. We more or less understood each other, and not only did the two of us understand it, but also the girls and my gang—my pals. Lyusya asked me how things were going, Dora and Ida congratulated me. Avremke asks me how things stand on that front:

"The attack is still going on," I answer, "but we are advancing gradually step by step and the first troops apparently have entered the suburbs. I will provide you with further commentary on the situation in a separate communiqué. . . ." [. . .]

Several evenings she and I walked arm in arm. I felt extremely happy. She was coming closer to me, becoming more a part of myself. How often, when she would pause near a tree and lean against it, she would be so beautiful, so attractive, that I would have to restrain myself not to take hold of her and kiss her all over. Heni! I loved her! And I love her!

Ilya Gerber

Friday the 11th [September 1942]

I lay in bed until exactly seven o'clock in the evening. I had no more patience to lie in bed like a dead fish or the most gravely ill patient and got up, got dressed, and went out into the street. First, I went over to Heni's. I was told that she had left just five minutes earlier, so I went to Lyusya's. I stayed a couple of minutes with her, and noticed in the distance Dora, Ilik, Avremke, and Izke. Avremke was a bit upset and was walking with Ilik. We greeted each other from a distance. Dora and Izke came over to Lyusya and me and the other two turned down a side street. [. . .] "Kids, go home quick, do you hear? They are nabbing people in the streets!" We turned around. Several men were standing behind us and repeated their words. We slowly started to move away.

"Good-bye, Lyusya and Dora, I'm running over to Heni's!" I quietly said to them.

"Good-bye, Lyusik" [diminutive for Ilya].

With rapid steps I went to her. If the times are unsettled I wanted to warn her to take precautions. She was not at home. [. . .] All of a sudden I remembered that the notebook with the ghetto songs was at Ida's (I have a special notepad in which I collect all the songs that the ghetto creates—the first person I gave it to was Heni, later Ida), so I went over to her place and brought it back.

[Sunday, September 13]

I could not sit still at home. I feel drawn outside . . . [. . .] Right after lunch I went to Heni's. I "coincidentally" found her at home. (I say coincidentally, because usually when I come to her house, she is not at home.) Among the things we talked about, I asked her for a picture of herself. "I don't have any photos of myself," she answered. I know that from before, because I had looked through her two albums and I found no pictures of her there. But [now] I see her take out a new album with several big pictures of young people. At first she holds the photographs on her knees, but the album is turned with the good side to me. She explains to me who is in the pictures. In the middle of explaining she turns the album toward herself.

In order to see the pictures, I was forced to get up and stand near her to look into the album. I bent over. Her hair touched mine, they tickled me. . . . I became restless. I felt that my hand, which was leaning against her chair, was nervously trembling. That is the first time this has ever happened to me. A light and quiet voice continued to explain [the pictures]. I did not hear the words. I felt that I was not myself. I restrained myself: with one quick move I was sitting on the sofa opposite her. My breath was hot. I still felt the touch of her beautiful hair. She had control over me, but I also controlled myself.

Ilya Gerber

"Heni," I said to her, "when will you have time for me? I want to ask your advice about something . . ."

"You can't talk about it now?"

"No, not now. It's about a girl . . ."

"Lyusinke [diminutive for Ilya], if this is some gossip about a girl, then better don't tell me, because I dislike things like that."

"No, that didn't even cross my mind!" I exclaimed. "Have I ever talked to you about a girl behind her back? I don't think I ever have. I mean something quite different. I hate backbiting—it's not in my nature! If you ever have time," I draw out my words, "let me know, and then I will ask your advice."

I spoke, and my heart was beating with anxiety. I want to try myself out on her! The girl I want to speak to her about—is she herself! I want to tell her that I have fallen in love with a girl, and that my love endures to this day in the depths of my heart. I will tell her that I had happy evenings with the girl, despite the fact that I never declared my love for her. I kept my love stifled within myself. I wanted to turn away from the girl, I did not want to suffer pain, but no, I couldn't do that, or rather, I wasn't able to do it. I stifled my love inside me, and it choked me. It overcame me. That is what I will tell her and ask her advice. Let her show me the correct way: should I continue to suffer and even perhaps try to forget the girl who has not revealed her feelings for me, neither good nor bad. Or should I say to her that I love her, that I adore her more than any other? I would like to know the answer. It is important for me.

September 18, 1942

Among those rounded up for work at Palemon, my friend Beke Kot was caught. Beke was a schoolmate of mine, a merry fellow. In town he lived near us, in the same street. They had a bakery on Nemuno Street. His sister was run over by an automobile and killed. In the ghetto, during the Great Aktion [of October 28, 1941], his mother, who was ill, and his father were taken away to the [Ninth] Fort. Beke remained alone. His father had money. He buried it, but Beke did not know where it was. However, he did not lose his bearings. He even supported an aunt. He even had fights with the Jewish police and for that he frequently sat in jail—he could not tolerate their misdeeds. Since mostly it was single people who were sent to Palemon, he was dragged out of his bed in the middle of the night.

The next morning, the day after Beke was put in the jailhouse (it was from there that people were sent to Palemon) Izke was walking past the so-called prison:

"Izke, help me! Try to get me out of here! Save me!"

Izke raised his head to the iron-grated window. A pair of dark, sad eyes looked out to him. Both school friends gazed at each other—one of them with a pleading look, calling for help, the other with astonishment and sympathy. But Izke was unable to help Beke. How? In what way?! It was impossible at that moment. Beke has no one and is without pull, so he was taken away. . . .

September 24, 1942

Rosh Hashanah and Yom Kippur have already passed; we have them behind us. I want to mention that the population tried to be devout during this time of repentance. People organized *minyanim* [religious quorums] in private homes (the synagogue was closed [by the Germans] on the twenty-sixth of last month). Thus, for example, at the Santotskis there was a *baal-tefila* [prayer leader] and the main thing—the elite of the town were here, such as [Karl] Natkin [an official of the ghetto labor office], Lipzer, and many other big shots. People tried to fast, some of them did in fact fast, while others ate like in the good old days. Finished praying, finished beating their breasts, people had a bite to eat, and Yom Kippur was gone without a trace. Gone, left behind, people have forgotten about it. . . .

We young folks get together almost every evening and enjoy ourselves like little children, and for us the ghetto is no ghetto. We do not feel it in each other's company and we do not wish to feel that we sit behind wire, separated from the world and from humankind.

The vocational school has officially reopened. Today I got a certificate (with hard covers, with a design, with dots, with dates, with little boxes, and little stamps, and there is no lack of signatures in Yiddish . . .).

The twenty-first of this month was Lyusya's birthday. Izke, Bubchik (a likable young fellow of about thirteen or fourteen, maybe even all of fifteen, who lives in the same flat as Izke), and I came to Lyusya's at seven-thirty in the evening. Here also, as at the birthdays of Ilik and Ida, there were red lights and the main thing—a nice, lovely, tasteful, interesting, and rich table was set. On the table—sponge-cake rolls of two kinds, and both filled with jam or cream, pastries light- and dark-colored, of two different flavors, candies of all kinds, two whole cakes, one a light-colored one with icing in the form of a wreath—and best of all you could lick your fingers from it. The second cake looked like an eight, round, dark, shiny, cream-covered, delicious. In short, it got eaten too, and the young folks definitely did not hold back. In addition—coffee (of the better kind) with sugar—that was on the table. Around the table the company of young people. [. . .]

In a few minutes the table was half empty. In another couple of minutes no trace would have remained of anything, but we spared some, so the Manevitsh family should get something too. . . .

Ilya Gerber

September 27, 1942: Latest ghetto news:

A month ago, the ghetto was talking about an eviction of the inhabitants of several streets in the ghetto. Which ones? There was talk about those streets and alleys that are located behind Demokratų Street or Demokratų Square. It was talked about so much that finally the inhabitants of those streets truly became alarmed and one night the Jews of those eight streets tried to move across to the other side, within the boundaries of the ghetto. For two days people quietly gathered, stole past the fence with pillows, with parcels and valises. . . . And all of a sudden, yesterday (Saturday the twenty-sixth) I look out the window and I see whole caravans of wagons and loaded backs and shoulders. In short, we understood at our house that what had been talked about the whole time had now come to pass.

I put on my work clothes and went out in the direction of the vocational school, which is located on the "lucky" side that has to move out. On the way I encountered children, women, men—all carrying loads, all dragging their remaining possessions. Imagine what a broken life that is! A while ago, when Jews lived on the other side of Demokratų Street, an order was issued that within such and such a period of time, such and such streets, together with the main street of the neighborhood, Vienozinskio Street, must be vacated, leaving empty the whole area on the other side. In wintertime, in freezing temperatures, Jews moved, labored like ants, hands on their noses [to protect them from the cold], hauling on sleds or directly on the snow, because in two hours the area around Vienozinskio Street had to be free of Jews. Later the deadline was extended. The neighborhood, the eastern part of the ghetto, remained empty—without inhabitants. At the time people in the ghetto said that the emptied quarter is intended for one thousand German Jews, who will arrive here. A week went by, and another, and no one was brought there. No one was brought, only led past! They were led [to the Ninth Fort to their deaths instead]. [. . .]

October 17, 1942

"What's new with the [ghetto] policemen who were brought into the ghetto [accused of smuggling]?" I ask [Dora Rabinovitsh].

"Three of the six were freed, and the other three . . . You could say . . ." Dora did not finish her sentence and just looked at me. I understood.

"To the Ninth Fort?" I ask quietly.

"Yes, there, together with their families . . ."

"How did their families come to be there?"

"At night they rounded them up. Three families, women, children, infants. . . . There they were all . . ." She falls silent.

Ilya Gerber

"Shot?" I ask, finishing her thought.

She remains silent. No use talking about it. People lived, they strived, they wanted to live and to let others live, till . . . till they were cut down before their time because they wanted to eat, they wanted to exist, they wanted to survive. . . . But I say it's no use talking. It has all become clear to everyone, and I am afraid to say it—it's becoming natural. People look at such facts as facts, as inevitable. That is how it is, and nothing can be done about it. People look at such facts with open eyes, they see what happens to this one, to that one. For the moment they feel sorrow, but inside they feel glad [it's not them]. Why is it so? Has the human heart become so hardened that it cannot sympathize with others?

October 18, 1942

Today it is exactly one year (according to the Jewish calendar), two weeks after Simchat Torah, since the Great Aktion was carried out. It was on October 28, 1941. In my first notebook I described over half of the events that took place that unfortunate day. I really don't know why I didn't describe it in its entirety. I regret that. But now to remind myself what happened later to the Jews who had been sorted out [in Demokratų Square] in the Small Ghetto, their sad night in the unheated dwellings of the previously deported Jews of the Small Ghetto, whose lives also ended at the Ninth Fort—that is now rather hard for me. But at the first opportunity I will deliver either my written account or a transcription from the diary of Lyusya Manevitsh. (It was I who asked each of the three girls to keep a diary. They jumped at the idea and immediately armed themselves with writing paper. But in fact it was only Lyusya M. who carried it out. With her, all the dates are exact, even more exact than mine are. A couple of times I have had occasion to read her diary. I will now borrow it for a third time from her.)

October 19, 1942

Today the ghetto is very uneasy. Various rumors are circulating. It is interesting who is responsible for these exaggerated rumors—it seems to me that the Germans are better friends of the Jewish people than the Jews themselves. If a chill wind blows through the ghetto, then even before the Germans have decided what they are going to do with us, a rumor goes out in the ghetto, let out by the Jews themselves: an *aktion!* A misfortune! Anything at all and already they're digging mass graves at the Ninth Fort!

I remember, a while ago, that the mood was so bad in the ghetto that it could drive you crazy. People imagined everything from little incidents up to an aktion. Just then some *yaale* [big shot] or other happened to arrive at the committee.

Some Jews, ghetto big shots naturally, were bold enough to ask him about this painful question. He burst out laughing and answered: "It's interesting, that you, Jews, know more than we do! We know nothing yet about any of this and you already know the exact date. . . ."

Today there was a rumor (started by the women standing in line for bread) that the arrested Jews in the jail at Krisčiukaičio 107 (where the workshops are located) broke open the doors and windows and escaped.

"How many people escaped?" one woman asks another.

"What do you mean how many?" comes the answer. "All of them! As many people as there were there!"

"What did you say? How many people escaped?" asks a third woman.

"You just heard," a fourth woman intervenes, "five hundred men and women! They fled down to the last one!"

The first woman, who had been recounting the whole "affair," saw that the attention of the women in the line was lessening toward her, and that everyone was turning to the one that mentioned the five hundred. That annoyed her and she burst out in a single breath, "What five hundred? Why do you bother us if you don't know what you're talking about? I've just come from there—seven hundred people ran away! And just imagine," she adds, wringing her hands, "when the Germans learn of this. Then there will be—woe is me!—there will be an aktion! They'll grab people in the streets, they'll take people neighborhood by neighborhood!!" Around this woman everything grew quiet.

In a couple of minutes there was a commotion in the rear of the line. The noise grew louder and louder and there was the sound of fast running and the loud cry, "They're grabbing people in the streets! They're taking people away neighborhood by neighborhood! They're dividing people into left and right" [as during the Great Aktion].

[. . .] It looked as if a bomb had been dropped—everyone fled in a different direction. The woman who had wanted to direct everyone's attention to herself remained all alone in the corridor and whispered distractedly: "Can it be true? Can it be?. . ."

November 1, 1942

Last night Papa received a commission from the Jewish ghetto police to arrange the Hebrew hymn *Hatikva* for a whole orchestra. This morning, lying in bed, Papa wrote it out. Today at ten o'clock (today, Sunday, the technical school is not working for the third Sunday in a row and I am free today all day) we were sent two notices at home.

[Entry written that night:]

Today I brought back from Heni the book *The Diary of Kostya Ryabtsev*. There were [between Heni and Ilya] short, abrupt words, silent, dull glances, a brief handshake and that was it—as if there had never been anything. . . .

Papa tells us his impressions of the ceremonial oath of the police officers in the Yeshiva. Everything was successfully performed. The police swore to the labor office that all the orders they receive from the higher [ghetto] authority they will carry out in a spirit of integrity, without regard to any external obstacles, because that is what is required of them. They swore that in case an extreme situation arises in the ghetto there will be no "this one is my brother, my sister, this one is a stranger"—all must be equal at such a moment. No favoritism must be shown. These are the obligations of the Jewish policeman.

November 2, 1942

Today I received an announcement that I have to go into town to work as a carpenter in the "Boston" factory. In general lately a lot of people from the vocational school have been sent to work in town. For example, thirty locksmiths and twelve carpenters. On one hand I am pleased and on the other hand it makes me sad. I am pleased that I will be able to bring a little bit of food from there and thereby help my family, and I am sad that I will have to part company with my fun-loving young companions, with whom I have been having a cheerful and happy time in the vocational school.

November 5, 1942

Since the third [of November] I have been working in "Boston." "Boston" is the name of a factory that dates from the good old [prewar] times. Now the machinery of the factory has been sent deep into Germany and the factory has been transformed into a big automobile garage. Here in the garage work thirty Jews, more or less skilled workers, and about five Lithuanians. The supervisor is a German *Meister* [specialist], a [Nazi] Party member, but still a decent person. He doesn't yell at you, jokes from time to time, and understands your feelings.

At quarter to seven we pass through the ghetto gate. We have no guard along the way. There is no disciplined marching either. The procession of thirty men stretches for two blocks. There are quite a few meters between each man and the next. When we arrive at "Boston" (about ten minutes walk from the ghetto) all the Jews go up to the window where the German Meister stands and hands each person a slip of paper. On the slip is marked each one's number (my number—146).

Ilya Gerber

Below that each worker at the factory has to fill out these question like: what did you work at, how many hours did it take you, what did you complete, and so on. We go to work, and work till eight-thirty. From then till nine o'clock it's breakfast.

At the appointed time a gong sounds, and everyone downs tools. Everyone runs up the hill to the special room that has been provided for the Jews. Here is the kitchen and the food hall. In the kitchen two women work. One is our neighbor Mrs. Britfeld and the other everyone calls Sheynele. I call her that, too. On three long tables cups of coffee are already standing ready. At nine o'clock everyone goes back to work. We work till twelve.

From twelve to twelve-thirty is lunchtime. The bowls of *yushnik* [swill] are already prepared. The lunch costs two marks [twenty rubles] per person. If you are hungry, you eat it and even digest it. There are not many who reject it. . . . Lunch is the time when business deals are made. Some daring fellows made a hole in the fence and from there they scatter in all directions. These men bring back with them hundreds of pounds of flour, beets, potatoes, macaroni, and green vegetables. Naturally, they want to be compensated for the risks they have taken, and you cannot blame them. For potatoes people here pay 15 rubles [per kilo], beets—20 rubles, butter—700 rubles, macaroni—140 rubles, rye flour—60 rubles, two kilos of bread—130 rubles.

We knock off work at four o'clock. We arrive at the ghetto about six. The inspection at the gate (we go through the Varnių Street gate) goes pretty well today. The Lithuanian policeman has been given forty marks and the brigade goes through without incident. The policeman (a high-ranking officer) pats everyone, but confiscates nothing. I am the last to go through. I had on me three kilos of rye flour, five kilos of potatoes, and two kilos of beets. The flour I hid around my stomach and the rest I carried in a bag. The policeman patted me from top to bottom, including my stomach, tapped my "compress" [a "girdle" with a compartment for smuggling food] thoroughly and shoved me into the ghetto without saying a word.

November 10, 1942

Father has obtained a new position in the ghetto. One no one had ever heard of before, and one he never sought—he has become the conductor of the Policemen's Chorus, now being formed. Papa has been appointed director and he must put together a four-voice chorus of about a hundred ghetto policemen. It sounds like a [bad] dream—the Jews in the ghetto, people condemned to death, no, not so much people as shadows of people, living corpses, future "daisy-pushers"—these are the ones who are to create a chorus in the ghetto? Why? To amuse the embittered public? For whom? For the Germans? Hebrew songs, cantorial laments,

Yom Kippur melodies, all for the Germans? Whom are they creating the chorus for—the labor office? For Margolis [head of recruitment at the labor office of the Jewish Council]? For Lurie [head of the airfield section of the labor office]? For the people whose friends, brothers, sisters, and nearest and dearest have gone to the [Ninth] Fort!? For whom . . . ?

November 15, 1942

[. . .] Ten minutes ago Fanye Dembovitsh ran into our house. She says [that] half an hour ago an assassination was attempted against the ghetto commandant. It happened this way—a certain watchmaker named Meck . . . tried to crawl through the fence with a package. The commandant noticed Meck and wanted to detain him. Meck shot at him but missed. Meck was arrested. . . . As soon as the higher ranks of the labor office found out about this, they closed the offices and convened the council members.

Fanye adds that Gestapo men have already entered the ghetto. . . . We all wondered: a Jew should have a weapon on him? Such a thing has never been heard of! Hard to believe that a Jew would have the audacity to hold a revolver in his hand and shoot from it, too!! It is more likely to be a provocation, either from the ghetto commandant or from the Lithuanians. I am reminded at once of the first provocation, which likewise sounded like this: "The then ghetto commandant Kozlovski was shot at from the ghetto." I remember that after the provocation (in a day or two) the aktion against the Small Ghetto was carried out. . . . And now yet again a provocation?! And will they deport again?

November 16, 1942

Today, Monday, the mood in the brigade was not at all upbeat. Yesterday's events had a strong effect on life inside the ghetto. There was the threat of a mass execution. As the Jewish police inform us, it was not a provocation, but something real— the young man Meck shot at the commandant, or perhaps into the air. Makes no difference.

November 18, 1942 [Drawing of a man hanging on a gallows, a skeleton with a bow and arrow, and a skull and crossbones]

Last night Dora told me that Meck will be hanged today. Today, coming back from my brigade through the Varnių Street gate, we were told that Meck is hanging near the committee [Jewish Council offices]. (Actually, we already knew it at about noon, working at the "Boston" factory.)

When I went through the gate, it was already very dark, and although I looked

Ilya Gerber

{353}

for the spot of the hanged Meck, I could not find it. My heart would not let me ask people, ask a Jewish passer-by. How can the words even be uttered: "Where is Meck hanging?" I couldn't do it. The words sounded too simple and at the same time too cruel. Brrrr. . . .

As my mother tells it they hanged Meck at exactly noon. There arrived many yaales in taxis, on horseback, on motorcycles, and on foot. They came with one object—to see the Jew hanging. The inhabitants of the surrounding streets were driven to the hanging place. Before the hanging, Meck was asked what he wanted before his death. He said: "I want to go as a sacrifice for my family. I ask—let my mother and sister go free." Poor Meck didn't know that his mother and sister had been sent to the Ninth Fort an hour before. . . .

November 19, 1942

Today at noon they took Meck down from the gallows. Yesterday evening I wanted to go over to him, but my heart did not let me. For a couple of minutes I looked from a distance at the black, swaying body and walked away whistling. Why whistling, of all things? To cheer myself up? I don't know. Maybe so.

This morning, on my way to work, I saw the body hanging again, but again went by without stopping. At twelve o'clock (precisely) he was buried in the Jewish cemetery. The whole time that Meck was hanging, two Jewish policemen stood by his body. Every two hours they were changed. That was a kind of "Garbės sargyba" [guard of honor].

November 27, 1942

I haven't written since the nineteenth because there was no very important Jewish news, except that brigades have lately been smuggling in [food] not in their pockets, and not in little packages, but in fact in whole bundles. Sometimes the passage through the Kriščiukaičio gate is successful and sometimes not. Mostly, when the ghetto commandant stands by the gate, the bundles or packages are confiscated and you sometimes feel his whip. But if he is not there it costs you whatever it takes to grease the palm of the partisan [Lithuanian auxiliary serving the Germans] or the policeman, and you pass through undisturbed. At the Varnių gate it's different—here the commandant does not come so often and naturally Jews take advantage of the opportunity to carry in hundreds of kilograms. Brigades coming laden with packages from the city make a detour and enter the ghetto via Varnių Street.

But the Varnių gate is very expensive. I know that as a worker at the "Boston" brigade. At first, the Lithuanian police used to ask about three hundred rubles [thirty reichsmarks] for letting you through. But the Jewish police or the people from the labor office want to earn something as well! So they come up with a new method of payment—the money is not handed over to the Lithuanian directly but goes through the Jewish policeman. You come to the gate and the Jewish guards at the gate demand:

"For going through the gate you have to pay four hundred rubles."

And a couple of days later:

"Today you pay six hundred rubles!"

A couple of days go by and there is a new demand:

"You pay eight hundred rubles!"

And we pay. Do we have a choice? What if they confiscate [our food]? And how often has it happened that they confiscated everything [anyway], the fine fellows!?

December 1, 1942

Today is the third day that winter has shown its true darkened face and its ice-cold character. Outside it's cold, the wind blows on all its wind and reed instruments to the accompaniment of the white snow. It is hard to keep your eyes open, and from time to time your breath is taken away, cut off by the sharp wind. [. . .]

Today I brought home the rations for my work at "Boston." You get these rations once a month: 2.8 kilograms of bread, 300 grams of butter, a bit of sugar and coffee.

Lately they have been talking about great victories for the Red Army. They are attacking on all the fronts from the Caucasus to the White Sea. Near Terek [on the Caucasus front] they have broken through the German lines. They are finishing up clearing them out of Stalingrad, the offensive between the Volga and the Don has brought good results for the Russians, as the German newspaper itself announces. In the ghetto there are already many rumors that there are battles on the Estonian border and that the deliverance of the Jews is rapidly approaching from the northeast. . . . In Africa, they say, the Germans are beaten down.

See! One more day, a couple of days and the liberation is near. You only need not to lose patience and then everything will be all right. . . . The day after tomorrow is Hanukkah!

December 4, 1942 [Drawing of a menorah with two candles]

Today is the second candle lighting of Hanukkah. Miracles are not evident in the present century. They took place or happened when we did not [yet] exist. Evidently the luck of the Jews of old was greater than our luck. It is not our luck, alas, for miracles to happen to us.[12]

The people creates bit by bit, writes down and expresses the pain of Jewish life

Ilya Gerber

in song. Here they tell, recite, and sing about the life of the Jewish ghetto dweller at work. Every song is a piece of life that embraces a very special period of our times. A ghetto song mostly starts with the pain and misfortune of the Jewish people and ends with the hope for better things, for a bright and happy future. [. . .]

Songs have been created whose content is: (1) leaving the ghetto and the way to the workplace, (2) the suffering, the psychological and physical pain of the work, (3) the making light of your troubles once you have the package [of food bought or bartered outside the ghetto] with you, (4) the way back from work in either a light-hearted mood, or the reverse.

December 20, 1942 [Drawing of three musicians in ragged clothes playing a drum, a violin, and a cello outside on the street]

Despite the fact that spirits in the ghetto are not very high—people are whispering about the aktions that are taking place in Hitler's empire—nevertheless the musical circles are working at 120 percent. They arrange concerts, they have rehearsals, they sing, they play, they blow and they tickle their instruments. Last Saturday there took place a concert for the Jewish police; last Sunday for the better aero-dromshchiks. On that occasion even the German commandant came, together with the Lithuanian one. They liked the concert a lot, and applauded a great deal. When the program had already ended, and everybody got up out of their seats, the aforementioned yaales were still sitting in their places and demanding more. . . .

Today, Sunday, there is a concert for the ghetto administration. The concert takes place at twelve o'clock noon. Until now, concerts used to take place about four o'clock. But since yesterday, when the wires were cut and no more electricity is provided, except for very important institutions and the workshops, leaving the ghetto in the dark, they happen earlier, when it is still light outside.

[. . .] At about noon I was at Salke's. Salke was still lying in bed. When he heard that there is a possibility of hearing the concert, he was ready in ten minutes. At quarter to one we were already at Jesubotų 16, near the former yeshiva. At the door there were a pair of [Jewish] policemen. [. . .]

We find ourselves inside. Quite a long and wide space, adorned with thick pillars in the middle. This is the concert hall. At the end—a platform. Along both sides a painted design representing two harps. In the middle of the platform, two Stars of David. One looked like this [drawing of a star with "J.G.P." in the middle] and the second [drawing of a star inscribed inside a capital G]. The first stands for Jewish Ghetto Police and the second Ghetto Community. We sidled our way into a corner. In the front row were sitting two Lithuanian big shots.

The orchestra performed several numbers, which in general were well received

Ilya Gerber
{356}

by the audience. The conductor Hofmekler bowed graciously to the applause. . . . The newly appointed Kolonnenführer [column leader of a labor brigade] of the airfield, Zaks, sang two songs and then just stopped. The next-to-last number that the orchestra performed was Kol Nidre. The concert was over.

[Later that day, Ilya was walking with his friends Salke and Bebke.]

"Halt!" we suddenly hear a command. Behind us are standing two [ghetto] policemen. I recognize officer Ika [Yehoshua] Grinberg [commander of the First Precinct of the Kovno Ghetto Police].

He asks Salke, "Where do you work?"

"In the vocational school," comes the reply.

"And you?"

"Also in the vocational school," says Bebke.

"And what about you, Gerber?"

"In 'Boston,'" I boldly reply.

"Did you work today?"

"Not today, but I did the whole week."

"Give me your [work] card," he says resoundingly.

That surprises me—a close acquaintance, a former Gimnaziye teacher of mine, a good friend of our family—he's the one who arrests me? I try to talk him out of it. It doesn't help.

"Go, Salya [Salke], tell them at our house that I've been nabbed." The boys disappear.

I walk with Officer Grinberg and am amazed. For the moment I was angry with him, but later I thought to myself that if all the yaales were so conscientious, if nobody had any *protektsiye* [pull], as is the case with him, things would be very different. As it is, as a result of all the protektsiye it is only the *amkho* [common people], those with few connections in the "well-known" circles, who suffer. If there were no protektsiye, the "Jewish catastrophe" would have fallen not only on the heads of the unknown, but on everyone generally. In this case I respected and esteemed Grinberg.

On the way, the "commander" [Grinberg] caught several other people who were not working on Sunday and led us all away to the office of the jail on the corner of Kriščiukaičio. We went through a small door in a high barbed-wire fence, and entered the narrow corridor of the former Jewish school. The low ceiling and narrow passageway are perfectly suited for a jail. The jail office is on the left. A four-sided room, the ceiling practically on top of your head, and filled with policemen. Opposite the door, against the wall, a rectangular table, weighed down with a big white lamp, tens of work cards of detainees, and the two hands of the secretary—also a policeman.

The noise in the crowded room was great.

"You're a stool pigeon! I brought in two people and you, scum, let them go!" one policeman screams at another.

"You're scum yourself! How can you accuse me of letting them out? Did you see it? Swine!"

"Silence!" Grinberg says to the two opponents in a quiet and authoritative tone.

Things gradually quiet down. But then all at once all the policemen go running over to the commander, exclaiming:

"Write down, Commander, I brought in two!"

"I brought four!"

"Me, one, write it down. . . ."

The disorder causes Grinberg to start shouting.

December 21, 1942

Every minute policemen arrived with "captives." Grinberg wrote down how many young men each brought with him and the other scribbler registered the people brought in. Every group of three people who were registered were handed over to the policeman Iserlis.

Among the family names that were called out was mine. They led us out into the corridor. Iserlis was already holding our cards in his hand. To me he looked uncouth and coarse. In one hand he held a flashlight and a whip and in the other our three cards. He called us out individually. At that moment he opened the door to the corridor and tried to push us in there. It was hard for him. On the open side of the door there stood squeezed together about ten men and behind them many more faces stood out. I understood that it is the threshold of the jail. The voices of the "jailbirds" were not musical and also could not be heard by the ordinary passer-by. Iserlis pushed us from behind and in the front stood a wall of Jews that would not let us in. Iserlis yelled, beat his whip against the ceiling, till the men there took fright and let us in among them.

The door closed behind us. The lock made a grating sound. I am in jail! I was surrounded by darkness. Voices echoed through the emptiness. Everyone was arguing, "blessing" the policemen and the yaales along with their mothers. . . . And all this in the dark while stepping on people's feet and corns. Through the grates and tall windows of the former school a little light penetrated, but that was too weak to overcome the darkness. I lit a match. Pale faces were standing around me and were looking at the spark. There were quite a few of my friends there. I got interested in examining the jail. On the right and left, near the wall and near the windows, stood long and wide double bunk beds. Six beds, three on each side, created a long, wide passageway. In the middle of the room stood a pathetic little stove. My heart sank.

[. . .] The door of the "prison" keeps on opening and closing—new "captives" come in. The noise level gets higher with every minute. Everyone is arguing and gesticulating in the dark, and several people have already quarreled among themselves because in the dark one hit the other in the back with his hands. [. . .]

Suddenly a voice is heard: "Gerber!"

The crowd repeats like an echo, each one individually: "Ge-e-e-r-be-e-r."

Iserlis called me and I went out from the jail to the corridor. I look up—Papa and Khaye [Ilya's sister]. Salke had informed them at my house than I was confined. So Papa came running right over with my sister. They brought my work clothes and some food. I immediately changed clothes and went back into the jail. But Papa did not rest. Since he is more or less known to all the functionaries and policemen, getting me out of jail was not too difficult. Aronshtam [ghetto police officer in charge of labor recruitment], Iserlis, and the police inspector of the Third Precinct and others were very helpful. Papa took his "darling boy" out of jail and transported me home. That was the first time that I was confined behind bars.

December 31, 1942

The notes for the [policemen's] chorus that Papa is being compelled to create are now ready. He has auditioned the voices, the list is ready and today is supposed to be the first rehearsal. Many of the policemen have little desire to be involved in the whole matter and individually they come to our house and try through their personal connections to be excused from singing. This one cannot, that one doesn't want to, his heart will not let him. One of them says, "The whole world is fasting because of our catastrophe, and we should go and sing? The pope, too, has been fasting, and we should amuse ourselves?! No!"

My father hears out such arguments, but he is forced to answer them with one word—no! He cannot excuse anyone. He is being forced to do it, and therefore he has to force others.

January 1, 1943

We, the Jews, stand on the threshold of 1943. Of this year it was said that the Jews will not see it—they will not survive that long. At the beginning of 1942 people were already saying in the ghetto that the Führer had stated that in 1943 you would have to look in a museum to find a Jew. The Jew, the people cursed by *Der Stürmer* as the criminal of all crimes, the one responsible for the world war, the betrayer of nations, the enemy of the people, the parasite who lives at the expense of others, the Bolshevik, the capitalist, the eternal exploiter, upon whose head all curses are heaped, guilty of everything—he, yes he, has survived to a new year, the year 'forty-three!

That is why our little Jews smashed glasses, said "mazel tov" to one another, and caroused. For a whole week they did not despair—they lived well, they ate, they gulped down, they snacked (they overcame their hard-heartedness), they didn't get enough sleep. Let alone the young people. They want to take in everything (an old story: *Der Stürmer* writes the same thing—"Jews want to take over the world and enslave and destroy everyone . . .") and to carry on and dance and sing like in the good old days . . .

January 23, 1943

My final concern at the moment of writing these lines is—where do I find a new notebook, a new diary? Hmm?! Tell me, maybe you know where to get it? I will be most grateful to you for it . . .

BASTA!

13

Anonymous Boy

ŁÓDŹ GHETTO

If there is one diary that captures most vividly the urgent, desperate race for survival that so many Jews shared in the waning years of the war, it is that of an anonymous boy writing in the Łódź ghetto in the spring and summer of 1944. The notes, scribbled in the endpages and margins of a French book titled *Les Vrais riches* [*The Truly Rich*] by François Coppée, were written in Hebrew, Yiddish, Polish, and English. The book seems to have had at least one previous owner, for on the first page there is an affectionate inscription in French, dated February 5, 1918, which reads, "To my dear sister, in remembrance of the good times." In the book's pages, however, the nameless writer who had taken possession of it poured out instead his fury and rage at the Germans and at all humankind, his despair and anxiety about the immediate fate of the surviving Jews in Łódź, his reproaches and appeals to God, and, in the final days, his desperation at the ever dwindling prospect of survival.

By the time the writer began his diary, the ghetto in Łódź (or Litzmannstadt, as the Germans had renamed the city in 1939) was the only Jewish ghetto still standing in occupied Poland, the last of more than two hundred, all the rest of which had been liquidated. In the Łódź ghetto (which was sealed on May 1, 1940, with approximately 163,000 people in it), the German authorities had carried out a series of sporadic deportations between January and May 1942, during which they took away almost 55,000 people from the ghetto. During the final roundup (called the *Shperre,* or "curfew"), in early September 1942, the Germans had forcibly removed another 15,000 people, primarily children under ten years old, the elderly, the sick, and others deemed "unfit for work." Though not known to the ghetto inhabitants at the time, all of these people were taken to the death camp in Chełmno, where they were murdered. With the temporary halt of the deportations, Łódź (with a drastically reduced population of some 89,000 people) essentially became a labor camp, its inhabitants working ceaselessly for the German war effort, and dying not from carbon monoxide poisoning in nearby Chełmno but from starvation, disease, and exhaustion in the ghetto itself.[1]

The diary reveals little about the writer's personal history. He had a twelve-year-old sister, about whom he wrote often, reflecting on her courage in the face of the tremendous suffering she endured.[2] He was plagued by thoughts of her deprivation, her lost youth (often repeating in his diary the hopelessly fatalistic philosophy she had adopted in order to cope with her life), and the part he himself played in her suffering because of his "nervous confusion." It would appear that the two of them lived alone, their "sainted father" (as the writer called him) having died from starvation in the ghetto. Their mother, too, must have been deceased, although the diarist did not mention her, nor did he indicate whether he had ever had any siblings besides his sister. No information survives about the author's name, age, background, and schooling. Indeed, but for the fact that he used the masculine form of verbs when referring to himself in Hebrew and Polish, even his gender would be difficult to establish from the diary.

"Many times I resolved, many times I began writing memoirs, diaries, but after a few entries I dropped it," the diarist wrote in English in mid-May 1944. "It is the total lack of mental and phisical [sic] energy which accounts for it." This, his final attempt at the task, yielded an unusual result; indeed, the text bears only a faint resemblance to other diaries of this period. The entries, though most often dated, are not always written in sequential order; rather, they seem to have been jotted on various pages, wherever the diarist could find space.[3] His handwriting is sometimes neat and orderly (entries in various languages are carefully divided by a horizontal line across the page), and other times hastily scrawled, though still legible, in large, frantic letters woven around a block of printed text. As in the case of another young Polish diarist, Lejzer Silberman, who scribbled across salvaged paper of all kinds, this diary (written on probably the only paper the writer could find) expresses the urgency of committing his final thoughts to paper, no matter how improvised the form or chaotic the style.

It is not only the physical diary that is unusual, but the nature of the text itself. Rather than being a series of sequential diary entries that form a single narrative thread, the text is repetitive and almost elliptical, as an entry on a particular date in one language was often followed by similar text penned in another, and then by yet a third or fourth version. Sometimes, in the middle of the night when he had finished writing in one language, he would turn immediately to another, echoing virtually the same content and phraseology. His command of the four languages in which he wrote is impressive; he expressed himself with almost as much color and force in Hebrew and English as he did in Yiddish and Polish (which were most likely his native languages). The text is laced with German and French words, phrases, and expressions, revealing that he had at least some fluency in those languages as well. Perhaps he wrote in multiple languages to make certain that his ideas and feelings would be understood by anyone who found the diary, to communicate the collective story of life in Łódź to as wide an audience as possible. The multiplicity of language also seems to reveal his driving need to write and to keep writing, to ease his own inner anxiety, bringing himself some comfort during the long, sleepless nights that inevitably magnified worry and fear.

The diary opens in May with the following introduction: "I decided to write a diary, though it is a bit too late. To recapitulate the past events is quite impossible so I begin with the present." From the outset, the primary concerns of the present were, not surprisingly, bread and deportation, the same preoccupations of the anonymous girl writing in the Łódź ghetto two years earlier. But unlike the anonymous girl from Łódź, whose diary was almost entirely devoted to reporting on the specific details of her days, this writer turned his gaze to the wider devastation wrought on humanity by genocide and war. It is as if in the final moments of the battle (the news reaching the ghetto about German defeats and Allied advances) he stopped and took stock of the world as he saw and understood it. The resulting picture is a bitter one in which humanity emerges as a monumental failure. This is evident first and foremost in the dehumanization of the victims themselves, their dignity wrested from them together with their lives. Time and again he referred to all forms of the humiliation of the Jews, their "terrible inhuman state of mind," their "mere beastly craving for food," and their "tragic callousness." And while he usually wrote with tremendous pity and compassion for his "fellow-sufferers," sharing their common fate and desolation, he sometimes shifted his tone, capturing their degradation and indignity with an incomparable mixture of dark humor and caustic wit. "[We are] still far from being able even to dream about a human life, nay, a piggish life, even that is unattainable for us," he reflected in one entry. "Pigs eat and don't worry and we eat not, and worry much and work like asses." From time to time, his despair took still another form, turning from sympathetic solidarity into frank exasperation directed at the Jews themselves for their own dogged determination to live, no matter what the cost.

His portrait of the Jews and the price of their suffering ("us") is matched only by his unrelenting tirades against the criminality of the Germans ("them"). In contrast to most diarists, who were relatively tame on that score, this writer returned again and again to express his loathing for the perpetrators of the crime, assigning them a dizzying variety of insulting epithets. They were, in his words, "our disgustingly untiring oppressors," "abominable thugs," the "diabolical enemy of all humankind," the "cursed devillish [sic] foe," the "Germanohyena," the "uniformed, military Teutonic lice," and "murderous madmen," to name just a few. Their acts are labeled as "German artistry in Sadicisising [Sadism]," "barbaric German exaggeration," "invincible human folly," and the like. In one remarkable diatribe, the writer burst forth with the following: "Indeed! to kill so pointlessly, to continue to fight this hopeless battle, can only be done by these disgusting, sordid, perverted, devoid of all human feelings, slow-witted 'schwermütige' [melancholy] Prussians! Phew! Vampires, sharks, pirates, buccaneers, thugs—to what kind of incomprehensible, predatory species do you belong?"

Far from limiting his fury to the Germans, he also condemned the wider world, "this most conscienceless generation of all," for its part in the grim drama of genocide and war. Nowhere is the belief in the goodness of all people that Anne Frank expressed (and the interpreters of her diary so quickly and willingly adopted) more consistently and thoroughly contradicted than in this desperate, final outcry. He declared his disgust not only with the human beings of the present—the wretched victimhood of the Jews, the obscene criminality of the Germans, and the vaguely articulated "rest of the world"—but with humanity itself. Time and again he expressed the conviction that modern humanity had chosen a course of evil and indifference that could never be reversed. Even God himself was not exempt from reproach; indeed, for the diarist, God's failure to intervene, to take his rightful place as judge and arbiter in this most unequal of contests, was incomprehensible. Just as he condemned humanity for its indifference, so, too, he repeatedly—if rhetorically—confronted God, railing against his detachment from the very world he supposedly governed. "Almighty God, how can you do this?" he demanded in one entry. "How can you in face of such unheard of horrors (to speak with modern language) preserve such an unhesitating neutrality?"

As in even the most internal and meditative diaries, this writer's entries reflect the ebb and flow of events around him, the occasional reprieves and inevitable renewal of violence that characterized his days. In Łódź, a new set of deportations began on June 23, 1944.[4] This crisis prompted a desperate series of entries about the immediate fate of the deported Jews from Łódź and elsewhere, in which the diarist referred openly and directly to the fact of their annihilation. He also reported the news of the murder of hundreds of thousands of Hungarian Jews who were being deported to Auschwitz over the course of the summer of 1944. Far from adopting the comforting belief that this slaughter was an exception to the rule, he wrote of the recent deportees from Łódź: "Seven thousand of our hapless brethren have been exiled. It is difficult to believe that the murderers treated them differently than all other Jews of Europe."

To understand the astonishing frankness with which the writer referred to the mass murder of the Jews, it is essential to consider the particular moment in which the diary was written. By May 1944, after four and a half years of Nazi oppression, few Jews in Łódź (or elsewhere) could be deceived about the fate of the hundreds of thousands of Jews who had seemingly disappeared from the face of the earth. Even in Łódź, which was more dramatically cut off than any other ghetto, news of the fate of the deportees began to filter in during the summer of 1942. Further, the horrendous events of the September 1942 *Shperre* left few peoples' illusions intact.[5] Over time, the complex interplay of suspicion, inference, experience, and, occasionally, concrete information dispelled the hopes of even the most optimistic thinkers, and by this late date most were appallingly aware of the massive slaughter taking place around them. Acceptance of the unbelievable, however, was another matter. Far from being a linear process, the diary reflects the violent swings from incredulity to suspicion, skepticism to belief, and certainty back to doubt and disbelief again. This explains how it is possible that from time to time, even amidst entries that are brutally honest, the diarist occasionally voiced the hope—far-fetched though he knew it was—that perhaps deportation was not, by definition, synonymous with murder.

As if to confirm this faltering hope, the deportations were called to a halt on July 14, 1944. The diarist's joy at this development, however, was mitigated by the news (which apparently reached the ghetto via letter) that the seven thousand Jews had been sent to Koło (in the direction of Chełmno), which the diarist referred to as "the abattoir for the Jews."[6] The implications of this news, and the diarist's attendant shock and horror, are conveyed not only by the language of his next several entries but by the fact that he referred to the seven thousand murdered Jews no fewer than six times in six sequential entries written over the course of two days. The news led him to wonder whether it was at all possible that any Jews would survive from Łódź. His fears were well founded; the halt of deportations was not, in fact, a cessation, but rather a brief pause brought about by the rapid advance of the Red Army from the east, which had necessitated the Nazis' destruction of Chełmno. In the interlude, the German authorities in Łódź took stock of the worsening war developments and deliberated about the fate of the more than sixty-five thousand Jews remaining in the Łódź ghetto.

Hence, while much of the diary is about looking back and summing up the world as the writer saw and understood it, it was also written at a moment that was in itself a turning point, a pause, breath held, waiting for the decisive next step. Indeed, the tide of the war had finally shifted, the Allies were within striking distance of victory, and the cities and towns of the East were being liberated by the advancing Red Army. The complexities and nuances of that moment, caught between the ruins of the past and the potential, however frail, for the future, are captured in the pages of the diary. On one hand, the text is filled with news of the advancing Red Army and calculations about the moment of their arrival. On the other hand, these entries are composed of endless speculation and interpretation about the Nazis' plans, their likely conduct in the face of certain defeat. At the same time, the diarist's growing confidence was always tempered by a fierce realism and lingering doubt; he remained ever aware that hopes could be dispelled with a single gesture from the German authorities.

Toward the very end, the diary takes a poignant, unexpected turn. Seeing the signs of imminent deliverance, the writer began, perhaps unconsciously, to reflect on the future as it applied both to him (in particular referring to his dream of building a new life in Palestine) and to the emotional and moral imperatives facing all the surviving European Jews. A primary obligation was the acknowledgment of grief and bereavement, and the remembrance of lost loved ones. This long-awaited opportunity to grieve was impossible in the present, since, as he put it, "all our senses are geared toward the matter of eating." With grief, he wrote, would come healing, which was the second task of the future. Even in these more tender entries a trace of his cynicism is evident in his expectation that other nations would be indifferent to the Jews after the war. Indeed, so deep was his pain that he did not believe that other Jews who had not endured the Holocaust would be able to empathize fully with their suffering. Instead, he returned again and again to the dream of finding shelter in Palestine, where he imagined the handful of surviving Jews comforting one another in their loss and bereavement.

Finally, there was the monumental, and to his mind, utterly essential imperative to tell the world what had happened to the Jews. In his writing, he expressed at one and the same time this fervent need to speak and to be heard, and conversely the impossible limitations of language itself. Exasperated, he railed time and again at his inability to find words to communicate the depth of his loss and the magnitude of his suffering. Indeed, for him, the problem was not the talent of the writer but the poverty of language itself in the face of reality. "Oh! If I should be a poet," he wrote, "I should say that my heart is like the stormy ocean, my brains a bursting volcano, my soul like . . . forgiveness. I am no poet. And the greatest of poets is to[o] poor a fellow in word even to hint, only to allude at what we passed, and we are presently passing by." In his reflections on this theme, this diarist gave voice to the bitter truth that no speaker, even one with the greatest talents, would ever be able to fully express to any listener, even one with the greatest imagination, the true nature of the crime that had been committed against the Jews of Europe.

The final pages of the diary reach a feverish crescendo of hope and desperation. But on August 1, unbeknownst to the diarist, the decisive step was taken as the Red Army halted its advance on the banks of the Vistula River, not more than ninety miles from Łódź. The following day, the Germans announced the final liquidation of the ghetto. On August 3, he scrawled: "I write these lines in a terrible state of mind—we have, all of us, to leave Litz[mannstadt] Getto during a few days." In this final moment, faced with his own inevitable deportation, the diarist's harsh realism seemed momentarily to falter, as he was tempted to at least consider—if not to wholly believe—the lies once again being fed to the Jewish population of Łódź. "Evidently some pressure on the part of the victorious allies must have had some effect on the brigands and they become more lenient," he wrote. "[Hans] Biebow . . . held a speech for the Jews—the essence of which was that this time they are not to be afraid of being dealt with in the same way all the other outsettled have been." Seen in the context of the rest of the diary, in which this writer so doggedly struggled to avoid shrinking from the truth, this flicker of hope speaks especially poignantly to human fragility in the face of imminent terror and desperation. Still, though perhaps briefly drawn away from his determination to face the truth, the final lines of this writer's diary belie his momentary hopefulness. "I don't even know if I shall be allowed to be together with my sister!" he wrote in despair. "I cannot write more, I am terribly resigned and black spirited!"

Over the next several weeks, the ghetto was emptied, with the exception of about 800 people, some of whom had been retained by the Germans to clean the ghetto and others who had gone into hiding. The overwhelming majority of the 68,500 people in the ghetto were deported to the killing center of Auschwitz-Birkenau. The Red Army reached Łódź on January 19, 1945, finding 877 survivors in Łódź itself.[7] The following July, a former inhabitant of the Łódź ghetto, Avraham Benkel, returned to find his home in ruins. He came across the diary in the abandoned building next to his and took possession of it, keeping it safe for twenty-five years before giving it to Yad Vashem.[8] Nothing specific is known about the fate of the diarist or his sister, although they are both presumed to have perished.

5/5 [May 5] 1944 Litzmannstadt Getto[9] [in English]

I decided to write a diary, though it is a bit too late. To recapitulate the past events is quite impossible so I begin with the present. I committed this week an act which is best able to illustrate to what degree of dehumanisation we have been reduced—namely I finished my loaf of bread at a space of three days, that is to say on Sunday, so I had to wait till the next Saturday for a new one—I was terribly hungry. I had a prospect of living only from the "ressort" soups [those obtainable at work] which consist of three little potato pieces and two decagrams of flower [flour]. I was lying on Monday morning quite dejectedly in my bed and there was the half of a loaf of bread of my darling sister "present" with me. To cut a long story short, I could not resist the temptation and ate it up totally. After having done this—which is at present a terrible crime—I was overcome by terrible remorse of conscience and by a still greater care for what my little one would eat for the next five days. I felt a miserably helpless criminal but I was delivered of the terrible situation by the reception of a B. Talon [ration card]. I suffer terribly by feigning that I don't know where the bread has gone and I have to tell people that it was stolen by a supposed reckless and pitiless thief. And to keep up appearance I have to utter curses and condemnations on the imaginary thief. "I would hang him with my own hands had I come across him" and such like hipocritic [hypocritical] phrases—indeed I am to[o] nervous, to[o] exhausted for literary exertions at the present moment. All I can say is that I shall always suffer on the remembrance of this "noble" deed of mine. And that I shall always condemn myself for being able to become so unblushingly impudent—that I shall for evermore despise this part of "mankind" who were able to inflict such internal woes on their "co"-human beings.

15/5 1944 [in English]

Many times I resolved, many times I began writing memoirs, diaries, but after a few entries I dropped it—it is the total lack of mental and phisical [sic] energy which accounts for it. All I should like to have in life at the present moment is plenty to eat. I used to say lately—that the terrible, inhuman state of mind we are in may be best proved by the sad fact that a "Gettonian," when deprived of half a loaf of bread suffers more terribly than if his own parents had died—could a human being be reduced to such tragic callousness, to such a state of a mere beastly craving for food? Nay, it is only German artistry in Sadicisising [Sadism] which enabled this—which makes this possible. Nobody who didn't experience it will be able to believe it. I really feel too poor, too miserable even to attemp[t] to describe it.

Today is a remarkable day because of the taking out of the "przydział" [rations]. My mind is still further disordered. In this infernal conditions in which I am plunged, I trouble my mind and cannot decide if . . . o! fool that I am!—I shall go to Palestine or remain where I am. I want to go, Socialist cosmopolitist, and I still have many misgivings in nearest realisation of the World United States; and still, dear old Hebrew and ancient Palestine has an irresisstible [sic] fascination for me—alt[h]ough in my terrible wrath against nationalism caused by the barbaric German exaggeration—I rebuke myself as being a particularist, "a parochialist"— but after all I scarcely believe that, let us say, the Poles, would overnight forget their age long hate towards the group of people named Jews because of the "sobriety" which should be brought about by late history. What is most futile about it all is tha[t] I [am] a man who am entrapped in the German snare—out of which even the death cannot be quite sure of emerging unsee[n].

31/V 1944 [in Hebrew]

Our despair is deepening and the terrible hunger, the like of which has never before been suffered by human beings, is growing even more! We can say with full certainty that they didn't leave intact any part of body or soul. I do not waver from my crazy idea to get to Erez Israel [the Land of Israel]. I will not stay in Poland after the war ends. Oh! how bitter the irony of fate, my body is so weak, and my strengths so few, but the foremost condition for any action is to live! Without life we cannot act, see, or try. But I feel good with this because despite my worries and my delusions I lack a basis of realism—otherwise I would expire. Woe to those who fully realize the horror of our present situation. Woe to us if a feeling of reality should enter our ghetto! There are rumors that they are asking for volunteers for work outside the ghetto—each day with its own problem.

31/V 1944 [in English]

We are exasperated, despaired, dejected and losing hope. The hunger is getting continually stronger, our sufferings our [are] unimaginable, u[n]describable, to describe what we pass through—is a task equal to that of drinking up the ocean or embracing the universe! The question arises if after all that what is now happening—any hope is lef[t] for humanity. I am still hesitating in my mind if in case of survival I should go to Palestine—or remain here—how ridiculous—for to go, to do, to accomplish—you must live—and how can one be sure of life in L.G. [Łódź Ghetto] when everyone is almost sure of his death?

1/VI 1944 [in Hebrew]

I just finished my "loaf." Today was the third day since I received it. It was supposed to last me for another five days—but what can I do when I am so devoid of will power that I ate it in three days? Afterward I suffer terrible hunger. Is there no bread for me and for thousands like me, in this world, in this most corrupt of all worlds?

1/VI 1944 [in English]

I just finished my "loaf," which I had to have for eight days; today is the third. It may turn [out] to be lethal for me to behave in such a manner, but my will-power is so weakened and my ever increasing appetite so strong that I can't help it. Is there no bread, dry unsavoury bread enough for me and my fellow-sufferers in this world? Indeed a wise question, is it not? But the invincible human folly is dividing me from it! I just intercepted a talk between two Jews—one asks the other—will it ever finish? How long shall we go on being so incredibly tortured. The other an-

swers (it is Rabbi Silman) let us be satisfied with the present because the future . . .
who knows the future.

6/6 1944 [D-Day, the Allied landing in Normandy; in English]

Today the news of the . . . . penetrated into the Getto. Who knows?

7/6 1944 [in English]

It is true, the fact [of the Allied landing] has been accomplished, but shall we survive? Is it possible to come out of such unimaginable depths, of such unfathomable abysses?

[June] 9, 1944 [in English]

We are quite at sea about what is taking place, only roumouring and canarding—I am very hungry. I have to b[e] five days without the ration of bread because I finished it, as alas I usually do during three days. God be in our help.

11/6 Litzmannstad-Getto 1944 [in English]

And still Getto, and still subject to infernal sufferings, and still far from being able even to dream about a human life, nay, a piggish life, even that is unattainable for us. Pigs eat and don't worry and we eat not, and worry much and work like asses. I am just past my "supper." It consiste[d] of a few coffee-surrogate "cakes" (in bitterness able to compete with our existence) and some raw carrot leaves. In spite of this all I am still dreaming, thank heavens that I'm no realist, for to be a realist is to realise, and realising the whole horror of our situation would have been more tha[n] any human being could endure. I go on dreaming, dreaming, about survival and about getting fame, in order to be able to tell "the world" . . . to tell and "rebuke," to "tell and to protest," both seem at [the] present moment remote and unbelievable—but who knows maybe, perhaps. I dream about telling to humanity but should I be able? Should Shakespeare be able? And what yet I who am only a little proud of understanding Shakespeare?!

12/6 1944 [in Yiddish]

I suffer terribly but still I dream of a better future, of a more beautiful life, free and humane. I dream also of being able to tell the world of my suffering, at least as much as possible. In fact I should call it our suffering. For never before has suffering been felt so collectively as it is by us in the ghetto. After fantasizing of writing in various languages I return to my own language, to Yiddish, our charming mother tongue, because only in Yiddish can I hope to express my true inner self, directly and without contriving. I am ashamed when I think how I have neglected the Yiddish language until now. Like it or not, it is my language, and that of my fathers and my grandfathers, grandmothers and mothers. So I must and will love Yiddish—because it is my language.

14/6 1944 [in Yiddish]

Even if I were Homer, Shakespeare, Goethe, or Dante, called upon by their muses, it would be hard to describe our suffering, that which we find and experience in our life. Is it then at all humanly possible? One cannot however, under any circumstances, blame or hold our accomplishments responsible for our present life. Man can traverse seas and cross oceans, others fly toward the stratosphere, try to reach other planets, but to truly comprehend the suffering of human beings in Litzmannstadt would be an impossible task. The human language is too poor to describe the suffering of Jews in the ghettos of 1944. Where would the expressions come from, the descriptions, adjectives, that could only superficially describe our pain? Can one strum tunelessly what one hears when a musician plays a harmonious tune on a violin? With our writing we can only give an inkling of what

18/6 1944 [in English]

Cursed let be those who are able to cause such agony—as I suffer now—for their fellow-creatures. I write and I don't know if tomorrow I shall be able to read it—because our disgustingly untiring oppressors "want" some thousand of the unhappy Gettonians to be sent for "work." How one need understand "work" in teutonic interpretation, we already know! O heaven! For how long yet will this senseless cruelty be continued. What am I guilty or accused of? My little poor sister of twelve, it is already more t[h]an four years since you are toiling in the most unimaginable manner—since you are working harder, suffering more than an old Napoleonic soldier! Would all this horror, trouble, agony, fury, blows, tears and beastly fears be in vain? Oh, if it is to turn out this way, why didn't we die five years ago?

18/6 1944 [in English]

Truly it is difficult to believe that we shall escape! Such fiends relish the annihilating of their victims to the end. Why have we been born in this beastly generation? This most conscienceless generation of all?

19/6 1944 [in Yiddish]

We are living through a hard time now. Thousands of people are receiving orders sending them away to do labor. People know how to read these orders and are afraid, but they console themselves that perhaps they are being sent only to work. They would be happy if they could be sure that it is work. They hope that maybe it is. . . . Also, everyone feels detached, because we are so dead tired and exhausted.

20/6 1944 [in Hebrew]

We are in a terrible situation. At this time thousands are receiving orders to leave the ghetto to do work. We are unbelievably tense. But the amazing thing is that the affected are accepting the news unemotionally, almost indifferently. Because they are all convinced that the war is ending. Are they right? Will it be so? Who knows? But I am sure that the decision will be taken soon. Rumors are circulating. It is hard to believe that they are true. Some say that the Russians have already crossed the River Bug, and others go so far as to place the Russians in the suburbs of the capital city of Warsaw. I would give anything to be able to see, to be present at such a time when the wicked beast will be destroyed and our nation will be saved for all time.

22/6 1944 [in Hebrew]

Thousands are receiving tickets . . . inviting them to leave the ghetto. We dread and fear for our future. We are going through hard and horrible times that no human creatures had to suffer before. We are dying from deprivation and hunger, and who knows what is happening with the deportees? They [the Germans] say that the time for that has passed, that it has ended, but can we be sure? They say that the Russian and American governments have already sent their envoys to the Hebrew state that will be created in Palestine in the future. Oh, how wretched we are, we cannot know whether the abominable thugs will let us live so that we would have the privilege of seeing the hope of this unfortunate and bereaved nation: the Jewish nation.

25/6 1944 [in English]

Is any hope left for us? Thousands are once again being led away, outsettled [resettled, or deported], and taken away from their getto "homes." Numberless rumours are current: "they have not drunk their coffee," "ten hours after they departed the train came back quite emptied," et cetera, et cetera. No living soul is able to imagine what terrible anguish all this [these] rumours cause us, cannot our enemies ever be surfeited? Are they "Nimmersat[t]s" [gluttons] when it comes to the blood of the their innocent Jewish victims? Even my sister of twelve must help herself with the fatalistic philosophy "that really life is not worth living," that "so or so [one way or another] one must die" and that death would be "our liberation" and "Father died by starvation, so why should we live?" Really, if the world had a face, how should it blush that such philosophy is being the only "escape" of its horrors, even by little children!

26/6 1944 [in Hebrew]

My friend and I spent a few hours discussing the situation in Chełmno. We shudder with fear and feel, in every bone in our bodies, revulsion toward this accursed "European civilization," which elevates itself above others, to a "moral level." Woe and woe! to such a level. We all said that at the present moment we cannot feel the depth of the tragedy because all our senses are geared toward the matter of eating. The suffering is continuing on its terrible journey and is the biggest we have ever felt. One can feel small pain, but who could feel this terrible pain caused by bereavement?

26/6 1944, 11 A.M. [in Polish]

Actually I have nothing to "diarize" but a diary is supposed to be a friend to whom you tell everything, even unimportant things. I am overwhelmed by a terrible fatigue, I am terribly "Kriegs und lebensmüde" [weary of war and life]. One would like to just cease existing, to close one's eyes, to fall into some sort of liberating unawareness because reality is too murderously and incredibly unbearable!

26/6 1944 [in Hebrew]

I am writing these lines in a terrible mental state. Twenty-five thousand of the remaining inhabitants of the Litzmannstadt ghetto are slated for deportation. Every day about five hundred people leave the ghetto. We would be happy if we knew that our brethren were destined for work, for being slaves . . . because if so . . . Can we believe that despite promises of work they won't be sent to a fate that they already meted out to millions of our brethren? They say that the transport wagons returned after eleven hours. Some say one thing, others another. This one cried, and that one cried, and I belong to the generation that "merited" this! Woe to the world in which children like my little twelve-year-old sister have to ponder matters of life and death!

27/6 1944 [in Polish]

The situation is becoming more and more critical. As I write these words I don't know if I will ever read them. Moreover, will anyone ever read them? They searched the places of the "Old One" [Mordechai Chaim Rumkowski, head of the Jewish Council] and [Aron] Jakubowicz [director of the Central Workshop Bureau],

[Pinchas] Gierszowski [director of the ghetto bank], et cetera. Dawid Warszawski [head of the Tailors' Central Office] was arrested and taken away with his entire family. These are events that make one ponder, events that (may this not come true!) are ominous and sad. It is impossible to describe my emotional state at present. I am angry and terribly embittered about this diabolical enemy of all humankind, the human race, my nation, the world, universe. Well, I guess that about covers it because I am already unfortunately unwaveringly convinced that humanity (without exception, I believe, and the rest of it could behave in similar circumstances much like the Germans) is a sordid rabble of greedy beasts devoid of any pity or mercy. I firmly believe that man is only able to do good when he abounds with the best the earth can produce; only then, in order to flatter himself, he wants to be known as good. When he is deprived of such circumstances, when the desire to be called "good" is pushed to the background, man becomes worse and more despicable than the worst kind of animal. Damned nationalism is only a vent for disgusting egoism and self-love. What kind of a world is this, and what kind of people are these who can inflict such unbelievable and impossible suffering on living beings?

Our nearest ones have been murdered, some by starvation, some by deportations (modern civilian death). We have been crippled and degraded physically, emotionally, and reduced to an existence of the most horrible misery and privation, unprecedented in history. We are slaves, devoid of free will, who are happy when trodden upon and beg only that they not be trodden to death. We are, without exaggeration, the most miserable creatures ever under the sun—and all that is still not enough for the "mighty man." Still we are being deported, still our hearts are being torn to pieces. We, who would be happy if only they let us live, even as enslaved, wretched insects, as sordid, crawling reptiles—only to live . . . live . . . live . . . we truly deserve all those names! Because we do not, ourselves, put an end to our disgraceful torment but hold on to this miserable existence on this wretched earth. Even a fatalistic philosophy does not help survive a single moment in the Litzmannstadt Ghetto with indifference. We are no longer human beings, nor have we become animals—we are simply a strange psycho-physical creation "Made in Germany." Has modern humanity not proved wrong some preconceived plan in the creation of the universe? What kind of benevolent and provident intelligence could create something so monstrous?

When I observe my little sister in her suffering—in her modest and heroic effort—when I watch this twelve-year-old orphan struggle constantly and without hope—a vile and persistent thought occurs to me—that she too could be dep[orted]. . . . I feel my heart torn into pieces and I wish for the sun to be extinguished and for our earth to be pulverized!

Anonymous Boy

30/6 1944 [in Hebrew]

[. . .] The hunger is getting worse. Happy is the one who received six tiny pieces of potato for lunch. They count, measure, and weigh the pieces of potato as if it were pure gold. Executions, hunger, exile, investigations, hard labor, struggles, et cetera, et cetera, et cetera, cause the extermination of the last remnants of the people of Israel. And you, silent God? How can you look on? Send your wrath upon the wild beasts, the sickness of the human race and shame them. Deprive them of their faith. As they deprived the Jewish mothers in vain and for no purpose. We now know that there is no peace without war, there is no human happiness, no safety, as long as they live on this earth!

1/7 1944 [in Polish]

I haven't had breakfast and I don't want to live any longer. I don't have the courage to commit suicide but if I could cease existing in some painless way, if I could do this—I certainly would not hesitate.

2/7 1944 [in Hebrew]

Time goes on, month after month more and more of our blood is being spilled. We are full of dread at the thought that the loathsome thugs will deport us. They are themselves afraid now because the Russian front is approaching. They are not satisfied with our blood and our tears. The mood in the ghetto is getting worse.

2/7 1944 [in English]

Time is passing on and on and our suffering don't seem to be ever finished, the cursed, devillish foe is further annihilating the last remnants of our unhappy nation. They are afraid now of the approaching of the Russian front and therefore they began to outsettle [resettle] again. Spirits are terribly low—God be in our mercy—and destroy them—who seem never to be satiate[d] with human blood and tears.

3/4 [probably 3/7, or July 3] 1944[10] [in Polish]

1/2 in the morning. I am in a bad mood because I spilled a few grams of flour, because a few slices of my bread were stolen, and . . . because the deportations are continuing. In our present situation it is not preposterous to compare the disappearance of bread with deportations, as one and the other could prove fatal for us. It is the best indicator of our unbelievable psychological degradation that in the ghetto people are equally upset by the disappearance of a few bites of bread and by the death of their own father. Truly, never and nowhere has a piece of hard, black, chestnut-colored bread made such a "career" as here in Litzmannstadt, Anno Domini 1944.

3/7 1944, two o'clock in the afternoon [in Polish]

Our situation is more and more insecure. New lists are being compiled in all the workshops—again thousands more victims are being readied. It seemed that there was an easing of tension yesterday but it turned out to be an illusion. Preparations for deportations are continuing without stop. Oh! how sad our situation! I am so sorry for my little sister, who has suffered so much, more than one of Napoleon's old guard! The child is deprived of everything: a tender mother's heart, clothing, from dresses to stockings, to say nothing of constant hunger. She has to take care of herself, make do with substitutes; wooden "inventions" instead of shoes, rags sewn together instead of stockings, hunger instead of food, hard school of waiting in line and the "art" of ghetto cooking instead of motherly love. I am not ashamed to add that she has suffered because of me, because of my complete nervous confusion. Oh God! Is all this going to be in vain, for no purpose at all? Oh, how horrible, how heartbreaking! Oh God, how can you, how are you able to watch all this as if you were a neutral spectator?

3/7 1944, three o'clock in the afternoon [in Polish]

I am sitting here and dreaming . . . dreaming and floating in the clouds—I am overwhelmed with an indescribable longing for life—life as I understand it—filled with beautiful things, spiritual interests, craving for a book, theater, movies, radio, oh! (it is not nice to sigh)—and in this swamp yet.

4/7 1944 [in English]

Insecurity increasing steadily—because of the fresh demands—for victims—besides the twenty-five thousand, new three thousand are needed—they seem to enjoy the fun, our hideous enemies—otherwise it is not to be understood how they are not yet satiated—even German "thoroughness" could already have been surfeited. Curious if there would anybody be able to explain this madness of theirs. I just finished my breakfast consisting of some coffee-ersatz-cakes, a terrible meal—even to unsatiables as we are. [. . .] God seems to have abandoned us totally and left us entirely to the mercy of the heartless fiends. Almighty God, how can you do this? How can you in face of such unheard of horrors (to speak with modern language) preserve such an unhesitating neutrality?

Anonymous Boy

4/7 1944 [in English]

When I write these lines—I am almost certain that they will not allow us to stay—who knows if all our pains were not in vain—I am already getting gradually accustomed of imminent death—or rather wanton assassination. I repeat always the well known proverb that when dead, one is equal to Napoleon, Alexander the Great, Caesar. A nice philosophy is not it? But one can do otherwise in a world which is killing its sucklings!

5/7 1944 [in English]

I write these lines in the greatest disturbance of mind—because of our decidedly badly turning fate—it is sure the[y] will drive us from our poor wretched home—and even if they should [not] handle us immediately in their "human" way—we are exposed to mortal danger because of our utter phisical [*sic*] exhaustion—so that they in their "mercy" might "help" us die.

Registers are being [made] uninterruptedly of those to be sent away—everybody is anxious not to find his name on the "liste"—because this means expulsion—terrible "Strapazen" [exertion]—et cetera, et cetera (impossible to enumerate).

5/7 1944 [in Hebrew]

I write these lines with anxiety and terrible grief—who knows what the next few days will bring us? Thousands have already been deported, tens of thousands more are going to be deported. In our present situation, when we have no strength left for walking on our feet, literally—deportation is a mortal danger for us—even if they don't kill us right away, we will die from the hardships along the way—and from starvation.

6/7 1944 [in Hebrew]

It is not possible to estimate the distress in which we are presently living. The terrible uncertainty makes our bodies and souls quiver. The evil madmen (were they not mad they would not fight and kill), the accursed continue to do their job, the ones who remain continue to shrink. Not even one house remained untouched. One can say with certainty that there is not one family left intact in the Jewish Diaspora in all of Europe.

8/7 1944 [in Polish]

All signs point to the fact that this diabolical game is decidedly coming to an end—as they are being unbelievably defeated—but what of it, since for us the deportation lists are continuing to be compiled. Even if—in the best scenario—the deportations were for labor, one's life is in grave danger. I was able to witness with my own eyes yesterday several "volunteers for labor" who had been taken away a few weeks ago—they made a terrible impression on me. They were horribly battered, swollen, and totally exhausted—all this after only a few weeks of labor.

The distribution of all rations has been suspended for some time—this worries and terrifies me tremendously—death from starvation, although "rational" (caused by eating only one's rations)—is the worst, the suffering is the most horrible one can imagine. We are now, if I can put it this way, full of hope and despair, stoic resignation and, at the same time, some kind of heartened spirit and expectation! One thing is certain, that we have lived long enough to see the "black end" of our enemies; although the road to our liberation is still most dangerous.

9/7 1944 [in Hebrew]

Everything now depends on the news that reaches our ears. "They" are leaving Warsaw. The news is spotty, truth is mixed with lies, we don't know what to believe and what not to believe. Our situation from the point of view of food is getting worse and worse. In the future people will wonder how human beings could survive on such meager quantities of food. We are finally seeing their defeat, but our liberation, our salvation—not yet. But who will describe the next few days that are allotted us? If, God forbid, we will not survive, why was this not given to us in the first days of the war? It is astonishing to what terrible degree they reduced us—to such an extent that we are happy in our degradation—oh, if only we could live.

9/7 1944 [in English]

There are different rumours current, "good" ones and also bad ones. One cannot know what to believe and what not. The approvisational [provisional?] situation gets with every moment worse—it is now impossible for me to write down a few decent lines because of the utter destruction of my nervous system.

10/7 1944 [in Yiddish]

I am exhausted, I have no more patience, my nerves are frayed. What I do have is an indescribable disgust toward the world and mankind, toward the masses and people, toward doctrines and dogmas. I do not believe, I do not believe in any change in the world, no! Anyone who can sink as low as the modern man has can be nothing more than an unsuccessful experiment of nature, which certainly regrets it!

Anonymous Boy

11/7 1944 [in Yiddish]

It is three o'clock in the morning, for all generations, we have the beautiful month of July—Tammuz [the month according to the Jewish calendar], the lice are climbing in earnest and make sleep impossible. I curse them with the most bitter curses! They should be sent to Verkhoyansk-Irkutsk! But they don't listen and they are eating me alive. We suffer so much and so terribly. I cannot lie down on my bed. Also, I don't want to be a victim of the Germans in any form. Flies have no sense and know no nourishment other than human blood. The uniformed, military, Teutonic lice are as vacuous as they are.

11/7/ 1944 [in English]

It is three o'clock A.M. I am nearly devoured by "my" (the only property allowed by Ger. "law" for Jews) bugs. Visibly they too undertook some invasion—they besiege, destroy, occupy, penetrate into the most hidden places of my body and nerves. They ressemble awfully to their Berlin brethren—who are even more senseless beings than my bedbugs. I curse them both, the first I want to have sent to Wierchojansk or Jakuck, the latter to "Hambursh" [Hamburg]—but it is good for nothing; they don't obey—for really, why be obedient, gratifying and just—while you are numerous and strong and able to form the so-called "zahllose Divisonen" [innumerable divisions].

11/7 1944 [in English]

We suffer terribly as usual. Today morning we had a visit of the so called "Kripo" (criminal police), the most brutal beasts humanity has ever seen. They came to look for "their" jewels, they made a noise, beat, thre[a]tened. An old man was seriously wounded by the "gentlemen." He was told to run away by [through] the window (German invention). We all felt as if looking into the proverbia[l] death's eyes. The fiends have stayed more than an hour; they robbed some trifles and went away.

11/7 1944 Litzmannstadt-getto, ten o'clock in the evening [in English]

I could not resist the temptation of reading my little dear sister's introduction to her diary. It touched the deepest strains of my soul. I wondered how it was possible that such a mere child should write so philosophically and wisely about her suffering. It runs as follows:

"Many a time in the past I began to write my memoirs, but by unforseen circumstances, I was prevented from putting this mind-easing and soul-comforting practice into reality—to begin of those days when cares and suffering were unknown for me, I must look back to those days gone by—for my today is quite dissimilar to those which went away." She tries to write in verse:

> "Childhood's dear days
> Alas so few they were!
> That dimly only I remember them.
> It is only in my dream that I'm
> allowed to imagine days bygone.
> Short indeed is human happiness
> in this world of ours."

So write children whose only school was Teutonic "life" in A.D. 1944.

12/7 1944 [in Hebrew]

I long for a Jewish life in a Jewish state. If the Jewish nation had no history but for the past five years it would suffice to turn it into a special group, separate from any other. I doubt that even Jews will have enough talent to understand all that happened to us, let alone other nations. The hunt for our brethren continues to grow.

12/7 1944 [in Yiddish]

I have been to the only pleasurable place in the ghetto, an old-book storeroom. A woman came in, and wanted to buy a buckle for her backpack, which she was preparing for resettlement. She didn't like the buckle shown to her. After she left, the merchant said: "She is a stupid woman, because one way or another she won't have much use for it." I stood there, stricken, filled for the thousandth time with the fear of death, the kind of terror that one can only experience in Litzmannstadt. Oh woe, how terrible is our suffering! If only our persecutors had at least enough mercy for us to have killed us all at once. I remember the words of my dying father: "Woe to us, how can one torture living beings like this!" I want to scream to God, to humanity: Woe to us!! Woe!! How can you look on? Aren't we all human beings? How can one torment living creatures like this? How can any philosophy, religion, theory, justify this? The great God destroyed the world once already. Who would imagine that living beings would perform, for their greatest pleasure, sadistic vivisection on their own kind? God! Take back the oath that you have sworn that you will never again bring deluge to the beautiful world with its disgusting creatures!!! God, don't leave behind any more Noahs, Noah's children annihilate, Noah's children have made this war. We need another deluge, but without Noah—annihilation—it has to be fundamentally different, thorough and complete.

Anonymous Boy

12/7 1944 [in English]

Though I am quite unable to write, let alone to concentrate my disturbed mind as to be able to produce any literary description of what I feel at the present mom[ent], I can not forbear of putting some scattered words upon paper. I have been in my only recreation-place in the getto—at the old book shop: a woman came in to buy a buckle to her rucksack which she prepares for her exile—she was displeased with the pattern she was shown by the seller and went away without finishing the purchase—then the merchant uttered a few words which made me shiver, and shudder all over: "She will not have to carry long a time her rucksack because those who go to heaven have no need of the like." To say that it is unimaginable, undescribable, unspeakable, un . . . un . . . un . . . et cetera, is to have said nothing! Such terrible showers on the poor platform of the human heart can only be experienced in modern gettos. (There is no proper plural indicated in non-Hitlerite grammar.) I remember my father dying uttered with a scarcely audible voice: Oh! How is it possible to torment living creatures in such a way—Oh! Woe to us. Now I repeat it also agonisingly: oh! Is it possible to be so tormented? How is it possible to suffer thus?

If a Gettonian should get power over the universe—he would undoubtedly not hesitate a moment and would have destroyed it and indeed! he would have done the only right thing!

15/7 1944 [in Hebrew]

News arrived that the deportations have stopped. The rumor gripped everyone in the ghetto. People are kissing one another. The Jews drink in their imagination, because there is nothing to drink in the ghetto. But what shall I do, I can't believe these rumors because we have been disappointed so many times before. One thing is sure, the deportations have been postponed for a time, and that too is a great thing.

[Undated addition in English]

When I write these lines, I don't know for sure if the outsettling has been wholly stopped—or partly only, but it is after all good news, because time plays a considerable part at present.

15/7/ 1944 [in Polish]

I am writing these words at ten o'clock in the morning. All around me I hear only moans and sighs of the tormented, tortured, starving exiles—and yet no one commits suicide, no one is inclined to put an end to this inhuman suffering with his own hands. Good news is coming . . . I used to say that we have already lived long enough to see their defeat but not long enough to be liberated. Future generations will wonder one day about this strange creature, devoid of all sense, the German!

Why have they not yet [capitulated] when they see with their own eyes, can practically feel it, that the "Deut[s]ches Soldatentum" [German soldiers] have been smashed, when even the hard-headed and hard-minded "Kämpfer" [warriors] have only one possibility—to fall "für Führer und Fatherland [*sic*]" [for Hitler and the fatherland]? Indeed! to kill so pointlessly, to continue to fight this hopeless battle, can only be done by these disgusting, sordid, perverted, devoid of all human feelings, slow-witted, "schwermütige" [melancholy] Prussians! Phew! Vampires, sharks, pirates, buccaneers, thugs—to what kind of incomprehensible, predatory species do you belong?

15/7 1944 [in English]

Today morning rumours spread throughout the Getto with the speed of electricity: "the outsettling stopped" . . . People fell to kissing each other. I didn't give much credit to this information but afterwards it became evident that it is true. I was overcome with joy but a few hours later this joy of mine was spoilt by being told tha[t] someone read a letter which was hidden in the waggon of the outsettled—that they were travelling to Koło; and this is a terrible name for us, the name of this town, because there was the abbattoir [*sic*] for the Jews. . . . But after all it is bette[r] that it was stopped. How terrible to think of it that also the seven thousand sent away were to be barbarously killed—should our enemy have the wickedness, audacity, folly, to accomplish such acts even now, at this very moment which is decidedly his last? Should he? Yes! German folly is unfathomable!

15/7 1944, ten o'clock at night [in Yiddish]

It turns out that the news about the suspension of "wysiedlenie" [deportations] is true—at the same time, the thought gnaws at me that seven thousand people who have been deported in the past four weeks have been murdered. That these thugs should, in their last moments, have so much evil, insolence, and stupidity within them? If they could do this with this knowledge, what will they do with us? The loathsome thought is eating at me—will we live or not? And unfortunately I do not belong to those who are satisfied with life "for the time being," especially because life "for the time being" is very hard. Moreover I cannot rejoice so much in the "provisional news" while I am convinced that, as long as Adolf Hitler is alive and in power, we will not be more than a poor bundle of bones.

Anonymous Boy

16/7 1944 [in Hebrew]

The deportation has stopped. Seven thousand of our hapless brethren have been exiled. It is difficult to believe that the murderers treated them differently than all other Jews of Europe. News has reached the ghetto that 400,000 Hungarian Jews were brought to Poland and were annihilated. Woe is us! It is impossible to describe the feelings in our midst on hearing such news.

16/7 1944 [in English]

It is almost sure that also this 7000 thousand [*sic*] of our in the last month outsettled brethren have been "treated" in the "well known way" . . . A letter was found in the wagon which was cleansed after the travell in the getto—a letter whose contents made us shudder, it stated that the outsettled were driving by near Koło! . . . the place of the "abbattoir" . . . .

Rumours penetrate about four hundred thousand Hungarian Jews who have been brought to Poland and have been offered to Hitler. . . .

17/7 1944 [in Hebrew]

The idea that also seven thousand Jews were sent out of the ghetto in the past few days is killing me. I was sure that they would not dare, at the last minute, but who can descend into the depths of the mind of these murderous madmen (do they have a mind at all?). There is joy because the *wysiedlenie* has stopped. There is joy because all inhabitants of the ghetto received one and a half kilograms vegetables. If [a spot obscures the words—possibly "anyone outside"] of the ghetto wonders what brought joy to the inhabitants of the ghetto, he will certainly say: woe to them, to these creatures that this caused their joy!

17/7 1944 [in English]

The thought that also these seven thousand of our co-sufferers have been led away to be handled with in a "Germanly" way . . . haunts me with a ghastly obstinacy . . . Many among us were sure that in their last minutes (which are certainly now) they will be if not more merciful, at least more prudent! But it seems undeniably that prudence i[s] made of stuff eternally irreconcillable with a German pate . . . [. . .] They are "plein d'esprit," the German gentlemen, ain't they?

17/7 1944 [in Polish]

I am terribly worried about a stupid argument I had with my little sister—when I look at her poor little face, full of suffering, I am overcome with unspeakable pain.

[. . .] I am sick of everything—the world, people, all became for me "intolerable." Truly, human stupidity is infinite and everlasting. Man is a wretched beast, which evidently delights in putting itself to a tormented death—be it "heroic" for the "Fatherland," be it "disgraceful" for racial outcasts. In any case, to mangle themselves to death is the biggest pleasure for two-legged Huns. A bullfight would only satisfy humble medieval Spaniards, devoid of any imagination. A modern man equipped with the proper means and imagination can do more, much more.

18/7 1944 [in Polish]

What do these loathsome men want from us? Why did they not kill us on the first day of the war? Why don't they grant us, even now, this "coup de grâce"? How can they take such diabolical delight in the murder of the innocent? Can a Germanoid truly find no other pleasure than senseless murder? Again they have ordered compiling a list of inhabitants; what do they want to accomplish? Who else would they murder but us, the remaining Jews? Unless it is their own children—that would bring the world only good! The German brat is a warrior and a murderer—a German female is a candidate for an overbearing woman who informs the world about a son who was killed for the "Führer und Fland [Fatherland]."

18/7 1944 [in English]

A new Order reached today the Getto Authorities, according to which a register of the number of the getto population is to be compiled! . . . What mischief are they up to, these God forsaken creatures with this new demand of theirs. How disgracefully abominable they are, our German friends! They don't even want to inflict [upon] us the ultimate "coup de grâce," but to deleck [delight] in this horrible blood-sucking, in this gradual massacre of children and woman—in this annihilation of a whole guiltless nation!

19/7 1944 [in Polish]

Regarding the food supply we are now in one of the golden periods in the ghetto. They are giving out as much as five kilograms of vegetables per person. When a future historian notes what made people happy in the ghetto, he will undoubtedly think: oh, how unhappy must these people in the ghetto have been, if five kilograms of vegetables could put them in such a good mood.

19/7 1994 [in English]

We have now "good" times in the Getto. We can get some cabbage with what to lessen our mortal hunger. The only care is about our future, because everyone i[s] convinced that the war is decidedly approaching its end. Fears are aroused by rumours according to which the G. [Germans] destroyed tens of thousands of Hungarian Jews. When will this question of "to be or not to be" be taken off our shoulders?

20/7 1944 [in Yiddish]

I feel such a need to open my diary and to write in order to ease my bitter heart, about what hell we go through, how terribly we suffer. During the time when we had literally nothing to eat, we were willing to believe that the physical annihilation of men, women, and children of our nation had appeased the blond beast. But now it looks as if they have not had enough, and that they want to satisfy their thirst with the blood of the innocent. Yes, we had believed that the German stomach was already satiated—now that we have already a bit to eat, even if no more than just cabbage, we have received news that the physical annihilation has resumed. One is inclined to believe that God and fate let themselves be persuaded by Satan and are deriving pleasure from some sort of sadistic hunt and crushing our remaining will to live and digging into the depths of our tormented hearts.

21/7 1944 [in Polish]

[. . .] News has reached us about concentrating Hungarian Jews at a Hitlerian German ritual slaughter place [Auschwitz-Birkenau]! Many of them have already perished a truly heroic and martyred death. I think that these . . . (how do I find the right expression) dealt with the wretched seven thousand Jews in the same way, deported them in such a cowardly way from Łódź (pardon, Litzmannstadt . . .). At present we are possessed by mixed feelings, one moment we are full of hope, the next we are gripped by that well-founded resignation, to the point of feeling stifled. Do you believe that they will let us live? These "gentlemen" were not embarrassed by hundreds of thousands of children—have they not destroyed, in a manner unknown to humanity, half of our nation which was under their grip? All the same, it is hard to foresee what the next few days will bring us! Even a mortally wounded hyena might feel lightheaded—will want to [carry on] but will not be able to, will have to deal with its own dying.

21/7 1944 [in Polish]

Half an hour later—news arrived of an attempt on Hitler's life! Apparently the attempt succeeded only partially. According to a German newspaper he was only wounded. At this moment I cannot fully comprehend the importance of this first-rate event, I only regret, together with all of humanity—that he has not lost his life. But it is obvious that they have had enough, they are fed up with the *stolze Trauer* [proud suffering] and the "easy" laying down of their lives for the Führer.

22/7 1944 [in Polish]

Unfortunately it is not yet certain what happened to him—enemy of mankind number one—apparently he is severely wounded. What kind of satanic force guards him, takes care of him? I had a sad day yesterday, sad and joyous at the same time. Sad—because if he had been killed, the war would have ended; it is clear that he is the "life" of the war and all of these atrocities. I was also glad because there are already signs of what must, irrevocably, happen in the nearest future. Even the murderous determination of the Führer cannot prevent this. Something went wrong in this satanic kingdom! It is beginning to ferment and it will inevitably explode! Because if the world allowed itself to be conquered and then murdered . . . so be it . . . But the naughty world did not show any desire to be subjugated, it took up arms and now threatens the Fatherland in an *unerhörte Weise* [unheard-of manner]—so that even the "dull-witted" Hitlerite generals have had enough.

[. . .] What will happen to us? Won't this madman want to harm us before the power definitively falls from his hands? Who can guess? In any case, it is not difficult to come to the realization that our chances have improved considerably. As soon as this satanic madman disappears—our lives will no longer be threatened. There will not be another Führer, even if one of his favorites takes over: "Heil Göring" or "Heil Himmler" does not sound right. And so we have lived to see their twilight—we must only survive till our dawn, and that of all humanity!!!

23/7 1944 [in English]

It is two o'clock after midnight—I cannot lie in my Getto-bed for it is full of merciless bugs with whom I have no means to fight—so I have time for sombre thinking—I think about the [illegible] which is going to take place in the nearest future—but if we shall be present . . . if we shall live? This is the rub, this is what makes us shudder all over [. . .].

23/7 1944 [in Hebrew]

There are rumors in the ghetto that make us happy and encourage us. General Keitel, head of the general staff, resigned. The Russians are approaching Warsaw. The revolt in Germany is growing stronger to such an extent that the Gestapo is no longer in control of many towns. Apparently the revolt is spreading to army units. There are also other rumors that are difficult to believe. But the war is coming to an end. And if it is coming to an end, surely this will also be an end to our horrible suffering—will we live? Who knows? I talked with Rabbi Silman about liberation. I shudder when I think how my little sister and I sought shelter from the beasts and how my sainted father was overcome by inhuman fear—who will avenge us?

[Undated entry in Yiddish]

We can feel it in the air that the war is in the last shudders of its agony. There is no more doubt that this time the Hitlerian beast is being beaten and will not be able to withstand it. In a conversation with Rabbi Silman we have recalled some details of the *Shperre* [mass roundup, deportation, and murder of fifteen thousand ghetto residents, primarily children and the elderly, of September 5–12, 1942]. I remembered how terrible it was when the thugs came to our homes and how terrified we felt when we tried to find hiding places! No! I cannot write any more—because this is indescribable!

24/7 1944 [in Hebrew]

Rumors abound about their total defeat. They retreated from Lublin, Białystok, et cetera. Their anxiety is terrible. [. . .] We can't say that we are not glad—it is truly a great consolation for us when we see their total defeat with our own eyes. But at the same time we are consumed with a dreadful worry—will they really let us live and testify? This question occupies our minds like an annoying fly. Don't we know with whom we are dealing? We do know for sure what they are capable of doing, those disgusting thugs, those ugly abominations who have no conscience, no mercy, and no sense of responsibility. Yes, is this madman who is in power now not responsible for his deeds? In his hatred of us he can do us harm at the last moment—but let's not give up hope—it is quite possible that he will not achieve his purpose and will leave us alive. For he and his are approaching total annihilation. Woe to him who lives in insecurity as we have lived these five years—years of . . . what can I say and what can I tell, my language is so impoverished.

25/7 1944, two hours past midnight [in Hebrew]

I can't sleep because of bedbugs and my agitated state of mind. I was patient for five years, and now my patience is gone. We can feel the coming liberation in the air. The Russians have captured Lublin. In Germany war is being waged, there was an attempt on Hitler's life. They definitely oppose the war and want to end it. Even for them it is no longer a pleasure. The end is knocking on our doors. Another mo-

Anonymous Boy
{388}

ment and we will be free. Just thinking about it makes me cry. They might leave us alone before liberation because Hitler's power has waned. He is no longer so sure of himself, the opposition is strengthening. Really this whole awful war is so senseless and crazy for every person killed on the front, when the Germans are already convinced of total defeat. It is hard to believe that they will harm us but we are fearful because who can foresee the depth of the intentions of the crazy Hitler! He is irresponsible with regard to his own nation's future. We are full of hope and impatience. Rumors are being spread in the ghetto that are simply lies—that Hitler was arrested by the rebels and that he was killed! But let's hope that this will happen in the near future.

26/7 1944, morning [in Hebrew]

This morning my friend Fogel came to visit me and told me that when they retreated from Vilna, they beat up a great number of the inhabitants in great anger, as is their beastly habit—will they treat us differently? The Jews? Will they forgo their "beautiful" habit of killing quiet civilians? We need a great miracle so that they will not be able to turn against us! Who knows what the next days will bring? What surprises, adventures, troubles? Will the time come when I will say: this is the end of our long suffering? When will we too breathe air into our lungs, without being troubled by terrible worries about matters of death!

26/7 1944 [in Polish]

On the whole today has not brought us anything in particular. Thank God for that—for we are playing for time. Rumors are spreading, one more sensational than the other! [. . .] In the past few days I have completely lost the patience that characterized me throughout the entire war. I would so badly like to be on the other side of the barrier that I get sick just thinking about it. Regarding the food supply in the ghetto, it is not too terrible right now. We receive sufficient amounts of cabbage. For us, whose aspirations have been so greatly reduced, this is indeed unbelievably fortunate. We cannot foresee what the next few days will bring us but one can feel that they will be loaded with significant events. We expect, more than ever before, that we will be allowed to live. But every one of us knows that we cannot be certain. Can one expect logic from beasts of prey?! negotiate with a tiger? I spend my days feeling very tense and excited. Everyone is trying to guess what the future will bring. Only our imagination can find a solution to this impossible situation! There is talk of a hurried departure of the Reichs-Germans from Litzmannstadt. May the next few hours bring us liberation from our inhuman bondage! [. . .]

Anonymous Boy

27/7 1944 [in English]

All during this period of five years, which have been five ages I have been tolerably patient and calm—I supported all the interminable, innumerable, innamable sufferings which bothomless [bottomless], fertile German inventiveness heaped on us so lavishly—with an uncomparable stoicism. But now, whe[n] the solution is near, I am quite at my wits end, and got to be very impatient and nervous, full of anxiety. I meditate over the future—if we have any at all! Then if we should walk the same path our heroic brethren have gone—can we speak about any future— eternity has no future whatever! The death and merdered [dead and murdered] don't have any calendar! But sure of either life or death we can't be—maybe that they would be thwarted in their "noble" plan, our infernal, devillish, satanic German fiends—and we shall have the narrowest of escapes?—to tell decent un-German humanity about their deeds! And curse their abominable name for evermore!

28/7 1944 [in Polish]

My excitement and terrible impatience grow with every moment—I would like to find myself on the other side of the barrier. I want this so badly I can hardly breathe. Can anyone imagine a condemned man in his awful dungeon—when he can clearly hear the hammering on the other side of the walls of his prison? We can also hear the hammering—every night we have several alarms. No wonder, they themselves admit that there is fighting in *östlich Warschau* [eastern Warsaw]. What magic words—what times we live in. Perhaps our relentless fate has become more kind to us and we will survive nevertheless!

20/7 [probably 29/7, or July 29] 1944 [in Polish]

Yesterday, at twelve o'clock, we could hear loud machine-gun fire and an explosion. We all thought that those were "our people" but unfortunately it turned out to be an illusion. Even if we don't believe in all the exaggerations, according to what even the Germans admit, we have reached quite far. Lublin, Białystok, Dinanburg are definitely torn out of the ethnic "Europas"—it is not difficult to imagine this graveyard order that would rule Europe after a Nazi victory, it would be an order reigning in a cemetery! where it is quiet and cozy as it is in the Third Reich . . . Oh! When will it finally happen this . . . this . . . liberation? If one can become ill from lack of patience—I am a candidate for becoming gravely ill in this case—impatience . . .

29/7 1944, Litzmannstadt-Ghetto (once Łódź) [in English]

I am in a state of terrible excitement mixed with disbelief and fear. Who of us who are subject to such sufferings could believe it that we should get out, that we should be among those who survive! Oh! If I should be a poet, I should say that my heart is like the stormy ocean, my brains a bursting volcano, my soul like . . . for-giveness, I am no poet. And the greatest of poets is to[o] poor a fellow in word even to hint, only to allude at what we passed, and are presently passing by. Never has any human being been put into such a state of "the profundis" as we have been. Imagine a Jew of Litzm[annstadt] Getto not wholly deprived of imagination when he is being told the few magic words of the OKW [Oberkommando der Wehr-macht, or Supreme Army Command], which run as follows: "Am rande der Stadt Warschau!!! kam es zur verbitterten Kampfen" [Am Rande der Stadt Warschau kam es zu erbitterten Kämpfen: Bitter fighting has reached the outskirts of War-saw]. At last it is not in Asia, it is not in Africa . . . but in Europe, in Poland, in Warschau. . . . If we lived up to this time perhaps shall we live up to the moment of our dreams, to the moment of our deliverance, which seems so discouragingly "in-croyable" [incredible] perhaps. . . .

I have been saddened by the fact that a Getto inhabitant has been wantonly murdered by being shot at by the Nazi "Kripo" (what fiends). I, with my easily im-pressed mind begun to reason if they could, what will they do with us at the last moment? But away with such thoughts. If we live up to the time when our capital is taken, it is nearly sure that we shall see also Litzmannstadt delivered. Meanwhile I am walking along as a lunatic, fevered with impatient expectation, full of hope and fear, I should like to become a few weeks older and still be alive!!

[Undated addition in Polish]

It is impossible for anyone who has not been with us to imagine what we went through. The human language is too poor to describe this. There are no words necessary to even allude partially to our sufferings, not to mention the intent to de-scribe our reality.

29/7 1944 [in Hebrew]

I am now in a state of anticipation which is hard to describe. My God who art in heaven, if we were able to live long enough to hear the Germans announce "Kämpfe am rande der St. Warszawa" [*sic*] [fighting on the outskirts of the city of Warsaw], that means salvation is near. Another little while and we will be liberated. We can hardly believe, and will not believe till the last moment, that we will survive. Can anyone imagine the feelings of the Jews from the ghetto when they heard the news of the capture of Warsaw? We can see the realization of our dreams. If only the thugs won't do us harm! They now have so many worries of their own that they may not do to us what they intended. When I look at myself and at my little sister, who has suffered so much in the last years, it is hard to believe that tomorrow will bring us life. We will see, and we will tell, we will remember and mourn our relatives, the murdered ones, victims of starvation, martyrs of the holy nation, which was annihilated in such a terrible way. Is that not so?! I joked with Mr. Bohon that I don't know what transgressions helped us survive. Because all the honest, timid, righteous people are gone, all of them (also my father, honest, warm, wise, a real man). How happy I would be, my little sister if I did not have to see you so unhappy, mending your clothes, full of worries. I can say that certainly you have no more than one of Napoleon's soldiers.

People say that if we survive, we must settle only in Palestine. Without any doubt, the nations of the world that commiserate with us to our faces will forget what has been done to us. Some may even be pleased. This "do not forget," understanding of our sorrow, can only happen in our Hebrew state. Because every utterance, every word out of our mouths will be devoted to our sorrows, to the suffering of the Jews of Europe under Hitler's rule. Others, outsiders, will not be interested in those matters, they will turn to their own business and take care of their own losses.

29/7 1944 Litz. Ghetto [in Hebrew]

Rumors have reached us about the capital city of Warsaw. Is that so? Could it be true? None of us can wait any longer, not even a short little while! Because we know that as long as we are in their grasp, we are exposed to all . . . and our lives depend on it. We can see their defeat but our deliverance has not arrived yet. We have strong hope that we will survive, that we shall overcome, that we will pass through this, that we will rise above this. We strongly believe that this will happen! They have their own worries now, and problems. There is hope that they will forget us, that they will not bother with us. Days come and go, rumors about rumors keep coming to us but we cannot depend on them. But there is no doubt that we won't have to wait long this time because the Germans themselves admit they have retreated from Lublin, Białystok, Brisk [Brest-Litovsk], Dinanburg—and other towns. If it were not for the crazed obstinacy of the "Leader" it would be all over. Sometimes I suffer great doubts because our situation is precarious and not at all clear. Could I possibly forget in whose hands we find ourselves! But who can predict our future—will they not kill us, will they let us live—my blood freezes at the thought. I would be so happy if I would have the privilege of going to Palestine—there are no more Jews in the Diaspora! For who will acknowledge our distress, and who will console us in our grief—the Poles, Hungarians, Romanians? Only a Jewish heart is able to feel the sadness of our troubles, the depth of our pain. We have no more strength, no more patience. If God will let us live, we will console ourselves!

31/7 1944 Litz-Ghetto [in Hebrew]

Tension and anxiety among us have increased to an indescribable level. There are rumors that heavy fighting is taking place in eastern parts of Warsaw and that the Russians crossed the Vistula River and that they [the Germans] were compelled to abandon the eastern front. Will we be liberated, will we be human again? Is it possible? Those who are not with us here will never believe that it was possible to live as many years as we did. If we survive and live without worry about filling our stomachs surely we will remember the holy ones, the pure ones, the guiltless heroes. We will remember our fathers, our relatives, acquaintances who were murdered, who starved to death and suffered indescribable torment. We will remember those who were buried, those who were burned alive—we will remember our brethren who were cut into pieces, destroyed in pits, hanged, crucified, drowned. The people of Israel will remember its heroes, its martyrs who suffered as no other human beings ever suffered on this earth. We fear that they will do with us what they usually do, for every Jew is a burden in their foul hearts. Because they know that we would enjoy the celebrating of our second Purim. But maybe they will be forced to leave our city in panic and confusion without being able to harm us? We are living through great and awesome days now, days in which the thugs are being destroyed, days of ruin, shame, and defeat for the enemy of humanity.

Even though I write a broken and dubious Hebrew, I cannot but write in Hebrew, because Hebrew is the language of the future. In Hebrew we will be proud Jews in Erez Israel.

3/8 1944 [in English]

I write these lines in a terrible state of mind—we have, all of us, to leave Litz. Getto during a few days. When I first heard of it I was sure that this mean[t] the end of our unheard of martyrdom equatanously [together] with our lives, for we were sure that we should be "vernichtet" [annihilated] in the well known way of theirs. People were regretting that they didn't die on the first day of the war. What for to have suffered five years of "ausrottungsKampf" [war of extermination]. Couldn't they give us the "coup de grâce" in the very beginning?

But evidently some pressure on the part of the victorious allies must have had some effect on the brigands and they become more lenient—and [Hans] Biebow, the German Getto Chief, held a speech for the Jews—the essence of which was that this time they are not to be afraid of being dealt with in the same way all the other outsettled have been—because of a change in war conditions "und damit das Deutsche Reich den Krieg gewinnt, hat unser Führer befohlen jede Arbeitshand auszunützen" [and in order that the German Reich should win, our Führer has ordered to use every worker]. Evidently! The only right which entitle[s] us to live under the same sky with Germans—though to live as the lowest slaves, is the privilege of working for their victory, working much! and eating nothing. Really, they are even more abominable in their diabolic cruelty than any human mind could follow. He further said "Wenn Zwang angewendet werden muss, dann überlebt niemand!" [If force has to be used, no one will survive!] He asked the crowd (Jewish) if they are ready to work faithfully for the Reich and every one answered "Jahwohl" [Yes, indeed!]—I thought about the abjectedness of such a situation! What sort of people are the Germans that they managed to transform us into such low, crawling creatures, as to say "Jahwohl." Is life really so worthy? Is it not better not [to] live in a world where there are 80 millions of Germans? O, [is] it not a shame to be a man on the same earth as the Ger-man? Oh! shabby, miserable human, your meanness will always surpass your importance!

When I look on my little sister, my heart is melting. Hasn't the child suffered its [her] part? She, who fought so heroically the last five years? When I look on our cozy little room, tidied up by the young, intelligent, poor being, I am getting saddened by the thought that soon she and I will have to leave our last particle of home! When I come across trifling objects which had a narrow escape all the time—I am sad on the thought on parting with them—for they, the companions of our misery, became endeared to me. Now we have to leave our home. What will they do with our sick? With our old? With our young? Oh, God in heaven, why didst thou create Germans to destroy humanity? I don't even know if I shall be allowed to be together with my sister! I cannot write more, I am terribly resigned and black spirited!

[Undated entry in Hebrew]

My God, why do you allow them to say that you are neutral? Why will you not punish, with all your wrath, those who are destroying us? Are we the sinners and they the righteous? Is that the truth? Surely you are intelligent enough to understand that it is not so, that we are not the sinners and they are not the Messiah!

14

Alice Ehrmann
TEREZÍN GHETTO

Alice Ehrmann (later Alisa Shek) was born on May 5, 1927, the second daughter of an upper-middle-class family in Prague. Her father, Rudolf Ehrmann, was an assimilated Czech Jew, and an architect by profession. Pavla Ehrmann, Alice's mother, had been born into a Catholic family in Vienna, but after her marriage she did not practice any religion. Alice and her sister, Ruth (almost three years her senior), did not have a Jewish upbringing, nor did they attend religious school, but she recalled many years later that she "always knew [she] was Jewish." She attended a Czech primary school in Prague and completed two grades of high school before, at age thirteen, she was forced out of school because she was Jewish.[1]

The Nazis had taken power in Prague two years earlier, in September 1938. According to the definition put forth in the Nuremberg Race Laws, upon which the Czech laws were based, the Ehrmann children were classified as mischlinge of the first degree, children of a mixed marriage in which two grandparents were Jewish. Like the Ginz children, Alice and Ruth were deported to Terezín without their parents; they left Prague on July 13, 1943, when Alice was sixteen and Ruth was nineteen. Because their mother was non-Jewish, she was able to remain in Prague for the duration of the war. Their father was arrested in Prague in the spring of 1944 and imprisoned in the so-called Small Fortress at Terezín, where he remained for several months until he was deported to Auschwitz.

In Terezín, Alice encountered Ze'ev Shek, whom she had met during the summer of 1942 in Prague. It is clear from the very first pages of her diary that they were deeply in love. Seven years older than Alice, Ze'ev had been born into an Orthodox Jewish family in the Moravian town of Olomouc, and though he was not religious himself he had been deeply involved in working with Jewish young people during the prewar years, especially as a leader in the Zionist youth movement, Maccabee Hazair. In the ghetto, Ze'ev worked in the youth welfare department of the Jewish Council in Terezín under the leadership of Gonda Redlich and with Fredy Hirsch, mainly teaching Hebrew in the children's homes. He was also secretly engaged in collecting and preserving documents related to the history of Terezín. When Ze'ev was deported from Terezín in October 1944, Alice continued his work, adding to his stockpile of orders issued by the Jewish Council, and hiding the suitcase that held them in an underground passage leading out of the ghetto. In addition, just after Ze'ev's deportation Alice began to keep a diary, writing in German but camouflaging it by using Hebrew letters.[2]

Early in her diary, Alice voiced the imperative that had given rise to her writing. "I will try to bear written witness as best I can so that it will survive me. That is what occupies my thoughts," she wrote: "to say to the world and time what was accomplished here; to read to them a chapter out of the *Golah* dated 1944." To this end, Alice sketched scenes of everything she saw around her, creating a rich chronicle of the major events in the ghetto. The "chapter out of the Golah" (the exile or Diaspora) that her diary thus records is the final one as it unfolded in Terezín: the deportations to Auschwitz in the fall of 1944, the gradual unraveling of German authority over the late winter and early spring of 1945, and the chaos, confusion, and ugliness of liberation in May 1945, which brought with it the first knowledge of the death camps and the unthinkable reality of constructing a new life.

The diary opens in October 1944, almost a month after the Nazis had resumed deportations from Terezín to Auschwitz, gathering the ill, the weak, children without parents, and others to send them off to what was for them the unknown. Alice recorded in her diary these horrific scenes, documenting the names or ages of the deportees, their physical and mental states, the violence meted out to them by the Nazi guards, and the conditions inside the train. It was not only the weak and the ill who were sent away on these transports. Many members of the Jewish Council were deported as well, leaving the ghetto bereft of its leadership and the structures that had sustained it. In November, after the deportations from the ghetto had ceased, Alice reflected on the eerie vanishing of thousands of people whose fate remained a mystery, writing, "All the people have disappeared somewhere; here and there an unclear message from somewhere—like far calls from a ship wandering the ocean."

As Terezín was depleted by transports to Auschwitz, the Nazis continued to force new arrivals through the gates. Often, these people were Jews married to non-Jews living in the Protectorate, who had for a time been exempt from deportation by virtue of their marriages. These transports in, like the transports out, carried with them the curse of repetitiveness, as time and again bewildered Jews arrived in Terezín, caught between having lost the bearings of home but not yet familiar with the crude reality of ghetto existence. Alice voiced her despair in the face of this cycle, writing, "We are so tired of teaching our captivity to others." Still, the arrivals from Prague brought something strange and new into the ghetto, reminding the ghetto dwellers of home and momentarily linking them with it, while at the same time underscoring how deeply divided they were from the outside world.

Alice was among many writers who witnessed and described this ceaseless movement of individuals, families, and communities as they were displaced from their homes to ghettos and often from there to the death camps of the East. Whereas many diarists wrote in the midst of the war, expressing not only pathos and pity for the deportees but also panic and fear for their own fates, Alice wrote her diary very late in the war, as the prolonged, protracted struggle for Allied victory and Jewish survival dragged on. Thus, it was not desperation for her own survival that she voiced in her diary, but exhaustion, resignation, and despair. Her entries are infused with the futility of it all, the disbelief that even after it was no longer bearable, it still had to be borne. "The city lives on," she wrote. "It lives with bated breath, a lull between two catastrophes; but it lives on. . . . The city is so exhausted; we will bear all this, I and the city and you and you."

The diary itself mirrors Alice's state of being; it is composed of short clipped phrases, succinct sketches and images, notes in fragmentary form, grammatical details such as definite articles and personal pronouns abandoned. Line after line of her text suggests her utter fatigue, as if she was simply too tired to form whole sentences, to explain matters in detail, and to create a cohesive, seamless account. Paradoxically, its stylistic informality and the mixture of reflections and observations on a myriad subjects also communicates the urgency of forsaking all

Alice Ehrmann
{397}

formalities in the pursuit of her central goal to accumulate the facts, details, images, names, and specifics of the crime being committed against the Jews. That Alice was able to record such specifics (unlike most diarists, who did not have access to so much information) was another matter; it was attributable to her closeness to members of the Jewish Council, especially her cousin Georg Vogel, who was in charge of heating and plumbing in the ghetto. Living as she did with his in-laws, she had access to information that many ghetto dwellers would not have known.[3] And though it is sometimes difficult to decipher the exact sense or precise historical meaning of this flood of seemingly unrelated, cryptic notations, the text itself evokes an image of Alice, overwhelmed with the weight of knowledge and responsibility, unburdening herself in the pages of her diary.

As the fall of 1944 turned into the winter of 1945, the tone of Alice's diary gradually shifted from despair and resignation to a cautious, half-believing, half-skeptical acknowledgment that things were changing. In February 1945, she remarked on a transport that was leaving the ghetto, allegedly to take its passengers to safety in Switzerland. Naturally, many ghetto inhabitants were reluctant to volunteer for this transport, having been lied to and deceived innumerable times during the German occupation. Still, two thousand people applied (though intellectuals, prominent personages, and those whose close relatives had been deported East were excluded for fear that they would talk too much upon arrival in Switzerland), and when the transport left Terezín on February 4, 1945, twelve hundred Jews were on it.[4] Whatever her misgivings about the veracity of the claim that the deportees were bound for Switzerland, Alice's description of the transport stands in undeniable contrast to those of the previous fall. The deportees traveled on passenger trains, the cars were uncrowded, windows were left open, and bread, jam, and margarine were provided for the journey. Indeed, it was not a ruse; Alice noted in her diary a few days later that reports had reached Terezín of the safe arrival of the Jews in Switzerland.

At around the same time, another unthinkable event occurred. A group of Jews who had been sent from Terezín to Zossen, Germany, in March 1944 as a labor brigade assigned to build new headquarters for the Gestapo was allowed to return to the ghetto.[5] Just as it was impossible to imagine that any Jew would be sent by the Nazis to safety in neutral Switzerland, so too it was unheard-of for those deported from the ghetto to return. In her diary, Alice summed up the mixture of joy, disbelief, and hope, writing: "There has been a second miracle. The fact that a few people have been tossed ashore puts us in a most unusual state. . . . It puts us into something like a state of rapture, and that stubborn little knot of hope that is divorced from all reality breaks loose."

Still other signs within the ghetto itself pointed to the fact that the Germans were losing ground. Most notable was the effort on the part of the SS to cover up the crime that had been committed there, to bury its traces in the face of eventual defeat. The beginnings of the cover-up had taken place the previous fall with the removal of the ashes of the dead, whose bodies had been cremated after they died in the ghetto.[6] In part, the task signaled the Germans' apparent recognition of inevitable defeat and the fear of public exposure of the staggering death rates in Terezín. But this was not Alice's concern; instead, she wrote about the shameful disrespect to the dead, the loss of evidence, and the burden placed on the survivors to stand in as witnesses. She described, too, the grimly surreal process by which prisoners lined up and passed the urns containing the remains of their friends and family members from the chamber where they were stored to the trucks that were to dispose of them.

The following spring, the Nazi effort to destroy evidence took the form of burning documents and papers and carting away files from their administrative offices in Terezín. Alice, writing from the perspective of one who struggled to preserve and safeguard such records, witnessed and documented this irreparable loss of evidence. In these entries, she reflected on the practical matter of losing valuable information, and also on the deeper injustice of the oppressor's power to "erase" not only the living and the dead, but to suppress the very story of their lives and deaths. "I watched as thousands of pages of documents flew up in flames," she wrote. "I saw the numbers, digits, dates, and names of which our misery is composed, in which it is mirrored, flicker dully and turn to ashes. Who can comprehend this?"

The Nazis' attempt to cover up their crimes was inevitably linked to their own tacit acknowledgment that the war was lost and that, sooner rather than later, the truth would be exposed. This threat loomed ever nearer in the spring as the International Red Cross demanded not only to send supplies into the ghetto but to be allowed to inspect it, and to install a representative there until the end of the war. Though not all of the Red Cross demands were met, members of the organization were allowed to visit the ghetto in April 1945. This was not the first time representatives of the Red Cross had been permitted to enter Terezín; another commission had been allowed to visit during the summer of 1944. The intensive "beautification" campaign that the Nazis undertook to pull the wool over the eyes of the Red Cross on this occasion, and its chilling success as a propaganda stunt, is by now well known. The Red Cross left in 1944 satisfied that Terezín was a "Jewish settlement" whose inhabitants were well cared for and well fed, that children played in parks and attended school, and that rumors of Nazi brutality had been wildly exaggerated.[7] This farce was repeated in the spring of 1945, though to a lesser degree. But unlike Alice's sobering account of the destruction of human and paper evidence, her reports on this late attempt to cover up the real nature of Terezín with cosmetic improvements reflected the gruesome absurdity of the project. The images she sketched in her notes are abrupt, pointed, and ironic. "Plan to convert a shooting range into a bowling alley," she wrote. "The children in *Fireflies* [a play to be performed for the Red Cross] get a tan daily under two sun lamps."

As the spring arrived, Alice finally witnessed the long-awaited reversal of fortune for the SS. On April 16, Swiss politician Jean Marie Musy's son Benoit visited Terezín, followed by Rudolf Kasztner of the Jewish Rescue Committee in Budapest, who arrived to inspect the ghetto.[8] As Alice reported it, the captor, the all-powerful, terrifying oppressor, was reduced to ridiculousness as the inspectors ignored the Germans and interviewed the members of the Jewish Council instead. But perhaps what left Alice and the ghetto inhabitants most speechless of all was the change in the attitude of the SS toward its Jewish victims. Even a false rumor of the liberation, which caused pandemonium among the ghetto inmates, did not result in the expected violence. Instead, Alice noted with shock, the camp commandant, Karl Rahm, "made an announcement that began, 'Gentlemen! Please quiet down. This is premature; you will be informed when appropriate . . . ' et cetera. Unbelievable."

In early 1945, faced with the imminent arrival of the advancing Soviet army, the Nazis were forced to evacuate the death camps in the eastern territories and transport their prisoners westward toward Germany. In late April, the first of these prisoners from the "death transports" began to arrive in Terezín. If the diaries in this collection exist on a spectrum of knowledge and belief about the unprecedented nature and scope of the genocide of the Jews, the early refugee diaries,

Klaus Langer's and Elisabeth Kaufmann's, for example, are at one extreme, written before the crime had fully been conceived, let alone carried out. Other diarists, like Moshe Flinker, wavered between belief in the Nazi fictions about deportation for forced labor and dawning knowledge about the mass death in the East (though unaware that the deaths were caused by outright murder, rather than by illness or exhaustion from hard labor). Still others, like Yitskhok Rudashevski and Elsa Binder, acknowledged frankly the fact of murder, but did not explicitly reveal any knowledge of the full scope of the crime. The diary of the anonymous boy from the Łódź ghetto occupies the far end of the spectrum, when many were aware of the Nazis' intention to murder not only the Jews of their own communities but of Europe as a whole. It is Alice's diary, however, that most fully captures the first moment of confrontation with the reality of the crime that had been committed against Europe's Jews.[9]

The death camp survivors arrived in Terezín starved, disease-ridden, half-naked, and insane with the horror of their journey. Over the course of ten days, more than twelve thousand of these prisoners flooded the ghetto, pushing its already strained resources beyond measure.[10] Alice's diary entries express her shock and disbelief as she struggled to record what she witnessed and to put down on paper the onslaught of gruesome details. The information pouring in about the death camps was in itself difficult to absorb. In these entries, Auschwitz begins to emerge as the defining locus, the focal point of her comprehension of the death camps. "The news crashes down on us like a waterfall," she wrote. "It is hopeless, trying to grasp everything. I will write pell-mell, like a stuttering of fright and hopelessness. The key word: Auschwitz—aka labor camp Birkenau (death camp Auschwitz, international slaughtering block, sieve)."

As the SS and Nazi guards prepared to flee, the remaining structure of the ghetto disintegrated, leaving chaos and anarchy. At a loss for how to deal with the death camp survivors, the Jewish ghetto authorities fed them like animals, throwing food into the barracks where they were kept locked inside. As Alice reported it, riots erupted inside the barracks as people fought and killed one another over food; they ransacked and robbed kitchens and pharmacies in their desperation. Alice understood and described the pathos before her not only as the dehumanization of individuals, but as a representation of the very consequences of Nazi barbarism. Her entries are a potent reminder that the Nazi period was not a parenthesis in time or a self-enclosed epoch, after which the normal current of life and civilization could resume as before. To the contrary, the violence, chaos, and brutality of the Nazi years had forever altered and damaged not only the individuals who endured it but the fabric of European civilization itself. Most of all, however, Alice's diary shatters the common myth of the liberation as a time of universal joy, celebration, and relief for the survivors. For though many were grateful to have escaped with their lives, their worlds lay in ruins. In a line that sums up perhaps more eloquently than any other the horrifying contradictions of the liberation, Alice described the ghostly quality of the decimated ghetto: "Here and there a bent-over figure drags himself from barracks to barracks. . . . almost everyone has died. Only a few are still groaning, whimpering, and sobbing. And peace is breaking over this field of death."

In the context of the almost total destruction of the Jewish communities of Europe, Alice had become committed to the Zionist ideal of building a Jewish homeland in Israel. This was connected to her relationship with Ze'ev, who was a devout Zionist himself. She returned to the subject many times in her diary, always linking the dream of making aliyah with the desire to escape the brutal history of anti-Semitism that had plagued Europe's Jews for so many centuries. With the arrival of liberation, Alice voiced the desire to create a life in Palestine not only as an imperative for herself but as the only possible option for the embattled, meager remains of the European Jewish community. "I want to call out to the young Jews all over the world and tell them: this was the form that our *galut* [exile] took," she wrote early in the diary. "The essence is within you, in your Jewishness. . . . I beseech you in the name of our children who have been denied us—arise and go to Zion. No one should ever experience this again. No one. Away, away from here— do not believe in a 'finality'; create a beginning."

Alice and her sister Ruth returned to Prague from Terezín in mid-June 1945. Although Alice had heard conflicting reports about Ze'ev toward the end of the war, and had indeed been informed by several of his friends that he had died, she found his name among the survivors as she checked the lists posted daily by the Prague Jewish community. He had been found ill, delirious, and nearly unconscious by American soldiers in Dachau. They rescued him, and three weeks later he returned to Prague to find Alice.[11] At about the same time, the Ehrmanns received a letter from Alice's father, who had ended up in Slovakia with the Red

Army. He, too, returned home safely. Though the Ehrmann family had survived the Holocaust intact, Alice's sister Ruth, who had nursed the ill in Terezín and had risked her life to care for patients during a typhus epidemic that broke out during the final weeks of the war, became stricken with polio and died in Prague in 1945. Two years later, Alice married Ze'ev Shek in Prague; they emigrated to Israel in 1948, where they lived together until Ze'ev's death in 1978.

October 18, 1944

Transport. Train cars set at nine o'clock in the evening; departure at two o'clock at night. The last—a seventeen-year-old deaf-mute boy. Sixteen hundred sick, those who can't walk. Chain interrupted—about two wagon loads left behind. The first transport where [Rudolf] Haindl [deputy camp commandant] didn't slap people about the ears.

October 20, 1944

Orders. The last section heads (Elbert, Klapp, Gonda Redlich), 80 percent of the doctors, complete cripples, deathly tuberculosis, deathly ill children without their parents; mothers of deathly ill children left behind. It is too terrible to even feel unhappy. Father left [the small] fortress (about) fourteen days ago; destination unknown. Mother without regular signs of life—laundry—is she as incapable of remembering as we? Or has her grieving taken another direction—who knows. . . . Except that in this damned mouse trap—eighty kilometers away (in central Europe), I can't even say that all this isn't at an end. I am so terribly calm in the face of all these offenses as if I had a strange preview of all that lies beyond, even, I feel justified in saying, what lies beyond my own death. [. . .]

The path I am following is already beyond interruption. I am following the path of deliverance. I have come to terms with it, and if I die tomorrow, my life will have been that of one who came to terms as if I died sixty years hence. Today I understand that. This is how it is. And when the *golah* [exile] takes everything from me—and so it must be—when my parents have been taken from me in the most horrible way and my friends are lost to each other in the world; when my home is destroyed and the house of my birth and childhood lies in rubble and I must roam among strangers alone with my knowledge; when the last book has been burned in the fire and the last picture that is drawn—when all this has disappeared from my eyes and nothing, nothing remains for me on this earth—then I will have ended my thousand-year wanderings; the hour will be the hour of the Messiah—then I will go out into the world and bear children. And build a life—a life; life. You alone

Alice Ehrmann
{403}

know that I am tranquil, that I go tranquilly through my days, through our sorrows so that I may be delivered. So that I may deliver myself. All of a sudden, every prayer, every psalm, every song to Erez [Israel] makes sense. [. . .]

October 22, 1944

The sluice-gate [collection point for the deportees]: Swarms of six- to seven-year-old children alone on the transport. Sick children. Professor Lieben has tuberculosis. Hans Steckelmacher, completely lamed; enteritis. There are no uniforms. It is hopeless. I long for you, and you gradually become unattainable, your present existence too foreign. I start to gnaw at the certainty of our reunion. I have terrible fears for you. Please—stay healthy. All belief in purpose disappears in the Apocalypse of the sluice-gate.

October 23, 1944

Night time in the sluice-gate. At nine-thirty getting people into the cars. The sick, the sick, the sick, stretchers without end. And all this, including loading luggage, is done by forty people with white caps. Luggage everywhere. Luggage in front of the sluice-gate, luggage in the sluice-gate, on the platforms, in the cars. And everyone has so ridiculously little, and even that will probably be taken from them. Why these heaps of energy, which really is the last.

Came into the room; small children, three to ten. Screaming. Each has a little backpack, with cried-out eyes; some a mature and self-possessed expression that could shoot fear into one. They will have their bags, but probably never again their childhood. All are alone; most of their parents were murdered in the KZ [concentration camp]. Infants. A woman has birth pains. The Germans think she's faking. People walk in a long eddy, drag their bags and lay them down; and drag. They walk and are brave. Terribly brave. There is not a person here whose history is not a tragedy; all have been abandoned to terror—by men, parents, siblings, loved ones. Now they go without hope of reunion. One stares peculiarly at those with cried-out eyes. One is brave. Those who walk have turned to stone; those who remain swallow their tears. In the end, the luggage remained; there was no space. [. . .]

October 24, 1944

[. . .] Tomorrow a march for all men between sixteen and sixty-five. Think we'll be going along this time. Schmidt expelled from the ghetto. All the same—to go or not to go. Know it all—I can't lose more than everything on the straight path to deliverance. Possible that I will die—even then I have my bearings. Have no fear anymore; have learned to be economical with my feelings. Am exhausted; I yearn to wake up in your arms.

October 28, 1944

Into the cars. Orders—the last [Jewish] leaders [of the ghetto] are to go. Sections completely empty. Where there were a hundred before, now there are three people. All kitchens closed except two. The work of three years. [. . .] All who had such un-human responsibility for the life and death of thousands; squandered energy, risking their lives daily when the command paid a visit.—2,038 persons; in cattle cars, 50 and more. [Hans] Günther [head of the Central Office for the Regulation of the Jewish Question in Bohemia and Moravia] had the last tiny little windows nailed shut with tin so that people had to sit on that heap of luggage for twenty-four hours without an atom of air or light, with one pail for 50 people. It is too terrible, and we are much too brave. I am completely exhausted. Here there is no one who loves me. And there is one who loves me, but he is far away, and I would have to cry today if I thought of him.

October 28, 1944 [second entry on this date]

Ghetto being reorganized. No more transports for the time being. Everyone is too exhausted to start over again. But we will do it. We are the god-appointed slaves of our eternally unfailing energy who are condemned to rebuild what has been destroyed, to rebuild what was previously destroyed, to rebuild everything. It is like trying to hold back a waterfall with two outstretched hands. We are all so exhausted—although our wakefulness never ends—that is the exercise that will last a thousand years. . . .

October 31, 1944

Beginning of the reorganization. [. . .] But everything is at such finality that there can be no beginning. Life continues out of habit its old ways, its ancient well-trodden ways. One numbs oneself and lives sparingly. It's all over; outwardly nothing has changed except everything has grown a few shades darker and deeper. All of us have already climbed silently below some demarcation line, and now we are here. But the law, the spirit, nature—however you might name it—can never be violated. Never, never . . . [. . .]

November 1, 1944

The urn chamber is being cleared. Thirty thousand urns, thirty thousand cardboard boxes, thirty thousand remains of people, mothers, children, loved ones.

Alice Ehrmann

What is the point . . . More importantly, it is the knowledge that dead witnesses, substance, is being destroyed—and we are the witnesses, we who still live, I and you, my sister—and all those who are gone.

It is not a technical problem, but I cannot imagine it—and still—I am afraid to admit that I have understood it. And still I go to work in the morning, will eat, sleep, wash my hands, brush my teeth. Maybe even laugh. I will not think about it, but it will inform all my thoughts. Perhaps everything will grow quiet, and it will retreat into the background, and I will be permitted to "not think" once again. Or will it grow huge so that all my thoughts end in it, even my life and my time, until I myself come to an end in it?

O my Mother and you—am I afraid? I will read *Faust* and Isaiah and Jeremiah, and I will try to bear written witness as best I can so that it will survive me. That is what occupies my thoughts—not to have the world take notice of me—not to say: there was one who was beautiful and smart and open to the world, and she was seventeen and was snuffed out before her life could even start. No, to say to the world and time what was accomplished here; to read to them a chapter out of the *Golah* dated 1944—above all, I want to call out to the young Jews all over the world and tell them: This was the form that our *galut* [exile] took—the form. The essence is within you, in your Jewishness; what do you want to hear? If you want to hear it? Deliverance has not been granted to us. We didn't have any children, either. We beseech you; the path lies open. That is not pathos, not posturing; no, I beseech you in the name of our children who have been denied us—arise and go to Zion. No one should ever experience this again. No one. Away, away from here—do not believe in a "finality"; create a beginning.

November 2, 1944

Urns are taken away in numerical order. In all probability, they will be dumped into the Eger. A pontoon bridge is being built there so that tractors can be driven out on it. A chain of people goes from the urn chamber to the trucks. Early shift—children eight and over. Afternoon shift—seniors over sixty-five. We've already laughed about it today; we cannot do otherwise or else we would die.

We live holding our breaths. We don't wait—we endure. I live as if at the brink of a finality. My mother, without news from us, nor from father, alone like me, so terribly, cruelly alone so that one knows that it can only be borne so long and yet time has no end, ebbs away and then once. . . . My father, after all the unknown things he has endured, which only reveal themselves in nightmares.

Who knows in which concentration camp my love, my only true friend is, to whom I gave my life, no—wanted to give (since I haven't yet lived that much). I saw that last night, that it cannot be survived. I said that to myself in accordance with my best understanding, logically. I tried to simply think this out to the end and to carry it within me like a child until its birth. Can I go on? To look at all my infinite days and ask: are you the day that will bring my end? If I had alcohol, I would drink myself into unconsciousness. If I could only say: I want to live! without thereby losing my balance and sense of resignation, I could be one of the naive ones who calls to you the way one calls one's nursemaid after a nightmare. I am exiled in my knowledge, on one hand; in my seventeen years on the other. Am too exhausted since I may not wait.

November 5, 1944

They are stopping at urn number 17,000. One senses where they are going. Except, a few say that the ashes are being strewn on the vegetable fields in Trabschitz. It is so hard to find the strength to live one's life to the end, without simply letting oneself be killed. . . .

November 8, 1944

When one hears that the world lies in flames and rubble, one has to think that there really will be no refuge in the future. I am so exhausted. This is where we stand in our best hopes for life. Already they have become hushed dreams, already homeless. Our homes no longer exist; we Jews can bear this since we are born to that reality. That is why I pity the *goyim* [non-Jews] who think that the bombs could just as well have fallen two meters farther on. Poor them; how I pity them, who have been removed from the reciprocity of fate.

November 19, 1944

All the people have disappeared somewhere; here and there an unclear message from somewhere—like far calls from a ship wandering the ocean. The city lives on. It lives with bated breath, a lull between two catastrophes; but it lives on. People carry their heroism masked behind an everyday face; they no longer even talk about it. Every loved one is alone with their—waiting? cares? fears? What should one call it? They say that many people are coming. Who knows? The city is so exhausted; we will bear all this, I and the city and you and you. . . .

Forty people just arrived from Prague. Widows from mixed marriages, prisoners. No one talked to or saw them as they were being transported. They come from the world outside and are quarantined. They have parents and siblings here; they bring news but are inaccessible. Because of that they are unearthly, and how un-

Alice Ehrmann

earthly must this city seem to them! This is how it is done: this is how psychosis is created, fear of ghosts.

Forty-nine children from Westerbork via Celle, alone with two caretakers; the oldest seven and a half years. Among them are children who cannot walk, famished, four cases of scarlet fever, one each of diphtheria and measles.

January 23, 1945

Women drag sections of the barracks up the stairs to the ramparts. Ice, wind; some are bent down to the ground. Some break out in hysteria, scream that they can no longer hang on. The psychosis grows and can only be suppressed by great effort. Haindl and Rahm are there almost the entire day. Even if your hands fall off, you are not permitted to let go; even if you croak. And you won't either; the two of them are in front of you and behind you constantly. Just seeing them, you know that their mere presence will drive you on until you drop dead. Galleys. We are not merely enslaved; we are slaves, drudges, our strength in the possession of murderers.

January 29, 1945

A rumor is making the rounds. Supposedly, a transport went through Bauschowitz with people from Auschwitz in open cattle cars. The camp must have been occupied at least a week ago. And today it is minus thirteen degrees Celsius. That's all you have to know. My father was there; perhaps he rode by. Maybe he still knew this. Maybe . . . Don't think.

January 30, 1945

We are awaiting a transport with a thousand people from Prague. Whoever has never experienced this tiresome waiting for some finality cannot know what this means. Poor Jews.

February 1, 1945

Transport arrived. More than a thousand halves of mixed marriages (men) have come from Prague. We are so tired of teaching our captivity to others. And still— we see them through the eyes of others, and then the barrier is gone and we see: a glimpse, a foretaste of return, into a future, whose mere existence means an unending flood of emotions, of life.

February 3, 1945

A transport to Switzerland has been planned for Monday, February 5, twelve hundred people. There are a thousand versions: Danes and Dutch. Whole families, people up to twenty-five years, people whose families haven't been taken away, and so on. Those who are not eligible for these transports include those who are important for the ghetto and those for whom there has been an appeal based on family kinship. Who can survive this range of feelings that coursed through us a thousand times during these hours?

February 4, 1945

[. . .] At eight, the first group; headquarters, Rahm, Günther. Until ten at night. Stamp and not summons. Guidelines: one suitcase and one bag. No wooden shoes; be well dressed. Equip, but give no shoes; shaved, haircut, appear before [Dr. Benjamin] Murmelstein [the head of the Jewish Council] at the sluice-gate. Medications and condensed milk. Passes without stamps. [Leo] Baeck [a prominent rabbi and leader from Berlin]—signature, tickets—start the trip. In the morning, load the railroad cars, express trains, eighty per car. Five empty seats per car, open windows, food parcels: two large breads, four yeast dumplings, one plait [jar of jam], 120 grams of margarine, condensed milk. Escorts: three men from the Ministry of the Exterior. Hand over in Bauschowitz. There is talk of further transports. Arrival of twelve hundred mixed marriages—men.

February 10, 1945

Three transports filled with those with Aryan kin. The transport with the Zossen barracks builders returned (250 min[us] 40). Nine days in cattle cars from Zossen via Pilsen and Prague. There has been a second miracle. The fact that a few people have been tossed ashore puts us in a most unusual state. Of the thousands who have waited and suffered, there are maybe 10 or 15 whom fate has now given an immeasurable gift. It puts us into something like a state of rapture, and that stubborn little knot of hope that is divorced from all reality breaks loose. What nonsense: fate has given us 250 people—nothing more.

February 14, 1945

What they told us was merely a final chord to the hundreds of wild notes that accompanied our days and nights. They suffered; they are alive by chance. That initial intoxication of hope, which even in its embryonic form was without shape within us and for a moment loosened the bonds. Whatever may happen, I know one thing about these days: it will only end in the same certainty, in the same constriction that tightens around us to the point of screaming but already contains some sense of resignation within it.

Alice Ehrmann

February 17, 1945

Thirty-one cards (postcards) from St. Gall from those who were rescued [in the Swiss transport of February 4], from those given the gift of freedom. And still, I would not want to be among them.

March 5, 1945

Plan to convert a shooting range into a bowling alley—one year's work. Beautifications taking place. [. . .]

March 10, 1945

Thirty-six men sought out by [Franz] Stuschka [head of the work brigades in Wulkow]. What does this mean? Ask the crazed eyes of the boys, the dumbstruck laughing ones. Among them Mugden, who was slapped about the ears most often. It had to be so; slowly the cup of cruelty is being filled to the brim, very slowly. I have given myself over to thought of you and find no entry into this life and forget its meaning—what for, O God.

March 12, 1945

Five hundred from Sered, including men—not to the Reich. The seventeen hundred from Vienna are Hungarians and Slovaks, all Orthodox, Agudists. For them, Zionists are goyim. Two versions of the golah: the one that awaits the Messiah, that prepares for a birth with all their reserved strength; the other the defections from this process of crystallization.[12] That which remains on both sides of the path. Judaism; timeless—it certainly is.

March 17, 1945

[Karl Hermann] Frank [Reichsminister for Bohemia and Moravia and high-level SS officer] announced for tomorrow. all shop windows decorated. Sidewalks washed. Rain at night; bottomless dirt. Curtains are mandatory, et cetera.

March 25, 1945

A transport with three thousand Hungarians has been en route for thirteen days. Only we who have unloaded the transports know what that means. Thirteen days and nights; how many insane? The air raid alerts get longer every day, three to four hours.

March 26, 1945

It's [Dr. Rudolf] Freiberger's turn [member of the Jewish Council]; how could we have doubted it would happen. How can we doubt that Georg's [Vogel, her cousin] number will also come up. The last one. The thought presses down on me like a curse. It is terrible, this erasure of people, without a word, in silence, without hatred and without passion. One day while inspecting the apartments in the Magdeburg barracks, the room is sealed; and he is called to headquarters directly from the south barracks. And then we hear nothing more, absolutely nothing. Just incidentally, on one's daily rounds, the fate of a living human being is executed, a long-sealed fate. He falls silently into the maelstrom and is killed off.

April 1, 1945

Frank is expected; on the fifth the [Red Cross] Commission. The children in *Fire-flies* get a tan daily under two sun lamps.

Three trucks with food from Switzerland arrived. White tents with red crosses. Chocolate, rice, sugar, matzoh, peas, cigarettes. The drivers stayed in the fellowship house. While they were talking to the SS, Georg [Vogel] was sweating in the boiler room trying to get the boiler to work so that the men could have a hot bath—as if that were usual here. Since it was broken, Georg expected shit this evening. That's the picture. They, however, don't know.

Sometimes I think that if they did know . . . well, they still wouldn't be able to understand. And even if they could understand—I hate their pity because we are not pitiable—not, in any case, by them. How much higher we stand in our misery than they in their prosperity. I hate their pity and sympathy and laugh in this merciful one's face: are they not the ones who instigated torture upon torture upon us for thousands of years; bloodbath upon bloodbath, humiliation upon humiliation for hundreds of years? Are they not the ones whose children will become the carriers of a new Jew hatred? O God, a plaything in their hands, we in their hands; an object of their mood, their interest—always an object. Here I know: I am in the middle of a development that is cruelly true and necessary. I am permitted to hate all of them, and since I can expect nothing except death and torture at their hands, I never have to be grateful. Never.

April 6, 1945

A few ridiculous moments in the current theater: if asked, people were not permitted to say anyone had gone away or died. All the gendarmes were at their posts in civilian dress. Only inside did everyone wear uniforms. All local SS in civilian dress. Displays stuffed with merchandise. Invalids and elderly—house arrest. The "babičky" [grandmothers] in the old-age homes are given makeup. Leisure program from nine in the morning. Lunch: a double helping of grilled meat and potatoes and pea soup. Dinner: salami, barley with peas, *lebkuchen* for dessert. Yesterday, half a kilogram of sugar; day before, too. All the while: Vienna, Pressburg, Hannover [fallen]; it leaves one speechless.

April 8, 1945

Forty people building barracks, one disappears, is found; nothing happens. It's all a foretaste of *sof* [the end]. [. . .]

April 12, 1945

All card files, documents up to the end of 1944 burned; smoke coming out of all the chimneys. Things are being burned that can never be replaced. Ze'ev's documents gain in value minute by minute.[13]

April 13, 1945

Trucks with trailers as well as tractors driven away with files and file cabinets. All the material regarding this stage of the golah is being burned in Ravelin 20. Today I saw the enormous pile of ashes. I watched as thousands of pages of documents flew up in flames; I saw the numbers, digits, dates, and names of which our misery is composed, in which it is mirrored, flicker dully and turn to ashes. Who can comprehend this? [. . .] The end, the end, the end; that is what everything sings to me.

April 14, 1945

Today I saw the boys going through town, how they tried to absorb every little stone in their attempt to take with them everything that they experienced here; everything. How well I understood them. Then, they stood at the window of the sluice-gate and handed cigarettes to the girls, from the window of the same sluice-gate in which I was sluiced. They were in a state of complete intoxication. They have lost their senses. [. . .] I am so stuffed with experiences that I can no longer write objectively. Everything flows together in the overwhelming excitement that agitates us. I wish I didn't have to sleep or work so that I could just drink in these days. Sometimes I wish they wouldn't come to an end. Only one thought makes me shudder.

April 15, 1945

This morning I saw twenty-four white cars with the insignia of the Red Cross. Twenty-four drivers from Sweden drove slowly out of the ghetto, taking 420 [Danish] Jews to a new life, to freedom. People stood there intoxicated; they yelled and made signs; they surged as far as Q-7, the "Victoria," the closed quarter where one can only go with a pass. The band played, and a spring morning presided in all its glory over the event.[14]

Airplanes fly over from the north, one after the other; sirens day and night. People say that Dresden has fallen. Buchenwald with its twenty thousand people is supposed to have fallen into the hands of the Americans. Celle, too, with its fifty thousand, although with typhus. [. . .]

April 16, 1945

Inspection. [. . .] They questioned and talked only with Murmelstein, completely ignoring the SS. The way Rahm looked was worth money; he walked behind carrying his hat in his hands—the dog and slave holder, the same one who galloped through his settlement on horseback and who made trouble for people wherever he went, bringing them closer to death or insanity; the same one who was once preceded by a wave of ashen-faced silence. How can one think this single detail to its conclusion, given such excitement. The city is intoxicated.

In the afternoon, air raid on Leitmeritz and one of the roads or railroads. It was tremendously exciting for us; five airplanes, silver with red cockpits dove down low, circled, and flew in a wave toward the ground. They dropped their payload and aimed directly at their target. One had the feeling that one was well protected. [. . .]

April 17, 1945

[. . .] All of a sudden we feel so secure and guarded and protected by a world that knows about us. The Germans are getting prepared. At the train station, everything that has wheels is being repaired: crates and trailers, a field kitchen, a railroad car for poultry, rabbit cages, et cetera. [. . .]

There is a bonfire in the courtyard of the Sudeten barracks. Sweating SS men are throwing ten- to twenty-kilogram packages of files down from the windows. They stand there in a line, like the Jews a year ago, and sweat it out. Above, they patrol and collect stray pages blowing about.

Haindl slapped someone about the ears today, but that is no longer the way things go. Nothing more is known about the Commission; Murmelstein is very satisfied. Rumors of surrender circulate. Everything is topsy-turvy, and time moves so slowly.

Alice Ehrmann

April 18, 1945

The psychosis has gone so far that tonight rumor spread that the SS had already left the city. Immediately, the people with Aryan kin surged out of the barracks, woke up everyone else, and ran through the city, beating against the windows and yelling, "Wir sind frei . . . At' žije Československo" [We are free . . . Long live Czechoslovakia], and so on. Within a half hour, the entire city was up and noise filled the streets. Lights in the windows; people ran every which way in the same state as when they got up out of bed.

When everything had quieted down a little, Murmelstein came into the barracks and gave the jubilant patriots, who by this time were singing nationalist songs, a good dressing down. Haindl and Rahm had also arrived with submachine guns. Rahm had everyone line up in six rows, and all thought . . . But he made an announcement that began, "Gentlemen! Please quiet down. This is premature; you will be informed when appropriate . . ." et cetera. Unbelievable. [. . .]

April 19, 1945

[. . .] It was all empty talk about Buchenwald and Celle; the tendency is downward, or rather, it just continues. How could we have given in to this craziness, how could we have thought that such a thing could be so that we could simply discard a line of thought in the face of a few facts. How drunk and hysterical was our loosening up. Well, it was the second stage of all developments, the second extreme. Now the balance will be equalized, now comes the dissolution. I see it clearly before me. And so, this sof will become an entr'acte between all hopelessness and all the intoxication of these days. It is all bitter, but really a bitter reality, but of this planet.

April 20, 1945

At six-thirty a transport arrived consisting of twenty-five railroad cars, eighteen hundred people. The news flew through the ghetto: people from the camps. As they passed by [. . .] they yelled out "Auschwitz," "Birkenau," "Hannover," "Buchenwald"; they yelled out the most frightful phrases from the train. The heart of the city stood still, and now they are here. Stinking, befouled cattle cars, stinking, befouled people within them, half-living, half-dead or corpses. They pressed themselves against the windows; horrible faces, bones and eyes. Eighty women from Teres [probably Terezín]; other than that, mostly men. And how they looked. Now they were coming, what for months had made us tremble the most. It is a matter of life and death for us, of countless sufferings without deliverance and now it is here. Now it is here. The little remainder of the mass, the remains of human beings. They threw out cigarettes, they pointed to their mouths, they fell to the ground—drink, eat. They

Alice Ehrmann

were unloaded in the sluice-gate—*unloaded*. So-and-so has arrived, names—mother, daughter, loved one of so-and so. Everyone is horrified. They are taken on flatbed carts to the hastily constructed sick rooms. Mothers don't recognize their own children, their eyes are so deadened. People throw bread to them; they throw themselves upon it and fight one another for it. They have been under way for days. They are starved. The cars—I will never forget it. The half-dark, the wooden crates and cellulose, filth, articles of befouled clothing—and yet so empty. A stench that is just too horrible of old excrement, and on the slippery floor, behind a crate, in the dark, the white gleaming foot of a dead person, of one who had been alive a week before. And in all this misery, it became clear to me how good it is to be dead. Carried out on stretchers . . . In the middle of the night, six cars from Hungary.

April 21, 1945

[. . .] Women, too, arrived by foot this afternoon. Eight days under way. All crippled, shrunken beings with tiny heads and burning eyes. Hunger, animal fear, insanity. In striped uniforms, barefoot; feet with pus-covered wounds wrapped in rags, some wearing wooden clogs . . .

Fifteen hundred who simply couldn't go on, shot. Of these, five hundred remained. They point to their mouths, "hunger"; they keel over. They are no longer human beings; and when you hear the names of these ruins—Dr. Schaff, Dr. Österreicher. They will fight and beat one another over a tidbit. [. . .] Eight hundred skeletons with hanging breasts and stomachs, legs like sticks, bones and wrinkles—elderly-looking women who are younger than I am, a single child.

Another group of 170 arrived this evening. Days under way without food, without sleep, from Eudendorf near Chemnitz—KZ. Two hundred from the Et transport, all acquaintances, Dvory, Kitty, Gerda, Cvok Winternitz, Putka, Lydia, Vera Slv and others. A wave of insane joy—complete, Eva Tutsch, Deborah. No lice! Eight days under way from Leitmeritz to Theresienstadt [Terezín]. Waited for five days on the road, Prominents' ghetto.

[. . .] God, this bitterness and this thankfulness, this hopelessness and desperation and eternal hope without end, pulverized and exhausted, brave and broken, and you—I feel completely empty inside; everything has been torn out, perhaps even my heart. Only a suffocating feeling, a prayer and a curse simultaneously directed at heaven. Everything, everything is over, and I can't believe it.

April 22, 1945

Early, a train, Hungary, Poland, Balkans—men in open cars, seventy dead, striped. Eyes, eyes. From Zeiss, before that Buchenwald they say, most scattered about

Alice Ehrmann

Germany, many on the way here. Hunger, wildness. [. . .] Peter Lang. Says that Ze'ev was with him in Gleiwitz. Had some sort of "good" position. [. . .] I tremble all the more for your fate, which for the moment has interrupted hell. Underground factory.—Afternoon Hungary, all have "KZ" on their backs, numbers sewn to their sleeves; all together—children . . . They have children with them!!! [. . .] Steal everything; how is one to distribute food? This afternoon in front of the riflers' barracks, the handsome Greek in my arms—a whimpering old man of fifty-two. His clear eyes. The whimpering and roaring continues through the night. The gray masses under blankets. Hail, snow.

April 23, 1945

Nobody arrived today. At night, the Dresden [barracks], transfer, five thousand Hungarians in there. Distribution of food, half sated, discipline. On the other hand, in the Hamburg [barracks] those from the KZ in striped "pajamas," among them Aryans (murderers and criminals serving up to twenty-five years). It is horrible. Yesterday we searched for our people among them; today we are at our wit's end how to protect ourselves from them. We have a creepy feeling down our backs, and we are afraid . . . Because they are insane and three thousand, and we have no men, except for the kin of Aryans. And no weapons, and no SS, and no gendarmes.

It is no time to think about our misfortune. Now I understand why they held fast to life, these mothers without children and people with a shattered life purpose. It is out of calculation that they hang on to purpose—about you, you far-flung ones who are the content of their lives. But not calculation, from a dark animal urge that they all have and we feel already. I see the development that leads there and begins with us. I think that the germ of all evil is violence and fear, perhaps fear even earlier, and then they alternate.—They sit in the Hamburg [barracks], food is shoved through the door and then slammed shut. And inside, they beat each other. Today there were several deaths. How can this continue? It is too horrible, and nobody knows a way out, and something will have to happen, God, oh God . . .

And then Oświęcim [Auschwitz]. Barbed wire all around. Disinfestations, crematorium, seven chimneys, fire. Luggage in the car; change outside, Jewish sluice-gate team, naked hour after hour. Then a bath; then standing naked again. Scissors. Selection immediately after getting off the train; men, women, old people, young, et cetera. Then to work. In the disinfestation bath, water + gas . . . [. . .]

April 24, 1945

The news crashes down on us like a waterfall. It is hopeless, trying to grasp everything. I will write pell-mell, like a stuttering of fright and hopelessness. The key word: Auschwitz—aka labor camp Birkenau (death camp Auschwitz, international slaughtering block, sieve). [. . .] There was a massive slaughter of Czechs on March 7, 1944 (Masaryk's birthday); the September transport completely gassed. Epidemic—red spots; everyone with a red spot, straight to the crematorium, alive.—Minsk: of the entire transport (one thousand), only three survived, purely by chance. Shot, pogroms.

News from Ze'ev: Klinger—Kaufering (Munich and Innsbruck), there with him until January 5. He sang in the cabaret; he was doing very well, enough to eat, looked unchanged. Who can understand what that means for me. Save him, O God, that we may have many children—nothing more than that, nothing.

April 25, 1945

Early morning 250 women from Dresden. Afternoon men from Dresden, Poland, and Hungary; "very good." Early, barracks construction, headquarters. Forty are to go. To where, they have known for the past four days . . . Saw the first ear beatings. Early morning canceled; the Germans take all their grub with them. Details go back and forth; everyone thinks they know, but nobody knows. Only dread, dread, dread. I can't think anymore; the same narcosis as in October. Only now I know that in the end I will wake up. Every day brings more pain; a new wound is opened up. I pray that sof will happen now so that I won't have to wake up.

April 27, 1945

More small groups. Disinfestation continues; the new arrivals get double portions. Slowly they are reviving; slowly, slowly they are becoming beings similar to us. The Germans are completely packed. Fifteen cars from yesterday stand empty; the final travel preparations.

April 29, 1945

Six hundred and fifty Hungarian and Slovak women from Leipzig (Hawrik?), on foot sixteen days (wooden clogs)—very good. [. . .] In the ghetto there is a partial resurgence of excitement, but skepticism as well. Even if they are wrong, the news reports are just too good. [. . .] Will I celebrate my birthday in peace? My fears about you are frantic, like when there is a race with a minute or two left and you have bet everything, everything, and I have too.

April 30, 1945

[. . .] We've been waiting for six endless, unbearable years for this moment. And now everything is so shabby and has lost the appearance of glory because every-

has become so superfluous and so pointless. Everything just goes around
es. Those who destroyed us saved the remnants and now want to be cele-
Everything, everything is so pointless. We sit there and see: the worst thing
that they did to us was to rob us of reality, of the concept of reality. We know a tortured, horror-filled world of cruelty in which we are the objects of events. And
dreams. And between them lies the only thing capable of being reality and of being
lived as such, darkness. They bound our eyes shut for so long, and now we are
blind. We shatter in eternal flight between dream and cruelty upon the rocks of a
reality that is shrouded by eternal night. It is too late for everything. Does anything
remain that might make sense in this senselessness? Things reveal themselves in
their senselessness. And that, precisely at the moment that we harbor hopes for life
after an endless dying between our twelfth and eighteenth years.

May 1, 1945

[. . .] The excitement is unbearable. I wish I could either cry or die; it simply cannot become more intense; it must end somewhere. I can do nothing anymore. I am
unhappy and abandoned and alone and have prospects of a disillusionment that is
perhaps called life. It could come any time now. Dachau—150 boxcars of the dead.
In us there is a collision between the dread of the unfinished struggle and that
which is finished. It is horrible.

May 2, 1945

[. . .] In the evening a rebellion in the West barracks; at night in the Hamburg barracks. Kitchen smashed, pharmacy destroyed, sanitation room robbed. It's true;
these people have taken Europe's destructive insanity into their blood. They are
the unfortunate carriers of all of this war's meanness and unhappiness. Each of
them is a living personification of those characteristics and drives that brought
about this endless destruction and horror. They are the tragic, the endlessly tragic
product of these times. The war and the curse that is attached to the world are
manifested in them. [. . .]

May 4, 1945

The psychosis is intensified hour by hour by the lack of discipline. People to
whom it had not yet occurred pack up and flee. Trying to stop them is like trying to
hold water in a sieve. The numbers can't be estimated. Aryans are moving all about
the ghetto. They pick up their spouses and children and then take off. No one tries
to stop them; there is no fear of the administrators—they simply no longer exist.
Hundreds of people and thousands of letters back and forth. The funny thing is

Alice Ehrmann
{ 418 }

that things still function. This is a magical capacity of the community: tasks are suddenly completed out of disorganization and anarchy and idleness . . .

[. . .] I received the forms for aliyah, wrote home, and invited Mother. Filled straw sacks until twelve and am exhausted. So, this is sof . . .

May 5, 1945

I spiked a temperature at night; it was a difficult night. And in the morning I awoke to the sounds of jubilation from the street. An automobile with two flags stopped in front of headquarters, a gendarme got in, and they drove through the city. People applauded loudly. Then, the flag was raised in front of our house and hymns were sung. Everyone walks around with tricolors. The guard consists of the Czech army with tricolor armbands. The Jews are happy; they once again have colors to wear . . . People flee in masses. Headquarters stormed, Rahm and Haindl fled into the SS guards' quarters. The gendarmes have taken over the city. A flag billows in front of the bakery, Hannover [barracks]—red flags. There are red placards on the headquarters door, and why? nobody knows. People talk of tank troops here and there and battles in Prague, et cetera.

Nobody knows what is actually happening. I see and hear everything and cannot suppress my bitterness: celebration—it is too late for that. And what the poor Jews celebrate, just learned the bloody way, they start all over again. And how they celebrate, rabble, riff-raff. I am sad and tired; it is all pointless. The years were for nothing [. . .]. Just one day after the end, and it says only one thing: for nothing. I think about how pointless, pointless this is and think with bitterness about which people fate has saved, and I think of you.

May 7, 1945

The absolute disorganization, or better put, no organization, reached its high point today. Everything is running on empty, if at all. There is no power to which one can turn. There is not a single person from here in the South barracks, and no one has taken it over. They have no food or anything else. In the morning, those in the hospital barracks were half dead or half dying. Not a single person. I went around today and peered into a wall of powerlessness and insanity, and I thought of all those to whom I had said, "We have everything."—of the individuals and the lousy masses who get nothing to eat and must think that we brought them here just so that they could die one after the other.

[. . .] I walked through the streets and in the middle of this "something has to be done" it slowly dawned on me, slowly came into my mind, and a cruel motionless stillness came over me before I even grasped the germ of the idea: Nothing has

Alice Ehrmann
{ 419 }

to be done. That none of this must lead to a solution and dissolution and deliverance, no, that everything in this endless confusion of instincts, feelings, standards, and human and earthly principles can all peter out like a sound without law. The fact that there is no one and nothing that still carries truth and honor and reality within it—now I felt completely lost for the first time. This day I saw an end to faith in a law on earth. I never experienced worse. Slowly, something is changing in me. Everything that until now held things together lies in shards. No, here it comes; I feel it: a ship without a rudder. What's the point . . . [. . .]

All the red crosses, posters, nurses, cars, doctors. It makes me sick. There is not a gram of human decency behind it. Not behind the crosses, not behind the peace. Nowhere. And the Jewish tragedy called golah just keeps on going. Anti-Semitism and complexes and all those unappetizing witnesses. I hate everything and everybody, and I despair and am abandoned and bitter; grief. Evening: surrender signed, no jubilation. Everything is still within me. The living thoughts that hoped for expression leave the desolate ship. I am tired; the world has made me tired. Forever?

May 8, 1945

[. . .] Everything is going to pieces; it has to. Evening at nine-thirty, the first Russians. Loud noise and cheers. Yesterday they sang Czech songs and wore tricolors; today they sing the *Internationale* and carry red flags through the streets. I have such bitterness inside me. I cannot go along with them anymore because something has broken and the burden of centuries weighs upon me, stirred up and alive. I have only one path, and all this disgusts me. People disgust me. Whenever I think about them, I am overcome with the hopelessness of one who must carry about all the undigested matter of all those who are singing.

May 9, 1945

Early morning and all day long, air raids, artillery, guns. Things can't go on; no one knows what to do. Raschek (Raska) went to Prague with the Russians during the night. The day lets us catch our breath. Prague destroyed? Now occupied and quiet. People are streaming in from all sides. Uniformed and wonderful looking Frenchmen and English; prisoners walk about with girls. The "pajamas" [concentration camp survivors in striped uniforms] are camped all about, and others from Leitmeritz, et cetera. South barracks: people are dying, ten to twenty per day. The number of sick in one barracks has risen from 100 to 180. They have become relatively disciplined (by their misery). No one there, ten girls distribute food; Ruth [Alice's sister] and Váva Schön alone with Dr. Schorsch, outpatient. Barracks filled, fore and aft, lousy rags, everywhere—cleaned in exchange for salami. Disinfestation station hasn't functioned all day because there is no water or electricity.

Nobody helps us. The only thing we wish for is that a bomb would burst this misery. Save? One sees only death and misery; the former is better because we can't give people life, even if they stay alive. Our hands are as nothing in these events, but then—are people worth it? The question arises whether it wouldn't be better to die and have peace. There is nothing to save; we are fighting apparitions, the human being remains. We are fighting symptoms; the essence remains the same. For what? The whole rigmarole starts over again. In the evenings, the kin of Aryans demonstrate in the streets. They want to go home. Of course, they are right. If only we revolted so that we wouldn't croak here . . . but we are the eternally silent; how could it be otherwise . . .

May 10, 1945

The Russians are in the ghetto. They came to pick up Russians [prisoners of war]. They broke through to Hamburg [barracks] but were more or less repelled. The Russians have disarmed the gendarmes; there is a tremendous increase in chaos. The kin of Aryans register; people run away; they go with the Russians. The Soviet flag flies over headquarters. Other than that, Czechoslovak flags and red crosses. The Jews are busy sewing; only the colors change. [Paul] Dunant [the representative from the International Red Cross] is gone; his mission has been accomplished. Gone. Jirka [Georg Vogel] is going to Prague. Meissner is in Prague. [. . .] And we . . . Surely, we're going to pay because we didn't care. The Red Cross sent five nurses—what a joke. Tomorrow there will almost certainly be nothing left to eat; it's a miracle that there is anything today. People are insane, used up. Is it any wonder after six years of all this?

[. . .] What are we to them? To the Russians, we are simply a hospital city. And there is no other nurse except Ruth and another one. South barracks: we drove beds and mattresses there by car for twelve Aryan sisters. Night. Below, the barracks with half-lit windows, barbed wire, and skulls and crossbones everywhere: "Typhus," rags, lousy blankets and shoes lying about. And the stench, the endless stench of cattle cars and sluice-gates. Here and there a bent-over figure drags himself from barracks to barracks. [. . .] Almost everyone has died. Only a few are still groaning, whimpering, and sobbing. And peace is breaking over this field of death. One can see fireworks in the distance; people are celebrating freedom, freedom—happiness. They are building happiness out of the misery they brought about, and they are having a good time—and for that one is supposed to go home.

Alice Ehrmann
{ 421 }

May 11, 1945

Relative order; the ghetto is functioning more or less. Many are leaving. [. . .] Order is slowly being restored; the Russians are here—they come and go. They are tonic for our confused Central European senses that have been burdened by hysteria and insanity. [. . .] The promised transfer to the field hospital has not materialized. The doctor doesn't dare go inside—he promised them he would. All those who are ambulatory have been disinfested and are in the Bodenbacher [barracks]. Two hundred and fifty who were not able to move met a cruel death in the barracks, in their own filth beneath other corpses. It is horrible. My sister is there and cannot drag herself away—I can understand her. To decide to leave the barracks behind and to know that you are just letting 250 young and living people croak, and how—who could do that? Even if one knows that one can't help. I am so endlessly exhausted. I think it must be glorious not to have to do anything, ever again.

May 12, 1945

Ruth outside all night. [. . .] A new picture in the album of the war. "Organizing" out of a need to be active, not for use value (coffee . . . Josef). At night two Russian officers—Ruth shows them the crematorium. One pile, a hundred corpses, naked. Horror. And? In the evening, visiting the four in their barracks. An experience. Surroundings—grotesque? We sat and talked about things with great effort—trying to get past the KZs. However, we realized that they have become our starting point and motif.

Josef, temperament (nervous shock), unfortunately: gentleman and robber; perhaps a child and a criminal. A bright spirit and a warped character; a child of tender years and a destroyed person. All this combines and alternates. Motek, thirty-four years old, is tired of living, and after five years in a KZ, he has arrived at a terrible "What's the point." He needs love, fears aloneness, awakened thinking. Thirty-four, wife and children—crematorium. A bitter and awake heart under the crust of disinterest. Max, perhaps the most tragic—a handsome thirteen-year-old boy with sparkling eyes; parents dead, everything passes—prisoner, wants to go to Erez Israel.

May 14, 1945

Thanks to Russian intervention, work is again being accomplished. Slowly, anarchy and hysteria are giving way to order. Lately, I have gotten detailed insight into the state of organization, or, better said, disorganization, and everything connected to it. I have experienced the total powerlessness of those exercising responsibility who have oversight of the entire situation, above and beyond their own interests—from the details to the whole. That is why I appreciate the good fortune that it is happening. The idiot masses see only that soldiers are molesting girls. These days, I am experiencing the entire burden of responsibility, the entire burden that has been transferred to me by the ignorant as a result of my knowledge. The West barracks cleaned up at night; seven girls, three barracks, from ten-thirty to four. Unimaginable filth.—Georg [Vogel] has been entrusted with administration.

May 15, 1945

The Russian commanders are first class, but it is difficult. Are childish, make crazy demands; they have no concept of technical difficulties. They can do everything—how come we can't? They send huge shipments of food; soon we will be supplied as well as the Russian army. We've had 600 grams of bread, 180 grams of sugar, now up to 250. They place the infection barracks under their control. Dysentery in the "Genius" [engineer corps] barracks. West barracks—typhus, L-504—internees, house arrest from 10 P.M. to 5 A.M. Names of KZ prisoners are reported daily.

May 18, 1945

In the evening, Mařka Pick, Honza Meissner, father in Slovakia. I think that everything is turning within me, all the crushed thoughts of horror about him pass before my eyes. It is like a storm breaking, terrible yet harmless; all black shadows and spirits of the night—I extinguish them with a motion. This light is too bright and I am blind. And all around is dense darkness. In the evening, a letter. I have my mother again.

May 19, 1945

Hans Schimmerling. We have played it out to the end. You were right.

Appendix I

YOUNG DIARISTS OF THE HOLOCAUST

Editor's note: Many diaries and journals have come to light since the first edition of *Salvaged Pages*. The collections of major institutions such as the United States Holocaust Memorial Museum in Washington, D.C., and Yad Vashem in Jerusalem contain unpublished manuscripts written during the war years by Jewish youngsters and teens. Unfortunately, it was beyond the scope of this revision to review and incorporate all of those texts in this appendix. I have therefore updated information to the existing entries where relevant, and added several important published young writers' diaries to this list.

Werner T. Angress

Werner T. (or Thomas) Angress (nicknamed Töpper) was born on June 27, 1920, in Berlin. He was the eldest son of Ernst Hermann Angress and Henny Angress (née Kiefer), and had two younger brothers, Fritz and Hans. He was a resident at the non-Zionist agricultural training farm at Gross-Breesen from May 1936 until late October 1937, at which point he was summoned back to Berlin and emigrated with his parents and brothers from Germany to England via Amsterdam. He subsequently returned to Holland with his family for reasons related to his father's business. He began his diary in 1935 in Berlin, wrote in 1936 in the camp at Gross-Breesen, and wrote diary entries and letters as a refugee in Amsterdam, reflecting on the conflicting nature of his German-Jewish identity, reporting on the news of Kristallnacht as it reached him in exile, and recounting his desperate attempts to help his friends in Germany to emigrate as quickly as possible. He immigrated to America in October 1939 and joined the U.S. Army, serving in active duty between May 1941 and September 1945. He was reunited with his mother and brothers after the war; his father had been arrested in April 1941 and deported to Auschwitz, where he perished. The diary is in a private collection. Excerpts of his diary and letters (under the name Töpper) were translated into English and included in Werner T. Angress, *Between Fear and Hope: Jewish Youth in the Third Reich* (New York: Columbia University Press, 1988).

Anonymous Boy, Łódź. See Chapter 13

Anonymous Girl, Łódź. See Chapter 8

Janina Bauman. See Janina Lewinson

Mary Berg. See Appendix II

Helene Berr

Helene Berr, born in Paris in 1921 to a French Jewish family, studied English at the Sorbonne in Paris as a young woman. She began her diary on April 2, 1942, at age twenty-one and wrote until February 15, 1944, amid escalating restrictions and humiliations for Jews in Paris. She and her family were deported to Drancy in March 1944 and from there to Auschwitz-Birkenau. Helene was forced on a death march to Bergen-Belsen in November 1944 and died of typhus there in April 1945, just days before the liberation. The original diary resides in the Mémorial de la Shoah in Paris. It was published in France in 2008 and in the United States, under the title *The Journal of Helene Berr,* in 2009.

Elsa Binder. See Chapter 11

Berthe Jeanne Bloch–van Rhijn

Berthe Jeanne (Bertje) Bloch–van Rhijn kept her diary while in hiding with her family in Holland. According to Debórah Dwork, who interviewed the writer in 1984, the diary was buried in the garden of the home of a woman who sheltered Bertje and her family. It was taken out from time to time to allow Bertje to write in it and then buried again for safekeeping. The original diary is apparently in a private collection and has never been published, with the exception of two short entries excerpted in Dwork's book, *Children With a Star: Jewish Youth in Nazi Europe* (New Haven: Yale University Press, 1991), xxiii, 24–25, 72, 76.

Anita Budding. See Anita Meyer

Lilly Cohn

Lilly Cohn (later Lillyan Rosenberg) was born on January 30, 1928, in Halberstadt, Germany. She began her diary on her eleventh birthday in Halberstadt, where she lived with her parents and her older brother, Werner. She wrote throughout 1939, capturing details of her daily life playing with friends and visiting with family members. In July 1939, she left Germany for safety in England, describing the bureaucratic details of the emigration in her diary. She did not write again until June 1942, when she recounted the story of her emigration and her adjustment to a new life in England. She continued to write sporadically until mid-1944. Her brother Werner had also reached safety in England; in 1946 they immigrated to America. Her parents were killed during the Holocaust. Her diary is on loan to the United States Holocaust Memorial Museum, Washington, D.C., which also holds a translation of the text in English in its collections.

Věra Diament

Věra Diament was born on July 4, 1928, and grew up in the small Czechoslovakian town of Čelákovice with her parents, Karel and Irma Diament, and her older sister Eva. During her childhood, she was surrounded by a close extended family, including her maternal grandparents, aunts, uncles, and cousins. The family was middle class and assimilated and, like many Czech Jews of its generation, not deeply religious or observant. In 1938, Karel Diament had his daughters baptized as Christians to protect them from the rising threat of Nazi persecution. In late June 1939, Eva and Věra were sent to England under the auspices of the British Refugee Committee. Given her diary by her father shortly before her departure, Věra began writing on the journey and continued throughout her years of exile. She was welcomed into the home of the Rainford family in Liverpool, who cared for her, sheltered her, and brought her up as a daughter. Her sister Eva lived with a different

British family, but the two girls visited each other and maintained a close relationship. In autumn 1941, Věra began school at Hinton Hall in Shropshire, a Czech school aimed at helping refugee children maintain their ties to their native language and culture. Her sister Eva went on to become a nurse, caring for wounded and sick soldiers returning from the front. Věra's parents, to whom she was deeply attached, perished in the Holocaust. Her father was apparently shot on a death march, although exact details of his fate are not known, and her mother died of typhus two days after liberation in Bergen-Belsen. Much of her extended family, including her grandfather and two cousins, also lost their lives. In August 1945, she was repatriated to Czechoslovakia to be reunited with her mother's sister Berta, who had survived Auschwitz and Bergen-Belsen. Though some of her diaries are lost, excerpts of the diaries from 1939–40 and 1945 and beyond, as well as a number of letters exchanged between the Diament daughters and their parents, are reprinted in the diarist's memoirs, published under her married name, Vera Gissing, as *Pearls of Childhood* (New York: St. Martin's, 1988). In 1949, disillusioned by the mixed treatment of Jews in postwar Czechoslovakia, she returned to Britain, which she adopted as her permanent home. The diaries are in a private collection.

Lilla Ecséri. See Lilla Kánitz

Alice Ehrmann. See Chapter 14

Peter Feigl. See Chapter 3

Sarah Fishkin

Sarah Fishkin was eleven years old when she first began writing in her diary. In 1941, when she was seventeen, the Nazis occupied Rubezhevichi, in Belarus, where she and her family were living. She continued to write in her diary until she was deported from Rubezhevichi in 1942. Her youngest brother and sister were killed in Rubezhevichi. Her father and brother Jacob were deported to a death camp. She was sent, together with her mother and aunt, to Dworzec; her mother died there and Sarah was executed together with the majority of the prisoners shortly before liberation. Her aunt survived and recovered the diary from Rubezhevichi after the end of the war. She gave it to Sarah's only surviving sibling, Jacob. The original diary and English translation are in a private collection. Short extracts of it were published in Laurel Holliday's *Children in the Holocaust and World War II: Their Secret Diaries* (New York: Washington Square Press, 1996). Sarah's brother Jacob incorporated portions of the diary in English in a memoir titled *Heaven and Earth: The Diary of Sarah Fishkin,* published by YIVO Institute for Jewish Research in 2005.

Moshe Ze'ev Flinker. See Chapter 4

Anne Frank

Anne Frank began writing her diary on June 12, 1942. Anne was born in Germany, and she and her family moved to Holland in 1933. In 1942, they went into hiding in the "secret annex" in Amsterdam. Her last entry was written on August 1, 1944; three days later the hiding place was discovered and all the inhabitants were arrested. Anne, her sister Margot, and her mother Edith perished. After the war, Anne's father, Otto Frank, retrieved her diary from Miep Gies and, in 1952, published the first English edition. The original diary is housed at the Anne Frank House in Amsterdam. There have been innumerable editions and versions of the diary; the two most significant are the Critical Edition, prepared by the Netherlands State Institute for War Documentation and published by Doubleday in 1989, and the Definitive Edition, published by Doubleday in 1995.

Raymonde Frazier. See Raymonde Nowodworski

Ilya Gerber. See Chapter 12

Petr Ginz

In the spring of 2003, two volumes of Petr Ginz's diaries, written from February 24, 1941, until August 1942, and four additional notebooks containing his written manuscripts, surfaced in Prague. The following year, Petr's sister Chava Pressburger edited a volume titled *The Diary of Petr Ginz, 1941–1942* (New York: Atlantic Monthly Press, 2003). Petr infused his diaries with his unique voice and writing style, and filled them with observations on all aspects of life under German occupation, adding immeasurably to his story and the wider picture of Jewish life in Prague at this time. The volume is an indispensable companion to Petr's short diary and journal from Terezín that are included here.

Petr Ginz and Eva Ginzová. See Chapter 6

Vera Gissing. See Věra Diament

Irena Glück

Irena Glück was an only child born on July 25, 1924. She began writing her diary in May 1940 in Cracow, Poland; her diary also records her experiences in the town of Niepolomice. She wrote until August 19, 1942, at which point her diary breaks off abruptly. According to Tadeusz Pankiewicz, author of *The Cracow Ghetto Pharmacy,* he witnessed the Glück family in the Cracow ghetto on October 28, 1942, and saw Irena and her mother boarding the train for Auschwitz on that day. Irena's father, who was a doctor, apparently remained in Cracow. (This information was confirmed by another eyewitness, a Dr. Biberstein.) Irena and her mother are presumed to have perished; no further information is known about the survival or postwar whereabouts of her father. The diary was found in Niepolomice, where Irena left it before fleeing to Cracow. According to the Jewish Historical Institute in Warsaw, the original is in a private collection, though I have not been able to confirm with certainty its whereabouts. A typescript of the diary is in the holdings of the Jewish Historical Institute in Warsaw. A duplicate copy is in the microfilm collections of the United States Holocaust Memorial Museum. An English translation of the diary was made by Małgorzata Markoff for this project and is in the collection of the editor.

Mina Glucksman

Mina Glucksman (later Mina Perlberger) was born in Tyczyn, Poland. She was interned in the ghetto in Rzeszów, Poland, and escaped with her younger sister Sabina. They hid for two years in a bunker near the farmhouse of a Polish family. She began her diary in March 1943. She and her sister survived the war, but almost all their family perished, including their siblings, parents, grandparents, aunts, uncles, and cousins. The original diary is in the Yad Vashem archives. An English translation made by the author of the diary is in the microfilm collections of the United States Holocaust Memorial Museum.

Riva Goldtsman

Riva Goldtsman was in her mid-teens when she kept her diary in the eastern Ukrainian city of Dnepropetrovsk. Written in Russian, her diary spans the outbreak of the war between the Germans and the Soviets, beginning on June 21, 1941 (it may have begun even earlier), and continuing until December 31, 1941. At some point in 1942, her family was rounded up and executed by the Germans; Riva, who was wounded but not killed, was able to escape from the mass grave after nightfall. She was hidden for some time by a Ukrainian teacher; this teacher later made contact with members of the Communist underground in the area who planned to take Riva to another hiding place. When the members of the underground arrived at the teacher's home to meet Riva, they learned that the Gestapo had arrested the teacher and Riva, both of whom were subsequently executed. The diary is in a private collection. Excerpts of the diary were published in Feliks Levitas, *Ievreï Ukraïny v roky drugoï svitovoï viiny* [Jews of Ukraine in the Second World War], published in Kiev in 1997. The diary apparently has never been translated or published in English and the excerpts in Levitas's book are the only published fragments of the diary.

Zimra Harsanyi

Zimra Harsanyi (later Ana Novac) was born in Dej, in northern Transylvania, on June 21, 1929. She lived with her parents and younger brother in Nagyvárad (now Oradea). She was sent to a Jewish school in Miskolc, Hungary, and remained there until the Germans took over Hungary in March 1944. She tried to return home but was arrested, taken off the train, interned in a ghetto, and then deported from there to Auschwitz in the early summer of 1944, at age fifteen. According to the author, her notes were written over a six-month period while she was in Auschwitz and Plaszów, among other camps. The diary, written in a thick notebook, was smuggled out of the camp with the help of a kapo. She reports that after that time she was able to keep additional notes of her daily experiences by writing on scraps of paper salvaged in the camp, and hiding her papers in her shoes. She was ultimately liberated at Kratzau in Czechoslovakia in May 1945. Her parents and her brother perished. The diary was published under its author's current name, Ana Novac, in multiple languages, including French, German, Italian, Dutch, and Hungarian. It was published in English as *The Beautiful Days of My Youth*, translated from the French by George L. Newman (New York: Henry Holt, 1997). The original diary is in Mrs. Novac's possession. Mrs. Novac went on to become an author, publishing many books and producing a number of plays.

Gabik Heller

Gabik Heller was the son of Moyshe Heller, a well-known Vilna history teacher who worked in the ghetto library and perished in November 1942. Gabik was a close friend of Yitskhok Rudashevski, and is mentioned frequently in Rudashevski's diary. Gabik wrote his diary in Yiddish; his notes cover the period of February to September 1943. He perished during the liquidation of the Vilna ghetto in September 1943. The original diary is in the collections of the YIVO Institute for Jewish Research in New York. An English translation of the diary was made by Dr. Solon Beinfeld for this project and is in the collection of the editor.

Janina Hescheles (also Yanka Heszeles). See Appendix II

Edith van Hessen

Edith van Hessen (later Edith Velmans) was born on July 3, 1925, in The Hague. She grew up in a middle-class home with her parents and her older brothers, Guus and Jules. In 1938, her maternal grandmother came to live with the family and gave Edith the first of her many notebooks, which she began on September 19, 1938. She continued to write in her diary until July 13, 1942, one week before she assumed a false identity and went into hiding with a non-Jewish family in Breda, near the Belgian border. She remained with Tine and Egberg zur Kleinsmiede and their daughter Ineke until the liberation. During this time, she was forbidden to keep a journal because of the danger it would pose to her and her rescuers. Edith's brother Jules, her mother, and her grandmother were all deported to the death camps in the East, where they perished. Her father died of cancer in a hospital in Holland in June 1943. Edith was liberated in Breda on October 29, 1944, and was eventually reunited with her brother Guus (who had immigrated to America in March 1940 and joined the U.S. Army). After the war, she recovered her diaries from her friend Miep Fernandes, who had kept them during her absence. Extensive excerpts of her diary are included in her memoir, published under her current name, Edith Velmans, and titled *Edith's Story* (New York: Soho Press, 1999, and Bantam, 2001).

Éva Heyman. See Appendix II

Etty Hillesum. See Appendix II

Susi Hilsenrath

Susi Hilsenrath (later Susan Warsinger) was born on May 27, 1929, in Bad Kreuznach, Germany. She had two younger brothers, Joseph and Ernest. In April 1939, she and her brother Joseph were sent to France in the care of a woman paid by Susi's father. They lived with various people in Paris until the German invasion in June 1940, when they were taken to Versailles. She and her brother eventually were sent to an improvised home for displaced children at Château de Morelles, located in the southern, unoccupied zone of France. She began her diary, written in German, on May 29, 1941, and completed it in August of the same year. In September 1941, her parents and her youngest brother (who had safely arrived in the United States) sent for Susi and Joseph. They traveled via train to Marseilles and through the Pyrenees mountains to Lisbon, where they boarded a boat for America. They arrived in Ellis Island on September 21, 1941. The original diary is in the collections of the United States Holocaust Memorial Museum.

Helga Hošková. See Helga Weissová

Ingrid Jacoby. See Inga Pollak

Leja Jedwab

Leja Jedwab (later Lena Rozenberg) was born on November 30, 1924, in Białystok to Freyde Rive Ryba and Leib Jedwab. She was the oldest of three children; her siblings were Moishe (born in 1925) and Sarah (born in 1927). On June 15, 1941, one week before the Germans attacked the Soviet Union, she left Białystok to be an assistant counselor in a summer camp in Druskenik. With the onset of war, the summer camp was turned into an orphanage, its inhabitants evacuated first to Sarapul in the Soviet Union for a few weeks, then to Karakulino in the Urals for the duration of the war. The diary starts on October 8, 1941, and ends on July 24, 1945. Lena (the name the diarist used in Russia) lived for two years in Karakulino, after which she went to Moscow, where she attended university. She was in Moscow at the time of the liberation. The original is in a private collection. The diary was published in Yiddish under the title *Fun Heym tsu Navenad* [From Home to Wandering: War Diary, 1941–1945] (Paris: 1999). It was published in English by Holmes and Meier in 2002 under the title *Girl with Two Landscapes: The Wartime Diary of Lena Jedwab, 1941–1945*.

Isabelle Jesion

Isabelle Jesion was born on December 23, 1926; she was an only child, living with her parents in Paris. She began the first of her two diaries at age fourteen on September 12, 1941, and continued to write until May 5, 1942. Her second diary runs from May 6 to November 27, 1942. She added three final entries to the second diary in March and April 1944. Isabelle's parents were deported to Drancy on July 16, 1942, leaving her alone in Paris. They wrote her three postcards from Drancy before being deported to Auschwitz, where they were murdered. Isabelle's diaries are filled with deeply personal reflections about friendship, love, and her relationships with her schoolmates and teachers. Often feeling alienated and lonely, Isabelle poured her feelings into her diary, calling it her confidante and her friend. She only occasionally alluded to the repression of the Jews in Paris, remarking in passing on the decrees restricting the freedom of the Jews, the imposition of the Star of David, and the roundups in the city. She also wrote poignantly about her separation from her parents after their deportation, her loneliness, and her anxiety for their well-being. Though she was evidently born Jewish, her diary reveals her growing attachment to Catholicism, as she attended mass, briefly considered becoming a nun, and signed her name "Isabelle, La Catholique" in the last entry of the first journal. She apparently returned to Judaism sometime in 1943 or 1944, and maintained some relationship with the Jewish Scouts in Paris. After the war, Isabelle immigrated to Palestine; she died in 1951 of cancer, at the age of twenty-five. The two notebooks of the original diary, written in French, are in the archives of the Ghetto Fighters' House (Beit Lochamai Haghetaot) in Israel, as are the postcards written to Isabelle by her parents in Drancy and a photograph of her.

Inga Joseph. See Inga Pollak

Lilla Kánitz

Lilla Kánitz (later Lilla Ecséri) was born on June 30, 1928. She had an older brother named György. She was of Jewish origin but had been baptized as a Roman Catholic, presumably to protect her from the threats of rising Fascism in Hungary. The fact of her family's conversion was kept a secret from much of her large extended family. She began her diary on January 1, 1944, in Budapest at fifteen and a half. She wrote sporadically throughout the year, documenting the rising tensions in the city, increasing restrictions leveled against Jews, and her life in the ghetto after August 1944. The following October, with conditions worsening in Hungary, Lilla ceased to write in her diary, depositing it in safekeeping with a Christian friend. She wrote a second account of her family's experiences between

October 1944 and February 1945, during which time Lilla was almost constantly on the move and in hiding, under threat by the Hungarian Nazi party, the Arrow Cross. She was liberated in February 1945 and returned home to find that her mother, who had long suffered from diabetes, had died. Her father and brother (who escaped to America sometime in 1939–40) survived the war. In 1995, the diary was published in Hungarian under the title *Napló, 1944*. Mrs. Ecséri died in 1986.

Anneliese Katz

Anneliese Katz (later Anne Ranasinghe) was born in Essen, Germany, on October 2, 1925. In January 1939, when she was thirteen, her parents sent her to England, hoping soon to join her there or in America. Upon her arrival in England, Anne began keeping a diary, which captures her loneliness and her struggle to adjust to a new life in a foreign culture. Anne survived the war in England, but her parents were deported from Essen to the Łódź ghetto and from there to Chełmno, where they were murdered. The diary, as well as correspondence between Anne and her parents from the time of her immigration to England until May 1940, and five postcards written by Anne's mother to her own half-sister, survived the war and are in the Łódź section of the Yad Vashem archives. A copy of selected extracts of the diary is in the archives of the Alte Synagogue in Essen, Germany, as are other papers belonging to the diarist. Mrs. Ranasinghe is the author of several books of poetry and prose, among them *At What Dark Point* and *Desire and Other Stories*.

Elisabeth Kaufmann. *See* Chapter 2

Helga Kinsky. *See* Helga Pollacková

Renia Knoll

Renia Knoll was thirteen when she began writing her diary in May 1940 in Cracow. Little is known about her personal history, except that she lived with her parents and her younger sister Sabina. An uncle of Renia's was apparently in the Jewish Police in Cracow, which may have allowed for some limited protection of the family. She kept her diary over a period of one year and four months, during which time the family was forced into the Cracow ghetto. Her diary appears to break off on August 18, 1941 (no other notebooks have been found). She and her family are presumed to have perished. According to the records of the Jewish Historical Institute in Warsaw, the diary was found in March 1943 by a Mr. Kazimierz Paciorek in a pile of paper trash at a paper factory in Jeziorna, near Warsaw. Mr. Paciorek, who worked at the factory, retrieved the diary and in 1958 (on the occasion of the fifteenth anniversary of the Warsaw ghetto uprising) donated it to the Jewish Historical Institute. A duplicate copy of the handwritten original is in the microfilm collections of the United States Holocaust Memorial Museum. An English translation of extensive excerpts of the diary was made by Małgorzata Markoff for this project and is in the collection of the editor.

David Koker

David Koker was born on November 27, 1921, and grew up in a Jewish family in Amsterdam, Holland. He and his family were captured by the Germans and deported to the Vught concentration camp in February 1943, after nearly three years of life under occupation. David began keeping a diary in Vught on February 11, 1943, recording valuable and rare details of daily life inside a concentration camp, in addition to documenting his personal evolution as a writer. He successfully smuggled the pages of the diary from February 1943 to February 1944 out of the camp and into safekeeping with his best friend, Karel van het Reve. Another set of pages kept from February to June 1944 was lost. David, his brother Max, and his parents were deported to Auschwitz-Birkenau in June 1944. David died en route to Dachau in February 1945. His father also perished, but his mother and brother survived. The original diary is housed in the Dutch Institute for War Documentation. It was published in Holland in 1977, but an English edition did not appear until decades later. Edited and introduced by eminent Holocaust scholar Robert Jan van Pelt, the diary was published as *At the Edge of the Abyss: A Concentration Camp Diary, 1943–44,* by Northwestern University Press in 2012.

Miriam Korber. See Chapter 9

Clara Kramer. See Clara Schwarz

Michael Kraus. See Appendix II

Klaus Langer. See Chapter 1

Ruthka Laskier

Ruthka Laskier, born in Danzig in 1929, moved with her parents to Bedzin, Poland, in the early 1930s. Imprisoned in the ghetto established there by the Germans during the occupation, she kept a diary from January 19 to April 24, 1943, describing German atrocities against the Jews and her fears and anxieties about her fate. She was deported from the ghetto in August 1943 and perished with her parents in Auschwitz-Birkenau in the same year. Before leaving Bedzin, she hid her diary in the floorboards of her home with the knowledge of a Polish Christian friend named Stanisława Sapinksa. Her friend rescued the diary and kept it for more than sixty years before allowing it to be published in Poland in 2006. The diary is now in the archives of Yad Vashem. It was published in Hebrew, and in English under the title *Ruthka's Notebook: A Voice from the Holocaust,* by Time, Inc., and Yad Vashem in 2008.

Tamara Lazerson

Tamara Lazerson (later Tamara Rostovsky) was born to a highly assimilated and acculturated family in Kovno, Lithuania, on March 6, 1929. In the summer of 1941, Tamara, her brother Victor, and her parents were forced into the Kovno ghetto. Her eldest brother, Rudolph, had been captured in June 1941 by Lithuanian Fascists and was subsequently turned over to the Gestapo. The family never heard from him again. Tamara's diary comprises two notebooks; the first covers the period from July 19, 1941, to September 13, 1942, and the second from September 19, 1942, to April 4, 1944. On April 7, 1944, she escaped from the ghetto and was sheltered first by her former history teacher, Petronele Lastene, and subsequently by that teacher's sister, Vera Efertene. During the deportations of the summer of 1944, her parents were deported; her father subsequently perished in Dachau and her mother perished in Stutthof. After the liberation, Tamara and her brother Victor returned to Kovno, where they found the only surviving notebook of the diary (the second one, beginning on September 19, 1942), together with some of Victor's notebooks. The original diary is in a private collection. It was published in the original Lithuanian and also in Hebrew under the title *Yomanah shel Tamarah* in 1975. The full diary has never been published in Russian or English, but in 2011, Russian director Evgeny Tsymbal released a documentary film titled *Dnevnik iz sozhennogo getto* (Diary from the Burned Ghetto), which includes translated excerpts of the diary and interviews with Ms. Lazerson. It is in Russian with English subtitles. Short extracts of the diary were published in English in *The Hidden History of the Kovno Ghetto* (New York: Little, Brown, 1997).

Denise Lefschetz

Denise Lefschetz (later Denise Weill) was born in Paris in 1926. Her parents were of Russian origin. She lived in Paris throughout her childhood and as a young girl participated in the Jewish youth movement under the auspices of the Eclaireurs Israélites de France, or the French Jewish Scouts. After 1942, she and her youth group became involved in clandestine resistance activities, with the direct involvement and oversight of her father, Emmanuel Lefschetz. They fabricated false identity papers and hid children who were left alone after the deportation of their parents. In her diary, which Denise wrote during one week in mid-July 1942, when she was fifteen and a half, she mentioned (in veiled terms) the activities of this youth group and alluded to the repression of the Jews in Paris, including the imposition of the yellow star and the massive roundup at the Velodrôme d'Hiver. After January 1944, Denise herself lived under a false identity, moving from place to place, and so survived the Holocaust. After the war, she passed her baccalauréat and went on to become a psychoanalyst. The diary is in a private collection and has never been published.

Jutta Levy. *See* Jutta Salzberg

Janina Lewinson

Janina Lewinson (later Janina Bauman) was born on August 18, 1926, in Warsaw. From 1941 to 1944 she kept notes of her life with her mother and sister, first in the Warsaw ghetto, then in hiding on the so-called Aryan side of the city. After the Warsaw ghetto uprising, when all of the non-Jewish inhabitants of the city were evacuated in October 1944, she hid her notes and short stories in a hole in the floor of a stranger's apartment. After the war, she returned to find her papers still intact. When she and her husband emigrated from Poland to Israel in 1968, her diary and stories were removed from her luggage by the Polish customs authorities. She was never able to recover them. However, in 1980, after the death of her mother, the diarist found portions of the diary that her mother had copied by hand in 1959. These excerpts were translated into English and published in Mrs. Bauman's memoirs, *Winter in the Morning: A Young Girl's Life in the Warsaw Ghetto and Beyond* (London: Virago Press, 1986).

Ruthka Lieblich

Ruthka Lieblich was born on December 6, 1926, in the shtetl of Andrychów in Polish Silesia. She grew up there with her parents and her younger brother. She began her diary at age thirteen on August 13, 1940, less than one year after the Germans invaded and occupied

Poland. In late September and early October 1941, the Jewish inhabitants of Andrychów were forced into a ghetto established there. Ruthka continued writing until December 28, 1942. In July of the following year, she and her family were deported to Auschwitz, where they were murdered. Prior to her deportation, she had entrusted her three notebooks to a non-Jewish friend, who in turn gave them to Ruthka's cousin Renia Ringer after the war. The diary was published in English under the title *Ruthka: A Diary of War,* translated and edited by Jehoshua and Anna Eibeshitz (New York: Remember, 1993).

Rywka Lipszyc

Rywka Lipszyc was born in Łódź, Poland, in September 1929. The eldest of four children, she and her family were forced into the Łódź ghetto, where her father died in 1941 and her mother in 1942. Two of her siblings, as well as her uncle, were deported from the ghetto during the infamous Shperre in September 1942; they were all murdered by carbon monoxide poisoning in the death camp of Chełmno. Rywka remained with her younger sister, Cipka, in the care of three older cousins. She wrote her diary from October 3, 1943, until April 12, 1944, recording all aspects of her daily life, especially her work, her complicated relationships with her cousins, and her deep and abiding faith in God, which sustained her amid her suffering. She reflected on her parents' and siblings' deaths, reported on her efforts to study and learn in the ghetto, and dreamed of a future as a writer. In August 1944, Rywka was deported from Łódź to Auschwitz-Birkenau as part of the final liquidation of the ghetto. She brought her diary with her. Rywka's exact fate is not known, though she is thought to have died in a hospital in Germany shortly after the liberation. In June 1945, the diary was found at Auschwitz-Birkenau by Zinaida Berezovskaya, a doctor with the Soviet Army that had liberated the camp. It was kept with the Berezovskaya family for more than sixty years, until it was brought to the United States and came to the attention of the staff of the Tauber Library at Jewish Family and Children's Services in San Francisco. Through the efforts of the archives staff, the diary was thoroughly researched, authenticated, and translated. In 2013 it was published in English under the title *The Diary of Rywka Lipszyc* (ed. Alexandra Zapruder).

Ruth Maier

Ruth Maier was born in 1920 to a middle-class Jewish family in Vienna. She began writing a diary in 1934, at the age of fourteen, and continued for eight years, making hers one of the longest and most comprehensive records of a young girl coming of age during the 1930s and early 1940s in Nazi Europe. Following the German invasion and occupation of Austria in March 1938, Ruth's sister immigrated to England. In early 1939, Ruth left Vienna for a town near Oslo, Norway, where she lived as a refugee with a Norwegian family. When the Germans occupied Norway in April 1940, Ruth again found herself in imminent danger and attempted to reunite with her family in England. In November 1942, she was deported to Auschwitz-Birkenau, where she was murdered on arrival. Her extensive notes, which offer a rare glimpse of the experience of occupation and Jewish persecution in Norway, were kept by her close friend Gunvor Hofmo, who went on to become a celebrated poet. The diary was found among her papers after her death. In 2010, it was published in English by Vintage Books under the title *Ruth Maier's Diary: A Young Girl's Life Under Nazism.*

Eva Mándlová

Eva Mándlová (later Eva Roubíčková) was born in the town of Žatec in northern Bohemia on July 16, 1921. She was an only child, living in a comfortable middle-class home with her parents, maternal grandmother, and uncle. In September 1938, at the time of the German occupation of the Sudetenland (where Žatec was located), Eva's family was forced to escape to Prague. In March 1939, after the Germans occupied the rest of Czechoslovakia, Eva's fiancé, Richard Roubíček, was able to flee to England, intending to arrange for Eva, her family, and his own relatives to follow. However, despite his efforts, she and her family were not able to leave Prague. Her grandmother committed suicide in March 1939. Eva and her mother were deported to Terezín on December 17, 1941. Her father followed about six months later. She wrote from December 1941 until September 1944, creating one of the most detailed and complete records of the daily life of a young person in Terezín. After the deportation of her parents to Auschwitz in September 1944, she ceased writing. In January 1945, she resumed her diary and wrote brief daily notes through the liberation of the camp in May 1945. Her parents perished in Auschwitz. She survived the war in Terezín and later married Richard Roubíček. The original diary is in the collections of the United States Holocaust Memorial Museum. It was published in English under the diarist's current name, Eva Roubíčková, as *We're Alive and Life Goes On: A Theresienstadt Diary* (New York: Henry Holt, 1998).

Günther Marcuse

Günther Marcuse was born in Berlin on September 4, 1923, to Herbert and Erna Martha Marcuse. He lived in Berlin with his parents and older sister Rachel (Ursula), attending elementary and secondary school there. After Kristallnacht, Günther was forced out of the Victoria State Secondary School, where he was in his fifth year. His father was arrested and imprisoned for more than three months, his release conditional upon his emigration from Germany. In February 1939, Günther's parents left Germany and Günther entered the Gross-Breesen Jewish Emigration Training Farm, a non-Zionist organization established to provide agricultural training to Jewish boys wishing to emigrate abroad (not to Palestine). He lived there for four years, witnessing its gradual transformation from a training camp run by the Jewish leader Curt Bondy to a forced labor camp run by the Gestapo beginning in late August 1941. In March 1942, Günther began writing in his diary, recording the details of daily life in the labor camp and the mounting tension as to its fate. Günther's diary breaks off on February 26, 1943. A few days later he was deported to Auschwitz, where he perished on March 23, 1944. His original diary is in the Yad Vashem archives. Excerpts of the diary were published in English in Joseph Walk's "The Diary of Günther Marcuse: The Last Days of the Gross-Breesen Training Center" in *Yad Vashem Studies* 8 (1970): 159–81; and in Werner T. Angress, *Between Fear and Hope: Jewish Youth in the Third Reich* (New York: Columbia University Press, 1988).

Anita Meyer

Anita Meyer (later Anita Budding) was born in The Hague on July 30, 1929. She was in grade school in May 1940 when the Germans invaded and occupied Holland. Forbidden to attend public school, Anita went to a Jewish school instead. In 1942, the Meyer family lost possession of their home and moved to Amsterdam to live with a cousin. In

1943, Anita went into hiding with a non-Jewish family in Eindhoven in southern Holland. Her move was organized by Anna Gisela Soehnlein, who used her father's position in the Dutch railway system to smuggle Jewish children into hiding. Anita's sister was also sent into hiding. Anita's diary spans the latter years she spent underground, beginning in January 1944 and ending in May 1945, when she was liberated in Eindhoven. Her daily notes are terse and dry, but they nevertheless offer a glimpse of the routine of her daily life in hiding, including what she ate, the many chores and errands she performed, and her comings and goings. She also closely followed and recorded the progress of the war, including the breathless excitement of the impending liberation in the spring of 1945, which brought with it her joyful return to school and her long-awaited reunion with her parents. The original diary and a working translation of it are in the archives of the Museum of Jewish Heritage in New York. To my knowledge, the diary has never been published.

Halina Nelken

Halina Nelken was born in Cracow, Poland, on September 20, 1924, and lived throughout her childhood with her parents and older brother, Felek, in a middle-class home. A few pages from one of her early diaries survived, spanning the period from July 1937 to January 1938. She began another diary in July 1939 and wrote until March 1942, covering the German invasion and occupation of Cracow, the early months under German rule, the establishment of the ghetto and the move into it, and her family's first year there. In May 1942, she completed that notebook of her diary, but she continued to write stories and sporadic journal entries throughout the rest of her imprisonment in the ghetto and through the early months of life in the Fliegerhorst airfield base in Cracow, where she was sent in December 1942. According to the diarist, she also later wrote poems in a small notebook she smuggled with her through her internment in the concentration camps of Auschwitz, Ravensbrück, Malchow, and Leipzig. She survived the war, as did her mother and brother. Her father perished in Auschwitz. The original diary is in a private collection. Her diary has been published in Polish (Toronto: Polish-Canadian Publishing Fund, 1987), in German (Gerlingen: Bleicher Verlag, 1996), and most recently in English under the title *And Yet I Am Here!* translated by Halina Nelken with Alicia Nitecki (Amherst: University of Massachusetts Press, 1999).

Ana Novac. *See* Zimra Harsanyi

Raymonde Nowodworski

Raymonde Nowodworski (later Raymonde Frazier) was born in Nowy Dwor, near Warsaw, on March 15, 1929. Her parents immigrated to France in 1930; her mother returned home briefly in 1932 to give birth to her second daughter, Suzanne-Sara. In 1933, the family settled in Montargis, where the third and fourth daughters were born: Flora in 1935 and Monique in 1941. Raymonde's parents' clothing and shoe business was confiscated in 1941 as a consequence of the German occupation and the promulgation of anti-Semitic legislation in France. Her mother, Golda Kalina, was arrested by French police in Montargis on July 14, 1942, and deported to Auschwitz-Birkenau, where she was killed on July 21 at age thirty-eight. The children were entrusted to "half-Jewish" families (in which the husband or wife was not Jewish) until October 8, 1942. On that date, the three eldest daughters were arrested, imprisoned, and ultimately interned in the

French camp Beaune-la-Rolande. On December 10, 1942, the Nowodworski daughters (except the youngest, Monique) were sent to Paris and placed in the care of UGIF. They were separated and put in "children's homes," where the Germans planned to gather Jewish children and then deport them to the East. Raymonde was in the Centre Vauquelin, where she wrote her diary from July 5 to August 24, 1943. The diary includes the thoughts and observations of the young writer, who desperately missed her family and struggled with the existential questions raised by her suffering. After seven failed attempts to find one another and flee, the Nowodworski girls were finally able to leave Paris with the help of an uncle. They found their father (who had himself been interned in a camp), and he arranged for them to be hidden in a Catholic school. There they remained from October 1943 until August 1944, when they were liberated. The family returned to Montargis, and the daughters reentered school in October 1944. Raymonde went on to become an educator; she married and had two daughters of her own. She donated her diary to the archives of the Centre de Documentation Juive Contemporaine in Paris.

Elisabeth Ornstein

Elisabeth Ornstein (later Elisabeth M. Orsten) was born in Vienna on November 8, 1927. She was raised in a well-off middle-class family, living with her parents, her younger brother George, and her nanny. She was ten years old when the Germans annexed Austria in March 1938. Ten months later, she and her brother were sent to safety in England through the English Quakers. Given her diary by her nanny before departing, she began writing upon her arrival in England. She continued to write in her diary throughout the first years of her life in exile, describing, among other things, her homesickness and her difficulties getting adjusted to life as a refugee. In mid-September 1940, arrangements were confirmed for Elisabeth to travel to the United States (originally with her brother George, who had been living apart from her during his years in England), where they were to be reunited with their parents. Her diary covers the events of her last days in England, her pain at leaving her by-now familiar life, and the voyage via ship to America without her brother, who traveled later. She stopped writing in her diary after her arrival in the United States, where she was eventually reunited with her parents and her brother. The diary is in the collections of the United States Holocaust Memorial Museum. Except for a few minor omissions, the entire diary is translated and commented on in Ms. Orsten's memoirs, *From Anschluss to Albion: Memoirs of a Refugee Girl, 1939–1940* (Cambridge: Acorn Edition, 1998).

Elisabeth M. Orsten. *See* Elisabeth Ornstein

Mina Perlberger. *See* Mina Glucksman

Adèle Louise Pinkhof

Adèle Louise Pinkhof (nicknamed Detje) was born on March 20, 1924, in Amsterdam. She lived with her parents and three sisters in Amsterdam. After finishing high school in 1942, Detje began working in a Jewish day care center. The diary that survived began in September of the same year; in it, Detje primarily recorded the details of the daily lives of her young charges. On September 16, Detje and her family were arrested and sent to the Westerbork transit camp. While there, she did not write in her diary, but wrote a "fairy tale" for her fourteen-year-old sister which reads much like an allegory of life in Westerbork. She and her family were allowed to return to Amsterdam in October and Detje wrote for a few more weeks in her diary, ceasing her entries on October 22, 1942. In May 1943, the family was arrested and again sent to Westerbork. On July 20, 1943, they were deported to the Sobibór death camp. Detje's eldest sister, Esther, who was married and did not live with the family, survived Bergen-Belsen; she was the only survivor in the family. The diary was cared for during the war years by a family friend, Jan Willemse, who gave the diary to Esther after the liberation. The diary is now in Israel in the safekeeping of Mirjam Pinkhof, the widow of Detje's cousin Menachem Pinkhof. The diary was published in Dutch under the title *Een dagboek met sprookjes uit Kamp Westerbork* (Netherlands: Herinneringscentrum Kamp Westerbork, 1998).

Helga Pollacková

Helga Pollacková (later Helga Kinsky) was born in Vienna on May 28, 1930. Her parents divorced in 1936, and Helga lived with her mother in Vienna. In the summer of 1938 (a few months after Germany annexed Austria in March), Helga was sent to her grandmother, aunt, and other relatives in Kyjov, Moravia, for vacation. Because of the dangerous circumstances in Vienna, she remained in Kyjov and Brno with her extended family. In March 1939, Helga's mother was able to leave Vienna on a domestic servant visa; Helga was supposed to join her, but in the meantime the war broke out, preventing her escape from Europe. In the autumn of 1941, Helga's father joined her and her relatives in Kyjov. It was from there in January 1943 that she was deported together with her father, aunts, uncles, and other relatives to Terezín. She began writing in January 1943 and continued throughout the duration of her internment in Terezín, until October 1944. At that time, she was deported to Auschwitz, and subsequently to a forced labor camp that was a satellite of Flossenberg, and then again to Terezín, where she was liberated. Her father had hidden her diary for her at the time of her deportation, and Helga was able to recover it after the war. Her father also survived the Holocaust, and the two of them returned to Kyjov after the liberation. The diary is held in a private collection. A copy of the original is in the archives of Beit Theresienstadt, and a version on CD-ROM is held in the archives of the Jewish Community in Prague. Excerpts of her diary were published in English in *Terezín* (Prague: Council of Jewish Communities, 1965). An English translation of extensive excerpts of the diary was made by Madeline Vadkerty for this project and is in the collection of the editor.

Inga Pollak

Inga Pollak (later Inga Joseph) was born in Vienna on March 9, 1927. She lived there with her parents and older sister, Lieselotte, until 1939, when the two girls were sent via Kindertransport to Britain, where they lived with a foster family in Falmouth. The first part of Inga's diary spans the period 1937–39, when she was still in Vienna. The second part, from 1939 to 1944, covers the years she spent as a refugee in England, trying to adjust to a new culture, language, and foster family. Inga and Lieselotte were reunited with their father, who had fled to England after the fall of Paris, in Falmouth on August 9, 1940. He went on to serve in the British army, while the girls remained in foster care in Britain. The girls' mother and grandmother were deported from Vienna to Minsk in November 1941.

The details of their deaths are not clear; they either perished due to the horrendous conditions during the journey or were shot on arrival in Minsk. The diary was published in English under Mrs. Joseph's pen name, Ingrid Jacoby, as *My Darling Diary: A Wartime Journal, Vienna 1937–1939, Falmouth 1939–1944* (Great Britain: United Writers Publications, 1998).

Anne Ranasinghe. See Anneliese Katz

Macha Rolnikas (also Masha or Maria Rolnikaite). See Appendix II

Lillyan Rosenberg. See Lilly Cohn

Tamara Rostovsky. See Tamara Lazerson

Eva Roubíčková. See Eva Mándlová

Lena Rozenberg. See Leja Jedwab

Dawid Rubinowicz. See Chapter 10

Yitskhok Rudashevski. See Chapter 7

Jutta Salzberg

Jutta Salzberg (later Jutta Levy) was born on September 28, 1926, in Hamburg, Germany. She began her diary on September 28, 1938, her twelfth birthday. The family, including her father Isaac, her mother Rose, and her sister Ruth, left Hamburg for Paris via midnight train on November 7, 1938, just hours before SS troops stormed their home during the course of Kristallnacht. After four days in Paris, the family boarded the *Queen Mary,* which took them safely to America. Jutta wrote during the voyage from her native Hamburg to America, and continued to write in her diary after her arrival in the United States. In the summer of 1939, she and her family moved from New York to Washington, at which point the diarist began writing in English. She continued to write the diary until January 1944. In 1952, Jutta married Harold Levy, who had fought in World War II and earned the Legion of Merit for his heroic rescue of wounded soldiers. The diary is in a private collection.

Gertrude Schneider

Gertrude Schneider (née Hirschhorn) was born on May 27, 1928. As a young girl, she lived in Vienna with her parents and her younger sister Rita, surrounded by a large extended family. Following the German annexation of Austria, Gertrude was expelled from school in May 1938. She and her family experienced the violence and vandalism of Kristallnacht in Vienna and were forced to wear the yellow star beginning in September 1941. On February 6, 1942, Gertrude and her immediate family were deported to the Riga ghetto. They remained there until September 25, 1943, when the family was sent to the Kaiserwald concentration camp. In August 1944, the family was displaced again, this time to Stutthof. Gertrude's father was separated from his family and sent to Buchenwald. From there, he was transferred to the satellite camp of Bochum to perform hard labor, and in March 1945 was brought back to Buchenwald, where he perished on the very day of the liberation. On August 24, 1944, Gertrude's mother and sister were sent from Stutthof to the Sophienwalde labor camp, and on September 16, Gertrude was able to join them there. Gertrude and her mother and sister all survived the Holocaust and returned to Vienna on June 1, 1945. The first diary, kept in Vienna from May 27, 1938, until February 1, 1942, was buried in the Riga ghetto shortly before Gertrude and her family were sent from the ghetto to Kaiserwald. She returned to Riga with her mother in 1971 and recovered the diary, wrapped in oilcloth, from its hiding place. She started a second diary on February 1, 1942, writing during the course of her family's deportation from Vienna to Riga, and in the Riga ghetto, Kaiserwald, Stutthof, and Sophienwalde. The only break in the diary occurs from August 24 to September 16, 1944, when Gertrude was alone in Stutthof and the diary was in the possession of her mother. Upon her arrival in Sophienwalde, and her reunion with her mother and sister there, she resumed writing and continued her diary during and after the liberation. The diary is in a private collection.

Clara Schwarz

Clara Schwarz (later Clara Kramer) was born in Zolkiew, Poland, on April 9, 1927. She was fifteen in the autumn of 1942 when she, her family, and fourteen other Jews went into hiding in a bunker outside Zolkiew. They were sheltered by an ethnic German family named Beck. The early part of her diary is a summary of the events from the summer of 1942 until the end of the summer of 1943, during which time her sister Mania had been caught and killed. Her daily diary entries began on August 31, 1943, and end on July 26, 1944, after she and the survivors from the bunker were liberated. The original diary is in the collections of the United States Holocaust Memorial Museum, and an English translation of the diary, made by its author, can be found in the museum's library under the title "Wartime Diary, 1942–1944."

Vera Segerová

Vera Segerová was born on November 13, 1927, to Josef and Františka Seger. She lived in Prague and began her diary in July 1942, when she was fifteen. She wrote for less than a month, penning in her diary the details of her daily life and the activities and discussions held in the Jewish youth group of which she was a part. She also occasionally mentioned, in veiled form, the deportations to Terezín and the scenes of humiliation she witnessed on the streets of Prague. Despite the brevity of her diary, it captures the writer's sense of humor and self-possession, especially in matters relating to her personality and character. Her diary ended on August 14, 1942; less than a month later, on September 8, 1942, she was deported from Prague to Terezín. On February 1, 1943, she was deported from Terezín to Auschwitz, where she perished. Her original diary, written in Czech, is in the archives of Beit Theresienstadt in Israel, as is a Hebrew translation of the diary. An English translation was made by Benjamin Herman for this project and is in the collection of the editor. A duplicate copy of the English translation is in the archives of Beit Theresienstadt.

Hannah Senesh. *See* Appendix II

Dawid Sierakowiak

Dawid Sierakowiak was born in 1924 in Łódź, Poland, where he spent his childhood with his parents and younger sister Nadzia. He began his diary in the summer of 1939, shortly before the outbreak of war, and continued writing in his first of five notebooks during the period of the German invasion of Poland and the early months of German occupation.

His other four notebooks span two years in the Łódź ghetto (with intermittent gaps presumably because of lost notebooks) beginning in April 1941 and ending in April 1943. His mother was deported to Chełmno in September 1942 and murdered; his father died in the ghetto on March 6, 1943. Dawid ended his diary in April 1943 and perished four months later, at the age of nineteen, due to tuberculosis, starvation, and exhaustion. His younger sister Nadzia, the only surviving member of the family, was presumably deported to Auschwitz during the liquidation of the Łódź ghetto in August 1944, where she is assumed to have perished. Dawid's notebooks were found in the Sierakowiaks' ghetto apartment after the war. Two of the notebooks are in the archives of the Jewish Historical Institute in Warsaw; the remaining three are in the collections of the United States Holocaust Memorial Museum. The diary was published with the title *The Diary of Dawid Sierakowiak: Five Notebooks from the Łódź Ghetto*, edited by Alan Adelson, translated by Kamil Turowski (New York: Oxford University Press, 1996).

Lejzer Silberman

Lejzer (later Leo) Silberman was born on December 13, 1928, the middle child of seven born to Josef and Dresla (née Krieger) Silberman in Przemyśl, Poland. His father was in the dairy business and his mother was a housewife, raising the children and helping her husband in his work. Lejzer's family was decimated by the German occupation of Przemyśl; much of his immediate family was deported from the Przemyśl ghetto to the killing center at Bełżec, where they were murdered. Lejzer had been on the train bound for Bełżec but escaped and returned to the ghetto to look for his siblings Cyla and Israel, who had not been deported. During the winter of 1943–44, Lejzer, his sister Cyla and her husband, his brother Israel, a cousin, and thirteen other Jews hid in a bunker until they were discovered. All except Lejzer were shot and killed. During the final months of the war he hid in a cellar beneath the stairs of an apartment building in Przemyśl, aided by a Polish woman named Zofia Mikula; it was there that he wrote his diary. The first part, written on scraps of paper and the backs of notices, is a detailed account of his experiences until that time; the second, shorter part, written in an address book, is a terse but powerful contemporaneous series of entries about his last months in hiding, the liberation, and his grief over the loss of his family. He survived the Holocaust and immigrated to the United States. The original diary is in a private collection. An English translation of the diary was made by Kristine Belfoure for this project and is in the collection of the editor.

Tereska Torrès. See Appendix II

Jerzy Feliks Urman

Jerzy Feliks Urman was born on April 9, 1932, in Stanisławów, Poland, to Sophie and Izydor Urman. He and his parents were imprisoned in the Stanisławów ghetto in December 1941 and remained there throughout the various roundups and mass killings that took place sporadically during 1942. In October of that year, Jerzy's father organized hiding places for his family outside the ghetto; Jerzy went first to the home of a Polish family outside the Drohobycz ghetto, followed by his mother in November and his father in December or January 1943. In March 1943, the family moved again, to the apartment of the former housekeeper of Jerzy's uncle Artur. It was here that Jerzy wrote his fragmentary diary, from September to November 1943. During a search of the home where the

Urman family was hiding, Jerzy killed himself with cyanide to avoid being caught and deported. He was eleven and a half. His parents survived the war in hiding. The original manuscript of his diary is apparently missing, but a typescript of it served as the basis for an English translation, published as *I'm Not Even a Grown-Up: The Diary of Jerzy Feliks Urman* (London: Menard Press/King's College, 1991). I have not been able to establish the whereabouts of the typescript, although it is presumably in a private collection.

Edith Velmans. See Edith van Hessen

Charlotte Verešová. See Appendix II

Werner Warmbrunn

Werner Warmbrunn was born on July 3, 1920, in Frankfurt am Main. He was the youngest of three children born to David and Lilly Warmbrunn. His mother's family was highly assimilated; some members of the family had converted to Christianity. By contrast, his paternal grandfather was an Orthodox Jew who had immigrated to Germany from Poland in the nineteenth century. Werner's family was comfortably middle class; they observed the major Jewish holidays but did not adhere to the strictest elements of Jewish ritual and law. As a young boy, Werner attended Jewish grade school and then went to German public school from 1930 until 1936. In 1936, the Warmbrunn family legally emigrated from Germany to Holland, in possession of their furniture and other belongings. Werner's parents left Holland by boat for Porto, Portugal, in December 1939; in late winter 1940–41, they reached safety in the United States. Werner remained in Amsterdam (returning to Frankfurt periodically from 1936 to 1938 for vacations) until June 1940, when he went to a Quaker school in Ommen. In March 1941, Werner went to Berlin, and then departed for Lisbon, Portugal, by plane. He left Lisbon on the SS *Nyassa,* arriving in New York City on April 25, 1941. He wrote the five notebooks of his diary between March 1935 and March 1941; in them, he wrote about his relationships with friends, the problems of a Jewish boy in German public school, and the difficulties of emigration and adjustment to life in a foreign country. Being deeply attached to his German home, Werner also reflected on his own identity as a German youth and his desire to return home after the fall of Nazism. All the members of Werner's immediate family survived the Holocaust, although some members of the extended family lost their lives in the concentration camps. Werner went on to earn a B.A. at Cornell University and a Ph.D. in history at Stanford University. He is professor emeritus in history at Pitzer College in Claremont, California. The diary is in a private collection.

Susan Warsinger. See Susi Hilsenrath

Denise Weill. See Denise Lefschetz

Pavel Weiner

Pavel Weiner (later Paul Weiner) was born on November 13, 1931, into a middle-class, assimilated Jewish family in Prague. He and his older brother Hanuš (nicknamed Handa) were deported to Terezín, together with their parents, in May 1942, when Paul was ten and Hanuš was fourteen. He began writing in his diary at age twelve in Terezín in April 1944 and continued to write on a regular basis until January 1945. The diary is filled with details about all aspects of his daily life in Terezín, including not only the physical and emotional hardships he experienced, but also his efforts to maintain an intellectual life by reading and writing. To this end, he led the efforts to create *Nesar,* a magazine made by the boys in Room 7 of Building L417, where he lived, and reported frequently on its progress in his diary. In September 1944, his father and brother were deported from Terezín to Auschwitz. After January 1945, there is a break in the diary; he resumed writing in April, recounting briefly the events of the previous months and writing again on an almost daily basis. He ended his diary on April 22, 1945, just a few weeks before the liberation of Terezín. His father and brother were sent from Auschwitz to Kaufering, a sub-camp of Dachau, where his father died in December 1944, and Hanuš in January 1945. Paul and his mother returned to Prague after the liberation. The original diary, written in Czech and consisting of several notebooks, is in the collections of the United States Holocaust Memorial Museum. Short extracts of the diary were published in *Terezínske listy* in 1998. In 2011, Pavel Weiner, with his daughter Karen, translated and published the diary in English, with an introduction by Debórah Dwork, under the title *A Boy in Terezin: The Private Diary of Pavel Weiner, April 1944–April 1945* (Evanston, Ill.: Northwestern University Press).

Helga Weissová

Helga Weissová (later Helga Hošková) was born on November 10, 1929, in Prague. She began writing her diary in March 1939, when the Germans partitioned Czechoslovakia and established the so-called Protectorate of Bohemia and Moravia. On December 10, 1941, she was deported to Terezín, where she remained until October 1944. Her diary spans the entire time that she remained in Terezín. She also created a great number of drawings in Terezín that survived the war. In October 1944, she was deported to Auschwitz, and subsequently to Freiberg and Mauthausen. She and her mother survived the Holocaust, but her father perished in Auschwitz. After the war, she reclaimed her diary, adding in 1945 an account of her experiences in the concentration camps. Excerpts of her diary in Czech were published in Jaromír Horec's *Deníky Detí: deníky a zápisky z koncentracních táborů* (Prague: Nase vojsko, 1961), and in English in *Terezín* (Prague: Council of Jewish Communities, 1965). More recently, Mrs. Hošková has published a book of her artwork titled *Zeichne, was Du siehst: Zeichnungen eines Kindes aus Theresienstadt* [Draw What You See: A Child's Drawings from Theresienstadt], with text in German, Czech, and English (Göttingen: Wallstein, 1998). The full diary has been translated into English by Dora Slabá. The original diary and English translation are in a private collection.

Leon Weliczker

Leon Weliczker (later Leon Wells) was born in the shtetl of Stojanov, near Lvov, on March 10, 1925. He was the second of seven children who grew up in a close-knit and very traditional and religious Jewish community. In March 1933, Leon's family moved to the nearby city of Lvov, where he attended school. At the time of the German invasion of Poland, Leon had completed one year of high school. The family remained in Lvov during the course of the next two years under the Russian occupation. Although Leon had been accepted to a technical school in Moscow for the school year 1941, the German invasion of Russia in June 1941 prevented him from leaving. With the onset of the German occupation, Leon and his family were subjected to the brutality and violence that characterized Jewish life under the Nazis. The family was forced into the Lvov ghetto in November 1941, and the following March, Leon was sent to the Janowska concentration camp. He managed a narrow escape from death in the early summer of 1942, and escaped from the camp to return home, where he recuperated from typhoid fever and double pneumonia contracted in Janowska. Once recovered, he went to Stojanov to stay with part of his family, while the rest remained in Lvov. His mother was arrested in Lvov and, with the exception of Leon, the entire family in Stojanov was killed during the aktion there. As one of the few survivors of Stojanov, Leon was moved from town to town and ultimately fled into the woods to hide. He returned to Lvov in mid-December 1942, only to find his father had been taken away and his two surviving brothers (Aaron, age fifteen, and Jacob, age thirteen) were left alone. He stayed with his brothers to care for them in the ghetto until June 1943, when the three boys were sent to Janowska. Both Aaron and Jacob were killed, leaving eighteen-year-old Leon the sole survivor of his family. Leon kept his extraordinary diary while he was a member of the Sonderkommando ("Death Brigade"), which was charged with the gruesome job of burning the bodies of the Jews killed by the Nazis and otherwise obliterating all traces of the mass murders perpetrated there. He wrote sporadically from June to November 1943, recording the chilling details of the task he was forced to carry out. In November 1943, he and other camp inhabitants organized a breakout that allowed him to escape Janowska for a second time. He was ultimately taken in by a non-Jewish farmer named Kalwinski and hidden in a basement under a barn with twenty-two other Jews until the liberation of Lvov by the Russians in the summer of 1944. Leon's notes from Janowska are translated into English and included in his excellently written memoirs, published under his current name, Leon Wells, and entitled *The Janowska Road* (Washington, D.C.: Holocaust Library, an imprint of the United States Holocaust Memorial Museum, 1999). *The Janowska Road* has been published in eleven different languages in twelve countries.

Leon Wells. See Leon Weliczker

Otto Wolf. See Chapter 5

Yarden

Little is known about this diary and its writer, whose identity remains a mystery. In fact, there are several complexities posed by the text itself, which was written in Poland between August and November 1939. The writer's gender in the Hebrew text changes from masculine to feminine toward the end of the diary; in addition, the writer of the early part of the text reported on his experiences fighting on the front lines with the Polish army, thus suggesting that he was a young man, but later in the diary quoted someone referring to him/herself as a girl. Finally, the dates are not consecutive and appear to be signed by multiple people, delineated by lines that separate seemingly distinct entries. These inconsistencies in combination with the fact that the writer or writers seemed to have a connection to the Zionist youth group Hashomer Hazair (which like many such groups stressed and cultivated communal and collective life in preparation for a future in Palestine) suggests that perhaps not one but several young people wrote their reflections and observations in this diary. Whatever the case may be, the diary includes horrific accounts of the battles on the front lines as well as a few chilling entries about the early weeks of the German occupation of Łódź in the fall of 1939. The handwritten text is in the Moreshet Archives, Givat Haviva, Israel. An English translation of the diary was made by Galeet Westreich for this project and is in the collection of the editor.

Appendix II

AT THE MARGINS

Although this book centers on the diary writings of young Jewish victims of the Holocaust, it is evident that the impulse to write and document the extraordinary events of the 1930s and 1940s in Europe was present in a great many people and took a great many forms. As I searched for diaries written by young people during the Holocaust, I inevitably came upon many texts that in terms of genre (diaries), subject (the Holocaust), or authorship (youth) did not fall strictly into the scope that I had defined for this work, but were not so unrelated that they could be simply set aside and considered wholly separate. Likewise, many of these distinctions have been blurred in other works on the subject, which mix diaries, part diary–part memoirs, rewritten diaries, and letters; the writings of victims of the Holocaust with those who were victims of World War II; and the writings of young people, young adults, and adults. Simply put, some texts fell squarely in the scope of my work, others fell squarely outside it, but many occupied what I informally termed a gray area, falling in neither one category nor the other and consequently demanding some examination and explication in this work.

To begin with the matter of genre, it was easy enough to define diaries (records of events recorded contemporaneously, usually composed of periodic dated entries) in relation to memoirs (a retrospective account of events, usually in the form of a long narrative). But between these two clear-cut distinctions, several permutations of diaries emerged. The journal of Mary Berg, for example, though consistently cited among diaries of this period, is in fact a hybrid text; the author wrote notes in the Warsaw ghetto and then added to them after her release (with a group of privileged prisoners who were exchanged for a group of German POWs) and her arrival in America. While her text reads like a diary and is indeed an invaluable source of information on the life of a young girl in the Warsaw ghetto, it is in fact part diary–part memoir, layered with the knowledge she gained and the perspective she acquired after her liberation.[1] Similarly, Charlotte Verešová kept a diary in Terezín, most of which was lost after the war when she lent part of it to a journalist who never returned it to her. A few fragmentary pages remained with the author, to which she added her memories and recollections. Like the diary of Mary Berg, the resulting text has at its core a diary written at the time, albeit a fragmentary one, and is amplified by the writer's postwar recollections.[2]

Not unlike the diaries of Mary Berg and Charlotte Verešová, the journal of Janina Hescheles is frequently included among the diaries of young writers of this period. According to Leo Schwarz, who introduced excerpts of the text in English (under the name Yanka Heszeles) in *The Root and the Bough,* the diarist made "jottings on scraps of paper" during the summer of 1943, then "completed the diary" when she was in hiding in Cracow subsequently. Whether the original notes were amplified or it was rewritten completely is unclear. What is clear from a reading of the text is that it is not a sustained daily account of events, like the diaries of Moshe Flinker or Alice Ehrmann, but more properly a wartime testimony, actually penned during the war while the writer was still in captivity, reporting on not the present but events of the recent past.[3]

Still other texts were written just days or months after rescue or liberation; among these are the diary of Guido Lopez, written just after his escape from Italy to Switzerland in 1943, and the diary of Yona Melaron, who wrote about her experiences in Romania after she had arrived in Tel Aviv in 1944. Other writers, like Michael Kraus in Terezín and Macha Rolnikas in Vilna, kept diaries at the time but found after the war that they were lost or destroyed. Michael Kraus rewrote his diary as soon as possible after his liberation from Auschwitz-Birkenau, recreating as much as possible of his diary entries from memory.[4]

Similarly, Macha Rolnikas wrote a diary documenting the early months of the German occupation and terror, as well as the establishment of the ghetto, and subsequently gave it to her teacher for safekeeping. Because of the danger of keeping a diary in the Vilna ghetto, her mother encouraged her to memorize her text so that she could recreate it if it happened to be lost or destroyed. So, based on memory, the author recreated it on paper after the war.[5]

Perhaps the most controversial of these "quasi-diaries" is the well-known journal of Éva Heyman, long considered the only surviving diary written by a young Jewish girl in Hungary (although in fact another diary of a Hungarian teenager, Lilla Kánitz Ecséri, was published in Hungarian; see Appendix I). Éva Heyman kept her diary in Nagyvárad, in northern Transylvania, during the spring and summer of 1944, recording the sudden and violent German onslaught there. She was deported to Auschwitz from the Nagyvárad ghetto, apparently entrusting her diary to the family's maid, Mariska Szabó, before her departure. Éva's mother, Ági Zsolt, had fled the ghetto with her husband, the well-known Hungarian writer Béla Zsolt, to find safety in Switzerland, leaving Éva behind. When she returned to Nagyvárad after the war, she reclaimed the diary.

In the 1973 introduction to the English edition of the diary, Dr. Judah Marton suggests that there has been some doubt about the diary's authenticity and implies that it could have been doctored by Éva's mother, who had the diary for more than three years before it was published and who was "an intellectual with a literary bent," married to a famous writer. Marton ultimately dismisses these doubts, citing the maturity of Jewish children in the prewar years in Europe and the recollections of some of Éva's family members and former classmates to account for Éva's precocious style. He concludes by citing the opinion of Éva's family and friends who, he writes, "had no reason to question the authenticity of any part of the diary."[6]

Still, a close reading of the English text (translated from the Hebrew edition of the diary, which was itself made from the 1947 Hungarian edition, not the original) reveals considerable inconsistencies in tone, style, and in a few cases content, lending credence to the suspicion that the text was altered. It is entirely likely that Éva did keep a diary at some point during the war years and that this diary was given to Ági by Mariska after the liberation. But it is also possible that those notes were too thin to be published on their own and that Ági (who was apparently plagued with guilt at having abandoned Éva in the ghetto) added to them in an attempt to ensure that the diary would be published and her daughter's memory would be preserved.

To further confuse matters, the original diary was apparently lost, having disappeared sometime after Ági Zsolt had the first edition published in Hungarian in 1947.[7] Without the original diary, it is impossible to compare the handwritten original notes with the transcribed text in the Hungarian publication. While it is likely that Eva wrote a diary and that parts of it are included in the published diary, it is difficult to escape the impression that other parts may have been altered by her mother in the years after the war.

Distinguishing diaries from memoirs and untangling parts of diaries from parts rewritten after the war is not as easy as it might seem, but not because the texts themselves are inherently confusing. In fact, the commonalities of style in diaries (most notably the consistent use of dated entries, the present tense, and other like indicators) make them relatively easy to distinguish from memoirs, even at a superficial reading. Rather, it is the fact that many editors and writers simply present these texts as "diaries" without being direct about the inconsistencies within them and the questions such inconsistencies should raise. While in some cases such misattributions are simple mistakes, it is striking how often editors and writers seem to gloss over perfectly obvious indicators that the text was written retrospectively, choosing to ignore rather than to probe the question. It is as if the acknowledgment of the practical realities of these texts, and an examination of their inconsistencies, would be disappointing, detracting from the romantic illusion of these diaries emerging whole and unblemished from the past.

One result of this unfortunate tendency is that a hierarchy has been constructed in which diaries are "real" and memoirs are "memories" and there is nothing in between. This in turn has led to the glorification of diaries as more authentic than other documents, for no other reason than because they were written at the time, rather than after events occurred. In reality, it was difficult to keep a diary and easy to lose one; the fact that people kept rough notes and added to them after the war is not surprising, since it reflects a continuation of that impulse to write that gave rise to the diary in the first place. The fact that people wrote immediately upon reaching safety is a signal of how important it was to mark down the details of the long imprisonment as soon as it was over. And the fact that people were devastated by the loss of their diaries and undertook the monumental and painful task of rewriting them is a reflection of how much they treasured their diaries and how essential they believed them to be as records of the war years. The end result—the form the writing took—naturally reflects a different perspective and contains different content from the original diary. But the sense that such writings are less authentic than diaries marginalizes these postwar writings, which are different but nevertheless valuable records of the writer's experience.

Before turning from the gray areas of genre to those of subject matter, it is important to mention the letters of this period, which, while surely different from diaries, nevertheless bear something in common with them, providing a window into daily lives and offering a contemporaneous account of circumstances as the writer saw and observed them. Collections of letters of young people may be, like diaries, more common than it seems, although few surfaced during my research. Louise Jacobson wrote a series of letters to her loved ones while she was imprisoned in Fresnes and Drancy; she ultimately perished in the gas chambers in Auschwitz. Her collected letters constitute a rare record created by a young person in a transit camp in France. Peter Schwiefert, a "half-Jew" from Germany, wrote letters to his mother while he fled from Nazi Germany to Portugal and Greece; he lost his life in 1945, at the age of twenty-seven, fighting in the ranks of the Free French. There are also four letters by Hertha Aussen (nicknamed Hetty), who wrote in freedom in Holland, then in Westerbork, and finally threw a postcard from the train that carried her to her death in Auschwitz. Last, Gita Hojtašová, who was ill in the ghetto hospital in Terezín, wrote a series of letters to her mother, who was in the ghetto itself; both of them survived the Holocaust.[8]

Then there are writings that are neither diaries nor letters, neither memoirs nor testimonies, but prose accounts written by young people during the war years. Among these are the writings of Moshe Kravec, who was ten when he began writing in the Kovno ghetto in Lithuania. While his writings are not a diary in the strictest sense, they are an unusual record, written in poetry and prose, of life as he experienced and witnessed it in the ghetto (roundups, public hangings, hunger and starvation, and hard labor) from 1942 to 1943. An extraordinary "collective" diary, led by twenty-one-year-old Aleksander Demajo between December 1941 and February 1943, documents the activities of a number of young Yugoslavian Jews interned in San Vincenzo della Fonte and subsequently in the Italian camp of Ferramonte. The "diary" is not a personal record of events but a public one, offering a contemporaneous account of the intellectual and cultural life led by the young Yugoslavian internees. Such a "publication" bears a resemblance to magazines made by young writers in ghettos (the most famous being *Vedem* in Terezín, though there were others), in which young people created their own new genre in which to recount the experiences of their lives.[9]

Just as there are distinctions between genres (diaries as compared to memoirs), so are there evident delineations between related but fundamentally different experiences of the war years. Thus, just as straight memoirs written entirely after the war fell outside the scope of my research, so did diaries written by non-Jewish youngsters living in countries occupied by or at war with Germany. These include the fascinating journals of Dirk van der Heide in Rotterdam, Holland, Tomi Ungerer in Alsace-Lorraine, and Colin Perry and Joan Wyndham in England; as well as the diaries of Nina Kosterina and Ina Konstantinova, both of whom lost their lives as Soviet partisans fighting the Germans. But just as there is a gray area between diaries and memoirs, there is also a gray area between diarists who recounted the events of the Holocaust as its victims (primarily Jews) and those who recorded the events of World War II (primarily non-Jews). This division does not take into account non-Jewish Poles and Slavs who were persecuted by the Nazis and denied freedoms and rights based on the hierarchy of so-called racial purity. Many were removed from their homes, forced to live in unsanitary and crowded dwellings, ill-fed, and exploited for slave labor. Some scholars argue that the Nazis intended eventually to annihilate the Poles and that they were kept alive only as long as they could work; in short, that they were seen as an expendable wartime resource, much like the Jews in ghettos, slave labor camps, and concentration camps throughout Europe. To my knowledge, as in the case of the wartime diaries of non-Jews, little scholarship has been done about these particular diaries; the few I have encountered were written in Poland and include the diaries of Janine Phillips, Maria Ginter, Jerzy Wolski, and Jerzy Świderski, though there are surely many others at large.[10]

A few diaries and collections of letters that were written by non-Jews who were engaged in the resistance surfaced, as well. In addition to the diaries written by Soviet partisans mentioned above, there are the writings of brother and sister Hans and Sophie Scholl of the German resistance organization called the White Rose, and of Kim Malthe-Bruun in Denmark. This is yet another shade of gray, for these young people were not targeted by the Nazis for annihilation for racial or biological reasons, yet they acted out against the repression of non-Jews and Jews, and died for their defiance. Their diaries speak less to the racial obsessiveness of Nazi ideology than to the nature of life in a totalitarian regime, in which to dare to protest meant danger, subjugation, and often death.[11]

Further, there are two diaries written by Jewish youngsters that, because of their content, did not fit into the category of "Holocaust" diaries but bear mention here. The first is that of Anni Hazkelson, who began her diary in Riga, Latvia, on January 27, 1934, when she was eleven years old. Her diary spans five years, ending on July 29, 1939, when Anni was sixteen. Her diary, written in German, is one of the very few to emerge from the prewar years, capturing both the rising tension of Europe in the 1930s and the daily life of a young Jewish girl. Though the Hazkelson family is presumed to have perished during the Holocaust, Anni's diary reflects not the events of the Holocaust itself but the tumultuous years leading up to it.[12]

The second is the very famous diary and writings of Hannah Senesh, who wrote in Hungary during the 1930s and subsequently when she immigrated to Palestine to live and work on a kibbutz there. The first part of it is essentially a prewar diary, like that of Anni Hazkelson. The latter part was written during the war years in Palestine. In March 1944, at the age of twenty-three, Hannah volunteered to join a parachute corps that had been formed by the British. She and her compatriots were dropped behind enemy lines in Yugoslavia and crossed into Hungary, where she was caught, put on trial, tortured, and executed by the Hungarian authorities. Her courage in sacrificing her life has tied her irrevocably to the Holocaust, though the diary itself captures a different moment in her life. It is for this reason that it is not included in this collection; it is not to redefine Hannah Senesh in relation to the Holocaust or to downplay her contribution to the resistance. Rather, it is to define the diary she wrote in relation to the body of material that is the subject of this work.[13]

The last set of gray areas is perhaps the most complex and problematic, for it concerns the matter of age. Although one may argue for a clear, definable difference between diaries and memoirs, and even between the Holocaust and the war, despite their evident interrelatedness, the definition of youth in relation to age is considerably more elusive. The diaries of full-grown adults were clearly outside the scope of my work, and the writings of teenagers were, of course, clearly in it. But there are quite a number of diaries written by young adults in their twenties that are neither clearly within the scope of this work nor clearly outside it. The well-known diary of Etty Hillesum, begun in Amsterdam when the author was twenty-seven and continued in the Dutch transit camp of Westerbork (together with a surviving collection of letters) is not the diary of a child or an adolescent, though it is the diary of a developing young woman, struggling to understand herself, her passions, and her character as she faced adulthood. Like so many of her counterparts, she did not live to see that adulthood, for she perished in Auschwitz at the age of twenty-nine. Similarly, Renata Laqueur was twenty-five when she wrote her diary in the Bergen-Belsen concentration camp; Lilly Isaacs was twenty-four when she wrote in the slave labor camp at Sommerda; Selma Engel was twenty-two when she wrote her diary in hiding in Poland after her escape from the Sobibór death camp with her husband Chaim; Aba Gefen started his diary in hiding in Lithuania when he was twenty-one and wrote until he was twenty-four; and Elsa Binder began her diary at twenty-one in Stanisławów. There are no clear-cut distinctions to be made here; how to argue for a quantifiable difference between the diary of a twenty-year-old as compared to that of a twenty-one- or twenty-two-year-old? In the end, I included Elsa Binder's diary in this work, although she is at the outer edge of what could be considered a "young writer"; I did not include Aba Gefen's diary, considering it that of a young adult, but another editor might have made the determination differently.[14]

In fact, what is most relevant is not the splitting of hairs over age itself, and thus which diary falls into which category, but the questions such distinctions raise about youth under the circumstances of the Holocaust, and how they are reflected in the diaries of the young. Because young writers' experiences of youth and age were layered by the extraordinary ordeal they faced, normal definitions of youth (living in the context of a family, dependent on parents or guardians) and its clichés (innocence, naïveté, and ignorance of the ways of the world) have no relevance here. A great many young children were orphaned and lived alone in hiding or on the streets of the ghettos, forced to adapt to circumstances and adopt an adult role early in life; conversely, many young adults in their early twenties who would normally have been living independently or studying at a university remained with their families, sometimes for material reasons or for the safety and security family life seemed to offer.

There is one diary that occupies the grayest of the gray areas, both in terms of subject and authorship, and as such poses challenging questions about the very purpose of making such determinations. Tereska Torrès was born in France to Polish Jewish parents who had converted to Catholicism before her birth. She was brought up as a Catholic, and according to her diary she seriously considered joining the convent before deciding against it. She was close to her Jewish extended family in Poland, and had vivid memories of her visits to her grandparents' homes in Łódź and Zgierz. Although Tereska herself was Catholic by conviction and upbringing, she would without question have been considered Jewish by both the German Nazis and the French, because she had four Jewish grandparents. And though she was deeply attached to her faith, she seemed in her diary to associate herself with the persecuted Jews of Poland, writing in one entry: "The news of Poland which my grandparents give us is atrocious, poor martyred Jews, my people, my poor people. I am so proud to be Jewish. If I were in Poland, I would proclaim it from the rooftops in order to die for my race." Although the question of whether or not Tereska was Jewish, or whose determination matters most (hers or the Nazis'), is complex, as it touches on the eternally confounding matter of defining Jewishness, it is only one part of the question. For Peter Feigl did not consider himself a Jew, yet he was persecuted as one in France and his diary is included in this work.[15]

Perhaps, then, the question can be refined. Perhaps what matters is whether the experience recounted in the diary is that of a victim of the Holocaust. For had Tereska and her family remained in France, they would have been persecuted as Jews and been as likely to have perished as any other foreign Jews on French soil at that particularly dangerous time. But they fled in June 1940 to safety in England (and in so doing never fell victim to anti-Jewish legislation in France), and most of Tereska's diary concerns her life there and her work in the ranks of the Free French fighting in the resistance with General Charles de Gaulle. In this, the diary itself does not so much capture a facet of life during the Holocaust as it sheds light on a facet of the war and the French resistance movement. On the other hand, the diaries of Jewish refugee children fleeing Europe to escape Nazism and living in exile are included in this work without question. Tereska's experience of fleeing France and leaving behind her dearly beloved Paris is in many ways no different than those accounts.

As if all this were not complex enough, Tereska was eighteen or nineteen in 1939, when she began the diary that concerns this study, and in 1940 she passed her baccalauréat, signifying the completion of her high school studies. In the beginning of the diary, her voice is very much that of a young girl, but in the spring of 1944, at the age of twenty-three, she married Georges Torrès. She soon became pregnant, and the following autumn she learned that her young husband had fallen in battle. She went on to deliver her daughter, who never knew her father. While the early part of the diary is the work of an idealistic, reflective young woman, the latter part is surely that of a woman, older not only in years but by virtue of war, exile, love, grief, and finally motherhood.

What is a diary, what is a Jew, what is a victim, what is youth? The questions and their answers have gray areas, nuances, and reflect to some extent subjective judgments. Indeed, what is the point of such minute classifications anyway? Only this: to be able to recognize that which is *like,* to group it, and to see what it as a body yields. The material at the margins thankfully complicates seemingly clear-cut distinctions and reveals nuances that exist but can be ignored until an aberration surfaces. In this, this material not only helps by its distinctions to define matters of genre, scope, and authorship, but it brings into relief the deepest questions about what we seek and hope to find in our investigations.

In the end, these "gray areas" themselves begin to take their own shape, as multiple writings of one or another kind surface and patterns emerge. Certainly their existence sharpened my own definitions about the scope of my research, raised provocative questions about what diaries written by young people in the Holocaust might yield as compared with other, similar documents, and suggested new ways of thinking about the material I found. Clearly, however, these texts are well worth investigating and reading for their own merits and on their own terms. All of them—diary-memoirs, letters, and prose, wartime journals by non-Jews, and diaries written by young adults—constitute valid contributions to the body of historical and literary material that has surfaced from World War II and the Holocaust.

Notes

Introduction

1. Lawrence Graver, *An Obsession with Anne Frank: Meyer Levin and the Diary* (Berkeley and Los Angeles: University of California Press, 1995), 16; Melissa Müller, *Anne Frank: The Biography,* translated by Rita and Robert Kimber (New York: Metropolitan Books, an imprint of Henry Holt, 1998), 274.
2. Graver, *Obsession with Anne Frank,* 16–17; Müller, *Anne Frank,* 275; Meyer Levin, *In Search* (New York: Horizon, 1950), 174. For this interpretation I am indebted to Lawrence Graver, who eloquently describes Levin's experiences in Europe, their impact on his understanding of the Holocaust, and his first vision for Anne Frank's diary (Graver, *Obsession with Anne Frank,* 1–15).
3. Graver, *Obsession with Anne Frank,* 25, 26.
4. Ibid., 95.
5. One notable exception is *The Diary of Dawid Sierakowiak* (Oxford: Oxford University Press, 1996), which carries a foreword by Lawrence Langer and an introduction by the editor, Alan Adelson, both of which are devoid of any of the clichés or sentimentality so often found among published diaries of this period.
6. Patricia McKissack, foreword to *We Are Witnesses,* by Jacob Boas (New York: Henry Holt, 1995), vii; Jehoshua and Anna Eibeshitz, translator's preface to *Ruthka: A Diary of War,* by Ruthka Lieblich (New York: Remember, 1993), ix; Serge Klarsfeld, preface to *Les Lettres de Louise Jacobson et de ses proches, Fresnes, Drancy, 1942–1943,* by Louise Jacobson (Paris: Editions Robert Laffont, 1997), 9 [editor's translation].
7. Derek Bowman, introduction to *The Diary of Dawid Rubinowicz,* by Dawid Rubinowicz (Edmonds, Washington: Creative Options, 1982), x; Jacob Boas, *We Are Witnesses,* 7; Klarsfeld, preface to *Les Lettres de Louise Jacobson,* 11 [editor's translation]; Eibeshitz, translator's preface to *Ruthka,* vii.
8. Bowman, introduction to *The Diary of Dawid Rubinowicz,* xiv; Geoffrey Wigoder, introduction to *Young Moshe's Diary,* by Moshe Flinker (Jerusalem: Yad Vashem, 1971), 16.
9. There have been so many books and articles written on this subject that a complete list would perhaps be impossible. But among the writers and historians who must be credited with having posed questions and voiced ideas and opinions that gave me much to consider are Hannah Arendt, Bruno Bettelheim, Denise DeCosta, Judith Doneson, Hyman Enzer and Sandra Solotaroff-Enzer, Lawrence Graver, Lawrence Langer, Ralph Melnick, Peter Novick, Cynthia Ozick, David Patterson, Alvin Rosenfeld, David Roskies, Marie Syrkin, and James Young. To this list, I must add the

many unnamed or little-known journalists who wrote about Anne Frank's diary during the 1950s in such magazines as *Life, Newsweek, The New Republic, Commonweal, Time Midstream, Jewish Frontier,* and *Congress Weekly.* In many cases, these articles served as informative primary sources, shedding valuable light on the birth of the American popular perception of Anne Frank's diary.

10. Primo Levi, *The Periodic Table* (New York: Schocken, 1984), 48–49.

1. Klaus Langer

1. Unless otherwise noted, biographical information about Klaus (Jacob) Langer and his family comes from unpublished correspondence between Mr. Langer and the editor.

2. Jacob Langer, letter to editor, February 6, 1997.

3. For a study of the persecution of Jewish children in Germany during the 1930s, the role and significance of Zionist and non-Zionist youth groups in Germany, and the Nazi responses to such groups, see Werner T. Angress, *Between Fear and Hope: Jewish Youth in the Third Reich* (New York: Columbia University Press, 1988), 1–42.

4. Avraham Barkai, "The Continuation and Acceleration of Plunder," *November 1938: From "Kristallnacht" to Genocide,* ed. Walter Pehle, trans. Walter Templer (New York: Berg Publishers, 1991), 116, 121. For a brief history of the Nazi persecution of the Jews of Essen, see Angela Genger, *Persecution and Resistance in Essen, 1933–1945* (Essen: Cultural Office of the City of Essen, 1984).

5. Saul Friedländer, *Nazi Germany and the Jews,* vol. 1, *The Years of Persecution, 1933–1939* (New York: HarperCollins, 1997), 248–49, 299–302.

6. Sandra Berliant Kadosh, "Ideology vs. Reality: Youth Aliyah and the Rescue of the Jewish Children During the Holocaust Era, 1933–1945" (Ph.D. diss., Columbia University, 1995), 213–14.

7. *Encyclopedia Judaica,* s.v. "Izbica Lubelska." In the Bundesarchiv's *Gedenkbuch,* which provides a register of the dead from West Germany, Erich Langer, Klaus's father, is listed as having been declared deceased (p. 809). Izbica is given as his last known location. Klaus's grandmother Mina Benderski is listed as "missing" in the *Gedenkbuch* (p. 93), with Minsk her last known location.

   Jacob Langer (after changing his name from Klaus) lived on a kibbutz in Ramat David for two years and then moved to another kibbutz called Ma'ayan Tzvi. He married in 1947 and remained on the kibbutz until 1956. He went on to study biology at Tel Aviv University and worked in Israel until his retirement in 1989.

8. In late October 1938, about sixteen thousand Polish Jews were expelled from Germany. They were sent to the Polish border town Zbąszyń, where Polish authorities refused to allow them to enter Poland. They remained between the two borders for days, before many of them were placed in a Polish camp in Zbąszyń. On November 7, 1938, a young Polish Jew, Herschel Grynszpan, whose family was among those expelled from Germany, shot a German diplomat, Ernst vom Rath, as a public protest against the treatment of the Jews. This was the alleged catalyst for Kristallnacht. (Friedländer, *Nazi Germany and the Jews,* vol. 1, 267–68.)

9. *Erez,* or *Erez Israel* (literally "the Land of Israel"), is the Hebrew term referring to the

Jewish homeland in Israel. At the time that the diary was written, the state of Israel had not been established. Throughout the diary, Langer uses the terms "Erez," "Erez Israel," and "Palestine" interchangeably.

10. The director of the Jawne School was Erich Klibansky, an energetic young principal who realized that his young students' lives were in danger and undertook to move the entire school to England. Although this plan was unsuccessful, he did succeed in arranging for the emigration of many hundreds of students and teachers from the school. He himself did not get out of Germany in time and was deported from Cologne in July 1942. He was sent with his wife and their three sons to Minsk, where they were murdered. For a detailed account of the history of the Jawne School and Klibansky's rescue of its students, see Dieter Corbach, *Die Jawne zu Köln: Zur Geschichte des ersten jüdischen Gymnasiums im Rheinland und zum Gedächtnis an Erich Klibansky, 1900–1942* [The Jawne in Cologne: The History of the First Jewish Grammar School in Rhineland, In Memory of Erich Klibansky, 1900–1942; text in English] (Cologne: Scriba Verlag, 1990).

11. Schniebinchen was an agricultural training camp *(hachsharah)* run by the Youth Aliyah. All young people seeking to go to Palestine through Youth Aliyah had to attend such a training camp as a prerequisite to their emigration. (Kadosh, "Ideology vs. Reality," 200.)

12. In July 1938, the German Ministry of the Interior issued a decree that required every Jew in Germany to apply for an identity card and to carry it at all times. These cards were marked with a "J" to indicate that the bearer was Jewish. (Friedländer, *Nazi Germany and the Jews,* vol. 1, 254.)

13. The Dutch had established the Nieuwesluis refugee camp in Wieringen, North Holland, which was an agricultural training facility for young Jews who had fled from Germany. (Angress, *Between Fear and Hope,* 78.)

14. On August 17, 1938, the Nazis had issued a decree stating that Jewish men and boys had to take the name "Israel" and Jewish women and girls had to take the name "Sara." There was an appendix that listed "Jewish" names—such as Abel, Abieser, Absalom, Ahaser, and so on. Those who already had such first names were not required to add Israel or Sara. (Friedländer, *Nazi Germany and the Jews,* vol. 1, 254–55.)

15. Anneliese Katz (later Anne Ranasinghe) wrote her diary after her emigration to England, documenting the first difficult months in a new environment, far from her family. See Appendix I.

16. Many of Klaus Langer's friends were able to escape Germany as well. Mr. Langer recalled that Bobby Ferse emigrated to England and went from there to Palestine; Kurt Melchior (Kume) emigrated to the United States; Lother Bierhoff (Lobi) emigrated to Montevideo, Uruguay, and went from there to Argentina; Wolfgang Rapp (Rotzig) emigrated to the United States; and Paul Rolman emigrated to Amsterdam and eventually to Palestine.

2. Elisabeth Kaufmann

1. Unless otherwise noted, biographical information about Elisabeth Kaufmann (Elizabeth Koenig) and her family comes from unpublished correspondence between the

editor and Mrs. Koenig, and from Elizabeth Koenig, videorecorded interview, January 29, 1990, conducted by and in the Collection of the United States Holocaust Memorial Museum, Washington, D.C.

2. For more on the particular problems facing German and Austrian Jewish refugees in France, see Lucien Lazare, *Rescue as Resistance: How Jewish Organizations Fought the Holocaust in France* (New York: Columbia University Press, 1996), 3–22.

3. During this time, Elisabeth filled a sketchbook with drawings and paintings depicting scenes from her life as a refugee in France. In many cases, the pictures correspond directly to the events she described in her diary, such that the sketchbook can in some ways be regarded as an illustration of it. Many of the charcoal drawings and watercolors are powerfully rendered, revealing Elisabeth's considerable talent as a young artist. The sketchbook is now in the Collection of the United States Holocaust Memorial Museum, Washington, D.C.

4. Le Chambon sur Lignon was the Protestant town where Pastor André Trocmé led an effort to shelter and hide thousands of refugees, including hundreds of Jewish children. Elisabeth first cared for Pastor and Mrs. Trocmé's children as their au pair, and later helped to care for some of the children who had arrived in Le Chambon and were being hidden there. Many of these were German Jewish children who did not speak French and had been separated from their parents, who had been deported. One of the many children who were sheltered by the Trocmé family was Peter Feigl, who kept a diary beginning in August 1942. His diary is included in this collection. An illustrated autograph book signed by many of the children in Le Chambon and given to Elisabeth when she departed is in the Collection of the United States Holocaust Memorial Museum, Washington, D.C. For more on the rescue efforts of the Chambonnais, see Phillip Hallie, *Lest Innocent Blood Be Shed: The Story of the Village of Le Chambon and How Goodness Happened There* (New York: Harper and Row, 1979), and Pierre Sauvage's excellent documentary film, *Weapons of the Spirit*.

5. The visas had been secured through the efforts of an American in France, Varian Fry, who was working under the auspices of the Emergency Rescue Committee. He had been sent especially to help those German refugees in particular danger as a result of Article 19 of the Franco-German Armistice signed on June 22, 1940. This article required the French to "surrender on demand" any German national wanted by the Gestapo. Anti-Nazi German intellectuals, writers, liberal thinkers, artists, musicians, and others who had fled repression in Germany were therefore in grave danger of extradition. Elisabeth's father, as a liberal journalist, thus found himself in the same company as such distinguished writers and artists as Lion Feuchtwanger, Heinrich Mann, Walter Mehring, and André Breton. As it happened, by the time the Kaufmanns got their American visas in November 1941, Varian Fry had been expelled from France, but during the thirteen months he spent there he rescued more than a thousand German refugees and provided monetary support, relief, and advice to many more. For a detailed account of Fry's rescue activities, see Anita Kassof, "Intent and Interpretation: German Refugees and Article 19 of the Franco-German Armistice" (master's thesis, University of Maryland, 1992).

6. This was a prevailing attitude among many in the French establishment who feared the rise of Bolshevism and, consequently, looked to Hitler and the Nazis as an effective "bulwark" against it. (Lazare, *Rescue as Resistance,* 6.)

7. A decree of January 13, 1940, allowed some able-bodied male internees to leave the camps in order to join labor battalions, or *prestataires*. (Kassof, "Intent and Interpretation," 42.)

8. Gymnasium is similar to the French *lycée*, both of which are roughly equivalent to high school in American terms. However, the European high school system is more rigorous and competitive than the American one and graduation is contingent upon passing the baccalauréat examination or its equivalent. Elisabeth included her attendance at gymnasium as an example of the privileges of her life prior to the Nazi takeover in Austria because it signified the value she and her family placed on higher education.

9. Ernst Koenig's diary was lost sometime during or after the war.

3. Peter Feigl

1. Unless otherwise noted, biographical information about Peter Feigl and his family comes from unpublished correspondence between the editor and Mr. Feigl; from Mr. Feigl's unpublished preface and epilogue to the diary; and from Peter Feigl, videorecorded interview, August 23, 1995, conducted by and in the Collection of the United States Holocaust Memorial Museum, Washington, D.C. An extraordinary wealth of documentation about Peter and his wartime experiences has surfaced since the first edition of *Salvaged Pages* appeared. Many of Peter's personal papers, including letters between his mother and grandmother written in 1941–42, as well as documentation from the American Quakers and records related to his immigration to America, have been donated to the United States Holocaust Memorial Museum in Washington, D.C. Peter has given several videotaped interviews, which can be found at the United States Holocaust Memorial Museum and at the USC Shoah Foundation Visual History Archive. For an excellent educational resource about the diary, see *One Man, Two Voices: Peter Feigl's Diary and Testimony,* written by Sheila Hansen and located online at the USC Shoah Foundation website. For another published account of Peter's life and diary, with extensive documentation, see Gisele Polya-Somogyi, *Enfants Deportés, Enfants Sauvés: Les Petits Refugies Juifs du Gers, 1940–1944* (Saint-Cyr-sur-Loire: Sutton, 2011).

2. Peter Feigl, unpublished preface to the diary, 1.
   Ernst Feigl's decision to have Peter baptized as a Catholic is deeply suggestive of the plight that faced many highly assimilated Central European Jews who did not initially understand that Nazi anti-Semitism represented a dramatic break from the "traditional" anti-Semitism of the past. Whereas conversion had always been the desired result of centuries of Church-sponsored oppression of Jews, the Nazis had shifted the paradigm completely, defining the "Jewish problem" not as one of religious practice (and thus remediable by conversion) but as one of racial identity and heredity. This shift precluded any preemptive act on the part of the Jews. It is one of the many ironies embedded in Peter's story that the decision to have him convert to Catholicism was taken not to "save" him religiously but to save him physically, and yet, ultimately, this decision had no power to alter his destiny as the Nazis decreed it. (Raul Hilberg, *The Destruction of the European Jews*, 3 vols. [New York: Holmes & Meier, 1985], 5–22.)

3. Feigl, unpublished preface, 2.

4. Peter was helped by Mme. Cavailhon, a French woman who operated the Catholic summer camp at Château de Montéléone. She made contact with the American Friends Service Committee (the American Quakers), who were organizing a transport of Jewish children to immigrate to America. After considerable effort, she succeeded in getting Peter on the list, but the ship did not end up sailing. Instead, Peter was sent to a temporary refuge run by a couple called the Brémonds at Les Caillols and from there to Les Grillons, a boarding school for Jewish refugee children established by the American Quakers in Le Chambon sur Lignon. There, Peter was under the care of Daniel Trocmé, the nephew of Pastor André Trocmé. In addition to these identified people and organizations, there is a vague cadre of others, sometimes named but often not, who were occupied with trying to save Peter, among other children in similar situations.

5. Serge Klarsfeld, *Memorial to the Jews Deported from France 1942–1944* (New York: Beate Klarsfeld Foundation, 1983), 243–45.

6. Michael R. Marrus and Robert O. Paxton, *Vichy France and the Jews* (New York: Basic, 1981), 343.

7. See Hallie, *Lest Innocent Blood Be Shed.*

8. Feigl, unpublished preface, 2.

9. Ibid.

10. In midsummer 1943, the only successful raid on a home in Le Chambon took place. Daniel Trocmé and a number of the boys in his care were arrested, interrogated, and deported. Daniel Trocmé was murdered in the Majdanek death camp. (Hallie, *Lest Innocent Blood Be Shed,* 203–17.)

11. Peter Feigl, interview, U.S. Holocaust Memorial Museum, 35.

12. Peter Feigl, unpublished epilogue to the diary, 1.

13. The school was probably the Cévenol Normal School in Le Chambon sur Lignon, the Protestant enclave on a high plateau in the Haute-Loire region of France.

14. Mrs. Cavailhon's appeals to the emigration board on Peter's behalf were apparently hampered by the fact that, as a Catholic, Peter was not considered an urgent candidate for emigration. This of course failed to take into consideration the fact that the Nazis defined Jewishness on a so-called racial basis, not a religious one, and consequently Peter was in as grave danger as any other Jew in Europe. Mrs. Cavailhon wrote a long letter to the board explaining his status and pleading his case. In 1996, Peter Feigl obtained from the OSE (Oeuvre de Secours aux Enfants) in Paris a copy of his file, which contained the letter, and Mrs. Cavailhon's reply.

15. On November 11, 1942, the Germans occupied the southern, formerly "free" zone of France in reaction to the Allied landing in North Africa several days earlier, on November 8. (Marrus and Paxton, *Vichy France and the Jews,* 302–3.)

16. Peter was temporarily sent away from Les Caillols as punishment for having gotten into a conversation with some German soldiers stationed near there. Such conversations had the potential of endangering him and the other children who were hiding from the Vichy authorities and the Nazis.

17. This is a reference to Daniel Trocmé, director of Les Grillons [The Crickets], a home for Jewish refugee children established by the American Quakers at Le Chambon sur

Lignon in the Haute-Loire. Peter was sent there on January 16, 1943. Daniel Trocmé was the nephew of Pastor André Trocmé, the spiritual leader of the Protestant community of Le Chambon sur Lignon.

18. Peter said that this might have been a reference to his birth certificate, the back of which had an endorsement from the Catholic Church in Vienna acknowledging his baptism.

19. Referred to in the entry for September 21, 1942.

20. Peter recalled that the Germans moved a number of their trucks into the school courtyard and some of his friends decided to sabotage the trucks by slashing the tires and pouring sugar, which was hard to come by during those times, into the gas tanks.

21. This page contains a sketch of the border crossing point showing the two rows of barbed-wire fence between France and Switzerland, the no-man's land between the two, the crossing point, the direction of Geneva, the Swiss border guard building, a garden behind it and vineyards on one side of the building, and mountains in the background on the Swiss side.

22. Peter said that he used this term to show anyone who might look through the diary that he was not Jewish, as there were rumors that Jews would be sent from Switzerland back to France.

4. Moshe Flinker

1. Until 2013, I knew very little about Moshe Flinker and his family. The biographical information in the first edition of *Salvaged Pages* came exclusively from Shaul Esh and Geoffrey Wigoder's introductions to the English edition of the diary (*Young Moshe's Diary: The Spiritual Torment of a Jewish Boy in Nazi Europe* [Jerusalem: Yad Vashem, 1971]). In 2013, I was contacted by Leon Schwimmer, the son of Moshe Flinker's eldest sister, Esther Malka. Thanks to his considerable efforts and generosity, I learned many more details about the family history, first from an article written by David Damen, entitled "Diaries of Love and War" (*Mishpacha*, October 20, 2013), and then when I traveled to Israel and interviewed Moshe's only two surviving sisters, Leah Levy and Rebecca (Rivka) Schweber, in July 2014. Copies of that interview may be found at the United States Holocaust Memorial Museum, Yad Vashem, and the USC Shoah Foundation Visual History Archive. In addition, the Raab Holocaust Education Center in Jerusalem made a documentary film about Moshe and his diary titled *Under Your Wing: The Journal of Young Moshe. Young Moshe's Diary*, which is out of print, still contains the most complete English version of the text, with omissions indicated by an asterisk. Those edits are indicated in this edition with a bracketed asterisk. The diary was recently published in a new Hebrew edition and is currently being translated by Guylain Sitbon for a French edition.

2. Esh, introduction to *Young Moshe's Diary*, 8.

3. Although these two ideas are related in the diary, he did not introduce them at the same time. The concept of the Nazi oppression of the Jews as a "link in a long chain of suffering" is first expressed in the entry for November 30, 1942; the notion of their suffering as the "birthpang of the Messiah" is first articulated in his entry of December 28, 1942.

4. Wigoder, introduction to *Young Moshe's Diary*, 14.
5. A similar point is made in Esh, introduction to *Young Moshe's Diary*, 9.
6. By the end of 1941, more than a million Jews had been killed, most of them during "Operation Barbarossa," as the Einsatzgruppen (mobile killing squads) followed behind the advancing German army as it penetrated Russian territory. Moshe's confrontation with the fact of the mass murder of the Jews took place a full year later, by which time more than two and half million additional Jews had been killed. (Hilberg, *Destruction of the European Jews*, 1220.)
7. According to Shaul Esh, Moshe's idea that the Jews who hid from the Nazis would be punished like those who "perished in the darkness of Egypt" stems from a well-known Midrash, or commentary on the Torah. (Esh, introduction to *Young Moshe's Diary*, 9.)
8. Ibid., 7–8.
9. In the first edition of this book, I took my information about the fate of the Flinker family from Shaul Esh's introduction to *Young Moshe's Diary*, which mistakenly states that the family was deported to Auschwitz, where Moshe and his parents were murdered upon arrival and the rest of the family survived. The corrected details here come from my interview with Leah Levy and Rebecca Schweber and also from John Braat, who conducted extensive research on the Flinker family and wrote a chapter about them in his Dutch-language book *De Joodse Gemeenschap in Roosendaal* [The Jewish Community in Roosendaal before and during the Second World War]. He provided me with the information regarding Moshe and his father's deportation from Auschwitz-Birkenau to the slave labor camp Echterdingen and then, amid the typhus epidemic, to Bergen-Belsen in January 1945, where they perished. I am immensely grateful to Mr. Braat, who shared his research and records with me. Finally, through the State Archives of Belgium and the Directorate General of War Victims in Brussels, I found extensive files relating to all members of the Flinker family.
10. Being "invited to the wedding" was a code used by Jews throughout German-occupied Europe. It meant that one had received a summons for deportation.
11. This is surely a reference to one of the concentration camps—Buchenwald, Dachau, and Mauthausen—about which the European public was generally aware by the time Moshe wrote this entry in November 1942. It most likely refers to Mauthausen, where 430 Dutch Jews had been sent in February 1941, followed by 230 more in June of the same year, in a high-profile reprisal for an "attack" on Nazis patrolling the Jewish quarter in Amsterdam. (Hilberg, *Destruction of the European Jews*, 581–83, and Jacob Presser, *The Destruction of the Dutch Jews* [New York: Dutton, 1969], 51–54.) Whatever Moshe specifically meant, it is important to stress that it was surely not a reference to the killing centers in the Eastern territories, about which Moshe could not have had any knowledge at the time that this entry was written.
12. *Jud Süss* was an anti-Semitic propaganda film, released in Germany in September 1940, which depicted the alleged moral and financial misdeeds of Joseph Süss-Oppenheimer, the Jewish adviser to Duke Karl Alexander of Wurttemburg. By focusing on the "typically Jewish" characteristics of greed and immorality as they manifested themselves in the "Jew Süss," the film was intended to present a historical basis and justification for the anti-Jewish legislation of the Nazi regime.

5. Otto Wolf

1. Biographical information about Otto Wolf and his family comes primarily from Otto's sister, Felicitas Garda, interview by editor, March 4, 2000, Miami, Florida, and from unpublished correspondence with Mrs. Garda and with Mr. Thomas Mandl. Additional information comes from Ludvík Václavek, introduction to *Deník Otty Wolfa: 1942–1945,* by Otto Wolf (Prague: Sefer Nadace Terezínská Iniciativa, 1997; English translation by Madeline Vadkerty). Beginning in 2007, an American teacher, Colleen Tambuscio, with help from colleagues Lisa Bauman and Bonnie Sussman, embarked with a group of students on a project to conduct additional research on Otto's story, to locate some of the rescuers who had aided his family, and to make a personal connection with the existing community in Olomouc. As part of an annual, intensive two-week study tour in Berlin, the Czech Republic, and Poland, Colleen, with her colleagues and students, eventually created two permanent memorials—one for the Wolf family and a second one for those who sheltered them. I was very pleased to be present in 2012 for the dedication of the memorial to the Wolf family, which took place in the forest outside of Olomouc, at the site of the family's hiding place. For a more detailed account of the project and its educational significance, see Colleen Tambuscio's article, written with Lisa Bauman and Bonnie Sussman, entitled "Making History: Beyond the Text," in *Prism: An Interdisciplinary Journal for Holocaust Educators,* vol. 6 (Spring 2014: 101–6.)
2. Felicitas Garda, unpublished preface to English translation of Otto Wolf's diary, 1.
3. Václavek, introduction to *Deník Otty Wolfa,* 16.
4. Ibid., 16–17.
5. Erich Kulka, *Jews in Svoboda's Army in the Soviet Union: Czechoslovak Jewry's Fight Against the Nazis During World War II* (Lanham, Md.: University Press of America, and Jerusalem: Institute of Contemporary Jewry, 1987), 194–95. Details about Kurt Wolf's role in General Svoboda's army, recollections of his fellow soldiers, and further information about his heroic death, for which he was posthumously awarded the Order of the Red Flag by the Soviet government, can be found in Kulka, *Jews in Svoboda's Army,* 114, 126, 194–95, 206, 414, 417.
6. Mr. Blaha's knowledge of the Wolfs' presence in the forest compromised his own safety, as helping Jews to hide was strictly forbidden by the Germans. He thus needed not only to give his promise that he would not betray the Wolfs but to secure a promise from them that they would never reveal that he knew of their whereabouts.
7. During periods when the Wolfs stayed inside Slávek's hut at the edge of the forest, he locked the door from the outside so that passers-by would not open it and discover them. They were unable to get out for fresh air, food, or to relieve themselves until he unlocked the hut.

6. Petr Ginz and Eva Ginzová

1. Biographical information about the Ginz family comes primarily from unpublished correspondence with Mrs. Chava Pressburger (née Eva Ginzová), and from Marie Rút Křížková, Kurt Jiří Koutouč, and Zdeněk Ornest, eds., *We Are Children Just the*

Same: Vedem, the Secret Magazine by the Boys of Terezín (Philadelphia: Jewish Publication Society, 1995), 62–77. In the spring of 2003, two volumes of Petr Ginz's diaries, written from February 24, 1941, until August 1942, and four additional notebooks containing his written manuscripts, surfaced in Prague. They had been found in an old home and kept untouched until the *Discovery* space shuttle exploded on reentry into the Earth's atmosphere, killing all the astronauts on board. Among the crew was Ilan Ramon, an Israeli astronaut and son of Holocaust survivors, who had brought a copy of one of Petr's drawings, *Moon Landscape,* into space with him as a symbol of the tragedy of the Jewish genocide. When the news appeared in the Czech Republic, the person who held the diaries in his possession approached Yad Vashem to see if they would buy them. Eventually, the diaries found their rightful home with Petr's surviving sister, and many of the manuscripts and drawings were added to the collections of Yad Vashem. In 2004, Petr's sister Chava edited and published a volume of Petr's diaries from Prague, which includes family photos, excerpts of his other writings, images of his artwork, and other documentation. She also wrote a beautiful, detailed, and immensely valuable introduction to the book, which adds significant information about Petr's life and work and the families' prewar and wartime experiences. It is an indispensable companion to Petr's short diary and journal from Terezín that are included in this volume. See *The Diary of Petr Ginz, 1941–1942* (New York: Atlantic Monthly Press, 2003.)

2. František Ehrmann, Otto Heitlinger, and Rudolf Itlis, eds., *Terezín* (Prague: Council of Jewish Communities, 1965), 15.

3. Hilberg, *Destruction of the European Jews,* 169–70, 178.

4. Of the Ginz family, Otto was the only survivor among his siblings. His mother perished in Terezín and one of his sisters and her husband were deported directly to Poland. The others passed through Terezín but did not survive the Holocaust. Otto's brother Miloš was deported to Auschwitz in October 1944, where he passed the "selection" and went into slave labor. When the camp was liquidated in January 1945 and the surviving prisoners were transported toward the interior of Germany to avoid the Red Army troops advancing from the East, Miloš Ginz was sent with them. There are conflicting reports from witnesses as to his fate; one survivor claimed to have seen him at slave labor in Dachau and another reported that he had been killed by a fellow prisoner over a struggle for bread. The date of his death is not known, though it must have been in the late winter or early spring of 1945. Of the children, Eva and her cousin Hanka were the only survivors. Eva's mother and Aunt Nad'a (Pavel and Hanka's mother) both survived the war in Prague. (Pressburger, letters to editor, December 12, 1999, and June 22, 2000.)

5. See *The Terezín Diary of Gonda Redlich,* ed. Saul S. Friedman, trans. Laurence Kutler (Lexington: University Press of Kentucky, 1992), and Shlomo Schmiedt, "Hehalutz in Theresienstadt—Its Influence and Educational Activities," *Yad Vashem Studies on the European Jewish Catastrophe and Resistance,* ed. Livia Rothkirchen, vol. 7 (1968).

6. A great many of Petr's works of art (watercolors, drawings, linoleum cuts, and more) survived the Holocaust. In the spring of 1984, Yad Vashem organized and exhibited a collection of Petr's Terezín paintings and drawings, together with the postwar art-

work of his sister Eva (Chava Pressburger). The exhibit and accompanying catalogue-brochure were titled *"The Road Through Theresienstadt": Petr Ginz, 1928–1944, Chava Pressburger (Eva Ginz)*. Most of Petr's artwork was donated to Yad Vashem by his father, Otto Ginz.

The proliferation of creative and intellectual projects recorded in the journal speaks not only to Petr and his interests, but also to the particular character of Petr's immediate surroundings—that of Home 1 in Building L417. Home 1 was clearly an exceptional place, led by Professor Valtr Eisinger, a man who seems to have been universally loved and admired by his young charges. Inspired by Professor Eisinger, the boys organized themselves into a self-governing body, called the Republic of Shkid, and vowed to live a communal life based on decency, honesty, and mutual respect. Their educational goals were equally ambitious; according to Petr's journal, classes offered in the "program" there included not only poetry, grammar, literature, Russian, and Latin, but also Sanskrit, Esperanto, and Sinhalese. In addition to classes, the boys organized and delivered lectures to the group on a variety of subjects.

7. Křížková, Koutouč, and Ornest, eds., *We Are Children,* 42, 64.

8. Pressburger, letter to editor, December 12, 1999.

9. George E. Berkley, *Hitler's Gift: The Story of Theresienstadt* (Boston: Branden, 1993), 240–43. See also the diary of Alice Ehrmann, entries beginning on April 20, 1945.

10. An English translation of Petr's excellent essay about insults, titled "The Life of an Inanimate Object," can be found in Křížková, Koutouč, and Ornest, eds., *We Are Children,* 66.

11. In preparation for the visit of the Red Cross to Terezín in the summer of 1944, and to avoid the appearance of overcrowding and the embarrassing presence of sick or weak people and orphaned children, ghetto commandant Karl Rahm ordered the deportation of seventy-five hundred Jews to take place over three transports in May. Although the camp inmates were told that these deportees were headed to the Dresden area, they went instead to Auschwitz-Birkenau to the so-called Family Camp. Though Eva frankly acknowledged that these deportees were being sent to Birkenau (as her brother had done in his diary entry mentioning other transports in December 1943), and though she mentioned the camp in other contexts throughout the early part of the diary, there is no reason to suppose that either of them knew anything about the true nature of the camp or the mass killings there at this time. Indeed, it was not until the spring of 1945, when twelve thousand death camp survivors came to Terezín, that the true nature of Birkenau and the other death camps became known to the population at large. (Berkley, *Hitler's Gift,* 169–70, 200.)

12. In a related entry from Petr's "plans" of August 1944, the same month as this entry in Eva's diary, he had noted to himself to "borrow a stenography textbook."

13. In his history of Terezín, George Berkley mentions that postcards arrived in Terezín from some deportees who had left the ghetto during the fall 1944 transports. This was a ruse that had been employed by the Nazis many times before to deflect suspicion about the fate of the deportees. In this case, the train carrying the prisoners stopped in Dresden, where the cards were issued, filled out by the prisoners, and collected before the train resumed its course, changing its direction for Auschwitz. The correspondence was then sent from Dresden, carrying the reassuring postmark to the

deportees' loved ones in Terezín. It is most likely that this correspondence from Milos Ginz to his daughter and niece was one such letter. (Berkley, *Hitler's Gift,* 200.)

14. In fact, the Danish Jews in Terezín did depart the camp in mid-April 1944, escorted home on Red Cross buses driven by Swedish workers. (Berkley, *Hitler's Gift,* 233–34.) This and subsequent events in the ghetto are also described in Alice Ehrmann's diary, in entries beginning on April 15, 1945.

7. Yitskhok Rudashevski

1. Biographical information about Yitskhok Rudashevski and his family comes primarily from Zvi Shner, introduction to *The Diary of the Vilna Ghetto,* by Yitskhok Rudashevski (Israel: Ghetto Fighters' House, 1973). This edition, the only complete English version of Rudashevski's diary, includes two introductions to the text and extensive discursive notes about him, his circle of friends, local ghetto inhabitants, and events mentioned in the diary. It is currently out of print. In 2014, I traveled to Israel and interviewed Sarah Kalivatsch (née Sore Voloshin), Yitskhok's first cousin and dear friend. In her interview, she shared her personal memories of her cousin and details about their experiences before and during the war years. Copies of the interview can be found at the United States Holocaust Memorial Museum, Yad Vashem, and the USC Shoah Foundation Archives.

2. Yitzhak Arad, *Ghetto in Flames: The Struggle and Destruction of the Jews in Vilna in the Holocaust* (New York: Holocaust Library, 1982), 10, 20–21.

3. One entry, written on March 23, 1942, seems to belong to the second part of the diary, though the main body of sequential dated entries did not begin until seven months later.

4. Whether Jews in the ghetto had any knowledge of the mass murders at the Ponar killing site is a complex matter that is outlined in detail in Arad, *Ghetto in Flames,* 172–99. Arad concludes that most of the Jews in the ghetto knew nothing of the murders until November 1941 and that widespread acknowledgment of the fact did not penetrate the Vilna ghetto until December 1941 or January 1942. (Arad, *Ghetto in Flames,* 178, 182.)

   Yitskhok's references to the existence of a Soviet youth group (called the "pioneers" and carried out secretly under the Germans' noses) are subtle and easy to confuse with references to the Soviet youth organization called the Young Pioneers, participation in which was required under the Soviet regime. Indeed, they appear in the context of Yitskhok's description of the last attempted meeting of the Young Pioneers on the day the Germans attacked Lithuania. Though that meeting was aborted because of the bombings, he wrote, *"Now as I write* I think we have become quite different pioneers. I feel that if they will need us, we shall come, even if it will be our last pioneer meeting" (June 21, 1941). While at first this was a gathering of young people who were supportive of the Soviet regime, it was transformed into a resistance group after the renewal of deportations and mass murders in March 1943. Hence Yitskhok's reference to having become "quite different pioneers" and the allusion to a possible "last pioneer meeting" in which the members might be killed defending themselves. The presence of these references in his June 21 entry places the actual writing of the entry, or some parts of it, after February or March 1943.

5. There are some discrepancies in the death toll for this period of the ghetto's history. Arad concludes that the total number was 33,500, but for a fuller examination of the matter, see Arad, *Ghetto in Flames*, 209–17.

6. Ibid., 359, 360–61.

7. Rudashevski, *Diary of the Vilna Ghetto*, 149, 12.

8. Gabik Heller, a close friend of Yitskhok's, also kept a diary in the Vilna ghetto; see Appendix I.

9. See the entries for February 27, March 28, and April 5, 1943.

10. There were several consecutive orders regarding the badge identifying the Jews in Vilna. The first was issued on July 3, 1941, by German military commander Von Ostman of Vilna, requiring Jews to wear white armbands with a yellow Star of David on the right arm. It was followed on July 4 by a decree issued by the Lithuanian authorities ordering the Jews to wear a badge on the chest and shoulder. A few days later the new military governor, Zehnpfenning, decreed that Jews must wear a white armband with yellow star or yellow circle containing a "J." On August 2, the final decree was issued by Gebeitskommisar Hingst, the German head of the civil government in Vilna, requiring a yellow star on the chest and back shoulder. (Arad, *Ghetto in Flames*, 54–56, 94–95.)

11. During the "Great Provocation" of August 31 to September 2, 3,700 Jews from Vilna were taken to Ponar and murdered. (Ibid., 101–7.)

12. Yitskhok and his immediate family were in the so-called first ghetto. The "second ghetto" was smaller in size; the two were separated by Niemiecka Street and had separate entrances and exits, which were far apart to prevent contact between those imprisoned inside. The Germans frequently used the technique of creating multiple ghettos so that it would be easier to carry out repeated "selections," each time isolating those who were deemed fit to live from those slated for murder. (Ibid., 108.)

13. During the *aktion* [raid] of September 15, 1941, those without work permits were expelled from the first ghetto. According to Arad, 600 of them reached the second ghetto; 1,271 were taken to Ponar and murdered on September 17, 1941. (Ibid., 133–34.)

14. During the Yom Kippur aktion of October 1, 1941, which took place in both ghettos, 3,900 Jews were taken to Ponar and murdered. (Ibid., 137–39, 215.)

15. The liquidation of the second ghetto took place during three *aktionen* from October 3 to 21, 1941. Approximately 5,500 Jews were taken to Ponar and murdered. (Ibid., 139–42.)

16. The issuing of the "yellow certificates" took place in mid-October 1941. The distribution of passes was completed on October 23. (Ibid., 143–49.)

17. Rudashevski is referring to the distribution of blue slips to the holders of yellow passes, which took place on the evening of October 23, 1941. These people left the ghetto before the ensuing aktion of October 24–25. (Ibid., 149–50.)

18. During the course of this aktion, 3,781 Jews were taken to Ponar and murdered. (Ibid., 152.)

19. This is the aktion of October 29, 1941, in which 1,533 Jews were murdered at Ponar. (Ibid., 153.) It seems that Yitskhok and his family did not go to the second ghetto as they were supposed to but stayed illegally in the first ghetto. According to Arad, there were no searches in the first ghetto during that night, which accounts for their

survival. Yitskhok's uncle (Sore Voloshin's father) went to the second ghetto but hid in a maline and thus survived.

20. This was November 3–5, 1941, the so-called second "yellow-pass aktion," during which 1,532 Jews were taken to Ponar and murdered. (Ibid., 153–56.) Since only spouses and children could be registered on passes, Yiskhok's grandmother was not allowed to leave the ghetto. She was taken to Ponar and murdered.

21. The "pink-pass aktion" was the last one during this period. In early December pink passes were distributed, and on December 20–21 the aktion against those without pink passes was carried out. Four hundred Jews were murdered at Ponar. (Ibid., 161–63.)

22. The full text of Yitskhok's essay in memory of his teacher Gershteyn appears in Rudashevski, *Diary of the Vilna Ghetto*, Appendix A.

23. This is a play on words related to the Purim tradition of eating Hamantashn, a three-cornered cake named for the Persian minister Haman whose persecution of the Jews is recounted in the Book of Esther and who was ultimately defeated, bringing deliverance and renewed freedom.

8. Anonymous Girl

1. Lucjan Dobroszycki, ed., *Chronicle of the Łódź Ghetto, 1941–1944* (New Haven: Yale University Press, 1984), xxiii–xxv, xxxiv–xxxvi; Hilberg, *Destruction of the European Jews*, 205–14.

2. In particular, the diary of Dawid Sierakowiak, also written in the Łódź ghetto, reflects this struggle as it was played out between the diarist and his father. (Dawid Sierakowiak, *The Diary of Dawid Sierakowiak: Five Notebooks from the Łódź Ghetto*, edited by Alan Adelson, translated by Kamil Turowski [New York: Oxford University Press, 1996].)

3. Dobroszycki, ed., *Chronicle of the Łódź Ghetto*, 128, 133.

4. Ibid., xx.

5. Lucjan Dobroszycki, "Polska Anna Frank: Nazywała się?" [A Polish Anne Frank: Her Name Was?], *Mówią wieki* 7 (1958), 4–5.

6. Following the fragmentary undated entry at the beginning, the first dated entry, given in the diary as Friday, February 24, appears to have mistaken the date. The following entry is dated Saturday, February 28, followed by Sunday, March 1. All the rest of the entries are correctly and sequentially dated. It seems likely, therefore, that the correct date of the first dated entry is Friday, February 27.

9. Miriam Korber

1. Biographical information about Miriam Korber and her family comes from Miriam Korber Bercovici, *Jurnal de Ghetou; Djurin, Transnistria, 1941–1943* (Bucharest: Editura Kriterion, 1995) and from unpublished correspondence with Mrs. Bercovici.

2. Hilberg, *Destruction of the European Jews,* vol. 2, 759.
3. Radu Ioanid, *The Holocaust in Romania: The Destruction of Jews and Gypsies Under the Antonescu Regime, 1940–1944* (Chicago: Ivan R. Dee, in association with the United States Holocaust Memorial Museum, 2000), 4–14.
4. Ibid., 28, 19–23, 43–51; Paul A. Shapiro, "Prelude to Dictatorship in Romania: The National Christian Party in Power, December 1937–February 1938," *Canadian-American Slavic Studies* 8, no. 1 (Spring 1974), 72–73.
5. Bercovici, *Jurnal de Ghetou,* 114–15.
6. Hilberg, *Destruction of the European Jews,* 768–69; Ioanid, *Holocaust in Romania,* 155–70.
7. See Ioanid, *Holocaust in Romania,* chapters 5 and 6.
8. Ibid., 289–95.
9. Bercovici, *Jurnal de Ghetou,* 119–20.
10. In her diary, Miriam often referred to the brutally exploitative economy that existed in Transnistria and that allowed members of the local population to profit from the desperation of the Jews. Although very often people traded valuables for food or medicine, the value of money itself depended on many factors, including the availability of provisions, the prices set by local traders, and the strength of the black market. Often the inflation caused by a shortage of provisions made the most basic necessities far too expensive for the poorer ghetto dwellers. In Transnistria in December 1941, according to Miriam's diary, forty lei were worth about one ruble; in July 1942, sixty lei were worth about one mark.

10. Dawid Rubinowicz

1. Biographical information about Dawid and his family comes from Derek Bowman, introduction to *The Diary of Dawid Rubinowicz,* by Dawid Rubinowicz (Edmonds, Wash.: Creative Options Publishing, 1982), and from Maria Jarochowska, epilogue to *Pamiętnik Dawida Rubinowicza* (Warsaw: Książka i Wiedza, 1987; translated by Małgorzata Markoff).
2. Until beginning work on the new edition of *Salvaged Pages,* I did not have the full story about how Dawid's diaries were discovered. Thanks to Ewa Wymark, the editor of Bodzentyn.net, I learned more details. At some point between June 1942, when Dawid wrote his last entry, and September of the same year, when the ghetto was liquidated, Dawid left the five notebooks of his diary in the safekeeping of his Polish friend and next-door neighbor Tadeusz Waciński. The notebooks were later passed on to Antoni Waciński, together with some other school papers, and remained in the home for fifteen years, during which time the home was rented to Krystyna and Stefan Rachtan. In 1957, the owner of the home found the diaries while cleaning out the attic and passed them to Krystyna's father, Artemiusz Wołczyk, who was a former secretary of the Bodzentyn town council and director of a local radio station. Mr. Wołczyk and his wife, Helena, began reading the diaries out loud on the local radio. Two years later, in 1959, journalist Maria Jarochowska learned about the diaries, and in 1960 she published the first Polish edition, titled *Pamiętnik Dawida Rubinowicza.* Sadly, the whereabouts of the original manuscripts of Dawid's diary are currently unknown.

More information about the diary and images related to it can be found at Bodzentyn .net.

11. Elsa Binder

1. Andrea Axt led the first efforts to research and gather information about the diary of Elsa Binder and completed the first translation of it in English (in the archives of the Jewish Historical Institute in Warsaw). She generously shared her material with me (including copies of the original handwritten diary, details about the history of the diary and the identity of the diarist gathered from surviving members of Stanisławów's Jewish community, photographs of the diarist and her friends, as well as research about Stanisławów and copies of related diaries) and agreed to be interviewed at her home in Montreal. Consequently, all biographical information about Elsa Binder and her family, as well as knowledge of the history and provenance of the diary, comes from this source. Others who participated in various aspects of work on Elsa's diary and helped to pinpoint her identity include Karoliny Ely, Adam Rubaszewski, Aza Gilad (née Blumenstayn), and Pini Goldencail. The latter two are included in the photograph of the Hashomer Hazair youth group with Elsa.

   The only other diary from Stanisławów that has surfaced thus far was written by eleven-year-old Jerzy Feliks Urman; see Appendix I.

2. Hilberg, *Destruction of the European Jews,* vol. 2, 496.

   Karoliny Ely, a friend of Andrea Axt, translated the diary into Hebrew from the Polish original. After completing it, she shared it with Aza Gilad, a member of her kibbutz in Israel, who had also lived in Stanisławów. In reading the text, Aza Gilad realized that she knew who Eliszewa was and that in fact they had been in the same Zionist youth group in the prewar years. She was able to identify her as Elsa Binder and to clarify the identities of some of the people mentioned in the diary.

3. For this information, I am again indebted to Andrea Axt, who shared it with me based on a reading of the original diary.

4. *Encyclopedia Judaica,* s.v. "Stanisław."

5. Hilberg, *Destruction of the European Jews,* vol. 2, 496.

   According to Andrea Axt, the diary was found in the ditch in July 1943 by Karol Różycki, who was a teacher in the secondary school in Stanisławów. Toward the end of his life, Mr. Różycki gave the diary to the Kwaśniewski brothers, who were editors of the *Stanisławów Gazette.* They in turn gave it to Adam Rubaszewski, who made a Polish transcription of the diary and attempted to have it published in Poland to no avail. In October 1987, Mr. Rubaszewski gave the diary to Mrs. Axt, who ultimately donated it to the Jewish Historical Institute in Warsaw. The archives also hold a copy of the Polish transcription and Mrs. Axt's original English translation. Copies of the handwritten diary and the Polish transcription can be found on microfilm in the Collections of the United States Holocaust Memorial Museum in Washington, D.C. (*Pamiętniki Żydów,* 302/267.)

6. This refers to posters that were part of a massive German propaganda campaign to equate Jewry and Communism. This propaganda effort was designed to keep Ukrainians, who were to a certain degree anti-Soviet and also anti-Semitic, on the side of Nazism.

7. Simon Petlura was a nationalist Ukrainian leader held responsible for allowing mass killings and violent pogroms against Jews in towns throughout the Ukraine in 1919.

8. The reference here (and in the entry for May 14, 1942) is to a small group of Hungarian Jews who were incarcerated in the ghetto. They were among about 18,000 "foreign" Jews (Polish and Russian, as well as some Hungarian Jews who could not prove their citizenship) who were deported in July and August 1941 from Hungary and Carpatho-Ruthenia to the Kamanetz-Podolsk area in then German-held Ukraine. According to Randolph Braham, approximately 14,000 to 16,000 of these Jews were murdered by the Einsatzgruppen, together with 7,000 to 9,000 local Jews from the region. According to Raul Hilberg, several thousand of these Hungarian deportees were confined in the Stanisławów ghetto and were murdered during 1942. (Randolph L. Braham, *The Politics of Genocide: The Holocaust in Hungary* [New York: Rosenthal Institute for Holocaust Studies, 1994], 211, 213; Hilberg, *Destruction of the European Jews,* vol. 2, 810–12.)

9. The sense of "St." in the heading of this entry is unclear. The most obvious guess is that it stood for Sobota, or Saturday, but the entry is dated March 13, 1942, which was a Friday. It is possible that the writer misdated the heading (getting either the day of the week or the date wrong), which happens frequently in diaries of the period. It could also perhaps be an abbreviation for the writer's name or nickname.

10. The expression "gonzi li toyva," written out and in quotes in the original diary, is a version of "gam zu le-toyve," which is Hebrew but also used in Yiddish. Literally meaning "this, too, is for the best," the expression is used to indicate an optimistic outlook even when the news is not good. It could also be translated as "let's look on the bright side."

12. Ilya Gerber

1. Throughout *Salvaged Pages* and in other records relating to this diary, the writer is known as Ilya Gerber. However, I learned from my colleague Bret Werb, senior musicologist at the United States Holocaust Memorial Museum, that he should also be identified as Lusik Gerber, which is how the Vilna poet Shmerke Kaczerginski referred to him in his postwar anthology of ghetto songs. Indeed, the writer himself uses the diminutive Lyusik and the initials L.G. to refer to himself in his diary. Kaczerginski also writes that Ilya/Lusik was deported to Dachau and murdered there, which is more than I previously knew about his fate. Although we could not change his name throughout the new edition of the book, I am adding this note for the sake of clarity.

   The historian Dov Levin, a Kovno survivor who went to a Hebrew high school with Ilya Gerber prior to the war, recalls that he was tall, dark, and physically attractive, athletic and aggressive in team sports. He also remembers that Ilya was not a particularly strong student and that his primary interests were music, drawing, and girls—information that seems to be confirmed by the content of the diary. (Telephone conversation between Dov Levin and translator Solon Beinfeld.)

   For a short essay describing Ilya Gerber's diary and that of Tamara Lazerson Rostovsky, who also wrote in Kovno, and for excerpts of the diaries in English and excellent color reproductions of several pages of the diaries, see *The Hidden History of the Kovno Ghetto* (New York: Little, Brown, 1997), 172, 174, 179, 183, 192, 195–98.

2. Jürgen Matthäus, "Assault and Destruction," in *The Hidden History of the Kovno Ghetto* (New York: Little, Brown, 1997), 18; Avraham Tory, *Surviving the Holocaust: The Kovno Ghetto Diary*, ed. Martin Gilbert (Cambridge: Harvard University Press, 1990), 4–12, 23, 28.

3. William W. Mishell, *Kaddish for Kovno: Life and Death in a Lithuanian Ghetto, 1941–1945* (Chicago: Chicago Review Press, 1988), 381; Tory, *Surviving the Holocaust*, 17–18.

4. Tory, *Surviving the Holocaust*, 59; Solon Beinfeld, "Life and Survival," in *Hidden History of the Kovno Ghetto*, 32–33.

5. The surviving notebook is the third one. We know from Ilya's entry of October 13, 1942, that the first notebook contained an account of the Great Aktion of October 28, 1941, which means he was writing during the early months of the ghetto's existence. The first and second notebooks have been lost, as have any that Ilya might have kept subsequently.

6. The second volume of Ilya Gerber's songbook, together with his diary, is held in the archives of the Vilna Gaon Jewish Museum in Vilnius, Lithuania. Thanks to Bret Werb, senior musicologist at the United States Holocaust Memorial Museum, I learned that the great Vilna poet Shmerke Kaczerginski used Ilya's songbook in his research for his anthology of ghetto songs. In the introduction, Kaczerginski wrote, "A great many devoted friends, recognizing the importance of such a publication, spared no effort to help me with this collection of texts, melodies, and corresponding photos. I am honored to mention the martyr Lusik [Ilya] Gerber (deported from Kovno ghetto to Dachau, and murdered there), whose notebook of Kovno ghetto songs was found in the ghetto ruins after the war. These songs are included in the collection." (Shmerke Kaczerginski, *Lider fun di getos un lavern* [New York: CYCO, 1948], xxv.)

7. Tory, *Surviving the Holocaust*, 507; Beinfeld, "Life and Survival," 38–41.

8. Ilya's information about the content of these meetings is flawed, but Avraham Tory in his diary of the Kovno ghetto did mention (on August 14, 1942) visits by Cramer and others to the ghetto. Tory also mentioned high-level German consultations at Cramer's office the previous day concerning the future of the ghetto. (Tory, *Surviving the Holocaust*, 125, 124.)

9. Dr. Chaim Nachman Shapiro was actually the principal of the vocational school, and the founder and head of the Jewish Council's cultural department. (Tory, *Surviving the Holocaust*, 247.)

10. Leon (Leib) Garfunkel was the deputy chairman of the Jewish Council. (Tory, *Surviving the Holocaust*, 12.)

11. "The first 530" who were taken away refers to the roundup on August 18, 1941, of 534 members of the Jewish intelligentsia in Kovno. They were supposedly taken away to perform work in the municipal archives; in fact they were taken to the Ninth Fort and shot the same day. (Tory, *Surviving the Holocaust*, 33.) The dance records at Ilik's party were probably obtained through someone who worked at the Gestapo offices as a laborer.

12. Moshe Flinker's entries written during Hanukkah in 1942 (December 3 and 7, 1942) echo the sentiments of Ilya on this occasion.

13. Anonymous Boy

1. Dobroszycki, ed., *Chronicle of the Łódź Ghetto,* lx, xxxviii–xxxix, xx–xxi.
2. The writer's younger sister apparently kept a diary, too. Her name and identity are unknown and her diary is lost, except for a few surviving passages that her brother copied into his journal.
3. It appears that the diarist wrote simultaneously from the front of the book inward (left to right, as in English and Polish) and from the back of the book inward (right to left, as in Hebrew and Yiddish), so that the early entries written on the same date in different languages appear in the front of the book and at the end. In general, he seemed to continue this way so that he was writing from both directions simultaneously, moving progressively toward the middle of the book. Some entries appear randomly, out of this "order," but this structure exists to some degree throughout the whole diary. It seems likely that he wrote this way because he was (at least initially) looking for pages that had more white space in which to write and he was gradually was forced toward the center of the book.
4. Dobroszycki, ed., *Chronicle of the Łódź Ghetto,* 506.
5. Ibid., xx–xxv.
6. The news of this letter, mentioned in the diary on July 15, 1944, also appears in the Łódź Ghetto Chronicle entry for June 24, 1944. The chronicle indicates that a note found in one of the freight cars reported that the train had stopped at Kutno, thirty-three kilometers from Łódź, where the deportees were unloaded into passenger cars. The chroniclers speculated that perhaps a "further transportation is being staged in Kutno," though they also acknowledged that the news had given rise to renewed anxiety and rumors in the ghetto. (Dobroszycki, ed., *Chronicle of the Łódź Ghetto,* 514–15.)
7. Ibid., lxiv–lxvi.
8. "The Unknown Diarist of the Łódź Ghetto," *Jerusalem Post,* May 3, 1970.
9. Entry dates appear as the author wrote them in the European form, beginning with the day, followed by the month (sometimes in Roman numerals), and ending with the year. The diary entries were not written in sequential order in the original text, but for the sake of clarity they have been arranged chronologically in this edition. The diarist's English entries have been transcribed as he wrote them and marked *sic* where necessary. Corrections essential to the comprehension of the diary appear in square brackets.
10. The heading for this entry appears to read 3/4 [April 3], but its placement in the original diary between entries dated 2/7 [July 2] and 3/7 [July 3] suggests that it was in fact written on July 3 and that the entry was misdated by the diarist.

14. Alice Ehrmann

1. Biographical information about Alice Ehrmann (Alisa Shek) and her family comes from the introduction and endnotes to the German edition of her diary (written by Mrs. Shek and Miroslav Kárný, and translated by Kenneth Kronenberg) and from unpublished correspondence with Mrs. Alisa Shek.
2. Alisa Shek, letter to editor, January 30, 2000. For more about Ze'ev Shek, see Redlich, *Terezín Diary,* 13, 78n; and Berkley, *Hitler's Gift,* 112, 156, 194, 214, 258, 261.
3. Shek, letter to editor, January 30, 2000. Mrs. Shek and Mr. Kárný provided detailed notes to the German publication of the diary in which they explicated many of the events mentioned. Further, Mrs. Shek reviewed the English translation of the diary, clarifying many passages and notations. Still, despite her extensive knowledge of the history of Terezín, she acknowledged that even she could not always remember or clarify the meaning of phrases or entries in her diary. (Shek, letter to editor, March 22, 1999.)
4. Berkley, *Hitler's Gift,* 222.
5. Ibid., 189, 205.
6. Ibid., 209–10.
7. Ibid., 229–30, 164–79.
8. Ibid., 234–35.
9. Eva Ginzová also vividly described the prisoners arriving in Terezín. See in particular her entry dated April 23, 1945.
10. Berkley, *Hitler's Gift,* 240–43.
11. Shek, letter to editor, January 30, 2000.
12. Moshe Flinker's diary (Chapter 4), embodies the first perspective described here, "the one that awaits the Messiah, that prepares for a birth with all their reserved strength."
13. Alice took the documents that Ze'ev had collected in Terezín back to Prague with her after the liberation. Shortly after returning to Prague from the camps in the summer of 1945, Ze'ev established a project to gather additional documents from the ghetto. One year later, he transferred the material to the National Library in Israel for safe-keeping. In 1976, Ze'ev donated the papers to Yad Vashem, where they are held as the Ze'ev Shek Collection.
14. See Berkley, *Hitler's Gift,* 233–34.

Appendix II: At the Margins

1. S. L. Shneiderman, preface to *Warsaw Ghetto,* by Mary Berg (New York: L. B. Fischer, 1945), 9.
2. Alisah Schiller, Beit Theresienstadt, letter to editor, July 6, 1997. A few fragments of Charlotte Verešová's diary, apparently the only surviving pages from the original diary, were published in *Terezín,* edited by František Ehrmann et al. (Prague: Council of Jewish Communities, 1965). Her diary-memoir can be found in the archives of Beit Theresienstadt, Givat Chaim Ichud, Israel.
3. Leo W. Schwarz, *The Root and the Bough: The Epic of an Enduring People* (New York: Rinehart, 1949), 277. Schwarz included a few pages of the text in English (un-

der the name Yanka Heszeles), entitled "As I Remember," in *The Root and the Bough;* Laurel Holliday included a short translation of several of the same pages (under the name Janina Heshele) in her book *Children in the Holocaust and World War II,* taken from a translation by Azriel Eisenberg in his work, *The Lost Generation: Children of the Holocaust.* There are small but significant discrepancies between the two translations; Schwarz's contains no present tense passages, suggesting that the entire text was written or revised while the diarist was in hiding in Cracow; Eisenberg's translation overlaps with Schwarz's but some passages are translated in the present tense, suggesting that at least part of it was written contemporaneously.

A typescript of the manuscript (under the name Janina Hescheles) can be found in the archives of the Jewish Historical Institute, Warsaw (Pamiętniki Żydów, 302/24) and in the microfilm collections of the United States Holocaust Memorial Museum under the same designation. The "diary" was published in Polish (also under the name Janina Hescheles) as *Oczyma dwunastoletniej dziewczyny* [Through the Eyes of a Twelve-Year-Old Girl] (Cracow: Cracow Jewish Historical Commission, 1946). A copy of it can be found in the Library of Congress.

4. Fondo Guido Lopez, Archive CDEC, Milan, Italy; Yona Melaron, 033/787, YV Archives, Israel; Michael Kraus, telephone conversation with editor, March 19, 1994. A copy of the Kraus diary in Czech can be found under the title *Pod nem nadvladou* [Under German Yoke] in the archives of Beit Theresienstadt, Givat Chaim Ichud.

5. Macha Rolnikas (also called Maria or Masha Rolnikaite), telephone conversation with editor, via translator, February 4, 1997. This account contradicts the report in Laurel Holliday's *Children in the Holocaust and World War II,* which says that the diarist "found the early parts of her diary where she had hidden them and was able to put them together with what she had written since deportation" (pp. 185–86), which implies that the surviving text is the original diary rather than a rewriting of it. Although there has apparently been some confusion about the nature of this text as a diary-memoir, it was published in French with a foreword by Ilya Ehrenberg that states very clearly that the diary was rewritten after the liberation. Ilya Ehrenberg, foreword to *Je devais le raconter (ce qu'Anne Frank n'a pu pas dire)* [I Must Tell You: What Anne Frank Was Not Able to Say] by Macha Rolnikas (Paris: Les Editeurs Français Réunis, 1966), 8.

6. Judah Marton, introduction to *The Diary of Éva Heyman: Child of the Holocaust,* by Éva Heyman, translated from Hebrew by Moshe M. Kohn (Jerusalem: Yad Vashem, 1988), 16–17. In 2014, at Yad Vashem, I met Gabriel Mayer, M.D., who is a scholar in Holocaust Studies at the University of Haifa. He was preparing a paper to deliver to the American Jewish Studies Conference in Baltimore, Md., in December of the same year about Éva's diary, the Hungarian edition of which he has compared with the Hebrew and English translations. He believes the diary is entirely authentic and an important contribution to adolescent writings of this period. While it is very difficult to establish the authenticity of a diary when the original manuscript is lost, Dr. Mayer presents an alternative explanation for the diary's linguistic peculiarities, and his scholarship adds to an understanding of the controversy surrounding it.

7. Ibid.

8. Louise Jacobson, *Les Lettres de Louise Jacobson et de ses proches, Fresnes, Drancy*

1942–1943 (Paris: Editions Robert Laffont, 1997); Peter Schwiefert, *The Bird Has No Wings* (London: Search Press, 1976); the letters of Hertha Aussen, in the archives of Herinneringscentrum Kamp Westerbork [Museum Camp Westerbork], Netherlands; the original letters of Gita Hojtašová and rough English translations, in the archives of the Museum of Jewish Heritage, New York (Kauffman/Pinsky Collection).

9. Aleksander Demajo "diary" (3407, K26-9-2/3, Jewish Historical Museum, Federation of Jewish Communities in Yugoslavia, Belgrade).

Moshe Kravec's prose and poetry were buried, together with other documents and photographs, in a bunker underneath the Kravecs' ghetto house. His mother returned to Kovno after the war and recovered the box. Moshe was able to hand-copy all of his writings after the war, which are in a private collection. He sent the originals to an archive, but their whereabouts are not currently known.

10. Dirk van der Heide [pseud.], *My Sister and I* (New York: Harcourt Brace Jovanovich, 1941); Tomi Ungerer, *Tomi: A Childhood Under the Nazis* (Boulder: Roberts Rinehart, 1998); Colin Perry, *Boy in the Blitz* (London: Leo Cooper, 1972); Joan Wyndham, *Love Lessons: A Wartime Diary* (London: William Heinemann, 1985); *The Girl from Kashin: Soviet Women in [the] Resistance in World War II*, edited and translated by K. J. Cottam (Manhattan, Kan.: MA/AH Publishers, 1984); *The Diary of Nina Kosterina*, translated by Mirra Ginsburg (New York: Crown, 1968); Janine Phillips, *My Secret Diary* (London: Shepheard-Walwyn, 1982); and Maria Ginter, *Life in Both Hands,* translated by P. C. Blauth-Muszowski (London: Hodder and Stoughton, 1964). Information in English about the diaries of Jerzy Wolski and Jerzy Świderski can be found in Richard C. Lukas, *Did the Children Cry? Hitler's War Against Jewish and Polish Children, 1939–1945* (New York: Hippocrene, 1994), 12, 14, 135–36. The text of both diaries in Polish can be found in Marian Turski, *Byli wówczas dziećmi* (Warsaw: Książka i Wiedza, 1980).

Two important volumes published since the first edition of *Salvaged Pages* bear particular mention here. First is *Hilke's Diary: Germany, July 1940–August 1945*, translated and edited by the author's sister, Geseke Clark, and published by the History Press in 2009. In 1940, Hilke, a German teenager, was evacuated from her hometown of Hamburg to avoid the Allied bombings and went to live with her aunt and uncle in Meisenheim; in 1942, she was sent to live on an estate in the country; and in 1944, she was sent to a boarding school in Lake Constance. When the war ended, Hilke walked back to Hamburg, describing her difficult journey in her diary. The perspective captured in her diary of a German teenager—one who participated in the Hitler Youth and viewed the Allies as her enemies—offers an important and unfamiliar view of coming of age during the war years in Germany. Second, Sarah Wallis and Svetlana Palmer edited a collection titled *We Were Young and At War: The First-Hand Story of Young Lives Lived and Lost in World War II* (London: Collins, 2009), which includes a significant number of previously unpublished diaries and letters by young non-Jews during World War II. Many of the diaries and letters in this collection were unknown to me, and they are meticulously researched and carefully presented. It is one of the few sources in English for diaries and letters by non-Jewish adolescents in Europe and the Pacific; as such, it makes an important contribution to our overall understanding of the lives of young people during World War II.

11. Inge Jens, ed., *At the Heart of the White Rose: Letter and Diaries of Hans and Sophie Scholl* (New York: Harper and Row, 1987); and Kim Malthe-Bruun, *Heroic Heart: The Diary and Letters of Kim Malthe-Bruun, 1941–1945,* edited by Vibeke Malthe-Bruun, translated by Gerry Bothmer (New York: Random House, 1955).

12. The diary was found in the Hazkelson apartment by a soldier of the invading German army during the summer of 1941. This soldier, whose identity is unknown, sent it to a friend in Berlin, who in turn entrusted it to his own daughters. The original diary and an English translation, made by Mr. Ernie Meyer in September 1987, are in the holdings of Yad Vashem, Jerusalem, Israel (033/2187, YV Archives, Israel). See "The Diary of Anni," *Jerusalem Post,* November 28, 1986, and "Anni X Gets a Surname," *Jerusalem Post,* December 12, 1986.

13. Hannah Senesh, *Hannah Senesh: Her Life and Diary* (New York: Schocken, 1971), 2–3.

14. Etty Hillesum, *An Interrupted Life: The Diaries of Etty Hillesum, 1941–1943* (New York: Pocket, 1981) and *Letters from Westerbork,* translated by Arnold J. Pomerans (New York: Pantheon, 1986); Lilly Isaacs diary, 1995.88, United States Holocaust Memorial Museum collections, Washington, D.C.; Selma Engel diary (private collection); Aba Gefen, *Hope in Darkness: The Aba Gefen Holocaust Diaries,* translated from the Hebrew by Ina Friedman (New York: Holocaust Library, 1989).

15. Tereska Torrès, *Une Française libre: Journal, 1939–1945* (Paris: Editions Phébus, 2000), 30; translation by the editor. According to her published journal, which is fascinating and well worth reading, Tereska began writing her first diary at age nine.

Sources and Translators

1. Klaus Langer: Excerpts translated and published with the permission of Mr. Jacob (Klaus) Langer. The English translation was made by Gerald Liebenau and authenticated by Mr. Langer.
2. Elisabeth Kaufmann: Excerpts translated and published with the permission of Mrs. Elizabeth Koenig (née Elisabeth Kaufmann) and the United States Holocaust Memorial Museum, Washington, D.C., which houses the diary and holds the copyright to it. The English translation was made by Gerald Liebenau and authenticated by Mrs. Koenig.
3. Peter Feigl: Excerpts of the English translation, made by Mr. Peter Feigl in 1993, published with his permission. In 1998, Mr. Feigl provided extensive annotations to the English translation of the diary, which, with the permission of the author, have been modified by the editor for this volume.
4. Moshe Flinker: Originally published in Hebrew under the title *Hana'ar Moshe— Yomano shel Moshe Flinker* [The Lad Moses: The Diary of Moses Flinker] (Jerusalem: Yad Vashem, 1958). Subsequently published in English, Yiddish, and Italian. Excerpts from the English edition, entitled *Young Moshe's Diary: The Spiritual Torment of a Jewish Boy in Nazi Europe,* by Moshe Flinker (Jerusalem: Yad Vashem, 1971), reprinted with the permission of Yad Vashem and the family of Moshe Flinker.
5. Otto Wolf: Excerpts of the English translation, made by Michael Kubat, published with the permission of Mrs. Felicitas Garda (née Wolfová), Otto Wolf's sister.
6. Petr Ginz and Eva Ginzová: Excerpts of both diaries translated and published with the permission of Mrs. Chava Pressburger (née Eva Ginzová). The English translations were made by Ivo Řezníček and authenticated by Mrs. Pressburger.
7. Yitskhok Rudashevski: Excerpts from *The Diary of the Vilna Ghetto,* by Yitskhok Rudashevski (Israel: Ghetto Fighters' House, 1973), reprinted with the permission of the United States Holocaust Memorial Museum. The English translation was made by Percy Matenko.
8. Anonymous Girl (Esterka or Minia): Translated and published with the permission of the Jewish Historical Institute, Warsaw. The English translation was made by Małgorzata Markoff.
9. Miriam Korber: Excerpts translated from Miriam Korber Bercovici, *Jurnal de Ghetou: Djurin, Transnistria, 1941–1943* (Bucharest: Editura Kriterion, 1995), and published in English with the permission of Mrs. Miriam Korber Bercovici. The translation was made by Julie Donat.

10. Dawid Rubinowicz: Excerpts from *The Diary of Dawid Rubinowicz,* © 1982 Norman Bolotin, reprinted courtesy of Laing Communications, Inc., Redmond, Washington, and Edmonton, Alberta. Originally translated into English by Derek Bowman, University of Edinburgh, Scotland. With the permission of the publisher, Scottish terms and expressions have been replaced with American ones and minor corrections to the translation have been made.

11. Elsa Binder: Excerpts translated and published with the permission of the Jewish Historical Institute, Warsaw. Originally translated into English by Andrea Axt. Translated into English for this volume by Malgorzata Markoff.

12. Ilya Gerber: Excerpts translated and published with the permission of the Vilna Gaon Jewish Museum, Vilnius, Lithuania. The English translation was made by Dr. Solon Beinfeld.

13. Anonymous Boy: Excerpts translated and published with the permission of Yad Vashem. The English translation was made by Dana Keren.

14. Alice Ehrmann: Excerpts translated and published with the permission of Alisa Shek (née Alice Ehrmann). The English translation was made by Kenneth Kronenberg from Alisa Shek, "Ein Theresienstädter Tagebuch 18 Oktober 1944–19 Mai 1945," *Theresienstädter Studien und Dokumente 1994,* ed. Miroslav Kárný, Raimund Kemper, and Margita Kárná (Prague: Verlag Academia, 1994), 169–205. Mrs. Shek and Mr. Kárný provided an introduction to the German edition of the diary and included extensive endnotes, which, with the author's permission, have been modified for this volume by the editor.

Index of Names

Cohn, Lilly (later Lillyan Rosenberg), 426
Cramer, Hans, 336, 472n.8

Demajo, Aleksander, 450
Diamant, David, 68
Diament, Věra, 426–27
Dobroszycki, Lucjan, 230, 468n.5, 473n.6
Dunant, Paul, 421
Dwork, Debórah, 426, 444

Ecséri, Lilla. *See* Kánitz, Lilla
Ehrmann, Alice (later Alisa Shek),
    403–23, 448; on arrival in Terezín of
    death camp survivors, 401, 414–16, 417,
    418; on deportations from Terezín,
    396–97, 403–5; on deportations to
    Terezín, 397, 407–8, 410; on despair,
    397, 398, 405, 407; and Erez Israel,
    402, 403, 404; on hope, 396, 398–99,
    409; on liberation, 396, 401–2, 416,
    417–23; on Nazis' efforts to conceal
    evidence, 399–400, 405–6, 407, 410,
    411–12, 413; relationship with Ze'ev
    Shek, 395–96, 402, 416, 417; on testify-
    ing, 399, 406; on transports to Swit-
    zerland, 398, 408–9, 410; on war news,
    410, 413; Ze'ev's documents preserved
    by, 412, 474n.13
Ehrmann, Ruth, 395, 402, 403, 421, 422
Eisinger, Professor Valtr, 464–65n.6
Elkes, Dr. Elkhanan, 330
Engel, Selma, 452
Esh, Shaul, 91, 461n.1, 462nn.7 and 9

Feigl, Peter, 69–89, 91, 452; and Catholi-
    cism, 63, 67–68, 73, 85, 91, 459n.2,
    460n.14, 461n.18; in Claparède refugee
    camp, 67; at Collège Champillion in
    Figeac, 66–67, 79–87, 456n.20; escape
    into Switzerland, 67–68, 87–89,
    461n.21; fate of parents of, 65, 67,
    69–71; first diary of, 64–65, 68, 69–79;
    hiding from French police, 65, 69, 71,
    73; in Les Caillols refuge for children,
    66, 74–77, 460n.16; at Les Grillons in

Le Chambon sur Lignon, 66, 77–79,
    458n.4, 460n.4, 461–62n.17; second
    diary of, 67, 79–80; in summer camp
    at Château de Montéléone in Con-
    dom, 64, 69, 460n.4
Feigl family, 63, 64, 65, 459nn.1 and 2
Fishkin, Sarah, 427
Flinker, Moshe Ze'ev, 6, 98–121, 445,
    474n.12; on Allies, 103, 104, 107–8, 109,
    113, 115, 118–19; on anti-Semitism, 114,
    118; on deportations from Brussels,
    110–11, 113, 115, 119; on despair, 108,
    112, 114, 115, 116, 117–18, 120; on guilt,
    110, 112, 113, 115–17, 121, 462n.7; on
    Hanukkah, 103, 105–6, 473n.12; on
    knowledge of mass murder, 107–8,
    401, 462n.6; on merit and sin, 111, 119;
    passing as a non-Jew, 90–91, 100; on
    persecution of Jews, 100–102, 105, 108,
    461n.3; on plans for the future, 104–5,
    117; on redemption of Jews, 102–3, 104,
    108, 109, 114, 115, 117, 119–20, 461n.3;
    on study of Arabic, 107, 110, 117;
    on war news, 100, 103, 109, 113, 115,
    118–19, 120
Flinker family, 90, 97, 99, 461n.1, 462nn.9
    and 10
Frank, Anne, 1–8, 364, 427–28, 455–56n.9
Frank, Karl Hermann, 410, 411
Frank, Otto, 1, 427
Frazier, Raymonde. *See* Nowodworski,
    Raymonde
Fry, Varian, 458n.5

Gabik. *See* Heller, Gabik
Gandis. *See* Zdařil, Mr.; Zdařilová, Mrs.
Garfunkel, Leon (Leib), 338, 472n.10
Gefen, Aba, 452
Gerber, Ilya, 330–60, 471–72n.1, 472n.5;
    arrest of, 332, 335, 357–59; drawings
    and sketches in diary of, 333–34;
    on the ghetto beach, 331, 339–40;
    on ghetto life, 331, 332–33, 336–37,
    352, 354–55; on ghetto rumors, 333,
    335–36, 348, 349–50; on hanging of

Meck, 333, 334, 353–54; on Hanukkah, 355; on murder of Jews, 348–49; on music, 333, 356–57, 472n.6; on parties and social life, 331, 340–41, 347, 472n.11; on Policeman's Chorus, 352–53, 359; on privilege, 330–31, 332, 335, 337–38, 359, 472n.10; on relationship with Heni, 334, 341, 342–46, 351; on swearing in of ghetto police, 333, 351; on war news, 355; on work, 330, 337, 338–39, 351–52

Gershteyn, Yankev, 193, 207, 211, 214, 468n.22

Gierszowski, Pinchas, 375

Gies, Miep, 427

Ginter, Maria, 450

Ginz, Miloš, 161, 166, 182, 464n.4, 465–66n.13

Ginz, Otto, 160, 161, 166, 464–65n.6

Ginz, Pavel, 160, 161, 165, 166

Ginz, Petr, 167–74; artistic interests of, 163, 164, 464–65n.6; deported to Terezín, 161, 395; diary kept by, 163, 164–65, 167–69, 463–64n.1; educational goals of, 165, 464–65n.6; and Eva, 168, 169, 173; plans and reports recorded by, 163–64, 166, 169–74, 465n.12; and *Vedem*, 165, 166, 170, 171

Ginz family, 160, 463–64n.1, 464n.4

Ginzová, Eva, 174–89, on arrival of father in Terezín, 180, 184, 185; on arrival in Terezín of death camp survivors, 187–88, 465n.11; on deportations from Terezín, 165, 175, 179, 181, 465n.11; on illnesses, 176, 178; and Judaism, 178; and liberation, 188; on loneliness and homesickness, 176–77, 182; and Petr, 165, 166–67, 176, 178, 179–80, 181, 182, 183, 185, 188; Petr's diary found by, 181–82; on work, 182, 183–84, 184–85

Ginzová, Hanka, 160, 161, 162, 165, 166, 464n.4

Gissing, Vera. *See* Diament, Věra

Glück, Irena, 428

Glucksman, Mina (later Mina Perlberger), 428–29

Goebbels, Joseph, 115

Goldtsman, Riva, 429

Graver, Lawrence, 2, 5, 455n.2

Grinberg, Yehoshua (Ika), 332, 335, 357, 358

Günther, Hans, 181, 405

Hácha, Emile, 151

Haindl, Rudolf, 184, 403, 408, 413, 414, 417

Hanka. *See* Ginzová, Hanka

Harsanyi, Zimra (later Ana Novac), 429

Hazkelson, Anni, 451, 477n.12

Heller, Gabik, 212–14, 429

Heller, Moyshe, 213, 429

Hescheles, Janina, 447–48, 474–75n.3

Heshele, Janina. *See* Hescheles, Janina

Hessen, Edith van (later Edith Velmans), 430

Heszeles, Yanka. *See* Hescheles, Janina

Heydrich, Reinhard, 123, 161

Heyman, Éva, 448–49, 475n.6

Hilberg, Raul, 459n.2, 462n.6, 471n.8

Hillesum, Etty, 451

Hilsenrath, Susi (later Susan Warsinger), 430

Himmler, Heinrich, 23

Hirsch, Fredy, 396

Hitler, Adolf, 6, 33, 49, 122, 188, 306; in the Anonymous Boy's diary, 383, 386–87, 388; in Moshe Flinker's diary, 106, 111, 114; in Otto Wolf's diary, 134, 146, 151

Hofmo, Gunvor, 435

Hojtašová, Gita, 450

Holliday, Laurel, 6, 427, 474–75n.3, 475n.5

Hošková, Helga. *See* Weissová, Helga

Isaacs, Lilly, 452

Jacobson, Louise, 6, 449–50

Jacoby, Ingrid. *See* Pollak, Inga

Marton, Dr. Judah, 448
McKissack, Patricia, 6
Melaron, Yona, 448
Mendele (Sholem-Yankev Abramovitsh), 192, 218
Meyer, Anita (later Anita Budding), 436–37
Murer, Franz, 218–19
Murmelstein, Dr. Benjamin, 409, 413, 414
Mussolini, Benito, 52
Musy, Benoit, 400
Musy, Jean Marie, 400

Natkin, Karl, 347
Nelken, Halina, 437
Novac, Ana. *See* Harsanyi, Zimra
Nowodworski, Raymonde (later Raymonde Frazier), 437–38

Ohera, Mr., 152, 154, 155, 156, 157
Oherová, Mrs., 152, 153, 154, 155, 157
Oleyski, Jacob, 337
Ornstein, Elisabeth (later Elisabeth M. Orsten), 438
Orsten, Elisabeth M. *See* Ornstein, Elisabeth

Pankiewicz, Tadeusz, 428
Pavel. *See* Ginz, Pavel
Perlberger, Mina. *See* Glucksman, Mina
Perry, Colin, 450
Petlura, Simon, 318, 471n.7
Phillips, Janine, 448
Pinkhof, Adèle Louise (Detje), 438–39
Pluhař, Alois, 125, 126, 133, 136–37, 138, 139–41, 142, 144, 146, 150, 153, 154
Pollacková, Helga (later Helga Kinsky), 439
Pollak, Inga (later Inga Joseph), 439–40

Rahm, Karl: in diary of Alice Ehrmann, 400, 408, 413, 414, 417; in diary of Eva Ginzová, 181, 465n.11; in diary of Petr Ginz, 169
Ranasinghe, Anne. *See* Katz, Anneliese
Rauca, Helmut, 336

Redlich, Gonda, 396
Rolnikas, Macha (also called Maria or Masha Rolnikaite), 448, 475n.5
Rosenberg, Lillyan. *See* Cohn, Lilly
Rostovsky, Tamara. *See* Lazerson, Tamara
Roubíčková, Eva. *See* Mándlová, Eva
Rozenberg, Lena. *See* Jedwab, Leja
Rubinowicz, Dawid, 6, 271–300, 469–70n.2; on arrest of father, 273, 275, 294–95; on exploitation of Jews by Germans, 272–73, 279, 281–82, 283–84, 285, 288, 290–91, 292–93; on exploitation of Jews by Poles, 273–74, 280, 281, 284, 286–87, 288, 294; on family tensions, 275, 293–94; father in Skarżysko Kamienna labor camp, 275–76, 296–300; on forced labor, 273, 280–81, 286–87, 288; on move to ghetto, 274, 289–90; on murder of Jews, 274–75, 282, 283, 284, 286, 290, 291, 299, 300; on oppression of Poles by Germans, 273; on raids by German police, 272, 278–79, 287, 291, 295–96
Rudashevski, Yitskhok, 191, 197–225, 429; awareness of mass murder of Jews, 193, 195, 196, 199, 204, 205, 207, 210, 224–25, 401, 466n.4, 467nn.5 and 11; commitment to Communism and the Soviet Union, 195, 197, 211–12, 222; first part of diary of (June–December 1941), 191, 193–94, 197–205, 460n.3; on imposition of badges worn by Jews, 199, 467n.10; on intellectual and cultural life of ghetto youth, 208, 210–11, 212, 214–15, 218, 219, 220–21, 222, 223; on Jewish ghetto police, 201, 209–10, 219; on the Lithuanians, 198; on the passage of time, 216–17; and the pioneer project (secret youth group), 195, 221–22, 224, 225, 466n.4; second part of diary of, 206–25; on self as a writer, 211, 468n.22; on war news, 195, 205, 215, 221, 222; on the Yom Kippur aktion, 201, 467n.14; and the Young Pioneers, 195, 197
Rumkowski, Mordechai Chaim, 238, 374

Index of Subjects

Dachau, 402, 433, 444, 462n.11

daily life: family tensions, 133, 135, 138, 238, 254, 256, 259, 293–94, 316–17; hunger in, 227–28, 230, 233; routine in, 42, 54, 79–83, 163, 253, 276–77, 381–82, 436, 437; in Vilna ghetto, 215; weather conditions, 130, 133–34, 153, 156, 157, 158, 199, 225, 232. *See also* cultural life; education; living conditions; schools

death: anonymity of, 250, 260–62, 266, 280; apathy toward, 252, 280, 308, 382; brutality of, 316, 420, 445; of collaborators, 312–13; for death camp survivors in Terezín, 422; desperation of the living, 314–16; disrespect for, 323, 399, 405–6; fear of, 55, 262, 266, 282; of friends, 314–15; of ghetto residents, 259, 442; of grandparents, 182, 260–62, 323–24, 327; hanging, 353–54; humor in the face of, 309; from hunger, 230, 235, 322, 442; indifference to, 241, 252, 262–63, 303, 316, 325; of parents, 213–14; reality of, 353–54, 378; selections for roundups, 270, 325–27, 348–49; of sister, 305–6, 325; Sonderkommando, 445; by starvation, 227–28, 235, 442; by suicide, 376, 382–83, 443; symbols of, 319; of teachers, 207, 213–14; in Transnistria, 245–46; treatment of bodies, 257, 280, 300, 303, 314, 323, 399, 445; urns of human remains, 399, 405–7; in Vilna ghetto, 203–4, 207, 213–14; wish for, 241, 263–64, 266, 303, 311, 322, 376, 381, 384–85, 393; work assignments as, 373, 374

death camp survivors, treatment of, 401–2, 415–16, 422

deception, fear of, 127, 131–32, 133, 135, 136, 146, 149, 154, 156, 463n.6

deportations: as death, 362, 373, 374, 375, 383, 384; exemptions from, 39–40, 49–50, 229, 232–33; for labor, 372–73, 374; from Łódź ghetto, 231; privileged mixed marriages, 160, 180, 395; ru-

mors of, 104, 110–11, 249–50, 262, 277, 373, 382; safe returns to the ghetto, 398–99; *Shperre,* 361, 365, 388, 435; suspension of, 383, 384; from Terezín (Thereisenstadt), 165, 175, 179, 181, 465n.11; to Terezín ghetto, 161–63; to Transnistria, 245–46; uncertainty, 377, 378–79; from Vilna ghetto, 203–4; witnesses to, 289

deprivation, 322; changes in economic status, 38, 40, 42, 43, 45–46, 48; children's, 25–26, 289–90, 293, 320–21, 372–73, 375, 377, 394; of comfort, 256; of death camp survivors, 415–16; of dreams, 312, 394; of grandparents' love, 260–62; in hiding, 129–30, 132, 133, 134, 140; hunger, 219, 227, 231, 234–38, 239–42; loss of dignity, 139, 141, 151, 177, 231, 245, 248–53, 263; loss of homes, 25–26, 251, 289–90, 293, 394, 403–4; sale of personal possessions, 17, 48, 242, 249, 251–52, 284–85, 289, 292, 296, 308

despair: after liberation, 402, 419–23, 442; aftermath of Vilna ghetto pogrom, 199–200, 203–5, 208; annihilation of the Jewish people, 359–61; bureaucracy of emigration, 26–28; of children, 112, 165–67, 179–80, 183, 262–63, 394; deportations, 165–67, 179–81, 373–74; food rations, 219, 227, 231, 234–38, 239–42; homelessness, 61, 162, 180, 397, 421, 438; homesickness, 176–77, 182, 252, 397; humiliation in Vilna ghetto, 218–19; idleness, 31, 76, 77, 100, 104, 117, 255; lack of correspondence, 9, 69–70, 71, 76, 77, 263; of the living, 291–93, 314–16; loneliness, 64, 116–17, 162, 176–77, 182–83, 260–61, 265, 279, 309, 431, 432; lost youth, 217, 311, 362, 363, 374; mass murders, 224–25; of new arrivals to ghetto, 194–95, 199–200, 397, 404, 407–8, 410, 414–18; news of murders of Jews, 108, 109; options for emigration, 24, 25, 26; over arrests, 155–56;

despair (*continued*)

physical weakness, 264; prayers, —105–6, 118; rumors of repatriation, 268, 269, 270; separations from family, 22, 39, 40, 43–44, 49, 54, 57–62, 77, 110, 155–58, 162–63; unemployment, 277

destruction of evidence by Nazis, 399–400, 412, 413

diaries: ages of authors, 13, 67, 272, 426, 427, 429, 431, 432, 434, 440, 443, 451–52; artwork in, 333–34, 355, 356; authenticity of, 448–49, 475n.6; badges, 90, 98, 129, 161, 194, 199, 434, 467n.10; biographical information in, 13, 34–35, 63, 98, 320–21, 362, 425–46; chronologies of, 44, 193–94, 362; as collections of letters, 449–50; confiscation of, 66; dating of, 451, 466n.4; diary genre defined, 447; as forbidden, 430; gaps in, 34, 120, 178, 369, 426, 432; historical context of, 8–11, 193–94; as hybrid texts, 429, 447; language of, 13, 37, 77, 93, 361, 363, 366–67, 371–72, 429; memoirs compared with, 426, 447–48, 449, 450, 453; as multi-authored works, 155–59, 305, 320–23, 445–46; need for expression, 6, 116–17, 302; non-Jewish authors of, 450–51; poems in, 381; postwar recollections in, 447, 449; question of merit and sin in, 92, 95, 101–3, 111, 119–20; ration lists in, 227–28, 231, 237–38, 239–40, 241–42; readers of, 184, 186, 236, 305, 374; recovery of, 68, 306, 309, 368, 425, 427, 428, 430, 432, 433, 434, 441, 442, 448, 469n.2, 470n.5; reviews of, 2–5; short stories in, 185, 438–39, 450; of siblings, 380–81, 473n.2; social discrimination in, 19, 21, 23, 26, 38, 41, 45–46, 68, 79–81, 90, 98, 106, 277, 321; styles of, 11, 64–65, 124–25, 163, 356, 361, 362, 449, 473n.3; translations of, 428, 429, 445, 448; trauma of reading

diaries, 181–82, 248; xenophobia, 39, 40, 41, 49, 60, 64

diarists: ages of, 13, 67, 161, 272, 426, 427, 429, 434, 440, 443, 451–52; arrests of, 155–56; awareness of political situation, 32–33, 44, 49–56, 75, 94–95, 400–401; as bearing witness, 367, 371–72, 390, 391, 393, 396, 406–7; biographical information, 13, 34–35, 37, 63, 98, 190, 302, 320–21, 362, 425–46; condemnation of humanity, 119, 364, 374; German identity of, 14, 443; historical perspectives of, 91–92, 101–3, 461n.3; identification of, 301–2, 470n.1; intent of, 23, 93, 363, 367, 368, 372, 391; mental state of, 374, 378–79; record of daily hunger, 227–28; reflections on life in Paris, 53–54; religious identity of, 14, 63, 67–69, 76, 81, 91–96, 122, 395, 426, 431, 432, 443, 452–53, 459n.2; self-description of, 3–4, 34, 44, 48, 211, 302, 310–11, 313, 322, 369, 463n.22; sophistication of, 38, 43, 453; unbelievability of evil, 9, 50, 61, 230, 299, 316, 319, 321–22, 364, 375, 382, 386

Diary of a Young Girl (Frank), 1–8, 364, 455–56n.9

Diary of Dawid Sierakowiak, The (Adelson), 442, 455n.5

"Diary of Günther Marcuse" (Walk), 436

Diary of the Vilna Ghetto, The (Rudashevski), 191, 466n.1

dignity, loss of, 139, 141, 151, 177, 231, 245, 248–53, 263, 322

discovery, fear of, 127, 131–32, 133, 135, 136, 146, 149, 154, 156, 463n.6

Djurin ghetto, 245, 248, 252, 254, 264, 265, 266, 267, 269

Drancy, 65, 71

Dresden, 413, 465nn.11 and 13

Easter, 18, 19, 81

Edith's Story (Velmans), 430

education: art school, 41–42; assignments, 214–15, 216; Bible study, 91, 94,

104–5, 107–8, 109; curriculum, 18, 21, 42, 82–83, 191, 243, 464–65n.6; deaths of teachers, 207, 213–14; emigration for, 25, 457n.10; in ghettos, 161, 168, 169–74, 175, 208, 217–18, 464–65n.6; goals and achievement, 18, 22, 42, 93, 163–65, 166, 169–71, 220, 464–65n.6; libraries, 217–18; sanctions against Jews, 21, 98, 244; in Zionist youth groups, 18–19

Einsatzgruppen, 462n.6, 471n.8

Emergency Rescue Committee, 458n.5

emigration: assistance from non-Jews for, 23, 25; border crossings, 67, 88, 90, 100, 112; bribes for, 32, 33, 51, 52; bureaucracy of, 26–27, 31–32; delays of, 28–29, 30, 31, 32, 53, 66, 72, 87; despair over, 24, 25, 32, 33, 56; destinations for, 15, 24, 31, 425, 430; for education, 25, 457n.10; expectations of, 77–78; financial considerations for, 22–24, 25, 26, 55; options for, 15–16, 17–18, 22–25, 26–29, 35; from Paris, 49, 50, 51–52, 56–59; restrictions on, 15–16, 29; routes of, 17, 30, 31, 53–54, 74, 430, 457n.16. *See also* aliyah; Palestine

England, 25, 103, 104, 107, 243, 425, 426, 432, 435, 436, 438, 439

Erez Israel, 26–29, 393, 404, 406, 456–57n.9, 457n.11

Estonia, 335

evacuations, 49–52; on foot, 40, 56–59, 129; illegal border crossings, 67, 88, 100, 112; from Krajno, 284–85, 289–90; non-Jews' indifference to, 289; from Paris, 56–62; to schools, 72

evil, unbelievability of, 9, 50, 61, 230, 299, 316, 319, 321–22, 364, 375, 382, 386

exploitation: bribery, 32, 33, 51, 52, 99–100, 252, 267, 328, 352, 354–55; of deportees, 49–50, 249, 277, 284–85; extortion by ghetto officials, 219, 274; food supply, 241, 242, 246, 251, 252, 278, 292; of ghetto residents, 246,

251–52, 253, 255–56, 264, 267; by helpers, 252–53, 255–56; inflation, 249, 255; of Jewish labor, 241; of Jews by Poles, 273–74, 280, 281, 284, 286–87, 288, 294; monetary exploitation, 255–56, 264, 274, 282, 292; of pending deportations, 249; by property owners, 255–56; raids by German police, 272, 278–79, 287, 291, 294–96; ransoms, 285–86; sale of personal possessions, 17, 48, 242, 249, 251–52, 284–85, 289, 292, 296, 308; seizures for forced labor, 273, 275, 276, 326, 333

false correspondence from Terezín deportees, 182, 466n.14

family: anxiety for safety of, 55; appreciation of parents, 48; arrests of family members, 39, 155–56, 157–58; changes in living arrangements, 25–26, 44; concern for parents during evacuation, 57–58; death of grandparents, 182, 260–62, 323–24; despair over emigration possibilities, 24, 25; disappearance of parents, 65, 212–14; escape with, 56–57; impact of hunger on, 228; parents' birthdays, 33; prison visits, 22, 43–44; release of prisoners by, 287; religious observances of, 63, 122, 160, 426; reunions with, 41, 44–45, 425, 426, 430, 438, 439; separation from, 22, 39, 40, 49, 54, 57–62, 110, 155–58, 162–63; sisters, 305–6, 325, 362, 368, 372–74, 375, 377, 380–81, 384, 392, 393–94, 473n.2; tensions, 133, 135, 138, 238, 254, 256, 259, 293–94, 316–17; tensions between spouses, 293–94, 320; transports out of Terezín ghetto, 165–67, 179–81; in Vilna ghetto, 200, 467n.12; worry for brothers, 163, 166–67, 178, 179–80, 185, 189. *See also* parents

fear: after Kristallnacht, 15, 19–21; air raids, 197; *aktion* in ghetto, 200–204, 330, 349, 467n.19, 468nn.20 and 21;

fear (*continued*)

arrival experience, 194–95, 199–200; of betrayal, 125, 127, 131–32, 133, 135, 136, 146, 149, 154, 156, 463n.6; blackmail, 282, 283; concentration camps, 99; of contagion, 262, 264; of death, 201–3, 230, 266, 381; of denunciation, 131, 132, 133, 463n.6; of deportation, 110, 252; of extermination, 266; for fate of siblings, 165–67, 179–80; for fate of transports, 165–67, 179–81; of future, 224, 246, 264; of gathering together for prayer, 262; Gestapo raids, 149, 155; of going to school, 21; in hiding, 130–31; of Jewish ghetto police, 209; raids by German police, 272, 278–79, 287, 291, 294–96; random violence, 241, 252, 266, 273, 276, 282–86, 299–300; of starvation, 231; worry for brother's safety, 163, 166–67, 178, 179–80, 185, 189

Final Solution, 329–30, 359–60

food: after liberation, 423; bribery, 354–55; for death camp survivors in Terezín, 415–16, 421; dreams of, 234, 312, 369; food lines, 212–13, 233–34, 336–37; German food policies, 336, 337, 379; meal preparations, 150, 253; paying for, 234, 239, 242; privileged access to, 198, 281, 283, 284, 307–8, 331, 332, 341; profiteering, 220, 230, 241, 242, 246, 251, 252, 292, 354–55; provisions in hiding, 129, 130, 132, 133, 134, 135–36, 137–38, 139, 141, 145–50, 154; quality of, 80, 188, 234, 242, 371; rationing of, 219–20, 227, 231, 234–42, 253, 291; ration lists in diaries, 227–28, 231, 237–38, 239–40, 241–42; sharing rations, 310, 368–69, 370, 371, 384, 385–86; smuggling, 219, 281, 348–49, 352, 354; wasting, 376–77; for workers, 231, 234, 297, 316, 351–52, 355. *See also* hunger; starvation

France, 44, 65, 243, 458n.6; German invasion and occupation of, 39–40, 50, 52, 55, 75, 460n.15; Jewish refugees in, 38, 39, 99, 459n.7; xenophobia in, 38–39, 64

friends, 35, 41; boyfriends, 34, 39, 45, 48, 50, 54, 55, 302, 313; decline of, 323; separation from, 112, 116

From Anschluss to Albion: Memoirs of a Refugee Girl, 1939–1940 (Orsten), 438

From Home to Wandering: War Diary, 1941–45 (Rozenberg), 431

future: aliyah as, 21, 23–25, 104–5, 366–67, 370, 393, 402; desire for plenty to eat, 369; dreams of, 234, 312, 369; Hebrew language as, 393; hopes for, 366–67; liberation, 304, 310; memorialization of martyrs, 393; repatriation, 247–48, 268, 269, 270, 427; sense of impermanence, 263–64; to tell the world about the crimes of Holocaust, 367, 371–72, 390, 391

gas chambers, 97, 187

gendarmes, 57–61, 272, 278–79, 281, 283, 287, 291, 295–96

German police, 272, 278–79, 281, 283, 287, 291, 295–96

Germans: blacklist of, 63; destruction of evidence by, 93, 399–400, 412, 413; expulsion of Polish Jews from Germany, 456n.8; food policies, 336, 337, 379; gendarmes, 57–61, 272, 278–79, 281, 283, 287, 291, 295–96; Gestapo, 127, 128, 149, 155, 210, 306, 327, 429; immorality of, 411; inhumanity of, 187, 336–37, 375, 377–78, 382–86, 415–16; Kripos, 380; Kristallnacht, 14–15, 19–21, 22, 24, 440, 456n.8; persecution of Poles by, 450; torture by, 285–86, 384, 385; vandalization and destruction of Jewish property, 20–21, 22, 37; war news of, 50, 51, 52–53, 86–87, 115, 142, 280, 355

Germany, 243, 447; Czechoslovakia annexed by, 122–23, 160; Lithuania invaded and occupied by, 329; Soviet

Union attacked by, 123, 191, 244, 271, 301

Gestapo, 127, 128, 149, 155, 210, 306, 327, 429

Ghetto Fighters' House, Israel, 431

Ghetto in Flames (Arad), 13, 466n.4, 467n.5, 467–68n.19

God: anger at, 112, 364–65, 394; faith in, 91–96, 108–9, 112, 121, 323; and redemption, 94–95; salvation from, 92, 94, 109, 112–14, 118–19, 323; silence of, 376, 377, 385; suffering and the existence of, 91–92, 100–101

grandparents, 34–35, 260–62, 323–24

grief: after liberation, 402, 419–23, 442; death of friends, 314–16; death of grandparents, 260–62, 323–24, 327; decimation of Jewish population, 314; deportations, 23, 270, 374; end of romantic love, 211, 313–14; evil as unbelievable, 50, 61, 230, 319, 321–22, 375; need for grieving, 367; over family members' arrests, 39, 155–56, 157–58; pain of reality, 374; wasting food, 376–77

Gross-Breesen Jewish Emigration Training Farm, 425, 436

guilt, 95, 96; humiliation in Vilna ghetto, 218–19; parents' arrests, 294–96, 297; selections for roundups, 325–27, 348–49; selfishness, 121, 326, 368–69, 370, 371; tensions with parents, 275

Gurs, 39, 64, 78

Habonim, 14. *See also* Zionist youth groups

hachsharah (agricultural training camps), 25, 26, 27–28, 29–30, 31, 457nn.11 and 13

Hague, The, 90, 98, 106

hangings, 333, 334, 353–54

Hanukkah, 103, 105–6, 183, 334, 355

Hashomer Hazair, 14, 301, 320, 443. *See also* Zionist youth groups

Hebrew language, 18, 19, 93, 393

hiders and rescuers: families as, 426, 429, 430, 436–37; fears of discovery and betrayal, 127, 145, 149, 156; homes for displaced children, 429; Jewish organizations as, 432, 438; relations with, 126–27, 132, 137, 139, 140, 145, 149, 151–52, 153, 460n.4; reliability of, 125–26, 130, 135, 136, 137, 138, 141, 152–53; reliance on, 125, 133–34, 139–40, 144; rescue networks, 66, 458n.4, 460n.4; teachers as, 429, 433

hiding: access to news, 127, 138, 148; changes in hiding places, 139, 145, 152, 440; from deportations, 123–24; deprivations in, 129–30; false identity, 430; fear of discovery in, 68, 127, 131–32, 133, 135, 136, 146, 149, 463n.6; in ghetto, 202, 467n.19; hygiene in, 139, 141, 151; illness as, 65, 70; Jews passing as non-Jews, 63, 66, 67, 68, 88, 90–91, 100; living conditions in, 130, 133–34, 153, 156, 157, 158, 437; religious observance in, 125, 132, 138, 139, 144; tensions in, 126–27, 133, 135, 137, 138, 139, 140, 150

Hitler Youth, 21

Holland, 90, 99, 106

Home I, Building L417 (Terezín ghetto), 168, 169, 464–65n.6

homelessness, 61, 162, 180, 397, 421, 438

homesickness, 176–77, 182, 252, 397

hope: for aliyah to Palestine, 21, 23–25, 28–29, 366–67, 370, 393; for better times, 259; daily life, 42, 54, 79–83, 276–77, 280–81, 381–82, 436; demise of Nazis, 379; deportations halted, 366; in *Diary of a Young Girl* (Frank), 5; for end of war, 387–88, 388–89, 390–93; frailty of, 306–7; for the future, 35–36, 50, 117, 217, 311, 371–72; good news, 142, 146–47, 149; illusions of, 365, 366, 379, 382–84, 390, 391–93; for liberation, 311, 319; perception of reality, 304; of postponed evacuation, 285, 289; prayers reflecting, 105,

hope (*continued*)
116, 125, 269; for redemption, 368; of
repatriation, 270; for return of family
members, 188, 189, 296; returns from
Zossen barracks, 398–99, 409; skills
learned in ghetto, 184–85; for survival,
267–68; transports to safety, 398–99,
409, 410

hunger: daily hunger, 227–28, 230, 233;
deaths from, 230, 235, 322, 442; as
deprivation, 219, 227, 231, 234–38,
239–42, 376–77; dreaming of food,
234, 312, 369; family tensions due to,
238; food rations, 219–20, 227, 231,
234–42, 235, 237–38, 239, 241–42, 253,
291; German food policies, 336, 337,
379; inhumanity of, 187, 336–37, 363,
370, 401, 415–16; privileged access to
food, 198, 307–8, 331, 332, 341; shame,
251, 310–12, 368–69, 370, 371, 376–77;
weight loss, 231, 242

idleness, 31, 73, 75, 76, 77, 93, 100, 104,
117, 255
illness: care of children by parents, 176; of
death camp survivors, 250, 404, 408,
414–15; disease and medical care, 179,
246, 250, 257, 259, 264, 318–19, 371,
380; fear of contagion, 262, 264; in
ghettos, 162, 178; as means of hiding,
65, 69, 71; parents', 263–64; profiteering from, 257, 264; as reason for
deportation, 229
*I'm Not Even a Grown-Up: The Diary of
Jerzy Feliks Urman* (Urman), 443
intellectual life: art, 41–42, 333–34, 444,
464–65n.6; club festival in Vilna
ghetto, 220–21; holiday celebrations,
223–24; libraries, 217–18; literary
groups, 191–92, 212, 215, 218, 222–23;
music, 19, 23, 29, 31, 333, 341, 350,
352–53, 355–57, 359; publications in
ghetto, 165–66, 444; reading, 19, 79,
80–81, 82, 85, 86, 169–74; in Terezín
ghetto, 163–65. *See also* education;
schools

International Red Cross, 399–400, 410,
411–12, 413, 421, 465n.11
Iron Guard, 244, 257
Izbica Lubelska, 17

Janowska concentration camp, 445
Janowska Road, The (Wells), 445
Jawne school, Cologne, 25, 26, 457n.10
Jewish Council: access to information,
398; apathy of, 295, 307–8; corruption
of, 297, 307–8, 322; deportation of
members, 396, 411; favoritism of, 302,
307; heroic efforts of, 330; imprison-
ment of, 327; inspections of ghetto,
400; prisoner release, 294, 295, 298;
privilege, 330
Jewish Council, Kovno ghetto: and Ilya
Gerber, 330, 472nn.9 and 10
Jewish Council, Krajno: and Dawid
Rubinowicz, 275, 294, 295, 297
Jewish Council, Łódź ghetto, 374
Jewish Council, Stanisławów, 275, 294,
295, 297, 322; corruption of, in Elsa
Binder's diary, 302–3, 307, 327
Jewish Council, Terezín ghetto: and Alice
Ehrmann, 396, 398, 400; deportations
of members of 396, 411
Jewish ghetto police: arrests by, 297, 332,
357–58; authority of, 351; burial of
murdered Jews by, 300; ceremonial
oath of, 351; as collaborators, 191, 201,
209, 210, 219, 297, 319; corruption of,
191, 201, 209, 210, 219, 220, 355, 432;
vulnerability of, 348–49
Jewish Historical Institute, Warsaw, 230,
428, 432, 442, 474–75n.3
Jewish identity: ambivalence toward,
68, 81, 88; anti-Jewish legislation, 23,
160–61; assimilation, 14, 63, 94, 122,
395, 426, 433, 443, 459n.2; authors as
victims of Holocaust, 452–53; badges,
90, 98, 100, 129, 161, 194, 199, 434,
437n.10; chosenness, 118; of diary
authors, 452–53; German identity
of diarists and family members, 14,
16–17, 443; *mischlinge*, 160, 180, 395;

names reflecting, 17, 26, 186, 457nn.12 and 14; passing as non-Jews, 63, 66, 67, 68, 88, 90–91, 100; practice of Catholicism, 67–68, 69, 76, 81; religious conversions, 63, 426, 459n.2; stars as symbols of, 90, 98, 129, 161, 194, 434, 467n.10; and status in Terezín ghetto, 169; youth groups, 13, 14, 17–19, 21, 35, 191, 192, 320, 434, 441, 445

Jewish youth groups. *See* youth groups; Zionist youth groups

Jews of Ukraine in the Second World War (Levitas), 429

Jud Süss (film), 106, 462n.12

Kaddish prayer, 260
Kaiserwald concentration camp, 440
Kindertransport, 439
Kovno ghetto, 224, 225, 330, 335, 336, 433; "Great Aktion" (October 28, 1941) in, 330, 472n.5; and Ilya Gerber, 330–60, 472n.5; mass execution of Jews of, 196, 329–30, 334–35, 472n.11; and Moshe Kravec, 450
Kristallnacht, 14–15, 19–21, 22, 24, 440, 456n.8

labor: access to food, 297, 336; certificates, 201–2, 305, 338–39; classifications for, 305, 326; as death, 372–73; deportations for, 372–73, 374, 379; food for workers, 231, 234, 297, 316, 336, 351–52, 355; registration for, 82, 165, 326; seizures for, 273, 275, 276, 326, 333; shoveling snow, 286–87, 288, 387; Sonderkommando, 445; vocational training, 337–38, 348, 351, 357
Le Chambon sur Lignon, 126, 460nn.10, 13, and 17; and Elisabeth Kaufmann, 40; and Peter Feigl, 66, 68, 458n.4; 460n.4
letters: codes in, 182; collections of, 449–50; destruction of, 265; diaries in form of letters, 64–65; false news in, 182, 306, 466n.14; family correspondence, 59, 69, 185, 267, 297–99, 427;

lack of, 9, 69–70, 71, 76, 77, 177; with prisoners, 297–99
Le Vernet, 39, 65
liberation: death as, 373–74; future, 304, 310; grief after, 402, 418, 419–23, 442; hopes for, 128, 188–89, 309–10, 311, 319, 321; rumor of, 371, 400, 413, 414
liquidations of ghettos, 224, 326–27, 367–68, 429
Lithuania, 190, 191, 201, 329, 335–36, 472n.8
Litzmannstadt. *See* Łódź ghetto
living conditions: disease and medical care, 179, 246, 257, 259, 263, 264, 318–19, 371, 380; in hiding, 130, 133–34, 153, 156, 157, 158, 161; no running water, 64; overcrowding, 251, 253, 266, 267, 407–8, 410; sanitation, 124, 139, 141, 151, 177, 245, 250–53, 257, 259; sharing living quarters, 25–26, 44; in Terezín ghetto, 161, 162, 177–78
Łódź ghetto, 187, 432, 435; Anonymous Boy in, 361–94; Anonymous Girl in, 226–42, 271, 302, 363; and Dawid Sierakowiak, 442; deportations from, 229, 361–62, 365, 366, 368; liquidation of, 367, 368; mortality in, 227, 228–29; Red Army arrival in, 368
loneliness, 64, 162, 176–77, 182–83, 260–61, 265, 279, 309, 431, 432
Luxembourg, 64
Lvov ghetto, 445

Maccabee Hazair, 396. *See also* Zionist youth groups
Majdanek death camp, 460n.10
Malines transit camp, 97
Maquis, 67, 79
mass murders: *aktion* in ghetto, 200–204, 330, 349, 467n. 19, 468nn. 20 and 21; awareness of, 193, 195, 196, 199, 204, 205, 207, 210, 224–25, 365–66, 391, 400–401, 466n.4, 467nn.5 and 11; confrontation with, 462n.6; liquidations of ghettos, 224, 326–27, 367–68, 429; massacres of Jews, 301–2, 307; mass

tected by, 17, 66, 71–74, 460n.4; Jewish relations with, 20, 23–24, 25; Jews passing as, 63, 66, 67, 68, 88, 90–91, 100; tensions with, 126–27, 137, 139, 140, 149, 151–52, 153

North Africa, 65, 75, 133, 460n.15

Nuremberg Race Laws, 160, 244, 395

Operation Barbarossa, 462n.6

Oświęcim. *See* Auschwitz-Birkenau

Palestine: and Alice Ehrmann, 402; and the Anonymous Boy in Łódź ghetto, 368, 369, 370, 392; desire for, 23, 25, 27, 30, 31, 369–70, 381, 404; as Erez Israel, 26–29, 393, 404, 406, 456–57n.9, 457n.11; *hachsharah* (agricultural training camps), 25, 26, 27–28, 29–30, 31, 457n.11, 457n.13; Jewish nation in, 373, 381, 402; and Klaus Langer, 17, 29, 30, 31–32, 456n.7; Zionist youth groups, 13–14, 17–19, 21, 25–26, 28, 32, 35–36, 320, 457n.11. *See also* aliyah; Zionism

parents: army service of, 47–48; arrests of, 15, 284, 294–96, 297; arrests of fathers, 273, 275, 294–95; care of children during illness, 176; deportations of, 17, 65; disappearance of, 65, 212–13; emigration decisions/options considered, 22–23, 25–26; fathers in labor camps, 275–76, 296–300; fathers' return, 276, 299–300; illnesses of, 246; intervention in children's work assignments, 337; Kristallnacht arrests of, 15; missed by children, 177, 180, 183; separation from, 33, 40–44, 47–48, 51, 56–62, 64–65, 67–70, 77, 176–77, 180, 183, 291–92; sharing food rations, 228, 239; son's relationship with, 294–95, 297, 299, 299–300; tensions with, 14, 256, 275–76, 282, 293–95, 297, 299–300, 308–9

passing as non-Jews, 63, 66–68, 88, 90–91, 100, 430, 433

Pearls of Childhood (Gissing), 427

personal possessions, sale/dispossession of, 16, 242, 249, 251–52, 284–85, 289, 308, 312, 323, 328–29

physical hardships: disease and medical care, 179, 246, 257, 259, 263, 264, 318–19, 371, 380; in hiding, 130, 133–34, 153, 156, 157, 158, 161; no running water, 64; overcrowding, 251, 253, 266, 267, 407–8, 410; sanitation, 124, 139, 141, 151, 177, 245, 250–53, 257, 259; sharing living quarters, 25–26, 44; in Terezín ghetto, 161, 162, 177–78

poetry, 212, 381, 437

pogroms, 202–4, 301–2

Poles: exploitation of Jews by, 273–74, 280, 281, 284, 286–87, 288, 294

police: destruction after Kristallnacht, 20; interrogations by, 57–59, 60–61; raids by German police, 272, 278–79, 287, 291, 294–96

police force, relations with, 280, 281

Policemen's Chorus, 333, 352–53, 359

Ponar killing site, 193, 196, 199, 204, 207, 224, 466n.4, 467–68nn.11–21

Prague, 123, 161, 395, 428

prayers: in hiding, 125, 132, 144; for High Holidays, 347; historical perspectives on, 118; Kaddish, 260; reflecting hope, 105, 116, 125, 269; for reunion, 76; for salvation, 92, 94; suffering in, 111, 113, 316; in Terezín ghetto, 178

prisons: descriptions of, 22–23, 46–47, 279; letters to prisoners, 297–99; release of prisoners, 22, 287, 296–98, 299–300; separations from family, 22, 39, 43–44, 275; visits with prisoners, 22, 46–47

privileged access to food, 198, 281, 283, 284, 307–8, 331, 332, 341

profiteering: bribery, 32, 33, 51, 52, 99–100, 252, 267, 328, 352, 354–55; extortion by ghetto officials, 219, 274; food supply, 241, 242, 246, 251, 252, 278, 292; by German government after

profiteering (*continued*)
Kristallnacht, 24; inflation, 249, 255;
from pending deportations, 249;
protektsiye, 220, 330, 332, 335, 357;
sale of personal possessions, 17, 48,
242, 249, 251–52, 284–85, 289, 292,
296, 308
propaganda, 49; anti-Jewish, 99, 312,
359–61; anti-Semitic caricatures
as, 288; beautification campaign in
advance of Red Cross visit, 399–400,
410, 411–13, 465n.11; on German
dominance, 115; in movies, 106,
462n.12; Nazi propaganda in schools,
21; rumors of war, 33; Soviet leaflet,
211–12; war effort, 52
prose accounts, 185, 438–49, 450
Protectorate of Bohemia and Moravia,
122, 123, 151, 444
protektsiye, 220, 330, 332, 335, 357
Przemyśl ghetto, 442
Purim, 134, 192, 223–24, 233, 468n.23

Quakers, 66, 71, 72, 438, 443, 460n.4

raids by German police, 272, 278–79, 287,
291, 294–96
random murders, 252, 266, 276, 282–84,
299–300
ransoms and fines, 285–86, 292
Red Army: advances of, 109, 142, 149, 150,
208, 366–67, 376; anniversary of, 222;
arrival in Łódź ghetto, 368; Djurin
liberated by, 248; evacuation of Vilna
ghetto, 197–98; liberation of Terezín,
188–89, 420, 421–23; in Stalingrad,
100, 134, 215–16, 221, 222; victories of,
109, 148, 195, 222, 307; in Yitskhok
Rudashevski's diary, 195, 196, 197, 198,
222
Red Cross, 399–400, 410, 411–12, 413, 421,
465n.11
relationships within Jewish community.
See Jewish Council; Jewish ghetto
police

religious life: Bible study, 91, 94, 104–5,
107–8, 109; Hanukkah, 103, 183, 334,
355; in hiding, 125, 132, 138, 139;
Passover, 144; Purim, 134, 192, 223–24,
233, 468n.23; rabbis, 388; Rosh
Chodesh, 155, 158; Rosh Hashanah,
138, 148, 206, 269, 347; secularism, 94,
95; Simchat Torah, 349; synagogues,
14–15, 19, 262, 347; Three Weeks
(period prior to Tisha be-Av), 267–68;
yahrzeits (death anniversaries), 145;
Yom Kippur, 201, 244, 269, 347. *See
also* Catholicism; Jewish identity;
prayers
repatriation, 247–48, 268, 269, 270, 427
reprieve: from fear, 146–47; hope for,
260, 262; hunger, 227–28, 230, 233,
384, 385–86; from illness, 276–77;
money received from relatives, 267;
and renewal of violence, 365, 366, 379,
382–84; social activities, 39, 45, 47,
53–54, 217, 339–40, 343
resistance: asylum to Jewish refugees, 458n.4; club festival in Vilna
ghetto, 220–21; communal meal in
Vilna ghetto, 217; daily routine as,
42, 54, 79–83, 163, 253, 276–77,
381–82, 437; hopes for the future,
221–22; illness as, 65, 70; intellectual
life of Vilna ghetto youth as, 191–92;
to police interrogation, 57–59, 60–61;
prayer, 269; resilience during evacuation, 57–59; surviving Vilna ghetto
pogrom, 203; Young Pioneers, 195–96,
197. *See also* cultural life; education;
religious life
Riga ghetto, 440
Romania, 243, 244, 245, 247–48, 249–50,
260
romantic relationships: boyfriends, 34,
39, 45, 50, 54, 302, 313, 396, 404, 405;
courtship, 334, 342–46, 351; end of,
211, 313–14; lack of, 263
Rosh Hashanah, 138, 148, 206, 269, 347
roundups, 269–70, 305, 306, 325, 330, 350

Rudolfsmühle, 305, 325, 327

rumors: Allied troops movements, 53; annihilation of the Jewish people, 359–61; of arrests, 20–21, 291; of concentration camp conditions, 169; credibility of, 335, 379; of deaths, 291; of deportations, 93–94, 110–11, 249–50, 262, 277–78, 373, 374, 382, 383–84; of end of war, 373, 387–88, 388–89, 390–93; of evacuation, 266, 267, 285; of eviction, 348; of fates of family members, 464n.4; German army movements, 55–56, 413; of liberation, 371, 400, 413, 414; liquidation of ghettos, 224; of mass murders, 94, 107, 322, 349–50, 353, 400–401, 462n.6; of police raids, 291; radio broadcasts, 307; of raids, 294–96, 295; of Red Army victory, 355; of repatriation, 247–48, 268, 269, 270; of reprieve, 262; of roundups, 94, 350; Soviet evacuation of Vilna ghetto, 197–98; as survival, 350

Ruthka: A Diary of War (Lieblich), 435

Saint Sauveur par Bellac, 40

sale of personal possessions, 17, 48, 242, 249, 251–52, 284–85, 289, 292, 296, 308

salvation, 92, 94, 112–14, 115, 118–19, 323

sanitation, 124, 139, 141, 151, 177, 245, 250–53, 257, 259

San Vincenzo della Fonte, 447

Şargorod ghetto, 257, 262

Schniebinchen, 25, 26, 27–28, 29–30, 31, 457n.11

schools, 338; acceptance of refugees in, 41, 78–80; achievement in, 42; art school, 41–42; classmates at, 21, 41, 45, 79–82, 85; Jews barred from, 21, 98, 277, 436; Nazi propaganda in, 21; social discrimination, 21, 26, 38, 41, 45–46, 68, 79–81, 321; youth groups, 35

secrecy, 127, 131–32, 133, 146, 463n.6

separation: anti-Jewish legislation, 160–61; anxieties of, 57, 64–65; from boyfriends, 34, 39, 45, 50, 313; from brothers, 166–67, 178, 179–80, 184, 189; death of grandmother, 182; during evacuation, 57–62; from family, 22, 39–44, 40–41, 49, 54, 57–62, 110, 155–58, 162–63; of friends, 30; lack of correspondence, 9, 69–70, 71, 76, 77, 177; military service, 34, 39, 45, 50, 54; from parents, 33, 40–44, 47–48, 51, 56–62, 64–65, 67–70, 77, 176–77, 180, 183, 291–92; pogroms, 203–4; from sisters, 305–6, 325, 372–73, 375, 377, 393–94; transports out of Terezín ghetto, 165–67, 179–81; trauma of, 68

shame: badges, 90, 98, 129, 161, 194, 199, 434, 467n.10; caricatures of Jews, 288; hunger, 251, 310–12, 368–69, 370, 371, 376–77; Jewish ghetto police, 209, 210, 219, 220; parents' arrests, 294–95, 297; selfishness, 121, 310–12, 326, 368–69

shoveling snow, 273, 285, 286, 288, 387

Shperre, 361, 365, 388, 435

silence, 241, 293, 376, 377, 385

Simchat Torah, 149, 349

Skarżysko Kamienna labor camp, 275, 295, 296, 299

smuggling, 219, 281, 306, 348–49, 352, 354, 429

Sobibór death camp, 439, 452

social discrimination, 19, 21, 23, 26, 38, 41, 45–46, 68, 79–81, 90, 98, 106, 277, 321, 436

Sommerda, 452

Sonderkommando, 445

Sophienwalde labor camp, 440, 441

Soviet Union, 123, 191, 244, 301, 329

Stalingrad, 134, 206, 215, 221, 222, 248

Stanisławów, 301, 305, 306, 311

Stanisławów ghetto: and Elsa Binder, 271, 301–28; establishment of, 301; and Jerzy Feliks Urman, 442; liquidation